REA

ORDER&
EXCLUSION

A volume in the series

CONJUNCTIONS OF

RELIGION & POWER IN

THE MEDIEVAL PAST

Edited by

Barbara H. Rosenwein

Medieval Cruelty:
Varieties of Perception from Late Antiquity
to the Early Modern Period
  by Daniel Baraz

Unjust Seizure: Conflict, Interest, and
Authority in an Early Medieval Society
  by Warren Brown

Ermengard of Narbonne and the
World of the Troubadours
  by Fredric L. Cheyette

Speaking of Slavery: Color, Ethnicity,
and Human Bondage in Italy
  by Steven A. Epstein

Surviving Poverty in Medieval Paris: Gender,
Ideology, and the Daily Lives of the Poor
  by Sharon Farmer

Order and Exclusion: Cluny and Christendom
Face Heresy, Judaism, and Islam (1000–1150)
  by Dominique Iogna-Prat

The Bishop's Palace: Architecture and
Authority in Medieval Italy
  by Maureen C. Miller

ORDER&
EXCLUSION

CLUNY AND CHRISTENDOM

FACE HERESY, JUDAISM, AND

ISLAM (1000 – 1150)

DOMINIQUE IOGNA-PRAT

Translated from the French by Graham Robert Edwards

Foreword by Barbara H. Rosenwein

CORNELL UNIVERSITY PRESS Ithaca & London

The publisher gratefully acknowledges the assistance of the French Ministry of Culture—Centre national du livre.

First published 2002 by
Cornell University Press

Printed in the United States of America

Library of Congress
Cataloging-in-Publication Data

Iogna-Prat, Dominique.
  [Ordonner et exclure. English]
  Order and exclusion : Cluny and Christendom face heresy, Judaism, and Islam, 1000–1150 / Dominique Iogna-Prat ; translated from the French by Graham Robert Edwards ; foreword by Barbara H. Rosenwein.
    p. cm. — (Conjunctions of religion & power in the medieval past)
Includes bibliographical references and indexes.
    ISBN 0-8014-3708-3 (alk. paper)
    1. Cluny (Benedictine abbey)—History—To 1500. 2. Peter, the Venerable, ca. 1092–1156. 3. Heresies, Christian—History—Middle Ages, 600–1500. 4. Peter, of Bruys, d. 1126. 5. Christianity and other religions—Judaism—History—To 1500. 6. Judaism—Relations—Christianity—History—To 1500. 7. Christianity and other religions—Islam—History—To 1500. 8. Islam—Relations—Christianity—History—To 1500. I. Title.
II. Series.
    BX2615.C63 I5613   2002
    271'.14—dc21

                      2002010491

Cloth printing   10 9 8 7 6 5 4 3 2 1

A la mémoire de

deux morts très spéciaux,

Dante Iogna-Prat et

Georges Duby,

et pour une vivante

bien aimée

CONTENTS

FOREWORD

Order and Exclusion introduces the English-speaking world to the French medieval historian Dominique Iogna-Prat. His debut is overdue. Already in 1988, in his first book, *Agni immaculati* (Undefiled Lambs), Iogna-Prat, a director of research at the French National Research Center (CNRS), mined with both delicacy and thoroughness a handful of saints' lives to reveal the ideals and claims of a group of virginal monks, the Cluniacs. Sacrificing their sexuality, the Cluniacs considered themselves to be the highest form of humankind, little short of the angels. Taking the analysis to a new level, *Order and Exclusion* shows how the power, prestige, and pretensions of the Cluniacs, whom Pope Urban II called "the light of the world," represented a decisive moment in the history of intolerance.

That the Cluniacs belong to this sorry story will surprise many. It was not long ago that historians were praising the same monks for their humane and moderate point of view. Peter the Venerable, in particular, was applauded for commissioning the first translation of the Qur'an and for taking the trouble to learn some stories in the Talmud. But Dominique Iogna-Prat shows that these pioneering efforts on Peter's part had far more ambiguous significance than has hitherto been recognized.

The key to that significance is the interaction between Cluny and its larger context. Ever since the 1950s, when the French theologian Marie-Dominique Chenu pioneered an integration of religious thought with social history, historians have realized that theology, religion, and spirituality could not be separated from society. But no historian before Iogna-Prat has shown in such stunning detail how one religious institution's ideas meshed with its material and political position in the world.

Among other things, Cluny's ideas defined, excoriated, and excluded others; *Order and Exclusion* is part of a now vast bibliography on the subject of the "Other." But it stands apart in demonstrating, as no other study has, that certain exclusionary ideas had a snowballing effect, that the very ways in which the Cluniacs understood the Christian Church led them to view Jews, heretics, and Muslims as outside human society itself. Here Iogna-Prat builds on R. I. Moore's *Formation of a Persecuting Society* (1987), which pointed to the commonalities in the perception and treatment of heretics, Jews, and lepers. By focusing on the Cluniacs, Iogna-Prat is able to show the inexorable logic that made the links.

Thus the contribution of Dominique Iogna-Prat, building to be sure on the work of Chenu, Moore, and a minor mountain of Cluniac studies, is to effect a revolution by firmly anchoring in its own world the institution that was—and continues to be—considered most unworldly. He does so precisely by analyzing Cluny's view of itself, its society, and its excluded.

"Order," the first word of the title, suggests the breadth of this study. *Ordo* was a word of many meanings in medieval Latin. It meant, for example, the way of life at a monastery, most specifically its liturgy, which included (by Cluny's day) not only two daily Masses but also a long round of prayer seven times a day and once at night. At the same time, *ordo* referred to social categories, the "orders" of those who pray (the monks and clerics), those who fight (the soldiers or knights), and those who work (the peasants). These were the categories by which medieval people imagined their social world. Beyond that, *ordo* referred to the arrangement of the cosmos created by God, a harmony that embraced not only the angels but also the resurrected, ranked in a hierarchy that was meant to be reflected on earth. Thus *ordo* had a political meaning as well: lordship began with God and descended to earthly powers, of whom the monks were the most prestigious.

Some of the social and political meanings of these notions of order have been mined by other historians, for example Heinrich Fichtenau, whose *Living in the Tenth Century* (1991) reviewed the various ranks in that society, and Georges Duby, whose *The Three Orders* (1980) pioneered new methods of social-intellectual history. But no book before *Order and Exclusion* has linked so inextricably the sophisticated medieval notions of order with the equally perfected medieval modes of exclusion.

Was the intolerance of the Middle Ages the ancestor of our own? Recent historians have rightly problematized any easy continuities. In particular it has been important to distinguish modern anti-Semitism from medieval anti-Judaism. But there is also the opposite danger: to deny any relationship between the medieval and modern altogether. *Order and Exclusion* belongs to a "new school" that recognizes that stereotypes remain embedded in cultures, reappearing occasionally and discontinuously, but always potently. It is telling that in the United States Robert Chazan published *Medieval Stereotypes and Modern Antisemitism* (1997), which argues connections between medieval and modern views, at the very moment that the French edition of *Order and Exclusion* was in press.

Order and Exclusion complicates and deepens our understanding of the nature of power and its guises. Just as Michel Foucault's *Discipline and Punish* reveals the genealogy of a scientific-legal complex that justifies itself precisely as it exerts its authority, so *Order and Exclusion* (the very title recalling Foucault's) uncovers the social-ecclesial matrix in which those who ruled worked out an astonishingly coherent, complex, and self-legitimating system of ideas and practices. In *Order and Exclusion* Dominique Iogna-Prat confronts the moral complexity of our past.

—*Barbara H. Rosenwein*

ACKNOWLEDGMENTS

The first part of this work, on the Cluniac "Church system," slowly took shape within the research group known as ARTeM (CNRS/Université de Nancy II), where I benefited from the kind solicitude of Michel Parisse. The main phase of writing came later, during my research at the Centre d'études médiévales d'Auxerre (Unité mixte 5605 of the CNRS and the Université de Bourgogne). I owe a particular debt to Monique Zerner, who invited me to deal with the subject of Peter the Venerable's *Contra Petrobrusianos* in a seminar on "l'invention de l'hérésie" (the invention of heresy) at the Centre d'études médiévales of the Université de Nice-Sophia Antipolis (1993–96). It was on Jacques Chiffoleau's advice that I extended the inquiry to those other objects of exclusion: Jews and Saracens. My gratitude goes to my translator, Graham Robert Edwards, who has had the courage to take on the very involved French of this son of an Italian immigrant. It is hard to find adequate words to thank my editor and friend, Barbara H. Rosenwein. She was on hand when I first put my thoughts down in French and has been an incomparable facilitator in enabling this work to be put before an English-speaking audience. I am extremely grateful to colleagues and friends—Maurice Kriegel, Michel Lauwers, Bruno Levallois, Eric Palazzo, Daniel Russo, Elisabeth Zadora-Rio—who agreed to read all or some of the first draft of this book, thereby enabling me to enrich and refine its argument. Nor must I forget the six official readers of the version of this work presented as a habilitation at the Université de Paris X-Nanterre: Henri Bresc, Gilbert Dahan, Alain Guerreau, Otto-Gerhard Oexle, Michel Sot, and Michel Zimmermann. Finally, I must make very special mention of two people without whom this work would never have come about: Georges Duby, to whose memory I dedicate this book—the fruit of endless exchanges with him in the flesh and even more within myself—and Anne Levallois, who taught me to look History in the eye and whose own thoughts are intimately woven into this essay on otherness.

—*Dominique Iogna-Prat*

ABBREVIATIONS

AASS	*Acta Sanctorum.* Ed. Jean Bolland et al. Antwerp, 1643–. Various editions and places.
AESC or *AHSS*	*Annales: Economies, Sociétés, Civilisations.* Paris, 1946–. From 1994 called Annales: Histoire Sciences Sociales.
AH	*Analecta Hymnica Medii Aevi.* Ed. G. M. Dreves, C. Blume, and H. M. Banister. 55 vols. Leipzig, 1886–1922; rpt., 1961
AJ	Peter the Venerable, *Adversus Iudeorum inveteratam duritiem.* (In the notes cited by part and line numbers.)
AMS	*Antiphonale Missarum Sextuplex.* Ed. René-Jean Hesbert. Brussels, 1935.
ASOSB	*Acta Sanctorum Ordinis Sancti Benedicti.* Ed. Jean Mabillon et al. 9 vols. Paris, 1668–1701.
BC	*Bibliotheca Cluniacensis.* Ed. Martin Marrier and André Duchesne. Paris, 1614; rpt., Mâcon, 1915.
BEC	*Bibliothèque de l'Ecole des Chartes.* Paris, 183940–.
BHL	*Bibliotheca Hagiographica Latina Antiquae et Mediae Aetatis.* Ed. Bollandists. Brussels. Main vol., 1898–1901; suppl., 1911; new suppl., 1986. In series *Subsidia hagiographica,* vols. 6, 12, 70.
Bullarium	*Bullarium sacri ordinis cluniacensis.*
CAO	*Corpus Antiphonalium Officii.* Ed. René-Jean Hesbert. 6 vols. Rome, 1963–70.
CCCM	*Corpus Christianorum Continuatio Mediaevalis.* Turnhout, 1966–.
CCM	*Corpus Consuetudinum Monasticarum.* Siegburg, 1963–.
CCMé	*Cahiers de Civilisation Médiévale.* Poitiers, 1958–.
CCSL	*Corpus Christianorum Series Latina.* Turnhout, 1954–.
CLU	*Recueil des chartes de l'abbaye de Cluny.* (In the notes cited by item number and date together with volume and page number.)
CP	Peter the Venerable, *Contra Petrobrusianos.* (In the notes cited by paragraph and line number.)
CS	Peter the Venerable, *Contra sectam Sarracenorum.*

CSEL	*Corpus Scriptorum Ecclesiasticorum Latinorum.* Vienna, 1866–.
DA	*Deutsches Archiv.* Weimar, 1937–.
DACL	*Dictionnaire d'Archéologie Chrétienne et de Liturgie.* Ed. Fernand Cabrol and Henri Leclercq. 15 vols. 1907–53.
Dekkers	*Clavis Patrum Latinorum.* 3d ed. Ed. Eligius Dekkers and Emil Gaar. Turnhout, 1995.
DHGE	*Dictionnaire d'Histoire et de Géographie Ecclésiastiques.* Ed. Alfred Baudrillart et al. 1912–.
DIP	*Dizionario degli Istituti di Perfezione.* Rome, 1974–.
DM	Peter the Venerable, *De miraculis libri duo.*
Ep.	Peter the Venerable, *Epistolae.*
FMSt	*Frühmittelalterliche Studien.* Berlin, 1967–.
LT	*Liber tramitis aevi Odilonis*
MEFRM	*Mélanges de l'Ecole française de Rome, Moyen Age*
MGH	*Monumenta Germaniae Historica*
	Auct. Ant.: Auctores Antiquissimi
	Cep: Capitulare episcoporum
	Ldl: Libelli de lite
	LNG: Leges nationum Germanicarum
	Pl: Poetae latini medii aevi
	PLAC: Poetae latini aevi carolini
	SS: Scriptores rerum germaniarum in usum scholarum separatim editi
PL	*Patrologia Latina.* Ed. J.-P. Migne. 221 vols. Paris, 1844–64.
RB	*Revue Bénédictine.* Vol. 8 on. Maredsous, 1890–.
RHC, hist. occ.	*Recueil des Historiens des Croisades, Historiens occidentaux.* 5 vols. Paris, 1841–95; rpt., Farnborough, England, 1967.
RHE	*Revue d'Histoire Ecclésiastique.* Leuven, 1900–.
RM	*Revue Mabillon.* Paris and Turnhout, 1905–.
SC	*Sources Chrétiennes.* Paris, 1940–.
SLD	Peter the Venerable, *Sermo in laude dominici sepulchri.*
SMGBOZ	*Studien und Mitteilungen zur Geschichte des Benediktiner-Ordens und seiner Zweige.* Munich, 1926–.
SSMI	Peter the Venerable, *Sermo de sancto Marcello papa et martyre.*
SSMII	Peter the Venerable, *Sermo cuius supra in honore sancti illius cuius reliquiae sunt in praesenti.*
Statutum	*Statuta Petri Venerabilis*
STD	Peter the Venerable, *Sermo de transfiguratione domini.*
Summa	Peter the Venerable, *Summa totius haeresis Sarracenorum.*
TRE	*Theologische Realenzyklopädie.* Berlin, 1976–.
"Two Studies"	"Two Studies in Cluniac History." Ed. Herbert E. J. Cowdrey.

Fuller details of works cited here only by title will be found in the bibliography.

TRANSLATOR'S NOTE

Bible quotations are from the 1609 Douay (Rheims-Douay) translation of the Vulgate unless stated otherwise. Biblical nomenclature follows the King James Version (1611) and related versions. The Psalms and books of Kings are numbered according to the Vulgate, with the KJV numbering in brackets, thus: Psalm 22(23); 4(2) Kings.

All quotations from Latin or other languages in the French edition of 1998 have been retranslated from the original for this edition and are the translator's own rendering unless otherwise stated.

Dates expressed with a forward stroke (e.g., 1078/81) refer to an occurrence at an indeterminate moment between those dates.

—Graham Robert Edwards

ORDER&
EXCLUSION

INTRODUCTION

A JOURNEY THROUGH
CHRISTENDOM VIA CLUNY

In its early centuries, Christianity was simply a religion that drew together a community of believers. Yet by the twelfth century it had become a spatial and structural entity that ordered an entire society, not only of believers but of unbelievers also. In short, Christianity had remodeled itself into Christendom. What historical conditions explain this transition from a community held together by belief to a social order coterminous with the Church? That, in brief, is the question that animates this book.

Peter, the apostles, and their disciples, foundation stones of the tradition of the Church, spread the "Good News" of Christ to the four corners of the Roman empire. At first persecuted and then tolerated, Christianity finally became a state religion at the end of the fourth century. Then began the long process whereby one term came to include the other, the culmination of which we shall attempt to trace here, the relatively short time in which, in the Latin west of the eleventh and twelfth centuries, Church and society ended up becoming coextensive notions. In the Roman context it was a question of defining the powers of the emperor as against those of Peter's successors; by contrast, at Byzantium the destiny of the "emperor-priest" was something different entirely.[1] Pope Gelasius I (492–96) maintained that the world was governed by two orders: clerics possessed authority (*auctoritas*), while the kings held power (*potestas*).[2] During the high Middle Ages, especially around 1050, when the notion of papal monarchy was reaching its height, this "hierarchical dyarchy" or twinship evolved in the direction of subordinating the *potestas* to the *auctoritas*.[3] In the 1140s, the decretalist Gratian held that "the priests of Christ are to be deemed the fathers

---

1. Gilbert Dagron, *Empereur et prêtre: étude sur le "césaropapisme" byzantin*, Bibliothèque des Histoires (Paris, 1995).

2. Gelasius I, *Ep.* 12 (to Emperor Anastasius), *Epistolae Romanorum Pontificum . . . a S. Hilaro usque ad Pelagium II*, ed. Andreas Thiel, vol. 1 (Braunsberg, 1868), p. 350.

3. The expression comes from Louis Dumont, *Essays on Individualism: Modern Ideology in Anthropological Perspective* (Chicago, 1986), pp. 45–52, esp. 52. [Rev. and augmented Eng. language ed. of *Essais sur l'individualisme: une perspective anthropologique sur l'idéologie moderne* (Paris, 1991 and 1993).]

and masters of kings, princes, and of all the faithful."[4] This development was linked to the emergence, during the eleventh century, of the all-embracing notion of Christendom, which no longer simply described a spiritual community but connoted a social and temporal structure. Institutionally, the Christendom (*Christianitas*) defined by eleventh- and twelfth-century clerics was a unitary whole with a center, Rome, and boundaries that were to be both defended against external enemies—the pagans and infidels—and extended until they encompassed the entire world (*Universalitas*).[5] The Church was like a mountain destined to fill all the space on earth, gradually eating up territory until it and the world were one. In this sense, Christendom was an institutional entity that steadily affirmed its differences against the outside—the Orthodox, Judaism and Islam—and a universalist utopia that accompanied, justified, and spurred on the expansion of the Latin west in the eleventh and twelfth centuries.

This study of that irresistible movement of inclusion focuses on a single monastic church, Cluny, and more particularly on the work of its ninth abbot, Peter the Venerable, whose abbacy ran from 1122 to 1156. By the twelfth century, the originally modest establishment founded by William III, duke of Aquitaine and count of Mâcon, had become a powerful network of houses that had expanded throughout the Latin world, extending as far as Christendom's limits, so that it confronted Islam in both the Iberian peninsula and the Holy Land. This awesome destiny was what led the Cluniacs to confuse their own church with the universal Church. The history of this confusion will occupy the first part of this book ("The Monks and the World Order"), which will give an outline history of Cluny in the eleventh and twelfth centuries and study at greater length the structure of this monastic church functionally identified with Rome.

The interplay of identity between the Church's members and head helps to explain how Peter the Venerable, a loyal Catholic whose vocation, as he himself put it, was not to stay silent, was drawn into defending the Church by writing and preaching against the Church's enemies, both outside and inside. Following in the footsteps of the Fathers, who had defined the main doctrines of Christian tradition by refuting aberrations and heresies, the abbot of Cluny attacked Peter of Bruis and the members of his sect, active in the regions of the Alpine arc and the south of Gaul in the years 1110–20. This shadowy figure, lost in the mists of a great wave of heresies contemporary with the great reform of the Latin Church in the eleventh and twelfth centuries, was refuted by our monk for undermining the very foundations of the order of Christendom. Peter of Bruis had struck at the bases of the institutional Church and the very conceptions of life and society that the clerics were establishing for themselves. Peter of Bruis rejected the baptism of children, on the grounds that salvation came through faith

4. Gratian, *Decretum*, Ia pars, dist. 96, cap. 9, in *Corpus Iuris Canonici*, ed. Friedberg (Leipzig, 1879), vol. 1, col. 340.

5. Jean Rupp, *L'idée de Chrétienté dans la pensée pontificale des origines à Innocent III* (Paris, 1939); Jan Van Laarhoven, "*Christianitas* et la Réforme grégorienne," in *Studi Gregoriani* 6 (1959–60): 1–98.

and that a young child was not sufficiently conscious to believe. He attacked the notion of sacred places, saying that the Church of God was not a building made of stones but a purely spiritual reality, the community of the faithful. He reviled and burned the Church's replicas of the Cross, arguing that the Cross was the hateful instrument of Christ's torture and suffering. He denied that priests had any powers of sacramental mediation, Christ's body having been consumed once only, by the disciples, at the Last Supper preceding the Passion; all further attempts to consume Christ's body, he contended, were therefore meaningless. Finally, Peter of Bruis considered that all funerary liturgy (offerings, prayers, masses, alms) was useless, since the deceased could expect to reap only what they had themselves sown in life.

In Part 2 of this book ("Christian Society"), we shall take a long look at how Peter the Venerable responded to these challenges in his first great theological treatise, *Contra Petrobrusianos*. In so doing, we shall see that his response is not limited to matters of doctrine alone, but that through his refutation of Petrobrusian error he reveals what he and others like him considered to be the conditions necessary to life in society. Peter the Venerable thus provides us with a sociology of Christianity in the twelfth century, a subject normally ignored in studies of feudal society because academic specialization has tended to force a separation between theology and social history. We, on the other hand, shall try here to follow Georges Duby in "disengaging from our habits of thought, from all the nostrums, the well-worn paths of traditional histories of Christianity" in order to ask "how to assign to the Church, and more generally to what we call the religious, its due place in feudal society, within 'feudalism.'"[6]

After the purgation of the Church within, defense of the Church spurred Peter the Venerable to address himself to the infidel. This is the subject of Part 3 of this book, "Christian Universality"—so-called because we shall seek to understand how Peter's all-or-nothing logic, first enunciated to demonstrate to the Petrobrusian heretics that all mankind shared a common destiny and that society was made up of necessary, obligatory forms of solidarity, entailed a similar challenge to those who did not believe in Christ. These were the Jews, who were to be found both inside and outside Christendom, and the Saracens, whose proselytism and warlike activity threatened Christendom from the outside during the period of the first two Crusades (1095–1149). In the struggles against the Jews and against Islam, Peter the Venerable was a protagonist of major importance. In order to argue against the infidel and write his two last theological treatises, *Adversus Iudeos* and *Contra sectam Sarracenorum*, Peter gathered together a great deal of documentation providing information on the authorities recognized by his adversaries. The abbot of Cluny was the first (or among the very first) in the medieval west to address the Jewish literary corpus of the exile, the

---

6. Georges Duby, *L'Histoire continue* (Paris, 1991), pp. 220–21, who gives concrete validation to Marc Bloch's aspirations.

Talmud, as well as to confront the Qur'an (Koran) and the legends relating to Muhammad. His war of ideas against the infidel was a perfectly logical extrapolation of his questioning of heresy. In this way, our monk was able to define not simply a sociology but also an anthropology of Christianity. Within the perspective of the Last Things, either humanity would be Christian or it would not. It was utterly imperative to engage in fierce combat with the different figures of Antichrist (the heretic, the Talmudic Jew, the Saracen, each in turn) and to define the structural basis and functioning of humanity saved by Christ. Certainly, Peter the Venerable helps us to see what rules organized the Christendom of the feudal age. But there is more. Looking into this distant and strangely exotic past of our own culture, we begin to grasp the price that was paid in tolerance when this society of Burgundian lords, lay castellans, and ecclesiastical grandees constructed its identity.

Before we begin, there are three points to be made. The first is about method, or more particularly conceptual ambiguity. Continental historiography during the 1980s was marked by a multiform return of the "religious."[7] Both Protestant and Catholic historians began to question openly their professional practice vis-à-vis their faith and trumpet a historiography described as "religious."[8] They therefore courted the risk of falling into teleology and ventured, as Georges Pérec once punned, to "écrire Histoire avec une hache"—do a hatchet job on history so as to write History. So let us dispel all doubt at the outset. The concept of "religion" is an eighteenth-century creation and its application to study of the Middle Ages wholly inappropriate.[9] Our aim is to provide a social history, to study the rules by which medieval society functioned during a time span (the eleventh and twelfth centuries) and a space (the Latin west) in which the production of ideas was the exclusive province of clerics.

Second, we shall not hear all the clerical voices of that period. The Cluniacs and Roman ideologues did not speak for the Church *in its entirety*. In discussing differences and the perception of otherness, more moderate voices were raised—and we shall hear them from time to time. Abelard and Peter the Venerable were close friends, yet differed hugely in their attitude to the Jews. We must therefore avoid presenting too one-sided a view of Latin Christendom during the period of the first two Crusades. There was a dominant tendency, and this is the chief focus of interest here; but not everyone, or at least not everyone

---

7. A European-scale assessment made in *Identités religieuses en Europe*, ed. Grace Davie and Danièle Hervieu-Léger (Paris, 1996).

8. This last, particularly striking example appears in *L'historien et la foi*, ed. Jean Delumeau (Paris, 1995).

9. In this connection, see Jean-Claude Schmitt's illuminating ideas in his "Une histoire religieuse du Moyen Age est-elle possible? (Jalons pour une anthropologie du christianisme médiéval)," in *Il mestiere di storico del Medioevo*, Atti del Convegno di Lugano, 17–19 maggio 1990, ed. Fernando Lepori and Francesco Santi (Spoleto, 1994), pp. 73–83. My thanks to Eric Palazzo for alerting me to this article.

to the same extent, regarded otherness as anathema. Then too, we would not have far to look among those who play the infidel role in this book, the Jews and Saracens, to discover equal and opposite instances of confessional intolerance. Take, for instance, the episodes of conversion or exile forced on the Jews in twelfth-century Spain when the reforming Muslim Almohads arrived. To explore the matter in further detail would fill a second book. Yet we cannot ignore this other facet of the problem. In our own day, versions of fundamentalism nourished by the soil of an often terrible common history have shown how obscurantism and intolerance can beset all the three religions of the Book and that none of them can arrogate to itself the mantle of the persecuted victim.

The third point has to do with our conception of the past. The eleventh- and twelfth-century Latin west and its relations with the different embodiments of otherness studied here are at once distant and familiar. It is true, of course, that all historical study amounts to making an "inventory of differences."[10] But it would be a great mistake if we interpreted our past in ways that so exaggerated the differences that the western Middle Ages remained a purely exotic phenomenon. The Islamic terrorists who, in the summer of 1995, shed blood in Paris claimed they were attacking the "Crusader capital" on the occasion of the nine hundredth anniversary of the call to the First Crusade. On 30 September 1997, the fifty-seventh anniversary of the Vichy regime's *Premier Statut des Juifs* (First Statute regarding the Jews), the French bishops made a declaration of repentance at the Drancy Memorial. A month later, on 30 October, a symposium of historians and Catholic theologians gathered at the Vatican to attempt to cast light on the Christian sources of anti-Semitism. Then on 16 March 1998, the Vatican Commission for Relations with Judaism published a Declaration on the Holocaust. On the eve of the two thousandth anniversary of the birth of Christ, the text called the faithful to a general examination of conscience regarding Christians' historic anti-Judaism (as distinct from Nazi anti-Semitism). The past thus continues to "break through the surface of the present" in bits and pieces that, whether we like it or not, allow us in varying and ever-provisional ways to construct an understanding of our own current circumstances.[11] A whole "imagined past," built up out of prefabricated concepts and schemes of interpretation, pervades our approach to today's questions of identity. Awareness of this phenomenon allows those who are distrustful of ready-made truths to gain a little autonomy and freedom.[12] It is little and yet much to ask. Such in any event is the modest ambition that drives the author of this book.

10. To quote the title of Paul Veyne's inaugural lesson at the Collège de France, Paris, 1976.

11. Alphonse Dupront, *Le mythe de croisade*, Bibliothèque des Histoires, 4 vols. (Paris, 1997), 1:17.

12. See discussion on these issues, which are crucial for the historian, in Otto G. Oexle, *Geschichtswissenschaft im Zeichen des Historismus*, Kritische Studien zur Geschichtswissenschaft, 116 (Göttingen, 1996), and "Die Moderne und ihr Mittelalter: eine Folgenreiche Problemsgeschichte," in *Mittelalter und Moderne: Entdeckung und Rekonstruktion der mittelalterlichen Welt*, ed. Peter Segl (Sigmaringen, 1997), pp. 307–64, to whom I owe the expression "imagined past."

I

THE MONKS
& THE
WORLD ORDER

I

THE "ORDERING" OF CHRISTENDOM

Civil society survives only by virtue of being above all a religious society. That is why a public religion of some sort is found to have existed among all peoples from the beginning of time. Religion is not simply necessary to the existence of society, it is society itself.
—Lamennais, *Le Conservateur*[1]

COSMIC ORDER AND SOCIAL ORDER

Order is "what we can see in the planets, inasmuch as each and every planet has its place and order and none is an impediment to another."[2] This pronouncement from Abelard's school in the twelfth century, suggesting that the cosmos and humanity as a group shared a common harmony, belongs to the distant conceptual heritage of the *ordo rerum* (order of things) bequeathed by Greek and Roman antiquity. Since the age of the Church Fathers, Christian authors had found among the ancients—the Stoics and especially the Platonists—an ancient framework of thinking about the social system that envisaged it as a concord of orders regulated after the model of the harmony of the planets. Augustine, who in his *De ordine* combined the cosmology of antiquity and the teachings of Scripture concerning Creation, made order the mover and regulator of the universe, which was defined as an ordered structure in a series of zones.

This chapter is a reworking (with significant cuts and additions) of my article, "Ordre(s), transcendance et mobilité sociale dans l'Occident médiéval (IVe–XIIe siècle)," in *Dictionnaire raisonné de l'Occident médiéval*, ed. Jacques Le Goff and Jean-Claude Schmitt (Paris, 1999), pp. 845–60. General treatments of the question of social orders in medieval society are: Giles Constable, *Three Studies in Medieval Religious and Social Thought* (Cambridge, 1995), pp. 251ff.; Otto G. Oexle's stimulating "Stand, Klasse," *Geschichtliche Grundbegriffe* 6 (1990): 155–200.

    1. Lamennais (Félicité Robert de La Mennais), *Le Conservateur* 3 (1819): 440, quoted by Jean-René Derré, *Le renouvellement de la pensée religieuse en France de 1824 à 1834: essais sur les ori-gines et la signification du Mennaisisme* (Paris, 1962), p. 385. My thanks to Anne Levallois for pointing out this text to me.

    2. *Quod possumus videre in planetis, quia unusquisque tenet locum et ordinem suum, nec unus inpedit alterum.* From *Sententie Parisienses, pars. I, De Fide*, ed. Arthur Landgraf, *Ecrits théologiques de l'Ecole d'Abélard: textes inédits*, Spicilegium Sacrum Lovaniense, Etudes et documents, 14 (Leuven, 1934), p. 19, ll. 4–6.

The Church Fathers, and subsequently medieval social theorists, presented this cosmological foundation (in a Christian environment simply the trappings of transcendence) in such a way that every member of society, whatever his or her place in the hierarchy, was deemed to conform to an order that had its origin in the divine.

To antiquity's ancient storehouse, Christianity added elements that were innovative, not to say revolutionary. The writings of Saint Paul, which were fundamental to all later thinking about the Church as a community in its social and juridical aspects (which specialists sometimes refer to as "ecclesial" considerations), contributed greatly to the decentering promoted by Christianity's organic ways of thinking. The unity of the faithful in the Church, conceived as the body of Christ, was an ordered assembly of "many members" corresponding to the graces and actions of the Holy Spirit (1 Corinthians 12:12). But these "many members" were transcended by an ecclesial dynamic that, in the perspective of the Last Things, ascribed to the lowest the greatest necessity and honor. Above all, the apostle insisted upon the equality of the faithful in baptism and the absence of respect of persons in the call of God. Thus he maintained in a passage of his Epistle to the Galatians (3:28): "There is neither Jew nor Greek; there is neither bond nor free; there is neither male nor female. For you are all one in Christ Jesus." In the *militia* (army) that constituted the Christian society on earth, each must keep to his place and estate. But the perspective was that of a subsequent reversal of condition: from being "called in the Lord . . . a bondsman" to becoming "the freeman of the Lord" and from being "called . . . free" to becoming "the bondsman of Christ" (1 Corinthians 7:22).

Early Distinctions within Christian Society (4th–8th century)

The Christians of the apostolic era were collectively the group of the elect—*kleros* in Greek, *sors* in Latin, both words synonymously meaning Christ's portion, lot, or heritage.[3] When it became apparent that the Parousia (the Second Coming of Christ) was not imminent, the disciples of Christ made a place for themselves in space and time, which included making ecclesial arrangements that enabled them to "order the brotherhood."[4] Hence the appearance of the very earliest distinctions between the *plebs*, the faithful people, and the *clerus*, the governors within the communities of "the Lord's portion." From the end of the first century, as exemplified in the *First Epistle of Clement*, the term *sors* was applied exclusively to the clergy. Very soon, Christian authors—for example Tertullian in his *Exhortation to Chastity*—appealed to moral criteria in drawing the distinc-

3. Cf. Acts 1:17, regarding Judas, *qui connumeratus erat in nobis, et sortitus est sortem [kleron] ministerii huius*—"who was numbered with us and had obtained part of this ministry."

4. The title is that of Alexandre Faivre's book, *Ordonner la fraternité: pouvoir d'innover et retour à l'ordre dans l'Eglise ancienne* (Paris, 1992); the expression comes from Gustave Flaubert, *Bouvard et Pécuchet* (unfinished, 1881; Paris: Livre de Poche, 1959), p. 216.

tion between laity and clergy. Thus those who gave themselves to God alone, fleeing the contaminating influences of marriage and earthly goods, were not to be confused with all the others who remained attached to these vanities. The appearance of monasticism in the fourth century entailed the superseding of the dual classification clerics/laity in favor of a scheme of three orders of life or degrees of perfection, corresponding to the Old Testament figures Noah, Daniel, and Job (cf. Ezekiel 14:14): the clerics, responsible for leading the Christian people, the continent (the monks), and the married (the laity). Nevertheless the basic division obtaining throughout the whole of the Middle Ages remained that between the "two orders of Christians" (*duo genera Christianorum*) defined canonically by Gratian in his *Decretum* during the twelfth century.[5]

During the later Roman empire, the order of clerics, the *ecclesiasticus ordo* invoked by the *Theodosian Code* (16.5.26), acquired privileges that defined its juridical parameters: exemption from military service, freedom from the civil law, and above all immunity, namely, exemption from public liabilities, thereby permitting the establishment of ecclesiastical enclosures symbolically dedicated to the divine. A little later, when the popes in Rome were affirming the powers of Peter's successors in the face of the emperor, Pope Gelasius I (492–96) added the ballast of political theory to the series of distinctions that would henceforth define the clergy. Two orders (*uterque potestas, uterque ordo*) governed the world. That of the clerics possessed authority (*auctoritas*); the other, that of the monarchs, held power (*potestas*).[6] Hereafter the question would constantly arise which of the two, the authority or the power, had the prerogative. Gelasius established a "hierarchical dyarchy" or twinship, whereby the "power" acknowledged the precedence of the "authority" in spiritual matters and the "authority" that of the "power" in temporal matters.[7] But Gelasius's pronouncement was

5. Gratian, *Decretum*, IIa pars, causa 12, quaestio 1, cap. 7, in *Corpus Iuris Canonici*, ed. Friedberg (Leipzig, 1879), vol. 1, col. 678.

6. Gelasius I, *Ep.*, 12 (to Emperor Anastasius), *Epistolae Romanorum Pontificum . . . a S. Hilaro usque ad Pelagium II*, ed. Andreas Thiel, vol. 1 (Braunsberg, 1868), p. 350: *Duo quippe sunt . . . quibus principaliter mundus hic regitur: auctoritas sacra [sacrata] pontificum et regalis potestas. In quibus tanto gravius est pondus sacerdotum, quanto etiam pro ipsis regibus [hominum] Domino in divino reddituri sunt examine rationem. Nosti etenim, fili clementissime, quod licet praesideas humano generi dignitate, rerum tamen praesulibus divinarum devotus colla submittis, atque ab eis causas tuae salutis expetis [expectas], inque sumendis caelestibus sacramentis, eisque, ut competit, disponendis, subdi te debere cognoscis religionis ordine potius quam praeese.*—"Two things there are . . . whereby principally this world is governed: the holy [hallowed] authority of the pontiffs and regal power. And the responsibility of the priests is so much the heavier in that they shall render account to the Lord in the divine judgment concerning the very kings [of men] themselves. For you know, most gentle son, that, although you command by office in the human sphere, nonetheless you bow necks to the protectors of divine things and seek [expect] from them the sources of your own salvation, and in the receiving and due arranging of the heavenly sacraments you understand by the order of religion that you must be subject rather than lead."

7. Louis Dumont, *Essays on Individualism: Modern Ideology in Anthropological Perspective* (Chicago, 1986), pp. 45–52, esp. 52. [Rev. and augmented Eng. language ed. of *Essais sur l'individualisme: une perspective anthropologique sur l'idéologie moderne* (Paris, 1991 and 1993).]

used in canonical collections, above all from the 1050s on, to move the agenda significantly away from the notion of hierarchical complementarity. The orders no longer governed the "world" but the "Church": the world had been absorbed into the Church; the power was henceforth subordinate to the authority. "The priests of Christ are to be deemed the fathers and masters of kings, princes, and of all the faithful," Gratian declared, reproducing words from a letter of Gregory VII to Hermann of Metz.[8] This development was linked to the gradual affirmation of papal monarchy from the middle of the eighth century—with the forged Donation of Constantine, whereby the first Christian emperor was supposed to have relinquished to Pope Sylvester I the exclusive use of the imperial insignia—and to the emergence during the ninth century of the all-embracing notion of Christendom.[9]

Mystical Hierarchy and Orders: The Carolingian Turning Point (8th–10th century)

The Carolingian period was of capital importance in the development of thinking about the order of things. Transcending the erosion of kingdoms and laws that characterized the early centuries of the Middle Ages, both clerics and monarchs—from Charlemagne to Charles the Bald—desired to gather the faithful within one structure, the empire, conceived as the "house of God." The intellectual framework within which this political purposefulness was articulated consisted in updated models taken from antiquity and late antiquity. Of primary importance was Saint Paul's organicism—modeling a system on a living thing—which Augustine elaborated in *The City of God*. Carolingian theologians like Claudius of Turin returned to the Pauline and Augustinian image of the Church as the Body of Christ. The Church thus came to be conceived as a unity within the diversity of its members operating through the workings of peace and charity, regulatory principles that integrated differences into harmony.

The Dionysian Hierarchies

This elementary organicism was enriched, from the ninth century on, by cosmological refinements drawn from Platonist thought. The Latin west had been familiar with Plato's *Timaeus* since its translation by Calcidius in the fourth

8. Gratian, *Decretum*, Ia pars, dist. 96, cap. 9, in *Corpus Iuris Canonici*, vol. 1, col. 340: *Quis dubitet sacerdotes Christi regum et principum omniumque fidelium patres et magistros censeri?*—"Who would doubt that the priests of Christ should be deemed the fathers and masters of kings, princes, and all the faithful?" The quoted sentence is from Gregory VII; see *Das Register Gregors VII.*, 8.21, ed. Erich Caspar, 2 vols., *MGH* Epistolae selectae, 2.1–2 (Munich, 1920), vol. 2, pp. 544–63, here 553.

9. Jean Rupp, *L'idée de Chrétienté dans la pensée pontificale des origines à Innocent III* (Paris, 1939); Jan Van Laarhoven, "*Christianitas* et la Réforme grégorienne," in *Studi Gregoriani* 6 (1959–60): 1–98. Yves Congar, *L'ecclésiologie du haut Moyen Age de saint Grégoire le Grand à la désunion entre Byzance et Rome* (Paris, 1968), esp. pp. 65, 239, and 259.

century. Thanks to Hilduin and above all the ninth-century translator John Scotus Erigena, the west now had access to the work of Dionysius the Pseudo-Areopagite, a Neoplatonist writer whom western intellectuals long confused with Saint Paul's Athenian disciple.[10] This Dionysius, who was doubtless active in Syria around the year 500, reflected powerfully on the structures of the universe. His view was that Creation was organized in a hierarchy, celestial then ecclesiastical, distributed by degrees in a series of encapsulated triads from the top celestial order (Thrones, Cherubim, Seraphim) down to the "initiates" (the purified, holy people, monks) who on earth constituted the last level of the pyramid. This ternary structure was consonant with the two-way movement energizing Creation: the "procession" (*processio*) of the One through the different triads from top to bottom of the hierarchy, then the return of the created toward the One by three steps (purgation, illumination, union) of transparency and adhesion to the primordial light. This theological "procession" primarily connoted spiritual emanation, analogous to the mode whereby the Holy Spirit "proceeded" from the Father and the Son. But as far as social classification was concerned, the speculations of Pseudo-Dionysius offered a conceptual framework (the ternary structures sustaining the world's harmony), a propaedeutic (the ways of returning to the One), and constructs like "procession" and "function" that would enduringly influence medieval anthropological thinkers from the intellectuals of the court of Charles the Bald to the Scholastic theologians. The secret behind the success of the Dionysian construction lay in the dynamic that energized the whole hierarchy. Each level participated in the "procession" both upward and downward; wherever located in the pyramid, it participated equally in the outpourings associated with the return to the One.

The Three Functional Orders[11]

The sociology of Carolingian writers was nourished by a second living source inherited from antiquity, namely, the memory of Roman classification

10. Cf. Acts 17:34. On Dionysius the Ps.-Areopagite and his world, see René Roques, *L'univers dionysien: structure hiérarchique du monde selon le Pseudo-Denys*, Patrimoines Christianisme (Paris, 1983); his reception in the west by John Scotus Erigena is authoritatively treated by Edouard Jeauneau, "Pseudo-Dionysius, Gregory of Nyssa, and Maximus the Confessor in the Works of John Scottus Eriugena," in *Carolingian Essays: Andrew W. Mellon Lectures in Early Christian Studies*, ed. Uta Renate Blumenthal (Washington, D.C., 1983), pp. 137–49; reprinted in *Etudes érigéniennes*, Etudes augustiniennes (Paris, 1987), pp. 175–87.

11. Within a vast, yet largely obsolete, bibliography it will be enough to name as the three main works of reference: Georges Duby, *Les trois ordres ou l'imaginaire du féodalisme*, Bibliothèque des Histoires (Paris, 1978)—Eng. trans., *The Three Orders: Feudal Society Imagined*, trans. Arthur Goldhammer, with foreword by Thomas N. Bisson (Chicago, 1982); Edmond Ortigues, "Haymon d'Auxerre, théoricien des trois ordres," in *L'Ecole carolingienne d'Auxerre, de Muretach à Remi, 830–908*, Entretiens d'Auxerre 1989, ed. Dominique Iogna-Prat, Guy Lobrichon, and Colette Jeudy (Paris, 1991), pp. 181–227; Giles Constable, "The Orders of Society," in *Three Studies in Medieval Religious and Social Thought*, pp. 279ff. Bernard Sergent, *Les Indo-Européens: histoire, langue, mythes* (Paris, 1996), conveniently helps to place the issue in an Indo-European context.

categories. It was long believed that the Indo-European framework elucidated by Georges Dumézil—that of the three functions: the religious, the bellicose, and the generative—had disappeared over a long period before reemerging via complex routes of Celtic, Anglo-Saxon, and Frankish oral tradition in the late-tenth-century medieval west. However, this was to neglect the learned Latin route, which in fact reveals the uninterrupted knowledge of this functional framework throughout the entire early medieval period. This realization prompts a different question. When, how, and why did the Indo-European tripartite functionality turn into a Christian theory about the organization of society? That indeed is the real question.

The Carolingian political project was worked out with a conscious eye on Rome or at least on what Rome was supposed to have been. Once upon a time, there was Romulus and Rome. In the fourth century A.D., the writer Servius, in his *Commentary on the Aeneid*, assembled the greater part of the Latin classics that dealt with the Romulean legend concerning the three primitive tribes of Rome (the Ramnes, the Tities, and the Luceres). In his *Etymologies*, Isidore of Seville (570–636) showed his antiquarian talent by revisiting Servius, but confused Servius's Romulean division with the three ranks in the Roman republic: senators, soldiers, and plebeians (*senatores, milites, plebes*). In the Carolingian period, *De rerum naturis* (*De universo*) by Raban Maur reworked Isidore's *Etymologies*, giving them an allegorical spin. The Christianization of the Indo-European social framework was thus under way. Haymo, the master of the Auxerre school, which was particularly active under Charles the Bald, was last in this line of textual transmission. He was the first to propound the medieval theory of the three orders. Haymo was a Carolingian intellectual who was both fascinated by Roman antiquity and keen to discover the structures of a Christian empire. He therefore scrutinized the truths contained in Scripture, essentially the works of the apostle Paul and John's Apocalypse, in which he sought to distinguish some historic rationality. The two fundamental figures for him were Christ and Romulus. When expounding *debita* (debts or dues) in his *Commentary on the Epistle to the Romans*, Haymo spoke of the *obsequium* (service or allegiance) that all Saint Paul's Christian contemporaries owed as Roman subjects. By the clever use of etymology, he passed from what was due, the "tributes," to the "tribunes" who collected them, and on to the "tribes," namely, the three parts of Roman society founded by Romulus: the *senatores* (senators), *milites* (soldiers), and *agricolae* (cultivators). Thereby Haymo adapted Isidore's antiquarian recollections to the needs of early medieval rural society; the plebeians had been replaced by peasants. This was, however, only a preliminary framework designed to describe a pagan institution that still needed integration into the Church. At the beginning of his *Commentary on the Apocalypse*, Haymo turned the three parts of Roman civil society into the three orders of the Church, who together constituted an "ordered battle line" (*acies ordonnata*) marching toward the Parousia. They were: the *sacerdotes*, the clerics led by the bishops; the men of arms led by the princes; the indistinct troop of producers.

After the 860s, the theory of the three functional orders became a commonplace of political theology. The all-embracing structure of Christian society had been durably elucidated for the whole of the Middle Ages. All further developments were but modifications probably reflecting a given interest and harnessing all the *imaginaire du féodalisme*—the mentalities and presuppositions of feudal society—authoritatively studied by Georges Duby. The matter cannot be exhaustively explored here, but it is possible to distinguish four main versions of the theory of the three orders, namely, the monastic, the episcopal, the monarchic, and the Gregorian.

Heiric of Auxerre, a disciple of Haymo but also of John Scotus Erigena, placed his master's theory within the framework of the Dionysian hierarchies and endowed the three orders with a cosmological dimension. His main contribution lay in turning the threefold framework round to make the first function the third. This was no mere scholar's whim. Humanity was seen to operate within a mystic circle that made possible a return to God; the logic of that return implied that the excellent should come after the better and the good. Above all, Heiric envisaged the order of monks as embodying this highest degree of excellence, to the exclusion of the traditional representatives of the function of prayer, the clerics guided by the bishops. As champions of the rights of monks against episcopal prerogatives, the Cluniacs of the year 1000 used this monastic version of the theory of the three orders as a real battle plan in favor of their exemption and temporal sovereignty.[12]

The theorizing of Adalberon of Laon in his *Carmen ad Rodbertum regem* and the opinions ascribed to Gerard of Cambrai in *Gesta episcoporum cameracensium*—sources long regarded as the earliest witnesses of the resurgence in the medieval west of Indo-European-style trifunctionality—were simply an episcopal response to the monks' attempts to gain independence. Both defended the old order and held to Haymo's theory. Their view was that the function of prayer resided with the clerics, who were subject to the bishops' power of order and jurisdiction. Moreover, within Christian society, the bishops fulfilled the role of guides and tutors to the monarchs, who by virtue of their anointing were similar to bishops.

The two other versions were distinguished preeminently by the differing roles they assigned to monarchs in their frameworks. An example of the monarchic version is to be found in the translation of Boethius's *De consolatione philosophiae* ascribed to King Alfred the Great (871–99). In this classic case of the

12. Dominique Iogna-Prat, "Le 'baptême' du schéma des trois ordres fonctionnels: l'apport de l'école d'Auxerre dans la seconde moitié du IXe siècle," *AESC* 1986.1: 101–26; *"Agni immaculati": recherches sur les sources hagiographiques relatives à saint Maieul de Cluny (954–994)* (Paris, 1988), pp. 351–54.

types discerned by Georges Dumézil, the king was seen as supported by the "tripod" of his anointed status, his strength, and his fertility; he thereby served all three functions at once. The Gregorian model, on the other hand, denied monarchs any prerogative. According to Humbert of Silva Candida in his *Libri tres adversus Simoniacos*, only one order could exist within the Church, that of the clerics led by the pope: kings and emperors were only the most celebrated representatives of the second function, the lay power. During the struggle of the priesthood against the empire, the pope's supporters, like Humbert, pointed out that, since true kingship was spiritual, it was a simple matter to do without the representatives of the temporal power by dating concrete acts not by reference to a monarch's accession but by the "reign of Christ."

From Orders to Order (11th–13th century)

Writing to the bishops of Rouen, Tours, and Sens in order to determine a simple matter of ecclesiastical hierarchy, Gregory VII gave a robust definition of the order of things:

> It was for this reason that the providence of divine dispensation established that the various grades and orders should be distinct: that the lesser (*minores*) might revere the greater (*potiores*), and that the greater bestow loving care on the lesser, that out of diversity there might be fashioned one concord and a linking and correct administration of the individual offices come to pass. Nor could the universe (*universitas*) subsist were there no order of difference (*differentiae ordo*) to serve it. The example of the celestial hosts informs us that Creation can neither be governed nor live in one and the same equal condition. For, since there are angels and archangels, it is apparent that they are not equal, but as you know one differs from another in power and order. If, therefore, among those who are sinless such a distinction is evident, what man will refuse to submit cheerfully to such an arrangement? Hence it is that peace and charity embrace each other, and purity of concord (*concordiae sinceritas*) in mutual love pleasing to God remains steadfast: because every office is wholesomely discharged when recourse is possible to one overseer (*praepositus*).[13]

13. *Das Register Gregors VII.*, 6.35, 2:450–52, here 450–51 (punctuation modernized): *Ad hoc enim divine dispensationis provisio gradus et diversos constituit ordines esse distinctos, ut, dum reverentiam minores potioribus exhiberent et potiores minoribus dilectionem impenderent, una concordia fieret ex diversitate, contextio et recte officiorum gigneretur administratio singulorum. Neque enim universitas alia poterat ratione subsistere, nisi huiusmodi magnus eam differentie ordo servaret. Quia vero creatura in una eademque equalitate gubernari vel vivere non potest celestium militiarum exemplar nos instruit, quia, dum sint angeli sint archangeli, liquet quia non equales sunt, sed in potestate et ordine, sicut nosti, differt alter ab altero. Si ergo inter hos, qui sine peccato sunt, ista constat esse distinctio, quis hominum abnuat huic se libenter dispositioni submittere? Hinc etenim pax et caritas mutua se vice complectuntur et manet firma concordie in alterna et Deo placita dilectione sinceritas, quia igitur unumquodque tunc saluberiter completur officium, cum fuerit*

This letter combines a useful summary of traditional teaching with some decisive novelties. Divine foundations, an eschatological perspective, hierarchical distribution imitating that of the heavenly orders, and the harmonizing of differences within the *universitas*—all these were classic eleventh-century themes. On the other hand, the care shown in distinguishing the orders and drawing attention to a hierarchical superior were signs of new times. It does not greatly matter that the *praepositus* referred to here was the primate of the Gallican bishops. Behind him we sense the presence of one who was even then gaining a hitherto-unimagined role, the pope. The demarcation of one status or estate in life from another and the primacy of Peter's successor—such was the construction the Gregorian movement laid upon the notion of order.

The Gregorian Divide

In his *Libri tres adversus Simoniacos*, Humbert of Silva Candida, one of the main Gregorian ideologues, resolutely described the boundary separating the lay condition from the sacred order:

> Just as inside the walls of basilicas clerics are duly distinguished and marked out from laymen by place and office, so too on the outside they ought to be set apart by their business. Therefore let laymen dispose and provide only for their own concerns, which are secular, and clerics see to theirs alone, which are ecclesiastical. On either side, they have their own predetermined rules.[14]

The distinction between the two estates in life was not new, but in the eleventh century Gregorian clerics downgraded the role of the laity. Meanwhile they gave hitherto merely moral precepts the force and inviolability of the law.[15] To be free of money and sex was no longer simply an ideal, in truth relatively little practiced by the clerics of former centuries. It now became a duty, accompanied by interdicts, to avoid what was dubbed "simony" and "Nicolaitism."[16] The canons of the Roman synod of 1059 specified that no cleric should receive a church from a layman, demanded that the laity should restore ecclesiastical property (tithes,

---

unus ad quem possit recurri prepositus. Cf. Erigena, *Expositions on the "Celestial Hierarchy" of Saint Diony-sius,* 9.2, *PL* 122:214D–215A—trans.

14. Humbert de Silva Candida, *Libri tres adversus Simoniacos,* 9, *De differentia clericorum et laico-rum et de studio beati Gregorii in talibus,* ed. Friedrich Thaner, *MGH Ldl,* 1:208, beginning: *Nam si-cut clerici . . . .*

15. On the definition of the laity as residual (*un reste*), see Michel Grandjean, *Les laïcs dans l'Eglise: regards de Pierre Damien, Anselme de Cantorbéry, Yves de Chartres,* Théologie historique, 97 (Paris, 1994), esp. the first part regarding Peter Damian.

16. A convenient guide to the enormous literature will be found in Johannes Laudage, *Gregori-anische Reform und Investiturstreit,* Erträge der Forschung (Darmstadt, 1993), here, pp. 59ff., and in his *Priesterbild und Reformpapsttum im 11. Jahrhundert,* Beihefte zu Archiv für Kulturgeschichte, 22 (Cologne and Vienna, 1984).

first fruits, and oblations), and condemned priests who had wives or concubines. At the same time, the sexuality of the laity was regulated by ruling marriage unlawful within seven degrees of consanguinity.[17]

This rigid regulation of spheres of activity within Christian society aimed to avoid all confusion between the material and the spiritual, considered to be as distinct from each other as body and spirit. According to this logic, there remained fundamentally only one order, that of the clerics; the laity occupied an inferior position. The *ordo clericalis* (clerical order), through its exclusive possession of the "sacred"—everything directly connected with divine service and, more generally, all property dependent on the altar—controlled all access to the Scriptures and all power of sacramental mediation. The evolution of the rite of ordination during the early Middle Ages is, from this point of view, highly instructive.[18] The ancient ordination liturgy was simple, but the ritual elaborated during the Carolingian period contained a group of rites whose aim was to show, with a profusion of symbols, what grace and sacramental power accomplished in those who received them. Three centuries later, Peter Lombard expressed, in one of his *Sentences*, the force of this evolution:

> Order [ordination] may be said to be a small sign, i.e., something sacred (*sacrum quiddam*), whereby spiritual power is conveyed to the one ordained, and office with it. The spiritual character, where promotion of power occurs, is called order or grade.[19]

The laity, on the other hand, now had only indirect access to the sacred, as Claude Carozzi has rightly noted.[20] In order to participate in the eucharistic sacrifice and gain, through donation and devotion, a share in eternal life, they were utterly dependent on those whose profession was to "transform" the earthly into the heavenly, the clerics.

In the twelfth and thirteenth centuries, this strict discrimination between the two estates in life was cloaked, it may be said, in the mantle of grace. We saw earlier that the apostle Paul regarded the Church as an ordered assembly of "many members" according to the actions of the Holy Spirit (1 Corinthians 12:12). But the "sacramentalization" of this assembly took shape only much later, during the Gregorian period, when significantly the Church was affirming itself in a new institutional way. It was at this time that the "mystery" of the "sacra-

17. *Nicolai II. Concilium Lateranense prius*, 1059, ed. Ludwig Weiland, *Constitutiones et acta publica imperatorum et regum*, vol. 1 (Hanover, 1893), no. 384, pp. 546–48.

18. Pierre-Marie Gy, "Remarques sur le vocabulaire antique du sacerdoce chrétien," in *Etudes sur le sacrement de l'ordre*, Lex orandi, 23 (Paris, 1957), pp. 125–45.

19. *Sententiarum Libri IV*, 4.24.10, many eds. including *PL* 192:904.

20. Claude Carozzi, "D'Adalbéron de Laon à Humbert de Moyenmoutier: la désacralisation de la royauté," in *La Cristianità dei secoli XI e XII in Occidente: coszienza e strutture di una società*, Atti della ottava Settimana internazionale di studio, Mendola, 30 June–5 July 1980, Miscellanea del Centro di Studi Medioevali, 10 (Milan, 1983), pp. 67–84, here 83.

ment" was being clearly defined as the efficient sign of the grace it produced. The elaboration of the synthesis of the seven sacraments instituted by Christ also dates from this time. These comprised baptism, confirmation, the Eucharist, penance, extreme unction, marriage, and "order" (*ordo*, ordination—note the Latin term), the sacrament that marked access to the priesthood. The received morality regarding estates in life, endlessly refined in the pastoral content of letters of spiritual direction and sermons *ad status* (to particular estates in life), became increasingly unchallengeable, as people's behavior, at their given place in the hierarchy, was monitored as an outward sign of grace. The clerics, as dispensers of the sacraments, were invested with considerable prerogatives. As Thomas Aquinas was to note in his *De forma absolutionis*, delivering the sacrament of order was a *traditio potestatis* (a handing over of power) clearly signified by the consecrating pontiff, who spoke in the imperative mood: "Receive the power to do this or that." *Ordo* (ordination) conferred the *potestas* (power) to exercise a precise office.[21]

Order's "Head"

From the eleventh to the thirteenth century, a head gradually emerged at the top of the hierarchy, and, through a series of minor adjustments, a doctrine with a fine future before it gradually took shape, namely, papal primacy.[22]

The principle that the Church's primal see might be judged by no one had already long reflected the spiritual prestige that Rome and Peter's successors enjoyed. But during the Gregorian period, this spiritual ascendancy expanded into the juridical field. In both theory and practice, the pope was increasingly levered into an unchallengeable position as the very cornerstone of order. During the twelfth century the pope's usual title changed from "Vicar of Peter" to "Vicar of Christ."[23] In his treatise *De consideratione*, addressed to his disciple Pope Eugenius III, Bernard of Clairvaux contributed strongly to this construction of papal inviolability. He notes the innumerable biblical types that the pope embodies and the multiplicity of his roles:

> Who art thou? The great priest, the supreme pontiff. Thou art the prince of the bishops, thou art the apostles' heir, thou art in terms of primacy Abel, steersmanship Noah, patriarchy Abraham, ordination Melchizedek, office

21. On the *potestas* conferred by *ordo* (ordination), see the analysis by Paul Peuchmaurd, "Le prêtre ministre de la parole dans la théologie du XIIe siècle," *Recherches de théologie ancienne et médiévale* 29 (1962): 61ff.

22. An excellent introduction to this vast subject is Klaus Schatz, *La primauté du pape: son histoire, des origines à nos jours*, trans. Joseph Hoffmann (Paris, 1992), here pp. 135ff., from German, *Der päpstliche Primat: seine Geschichte von den Ursprüngen bis zur Gegenwart* (Würzburg, 1990); Eng. trans., *Papal Primacy: From Its Origins to the Present*, trans. John A. Otto and Linda M. Malony (Collegeville, Minn., 1996).

23. Michèle Maccarrone, *Vicarius Christi: storia del titolo papale*, Lateranum, new ser., 18 (Rome, 1952).

Aaron, authority Moses, judgeship Samuel, power Peter and unction Jesus Christ.[24]

This play upon unity within plurality brought the pope transparently close to another synthesizing figure, the Virgin.[25] It was standard procedure in medieval spiritual anthropology to use the words of history in order to give a human face to figures from which sprang the principles of order (kinship and hierarchical distribution): the mother of the God who was made man, at once virgin and mother, daughter, sister, and spouse; or indeed the pope, who encapsulated the complementary types of Abel, Noah, Abraham, Melchizedek, Aaron, Moses, Samuel, and Peter, all themselves synthesized by Christ, whose "vicar" he was. Having thus described the pope, Bernard of Clairvaux went on to ascribe to him, as governor of the whole Church, a "plenitude of power" radically different from the simple "share in responsibility" that characterized bishops, those rectors of their own flock alone.

The effect of subsequent legal developments was to confirm and normalize the pope's anomalous position. The early Middle Ages did not always draw neat distinctions between canon law and theology or scriptural referents. Essential distinctions arose during the twelfth century, the great period of reflections about the *ius divinum* (divine law) and the *ius naturale* (natural law), that is, between immutable norms rooted in Scripture and changing norms not simply of canon law but of the human world with all its instabilities.[26] Laws were seen as being of differing levels according to their proximity to the divine. From Innocent IV (1243–54) on, the pope was regarded as subject to the *ius divinum* and therefore above changing norms.

All this explains how the management of ecclesiastical lawsuits and senior personnel came to be subject to increasing centralization. Already starting in the tenth century, the creation of new dioceses needed papal authority; over two centuries (between 1200 and the end of the fourteenth century), the nomination of bishops became a Roman prerogative. Reversing centuries of practical collegiality, synods and councils became, in the second half of the eleventh century, assemblies of the pope. Equally, during the same period the pope began to regulate access to sainthood and the divine hierarchies, with the institution of a procedure for canonization, which became an exclusively papal privilege starting in

24. *De consideratione*, 2.8.15, in *Opera omnia*, vol. 3 (Rome, 1963), pp. 379–493, ll. 8–12; Eng. trans., *Five Books on Consideration: Advice to a Pope*, trans. John A. Anderson and Elizabeth T. Kennan, Cistercian Fathers Series, 37 (Kalamazoo, 1976).

25. See further, *Marie: le culte de la Vierge dans la société médiévale*, ed. Dominique Iogna-Prat, Eric Palazzo, and Daniel Russo (Paris, 1996).

26. Rudolf Weigand, "Das göttliche Recht, Voraussetzung der mittelalterlichen Ordnung," in *Chiesa diritto e ordinamento della 'societa christiana' nei secoli XI e XII*, Atti della nona Settimana internazionale di studio, Mendola, 28 August–2 September 1983, Miscellanea del Centro di Studi Medioevali, 11 (Milan, 1986), pp. 113–32.

Innocent III's time. Similarly, important lawsuits were progressively "reserved" to the pope.

THE MONKS, THE "DIS-ORDERED," AND THE "EXCLUDED"

In his *De ordine*, Augustine noted, "Where all things are good, the question of order does not arise."[27] Order was necessary only where good existed alongside evil. Unassailable at the summit of the hierarchy, the pope, the vicar of Peter and ultimately of Christ, did not err, defined the course the ship should follow, and corrected all who turned aside from it. His power was claimed to be universal; its scope extended not merely to Christians but to all unbelievers.[28] He was the guarantor of order, and any derogation from obedience to him was reckoned a heresy. The strict internal bipartition imposed by the Gregorians drove out to the margins all who did not conform.

The eleventh and twelfth centuries did not see the invention of social deviancy. But they did see the creation of a quite new social category, that of the excluded. As R. I. Moore has shown, it is significant that the age in which the mighty machinery of the Gregorian Church went into action was precisely that which saw the virtually simultaneous appearance of "groups at risk": heretics, Jews, Saracens, sodomites, and lepers.[29] It is possible to discern this simultaneity by simply cross-checking the chronology. Pope Leo IX (1049–54) launched the reform of the Church; Gregory VII (1073–85) radicalized it. It was during Gregory's pontificate that the struggle between the empire and the papacy reached its climax with the famous episode of Emperor Henry IV's penance at Canossa in 1077, well before a compromise could be arrived at between the "two swords" at the Concordat of Worms in 1122.[30] The years 1049–1122 were not simply vital to the institutional construction of the Church; they were central within the longer period during which the Latin west defined those whom it excluded and put in place the structures that produced "deviants." The process

27. *De ordine*, 2.1.2, *CSEL 29*, p. *107*, ll. *26–27*.

28. Innocent IV, *Commentaria super libros quinque Decretalium*, 3.34.8 (Frankfurt, 1570), f. 430r2, quoted by Gilbert Dahan, *Les intellectuels chrétiens et les juifs au Moyen Age*, Patrimoine judaïsme (Paris, 1990), p. 106 and n. 36. See also Alberto Melloni, *Innocenzo IV: la concezione e l'esperienza della cristianità come regimen unius personae* (Geneva, 1990), pp. 177–87.

29. Robert I. Moore, *The Formation of a Persecuting Society: Power and Deviance in Western Europe, 950–1250* (Oxford, 1987), and "Heresy, Repression, and Social Change in the Age of Gregorian Reform," in *Christendom and Its Discontents: Exclusion, Persecution and Rebellion, 1000–1500*, ed. Scott L. Waugh and Peter D. Diehl (Cambridge, 1995), pp. 19–46.

30. The bibliography is vast, but see Gerd Tellenbach, *The Church in Western Europe from the Tenth to the Early Twelfth Century*, Cambridge Medieval Textbooks (Cambridge, 1993), who currently provides the best introduction to eleventh- and twelfth-century ecclesiastical issues.

reached its logical conclusion when, in 1231, the Pontifical Inquisition was instituted. But the chronology of exclusion began in the 1020s, with a first wave of heresy in Italy (Monteforte, near Asti) and in western Francia (Orléans; Vertus, near Châlons-sur-Marne; Arras).[31] Apart from a further flare-up recorded on imperial territory at Goslar in 1052, it was not until after the turn of the century that there was again talk of heresy. It was as if the struggle between the papacy and the empire left no room for other areas of polemic.

In order of appearance, the ecclesiastical censors first noted Tanchelm, in Flanders, in the early 1100s. Then, between 1120 and 1140, came Peter of Bruis and Henry of Lausanne in the Alpine arc, southern Gaul, then (in the case of Henry of Lausanne) Maine; a contemporary flare-up occurred in Italy, where Arnold of Brescia roused the people of Rome against both the pope and the emperor.[32] After the 1150s, heretical groups arose that were altogether more important and difficult for the Church: Waldenses in Lyon and Cathars in the Rhineland, Languedoc, and Italy. The chronology of the struggle against the "infidels" (Jews and Saracens) was strictly parallel.[33] The Jews began to be worried in the 1010s, when in different parts of the Latin west there were distinct rumblings about the sacking of the Holy Sepulchre by the "prince of Babylon." Shortly afterward, the Jews were accused of blasphemy against the Cross, for example at Rome in 1020. In return, the tradition arose—attested from the first three decades or so of the eleventh century—of the ritual blow dealt to a Jew on Easter Sunday in memory of the Crucifixion. The struggle against infidels took on a new dimension with the first two Crusades (1096–99 and 1146–49), expeditions launched to regain the holy places from Islam and that were inspired by the eleventh-century Reconquista undertaken in the Iberian peninsula. The Crusades provoked, in parallel, early examples of persecution of the Jews. From the 1140s, Jews began to be accused of the ritual murder of Christian children. In 1182 Philip II Augustus expelled the Jews for the first time from the kingdom of France.

The intention of this book is not to write (or rewrite) a general history of exclusion in the Latin west of the eleventh and twelfth centuries. Others have already done this, and done it well. My inspiration comes from recent English or

31. For handy and reliable guidance to the huge bibliography on eleventh- and twelfth-century heresy, with useful internal references, see Carl T. Berkhout and Jeffrey B. Russell, *Medieval Heresies: A Bibliography, 1960–1979*, Subsidia Mediaevalia, 11 (Toronto: Pontifical Institute, 1981); Moore, *Formation of a Persecuting Society*; Grado G. Merlo, *Eretici ad eresie medievali*, Universale paperbacks Il Mulino, 230 (Bologna, 1989); Merlo, *Contro gli eretici: la coercizione all'ortodossia prima dell'Inquisizione* (Bologna, 1996); *Eretici ed eresie medievali nella storiografia contemporanea*, ed. Merlo, Bolletino della Società di Studi Valdesi, 174 (Torre Pellice, 1994).

32. Arsenio Frugoni, *Arnaldo da Brescia nelle fonte del duecento* (Rome, 1954; 2d ed., Turin, 1989); trans. into French as *Arnaud de Brescia dans les sources du XIIe siècle* (Paris, 1993).

33. Essential authorities are Dahan, *Les intellectuels chrétiens et les juifs*; Claude Cahen, *Orient et Occident au temps des Croisades* (Paris, 1982); Norman Daniel, *Islam and the West: The Making of an Image*, rev. ed. (Oxford, 1993).

American works that have sought to throw light on "minorities" emerging from a "majority" assailed by doubt.[34] I want to try to apprehend the "logic of Christendom" at work in the exclusion of those who were "different" and thereby attempt to understand how persecution and demonization of the Other could become a "structural necessity" for Christian society.[35] This vast question will be approached by looking at a precise case, that of an abbot of Cluny particularly active in defending the Church in the years 1120–50, Peter the Venerable. In his *Contra Petrobrusianos*, Peter explained that the Church was historically placed in a dual movement of, on the one hand, *dilatatio* (a struggle against enemies without) and, on the other, *purgatio* (a cleansing through struggle within).[36] Anxious to remain faithful to tradition, Peter endorsed this program by joining the battle on both fronts, denouncing wayward lay people—the unruly castellans whom he lambasted in his *De miraculis* and the Petrobrusian heretics—no less than the Jews and Saracens. His defense of Christianity (or rather Christendom, conceived as a social order coterminous with the Church) was a global project realized in the theological triptych comprising his *Contra Petrobrusianos*, *Adversus Iudeos*, and *Contra sectam Sarracenorum*. This theological corpus was given narrative expression in the short, exemplary stories of *De miraculis*. Peter's efforts heralded Alan of Lille's *De fide catholica contra hereticos*, which was directed at the Albigensian and Waldensian heretics, the Jews, and the Muslims.

The chapters that follow will enable the reader to follow Peter's ideological campaign. But before plunging into the detail of his writings, we need to understand why the abbot of Cluny is so good a witness. This is all the more necessary inasmuch as Ludo J. R. Milis's somewhat iconoclastic *Angelic Monks and Earthly Men* has had the effect of making it acceptable to minimize the importance of monasticism within medieval society.[37] What could a monk contribute

34. In addition to Moore's *The Formation of a Persecuting Society* and "Heresy, Repression, and Social Change," this type of approach has been driven by Gavin I. Langmuir, *History, Religion, and Antisemitism* (Berkeley, 1990), and *Toward a Definition of Antisemitism* (Berkeley, 1990), esp. part 2, chap. 5, pp. 100–133: "Doubts in Christendom"; see also Robert Chazan, "The Deteriorating Image of the Jews—Twelfth and Thirteenth Centuries," in Waugh and Diehl, *Christendom and Its Discontents*, pp. 220–33. On homosexuality, see John Boswell, *Christianity, Social Tolerance, and Homosexuality: Gay People in Western Europe from the Beginning of the Christian Era to the Fourteenth Century* (Chicago, 1980).

35. The term "logic of Christendom" (*logique du chrétienté*) comes from André Vauchez, "Diables et hérétiques: les réactions de l'Eglise et de la société en Occident face aux mouvements religieux dissidents, de la fin du Xe au début du XIIe siècle," in *Santi e demoni nell'Alto Medioevo occidentale (secoli V–XI)*, Settimane di Studio del Centro Italiano di Studi sull'alto Medioevo, 36, 15–21 April 1993, 2 (Spoleto, 1989), p. 600. The term "structural necessity" comes from Robert I. Moore, "A la naissance d'une société persécutrice: les clercs, les cathares et la formation de l'Europe," *Heresis* 6 (1993): esp. 14ff.

36. *CP*, 212, ll. 15–19.

37. Ludo J. R. Milis, *Angelic Monks and Earthly Men: Monasticism and Its Meaning to Medieval Society* (Woodbridge, 1992). Needless to say I do not share Milis's view.

to the "purgation" and "dilatation" of the Church? At least two answers will be supplied here. The first has to do with the general evolution of monasticism in the eleventh and twelfth centuries. The second is connected to Cluny's gradual orientation toward a spirituality of combat that ascribed increasingly preponderant, not to say obsessive, importance to the fight against Satan and the defense of the Church.

In the ideal functional Christendom depicted in the ninth century, the monk was normally excluded from pastoral tasks and restricted to praying for the salvation of all in the isolation of the cloister. He was not—except in an extreme emergency—called upon to involve himself in the world in order to defend the Church; in the tradition of ancient Christianity, he confined himself to exercising his office and function in retreat from the world. The situation changed with the reform driven by the papacy in the middle of the eleventh century. As Rolf Zerfaß has rightly observed, the pressing need to purify the Church sometimes forced contemplatives to leave the isolation of the cloister or the hermitage and leap into the arena.[38] John Gualbert (died 1073) quit Vallombrosa in order to go and fight against the Florentine clerics tainted by money and sex. Ariald, an activist in the Pataria (the rising of the laity against the simoniacal and Nicolaitan clergy of Milan, 1057–circa 1075), justified his intervention by reference to the ineluctable logic of the *ordines*, the orders of Christendom. If the first order was not (or was no longer) capable of discharging its obligations and preaching by example, then the other two functions, those of the "continent and married," must take over and substitute themselves for the "preachers."[39] Around 1100, the hermits of western France—Robert of Arbrissel, Bernard of Tiron, Vitalis of Savigny, William Firmat, and so on—were accordingly not only itinerant preachers who advertised the holiness of their lives but also apostles zealous to spiritualize the world. Calls to crusade and preaching against heretics were for Bernard of Clairvaux and the Cistercians modes of intervention among others in service of the ecclesiastical hierarchy.[40] Even the Carthusians, for all their isolation, had a strong presence in the world. In the *Confessio fidei* (profession of

38. Rolf Zerfaß, *Der Streit um die Laienpredigt: eine pastoralgeschichtliche Untersuchung zum Verständnis des Predigtamtes und zu seiner Entwicklung im 12. und 13. Jahrhundert* (Freiburg im B., Basle, and Vienna, 1974), pp. 124ff.

39. *Vita Arialdi*, 10, *MGH SS* 30.2, p. 1056, quoted by Zerfaß, *Der Streit um die Laienpredigt*, p. 128, n. 480. On the *Pataria*, see Cinzio Violante's classic study, *La Pataria milanese e la reforma ecclesiastica*, vol. 1 (Rome, 1955).

40. Jean Leclercq, "L'hérésie d'après les écrits de saint Bernard de Clairvaux," in *The Concept of Heresy in the Middle Ages (11th–13th c.)*, Proceedings of the International Conference, Leuven, 13–16 May 1973, ed. Willem Lourdaux and Daniel Verhelst, Mediaevalia Lovaniensia, ser. 1, Studia 4 (Leuven and The Hague, 1976), pp. 12–26; he notes, pp. 24–25, that relatively little of Bernard of Clairvaux's corpus is devoted to antiheretical outreach. See also Beverley M. Kienzle, "Tending the Lord's Vineyard: Cistercians, Rhetoric, and Heresy, 1143–1229, part 1: Bernard of Clairvaux, the 1143 sermons, and the 1145 preaching mission," *Heresis* 25 (1995): 35. I thank Pilar Jimenez for drawing my attention to Kienzle's article.

faith) that he made on his deathbed concerning the Eucharist, Bruno, the founder of the Carthusian order, instituted the tradition whereby doctrinal soundness was expected of every reclusive religious person.[41] From the earliest generations, the notion of preaching through copying books had become established. Guigo I explained the purpose behind it in his own customary:

> For whenever we copy books we seem to be fashioning for ourselves public criers of the truth. We hope for a reward from the Lord for all who through them are corrected from error or advance in the Catholic faith, as well as for all who have compunction for their sins and vices or are stirred up by them to aspire to the heavenly fatherland.[42]

The task of scribal copying, which turned a solitary into a "silent preacher" (*taciturnus praedicator*)—as Peter the Venerable said of a recluse—was intended to fight "error" (including heresy) by the dissemination of orthodox literature.[43]

Alongside these new monastic and eremitic movements, the Cluny of the eleventh and twelfth centuries—regarded as a paradigm of traditional black (Benedictine) monasticism—made its own particularly radical contribution to the policy of ordering Christendom and of subsuming the world within the Church, in that it identified itself with the head of order and saw itself as Rome. Let us now see how this came about. We shall need first an outline history of the Burgundian sanctuary in the eleventh and twelfth centuries, analyzing in detail the Cluniac monastic model.

41. *Lettres des premiers Chartreux, SC*, 88 (Paris, 1962), pp. 90–92.

42. Guigo I, *Consuetudines Cartusiae*, 28.4, ed. and trans. anon. into French under title *Coutumes de Chartreuse, SC*, 313 (Paris, 1984), pp. 224–25.

43. *Ep.*, 20, 1:38–39.

2

A MONASTIC CHURCH
WITHIN THE CHURCH

A BRIEF HISTORY OF CLUNY IN THE
ELEVENTH AND TWELFTH CENTURIES

On 11 September 910, William III, duke of Aquitaine and count of Mâ-con, later known as William the Pious, presented Berno, the abbot of Baume-les-Messieurs and several other monastic establishments in the Berry and Jura, with a *villa* near Mâcon for the purpose of founding there a Benedictine monastery having the apostles Peter and Paul as its patrons.[1] In the foundation charter William gave up all rights over the establishment, yielded to the community the right to freely elect its abbot, and placed the monastery directly under papal protection. Such terms were to provide Cluny with conditions favoring the emergence and establishment of a form of monasticism that would be independent of spiritual and temporal authority down to the 1200s.

In his testament of 926 Berno nominated his disciple Odo as his successor at Cluny, and it was during Odo's abbacy (927–42) that the monastery really began to take shape. Cluny would bear the stamp of Odo's culture, ecclesiology, and reforming ideas for a long time to come. In 931, a privilege of Pope John XI gave to Cluny's abbot the right to take over and reform any monastery whose lay abbot requested it, as well as the right to admit any monk whose own monastery rejected reform. Odo was thus summoned to Rome, to Fleury-sur-Loire, to Aquitaine, and launched the Cluniac tradition of reform, which was to remain a personal activity and responsibility of the abbot until the close of Majolus's abbacy in 994.

Following the abbacy of Aymardus (942–54), significant for the increase in Cluny's property, the abbacies of Majolus (954–94) and Odilo (994–1049) rep-

---

1. Only a brief outline can be given here of Cluny's history in the eleventh and twelfth centuries. For more detail, see Joachim Wollasch, *Cluny, Licht der Welt. Aufstieg und Niedergang der klösterlichen Gemeinschaft* (Zurich/Düsseldorf, 1996). For the second half of the twelfth century, see Denyse Riche, "L'Ordre de Cluny de la mort de Pierre le Vénérable à Jean II de Bourbon. Le 'Vieux Pays clunisien,'" doctoral diss., 4 vols., typescript, Université Lumière-Lyon II, France, 1991.

resented a watershed in Cluny's development. Around the millennium, Berno's foundation became an important sanctuary round which a township, a *villa*, and a lordship took shape. When in 981 the second church (traditionally referred to as "Cluny II") was consecrated, the monastery acquired the relics of the apostles Peter and Paul and turned itself to some extent into a "little Rome." The same period saw Cluny become an autonomous sanctuary owing to a privilege of exemption granted by Gregory V in 998 and extended by John XIX in 1024 to all Cluniacs "wherever they may be." John's measure marked the real birth of the *Ecclesia cluniacensis* (the Cluniac Church) as an ecclesiastical network of abbeys and priories with the Burgundian sanctuary at its center. The autonomy of the Ecclesia cluniacensis was given concrete expression in writings intended to proclaim the monastery's sovereignty. The hagiography of its abbots, beginning with Majolus around the year 1000 and concluding with Abbot Hugh of Semur (died 1109), enabled the community, free from episcopal tutelage, to identify itself with a head figure who gained in majesty as one generation succeeded another.[2] The compiling of cartularies, begun toward the end of Odilo's abbacy but carried through essentially under that of Hugh of Semur, gave the Ecclesia cluniacensis an archive in which its assets and privileges could be recorded. They suggest how the modest monastery of the early days succeeded in expanding right across Latin Christendom by the early twelfth century.[3]

The usages of this monastic church were codified in customaries that updated and extended the Rule of Saint Benedict. The first such customs known, the *Consuetudines antiquiores* of the time of Majolus, were strictly liturgical; the second, the *Liber tramitis aevi Odilonis*, regulated both the internal life of the monastery and the community's relations with external powers (bishops, kings, emperors, etc.); the last we know of, the *Ordo Cluniacensis* and the *Antiquiores consuetudines cluniacensis monasterii*, often known simply as "Bernard's Customs" and "Ulrich's Customs" after their respective authors, contemporaries of the sixth abbot, Hugh of Semur, are in similar vein and undertake to give the monastery's sovereignty a legal form. This was all the more necessary as the Cluniacs had, by the turn of the millennium, become sovereign lords in their own right. Like

<hr />

2. Dominique Iogna-Prat, "Panorama de l'hagiographie abbatiale clunisienne (v. 940–v. 1140)," in *Manuscrits hagiographiques et travail des hagiographes*, ed. Martin Heinzelmann, Beihefte der Francia, 24 (Sigmaringen, 1991), pp. 77–118.

3. The best introduction to the complex issue of Cluny's three cartularies (A, B, and C) is by Maria Hillebrandt, specifically her "Les cartulaires de l'abbaye de Cluny," *Mémoires de la Société pour l'histoire du droit et des institutions des anciens pays bourguignons, comtois et romans* 50 (1993): 7–18. On the cartularies' commemorative aspect, their mix of transcribed charters with narrative, see Dominique Iogna-Prat, "La geste des origines dans l'historiographie clunisienne des XIe–XIIe siècles," *RB* 102 (1992): 135–91; also Patrick J. Geary, "Entre gestion et *gesta*," in *Les Cartulaires*, proceedings of conference jointly organized by the Ecole des Chartes and CNRS research group 121, Paris, 5–7 December 1993, ed. Olivier Guyotjeannin et al., Mémoires et Documents de l'Ecole des Chartes, 39 (Paris, 1993): 13–26, esp. 16, and Patrick J. Geary, *Phantoms of Remembrance: Memory and Oblivion at the End of the First Millennium* (Princeton, 1994), pp. 103–7.

other lay or ecclesiastical castellans, they had acquired the former prerogatives of royal power, particularly justice. The distinguishing feature of their lordship was the protection of their liberties by primarily "spiritual" means, such as defending church enclosures during the movements of the Peace and of the Truce of God, or later creating the Cluniac "sacred ban" during the papacy of the Cluniac pope, Urban II. Thus during the years of the Church's reform Cluny provided a small-scale trial of a much greater historical process, namely, the territorialization of the *libertas ecclesiae*, the "freedom of the Church" declared by the Gregorian Reform.

Under Abbots Majolus and Odilo—from 954 to 1049—Cluny's power was preeminently regional; it was present in Burgundy, the Auvergne, Provence, and in Italy along the road to Rome. But during Hugh of Semur's abbacy, from 1049 to 1109, Cluny's influence extended into the four corners of Europe and, after the First Crusade (1095–9), into the Holy Land. Toward the north, the Cluniacs established important dependencies in the Capetian kingdom—in particular the priory of Saint-Martin-des-Champs in Paris. After the conquest of England in 1066 by the duke of Normandy, the Cluniacs contributed to William the Conqueror's push for monastic reconstruction. In return, the English kings and their dependents gave Cluny financial support. Henry I of England (1100–1135) contributed to the building of the third Cluny church ("Cluny III"), the *maior ecclesia* (greatest church) of Christendom, whose construction was undertaken by Hugh of Semur. To the east, in spite of all the close and venerable ties with the empire from the time of the Ottonian and Salian sovereigns, the Cluniac push met with more difficulty. The independent spirit of the monks of Burgundy ran up against the logic of the imperial ecclesiastical system in which the emperor and his *fideles* (faithful men), particularly the bishops, had the upper hand over monastic establishments. It was therefore only quite late—during the second half of the eleventh century and often through the adoption of Cluniac customs by monasteries that remained juridically independent (Saint Blaise, Hirsau, Siegburg)—that Cluny penetrated the imperial world. Toward the southwest, the Cluniacs answered the call of Sancho III, the Great, of Navarre, and above all of Alfonso VI of Castile-León. They thus participated in the political and religious reconquest of the Iberian peninsula and contributed to the replacement of Mozarabic liturgy by the Roman. The sovereigns and aristocracy of the peninsula discovered Cluny to be not simply an instrument of ecclesiastical politics but also a "Roman" sanctuary under the patronage of Peter and Paul, whose ministrant monks, from the time of Abbot Odilo, originator of the Feast of the Dead on 2 November (All Souls), were great specialists in providing assistance in the afterlife. Conversely, the Cluniacs regarded Spain as a tributary land providing the hard cash necessary to their economy, one structurally dependent on gifts. Thus the construction of Cluny III was in large part financed out of the Spanish *cens* (tribute).

The development and growing organization of the Ecclesia cluniacensis dur-

.

ing Hugh of Semur's abbacy coincided with the great reform of the Church that tends to be described as the "Gregorian Reform" after Gregory VII, the pope under whose leadership it took place. This was also the time of the investiture controversy, the quarrel between the empire and the papacy during the course of which the papal authority strove to affirm and enforce its preeminence over the imperial power. The Cluniacs were directly involved in the reform movement as an instrument of the papacy. Various examples of the tendency may be cited: Hugh of Semur's goodwill mission as go-between for Henry IV and Pope Gregory VII at Canossa in 1077; papal delegations of Hugh and then of his successor Pontius of Melgueil (abbot 1109–22); admission of brothers of Cluny into the pontifical *curia*; participation in the constitution of a chamber of accounts (*camera*) by Peter Gloc after the Cluniac model; finally, the accession of Cluniacs to the episcopate and cardinalship, not to mention the papacy in the person of Urban II, the pope of the First Crusade. In return, Cluny's fate depended very much on Rome. The Cluniac network is often represented as constituting a sort of autonomous ecclesiastical state, structured hierarchically, pyramid-style, from the parent abbey at the apex down to the abbeys and priories that were its subjects below. Yet this is to overlook the pope, the essential intermediary who, from Gregory VII on, exercised the right to create or abolish religious institutions and was capable of going back on privileges conceded by his predecessors. The development of Cluny during the eleventh, twelfth, and thirteenth centuries was beset with endless disputes between the Burgundian monastery and this or that rebellious dependency, including some ancient and prestigious abbeys like Saint-Gilles-du-Gard, Vézelay, or Baume-les-Messieurs, which refused to submit to an "archabbot." In such quarrels between institutions belonging to Rome's direct jurisdiction, the pope would arbitrate in response to his own present needs, and these did not always necessarily coincide with those of Cluny.

During Pontius of Melgueil's abbacy, from 1109 to 1122, the Ecclesia cluniacensis underwent an earth-shattering experience whose exact character still largely eludes historical analysis.[4] Like other periods of inner confrontation that have riven the Church from time to time—in particular the crisis provoked by the opposition to Pope Innocent II by the antipope Anacletus II from 1130 to 1138—this troubled period in Cluny's history is dubbed one of "schism." It seems that there were two factions within the monastery, probably born of hostility between two castellan families represented at Cluny by family members among the brothers. That said, it is not clear who was against whom or indeed what role the inhabitants of the bourg of Cluny played in the affair. At all events, Pontius of Melgueil resigned as abbot and went off to Jerusalem on pilgrimage. On his return he had a change of heart and tried to reenter Cluny by force. He was condemned by the pope and ended his days in Rome.

4. A guide to the contradictory and voluminous bibliography concerning this subject is J. Wollasch, "Das Schisma des Abtes Pontius von Cluny," *Francia* 23.1 (1996): 31–52.

Pontius's "schism" coincided with a profound challenge to the Cluniac model of monasticism presented by newer religious movements of eremitic and monastic expression, such as the Cistercians and the Carthusians. After a brief interregnum of three months—the short abbacy of Hugh II—a dynamic young abbot was elected, Peter of Montboissier, who since the end of the twelfth century has been called "the Venerable." His governance, from 1122 to 1156, was another time of change. A series of statutes completed, or rather amended, the monastery's customs, and life at Cluny (whose lordly grandeur and liturgical splendor had given rise to criticism) was made more rigorous and austere. With the assistance of Henry of Winchester, Peter worked to convert the economy of the monastery from its structural dependence upon gifts to a direct, more rational exploitation of its own domain. Like Hugh of Semur, and to a degree Pontius of Melgueil, Peter was very involved in affairs of his day, though he differed from all his predecessors in the extent to which he also involved himself in doctrinal matters. In his *Contra Petrobrusianos*, he labored against the Petrobrusian heretics; in *Adversus Iudeos*, he joined his voice to the anti-Judaism associated with the Second Crusade; in *Contra sectam Sarracenorum* he demonized Islam. In his *De miraculis*, which blends edifying anecdotes with theological and ecclesiological teachings, and in his sermons and letters, which often amount to small treatises in their own right, he sought to depict Cluny as a universal Church, the ultimate ecclesial embodiment, both a refuge for the laity and a meeting place for all the various sorts and conditions of members belonging to the sacred order: priests, bishops, cardinals, popes, on the one hand; monks, hermits, and recluses, on the other. Among the recluses were those of Marcigny-sur-Loire, which was the personal foundation of Hugh of Semur.

The year 1132 saw Peter convene a general chapter, and this is often regarded as a first step toward greater collegiality and a less absolutist abbacy at the heart of the Ecclesia cluniacensis. Not, however, until the statutes of Hugh V, abbot from 1199 to 1207, did the practice of holding a yearly chapter-general become an institutional routine, in imitation of Cistercian usage. Thereafter it is possible to speak of an "order" structured by provinces whose establishments received periodic visits. Cluny would continue to play a core role in Benedictine monasticism right down to the end of the ancien régime in 1789. But it was never to recapture the measure of influence it attained in the tenth, eleventh, and twelfth centuries. The order's progressive retreat within the frontiers of the kingdom of France was, by an irony of history, accompanied by subjection to a twofold tutelage. The first was that of the king, who in the thirteenth century was granted protection of a fair number of Cluniac establishments, and who in 1281 assimilated the justice of the Cluniac lordship into the royal system of justice. The second and more important tutelage was that of the pope, who by the end of the twelfth century was acting within the order as a superior authority, able to dismiss the abbot as his own needs dictated. His control became even more radical in the fourteenth century, with the commendam system, whereby the pope could nominate the abbot of Cluny and the other abbots and principal priors of the order.

Such, in very rough summary, is the "received" history of Cluny, the foundations of which were laid out in his great synthesis by Ernst Sackur in the early 1890s, and which was criticized, corrected, altered, and extended over the twentieth century.[5] It is a product of the "philologico-combinatory method," the process of putting order into history, arranging—as if they were components of a coherent whole—sources of diverse dates, character, and reliability in such a way as to end up with an account with no gaps, in which the story's unbroken thread unwinds according to the implacable prescription willed by the historian in his role as deus ex machina.[6] Over the last twenty years a great many studies have facilitated a close reexamination of the documentary basis of the "received" version, and provided (or begun to provide) critical tools enabling historians to avoid the pitfalls of the philologico-combinatory method.[7] This reexamination has, among other things, made it possible to look afresh at the question of the exact nature and importance of the Cluniac monastic model in the framework of the Church's reform of the eleventh and twelfth centuries. In the absence of a satisfactory synthesis in the matter, we need for our present purposes to take stock by taking a detailed look at the Cluniac "Church system."

CLUNY AS A "CHURCH SYSTEM"

In his *Contra haereticos*, Hugh of Amiens, a monk of Cluny who became archbishop of Rouen from 1130 to 1164, reported that his adversaries rudely demanded the faithful to give a definition of the Church: "You who propose to follow the 'Church of God,' tell us what it is, where it is, and why it is."[8] Such an urgent call to elucidate the *quid, ubi,* and *quare* implicit in the constitution of the visible Church marks the beginning, in the antiheretical writings of the eleventh and twelfth centuries, of ecclesiological reflections that have conventionally been dated later, with the earliest treatises *de vera Ecclesia* around 1300.[9] The problem of the apostolic basis of the tradition and the question of mediation be-

5. Ernst Sackur, *Die Cluniacenser und ihrer kirchlichen und allgemeingeschichtlichen Wirksamkeit bis zur Mitte des elften Jahrhunderts*, 2 vols. (Halle, 1892–94).

6. On the dangers of such a method, see Arsenio Frugoni, *Arnaud de Brescia dans les sources du XIIe siècle* (Paris, 1993), pp. 1–2. [French trans. of *Arnaldo da Brescia nelle fonte del duecento* (Rome, 1954; 2d ed., Turin, 1989).]

7. For an attempted critical assessment based on major works published from 1984 to 1994, see Dominique Iogna-Prat and Christian Sapin, "Les études clunisiennes dans tous leurs états," *RM*, n.s., 5 (1994): 233–58.

8. *PL* 192:1294D.

9. Yves Congar, *L'église, de saint Augustin à l'époque moderne*, Histoire des dogmes, 3.3 (Paris, 1970), pp. 205–9; on the appearance of the earliest separate treatises of ecclesiology, circa 1300, see pp. 270ff.

tween *visibilia* and *invisibilia* (iconic, sacramental, or priestly)—such mediation being thought unnecessary by some, indispensable by others—were crucial issues in the history of a Christianity "long hesitating between the organization of a Church and that of a sect."[10] As Yves Congar has noted, Peter the Venerable's role in this prehistory was of prime importance, and his *Contra Petrobrusianos* in particular was effectively a *De vera Ecclesia* in outline and before its time.[11]

There are two questions to answer. First, what do we mean by a "Church system"? Second, in what sense can a monastic church like Cluny in its own right constitute a "Church system"? As to the first, historians interested in Cluny have learned from the "school of Münster"—and from Joachim Wollasch and Gert Melville in particular—to banish the term "order" from their vocabulary until around 1200 and opt instead when writing about the tenth to twelfth century for the term *Ecclesia cluniacensis*.[12] In truth the word "order" is an inadequate term to use prior to the reforms imposed upon Cluny by the papacy. Taking their cue from Cistercian customs, these papal reforms were to turn Cluny into an institution composed of a group of establishments structured by provinces in which the traditionally monarchic abbacy was henceforth tempered by the collegiality of an annual chapter-general, itself a representative and executive organ possessed of clearly defined areas of judicial competence.[13] Joachim Wollasch and his followers have much reflected upon the notion of the Ecclesia cluniacensis.[14] Its gradual restructuring from the informal network of its early days to the "body" so deeply involved in the life of the Church in the Gregorian age has been the subject of a careful analysis by Dietrich Poeck.[15] Elsewhere, excellent work has been done by Glauco Maria Cantarella and Jean-Pierre Torrell on Cluniac ecclesiology, that is to say on the theology of the *Ecclesia* developed at Cluny,

10. A distinction established by Ernst Troeltsch, *Die Sociallehren der christlichen Kirchen und Gruppen*, in *Gesammelte Schriften*, vol. 1 (Tübingen, 1912), pp. 358ff. (regarding medieval sects); the formula here is borrowed from Jean Séguy, *Christianisme et société: introduction à la sociologie d'Ernst Troeltsch* (Paris, 1980), pp. 174–75.

11. Yves Congar, *L'église, de saint Augustin à l'époque moderne*, p. 205, n. 29; Congar, "Eglise et cité de Dieu chez quelques auteurs cisterciens à l'époque des Croisades, en particulier dans le *De Peregrinatione civitate Dei* d'Henri d'Albano," in *Mélanges offerts à Etienne Gilson* (Paris and Toronto, 1959), pp. 173–202, here 191, n. 85.

12. Joachim Wollasch, *Mönchtum des Mittelalters zwischen Kirche und Welt*, Münstersche Mittelalter-Schriften, 7 (Munich, 1973), pp. 157ff.

13. Gert Melville, "Die cluniazensische *Reformatio tam in capite quam in membris*. Institutioneller Wandel zwischen Anpassung und Bewahrung," in *Sozialer Wandel im Mittelalter: Wahrnehmungsformen, Erklärungsmuster, Regelungsmechanismen*, ed. Jürgen Miethke and Klaus Schreiner (Sigmaringen, 1994), pp. 249–97.

14. Joachim Wollasch, *Mönchtum des Mittelalters*, pp. 157ff. and 178; the literature makes indifferent use of the terms *Ecclesia cluniacensis* and *Cluniacensis ecclesia*.

15. Dietrich Poeck, *"Cluniacensis Ecclesia": der cluniacensische Klosterverband (10.–12. Jahrhundert)*, Münstersche Mittelalter-Schriften, 71 (Munich, 1997).

essentially during Peter the Venerable's time as abbot.[16] Amid such a wealth of modern research, my aim here is to shift the focus somewhat and attempt a general appraisal of the notion of a Cluniac "Church system." Peter the Venerable's abbacy is a peculiarly apt moment for such an appraisal. First, the years of his abbacy, from 1122 to 1156, embody both an ending of sorts and a reorientation, prefacing the change from ecclesia to order and witnessing the beginnings of collegial mechanisms such as the chapter-general. Second, the rising power of new models of monasticism forced Cluny to reform while at the same time defending the excellence of its own tradition, especially against Cîteaux and Clairvaux. The task led Peter the Venerable not simply to describe but to theorize about the institution of Cluny. Last, Peter's period deserves special attention because no other abbot in Cluny's history had become so caught up in defending the Church, targeting the Church's enemies—the Petrobrusian heretics, the Jews, the Saracens—in treatises that constituted a coherent ecclesiological *Summa* far in advance of the tradition of treatises *de vera Ecclesia*.

Our second question remains: How are we to justify applying the notion of a "Church system" to a monastic church?[17] Indeed, what are we to understand by "system"? In his *Rules of Sociological Method*, Emile Durkheim stated the principle that any sociological analysis of an institution amounted to an elucidation of the causes that brought it into being and the function that enabled it to continue.[18] The task thus is "to explain an institution from the structure of the interaction system within which it appeared and is maintained."[19] System in effect equals function and vice versa. The society within which the Cluniac "Church system" arose was organized in "functional orders" whose interaction made up Christendom. As we saw earlier, the society of orders was a hierarchic organic structure stretching out toward the afterlife, at whose core the function of prayer tended to include the two other functions, the three "orders" being destined in the life to come to reduce themselves to the single "order" that was embodied already in the here and now by the clerics.

Here we need to pause a moment or two and consider the notion of "inclu-

---

16. Glauco M. Cantarella, "Un problema del XII secolo: l'ecclesiologia di Pietro il Venerabile," *Studi Medievali*, 3d ser., 19 (1978): 159–209; Cantarella, "Cultura ed ecclesiologia a Cluny (sec. XII)," *Aevum* 55.2 (1981): 272–93; Jean-Pierre Torrell, "L'Eglise dans l'oeuvre et la vie de Pierre le Vénérable," *Revue thomiste* 77 (1977): 357–92 and 558–91.

17. The notion of a "Cluniac system" was created by Georg Schreiber to describe the "congregation" having Cluny at its center (*Kongregationsmittelpunkt*). Schreiber, *Kurie und Kloster im 12. Jahrhundert*, 2 vols., Kirchenrechtliche Abhandlungen, 65–66 (Stuttgart, 1910).

18. Emile Durkheim, *Les règles de la méthode sociologique* (Paris, 1895), pp. 89–123: chap. 5: "Règles relatives à l'explication des faits sociaux" [Eng. trans., *The Rules of Sociological Method and Selected Texts on Sociology and Its Method*, trans. W. D. Halls, ed. Steven Lukes (London, 1982), chap. 5, "Rules for the Explanation of Social Facts"].

19 *A Critical Dictionary of Sociology*, ed. Raymond Bourdon, François Bourricaud, and Peter Hamilton (London, 1989), s.v. "function," pp. 176–80, here 178.

sion." Ernst Troeltsch and Max Weber considered that the "process of rationalization" that turned western society into a "totality" (*Einheitskultur*) reached maturity during the Gregorian period. At that time all areas of social life became Christianized (*Christianisierung*) and were subsumed by the Church (*Verkirchlichung*).[20] The rationalization process was marked by a dual movement of integration and exclusion. The latter term is as applicable to the experience of the heretics of the eleventh and twelfth centuries, who paid the price of the institutionalization of the Church, as it is to that of the "infidels," the Jews and Saracens, whom Christianity sought to reduce in the expansionary movements accompanying the first two Crusades (1095–1149). At the other extreme, integration is a force for inclusion and not for assimilation—which is a way of saying that the "society of orders" of the Middle Ages achieved unity in plurality.[21] Thus the "active otherworldly ascetics," the monks, found inclusion in the visible Church;[22] Max Weber goes so far as to regard this "active asceticism" as a force of intervention in the service of the papacy.[23] More recently, Louis Dumont has described the relationship between the phenomenon of renunciation and the world as one of an "ordered dichotomy" imaged as two concentric circles, the enclosed space between which ever expands in the course of history because "the paramount value will exert pressure upon the antithetical worldly element encapsulated within it. By stages worldly life will thus be contaminated by the otherworldly element, until finally the heterogeneity of the world disappears entirely."[24]

Taking our cue from Ernst Troeltsch, Max Weber, and Louis Dumont, we might say that the space enclosed between the circles became greater and greater in the Gregorian age; it was a period of active ecclesiastical intervention in the world, and the goal was a general conversion to "order." The program of action

20. For an excellent presentation of the problems, see Wolfgang Schluchter, *Religion und Lebensführung*, (Frankfurt am Main, 1988), 2:443–53.

21. Schluchter, *Religion und Lebensführung*, pp. 448–49, after Talcott Parsons, *Sociological Theory and Modern Society* (New York, 1967), pp. 23ff.

22. The description "active otherworldly ascetics" is used by Max Weber when discussing the phenomenon of "rejection of the world" in his chapter "Zwischenbetrachtung: Theorie der Stufen und Richtungen religiöser Weltablehnung," in *Gesammelte Aufsätze zur Religionssoziologie* (Tübingen, 1920), 1:536–73 [Eng. trans., "Religious Rejections of the World and Their Directions," essay 13 in *From Max Weber: Essays in Sociology*, trans. and ed. H. H. Gerth and C. Wright Mills with new preface by Bryan S. Turner (London, 1991), pp. 323–59]. The phenomenon of the monks' ecclesial "inclusion" is analyzed by Ernst Troeltsch, *Sociallehren* (see above, note 10), in a chapter (pp. 226–38, esp. 231) concerned with medieval asceticism.

23. See Schluchter, *Religion und Lebensführung*, p. 448, and Barbara H. Rosenwein, "Reformmönchtum und der Aufstieg Clunys. Webers Bedeutung für die Forschung heute," in *Max Webers Sicht des okzidentalen Christentums. Interpretation und Kritik*, ed. Wolfgang Schluchter (Frankfurt am Main, 1988), p. 280.

24. Louis Dumont, *Essays on Individualism: Modern Ideology in Anthropological Perspective* (Chicago, 1986), pp. 31–32 [rev. and augmented Eng. trans. of *Essais sur l'individualisme: une perspective anthropologique sur l'idéologie moderne* (Paris, 1991 and 1993)].

took various forms, but all are traceable to the one original way of designing and achieving "inclusion," namely, by taking over secular affairs. It owed its variety to the fact that in the Gregorian age and thereafter the Church was divided into so many branches: clerics, canons regular, traditional black monks (like the Cluniacs), reformed monks (like the Cistercians), eremitic orders (like the Carthusians), not to mention mendicant orders. Nevertheless it is possible to sort this multiplicity into just three modes of "inclusion": traditional monasticism; eremitism; the preaching orders. Our chief concern is with the first of these, but we need to mention the other two. The development of the last named, the preaching orders of Dominicans and Franciscans, coincided with the rapid development of towns in the medieval west. Their members were itinerant, and their sphere of action lay in the thick of secular life. Their action inspired, but it also excluded—witness the antiheretical pastoral effort of the Dominicans. In the midst of a world of urban turbulence, they created small societies of world renouncers ordered according to their degree of conversion, and comprising religious (men or women of the first and second orders) and laity constituting a "third order." This model, which thus "ordered" the laity, filtered into the other urban fraternities that were organized within the framework of guilds. The second, eremitic, model for renouncers of the world is epitomized by the Carthusians, who devised for themselves an inner space in the wilderness favorable to contemplation. But these renouncers remained in communion with the Church, in particular by means of prayer and pastorally via the written word. If need be, they might be invested with high ecclesiastical office, on the very ground that only the most pure could act effectively in the world. Thus it was that numerous Carthusians became bishops. Lastly, traditional monasticism, of which Cluny is indisputably the paradigm, envisaged the monastic community as a society of unblemished, poor, virgin individuals that offered a refuge to secular mankind. During the eleventh and twelfth centuries the accepted meaning of this refuge became such that in Peter the Venerable's writings the Ecclesia cluniacensis tended to become one with the "republic of the Christian Church." The community joined cenobitism with occasional eremitic practice, and a cloister was provided for women at Marcigny-sur-Loire. Close to Cluny's "little Rome" there grew up a whole army of attendants: the poor, penitents, pilgrims, and, more generally, any believer and his lineage concerned about properly managing their individual and family remembrance. This is the model of inclusion— so thorough that its propagandists, like Peter the Venerable, identified it with the Church itself—that I propose to analyze here.

Two narrative texts afford a brief insight into the Ecclesia cluniacensis as a structure of monastic and ecclesiastical inclusion. The first was composed at Gigny, one of the establishments of the network formerly set up by Berno and integrated by Gregory VII in 1075 into the Ecclesia cluniacensis.[25] Written be-

---

25. Gregory VII, *Epistolae extra registrum vagantes*, 22, PL 148:667D–668C.

fore the end of the 1150s, the *Translatio ad castrum Laudorum et ad coenobium Gigniacense* reports the circumstances in which the relics of Saint Taurinus were translated to sanctify Gigny. The anonymous writer treats this as an opportunity to praise the founder, Berno, and his "daughter," the modest Cluny of the early days destined to become the fabulous *monasterium omnium monasteriorum* (monastery of all monasteries), meaning the monastic church whose vocation was to include the totality of all other monasteries.[26] The second text, the *Vita sancti Morandi*, depicts a further stage on the road to inclusion. Morandus, who died in 1115, was the patron of the Cluniac priory of Altkirch in the diocese of Basle; he was also honored at Vienna in Austria, where some of his relics were deposited by Rudolph IV of Habsburg in Saint Stephen's Cathedral. Two *Vitae sancti Morandi* survive. The first and fuller account relates how Morandus, having been an oblate at Saint Mary's, Worms, entered Cluny as he passed through Burgundy on the way to Santiago de Compostela; he was subsequently sent by Hugh of Semur to the Auvergne, and then to Alsace. The second *Vita*, which is shorter, is a reworking of the first text. Doubtless it was a late composition, since Morandus did not gain admission to the Cluniac sanctorale until the fifteenth century.[27] It was clearly made in order to cut the local detail regarding the cult, while nevertheless rehearsing and extending the passages extolling Cluny. This is particularly true of the lengthy final passage devoted to the role of the Burgundian sanctuary in "building up the Church" (*in aedificationem Ecclesiae*) and the different offices—cardinal, bishop, abbot—that the brothers of the monastery were called upon to fill:

> The whole world [*universus orbis*] it seemed then had recourse to [Cluny], as to a communal asylum of piety, for the spiritual refreshment its places afforded. Truly, for those that lived there, subjecting the flesh to the spirit in a continual struggle, to live was Christ and to die was gain, as the Apostle says [Philippians 1:21]. Many of them were chosen and adopted to build up the Church, some as supreme pontiffs and cardinals, and others as bishops, abbots, and pastors. From the nard of spiritual virtues poured out hence, the whole house of the world was filled with the odor of the ointment [cf. John 12:3], and the ardor of monastic religion, which in those days had almost grown cold, grew warm again by dint of those men's example and zeal.[28]

26. *Translatio ad castrum Laudorum et ad coenobium Gigniacense*, indexed *BHL* 7995, text *AASS*, August II, pp. 645–50, here para. 13, p. 648CD.

27. "Coutumes liturgiques de l'Ordre de Cluny publiées par l'abbé Raymond de Cadoëne," MS, Bibliothèque Nationale, Paris, nouv. acq. lat. 1435, f. 3v: decree of chapter-general of Cluny, 21 April 1437; f. 6v: calendar, 3 June. Cf. Léopold Delisle, *Inventaire des manuscrits de la Bibliothèque Nationale, fonds de Cluni* (Paris, 1884), no. 13, p. 16. I thank Denyse Riche for this information. The two *Vitae Morandi* are indexed respectively as *BHL* 6019 and 6020.

28. *Vita sancti Morandi* (*BHL* 6020), *BC*, col. 506AB.

Here Cluny was seen as including no longer merely all monasteries but the entire Ecclesia. This brief apologia is of interest because it lays bare the two modes of inclusion. First is the movement of systole or contraction whereby "humankind universally" is received into the Cluniac "asylum." The second is the diffusion everywhere of the Cluniac "odor" because of the brothers' vocation to build up the Church by providing popes, cardinals, bishops, abbots, and pastors. Let us now look in detail at these two modes.

The Cluniac "Refuge"

The image of Cluny as a universal "refuge" or "asylum" occurs frequently in the Cluniac literature of the eleventh and twelfth centuries.[29] The passage cited from the *Vita sancti Morandi* was partly borrowed from the apology Peter the Venerable had placed in his own *De miraculis*.[30] Cluny, he explained, "is no inferior member of the universal Church." It is conspicuous, he says, by the severity of its discipline, the number of its brothers, the strict observance of the monastic rule, the efficacy of its suffrages, and its universal reach, like the "branches" stretching "unto the sea" spoken of in Psalm 79(80):12. Within his enumeration of the qualities constituting the excellence of Cluny, Peter recalls its role as "singular and common refuge for sinners," a function that drew folk of all orders, dignities, and professions, even bishops.

The term "refuge" or "asylum of piety for all" was no rhetorical exaggeration. It referred to an exact status in law. In 931 Pope John XI, in the first papal bull issued to Cluny, granted the monastery the right to admit monks from outside institutions if their motive was reform.[31] In January 1097, Urban II would renew this right of admittance, which outside institutions were not allowed to challenge, and extend it from monks to canons regular.[32] Meanwhile, in 1024, in the second bull of exemption issued to Cluny, Pope John XIX defined the monastery as a *domus pietatis* (house of piety), a *pietatis et salutis portus* (haven of piety and salvation), and a "stronghold of apostolic benediction and absolution."[33] In the bull of January 1097 just mentioned, Urban was to extend the scope of the description *pietatis et salutis portus* to all members of the Cluniac "corpus," which is why a dependency like Marcigny-sur-Loire, Hugh of Semur's

---

29. Dominique Iogna-Prat, "La geste des origines," pp. 175–76.

30. *DM*, 1.9, pp. 34–37, here 36, ll. 41ff.

31. *Papsturkunden 896–1046*, ed. Harald Zimmermann, Österreichische Akademie der Wissenschaften, Philosophisch-historische Klasse, Denkschriften, 174, 177, 198, 3 vols. (Vienna, 1984–89), vol. 1, no. 64, pp. 107–8. See Joachim Wollasch, "Königtum, Adel und Klöster im Berry während des 10. Jahrhunderts," in *Neue Forschungen über Cluny und die Cluniacenser*, ed. Gerd Tellenbach (Freiburg im B., 1959), pp. 97–111.

32. *Bullarium*, pp. 30–31 (*BC*, p. 520).

33. *Papsturkunden 896–1046*, vol. 2, no. 558, pp. 1053–54.

personal foundation, was also referred to as a place of refuge.[34] This collection of papal decisions made it legally possible for Cluny to admit any institution or individual. Thus to echo the words of Odilo's biographer, Jotsald, the monastery had become a *locus totius religionis* (place of total religion), a *terra repromissionis* (land of promise), open to the laity, to clerics, and to the religious.[35]

What Is a Cluniac Monk?

The term "Cluniac monk" is often used unspecifically and covers a wide variety of situations. This variety stems in large part from the universality of the monastery's recruitment, for it drew in not only monks from other establishments but also clergy and laity, adults and boys. Conversion at Cluny raises four major questions that we shall examine in turn: the type of conversion; unity in diversity; the radical division between seculars and regulars; the indelible character of conversion at Cluny.

Types of Conversion

The Cluniac "refuge" was much sought after in the eleventh and twelfth centuries. Peter the Venerable attempted by statute to regulate the flow of conversions so as to remedy the difficulties created by the "indiscriminate admission of useless persons."[36] The exponential growth in conversions, especially of the laity, dated from Hugh of Semur's time as abbot. Its success was due essentially to two factors: Cluny's role as a penitential asylum, and the monastery's pastoral work directed toward the laity.

In order to work effectively, the policy of control and reform of lay and ecclesiastical mores inspired by the papacy from the 1050s on needed to provide spaces for reconciliation where the faithful and clerics could be encouraged to amend their lives. In his *Monodiae*, Guibert of Nogent (1053–1124) cites an example of a conversion at Cluny related to penance. Guy, bishop of Beauvais, denounced for simony before the papal legate, Hugh of Die, is deposed for contumacy. He hears the news at Cluny, where finally he embraces the monastic life.[37] And there were others. In the last thirty years or so of the eleventh century, four other bishops accused of simony came to do penance at Cluny: Henry of Soissons, Geoffrey of Angers, Simon of Bourges, and John of Pampeluna.[38]

---

34. *Le cartulaire de Marcigny-sur-Loire (1045–1144): essai de reconstitution d'un manuscrit disparu*, ed. Jean Richard, Analecta Burgundica, 4 (Dijon, 1957), no. 288, pp. 165–71, here 166.

35. Iotsaldus, *Vita sancti Odilonis*, l.2 (Hebrews 11:9) and 2.27, ed. Johannes Staub, *MGH SS*, 68 (Hanover, 1999), pp. 149 and 271 (previous ed., *PL* 142:899D and 934A).

36. *Statutum* 35 (*De monachorum susceptione*), pp. 69–70.

37. Guibert of Nogent, *De vita sua sive Monodiae*, 1.14, ed. and French trans. Edmond-René Labande, Les Classiques de l'Histoire de France au Moyen Age, 34 (Paris, 1981), p. 100. [Eng. trans., *A Monk's Confession: The Memoirs of Guibert of Nogent*, trans. Paul A. Archambault (University Park, 1996), p. 44].

38. Joachim Mehne, "Cluniacenserbischöfe," *FMSt* 11 (1977): 270–71.

Cluny's asylum was also open to members of the laity in search of reconciliation. In a letter of 25 February 1079, Gregory VII congratulated Viscount Centullus IV of the Béarn for his piety, calling him "son of the Roman Church," yet none the less exhorting him to do penance for having contracted a marriage within the seven prohibited degrees of consanguinity.[39] Centullus heeded Gregory's pressing instruction: he proceeded to separate from his wife Gisla, while she, accompanied by two professed Cluniacs, William of Montaut, archbishop of Auch, and Aimé, bishop of Oloron, took herself off to the Cluniac nunnery of Marcigny-sur-Loire for a life of penitence.[40] In his *De miraculis*, Peter the Venerable paints a picture of this exemplary nun who, in the course of a fire and against the orders of the papal legate, Hugh of Die, staying there at the time, refused to flee and leave the cloister, because she said she could not cross "limits imposed on us in penance."[41] We do not know if Gisla really uttered these words. But it is not without interest that Peter the Venerable should have put them into the mouth of a woman who had gone into reclusion to cleanse herself of the spot of incest. With less success than Gregory VII had with Viscount Centullus, Hugh of Semur admonished King Philip I, anathematized for ten years for his incestuous liaison with Bertrada of Montfort, to repair to Cluny where Peter and Paul, "judges of emperors, kings, and the earth, are ready to receive you in their house, which our fathers have called an asylum of penitence."[42]

More generally, Cluny's pastoral effort contributed its own dynamic to producing many lay conversions. By pastoral is meant here the image the Ecclesia cluniacensis presented to the world and the way in which that image encouraged conversions. Later we shall be speaking of the important pastoral work relating to the dead that Cluny undertook for the laity from the turn of the millennium. Meanwhile we need to note the evolution of the notion of lay conversion during the eleventh century. In its earliest days Cluny had developed an image of the prince or Christian aristocrat that was faithful to the models elaborated in Carolingian "Mirrors of Princes." Odo's *Vita sancti Geraldi*, the passages devoted to the Ottonian sovereigns in Syrus's *Vita sancti Maioli*, and the epitaphs composed by Odilo in honor of Otto the Great and more particularly his widow Adelaide were all concerned to develop a prescriptive morality.[43] In

39. *Das Register Gregors VII.*, 6.20, ed. Erich Caspar, *MGH, Epistolae selectae*, 2, 1–2, 2:431–32.

40. On Gisla, see Else M. Wischermann, *Marcigny-sur-Loire. Gründungs- und Frühgeschichte des ersten Cluniacenserinnenpriorates (1055–1150)*, Münstersche Mittelalter-Schriften, 42 (Munich, 1986), pp. 367–69 and table 10, p. 501.

41. *DM*, 1.22, pp. 67–68.

42. Letter, "Two Studies," pp. 153–54, here 154. See Georges Duby, *Le chevalier, la femme et le prêtre: le mariage dans la France féodale* (Paris, 1981), pp. 7ff. [Eng. trans., *The Knight, the Lady, and the Priest: The Making of Modern Marriage in Medieval France*, trans. Barbara Bray, with introduction by Natalie Zemon Davis (London, 1984)].

43. For these last texts, consult D. Iogna-Prat, *"Agni immaculati": recherches sur les sources hagiographiques relatives à saint Maieul de Cluny (954–994)* (Paris, 1988), pp. 362–74; Patrick Corbet,

a functional Christian society, the princely model was not to be confused with that of clerics, still less with that of monks. The ideal prince, in the world, was like a "rhinoceros" breaking up the earth in the Church's service.[44] The Gregorian period marked a change from this relative ethic of good princes active in the world to an absolute ethic implying the world's conversion to the monastery, the antechamber to eternity. During Hugh of Semur's abbacy, important aristocratic laymen like Guy I, count of Albo and Vienne, and Hugh I, duke of Burgundy, decided to lay aside their sword belt, renounce secular life, and become monks.[45] Indeed, the abbot of Cluny was upbraided by Pope Gregory VII for allowing Hugh to convert, since it had the effect of leaving "a hundred thousand Christians without a guardian."[46] Hagiographic literature taught ways of individual fulfillment *in*, then *out of*, the world, to reach perfection. The *Miracula* of Saint Hugh speaks of the exemplary humiliation of the duke of Burgundy.[47] From the margins of the Ecclesia cluniacensis comes the famous case of Simon of Crépy-en-Valois, who died between 1080 and 1082.[48] Simon was the son of Raoul III, the count of Vexin and Crépy, the very model of a great lord ready to make use, by abduction if need be, of widows and heiresses to realize his political ambitions. Having reluctantly found himself head of his family line, he agreed to play the usual game of marriage alliances by wedding the daughter of Hildebert, count of Auvergne. Arriving in the nuptial chamber, he managed, in the tradition of the fifth-century Saint Alexis, to persuade his wife to renounce lust, avow virginity, and become a nun. He thereupon took himself off to the monastery of Saint Oyen (also known as Saint-Claude) in the Jura mountains where he distinguished himself in a life of asceticism and prayer interrupted only by diplomatic missions on behalf of Pope Gregory VII.

Les saints ottoniens: sainteté dynastique, sainteté royale et sainteté féminine autour de l'an Mil, Beihefte der Francia, 15 (Sigmaringen, 1986), pp. 59ff.

44. Barbara H. Rosenwein, *Rhinoceros Bound: Cluny in the Tenth Century* (Philadelphia, 1982), pp. 79, 81, 108. (The image was borrowed by Odo of Cluny from Gregory the Great's commentary on Job 39:10—trans.)

45. See various *Vitae* and *Miracula* of Saint Hugh: Gilo, *Vita*, "Two Studies," pp. 93–94; Hildebert of Lavardin, *Vita*, 40, *PL* 159:885C–886A; Reynold of Vézelay, *Vitae sancti Hugonis*, 40, in *Vizeliacensia II: textes relatifs à l'histoire de l'abbaye de Vézelay*, ed. Robert B. C. Huygens, CCCM, 42 Supplementum, p. 57 (Guy I); *Miracula*, *BC*, col. 459DE (Hugh I).

46. *Das Register Gregors VII.*, 6.17, 2:423–24.

47. *Alia miraculorum quorumdam S. Hugonis abbatis relatio*, *BC*, col. 459DE.

48. *Vita sancti Simonis*, *AASS*, September VIII, pp. 711–51; Herbert E. J. Cowdrey, "Count Simon of Crepy's Monastic Conversion," in *Papauté, monachisme et théories politiques*, Mélanges Marcel Pacaut, 1, Collection d'histoire et d'archéologie mediévale, 1 (Lyon, 1994), pp. 253–66. Regarding possible influence of Simon's example upon Hugh I, duke of Burgundy, see Armin Kohnle, *Abt Hugo von Cluny (1049–1109)*, Beihefte der Francia, 32 (Sigmaringen, 1993), p. 182.

Unity and Diversity

One of the chapters in Ulrich's *Antiquiores consuetudines* is devoted to the "diversity of novices."[49] The first category is composed of clerics and laymen "without the habit," as opposed to the novices who are already monks. The second category has several subdivisions. First are monks of other monasteries making a fresh profession at Cluny. Such recruits were a source of friction with other establishments, for example the monasteries of La Trinité at Vendôme and Clairvaux, which contested the canonicity of "double consecration" and of Cluny's right to admit monks from other houses, a right granted first in 931 and then with exceptional liberality during Hugh of Semur's abbacy.[50] Second are the members of any Cluniac dependency whom the abbot has already blessed but who must still come to Cluny itself to make their profession. A third subdivision points to brothers of a Cluniac dependency of abbatial status making their profession to their own abbot.

To such distinctions of "genetic" type, linked to provenance and profession, are added more radical differences related to the fact that certain brothers were offered as oblates at a tender age to the Ecclesia cluniacensis, which then fed them and brought them up, while others progressed in the world outside through the various ecclesiastical orders that led on to the priesthood. Some brothers were literate; others illiterate. Some lived a long conventual life; others were admitted to the monastery *in articulo mortis* (at the point of death). Such scenarios were not unique to Cluny. But one comes across few policies of inclusion during the eleventh and twelfth centuries as thoroughgoing as that adopted at Cluny in order to narrow the differences. To prove the point, let us examine two "extreme case" conversions: monks *ad succurrendum* (professing on their deathbeds) and the *conversi* or lay brothers.

The apologies *pro domo* composed at Cluny, such as the passage from Peter the Venerable's *De miraculis* quoted above, insist on the efficacy of the Ecclesia cluniacensis in the funerary sphere. The monastery's charter attests that lay donors in search of salvation were thronging to be buried in the cemetery at Cluny or, from 1097, in that of a dependent house. At the same time, the care of the dead primed the pump of the Cluniac economy, which was structurally dependent on gifts. In the numerous deeds regulating funeral undertakings by the monks it is not uncommon to see mention of details regarding the degree of

---

49. Ulrich, *Antiquiores consuetudines Cluniacensis monasterii*, 2.1, *PL* 149:700D–701D. On this subject see Giles Constable, "Entrance to Cluny in the Eleventh and Twelfth Centuries according to the Cluniac Customories and Statutes," in *Mediaevalia Christiana XIe–XIIIe siècles. Hommage à Raymonde Foreville de ses amis, ses collègues et ses anciens élèves*, ed. Colomon E. Viola (Tournai, 1989), p. 336.

50. Constable, "Entrance to Cluny," p. 345; also Giles Constable, "The Reception Privilege of Cluny in the Eleventh and Twelfth Centuries," in *Le gouvernement d'Hugues de Semur à Cluny*, Actes du colloque scientifique international, Cluny, September 1988 (Cluny, 1990), pp. 59–74.

pomp expected in the funeral and in the subsequent liturgical commemoration, as donors requested to be treated as a *familiaris* ("friend" of the monks), as a monk, or even as an abbot.[51] The inventory and analysis of these stipulations regarding the funerary honors due to benefactors remain in large part still to be done. For the moment, let us simply note that in the wide spectrum of possible arrangements, laymen coming to die *in extremis* in a monk's habit were an extreme case of monastic conversion. Within an atmosphere of general criticism of the "perverse effects" of monastic pastoral funerary practice, Peter the Venerable—whose own father, Maurice of Montboissier, had become a monk *ad succurrendum*—strongly defended these "laborers of the eleventh hour." In a passage of *De miraculis*, he explains that there is one monastic conversion, regardless of diversity of cases. Duration matters little; intention is everything: a moment, a few days, or long years, all avail for the same eternity.[52] Peter's defense of monks *ad succurrendum* tends to be viewed as a somewhat desperate rearguard action in the middle of the twelfth century. No doubt it was. But let us simply affirm that Peter was doing no more than articulating the strict inclusive logic of the Cluniac Church system: a logic of all or nothing, according to whose strictures what availed for one necessarily availed for all.

The same logic was at work in our second "extreme case" of monastic conversion, that of the *conversi* or lay brothers. The question of the exact status of Cluniac *conversi* has in the past excited plenty of controversy, now substantially superseded by the work of Wolfgang Teske.[53] A simple summary of his conclusions will suffice here. For Dom Kassius Hallinger, the *conversus* had no ecclesiastical order and no education in literacy (*illiteratus*), but was nevertheless a full member of the community. Bonifatius Egger and Guy de Valous, on the other hand, considered the status of the *conversus* to be "transitory," namely, while he was acquiring the literacy necessary to be a choir monk. As Wolfgang Teske has

51. *CLU* 3806, ca. 1100, 5.153–55: *et si in laycali vita obiret, delatus Cluniaco honorabiliter sepeliretur, et debitum missarum, et orationum, et elemosinarum, sicut pro uno monacho ita et pro eo ab omnibus persolveretur.*—Commented on by Maria Hillebrandt, "Le prieuré de Paray-le-Monial au XIe siècle: ses rapports avec le monde laïc et l'abbaye de Cluny," in *Paray-le-Monial*, Premier colloque scientifique international, 28–30 May 1992 (Paray-le-Monial, 1994), p. 121; *CLU* 3873, 1106, 5.226–27: *ita dumtaxat, ut [cum] uxor eius defunctus fuisset, honorifice in Cluniaco sepeliretur, monacho de Berziaco exhibente portitores et baiulos funeris . . .*; *CLU* 4279, 1180–81, 5.644–47, here 646: *Missam etiam unam cotidianam, pro ipso et antecessoribus eius sive successoribus ei concesserunt, et in fine suo tantum pro eo fiet, quantum solet fieri pro domno abbate Cluniacensi.* See Georg Schreiber, "Kirchliches Abgabenwesen an französischen Eigenkirchen aus Anlass von Ordalien," in *Zeitschrift der Savigny-Stiftung für Rechtsgeschichte, Kanonistische Abteilung*, 36 (1915), p. 442, n. 1.

52. *DM*, 1.7, p. 22, ll. 5–18.

53. Wolfgang Teske, "Laien, Laienmönche und Laienbrüder in der Abtei Cluny. Ein Beitrag zum 'Konversen-Problem,'" *FMSt* 10 (1976): 248–322 and 11 (1977): 288–339. Cyprian Davis's article "The Conversus of Cluny: Was He a Lay-Brother?" in *Benedictus: Studies in Honor of St. Benedict of Nursia*, ed. Ellen R. Elder, Cistercian Studies Series, 67 (Kalamazoo, 1981), pp. 99–107, though lacking detailed analysis, comes to similar conclusions to those of Teske. I am grateful to Denyse Riche for giving me access to Davis's article.

shown, the mobility of the *conversi* within the Cluniac monastery was real enough. One such case was Joceran III Grossus, who entered Cluny in 1074 and became prior in 1094;[54] another was Gerard, who, as Ulrich emphasizes at the beginning of his *Antiquiores consuetudines*, went on to become prior of La Charité-sur-Loire, although his knowledge of letters was limited.[55] But such cases were exceptional. For the most part, the *conversi* remained *illiterati*. The status of *conversus* was therefore not simply one of first-stage monastic education; some—in fact the majority—entered and died as *conversi* at Cluny. How does one distinguish these *conversi* within the monastery? Following the logic of Benedictine tradition as codified in chapter 63 of the Rule of Saint Benedict, the rank of a brother at Cluny would depend on his date of entry into the community. Yet other distinctions, to do with age, order, function, and office, disturbed this basic arrangement. The customs of Cluny thus mention a group of *seniores*, older brothers, or group of officers, who played the role of the *sanior pars* (more wholesome part) in electing an abbot.[56] Outside the monastery, as in the liturgy, the brothers were differentiated according to their ecclesiastical order: priests, deacons, subdeacons, minor orders, and then lay monks; thus in funeral rites they observed the rule of peer group (*similes in ordine*), whereby a priest would be interred by priests, a deacon by deacons, and a *conversus* by *conversi*.[57] The regroupings that might be demanded by the liturgy depended upon the degree of literacy; under that head distinctions existed among the *pueri* (boys), the *cantores* (choir monks), and the *conversi*, responsible for tasks suitable for the "unlettered," such as candle bearer. From 1088, in certain solemn circumstances, the abbot of Cluny wore *pontificalia*, which made him like a bishop;[58] thus the monastery of Cluny, with its liturgical arrangement of orders and functions, represented a sort of Church in miniature.

But these multiple distinctions were canceled out in the perspective of the Last Things. While some communities, in their liturgical commemoration, dis-

---

54. Wolfgang Teske, "Bernardus und Jocerannus Grossus als Mönche von Cluny. Zu den Aufstiegsmöglichkeiten cluniacensischer 'conversi' im 11. Jahrhundert," in *Ordenstudien I. Beiträge zur Geschichte der Konversen im Mittelalter*, ed. Kaspar Elm, Berliner Historische Studien, 2 (Berlin, 1980), pp. 9–24.

55. Ulrich, *Antiquiores consuetudines*, PL 149:632D–633A.

56. Giles Constable, "*Seniores* et *pueri* à Cluny aux Xe, XIe siècles," in *Histoire et société. Mélanges offerts à Georges Duby*, 3 vols. (Aix-en-Provence, 1992), 3:17–24.

57. Ulrich, *Antiquiores consuetudines*, 3.29, PL 149:773A; cited by Cécile Treffort, "Genèse du cimetière chrétien: étude sur l'accompagnement du mourant, les funérailles, la commémoration des défunts et les lieux d'inhumation à l'époque carolingienne (entre Loire et Rhin, milieu VIIIe–début XIe siècle)," doctoral thesis, typescript, Université Lumière-Lyon II (Lyon, 1994), 1:281.

58. *Bullarium*, pp. 22–23 (PL 151:291–93): Hugh of Semur was given permission by Urban II on major feasts to wear the dalmatic, episcopal shoes, gloves, and mitre. The privilege was renewed and extended by the same pope in 1095 (BC, cols. 516–18), by Pascal II in 1109 (*Bullarium*, pp. 36–37 [PL 163:260–61]), and Gelasius II in 1118 (*Bullarium*, p. 38 [PL 163:492]). On the subject of abbots' being allowed to wear *pontificalia*, see Philipp Hofmeister, *Mitra und Stab der wirklichen Prälaten ohne bischöflichen Charakter*, Kirchengeschichtliche Abhandlungen, 104 (Stuttgart, 1928).

tinguished between "external" and "internal" brothers, professed Cluniacs were all entitled to the same funeral provisions and the same mention in the necrology (*frater nostrae congregationis*—brother of our congregation).[59] Time in another way leveled the status of the brothers. The reforms driven by Peter the Venerable tended to establish clear distinctions between laymen and priest-monks by having all the monks become clerics and establishing a totally separate lay group. The lay brothers were henceforth confronted with a choice: acquire ecclesiastical orders, leave the monastery, or become *conversi* in the Cistercian sense of the term, namely, separate from the choir monks. By the thirteenth century, when the evolution summarized here had run its course, it is clear that a Cluniac monk was ipso facto a priest who had received instruction in literacy.

The Radical Division Regulars/Seculars

More and more systematically having the status of priest-monks, professed Cluniacs differed radically from secular clerics. In the history of the Ecclesia cluniacensis, instances of conversion from cleric to monk are numerous. Changing from the former state to the latter raised no particular problem. On the other hand, the Cluniacs opposed clerics who wanted to follow the life of a "regular" in the secular world.

For a long time Cluny appears to have had harmonious relations with the canons regular, an institution that, it is true, long had a marginal role compared with that of monasticism proper. Two of the earliest abbots of Cluny, Odo and Odilo, were former canons, from Tours and Brioude respectively, not to mention Majolus who came via the cathedral chapter of Mâcon. The only apparent example of a conflict between monks and canons regular is that reported by Rodulfus Glaber in his *Historiarum libri quinque* in relation to the reform of the monastery of Saint Paul outside the Walls (San Paolo fuori le Mura) in Rome embarked upon by Emperor Otto III at the instigation of Pope Sylvester II, pope from 999 to 1003. Glaber tells how Saint Paul appeared in a dream to the emperor in order to dissuade him from replacing the community of monks there with canons and thereby violating "order."[60] Only much later, in the context of monastic and canonical reforms at the end of the eleventh century, did relations between the two orders become embittered. In the portrait he paints of the ideal Cluniac Matthew of Albano in his *De miraculis*, Peter the Venerable attacks the canons regular in the sharpest terms.[61] Matthew, at the outset, had been a canon of the church of Reims attached to the *prévôt* and future archbishop Raoul le Verd; he then chose to renounce the order of canons and converted to Cluny on

---

59. Enlightening on this point is Joachim Wollasch's study, "A propos des *fratres barbati* de Hirsau," in *Histoire et société*, 3:37–48, esp. 43.

60. Rodulfus Glaber, *Historiarum libri quinque*, 1.4.14, *Works*, ed. John France et al., Oxford Medieval Texts (Oxford, 1989), pp. 28–30.

61. *DM*, 2.6, pp. 105–6.

reaching the priory of Saint-Martin-des-Champs in Paris, formerly an establishment of canons regular and granted to Cluny by King Philip I (1060–1108).[62] Matthew's passing from one order to another might have been calmly depicted as a step in the *cursus perfectionis* leading from the good to the better. However, Peter the Venerable saw fit to depict this conversion as a flight from a "pretended good" to the "true good." He speaks of Matthew abandoning "that canonical, nay almost secular and fallacious garb," so as to "serve God in the true and sincere order of monks." He says that Matthew "saw that those institutes of clerks are almost bereft of religion . . . that beneath the clerical tonsure or habit they can more accurately be described as mercenaries than canons."[63] What lies at the bottom of Peter's radical critique?[64] The heart of the matter is the question of ecclesiastical benefices. Matthew has accused himself, wrongly, of simony, thinking he has received his prebend as canon by uncanonical means. For him conversion to Cluny represents a radical rejection of "carnal benefices." For Peter the Venerable the example presents an opportunity to denounce what he sees as an equivocal category, regulars who, by continuing to live in the secular world, risk confusing physical goods with spiritual goods.

The Indelible Stamp of Cluniac Conversion

A radical separation from secular life, conversion to Cluny was indelible, even for brothers called to exercise a role outside the Ecclesia cluniacensis. The *Chronicon Mauriniacense* records the story of Macarius, former prior of Longpont and on that account a professed Cluniac.[65] The monks of Morigny elected Macarius as their abbot in 1142. But Archbishop Henry of Sens opposed the election on the grounds that Macarius was a Cluniac. The monks then went to Cluny to obtain from Peter the Venerable a release from obedience for Macarius. Later, Macarius became abbot of Fleury-sur-Loire. He remained none the less a Cluniac. He was commemorated on 15 March as a *frater nostrae congregationis* in the necrologies of Longpont and of Saint-Martin-des-Champs.[66]

62. On Saint-Martin-des-Champs, of which Matthew afterward became prior, see Cornelia Heintz, "Anfänge und Entwicklung des Cluniazenser-Priorates St.-Martin-des-Champs in Paris (1079–1150)," dissertation, Münster im W., 1982.

63. *DM*, 2.6, p. 105, ll. 4–8.

64. On this, see Glauco M. Cantarella, "Un problema del XII secolo: l'ecclesiologia di Pietro il Venerabile," *Studi Medievali*, 3d ser., 19 (1978): 189–90.

65. *Chronique de Morigny*, ed. Léon Mirot, Collection de textes pour servir à l'étude et à l'enseignement de l'Histoire, fasc. 41, 2d ed. (Paris, 1912), 3.4, pp. 77–80. Regarding this episode and the problem of release from obedience, see Poeck, *"Cluniacensis Ecclesia,"* pp. 127–28, on which my account here is based.

66. *Synopse der cluniacensischen Necrologien*, ed. Wolf-Dieter Heim et al. and Joachim Wollasch, Münstersche Mittelalter-Schriften, 39, 2 vols. (Munich, 1982), 15 March, 2:148, Longpont (1) and Saint-Martin-des-Champs (42): *Depositio domni M. abbatis Floriacensis;* see Dietrich Poeck, *Longpont: ein cluniacensisches Priorat in der Ile-de-France*, Münstersche Mittelalter-Schriften, 38 (Munich, 1986), pp. 188–90.

Those who answered the call to work as servants of the Church, as bishops, archbishops, cardinals, or even as pope, also remained Cluniacs. Pope Urban II, former grand prior of Cluny, figured in the Cluniac necrologies as *frater nostrae congregationis*.[67] When Peter the Venerable wrote to Gilo, cardinal archbishop of Tusculum, during the schism with Anacletus, he addressed the former professed Cluniac, now a schismatic bishop, as "most dear brother of the womb."[68] Theobald, former prior of Saint-Martin-des-Champs, who became bishop of Paris in 1144, is similarly called "dearest brother," whom ecclesiastical responsibilities and honors "have not cut off from the body of Cluny."[69] The case of Matthew of Albano is without doubt the best example, because the picture Peter gives of him is supposed to represent the model Cluniac monk.[70] Matthew's journey is described in terms of a fundamental breach (ceasing to be a canon and becoming a monk), followed by gradual progress in perfection—the simple professed monk giving himself up to contemplation within the community of Saint-Martin-des-Champs. He is the prior concerned for his subordinates and his guests, the restorer of Cluniac discipline during the schismatic period of Pontius of Melgueil, finally the Churchman, the cardinal of Albano. Yet at the peak of his ascension, beneath the cardinal's robes there still beat the heart of a monk. Until his death, Matthew abandoned no part of the copious Cluniac psalmody nor the "sacrifice of the altar," so that Pope Honorius II "reproached him almost for being too much of a monk."[71] Modeling himself upon Saint Martin, he chose to die as a monk on a hair shirt covered in ashes.[72] At his obsequies, "psalms were sung all round *more cluniacensi*" (in the Cluniac manner). His mortuary garb summed up his life's purpose: monastic, priestly, episcopal, without any one of these estates or orders effacing another. The professed Cluniac wore a hair shirt and cowl, the priest priestly ornaments, and the bishop pontifical insignia.[73]

Cluniac Eremitism

Alongside his treatment of Matthew of Albano, Peter the Venerable paints the portrait of several other model Cluniacs. Two of these, Gerard and Benedict, were followers of the solitary life, much prized in the medieval west around 1100.[74] The sort of eremitism then in vogue formed part of a general contesting of the traditional type of Cluniac monasticism. An excellent example of the opposition between the two ways of perfection, the communal (cenobitic)

67. *Synopse der cluniacensischen Necrologien*, 29 July, 2:420.

68. *Ep.*, 40, 1:134–6, here 134.

69. *Ep.*, 134, 1:338–9, here 339.

70. *DM*, 2.4–23, pp. 103–39.

71. *DM*, 2.14, p. 124, and 2.17, p. 129.

72. Paul Antin, "La mort de saint Martin," *Revue des études anciennes* 66 (1964): 108–120, here 112; the Cluniac liturgy was directly inspired by this example, see *LT*, 195.1, p. 272.

73. *DM*, 2.22, p. 137, and 23, p. 138.

74. *DM*, 1.8, pp. 23–34, and 20, pp. 58–63.

and the reclusive (eremitic), is Bernard of Tiron, a monk of Saint Cyprian's at Poitiers, who opted for a solitary life in Bas-Maine rather than witness his monastery reduced to the status of a dependency of Cluny, forced to yield obeisance to an *archiabbas* (archabbot).[75] However, we need to recognize that Cluniac monasticism, in tune with the wider reform movement in the Church, did in fact make room for the ideal of contempt for the world. It had a place for both cenobitism and eremitism.[76]

The first clear mention of Cluniac hermits dates from 1088. A charter of Cluny, still extant in the original, tells the story of Stephen and Ermenald, abbot and prior respectively of Saint-Rigaud at Ancise in the diocese of Mâcon, who decided to withdraw from the turbulence of the times and settle in the Gironde on the island of Cordouan, off the Pointe de la Grave.[77] To this end they obtained the authority of Hugh of Semur, the abbot of Cluny, to whose estates the island belonged. The two recluses were moreover joined by a monk of Cluny, a certain William, a "man of ingenuity" whose knowledge of pisciculture made their settlement viable. Soon there were crowds wishing to visit these men of God. In order that they could be reached without danger to their visitors, they decided to leave the island and settle on the Pointe de la Grave itself, where land was conceded to them by members of the laity. The new establishment was duly consecrated by the papal legate, Aimé of Oloron, accompanied by a representative of the church of Bordeaux, the dean and archdeacon Peter. The legate "solemnly chanted mass, exorcized the water, consecrated the cemetery, ate with us, gave us coins and other goods, and did not simply acknowledge and praise our building efforts, but actually commanded us as an act of obedience to pursue them strenuously." They set to work, assisted by brothers from Cluny, who persuaded them to place themselves within the obedience of the Ecclesia cluniacensis. This charter is particularly useful as a real-life demonstration of how hermits were integrated into Cluny. At the beginning of this episode the only link between Cluny and the establishment of Stephen and Ermenald was the monastery's ownership of the island of Cordouan. The later arrival of William on the island suggests that brothers of Cluny were authorized to lead an eremitic life. Finally the involvement of Archdeacon Peter and the papal legate Aimé of Oloron shows that the Church hierarchy was concerned to control the activities of recluses. The entry into Cluniac obedience is perhaps simply a sign of this desire for control.

75. Geoffrey Grossus records the words spoken by Bernard of Tiron at Rome: *Nunc vero Cluniacensis abbas . . . mihi qualicunque abbati tamen veluti archiabbas superba tyrannide dominari appetit*, *Vita sancti Bernardi*, 7.58, *PL* 172:1401D.

76. The basic study of Cluniac eremitism remains Jean Leclercq, "Pierre le Vénérable et l'érémitisme clunisien," in *Petrus Venerabilis, 1156–1956: Studies and Texts Commemorating the Eighth Centenary of His Death*, ed. Giles Constable and James Kritzeck, Studia Anselmiana, 40 (Rome, 1956).

77. *CLU* 3633, ca. 1088, 4.801–3.

It was doubtless during this same period that Ulrich of Zell and a certain Anastasius divided their life between the monastery and the desert. Ulrich of Zell, who died in 1093, was Emperor Henry III's godson.[78] The adoption of Ulrich's cult at Cluny, where he was celebrated on 10 July, testifies to the strength of the links forged in the eleventh century between the Burgundian monastery and the empire. Of the two known *Vitae*, one is very short and makes very little of the role of Cluny in the saint's career. The other, on the other hand, strongly emphasizes his stay at Cluny, where he quickly became a confidant of Hugh of Semur. Abbot Hugh made him both his chaplain and his counselor before entrusting him with the oversight of the convent of nuns at Marcigny, which he had founded with family wealth on family land. This *Vita* makes a point of mentioning that Ulrich was also the author of one of the accounts of the customs of Cluny. The tasks confided to him by Hugh of Semur also took him into the imperial circle. The account of this period of his life, and in particular the foundation of Zell in the diocese of Basle, highlights the three poles of the saint's activities: his cenobitic life; his love of solitude and eremitic practice in association with Cunus; his concern for women, on whose behalf he founded the monastic house of Bollschweil (transferred in 1115 to Sölden).[79]

Anastasius's history is known only through the *Vita* written by Galterius in support of the saint's cult, which was celebrated outside the Cluniac network, at Saint-Martin at Oydes, in the Ariège, where he was buried.[80] Born in Venice, Anastasius belonged to an informal group of "religious enthralled" by the personality of William of Dijon.[81] Having entered Mont-Saint-Michel at some indeterminate date, he left the monastery in 1057–58 after the allegedly simoniacal election of Abbot Renouf, and withdrew to the hermitage of Tombelaine. Passing through the region, Hugh of Semur called on the recluse, whose reputation had become widespread, as is witnessed by a letter written by Anselm of Bec to Robert of Tombelaine.[82] The names of Anselm and Robert place Anastasius in a circle of theologians of the first rank. As the author of a letter *De cor-*

78. Horst Fuhrmann, "Neues zur Biographie des Ulrich von Zell († 1093)," in *Person und Gemeinschaft im Mittelalter. Festschrift Karl Schmid zum fünfundsechzigsten Geburtstag*, ed. Gerd Althoff, Dieter Geuenich, Otto G. Oexle, and Joachim Wollasch (Sigmaringen, 1988), pp. 369–78.

79. *Vitae sancti Udalrici:* (1) indexed *BHL* 8379, text *MGH SS*, 12, pp. 251–53; (2) indexed *BHL* 8370, text *AASS*, July III, pp. 154–70. On Sölden, see *Helvetia Sacra*, 3.2, ed. Hans-Jörg Gilomen (Basle and Frankfurt am Main, 1991), pp. 35–39 and passim. On the "Gregorian" context within which he was led to speak, see Rolf Zerfaß, *Der Streit um die Laienpredigt: eine pastoralgeschichtliche Untersuchung zum Verständnis des Predigtamtes und zu seiner Entwicklung im 12. und 13. Jahrhundert* (Freiburg im B., Basle, and Vienna, 1974), pp. 132ff.

80. Galterius, *Vita sancti Anastasii*, PL 149:425–32. Matthieu Arnoux, "Un Vénitien au Mont-Saint-Michel: Anastase, moine, ermite et confesseur († vers 1085)," *Médiévales* 28 (1995): 55–78, now provides the in-depth study previously lacking.

81. The term is Arnoux's (*religieux subjugués*), "Un Vénitien au Mont-Saint-Michel," p. 73.

82. *S. Anselmi Cantuariensis archiepiscopi opera omnia*, ed. Franciscus Salesius Schmitt, vol. 3 (Edinburgh, 1946), no. 3, pp. 102–3; cited by Arnoux, "Un Vénitien au Mont-Saint-Michel," p. 52.

PART I. THE MONKS AND THE WORLD ORDER

pore et sanguine Domini, Anastasius was an early entrant into the eucharistic controversy sparked by Berengar of Tours. Abbot Hugh of Semur invited the hermit to come and give a good example of doctrine and morals to the brothers at Cluny. Anastasius agreed. At Cluny, he was an atypical monk who practiced the utmost asceticism and left the monastery once a year to spend Lent in solitude.[83] In obedience to Gregory VII and Hugh of Semur, he went off to Spain *ad praedicandum Sarracenis* (to preach to the Saracens). Seven years after his return he accompanied Hugh on a trip around Aquitaine, "in order to encourage certain brothers, laymen, and nobles, who, renouncing the world, wanted to become monks"; he was especially occupied in the district of Toulouse, where the count of Pamiers wished to convert together with his wife and children. When Lent came around, he sought his usual solitude in the Pyrenees. But this time he determined to stay on there and settled high up in a place called "Abriscola," where he built a hut and set an altar. As an *eremus,* he was in fact a dependent of the Cluniac priory of Saint-Antonin at "Fredelas," the two constituting a "double community."[84] Three years later, a letter from Hugh of Semur enjoined him to leave his hermitage and rejoin the *coenobium,* which was apparently in difficulties.[85] On arrival, he could find no trace of the community and continued his route northward, ending up dying at Saint-Martin at Oydes in 1083, on 16 or 17 October, the date on which his name appears in the necrology of Cluny. Anastasius exemplifies a half-cenobitic, half-eremitic life. The saint became a recluse within a strongly Gregorian movement fleeing from simoniacal contamination. At Cluny, where the abbot had no such taint, he was able to escape from the monastery during Lent, following the example given in the *Vita* of Saint Mary the Egyptian. His adoption of the solitary life was never irrevocable, since Hugh of Semur ultimately asked him to go back to his community. Among other advantages, the apparent coming and going made it possible for the half cenobite, half solitary to be employed by the Church as an itinerant preacher to laity contemplating conversion to the religious life, as well as, in Spain, to preach against the Saracens.

Next in the history of Cluniac eremitism come the two solitaries whose portraits are sketched by Peter the Venerable in *De miraculis.* Gerard, the first of these, Peter pictures as "worn out by the exactions of obedience over a long period in various parts of the world."[86] His mobility in office was typically Cluniac: he passed through numerous priories, notably Beaumont-sur-Grosne and Saint-Sauveur at Nevers, of which he was briefly in charge. A monk of eminence, he and several companions managed to find a wilderness near Cluny on the

83. Galterius, *Vita sancti Anastasii,* PL 149:428D–429A.

84. Arnoux's definition, "Un Vénitien au Mont-Saint-Michel," p. 69: the organization is envisaged as close to the Camaldolese model.

85. "Two Studies," p. 145. The Cluniac foundation was ephemeral; from 1095 the establishment was admitting canons regular: see Arnoux, "Un Vénitien au Mont-Saint-Michel," p. 67.

86. *DM,* 1.8, pp. 23–34, here 31, ll. 215ff.

heights of Aujoux.[87] The second, Benedict, is described as devoting himself day and night to contemplation in Cluny itself, in an oratory dedicated to the archangel Michael in one of the towers of Cluny III.[88] To these two examples may be added that of the recluse Gilbert, with whom Peter the Venerable was in correspondence.[89] But without doubt Peter's attraction to the solitary and contemplative life is most manifest in the attention he paid to the Carthusian model. Peter became acquainted with La Grande Chartreuse when he was responsible for the Cluniac priory of Domène, during the years 1120–22, just before he was elected abbot of Cluny. His attachment to the Carthusians was lifelong, as his correspondence testifies.[90] By engaging in land exchanges, Peter was able to assist the Carthusians in establishing the strict boundaries of their property in the small valley of Meyriat, near the Cluniac priory of Nantua.[91] In a statute dating from 1155, a year before his death, the Carthusians undertook to honor his memory as if he were a prior or a monk of their own order.[92] In the last part of his *De miraculis*, Peter lauds the Carthusians by describing them as having "a holier and more circumspect profession than many others of the same monastic purpose."[93] In the historical literature relating to the reform of the Church and the monasticism of the eleventh and twelfth centuries, the Carthusian movement is often portrayed as opposed to the traditional monastic model represented by Cluny. It is true that the basic option favored by the Carthusian founder Bruno and his followers, radical separation from secular society, contrasted strongly with the Cluniac system, which on the contrary was characterized by inclusion of the world. This specific trait of Carthusianism manifested itself notably in the refusal to hold any possession outside of the wilderness or to take any responsibility for the dead.[94] Even so, the two models were perhaps more complementary than antagonistic to each other. Such was at any rate the perception of the contemporary protagonists. In the logic of the Rule of Saint

87. On eremitic sites around Cluny, Belmont, Aujoux, Saint-Vital, Sainte-Radegonde, Saint-Jean-des-Bois, Cotte, Le Mont Saint-Romain, see Germaine Chachuat, "L'érémitisme à Cluny sous l'abbatiat de Pierre le Vénérable," *Annales de l'académie de Mâcon* 58 (1982): 89–96.

88. *DM*, 1.20, pp. 58–63, here 60–61, ll. 64ff.

89. *Ep.*, 20, 1:27–41.

90. *Ep.*, 24–25, 1:44–48 (Guigo I); 48, 1:146–48 (letter of condolence written in 1133/34 after an avalanche killed brothers of the Grande Chartreuse); 132, 1:333–34 (Anthelm, prior of the charterhouse of Belley); 170, 1:402–4 (to the prior of the charterhouse of Meyriat).

91. Jacques Dubois, "Le désert, cadre de vie des Chartreux au Moyen Age," in *La naissance des chartreuses*, Actes du VIe colloque international d'histoire et de spiritualité cartusiennes, Grenoble, 12–15 September 1984, ed. Bernard Bligny and Gérald Chaix (Grenoble, 1986), p. 19.

92. *Recueil des plus anciens actes de la Grande-Chartreuse* (1086–1196), ed. Bernard Bligny (Grenoble, 1958), no. 24, pp. 67–69; *Capitulum generale Basilii secundum*, ed. James Hogg, *Die ältesten Consuetudines der Kartäuser*, Analecta Cartusiana, vol. 1 (Berlin, 1970), pp. 136–37, the statute confirming an association of prayer between the Carthusians and the Cluniacs.

93. *DM*, 2.27–28, pp. 149–52, here ll. 9–10.

94. Guigo I, *Consuetudines Cartusiae*, 41, ed. and trans. anon. into French under title *Coutumes de Chartreuse*, SC, 313 (Paris, 1984), pp. 244–47.

Benedict, Peter the Venerable saw the contemplative life as the keystone of ceno-bitism. Viewed thus, the Carthusian model became complementary to the Clu-niac. Ralph of Sully, Peter's biographer, asserts that the abbot sought Carthusian solitude once a year.[95] Peter was in correspondence with Basil, prior of La Grande Chartreuse from 1151 to 1173/74, who had previously been at school at Cluny before "the Spirit that bloweth where it listeth" blew him from the "good to the better, from high to higher still."[96] Given the lack of a Carthusian hagiography, it is hardly surprising that Peter the Venerable, at the close of his *De miraculis*, should undertake to praise the institution that, so to speak, put the finishing touch to the exemplary character of Cluny.

The complementarity of Cluny and La Chartreuse makes it easier to under-stand the role of eremitism at Cluny. The recluses at Cordouan, Ulrich of Zell and Anastasius, Gerard and Benedict: all these examples speak of a *via media* that was half cenobitic, half eremitic. Peter the Venerable's fifty-third statute, *De clausura novi monasterii*, attempts to institutionalize this middle way by making provision even at Cluny for times and places that should be "holy and more se-cret," more suitable for personal prayer "as in a hermitage."[97] The advantage sought from this compromise between the communal and the reclusive life was to enable the brothers of Cluny to be counted among the most pure while re-maining present in the world. The question of the relatively late practice of eremitism at Cluny (leaving aside the early, isolated, and unimitated example of Adhegrin, a companion of Odo's) has never really been considered. It would ap-pear that the cenobitic and eremitic models remained mutually incompatible for the Cluniacs as long as the problem of the communion of solitaries with the rest of the *Ecclesia* had not been resolved, that is to say, until the second half of the eleventh century. Gregorian theorists expended a great deal of energy in showing that it was indeed possible to be at one and the same time "alone and together," a paradox pushed to its logical limit by the example of the hermit-priest blessing the faithful at the eucharistic sacrifice and uttering the formula *Dominus vobiscum*. When Peter Damian came to explain the paradox in a letter, he depicted the her-mit, at his nocturnal devotions, as in communion not simply with the Church but with the whole order of the world: "He contemplates the courses of the stars in the sky; even so the order of the psalms courses through his mouth."[98] The soli-

95. *Vita Petri Venerabilis*, PL 189:28BC.

96. *Ep.*, 186–87, 1:434–36. On the complementarity of the cenobitic and eremitic way, consid-ered by Peter to be two complementary poles within monasticism, see Gillian R. Knight, "The Lan-guage of Retreat and the Eremitic Ideal in Some Letters of Peter the Venerable," *Archives d'Histoire doctrinale et littéraire du Moyen Age* 63 (1996): 7–43. I am grateful to Eric Palazzo for drawing this article to my attention.

97. *Statutum* 53, p. 83.

98. Peter Damian, *Epistolae*, 28, ed. Kurt Reindel, 4 vols., *MGH*, Die Briefe der Deutschen Kaiserzeit (Munich, 1983–93), 4:248–78, here 274. See Michel Grandjean, *Les laïcs dans l'Eglise: re-gards de Pierre Damien, Anselme de Cantorbéry, Yves de Chartres*, Théologie historique, 97 (Paris, 1994), pp. 154ff.

tary thus in various ways remained present in the world: by prayer, by the copying of books (which was recommended to the recluse Gilbert and much practiced by the Carthusians),[99] but above all by the eucharistic sacrifice that was the foundation of the Church's community. Thus in *De miraculis*, Peter the Venerable draws attention to Benedict's devotions at the altar and Gerard's eucharistic ardor.[100]

The Cluniac "Noah's Ark"

The most extreme form of Cluniac reclusion was that practiced by the women of Marcigny-sur-Loire, which Peter the Venerable described in such terms as "prison," "permanent reclusion," "permanent, life-giving burial."[101] This last expression suggests the transmutation the holy women were supposed to effect by their isolation: they came to die to themselves so as to attain heavenly life and freedom. Strict enclosure was necessary for their preservation, for Hugh of Semur judged that like "vessels of the temple, . . . as precious stones of the sanctuary holier than any vessel, it would be a profanity for them to be gazed upon by defiling lights."[102]

The *Vitae* and *Miracula* of Saint Hugh go into much detail about his foundation of Marcigny. What emerges is a picture of the complementarity of Cluny and Marcigny that is important to our subject. The anonymous author of the *Miracula* emphasizes the twinning of communities within the Ecclesia cluniacensis: the men and the women; the cenobites and the anchorites; the cloister and the hermitage.[103] Gilo, author of one of the main *Vitae sancti Hugonis*, saw Hugh of Semur as a latter-day Noah choosing representatives of each kind to put in the "ship of Saint Peter," which he likened to the ark.[104] The image is a good illustration of how the Cluniacs saw themselves. They were a coming together of humanity whose different constituents had entered the "ship of Saint Peter" in order to be saved from the flood of the secular age.

"Branches unto the Sea"

In the fourth, fifth, and sixth chapters of book 3 of his *Historiarum libri quinque*, Rodulfus Glaber describes the renewal of the Christian world at the end

---

99. *Ep.*, 20, 1:27–41, here 38–39; Guigo I, *Consuetudines Cartusiae*, 28.4, SC, 313, p. 225.

100. DM, 1.8, p. 31, ll. 227–30; 1.20, p. 60, l. 57. Devotion at the altar is typically Cluniac, cf. Ulrich, *Antiquiores consuetudines*, 1.41, PL 149:687C.

101. DM, 1.22, pp. 65–66; *Ep.*, 20, 1:27–41; 107, p. 270; and 115 (to Héloïse), p. 306.

102. Gilo, *Vita sancti Hugonis*, 1.12, "Two Studies," p. 62.

103. *Alia miraculorum quorumdam S. Hugonis abbatis relatio*, BC, cols. 455C–457A, here 456C.

104. Gilo, *Vita sancti Hugonis*, 1.12, "Two Studies," pp. 62–63. Since patristic times the Church had been assimilated to Noah's ark; see Henri de Lubac, *Exégèse médiévale: les quatre sens de l'Ecriture*, 4 vols., Théologie, 41–42, 59 (Paris, 1959, 1961, 1964), 2.2, pp. 41ff. The extended application to the ship of Saint Peter is typically Gregorian: see Ian S. Robinson, "L'Eglise et la papauté," in *Histoire de la pensée politique médiévale*, ed. James H. Burns (Paris, 1993), pp. 244–46; on the single case of Peter Damian, M. Grandjean, *Laïcs dans l'Eglise*, p. 69.

of the first millennium. The Latin west was then being covered in a "white man-tle of churches," the monumental apparel of a renascent world that was the age of the monks, the age of Cluny. To explain the fabulous lot of the Burgundian monastery, Glaber resorts to etymology. "Cluny" comes, as he would have it, from *cluere*, "to grow." It was a fertile seed, that modest monastery of the early days with its mere twelve brothers; now it had come to fill "a great part of the earth."[105] In his apologia on behalf of Cluny at the heart of *De miraculis*, Peter the Venerable develops the same image, paraphrasing a passage in the Gospel of John and a verse of Psalm 79(80). From Cluny, "from the nard of spiritual virtues poured out from here, the whole 'house' of the world 'has been filled with the odor of the ointment'" (John 12:3); Cluny is a "vine," and its "monks 'the branches' that reach 'unto the sea'" (Psalm 79:12), in the west as in the east.[106]

The Ecclesia cluniacensis and the Cluniac "Nebula"

We need, of course, to recognize this image of Cluny's irresistible expansion for what it is: a shock argument in aid of a special pleading *pro domo*. The utility of such self-promotion of Cluny's "universalism" is that it forces the historian to ask a seemingly naive question: What precisely do we mean by "Cluny"?

Anyone who has needed to make a list of establishments constituting the Ecclesia cluniacensis (or worse, make a map!), or define "Cluniac" literature, knows that terms like "of Cluny" or "Cluniac" are actually rather hard to pin down.[107] To convince ourselves of this reality, it is sufficient to take the example of "Cluniac" literature.[108] Whom are we to include among Cluniac authors of the tenth to twelfth century? Simply the abbots and brothers of the monastery? To what extent can we consider the work of Rodulfus Glaber "Cluniac"? Glaber was extremely young when he entered the monastery of Saint-Germain at Auxerre, where his training brought him into contact with the works bequeathed by the Carolingian masters of this famous monastic school. His wanderlust and liter-ary gifts led him to frequent changes of religious house (among others, Moûtier-en-Puisaye and Saint-Léger at Champeaux). He attached himself to William of Dijon, disciple of Majolus of Cluny and abbot of Saint-Bénigne, Dijon, whose

---

105. *Works*, ed. J. France et al., Oxford Medieval Texts (Oxford, 1989), p. 124.

106. *DM*, 1.9, p. 36.

107. On the difficulties presented by cartographical representation of the Ecclesia cluniacensis, see I. Liebrich's contribution to the *Atlas d'Histoire de l'Eglise*, dir. Hubert Jedin, Kenneth Scott Latourette, and Jochen Martin (Turnhout, 1990), p. 47, and commentaries, pp. 35*–36* [French ed. of *Atlas zur Kirchengeschichte* (Freiburg im Breisgau, 1987)]. In view of the centrifugal movements to which the Cluniac body was periodically liable, no map can deliver more than a snapshot at best. The developments that I go on to outline below amply illustrate why I decided not to launch into so hazardous a venture.

108. The question was raised a long time ago by Jean Leclercq, *Aux sources de la spiritualité occi-dentale: étapes et constantes*, Tradition et spiritualité, 4 (Paris, 1964), pp. 105–6.

biographer he became. At Cluny, he began work on his *Historiarum libri quinque*, which he completed shortly before his death at Saint-Germain, Auxerre, in 1047. It consisted in an account of events taking place in the millennial anniversary years since the birth and passion of Christ, namely, from about the year 1000 to 1033, together with a profound meditation on the order of the world based upon a combination of the teachings of Ambrose of Milan and Maximus the Confessor.[109] Then what are we to say about Alger of Liège, who assumed the monastic habit late in life? Is he to be considered a "Cluniac" author? And what about Orderic Vitalis, whose *Historia ecclesiastica* is a precious source of information on the history of Cluny and its participation in the life of the Church in the twelfth century? The Anglo-Norman historiographer was a monk at Saint-Evroult, a house over which Cluny's influence was only indirect: some of its brothers were temporarily resident at the Burgundian sanctuary, and in the early 1060s it accepted the earliest Cluniac customs.[110] Then there is Gilo, monk of Cluny and later cardinal-bishop of Tusculum, the author of one of the *Vitae* of Saint Hugh and of a history of the First Crusade: Is he a "Cluniac" author? And are we to reject the important work of Hugh of Amiens, monk of Cluny and then successively prior of Saint-Martial at Limoges, prior of Saint Pancras's, Lewes, abbot of Reading, and archbishop of Rouen, whose writings were intimately bound up with Matthew of Albano and Peter the Venerable?

The difficulty of defining "Cluniac" in the literary sphere, as in others, presents the historian with a real problem of religious sociology. A possible way of solving the problem—such at any rate is my suggestion—is to draw a distinction between the Ecclesia cluniacensis and the Cluniac "nebula." Such a distinction makes it possible to show that to resort indiscriminately to the notion of a "Cluniac model" masks in fact very diverse realities. Narrowly conceived, it is a monastic church with a precise legal status; broadly conceived, it consists in more or less formal links generated by the spreading of the customs of Cluny—or indeed, in a still broader sense, a certain spiritual tone such as the obsession with funerary solidarity, which for want of a better epithet we call "Cluniac."[111]

109. Glaber's work is studied in the context of "Cluniac historiography" by Edmond Ortigues and Dominique Iogna-Prat, "Raoul Glaber et l'historiographie clunisienne," *Studi Medievali*, 3d ser., 26.2 (1985): 537–72; countered by Glauco M. Cantarella, "Appunti su Rodolfo il Glabro," *Aevum* 65 (1991): 279–94, who refuses to consider Glaber's work a Cluniac composition *stricto sensu*.

110. Orderic Vitalis, *Historia ecclesiastica*, 2.74, ed. and Eng. trans. Marjorie Chibnall, 6 vols., Oxford Medieval Texts (Oxford, 1969–80); and see Peter Dinter's introduction to *LT*, p. xxxii.

111. The "Cluniac tone" of charters *pro remedio animae* in the Milan diocesan area has been highlighted by Cinzio Violante, "Per una riconsiderazione della presenza cluniacense in Lombardia," in *Cluny in Lombardia*, Atti del Convegno storico celebrativo del IX Centenario della fondazione del priorato clunacense di Pontida, 22–25 April 1977, 2 vols., Italia benedettina, 1 (Cesena, 1979–81), pp. 521–664, here 626. See also Alfredo Lucioni, "Gli esordi del monachesimo fruttuariense nella diocesi di Milano: il priorato di San Nicolao di Padregnano," *Archivo Storico Lombardo* 116 (1990): 11–73, here 12.

The Ecclesia cluniacensis as a Structure

The Ecclesia cluniacensis was a juridical structure, the making of which has been well studied by Dietrich Poeck; it will suffice here to sum up the main conclusions of his research.[112] Under its early abbots, from Berno to Majolus, Cluny was a relatively informal network of establishments linked to the person of the abbot.[113] In this period it is very difficult to say precisely what was covered by the term *Sacrosancta ecclesia cluniacensis*, which regularly appears in the deeds. First and foremost it includes the properties that constitute the landed domain of the monastery and hence the churches and monastic dependencies, the patrimonial foundations of the first church of Cluny; beyond this first circle is a shifting, uncertain realm of monastic establishments that the abbot of Cluny reformed, spreading to them the models of discipline and liturgy in use at Cluny, although these houses did not become possessions of Cluny. Up to and including Majolus, such reforming activities were always considered matters personal to the abbot. For instance, at the reformed establishment of Saint-Germain, Auxerre, which Majolus took charge of in the 980s at the behest of Duke Henry of Burgundy, the abbot of Cluny represented only himself. At Fleury, Odo was abbot of Fleury: at Auxerre, Majolus was abbot of Saint-Germain.[114] This was an age of Cluniac ecclesiastical arrangements held on a life-interest basis. Like Benedict of Aniane and Berno, Odo and Majolus were "multi-abbots"; but their "multi-abbacy" remained personal to them. Much later, under Hugh of Semur's governance, the abbot of Cluny was functionally an *archiabbas*.[115] Between the two the Ecclesia cluniacensis had come into being as an institution; as Georg Schreiber said long ago, Cluny went from being a "Reformzentrum" (center of reform) to being a "Kongregationsmittelpunkt" (center of a congregation).[116]

From two points of view, Odilo's abbacy was a turning point in the develop-

112. Poeck, *"Cluniacensis Ecclesia."*

113. On the notion of monastic networks, see Cosimo D. Fonseca, "Typologie des réseaux monastiques et canoniaux des origines au XIIe siècle," in *Naissance et fonctionnement des réseaux monastiques et canoniaux*, Actes du premier colloque international du CERCOM, Saint-Etienne, 16–18 September 1985, CERCOR: Travaux et Recherches, 1 (Saint-Etienne, 1991), pp. 11–20.

114. On Majolus's reforming activities in northern Burgundy, especially at Saint-Germain at Auxerre, see Neithard Bulst, *Untersuchungen zu Klosterreformen Wilhelms von Dijon (962–1031)*, Pariser Historische Studien, 11 (Bonn, 1973), and Iogna-Prat, *"Agni immaculati,"* pp. 133–40.

115. I have used the term "multi-abbot" here rather than an equivalent of the *Oberabbas* Joachim Wollasch uses to describe Berno (*Mönchtum des Mittelalters*, p. 36), because *Oberabbas* is too close to the notion of "super-abbot" or "arch-abbot," which is not applicable before the abbacy of Hugh of Semur, when the Ecclesia cluniacensis as such was induced to take over other abbeys. On the "multi-abbacy," see also Michel Parisse, "Des réseaux invisibles: les relations entre monastères indépendants," in *Naissance et fonctionnement*, pp. 451–71, here 456–58. On the notion of reforming abbots' having their own personal networks in southern Gallia in the tenth and eleventh centuries, see Christian Lauranson-Rosaz, *L'Auvergne et ses marges (Velay, Gévaudan) du VIIIe au XIe siècle: la fin du monde antique?* (Le Puy-en-Vélay, 1987), pp. 242ff., and "Réseaux aristocratiques et pouvoir monastique dans le Midi aquitain du IXe au XIe siècle," in *Naissance et fonctionnement*, pp. 353–72, esp. 366ff.

116. Schreiber, *Kurie und Kloster*, p. 306.

ment of Cluny's constitution. First, Odilo developed a new conception of Cluniac reform, even if he had little success with it. Secondly, and most importantly, he obtained the first bull of exemption in the history of the monastery, a document that represented the first outline structuring of the Ecclesia cluniacensis. Unlike his predecessors or that other disciple of Majolus, William of Dijon, Odilo retained the title of abbot of Cluny in the very monasteries he was led to reform, such as Saint-Denis-en-France and Lérins.[117] His abbacy began a period in which the Ecclesia cluniacensis was structured along the lines of a cohesive group united around Cluny and its abbot, together with once-and-for-all integration (attempted in every case) of the reformed establishment.[118] This turning point in the conceptual development of Cluny as an ecclesiastical institution also explains the reluctance of princes and lay aristocrats to entrust the monasteries depending on them to so unaccommodating a reformer and the preference given to William of Dijon, who was not suspected of wishing to question the status of private monasteries (*Eigenklöster*). Thus a projected Cluniac implantation at Vézelay was rapidly aborted in 1026–27.[119] The case of Saint-Maur-des-Fossés is even more instructive. Reform of the establishment had previously been entrusted to Majolus by Count Burchard the Venerable with the agreement and support of Hugh, the new Capetian king.[120] Following his normal practice, Majolus had installed one of his disciples, Teuto, who had been confirmed by Robert II, the son and successor to Hugh Capet. Teuto was succeeded by Thibaud, abbot of Corméry and similarly a disciple of Majolus.[121] The account of this story, in the 1050s, by Burchard's biographer, Odo of Saint-Maur, is significant for revealing the distrust engendered by Cluniac "expansionism." Whereas Hugh Capet's original charter granting the *villa* of Maisons-Alfort to Majolus at the time of the reform of Saint-Maur-des-Fossés bore the words *Maiolo et congregationi eius* (to Majolus and his congregation), Odo sixty years later chooses to pass over all reference, even indirect, to Cluny and insists that the *villa* was given by the king to the "church of Saint-Maur."[122] Describing the

117. For Saint-Denis, see Léon Levillain, "Note sur quelques abbés de Saint-Denis," *RM* 1 (1905): 41–54, here 44, and Bulst, *Untersuchungen zu Klosterreformen Wilhelms von Dijon*, p. 215. For Lérins, see *Cartulaire de l'abbaye Saint-Honorat de Lérins*, ed. Henri Moris and Edmond Blanc (Paris, 1883 and 1905), 1.55, as well as Eliana Magnani Soares-Christen, "Monastères et aristocratie en Provence," 2 vols., doctoral thesis, Université de Provence (Aix-en-Provence, 1997), 1:49ff.

118. The phenomenon has been described by Marcel Pacaut as a "second Cluniac monastic network" in his "La formation du second réseau monastique clunisien (v. 1030–v. 1080)," in *Naissance et fonctionnement*, pp. 45–51.

119. On this obscure episode, see Bulst, *Untersuchungen zu Klosterreformen Wilhelms von Dijon*, pp. 190–2.

120. Described in Sackur, *Die Cluniacenser*, 1:247–50.

121. On Thibaud, see Olivier Guillot, *Le comte d'Anjou et son entourage au XIe siècle* (Paris, 1972), 1:168–70.

122. Eudes (Odo) of Saint-Maur, *Vita domni Burcardi*, chaps. 4–5, ed. Charles Bourel de la Roncière, Collection de textes pour servir à l'enseignement de l'Histoire (Paris, 1892), p. 12 and n. 1.

confirmation of Abbot Teuto by King Robert II, Odo notes the Cluniacs' sadness when the news was announced, because "they hoped to reduce the monastery to a dependency."[123] The "archabbacy" so dreaded by Odo of Saint-Maur and criticized by numerous opponents of Cluny in the twelfth century was contained in embryo in the Ecclesia cluniacensis developing during the abbacy of Odilo. The privilege of exemption granted by Pope Gregory V in 998 supplied the first clear definition of this monastic church.[124] The *enumeratio bonorum* (inventory of properties) contained in that document distinguished between two sections: first, Cluny itself and its immediate environs, essentially the *villae* and *curtes* constituting the lordship of Cluny; secondly, Cluniac property beyond the Mâconnais, which was described rather in "ecclesiastical" terms, as *ecclesiae, cellae, monasteria*. Given the longevity of legal definitions, the same basic distinction was reenacted in papal bulls down to Gregory VII, in 1076.

It was not until the abbacy of Hugh of Semur that the Ecclesia cluniacensis came to be described as a "body." In his "Customs," Bernard speaks of a *capitale monasterium*, considered as a head (*caput*), to which members (*membra*) belong. The distinction achieved force of law in a bull of Urban II issued in 1096.[125] Such an organic conception was not viable, however, until the papacy extended to the dependent establishments the privileges previously granted to Cluny alone, namely, those of exemption, exception from anathema and interdict, attribution of refuge status, and right of burial. This was achieved in the bull Urban II issued in 1097. Within the body thus defined, two levels of *membra* were gradually distinguished: the abbeys and the priories. First enunciated by Stephen IX (pope, 1057–58), this distinction became effective in the 1100s, when Paschal II decided that priories and abbeys currently without abbots should thenceforth remain so; certain ancient abbeys, like Charlieu, were reduced to priory status.

This short summary of the gradual structuring of the Ecclesia cluniacensis calls for several remarks. The Cluniac "body" was a hierarchic structure consisting of a head, the *monasterium capitale*, and members (abbeys and priories) of regional importance, to which in turn other priories or subpriories were subordinate at the local level. At its head, the abbot gave coherence to the whole; he represented the source of the customs of the *Ecclesia*.[126] This is what Gert Melville has termed the Cluniac abbatial "monarchism" rooted in the acknowl-

---

123. Ibid., chap. 5, p. 13. The relations between Cluny and Saint-Maur-des-Fossés in the years 1020–30 were in all probability not as bad as Odo of Saint-Maur, writing twenty years after the event, might lead his readers to believe. Odilo in fact, after 1027, acquired relics of Saint Maurus; see Peter Dinter's introduction to *LT*, pp. l–lii, and Dominique Iogna-Prat, "La geste des origines," 142–43.

124. *Papsturkunden 896–1046*, vol. 1, no. 351, pp. 682–86.

125. *Bullarium*, pp. 26–27, here 26 (*PL* 151:441–42). Bernard, *Ordo Cluniacensis*, 1.16, in *Vetus disciplina monastica*, ed. Marquard Herrgott (Paris, 1726), pp. 167–69, here 168, which is concerned with the benediction of novices *extra monasterium*.

126. Bernard, *Epistola ad Hugonem abbatem, Ordo Cluniacensis*, p. 135.

edged charisma of the abbots.[127] From the end of the tenth century, the time of Majolus, the tradition arose that the abbots of Cluny were holy.[128] More precisely, from this period, the abbatial function itself was seen as holy. For a long time the abbot of Cluny had been termed *venerabilis, venerandus,* even *reverendissimus.* But Majolus, in an act extant in the original, is the first abbot in office to be described as *sanctissimus.*[129] Sixty years later, another original act speaks of Abbot Odilo as a "man of highly renowned sanctity."[130] Gregory VII gave canonical force to the reality when, to the Roman synod of 1080, he declared that the abbatial office itself at Cluny was considered holy.[131]

The life of the Cluniac organism was ensured by the mobility of its members. Specifically this meant, first, the mobility of novices, who had to visit the "center," Cluny, to profess to the abbot, unless they were of a dependent house having its own abbot; secondly, the mobility of the abbot himself, most often journeying from one dependency to another; thirdly, the mobility of monastic officers, since the abbot would send officials from one house to another—like William of Roanne, named in *De miraculis,* who was successively prior of Saint-Martin-d'Ambierle, Charlieu, Sauxillanges, and Souvigny, grand prior of Cluny, abbot of Moissac, chamberlain of Cluny, then again prior of Charlieu.[132] Thus the Ecclesia cluniacensis was not a very centralized organism at all. Following in Dietrich Poeck's footsteps, we may ask to what extent the "head"—the abbot of Cluny—had any knowledge at all of the life of the most distant members, such as the subpriories. Cluny was not in fact to achieve organic coherence until the thirteenth century, the period in which the constituent administrative procedures of the order were put in place.[133]

The mobility of officers was not enough to check the centrifugal forces affecting the life of the congregation. The image given above of Cluny as a *monasterium omnium monasteriorum* is a fairly peaceful one. However, the integration of new members into the Ecclesia cluniacensis in the eleventh and twelfth centuries was often chaotic, uncertain, and never truly definitive, as Florent Cygler's

127. Melville, "Cluny après 'Cluny': le treizième siècle: un champ de recherche," *Francia* 17.1 (1990): 91–124. A general treatment of the question of the abbot's charismatic power is Franz J. Felten, "Herrschaft des Abtes," in *Herrschaft und Kirche. Beiträge zur Entstehung und Wirkungsweise episkopaler und monastischer Organisationsformen,* ed. Friedrich Prinz, Monographien zur Geschichte des Mittelalters, 33 (Stuttgart, 1988), pp. 147–286.

128. Iogna-Prat, "Panorama de l'hagiographie abbatiale clunisienne (v. 940–v. 1140)," in *Manuscrits hagiographiques,* pp. 77–118.

129. *CLU* 1461, 12 Nov. 978–11 Nov. 979, 2.515–16.

130. *CLU* 2927, 1039, 4.128–29.

131. Herbert E. J. Cowdrey, *The Cluniacs and the Gregorian Reform* (Oxford, 1970), pp. 272–73.

132. *DM,* 2.25, pp. 143–44.

133. Jörg Oberste, "*Ut domorum status certior habeatur* . . . Cluniazensischer Reformalltag und administratives Schriftgut im 13. und frühen 14. Jahrhundert," *Archiv für Kulturgeschichte* 76.1 (1994): 53ff.

study of the many thirteenth-century "rebellions" has shown.[134] Certain dependencies, like Lézat, retained their place in the Ecclesia cluniacensis over the long term; others, like Saint-Cyprien at Poitiers, Saint-Bertin, Saint-Gilles-du-Gard, or Vézelay, managed to throw off the yoke of the Cluniac "archabbacy"; still others, such as San Benedetto Po (Polirone) or Saint-Martial at Limoges, were able, by means of compromise, to keep a degree of independence within the Cluniac congregation; lastly, certain houses, such as the monastery of Saint-Rambert-en-Bugey, were but passing comets in the Cluniac firmament.[135]

In this complicated history, the role of the papacy was fundamental. In the second half of the eleventh century, Cluny represented an important quantity in the monastic politics of Rome. Thus Gregory VII and Urban II entrusted Hugh of Semur *vice nostra* (as our agent) with Saint-Gilles-du-Gard, San Benedetto Po (Polirone), Beaulieu, and Saint-Germain at Auxerre.[136] However, given the pope's recognized right to make "new laws,"[137] what had been granted might be withdrawn, even totally reversed. Thus Innocent II abrogated the earlier privileges that had placed Saint-Bertin within the Ecclesia cluniacensis.[138] The big problem lay in the "twin-headedness" of the Cluniac body. Dedicated to Saint Peter and Saint Paul, Cluny's fate was directly linked to that of the papacy. Dietrich Poeck has rightly stressed the importance of the bull granted by Urban II in 1096 in the history of the structuring of the Ecclesia cluniacensis, which thereafter was regarded as a body composed of a head and members. The problem was to know which—Cluny or the papacy—was its true head. Urban II's bull turned the Cluniac dependencies, regarded thus far as objects in the *enumeratio bonorum* of the Burgundian monastery, into actual subjects in law. But this new status was confirmed by privileges that the papacy granted directly to the estab-

---

134. Florent Cygler, "L'ordre de Cluny et les *rebelliones* au XIIIe siècle," *Francia* 19.1 (1992): 61–93.

135. Attached to Cluny in 1138–39, Saint-Rambert-en-Bugey had already departed from the ranks of Cluniac dependencies by the 1190s: see Cécile Treffort and Jean-François Reynaud, "Le berceau d'un culte: Saint-Rambert-en-Bugey," in *Saint Rambert: un culte régional depuis l'époque mérovingienne (histoire et archéologie)*, Monographies du CRA, 14 (Paris, 1995), pp. 25–39, here 29–30.

136. Saint-Gilles-du-Gard, 1076/77: Ulrich Winzer, *S. Gilles. Studien zum Rechtsstatus und Beziehungsnetz einer Abtei im Spiegel ihrer Memorialüberlieferung*, Münstersche Mittelalter-Schriften, 59 (Munich, 1988), pp. 58ff.; San Benedetto Po (Polirone), 1076/77: Leo Santifaller, *Quellen und Forschungen zum Urkunden- und Kanzleiwesen Papst Gregors VII.*, 1, Studi et Testi, 190 (Vatican City, 1957), no. 126, pp. 125–27; Armin Kohnle, *Abt Hugo von Cluny* (Sigmaringen, 1993), pp. 162–63; Beaulieu, 1096: *Bullarium*, p. 24 (*PL* 151:468), and Kohnle, *Abt Hugo*, pp. 204–5; Saint-Germain at Auxerre, ca. 1099: *CLU* 3717, 5.63–64, and Kohnle, *Abt Hugo*, pp. 177–79.

137. This right was established by Gregory VII in his famous *Dictatus papae*, 7, *Das Register Gregors VII.*, 2.55a, 1:203. There is a good synthesis of the subject of papal intervention in monastic church life in Ian S. Robinson, *The Papacy 1073–1198: Continuity and Innovation*, Cambridge Medieval Textbooks (Cambridge, 1990), pp. 236ff.

138. *Inn. II Papae Ep. et Priv.*, cap. 398, *PL* 179:459B–460A.

lishments concerned. The recognition of the members of the body was therefore achieved at the cost of the pope's intrusion into the procedures of the Ecclesia cluniacensis. The statutes of the thirteenth century, together with the change from an *ecclesia* to an order, in effect institutionalized his entry. Thenceforth it was no rarity to see the pope intervening, as Gregory IX did in 1231/33 and Nicholas IV in 1289, to reform the life of the order.

The Cluniac "Nebula"

From the margins of the Ecclesia cluniacensis, a legally defined structure, extended a "nebula" far more complex and difficult to examine. Gert Melville has spoken of "Cluny after 'Cluny'"[139] and Barbara H. Rosenwein of "Cluny before 'Cluny'";[140] perhaps we need to add here "Cluny beyond 'Cluny.'" Joachim Wollasch noted the phenomenon years ago, observing that, in the *Dialogus duorum monachorum Cluniacensis et Cisterciensis* written by Idung in 1154 or 1155, what in fact was meant by "Cluniac" was everything that was not Cistercian, in other words traditional Benedictine monasticism.[141]

How could they have reached such a point? The question is not amenable to an easy answer. The monastic reform was no doubt a catalyst in promoting the Cluniac model in the eleventh century. In the early years of the new millennium, at Fécamp, a monastery reformed by Majolus's disciple William of Dijon, Cluny was viewed as a source "from which the waters of holy monastic religion, dispersed already far and wide through many places, have in God's providence flowed on here."[142] The same recognition, without any direct reform on Cluny's part, was encouraged by Gregory VII, who cited Cluny, alongside Saint-Victor at Marseille, as a model of "Roman freedom" for other monasteries.[143]

The spread of Cluniac customs. Consideration of the customs of Cluny touches upon questions relating to the monastic reform. The history of the textual and manuscript tradition of the different Cluniac customs still largely remains to be written. The studies of Dom Kassius Hallinger, recently amended and complemented by those of Joachim Wollasch, Peter Dinter, and Burkhardt Tutsch, nevertheless give us enough information to draw up a stemma that provides an adequate summary of the spread of the Cluniac customs beyond Cluny.

Following Kassius Hallinger, we may differentiate three sorts of monastic customaries: those concerned with the liturgical use of a monastery; those relating to the organization of the physical life of the monastic community; "mixed"

139. Melville, "Cluny après 'Cluny.'"

140. "La question de l'immunité clunisienne," *Bulletin de la Société des fouilles archéologiques et des monuments historiques de L'Yonne* 12 (1995): 1–11, here 2.

141. Wollasch, *Mönchtum des Mittelalters*, p. 182.

142. *Recueil des actes des ducs de Normandie de 911 à 1066*, ed. Marie Fauroux, Mémoires de la Société des antiquaires de Normandie, 36 (Caen, 1961), no. 9, 30 May 1006, pp. 79–81, here 80.

143. Diploma of Gregory VII, dated 8 May 1080, to William of Hirsau for Schaffausen, *Das Register Gregors VII.*, 7.24, 2:502–5, here 504.

customaries, blending aspects of the former two categories.[144] Instead of the first two categories one might do better to employ Aimé-Georges Martimort's distinction between the "ordinary" and the "customary."[145] The *Consuetudines antiquiores* of Cluny belongs to the first type.[146] It is exclusively concerned with the liturgical life of the monastery, apart from very rare examples, such as articles dealing with bleeding or the time interval between eating and mass.[147] The date of composition of the *Consuetudines antiquiores* remains relatively uncertain. Kassius Hallinger, who has edited the text in volume VII/2 of the *Corpus Consuetudinum Monasticarum* by giving a synopsis of the base versions (B B[1]) and their derivatives, has in the end suggested a date somewhere in the 990s, but the margin of uncertainty may make it as late as 1015.[148] It seems therefore that these earliest Cluniac customs would have been composed near the beginning of Odilo's abbacy (994–1049). The other texts are hybrid. They are concerned as much with liturgical activity as with the organization of the life of the monastery; they thus deal as much with the "ordinary" as with the "customary." The first of these books is the *Liber tramitis aevi Odilonis* or "The Book of the Way." "The Way" is nothing other than the way that leads to heaven, which suggests the whole program of life contained in the customary. The *Liber tramitis*, in the form in which it has come down to us, was composed in three phases: the first, at Cluny, between 1027 and 1030; the second, after 1033, i.e., during the second part of Odilo's abbacy; the third, during 1050 and 1060, the period in which the copy of the text used at Farfa was composed.[149] It was due to the survival of the text used at this monastery of Sabina in Italy that the *Liber tramitis* was for so long known as "the customs of Farfa." Thanks to Peter Dinter's critical edition in the *Corpus Consuetudinum Monasticarum*, we now know that the text comprises the customs of Cluny together with an introduction and a few interpolations proper to Farfa. The *Liber tramitis* was composed on the foundations provided by the *Consuetudines antiquiores*. But it also includes the liturgical innovations introduced during the second part of Odilo's abbacy; most importantly, after the description of the liturgy comes a much shorter treatise on the offices of the monastery. Thus this codification contains the earliest written de-

144. Kassius Hallinger, "*Consuetudo*. Begriff, Formen, Forschungsgeschichte, Inhalt," in *Untersuchungen zu Kloster und Stift*, Veröffentlichungen des Max-Planck-Instituts für Geschichte, 68 (Göttingen, 1980), p. 148.

145. *Les "Ordines," les ordinaires et les cérémoniaux*, Typologie des sources du Moyen Age occidental, 56 (Turnhout, 1991), p. 66. Martimort (p. 75) considers the *Liber tramitis*, comprising "the ordinary strictly speaking (without title) and the consuetudinary (*Liber secundus*)," to be "the first complete monastic ordinary."

146. *CCM*, 7.1, pp. 81–115 and 206–329 (introduction); 7.2, pp. 3–150 (edition of the *Consuetudines antiquiores* and its derivatives) and pp. 151–233 (*apparatus explicativus*).

147. *CCM*, 7.2, 8–11, pp. 12–14.

148. *CCM*, 7.1, pp. 226, 246–48.

149. Peter Dinter discusses the different phases of composition of the *Liber tramitis* in his introduction to that volume: *CCM*, 10 (Siegburg, 1980).

scription we have of Cluny—of second-stage Cluny, Cluny II, consecrated in 981—and the life its monks led there.[150] During Hugh of Semur's abbacy, two more texts were composed. The first of these is the *Ordo cluniacensis*, the "Customs" of Bernard, which, in a first version dating from 1060–75, comprises two books, one liturgical, the other a treatise on the offices. As the author's letter of dedication shows, it was for internal use. The second is the *Antiquiores consuetudines cluniacensis monasterii*, the "Customs" of Ulrich of Zell, a monk of Regensburg who had stayed at Cluny and whose work was done at the request of Abbot William of Hirsau during the 1080s. Ulrich took Bernard's work as his model, at times reproducing it word for word, but not hesitating to complement and amend it. His main initiative consisted in introducing a third book (book 2 of his text) relating to disciplinary aspects of the life of the monastery. In return, Ulrich's "Customs" influenced the second redaction of those of Bernard dating from between 1084 and 1086. Such at least was the genesis of these customs as reconstructed by Kassius Hallinger.[151] Joachim Wollasch, taking a fresh look at the subject, has a significantly different interpretation.[152] He considers that Bernard and Ulrich both drew their inspiration from an earlier customary dating from the first part of Hugh of Semur's abbacy and no longer extant. According to this view, Bernard and Ulrich both worked in the same period, the former pre-1078 and the latter pre-1083, and there was no second redaction of Bernard's *Ordo*. Bernard's work was for internal use with a view to mediating between opposing parties within the monastery. Ulrich on the other hand sought a middle way suitable for the monastic life of outside communities drawn to the reforming vigor of the Cluniac usages.

The period 1085–90 saw an end to the composition of customaries at Cluny. What began then was an era of abbey statutes: precise provisions made by the abbot on points that had not been envisaged by the customs—in other words supplements to the customs—or else amendments to the older usages. The

150. For details of the reconstitution of Cluny II based on this description and the several soundings undertaken by Kenneth J. Conant, and for recent archaeological excavation, see respectively: Kenneth J. Conant, *Cluny: les églises et la maison du chef d'ordre* (Mâcon, 1968); Christian Sapin, *La Bourgogne préromane: construction, décor et fonction des édifices religieux* (Paris, 1986), pp. 67ff., and "Cluny II et l'interprétation archéologique de son plan," in *Religion et culture autour de l'an Mil: royaume capétien et Lotharingie*, actes du colloque, Hugues Capet 987–1987: la France de l'an Mil, Auxerre 26–27 June 1987, Metz 11–12 September 1987, ed. Dominique Iogna-Prat and Jean-Charles Picard (Paris, 1990), pp. 85–92; Neil Stratford, "Les bâtiments de l'abbaye de Cluny à l'époque médiévale: état des questions," *Bulletin monumental* 150.4 (1992): 383–411; Anne Baud and Gilles Rollier, "Abbaye de Cluny: campagne archéologique 1991–1992," *Bulletin monumental* 151.3 (1993): 453–68.

151. Kassius Hallinger, "Klunys Brauche zur Zeit Hugos des Grossen (1049–1109). Prolegomena zur Neuherausgabe des Bernhard und Udalrich von Kluny," *Zeitschrift der Savigny-Stiftung für Rechtsgeschichte, Kanonistische Abteilung* 45 (1959): 99–140.

152. "Zur Verschriftlichung der klösterlichen Lebensgewohnheiten unter Abt Hugo von Cluny," *FMSt* 27 (1993): 317–49.

statutes of Abbot Hugh of Semur belong to the former category. One of his statutes for example instituted a liturgical celebration in honor of Alfonso VI of Castile-León, a great benefactor of the monastery; the observance was to begin in his lifetime, then continue in his memory after his death, taking as its model that contained in the *Liber tramitis* regarding Emperor Henry II.[153] The statutes of Peter the Venerable are of a completely different order.[154] These did not simply complement the older usages; their chief character was to amend them within the context of reform of the Ecclesia cluniacensis. Each decision by the abbot was accompanied by a "cause" (*causa*), i.e., an argument explaining the statute's purpose.

Such, then, were the basic regulatory texts that, during the eleventh and twelfth centuries, constituted and modified the particular observance uniting the various members of the Ecclesia cluniacensis. Yet how are we to account for the vast influence the Cluniac customs exerted well beyond the Cluniac body without being forced to describe as "junior Cluniac" or "neo-Cluniac" the establishments that were thus influenced?[155] Peter Dinter has shown that the Cluniac usages codified in the *Liber tramitis* were treated at Farfa as a model to refer to without actually being followed on a day-to-day basis.[156] Burkhardt Tutsch's current research on how Bernard's and Ulrich's "Customs" were received points to similar conclusions. Within the Cluniac network, available texts were freely used: thus the brothers of Saint-Martial at Limoges made use of passages of Ulrich's work, comparing and contrasting them with Bernard's version. Meanwhile, outside the Ecclesia cluniacensis, at Nouaillé for instance, these customs were reworked and adapted to the local history and usages. On occasions, as at Cava, the Cluniac customs were used as a simple reference book, a sort of vade mecum for resolving this or that problem of practical life or liturgy.[157] One example of the influence of Cluniac usages, admittedly exceptional and limited in

153. Hugh's statute has been edited by H. E. J. Cowdrey, "Two Studies," pp. 159–60; the arrangement has been studied by Charles J. Bishko, "Liturgical Intercessions at Cluny for the King-Emperors of León," in *Spanish and Portuguese Monastic History*, 600–1300 (London, 1984), no. 8. Abbot Odilo's arrangements in honor of Henry II are in the *Liber tramitis*, 139, pp. 199–200.

154. Ed. Giles Constable, in *Consuetudines Benedictinae variae (Saec. XI–Saec. XIV)*, CCM, 6, pp. 39–106, with important introduction.

155. The notions alluded to come from Kassius Hallinger. The problem of defining links arising from the diffusion of the customs of Cluny is particularly acute in two studies of Cluniac influence in Italy: Giorgio Picasso, "Usus e consuetudines cluniacensi in Italia," *Aevum* 57 (1983): 215–26; Hubert Houben, "Il monachesimo cluniacense e i monasteri normanni dell'Italia meridionale," *Benedettina* 39.2 (1992): 341–61.

156. *LT*, p. xliii.

157. From a dissertation directed by Professor Joachim Wollasch at the Westfälische Wilhelms-Universität, Münster, which has been published as Burkhardt Tutsch, *Studien zur Rezeptionsgeschichte der Consuetudines Ulrichs von Cluny*, Vita regularis, 6 (Münster im W., 1998). See also Burkhardt Tutsch, "Die Consuetudines Bernhards und Ulrichs von Cluny im Spiegel ihrer handschriftlichen Überlieferung," *FMSt* 30 (1996): 248–93.

scope yet nonetheless particularly striking, is Odilo's decree inaugurating the feast commemorating the dead on 2 November (All Souls' Day). His decree, dating from at least the 1030s and incorporated into the *Liber tramitis*, concerned only the brothers at Cluny and its dependencies.[158] But soon, from the 1050s and by various routes, in particular collections of customs like Lanfranc's *Decreta*, the Cluniac commemoration spread from one place to another until it was observed throughout the entirety of Latin Christendom.[159]

Such examples make it possible to see how Cluny gained outside influence by a sort of capillary action. Its influence was spread as much by texts that transmitted the usages of Cluny as by men who were formed by them. We need only look at the monastic itinerary of Jotsald, Odilo's disciple and biographer, recently and convincingly reconstructed by Johannes Staub.[160] Both author and notary, the monk Jotsald had a lengthy period of activity under Abbots Odilo and Hugh of Semur; he is then lost sight of after 1051 or 1052, when he accompanied Hugh of Semur, who was then serving as papal legate, on a mission to Hungary.[161] Some Cluniac necrologies commemorate a Jotsald on 8 March, the very date on which the necrology of Saint-Claude (Saint-Oyand) in the Jura honors one of its abbots having the same name. The coincidence of the two names makes it more than probable that the two Jotsalds are one and the same. Having left Cluny in order to head an establishment not belonging to the Ecclesia cluniacensis, the former disciple of Odilo and companion to Hugh of Semur nevertheless retained his links with his former community. After his death, Jotsald's memory was honored at Cluny, just like that of any other professed monk of the monastery. Yet there is more: for it was to Saint-Claude that Count Simon of Crépy, one of Hugh of Semur's aristocratic connections in northeast Francia and founder of the Cluniac priory of Crépy-en-Valois, decided to go in order to lead the life of a hermit. The principal manuscript sources of the *Vita sancti Odilonis* also have Crépy-en-Valois as their provenance. Such were the commemorative and literary intricacies whereby the ideals of Cluny were diffused.

Inclusion in the Cluniac necrologies. Even at the heart of the Ecclesia cluniacensis, the term "nebula" allows us to plumb what is initially a surprising question: how one is supposed to identify the professed Cluniac. In a strict sense it is he who has made his monastic profession in the hands of the abbot or his representative. Yet is this true of all the *fratres* or *monachi nostrae congregationis* men-

---

158. *LT*, 126, pp. 186–7, and 138, p. 199.

159. The full details of the history of the spread of Odilo's decree still require research. I have attempted to offer some guidance in my "Les morts dans la comptabilité céleste des Clunisiens de l'an Mil," in *Religion et culture autour de l'an Mil*, pp. 59–60 [Eng. trans., "The Dead in the Celestial Bookkeeping of the Cluniac Monks around the Year 1000," in *Debating the Middle Ages: Issues and Readings*, ed. Lester K. Little and Barbara H. Rosenwein (Oxford, 1998), pp. 340–62].

160. "Die Vita des Abtes Odilo von Cluny (994–1049) von seinem Schüler Iostald, Abt von Saint-Claude und andere hagiographische Texte. Untersuchungen und kritische Editionen als Beitrag zur cluniazensischen Literatur," dissertation, Heidelberg, 1997, pp. 81ff.

161. Kohnle, *Abt Hugo*, p. 76.

tioned in the necrologies, in which case they are no more than simple *libri memoriales fratrum* (memorial books of monks)?

The Ecclesia cluniacensis, like any other eleventh- or twelfth-century monastic *familia* (the brothers and their *familiares* or lay friends), had inherited from the distant Carolingian period forms of solidarity—guilds, conjurations, and confraternities—that guaranteed to their members the advantages of brotherhood in this world and remembrance in the next.[162] Variously termed *libri confraternitatum, libri memoriales,* or *libri vitae,* registers were kept of the names of living or dead members so as to commend them to God at the eucharistic sacrifice. The Cluniac necrologies belong to this tradition of books of life.[163] Cluny's own necrology is lost, but Joachim Wollasch and his collaborators at the Institut für Frühmittelalterforschung at Münster have succeeded in reconstructing its tenor by way of a synopsis of necrologies deriving from nine member communities of the Ecclesia cluniacensis,[164] namely: Saint-Martial, Limoges (I)

162. Otto G. Oexle, "Gilden als soziale Gruppen in der Karolingerzeit," in *Das Handwerk in vor- und frühgeschichtlicher Zeit,* ed. Herbert Jankuhn et al., vol. 1, Abhandlungen der Akademie der Wissenschaften in Göttingen, Phil.-hist. Klasse, 3d ser., 122 (Göttingen, 1981), pp. 284–354; Oexle, "Conjuratio und Gilde im frühen Mittelalter. Ein Beitrag zum Problem der sozialgeschichtlichen Kontinuität zwischen Antike und Mittelalter," in *Gilden und Zünfte,* ed. Berent Schwineköper (Sigmaringen, 1985), pp. 151–214. In an analytical synthesis of Karl Schmid's work, Oexle has written a remarkable introduction to the *Gruppenforschung:* "Gruppen in der Gesellschaft. Das wissenschaftliche OEuvre von Karl Schmid," *FMSt* 28 (1994): 410–23.

163. On the genesis of the necrologies in the tradition of the books of life, see Nicolas-N. Huyghebaert, *Les documents nécrologiques,* Typologie des sources Moyen Age occidental, 4 (Turnhout, 1972), pp. 13–14.

164. *Synopse der cluniacensischen Necrologien.* The description that follows is based upon the introductory articles in the *Synopse* by Joachim Wollasch ("Die Synopse der cluniacensischen Necrologien als Arbeitsinstrument der Forschung") and Franz Neiske ("Die synoptische Darstellung der cluniacensischen Necrologien"), as well as studies by Axel Müssigbrod, "Zur Necrologüberlieferung aus cluniacensischen Klöstern," *RB* 98 (1988): 62–113, and Dietrich Poeck, "Formgeschichtliche Beobachtungen zur Entstehung einer necrologischen Tradition," in *Memoria: der geschichtliche Zeugniswert des liturgischen Gedenkens im Mittelalter,* ed. Karl Schmid and Joachim Wollasch, Münstersche Mittelalter-Schriften, 48 (Munich, 1984), pp. 727–49. Among items from the rich output of the Institut für Frühmittelalterforschung in Münster on this subject, particularly useful are Joachim Wollasch, "Les obituaires, témoins de la vie clunisienne," *CCMé* 22 (1979): 139–71; Franz Neiske, "Concordances et différences dans les nécrologes clunisiens: aspects d'une analyse statistique," *Revue d'histoire de l'Eglise de France* 68 (1982): 257–67; Dietrich Poeck, "La synopse des nécrologes clunisiens: un instrument de recherche," *RM* 60 (1983): 315–29. The three *Memoria* volumes of collected essays—the first just cited; the second, *Memoria in der Gesellschaft des Mittelalters,* ed. Dieter Geuenich and Otto G. Oexle, Veröffentlichungen des Max-Planck-Instituts für Geschichte, 111 (Göttingen, 1994); the third, *Memoria als Kultur,* ed. Otto G. Oexle, same series, 121 (Göttingen, 1995)—firmly place the Cluniac necrologies in the field of problems associated with memory in the high Middle Ages. Finally, two articles, one programmatic, the other an appraisal, consider necrological issues in the context of the confraternities: Karl Schmid and Joachim Wollasch, "Societas et Fraternitas: Begründung eines kommentierten Quellenswerkes zur Erforschung der Personen und Personengruppen des Mittelalters," *FMSt* 9 (1975): 1–48; Joachim Wollasch, "Das Projekt 'Societas et Fraternitas,'" in *Memoria in der Gesellschaft,* pp. 11–31.

from the years 1063/65;[165] Moissac/Duravel from 1070/77;[166] Marcigny-sur-Loire from 1092/93 (a necrology long thought to pertain to Villars-les-Moines, the provenance of the manuscript);[167] Saint-Martial, Limoges (II) from 1115/20; Saint-Saulve, near Valenciennes, from 1130/40; Saint-Martin-des-Champs, Paris, from 1174/76; Longpont, Ile-de-France, from 1190 /1200;[168] Beaumont, dependent priory of Saint-Martin-des-Champs, Paris, from about 1220; lastly, Montierneuf, Poitiers, from 1450. In so doing, they have assembled a vast mass of names—96,000 entries for 48,000 deceased persons—analysis of which, whether simple or cross-referenced with facts furnished by the charters, amounts to an extraordinary tool for studying the communities in question, the network of living and dead that made up the Ecclesia cluniacensis and its lay environment.[169]

When these nine extant sources are compared, there emerges a paradigm necrology containing two sorts of entry: a main category reserved for professed monks (*monachi nostrae congregationis*) and a secondary, not to say marginal category open to friends (*familiares, amici nostri*).[170] Two of the nine sources are from Saint-Martial at Limoges. The first bears witness to a tradition dating from

165. See Andreas Sohn, *Der Abbatiat Ademars von Saint-Martial de Limoges (1063–1114): ein Beitrag zur Geschichte des cluniacensischen Klosterverbandes*, Beiträge zur Geschichte des alten Mönchtums und des Benediktinertums, 37 (Münster im W., 1989); Jean-Loup Lemaître, *Mourir à Saint-Martial: la commémoration des morts et les obituaires à Saint-Martial de Limoges* (Paris, 1989).

166. *Das Martyrolog-Necrolog von Moissac/Duravel*, ed. Axel Müssigbrod and Joachim Wollasch, Münstersche Mittelalter-Schriften, 44 (Munich, 1988); see also Axel Müssigbrod, *Die Abtei Moissac 1050–1150: zu einem Zentrum cluniacensischen Mönchtums in Südwestfrankreich*, Münstersche Mittelalter-Schriften, 58 (Munich, 1988), and same author, "Quellen zum Totengedächtnis der Abtei Moissac," *RB* 97 (1987): 253–88.

167. *Das Necrologium des Cluniacenser-Priorates Münchenwiler (Villars-les-Moines)*, ed. Gustav Schnürer, Collectanea Friburgensia, n.s., 10 (Friburg, Switzerland, 1909); the reassignment to Marcigny is the work of Joachim Wollasch, "Ein cluniacensiches Totenbuch aus der Zeit Hugos von Cluny," *FMSt* 1 (1967): 406–43.

168. See Poeck, *Longpont*.

169. Among examples of simple or cross-referenced exploitation of this material, see the following three pieces by Joachim Wollasch: "Wer waren die Mönche von Cluny?" in *Clio et son regard. Mélanges d'histoire de l'art et d'archéologie offerts à Jacques Stiennon*, ed. Rita Lejeune and Joseph Deckers (Leuven, 1982), pp. 663–78; "Zur frühesten Schicht des Cluniacensischen Totengedächtnisses," in *Geschichtsschreibung und geistiges Leben im Mittelalter. Festschrift für Heinz Löwe zum 65. Geburtstag*, ed. Karl Hauck and Hubert Mordek (Cologne, 1978), pp. 247–80; "Prosopographie et informatique: l'exemple des Clunisiens et de leur entourage laïque," in *Informatique et prosopographie*, proceedings of conference, CNRS, Paris, 1984, ed. Caroline Bourlet, Jean-Philippe Genêt, and Lucie Fossier (Paris, 1986), pp. 109–18. See also Franz Neiske, "Der Konvent des Klosters Cluny zur Zeit des Abtes Maiolus. Die Namen der Mönche in Urkunden und Necrologien," in *Vinculum societatis: Joachim Wollasch zum 60. Geburtstag*, ed Franz Neiske, Dietrich Poeck, and Mechthild Sandmann (Sigmaringendorf, 1991), pp. 118–56; Maria Hillebrandt, "Stiftungen zum Seelenheit durch Frauen in den Urkunden des Klosters Cluny," ibid., pp. 58–67.

170. See chart in Poeck, "Formgeschichtliche Beobachtungen zur Entstehung einer necrologischen Tradition," p. 735.

before the abbey was "clunified" in 1062.[171] The deceased whose names are entered into the necrology are divided into two groups: the professed (*monachi nostrae congregationis*) and outside monks (*monachi peregrini*), i.e., brothers belonging to establishments in a communion of prayer with Saint-Martial. The second necrology, on the other hand, conforms to the professed/*familiares* style of division. The Cluniac necrological paradigm documented from the time of Abbot Hugh of Semur thus proves to be a memorial of the brothers that includes a selective and in sum marginal remembrance of lay people. The model followed goes back to the *Liber tramitis aevi Odilonis*, which stipulates that the names of the deceased should be entered chronologically in the "martyrology" ("necrology" is what the writer intended, a confusion that says much about its closeness, in his mind, to the saints' anniversary book) and read out in chapter on the anniversary of their death in order according to their group (professed/*familiares*).[172] The only distinction to appear in the memorials for the brethren relates not to their particular order but to the establishment to which they belonged: an *l* or *le* for Saint-Martial, Limoges, an *M* for Saint-Martin-des-Champs, or a simple cross for Saint-Saulve and Montierneuf, as opposed to other members of the Ecclesia cluniacensis. As for nuns, they are distinguished from the monks not merely at Marcigny-sur-Loire by means of the small mark *scm* (*sanctimonialis*), but also at Saint-Martin-des-Champs and Montierneuf where they constitute a third autonomous group beside the professed and the *familiares*. The parameters for the commemoration of the brothers also varied from place to place. Limoges I and Moissac/Duravel commemorated those of their community that had died before the establishment was "clunified." Some communities, like Montierneuf, took account of the whole of the Cluniac necrological tradition, including the names of professed Cluniacs prior to the foundation of their abbey at Poitiers in 1076. Others, like Saint-Saulve, limited their collective memorial to the professed of the Ecclesia cluniacensis who had died since the foundation of their particular establishment or its "clunification." It is possible, as Dietrich Poeck suggests, that this restriction in the case of Saint-Saulve (1130/40) resulted from an application of Peter the Venerable's statute of that period, which sought to limit the number of necrological entries per diem to fifty, so as to alleviate the liturgical and economic burdens relating to aid afforded to the deceased.[173]

The *memoriale fratrum* contains, upon analysis, several substantial surprises, so broad seemingly is the notion of who constitutes a *monachus nostrae congregationis*. Such for instance is the case at Saint-Martin-des-Champs and at Longpont, where Peter Damian is included among the group of professed Cluniacs—

171. Sohn, *Der Abbatiat Ademars von Saint-Martial*, pp. 134ff.

172. *LT*, 208, pp. 286–87. See Joachim Wollasch, "Zur Datierung des *Liber tramitis* aus Farfa anhand von Personen und Personengruppen," in *Person und Gemeinschaft im Mittelalter. Festschrift Karl Schmid zum fünfundsechzigsten Geburtstag*, pp. 237–55.

173. Poeck, "Formgeschichtliche Beobachtungen zur Entstehung einer necrologischen Tradition," p. 749.

a qualification that the hermit of Fonte Avellana, later raised to the dignity of cardinal-bishop of Ostia, assuredly did not have.[174] This example, which is particularly striking yet not exceptional, forces us to wonder whether all the *monachi nostrae congregationis* recorded in the necrologies and carefully distinguished from the *familiares* are truly brothers of Cluny. Joachim Wollasch considers that they are. But Neithard Bulst has noted that it was possible for monks who had never professed at Cluny to be enrolled in the necrology as *monachi nostrae congregationis*, such as Suppo, abbot of Fruttuaria and Mont-Saint-Michel (died 1061).[175] Finally, Axel Müssigbrod has relaunched the discussion about method by pointing out from the example of Bishop Peter of Pampeluna that the mere presence of a name on the necrology cannot be taken as proof of profession at Cluny. The truth is that many lay and ecclesiastical dignitaries were entitled to be commemorated at Cluny *quasi unus ex nobis* (as if one of us) by virtue of a necrological undertaking by the monastery that assimilated them to the status of brothers.[176] Are we therefore to conclude that the *plena fraternitas* (full fraternity) accorded to exceptional benefactors entailed incorporation into the Ecclesia cluniacensis as a *monachus nostrae congregationis*?[177] If so, and if as I believe the formula "monk of our congregation" cloaks many a lay or ecclesiastical grandee, then our entire conception of the Cluniac church as a structure of inclusion is ripe for revision.

The Ecclesia cluniacensis and the Wider Church

In order to perform a synthetic examination of the vast and complex question of Cluny's relations with the wider Church in the eleventh and twelfth centuries, we need to combine two complementary approaches: the microscopic and the macroscopic. Our first task therefore is to seek to understand the mechanisms whereby the Ecclesia cluniacensis managed to integrate itself into the web of institutional structures at the Church's base, the parish for instance. At a higher level, we need to look at how Cluniacs penetrated the ecclesiastical hierarchy. Lastly, we shall be interested in Cluny's "mimicry" of Rome, which enabled it to think of itself as a veritable Church in miniature.

"Incorporation" into the Parochial Network

In a Christian society defined by functions, the proposition of a "monastic *cura animarum* (care of souls)" ought, logically, to entail an internal contradiction.

174. Commemoration, 22 February. See Poeck, "La synopse des nécrologes clunisiens," 328.

175. Neithard Bulst, *CCMé* 13 (1970): 368–72, on the article of Wollasch, "Die Wahl des Papstes Nikolaus II." On Suppo, see Bulst, *Untersuchungen zu Klosterreformen Wilhelms von Dijon,* pp. 169–72.

176. Axel Mussigbrod, "Die Beziehungen des Bischofs Petrus von Pamplona zum französischen Mönchtum," *RB* 104 (1994): 346–78, esp. p. 353 and n. 27.

177. On the question of *plena fraternitas*, see Wollasch, "Das Projekt 'Societas et Fraternitas,'" pp. 18–19, which establishes a useful distinction between *societas* (participation) and *fraternitas* (membership).

According to the division of tasks decreed by the Carolingian legislators, it was the responsibility of monks to pray for collective salvation and that of the seculars to be directly responsible for the faithful. Yet theory was one thing and practice another. In the early Middle Ages monks did occupy themselves with pastoral activities, and the Cluniacs were right from the start implanted in the parochial network. During the period that interests us, the eleventh and twelfth centuries, the legal situation eventually came into line with the practical. At the end of an evolutionary process with many controversies along the way, it was finally recognized that "monks . . . like other priests" might legitimately exercise all the powers of the priestly office, "provided they have been chosen by the people and ordained by the bishop with the abbot's consent," as Gratian states in his *Decretum*.[178]

Several factors explain why the Gregorian opposition between ways of life came to be discarded and the Augustinian tradition of a unity of purpose between the cleric and the monk rediscovered. The first of these flows from the generalized access that monks gained to the priesthood. Though simply continent laymen when monasticism began, from at least the eighth century monks were admitted to the sacrament of ordination that turned them into priests.[179] Whatever secular clerics may sometimes have said of them, motivated by concern to preserve the monopoly of their own prerogatives and the revenues pertaining to the *cura animarum*, monks were not half-priests. The office of priest was indivisible; installation in that order conferred the power to exercise it wholly, be it in service at the altar or through the service of the word. The conflict between regulars and seculars (duplicated by the often-unedifying exchanges between the two sorts of regulars, monks and canons), plus the many debates sparked in eleventh- and twelfth-century councils about pastoral issues and monastic tithes, led to recognition of the right of monk-priests to ministry of the word; but it also made it possible to erect an essential distinction between the "power to preach" conferred by the sacrament of ordination and the authority to exercise that power, which only bishops and popes could confer. At the end of this long historical process, the monks passed beyond the simple ref-

178. Gratian, *Decretum*, IIa pars, causa xvi, quaest. i, cap. 19, in *Corpus Iuris Canonici*, ed. Friedberg (Leipzig, 1879), vol. 1, cols. 765–66. Within an abundant but often geographically circumscribed bibliography, the global parameters of the problem of the monasteries' pastoral outreach are best gauged from some of the older studies, such as Schreiber, *Kurie und Kloster*, 2:40–49; Ursmer Berlière, "L'exercice du ministère paroissial par les moines du XIIe au XVIIIe siècle," *RB* 39 (1927): 227–50; Philipp Hofmeister, "Mönchtum und Seelsorge bis zum 13. Jahrhundert," *SMGBOZ* 65 (1955): 245–62. See also the numerous references in Zerfaß, *Der Streit um die Laienpredigt*.

179. On the priesthood of monks, see O. Nussbaum, *Kloster, Priestermönch und Privatmesse: ihr Verhältnis im Westen von den Anfängen bis zum hohen Mittelalter*, Theophania, Beiträge zur Religionsund Kirchengeschichte des Altertums, 14 (Bonn, 1961), and above all, Angelus A. Häussling, *Mönchskonvent und Eucharistiefier*, Liturgiewissenschaftliche Quellen und Forschungen, 58 (Münster im W., 1973).

erence to "charisma" and saw their right to fulfill pastoral duties recognized, subject to episcopal or papal control.[180]

The monks' gradual access to the priesthood was linked in large part to the pastoral funerary role entrusted to them and to the fact that the service of the dead was in the first instance eucharistic.[181] From around the year 1000 the Cluniacs were effective propagandists in funerary matters. The monastery charters, analyzed in detail by Dietrich Poeck from the earliest period to the abbacy of Hugh of Semur, indicate an exponential growth in the number of gifts *pro remedio animae* (for the soul's relief) under Odilo.[182] The laity sought the companionship of Peter, bearer of the keys of heaven, close to whom they desired to be buried and whose votary they wished to become against the Day of Judgment. The attractiveness of the monastery's lay cemetery was extended to member establishments of the Ecclesia cluniacensis in 1097, when Pope Urban II recognized that the brothers of the Cluniac dependencies also had the right to bury (*sepulturae debita*).[183] These funerary duties in time revealed themselves to be both a powerful force integrating abbeys and priories dependent on Cluny into their regional environments and an essential factor in exchanges with the minor and middle-ranking aristocracy. Even if the phenomenon is well attested elsewhere, for instance at Monte Cassino,[184] the inclusion of members of the laity in the monastic *societas* was nowhere undertaken to such a degree as in the Cluniac network, a fact whose ecclesiological and sociological implications we shall be analyzing later on. This funerary preoccupation was all the more marked inasmuch as people sought the conjoined force of all the brothers of the Ecclesia cluniacensis, not simply the efficacy of the Burgundian sanctuary. The practice is attested from Odilo's time as abbot: donors whose gifts were made in connection with their death came to solicit the suffrages not simply of the monks at Cluny but of those of its dependencies also.[185] To its servants and friends the

180. On this development, here briefly summarized, see Maurice Peuchmaurd, "Le prêtre ministre de la parole dans la théologie du XIIe siècle," *Recherches de théologie ancienne et médiévale* 29 (1962): 52–76, but above all Rolf Zerfaß, *Der Streit um die Laienpredigt*, pp. 102ff.

181. On funerary pastoral work and the phenomenon of private Masses in the high Middle Ages, see the vital study by Arnold Angenendt, "*Missa specialis*. Zugleich ein Beitrag zur Entstehung der Privatmessen," *FMSt* 17 (1983): 153–221.

182. Dietrich Poeck, "Laienbegräbnisse in Cluny," *FMSt* 15 (1981): 68–179.

183. Bull of 17 April 1097, in *Bullarium*, p. 28 (*PL* 151:493–94). On this point see Kohnle, *Abt Hugo*, pp. 54 and 301–2.

184. Heinrich Dormeier, *Montecassino und die Laien im 11. und 12. Jahrhundert*, Schriften der MGH, 27 (Stuttgart, 1979), pp. 107ff.

185. On the possibilities of mobilizing the Ecclesia cluniacensis for funerary purposes, among other examples are Odilo's commitment to commemorate Count Lambert of Chalon, *CLU* 2921, 1037, 4.122–23, which speaks of suffrages *in Cluniaco monasterio vel in cunctis suis appendiciis Christo militantium*; Ulrich's *Antiquiores consuetudines*, 3.33, *PL* 149:777, speaking of undertaking for the laity before and after death *non solum apud nos, sed etiam in cunctis locis quae nostri iuris videntur*; Bernard's *Ordo Cluniacensis*, 1.26, p. 200, which speaks in similar terms; Peter the Venerable's commitment to

Ecclesia cluniacensis offered two types of funeral ceremonies: common or exceptional. The latter accorded the donor a *plena fraternitas*, the right to receive the same treatment as a professed brother. The chapter in the *Liber tramitis aevi Odilonis* that contains a model necrology distinguishes those members of the laity that possess titles, such as dukes, kings, or emperors.[186] Lording the heights of the lay memorials is the person of the "august" emperor Henry II, "most dear friend of our society and fraternity."[187] Following this model, Hugh of Semur took the step of honoring Emperor Henry III, Kings Ferdinand and Alfonso of Castile-León, and Empress Agnes and Queen Constance who followed in the wake of Empress Adelaide, the great benefactor of Cluny at the turn of the millennium.[188] The "Customs" of Bernard provide an echo to this by distinguishing two grades of anniversary, regular and exceptional. Exceptional ones were reserved to abbots, emperors, empresses, and kings, who were entitled to a maximum of ceremonial typified by, among other things, a full liturgical office, bread and wine for twelve paupers, and a full meal for the brothers.[189] From this point of view, the Cluniac commemorative sources (the necrologies, customs, and charters) were not simply the defining place of a society and brotherhood opening itself to the world, but the framework within which the laity endowed themselves with a memorial and called attention to the signs of their identity, their name and titles: they were in sum a mirror of aristocratic consciousness.[190] And thus we see just how important to contemporary society the funerary pastoral work undertaken by the Cluniacs was.

A second factor encouraging integration in the Church's local fabric stemmed from the early possession of altars, churches, and tithes. Cluny's readiness to build up its landed properties through gifts, exchanges, and sales meant that it came to own local churches. Marcel Pacaut has calculated that out of 5,500 charters in the *Recueil des chartes de Cluny*, 449 relate to the possession of churches and the revenues attaching to them; the years 1025–1109 are the most fertile period, yield-

<hr />

commemorate Raoul of Péronne *per universa monasteria ad Cluniacum pertinentia, ubi ordo tenetur,* CLU 4070, ca. 1140, 5.421–22. Other instances, cited by H. E. J. Cowdrey, "Unions and Confraternity with Cluny," *Journal of Ecclesiastical History* 16 (1965): 160, n. 1, are CLU 3233, 1049/1109, 4.359; 3393, 1063, 4.497–98; 3516, before 1078, 4.632–33; 3652, ca. 1090, 4.821–22; 3765, ca. 1100, 5.117–18.

186. *LT,* 208, p. 286.

187. *LT,* 207, p. 285.

188. Bernard, *Ordo Cluniacensis,* 1.51, p. 246; the statute relating to Alfonso VI has been edited by H. E. J. Cowdrey, "Two Studies," pp. 149–60.

189. Bernard, *Ordo Cluniacensis,* 1.74.27, p. 272.

190. On the general question, beyond the strictly Cluniac horizon, see Hubert Houben, "Autocoscienza nobiliare e commemorazione liturgica nel Medioevo," *Annali del Dipartimento di Scienze storiche e sociali* 4 (1985): 199–209, and Otto G. Oexle, "Adliges Selbstverständnis und seine Verknüpfung mit dem liturgischen Gedenken—das Beispiel der Welfen," *Zeitschrift für die Geschichte des Oberrheins* 134 (1986): 47–75. Nevertheless, one wonders how pertinent the notion of aristocratic "consciousness of self" can be in the context of exclusively monastic documents.

ing 210 documents, as against the 160 to 170 from pre-1025 and the 70 from the twelfth century.[191] Apart from monastic churches—priory churches and abbey churches—about 275 were acquired before 1109. Of these 275 churches, about 120 were properly speaking parish churches. The revenues of altars (*altaria*), which may be distinguished from the churches themselves, were no minor item in the Cluniac economy. In the twelfth century, tithes and offerings made up about a quarter of the resources of Cluny in grain and 15 percent of its cash revenue. In varying proportions, these proceeds were divided between the monks and the priests serving the church. Only in exceptional cases did a monk occupy himself with the *cura animarum* (pastoral responsibilities) of a church; normally it was the work of a priest who was maintained by the usufruct of some rural property, perhaps the land pertaining to an altar—a presbyteral manse or fief—and who paid to Cluny a fee of *vestitura* (investiture) and an annual rent.

In the history of tithes and more generally of monastic *spiritualia*, the years 1070–1130 were a period of vital evolution.[192] Like other monasteries, Cluny benefited from the repercussions of Gregorian policy regarding the restitution of churches and other *spiritualia*. In accordance with the logic already developed by Abbo of Fleury, of the "one Church of Christ," the traditional distinction between *altaria* and *ecclesia* was suppressed. From then on all *spiritualia* were regarded as one group belonging only to the Church.[193] The Church was therefore supposed to recover all ecclesiastical property in lay hands under penalty of sacrilege. In a bull of 1096 Urban II granted Cluny the unfettered possession of tithes "recovered from the laity."[194]

To be honest, the matter of tithes and *spiritualia* placed Cluny and traditional monasticism in a turbulent zone. Opposition came from both reformist monasticism and the episcopate. In their search for a new definition of monastic purity, the reformers (preeminently Cistercian and Carthusian) rejected all ownership of churches, *altaria*, burial dues, or tithes, so as not to "steal from the clergy."[195]

191. Marcel Pacaut, "Recherche sur les revenus paroissiaux monastiques: l'exemple de Cluny," in *Historia de la Iglesia y de las instituciones eclesiásticas: trabajos en homenaje a Ferran Valls i Taberner* (Barcelona, 1990), pp. 4025–42 and "Recherche sur les revenus paroissiaux: l'exemple des églises 'clunisiennes,'" in *Histoire de la paroisse*, Publications du Centre de recherches d'histoire religieuse et d'histoire des idées, 11 (Angers, 1988), pp. 33–42. Deeds from the years 814–910 make it possible to retrace the prehistory of property given to Cluny after its foundation.

192. On this very important question, see Giles Constable's contributions, especially his *Monastic Tithes from Their Origins to the Twelfth Century* (Cambridge, Mass., 1964) and "Monastic Possession of Churches and 'Spiritualia' in the Age of Reform," in *Il monachesimo e la riforma ecclesiastica (1049–1122)*, Atti della quarta Settimana internazionale di studio, Mendola, 22–29 August 1968, Miscellanea del Centro di Studi medioevali, 6 (Milan, 1971), reprinted in *Religious Life and Thought (11th–12th centuries)*, no. 8 (London, 1979).

193. Abbo of Fleury, *Apologeticus*, PL 139:465D–466A.

194. *Bullarium*, pp. 26–27 (PL 151:441–42).

195. The terms of the polemic are well summarized by Giles Constable in his "Monastic Possession of Churches," pp. 326ff.

The latter, dedicated as they were to tasks associated with the *cura animarum*, drew their living from the *spiritualia*, while monks, cut off from the world, were supposed to subsist on their own work. Such a radical position called into question the involvement of traditional monasticism in exchange networks. Thus we see Peter the Venerable, in one of his letters to Bernard of Clairvaux, defending Cluny's possession of parishes and parochial income.[196] Peter develops three arguments. The first is based on scriptural history. The monks are identified with the tribe of Levi, who have no material inheritance and whose sustenance is dependent on tithes and oblations. Peter's second argument is based on the excellence of the monks who intercede with God for their donors' sins, while the seculars, more concerned with the realities of this world (*temporalia*) than with spiritual things (*spiritualia*), are not occupied in saving souls. From this polemical starting point, Peter elaborates his thesis concerning the complementarity of tasks. The central function fulfilled by the secular clergy is that of saving the Church by the "divine mysteries." The main responsibility of the monks, who rarely administer the sacraments, is to pray for the salvation of the faithful, without encroaching upon the sacramental functions of the seculars. Such a partition of responsibilities—administration of the sacraments on the one hand, liturgical and charitable assistance oriented to salvation on the other—is intended to render to each his due. Thus monks are indeed intended to receive tithes, oblations, and revenues. Finally, Peter cites two canonical authorities intended to support the monks' claims: the Council of Toledo and Yvo of Chartres. Notable in Peter's prudent advocacy is the low profile he adopts as to the clerical status of monks, whereas in fact the eucharistic sacrifice had an essential role in Cluny's funerary pastoral work and Peter made every effort, as abbot, to see to it that every professed Cluniac was a monk-priest.[197] His position here is all the more surprising, because it was the new thinking about ordination during the twelfth century that enabled the old opposition between cleric and monk to be overcome, since monk-priests were acknowledged to have received a plenitude of power the day they were consecrated.[198] In book 6 of his *Dialogues*, Hugh of Amiens asserted the thesis of monastic completeness in far more clear-cut terms than Peter.[199] His view was that monks, possessing both the charisma of the pure and the ordained power of clerics, were doubly qualified to preach, confess, sacrifice, and thus also live off tithes and oblations.[200]

Episcopal claims regarding the churches possessed by monks were of a different order from the question of principle raised by a Bernard of Clairvaux.

196. *Ep.*, 28, 1:81–82.
197. See above, p. 44.
198. On this point and in particular the reflections of Rupert of Deutz, see Berlière, "L'exercice du ministère paroissial," 248–49.
199. *PL* 192:1219AB.
200. *PL* 192:1219BC.

From the turn of the millennium tithes were a bone of contention between bishops and monks.[201] It was still so in the twelfth century. The monastic party, led by Abbo of Fleury, had aired the matter at the Council of Saint-Denis in 997.[202] In 1119, at the Council of Reims, Pontius of Melgueil had to defend the Cluniac tithes against attack by the archbishop of Lyon.[203] Between the two dates, however, the ground of argument shifted substantially. At the end of the tenth century, it was about whether monks, as laymen, were entitled to receive tithes. During the first thirty years or so of the twelfth century, it was about the bishops trying to wrest back ordinary authority over the parishes. Between the two dates, a sort of status quo was arrived at. The ownership of tithes by monks was not canonical: yet it was an ancient practice and was current in the tenth century. Gregory VII at the Roman synod of 1078 and Urban II at the Council of Melfi in 1089 decided to confirm the existing situation and to make all future concessions of churches or tithes to monasteries subject to diocesan permission (*episcopo mediante*).[204] This decision, which was more clear-cut in theory than in practice, amounted to official recognition of monastic parishes.

A further step in Cluny's integration into the parish network came with the juridical recognition of the monastic community as a corporate body. Legal historians use the term "incorporation" to connote the act or deed "concluded by the bishop or his archdeacon, that legally confers on a collegiate church or monastery the pastoral care of a parish."[205] It was long believed that incorporation appeared during the twelfth century and that its diffusion was essentially a phenomenon of the thirteenth. But the work of Wolfgang Petke on the diocese of Toul, the diocese of Verdun, and the north of the ecclesiastical province of Reims has enabled its appearance to be dated to the very end of the eleventh century. The first known instance of incorporation is that of the church of Tours-sur-Marne, which in 1099 became a Cluniac possession *sine* or *absque persona*, a formula meaning that the Ecclesia cluniacensis was legally, through its abbot, the *persona* in charge of the church and the beneficiary of the income attaching to it, the *personatus*.[206] This vital development did not simply indicate that

201. Constable, *Monastic Tithes*, pp. 57–83.

202. Aimon, *Vita sancti Abbonis*, 9, PL 139:396–97. See Jean-François Lemarignier, "L'exemption monastique et la réforme clunisienne," in *A Cluny*, Congrès scientifique, 9–11 July 1949 (Dijon, 1950).

203. *Relatio de concilio Remensi*, MGH Ldl, 3, pp. 27–28; see Constable, "Monastic Possession of Churches," p. 321.

204. *Das Register Gregors VII.*, 6.5b, c. 9 and 25, 2:401–2; Mansi, *Amplissima collectio*, 20, col. 723B.

205. Wolfgang Petke, "Von der klösterlichen Eigenkirche zur Inkorporation in Lothringen und Nordfrankreich im 11. und 12. Jahrhundert," *RHE* 87 (1992): 34–72 and 375–404. See also *TRE*, 6, s.v. *Inkorporation* (Peter Landau).

206. The priory of Tours-sur-Marne was the scene of an event reported by Peter the Venerable in *De miraculis*, 1.5, p. 15.

PART I. THE MONKS AND THE WORLD ORDER

Cluny's parochial rights were officially recognized; it marked legal recognition of Cluny's *persona* at the heart of the parish network.

Cluny and the Ecclesiastical Hierarchy

From the microcosm of the parish we must widen our perspective to the macrocosm of the Church. In a letter addressed to Bernard of Clairvaux concerning the contested election of a Cluniac to the episcopal chair of Langres in 1138, we find Peter the Venerable sounding the obvious note that many episcopal, archiepiscopal, and patriarchal churches, even the Roman see itself, were wont to come and recruit (*assumere consueverunt*) their pastors from Cluny.[207]

As Dom Jacques Hourlier points out, there is striking "synchrony" between the growth in the power of Rome and the development of the religious orders in the eleventh and twelfth centuries, the one being at least partly explicable by the other.[208] Numerous monks and regular canons contributed to the reform of the Church, and the participation of Cluniacs in the ecclesiastical hierarchy was a part of that general movement. Hermann Diener's researches have made it possible to jettison the cliché of supposed Cluniac "anti-episcopalism."[209] On the contrary, it is possible to speak rather of "philo-episcopalism," given that the episcopate in the Gregorian age was substantially supplied from the cloister. Basing his work on necrological data, Joachim Mehne has studied with quasi-monographic precision both the flow of conversions of bishops to Cluny and, contrariwise, the accession of professed Cluniacs to the episcopate.[210] The two movements were synchronous. Though there were few examples in the 1030s, they multiplied very greatly during Hugh of Semur's abbacy, before decreasing again in the first half of the twelfth century. The abbot of Cluny acceded to the repeated demands of popes and princes, and permitted the creation of a group of bishops who might respond to such local needs of the Ecclesia cluniacensis as consecrating churches and altars, soliciting donations, and founding dependent establishments. More broadly, the appointment of professed Cluniacs as bishops meant that ecclesiastical networks, both secular and regular, became more involved and the aristocracies of the Church and lay life more interwoven. In the context of our enquiry into the identification of Cluny with the universal Church, we need only look at two examples in order to appreciate the importance of the phenomenon.

Adrald, who became bishop of Chartres in 1069, was a monk of Cluny.[211] He

207. *Ep.*, 29, 1:101–4, here 103–4. On this disputed election see Giles Constable, "The Disputed Election at Langres in 1138," *Traditio* 13 (1957): 119–52; reprinted in *Cluniac Studies* (London, 1980), no. 10.

208. Jacques Hourlier, *L'âge classique (1140–1378)*, Histoire du Droit et des Institutions de l'Eglise en Occident, 10 (Paris, 1974), p. 425.

209. Hermann Diener, "Das Verhältnis Clunys zu den Bischöfen vor allem in der Zeit seines Abtes Hugo (1049–1109)," in *Neue Forschungen über Cluny und die Cluniacenser*, ed. Gerd Tellenbach (Freiburg im B., 1959), pp. 219–393.

210. Mehne, "Cluniacenserbischöfe."

211. Ibid., pp. 255–56.

was a disciple of Odilo and, for a time, prior of Payerne.[212] He was subsequently put in charge of the abbey of Breme in Piedmont, an establishment that did not belong to the Ecclesia cluniacensis, but that had had a nephew of Odilo as its abbot in the late 1020s. In 1063, Adrald accompanied Peter Damian when Peter was entrusted by the pope with resolving the serious dispute between Cluny and the bishop of Mâcon over the monastery's exemption. Adrald died in 1075. His name is commemorated in the Cluniac necrologies under 10 February. In the absence of any book of confraternity, the customaries of Cluny reveal that the Ecclesia cluniacensis was accustomed to creating unions of prayer with other monastic or canonical communities.[213] Such was the case with the church of Chartres. An act inserted in the cartulary of Hugh of Semur attests that when Adrald was bishop of Chartres, links of spiritual fraternity were forged between the cathedral church and the Ecclesia cluniacensis. The Cluniac *societas* opened itself to the bishop and to the canonical community: in return the brothers of Cluny were granted a prebend that integrated them into the canonical community.[214]

Our second example is that of William, professed monk of Cluny, prior of Saint-Orens at Auch and archbishop of Auch from 1068 to 1096. William's family were the lords of Montaut, and they had extremely close links with the Ecclesia cluniacensis. Two female members of the family, Bernarde and Guillemette, entered the Cluniac convent at Marcigny-sur-Loire.[215] William played a prime role in the ecclesiastical policy conducted by Hugh of Semur in southwestern Gaul. He is the same William of Montaut who, along with Aimé of Oloron, escorted Viscountess Gisla of Béarn to Marcigny-sur-Loire.[216] During his archiepiscopacy, donations flowed into Cluny.[217] The archbishop him-

212. *Helvetia Sacra*, 3.3, p. 438.

213. Ulrich, *Antiquiores consuetudines*, 3.33, *PL* 149:777AB; Bernard, *Ordo Cluniacensis*, 1.26, p. 200. At the end of the *Bullarium*, pp. 225–30 (wrongly numbered 215–20), Pierre Simon prints a sixteenth-century *rotulus* stating the names of the churches in prayer union with Cluny. On this point see Cowdrey, "Unions and Confraternity with Cluny," 154, and Kohnle, *Abt Hugo*, pp. 49 and 52. To the cases mentioned in those studies may be added the unions concluded between Cluny, Bishop Almeradus, and the canons of Riez, *CLU* 1990, 4.201–3, dated by the editors to the years 993–1031 (on which see Joachim Wollasch, "Zur Datierung einiger Urkunden aus Cluny," *RM*, n.s., 3 (1992): 49–57), and that between Cluny and the church of Puy-en-Velay, *CLU* 4427, 5.800–801, at an indeterminate date but confirmed by a charter dating from 1207, which speaks of the ancient family ties (*quasi inveterata familiaritas*) joining the two churches.

214. *CLU* 3427, 1069/75, 4.537–39. Peter the Venerable alludes to this prebend in a letter to Atto of Troyes, *Ep.*, 2, 1:5–6, here 6. The cathedral church of Chartres is still mentioned in the sixteenth-century *rotulus*, *Bullarium*, p. 227 (erroneously numbered 217). This example along with others (the cathedral chapters of Autun in the time of Majolus and Orléans in that of Hugh of Semur) is analyzed by Joachim Wollasch, "Hugues Ier abbé de Cluny et la mémoire des morts," in *Le gouvernement d'Hugues de Semur à Cluny* (Cluny, 1990), pp. 79–80.

215. Wischermann, *Marcigny-sur-Loire*, pp. 337 and 421.

216. Ibid., pp. 367–69.

217. Diener, "Das Verhältnis Clunys zu den Bischöfen," 299ff.

self and his five brothers donated the church of Saint-Michel at Montaut with a view to being received into the Cluniac *societas*.[218] William and his family thus provide an exceptional illustration of how interwoven the networks of power were that united the Ecclesia cluniacensis with the great aristocratic families that supplied Cluny with monks, some of whom went on to become princes of the Church.

Cluny was also the source of a contingent of Roman cardinal-bishops. The monastic contribution to the origins of the College of Cardinals was considerable. Under Paschal II, a third of the cardinals created were monks.[219] Cluny's contribution, though less than that of Monte Cassino, was substantial.[220] Peter Pierleone, cardinal-deacon of SS. Cosma e Damiano, cardinal-priest of S. Maria in Trastevere (Rome), and subsequently pope—or rather, antipope—under the name of Anacletus II, was a former monk of Cluny.[221] So too were: two cardinal-bishops of Tusculum, Gilo and Imar;[222] a cardinal-bishop of Albano, Matthew;[223] a cardinal-bishop of the Roman church of S. Maria-in-Schola-Graeca, Adenulf; three, perhaps four, cardinal-bishops of Ostia, namely Gerald, Odo I (the future pope Urban II), possibly Odo II, and Alberic of Vézelay.[224] Most of the prelates mentioned took part in papal legations, as did the abbots of Cluny Hugh of Semur, Pontius of Melgueil, and Peter the Venerable.[225] Finally, going from one end of the hierarchy to the other, the *cursus honorum* of Pope Urban II gives a good idea of Cluny's contribution to the "building up of the Church."[226] Odo of Châtillon was at an early stage archdeacon of Reims cathedral.[227] Some

218. *CLU* 3416, 4.526–27. On William and his family, see Raphaela Averkorn, *Adel und Kirche in der Grafschaft Armagnac: das cluniacensische Priorat Saint-Jean-Baptiste de Saint-Mont (1086–1130)*, Europa in der Geschichte, 1 (Bochum, 1997), pp. 200ff.

219. Robinson, *The Papacy*, p. 215.

220. See Mehne, "Cluniacenserbischöfe," 263–64; *Letters of Peter the Venerable*, ed. Giles Constable, appendix J, 2:293–95; Rudolf Hüls, *Kardinäle, Klerus und Kirchen Roms 1049–1130*, Bibliothek des deutschen historischen Instituts in Rom, 48 (Tübingen, 1977).

221. Hüls, *Kardinäle*, p. 225.

222. Ibid., pp. 142–43; Heinz, "Anfänge und Entwicklung des Cluniazenser-Priorates St.-Martin-des-Champs in Paris (1079–1150)."

223. Hüls, *Kardinäle*, pp. 96–98.

224. Ibid., pp. 100–101 (Gerard), 102–3 (Odo I), 103–5 (Odo II).

225. Robinson, *The Papacy*, pp. 154ff. On the legations of Hugh of Semur, see Kohnle, *Abt Hugo*.

226. The Burgundian monastery provided a further pope—or rather antipope—Anacletus II, and this takes no account of offers that were made. In his *Vita sancti Maioli*, 3.10, ed. Dominique Iogna-Prat, in *"Agni immaculati,"* pp. 260–63, Syrus records that Otto II and his mother, Adelaide, offered the papacy to Majolus, which he declined. Gregory VII rose not via Cluny, but by way of Sainte-Marie-sur-l'Aventin, a monastery associated with Cluny. See Paul of Bernried, *Vita sancti Gregorii papae VII*, 9, ed. Johann M. Watterich, *Pontificum Romanorum qui fuerunt inde ab ex. saec. IX usque ad finem saec. XIII vitae*, vol. 1 (Leipzig, 1862), p. 477; also see Cowdrey, *The Cluniacs and the Gregorian Reform*, p. 148, n. 4. According to the *Historia Compostellana*, 2.9, ed. Emma Falque Rey, *CCCM*, 70 (Turnhout, 1988), p. 235, Pontius of Melgueil was a possible successor to Gelasius II when that pope died at Cluny in 1119.

227. On the career of Eudes (Odo) of Châtillon until his election as pope, see Alfons Becker, *Papst Urban II. (1088–1099)*, 2 vols., Schriften der *MGH*, 19, 1–2 (Stuttgart, 1964, 1988), 1:24–90.

time after 1070 he entered Cluny, becoming grand prior of the monastery about 1074. His abbot, Hugh of Semur, in response to Pope Gregory VII's appeal for "wise men" suitable to serve as bishops, sent him off to Rome. There he was promoted to the office of cardinal-bishop of Ostia in 1080. In 1084 Gregory put him in charge of a legation to Germany. Odo was elected pope in 1088, taking the name Urban II. Among a number of contributions to the establishment of a papal system of administration, he created a chamber of accounts (*camera*) along the lines of that at Cluny. The first official of the chamber whose name we know is Peter Gloc, a close relative of Hugh of Semur.[228]

Cluny and Its Mimicry of Rome

It was all the simpler for Cluny to contribute to "building up the Church" in the Gregorian age because it was a Roman monastery. In affirming their respective identities Rome and Cluny had a linked destiny. Brigitte Szabó-Bechstein has underlined the importance of the Cluniac contribution to the formulation of the notion of *libertas ecclesiae*.[229] In the matter of primacy, Cluny's role was no less significant. The monastery's foundation charter of 910 described the apostle Peter as the "administrator of the whole monarchy of churches" (*archiclavus totius monarchiae ecclesiarum*).[230] Defending the freedom of Cluny in a letter to Bishop Gauzlin of Mâcon in 1027, Pope John XIX was the first to describe Rome as the "head and cardinal point of the other churches" (*reliquarum ecclesiarum caput et cardo*).[231]

In return, Cluny's identity mirrored Rome. It was not a simple reflection. Cluny's exceptional status was rooted in the law of the Roman church. In a quit-claim of 1117, Bernard IV Grossus, lord of Uxelles and Brancion, swore on "the book known as the Register of Pope Gregory VII," which gives some idea of the place Roman texts had at Cluny.[232] The conjuncture *caput–membra* constituting the Ecclesia cluniacensis was purely and simply a transposition of that body of reference which, following a typically Gregorian exegesis of the notion of the Church as the "body of Christ" (1 Corinthians 12:27), had Rome as the head (*caput*) and the other churches as members (*membra*).[233] The "body" metaphor

---

228. Jürgen Sydow, "Cluny und die Anfänge der Apostolischen Kammer: Studien zur Geschichte der päpstlichen Finanzverwaltung im 11. und 12. Jahrhundert," *SMGBOZ* 63 (1951): 53ff.

229. Brigitte Szabó-Bechstein, *Libertas Ecclesiae: ein Schlüsselbegriff des Investiturstreits und seine Vorgeschichte 4.–11. Jahrhundert*, Studi Gregoriani, 12 (Rome, 1986), pp. 92–94; the author accords great importance to the terms used by King Raoul in his diploma of 937, without noting that the diploma was actually copied at Cluny: on this point see Jean Dufour, *Recueil des actes de Robert Ier et de Raoul rois de France*, Chartes et diplômes relatifs à l'histoire de France publiés par l'Académie des inscriptions et belles lettres, no. 12, p. 50.

230. *CLU* 112, 1.124–28, here 127.

231. *Papsturkunden 896–1046*, vol. 1, no. 573, p. 1088.

232. *CLU* 3926, 2 April 1117, 5.278–79.

233. See Robinson, "L'Eglise et la papauté," pp. 242–44.

worked both ways. As Peter's successor, the pope was the head of the Cluniac body. Inversely, the Cluniacs, who supplied members—bishops and cardinals—to the Church's body, were able to consider themselves a part of the papal body; the decree of 1059, which entrusted the pope's election to the College of Cardinals, actually established the college in a vacancy as the institutional body of the Church.[234] Lastly, Cluny could credit itself with being the last resting place of a pope, Gelasius II, who died and was buried in the monastery in February 1119.

The praises heaped upon Cluny by the papacy give a good idea of the "special" status enjoyed by the establishment, placed as it was from its foundation under Rome's protection. From what is a well-supplied tradition, let us note just three examples taken from the 1050s and after. In 1057 or 1058 Pope Stephen IX described Cluny as "the brightest sunshine of holy conduct . . . the form and mirror of sanctity to all the monasteries of the Latin tongue."[235] During the Roman synod of March 1080 Gregory VII vaunted Cluny's excellence in the service of God, observing, "There is no [monastery] that I know of in that land [beyond the mountains] that comes at all close to being its equal," and proclaimed that its holiness derived from the abbatial office itself.[236] In his bull of January 1097 Urban II reapplied Christ's word to the apostles in Matthew 5:14 to Cluny: "You are the light of the world."[237] Such literary hyperbole clothed a juridical reality. In his monumental *Kurie und Kloster,* Georg Schreiber examined the long and sometimes uncertain evolution of the epithet *specialis* in the history of medieval monasticism.[238] It was used at the outset to signify the nature of the ties that a monastery, the property of Peter, might have with Rome. Cluny was a case in point, having been subject to apostolic authority from its very foundation.[239] At the end of a slow process, which came to its maturity under Pope Alexander III (1159–81), the epithet *specialis* came to be applied to exempted establishments depending directly on the center, Rome, *nullo mediante* (without any intermediary). Such was Cluny's case from 998, and it was all the more so from 1024. The exempted monks were regarded as *speciales filii.* From 1024 the terms "daughter" or "son" were regularly used by the papacy to denote Cluny or the Cluniacs,[240] not simply out of "solicitude" but "in the plenitude of

234. On this fertile and complex question one can do no better than refer to A. Paravicini Bagliani, *Il corpo del Papa* (Turin, 1994), pp. 87ff.

235. *Bullarium,* p. 15G (*PL* 143:879–84).

236. Printed in Cowdrey, *The Cluniacs and the Gregorian Reform,* p. 272–73.

237. *Bullarium,* p. 30 (*BC,* p. 520); see Kohnle, *Abt Hugo,* p. 127.

238. Schreiber, *Kurie und Kloster,* 2:47–67.

239. *CLU* 112, 1.124–28; bull of John XI, March 931, *Papsturkunden 896–1046,* vol. 1, no. 64, p. 107; bull of Leo VII, end 936, ibid., no. 68, p. 126.

240. John XIX, 1024, *Papsturkunden 896–1046,* vol. 1, no. 558, p. 1053; Urban II, in 1095, *Bullarium,* p. 23, in 1096, ibid., p. 28, and in 1097, ibid., p. 30 (*BC,* p. 520). On the definition of Rome by Gregorian reformers as *mater specialis,* see Szabó-Bechstein, *Libertas Ecclesiae,* p. 110.

power."[241] In return, the Cluniacs spoke of the *sedes apostolica* or of the pope as of their "mother" or their "own, special father."[242]

This "family" context makes it easier to understand how Cluny came to identify itself with Rome. In a letter written some time between 1021 and 1023, Benedict VIII called upon the bishops of Burgundy, Aquitaine, and Provence to protect Cluny, emphasizing the importance of the monastery to the *status sanctae Ecclesiae* and considering wrong done to the Cluniacs as a "loss" affecting the entire Church—*commune omnium nostrum detrimentum*.[243] John XIX clarified the organic nature of the tie joining Cluny to Rome by using the "body" image of a head and its members; the pope, the vicar of Peter, referred to himself as the "head" and to his "sons" as *membra nostra*.[244] The organicist logic thus enabled the "members" to identify themselves with the "head"—with the pope or even with Saint Peter himself. Hugh of Semur was consecrated abbot on the feast of Saint Peter *in cathedra in Antiochia*, 22 February 1049.[245] Saint Peter was seen as miraculously intervening in person to ensure that the *maior ecclesia* of Christendom—Cluny III—was built in his honor.[246] Some of the *Vitae sancti Hugonis* record a miracle performed by the abbot in imitation of Saint Peter at the church of Sainte-Geneviève, Paris. Availing himself of the words Peter addressed to the paralyzed Aeneas of Lydda in Acts 9:34, Hugh, "as if his voice were Peter's own," chants the healing formula to the paralyzed Robert of Paris. The efficacious words of the abbot of Cluny thus fuse with those of the monastery's patron: through the lips of the one the other speaks.[247] On this occasion Abbot Hugh was regarded, like the pope, as the *vicarius Petri*.

The only thing that makes sense of this confusion of roles is the history of the

241. Nalgodus, *Vita sancti Odonis*, ed. Maria Luisa Fini, in "Studio sulla 'Vita Odonis reformata' di Nalgodo: il 'fragmentum mutilum' del Codice latino NA 1496 della Bibliothèque nationale di Parigi," in *Rendiconti dell'Accademia di Scienze dell'Istituto di Bologna, Classe di scienze morali*, Bologna 63.2 (1975), p. 146. On the context within which the *Vita* was composed, see D. Iogna-Prat, "La geste des origines," 185–86.

242. Such in particular is the term used, subject to slight modifications (such as *proprius pater*), by Peter the Venerable in his correspondence with the popes: *Ep.*, 1, 1:4; 11, 1:17; 17, 1:24; 22, 1:42; 23, 1:43; 27, 1:50; 32–33, 1:106–7; 39, 1:131; 46, 1:142; 63–64, 1:192–93; 72, 1:206; 92, 1:233; 97–99, 1:257–59; 101, 1:261; 103–4, 1:265–66; 112, 1:299; 113, 1:301; 116, 1:308; 118–19, 1: 311–12; 122, 1:315; 141–42, 1:348 and 350; 156–58, 1:375–77; 171, 1:404; 173–74, 1:410 and 413; 188–91, 1: 437–38, 440, and 442.

243. *Papsturkunden 896–1046*, vol. 1, no. 530, p. 1009.

244. Ibid., no. 572, pp. 1087–88.

245. Gilo, *Vita sancti Hugonis*, 1.4, "Two Studies," p. 52.

246. Ibid., 2.1, p. 90. The *Alia miraculorum quorumdam S. Hugonis abbatis relatio* speaks of the miraculous appearance of Peter, Paul, and the protomartyr Stephen, *BC*, col. 457.

247. Gilo, *Vita sancti Hugonis*, 1.24, "Two Studies," p. 72. In his own *Vita sancti Hugonis*, 14, "Two Studies," pp. 128–29, Hugh of Gournay mentions the "laudable controversy" generated by the miracle, between the Parisians, who regarded it as a miracle of Saint Peter with Hugh as intermediary, and the Cluniacs, who maintained on the contrary *quod Hugoni suo factum hoc debeat imputari; qui meritis Petri in nomine Christi debilem erexit.*

mutual substitutions of Cluny and Rome. By substitution, more is meant than the simple, classic role that the Cluniacs, like many other monks, fulfilled: that of being agents of the papacy *vice nostra* (in our place). Substitution here entails the wider issue of the Burgundian monastery's coming to see itself as a kind of substitute Rome. In a letter to Pope Urban II, Hugh of Semur maintains that many of the faithful, anxious to see the pope but prevented from doing so by various difficulties, choose to turn to the Cluniacs (*nos*), as to servants of the pope (*quasi ad domesticos vestros*).[248] The essential pull of these "servants" derived from the apostolic patronage of Peter and Paul. An act dating from Majolus's abbacy and preserved as a copy in the earliest cartulary of Cluny states that "in order to pray, Rostagnus came to Cluny *ad limina sanctorum apostolorum Petri et Pauli.*" We cannot be sure that by the time the act was written the monastery had acquired relics of the two apostles.[249] The *Liber tramitis aevi Odilonis* provides the first sure record of this, in that it contains a brief inventory of relics owned by the monastery during the first thirty or so years of the eleventh century, most of them being kept "in an image of Saint Peter" that served as a reliquary.[250] A late indication comes in a letter of Hugh of Gournay to Abbot Pontius of Melgueil in the 1120s, in which Hugh says that the earliest relics of Peter and Paul to come to Cluny from Rome were laid in the high altar of Cluny II, consecrated by Hugh, bishop of Bourges, in 981.[251] An act of Alfonso VI of Castile-León, dated 1079, describes Cluny as the basilica-reliquary of the two apostles.[252] Hugh of Semur similarly placed the nuns of his foundation of Marcigny-sur-Loire in the intimate orbit of the holy city by endowing it with relics of the Roman virgin Agnes.[253]

The apostles' relics helped to make Cluny a place of pilgrimage. To be frank, the history of pilgrimages to Cluny still remains to be written.[254] But there are many diplomatic and narrative sources dating from Hugh of Semur's time as abbot (1049–1109) to prove that from the mid-eleventh century Cluny was becoming a substitute destination for the pilgrimage to Rome. It was the period of

248. Ed. H. E. J. Cowdrey, "Two Studies," p. 150. Addressing the pope, Hugh describes Cluny as *congregatio vestra*.

249. *CLU* 367, 1.345–46: the editors' suggested date is pushed back by Maurice Chaume and Barbara H. Rosenwein to Majolus's abbacy (954–94), the period in fact when Cluny did acquire relics of Peter and Paul.

250. *LT*, 189, pp. 260–61.

251. Ed. Cowdrey, "Two Studies," pp. 113–17, here 116–17. See also Glauco M. Cantarella, "Per l'analisi di una fonte cluniacense: l'*Epistola ad domnum Pontium cluniacensem abbatem*," *Bulletino dell'Istituto Storico Italiano per il Medio Evo e Archivo Muratoriano* 87 (1978): 54–87.

252. Deed of donation of Saint Mary's, Nájera, *CLU* 3540, 4.665–66.

253. Wischermann, *Marcigny-sur-Loire*, pp. 71ff.

254. Until now this issue has essentially been the interest of art historians, concerned to highlight the role of Cluny on the pilgrimage route to Santiago de Compostela and to place Cluny III in the problem area of sanctuaries of pilgrimage. On this point, which will be further elucidated by publication of the proceedings of the Sahagún colloquium, *Cluny y el Camino de Santiago en España*, 27–29 May 1993, see Otto K. Werkmeister, "Cluny III and the pilgrimage of Santiago de Compostella," in *Current Studies on Cluny, Gesta* 27 (1988): 103–12.

a real "apostolic recentering on Cluny," to borrow Patrick Henriet's felicitous phrase.[255] The foundation charter of the priory of Saint Pancras's in Lewes, England, records the singular circumstances leading the founders, William I, count of Warenne and Surrey, and his wife, Gundrada, to seek Cluniac "society and brotherhood."[256] Prior to 1080, the date of the charter, William and Gundrada had tried to get to Rome in accordance with an ancient Anglo-Saxon tradition of pilgrimage *ad limina apostolorum* (to the home of the apostles).[257] However, the troubles connected with the strife between the empire and the papacy prevented them from fulfilling their intention. They determined to go instead to Cluny, whence sprang their "devotion and love for the order," whose propagation they assisted by founding Saint Pancras's Priory at Lewes. Another example is that of Guy of Faucigny, bishop of Geneva, who in a charter of 1083 tells how, in order to do penance and found the priory of Condamine-sur-Arve, he went *ad limina beatorum apostolorum Petri et Pauli, ad locum Cluniacensem* (to the home of the blessed apostles Peter and Paul at Cluny).[258] Dying on All Saints' Day in 1119, he again took the road to Cluny. In *De miraculis*, Peter the Venerable records how in the following year the deceased bishop appeared to a priest making his way to a synod at Geneva. The bishop told the priest of the aid he expected from the assembled fathers and that he intended to go to Cluny and Jerusalem in order to do penance.[259] Hugh of Semur's chief biographer, Gilo, describes how Saint Peter appeared to a pilgrim who had gone all the way to Rome, *ad limina*, and revealed to him that "the salvation he was seeking with his vows he might more readily [*paratius*] obtain in the monastery of Cluny than in the City."[260] Lastly, let us note that in 1132 Innocent II granted forty days' indulgence to pilgrims traveling to the *maior ecclesia* of Christendom.[261]

The "Ecclesia cluniacensis": A Polysemic Term

Incorporation into the parish network, recruitment into all levels of the ecclesiastical hierarchy, identification with Rome and substitution for it—elucidation of these three essential aspects of Cluniac monasticism in the eleventh and twelfth centuries makes it possible to take the measure of Peter the Vener-

255. "Les villes et la Ville (Rome) dans l'hagiographie clunisienne," in *Les moines dans la ville*, actes du colloque de l'université catholique de Lille, 31 March–1 April 1995, ed. Jean Heuclin and Philippe Racinet, Cahiers du CAHMER7 (1996), pp. 47–57, here 54.

256. *CLU* 3561, 4.689–96, This founding charter is a forgery, most probably dating from the thirteenth century; there are no doubts however regarding the *narratio* it contains—see Kohnle, *Abt Hugo*, p. 193.

257. Wilhelm Levison, *England and the Continent in the Eighth Century* (Oxford, 1946), pp. 15–44.

258. *CLU* 3599, 4.756–57, here 756.

259. *DM*, 1.24, p. 74, ll. 50–53.

260. Gilo, *Vita sancti Hugonis*, 2.2, "Two Studies," p. 92.

261. *Bullarium*, pp. 46–47 (*PL* 179:127–28).

able's imagery of Cluny's irresistible extension throughout the entire Church like "branches unto the sea."

In his study of Peter the Venerable's ecclesiology, Jean-Pierre Torrell reminds us that for a monastery to identify itself with the Church itself was historically not at all uncommon.[262] It stemmed from the fact that the monastic condition echoed the collective life of Christianity at its origins in the apostolic era. The case of Cluny is nonetheless exceptional by virtue of its particular links with Rome and the depth of its influence inside the Latin Church. As we have seen, the term *Ecclesia cluniacensis* is difficult to define, so much so that we resorted to the notion of a "Cluniac nebula" to describe any kind of Cluniac influence beyond Cluny's own narrow network of dependent establishments. For "Cluny" was more than just Cluny. The term *Ecclesia cluniacensis* is a polysemic one, capable of more than one signification. Narrowly defined, it would subsume the *ecclesia parochialis* (parish church) directly responsible to Cluny, whose rector was the community of Cluny in its corporate identity (*persona*). More often the term *Ecclesia cluniacensis* applies to the legally defined structure of establishments constituting a body with the abbot of Cluny as its head. In this second sense exemption placed the Ecclesia cluniacensis on a par with episcopal churches. In the hierarchic jockeying that had as much to do with charisma as with outward dignity, Peter the Venerable went so far as to claim Cluny as the first among the churches, "none before it in the Father's grace."[263] In this upward logic Cluny is ultimately identified with the universal Church. As Jean-Pierre Torrell rightly says, Peter the Venerable constantly and consciously transfers the "attributes of the universal Church" to Cluny.[264] One might say that his ecclesiology takes the form of a synecdoche, inasmuch as the part (Cluny) is taken for the whole (the Church) and vice versa. Like the universal Church, the Ecclesia cluniacensis is a *res publica* (republic).[265] Like the universal Church it may be riven by schism, such as that connected with Pontius of Melgueil; it is then seen, like the universal Church, as a mother who suffers to see her sons warring.[266] Peter the Venerable's image of Cluny spreading ineluctably like "branches unto the sea" is also nothing other than a variation on a theme dear to the Gregorian reformers, who viewed the papacy as a "great mountain filling the universe."[267] It now remains

262. Torrell, "L'Eglise," p. 583. The following account owes much to Torrell's study, especially his section on the Cluniacensis Ecclesia, 583–89.

263. *Ep.*, 34, 1:109–13, here 110, quoted by Torrell, "L'Eglise," p. 589.

264. Ibid., p. 583.

265. Ibid., p. 585; *DM*, 2.12, p. 117, l. 4; *Ep.*, 138, 1:345–46, here 346, and 178, 1:419–20, here 419, in which Peter finds a new role for Hugh of Amiens, the professed Cluniac who became archbishop of Rouen, *inter antiquos illos rei publicae nostrae senatores*.

266. Torrell, "L'Eglise," p. 584.

267. The imagery, which comes from Daniel 2:34–35, was used by Humbert of Silva Candida in his *De sancta Romana ecclesia;* see Percy E. Schramm, *Kaiser, Könige und Päpste,* Gesammelte Auf-

for us to see how these "branches" spread into contemporary secular life and what place was reserved for the laity in the Cluniac ecclesiastical system.

The Cluniac Ecclesia mater *and the Inclusion of the Laity*

In 1152 or 1153, Peter the Venerable intervened with Pope Eugenius III to help Count Guy of Domène to resolve his matrimonial problems. In his correspondence, the abbot of Cluny, himself a former prior of Domène—an establishment founded and maintained by the family bearing that name—presents the count's matter as "our own" and "domestic." In Peter's eyes, the benefactions of Guy and his ancestors to the monastery had made them "our people."[268] Such an undertaking on behalf of an aristocrat allied to Cluny is a perfect demonstration of the active policy to include the laity within the Ecclesia cluniacensis, of the monks' vocation to be responsible for the world, and of the theocratic proclivities that led clerics to merge the Church with society. Such intermingling of the cloister with secular life is hard to reduce to a schema that our age, one of firm distinctions between church and state, can readily appreciate. However, we shall usefully clarify our inquiry by distinguishing two areas that are in reality closely linked: the reception afforded lay people by the monastery and above all the interplay of lay and ecclesiastical networks within the seigneurial system. On the basis of these rapid considerations we shall then be able to consider, in the next part of this book, the theories elaborated by Peter the Venerable on the subject of the Christian society.

Open Doors

In a letter to King Roger II of Sicily in 1146 requesting material support, Peter the Venerable employs an arresting phrase to draw attention to the Cluniac tradition of openness to the world. Ever since it was founded, he says, the monastery has not simply been a hospice for outsiders or a refuge for those fleeing the life of the world or the storms of the seigneurial order: it has also been the "public treasure of the Christian republic," the Burgundian sanctuary that puts the interests of others before its own.[269]

Cluny the Hospice

Chapter 53 of the Rule of Saint Benedict laid down that all visitors were to be received as if they were Christ himself. Such unrestricted access for passersby, travelers of all sorts, pilgrims, messengers, and the like meant that Benedictine monasteries were the main and often only guest houses available in the early

---

sätze zur Geschichte des Mittelalters, 4.1 (Stuttgart, 1970), p. 156, quoted by Szabó-Bechstein, *Libertas Ecclesiae*, p. 111, n. 62.

268. *Ep.*, 189, 1:438–39, here 438.

269. *Ep.*, 131, 1:330–33, here 332. On Roger II, see Hubert Houben, *Roger II. von Sizilien, Herrscher zwischen Orient und Okzident*, Gestalten des Mittelalters und der Renaissance (Darmstadt, 1997).

Middle Ages prior to the appearance and development in the twelfth century of religious orders specializing in hospitality and the "assistance provided by municipal communities" in the thirteenth and fourteenth centuries.[270] In the Carolingian period, when the commentaries on the Rule and earliest customary adaptations of it were written, monastic hospitality was at the center of numerous debates. Was the monks' founding father's prescription to be taken at its full face value? If yes, how were the resulting burdens to be borne? How could the welcoming of outsiders be rendered compatible with the ideal of ascetic retreat? Following the tradition of the paradigm Carolingian monastery of Saint Gall, Cluny II and III included a guest house or *hospitium hospitum* run by an official of the monastery, the *hospitalarius*.[271] Peter the Venerable's letter to Roger II of Sicily, just quoted, makes clear that the provision of hospitality for strangers went right back to Cluny's foundation, a fact confirmed by the testament of its founder, Duke William of Aquitaine, whose own pious gesture was soon imitated by other lay benefactors earmarking a part of their gifts to pilgrims.[272] Indeed Cluniac historiography of the eleventh and twelfth centuries, in discussing the history of the monastery's origins, continually harks back to Duke William's example in this regard.[273] Not that the maximalist construction laid upon Saint Benedict's prescription at Cluny went uncontested. The rising generation of monks and hermits, the Cistercians and Carthusians especially, fought back with a conception of the regular life unsullied by distraction. In the *Consuetudines Cartusiae*, Guigo I vigorously asserted that he and his Carthusians had "fled into the remoteness of the wilderness not for the temporal care of the bodies of others, but for the eternal salvation of our own souls"[274]—hence the restrictions placed upon care for the poor and the Carthusian lack of guest houses. The Cistercians for their part put a minimalist interpretation on the fifty-third chapter of Saint Benedict's Rule. The monastery gate was kept closed and visitors were welcomed only subject to the abbot's authority. Even so, attempts were made to limit stays

270. An overview of issues relating to hospitality in the Middle Ages is given by Hans C. Peyer, *Von der Gastfreundschaft zum Gasthaus: Studien zur Gastlichkeit im Mittelalter, MGH* Schriften, 31 (Hanover, 1987), esp. pp. 116ff., and on changes at a regional level, Daniel Le Blévec, "Recherches sur l'assistance dans les pays du Bas-Rhône du XIIe siècle au milieu du XVe siècle," dissertation supervised by Georges Duby for the doctorat d'état, Université de Paris IV-Sorbonne, 1994, notice published in *RM*, n.s., 6 (1995): 317–20, from which the term quoted is taken.

271. On hospitality at Saint Gall, see Jutta Maria Berger, "Gastfreundschaft im Kloster St. Gallen im 9. und 10. Jahrhundert," *SMGBOZ* 104 (1993): 41–134 and 225–314. On Cluny, the account of Guy de Valous, *Le monachisme clunisien des origines au XVe siècle*, 2 vols., 2d ed. (Paris, 1970), 1:166ff., has been supplemented by Jutta Maria Berger, *Die Geschichte der Gastfreundschaft im hochmittelalterlichen Mönchtum. Die Cistercienser* (Berlin, 1999).

272. *CLU* 112, 1.124–28, here 126; *CLU* 1264, August 969, a gift by Berard to Cluny *ut peregrini et non habentes inde sustententur et recreentur*, 2.345–46; Georges Duby interprets this clause as founding a hospital, but may it not simply be financing the guesthouse? *La société aux XIe et XIIe siècles dans la région mâconnaise*, 2d ed. (Paris, 1971), p. 48, n. 15.

273. Iogna-Prat, "La geste des origines," 160 and 175.

274. *Consuetudines Cartusiae*, 20.1, *SC*, 313 (Paris, 1984), p. 206, and cf. 79.1, p. 286.

in the guest house to three days, to restrict the number of guests at any time to the symbolic number of twelve, and to exclude women. Hospitality was one of the issues in the controversy between Bernard of Clairvaux and Peter the Venerable.[275] The Cluniacs were charged with receiving too many—and badly. The abbot of Cluny rejoined, with good sense, that the Benedictine tradition was untenable if pushed to extremes. Either one put some restraints on hospitality or the abbot would be spending all his time receiving guests and washing their feet! And what about the liturgical life of the house if one could not entrust the main burden to a special official, the hosteler? For his part Peter's choice was to fulfill the one duty without neglecting the other, while taking all necessary measures to ensure that both remained viable. This meant remaining open to the world and respecting the regular life, while providing within the monastic space—open in part to pilgrims—areas and times that were totally separate, dedicated to prayer and solitary meditation.[276]

Cluny the Asylum

The distinction between temporary guests and those seeking assistance at the monastery was often a tenuous or essentially nominal one. However those seeking assistance can be usefully divided into three categories. First were those whose motives were spiritual. The monastery was first and foremost a spiritual refuge, the "house of piety" defined by Pope John XIX in his bull of 1024, to which clerics and laity in search of reconciliation retreated, as Abelard did at the end of his amorous and doctrinal tribulations.[277] It was also, in the proper sense of the term, an asylum where refugees from seigneurial unrest could benefit from the immunity the Burgundian sanctuary enjoyed. Lastly, and perhaps above all, it was a house of the poor.

In a Christian society ruled by *caritas* and traversing a period of slow economic growth in which basic food needs were still far from being universally met, the redistributive function of goods given to God in the great monastic sanctuary-lordships was essential to the survival of a mass of poverty-stricken people.[278] Throughout the eleventh century, until the crisis of the 1120s, the Cluniacs devoted themselves unreservedly to fulfilling this function, which was

275. *Ep.*, 28, 1:52–101, here 72–73 and 92; 111, 1:274–99, here 283–84; 150, 1:367–71, here 370–71.

276. *Ep.*, 28, 1:73; *Statutum* 23, p. 60, and 53, p. 83.

277. *Papsturkunden 896–1046*, vol. 2, no. 558, pp. 1053–54. On Abelard, see *Ep.*, 168, 1:401–2: Peter the Venerable to Héloïse.

278. On the charitable function of the monasteries in the eleventh and twelfth centuries, there is an abundant, yet extremely uneven, bibliography. The task is greatly facilitated by Michel Mollat, *Les pauvres au Moyen Age* (Paris, 1978); Otto G. Oexle, "Armutsbegriff und Armenfürsorge im Mittelalter," in *Soziale Sicherheit und soziale Disziplinierung*, ed. Christoph Sachse and Florian Tennstedt (Frankfurt am Main, 1986), pp. 73–101; Joachim Wollasch, "Konventsstärke und Armensorge in mittelalterlichen Klöstern," *Saeculum* 39 (1988): 193ff.

at times a heavy drain on the monastery's budget. During the famine of 1033, Odilo liquidated a part of the treasury in order to assist the poor.[279] In his "Customs," Ulrich gives an idea of the burden assumed by the Cluniac "refuge" in receiving guests, pilgrims, and above all the poor.[280] Eighteen paupers were permanently maintained at the monastery. On the eve of Lent, tradition dictated that all needy folk who presented themselves at the monastery gate should be given a piece of meat; 250 salted pigs were thus sacrificed to feed seventeen thousand poor people.[281] In his examination of the budget of Cluny between 1080 and 1155, Georges Duby calculated that the Cluniac deaneries devoted a third of their surpluses to alms distribution and receiving of guests.[282] Such were the realities inducing Peter the Venerable to describe Cluny as "in a manner of speaking the public treasure of the Christian *res publica*."

In the customs dating from Hugh of Semur's time, maintenance of the poor was the particular responsibility of a monastery official known as the *eleemosynarius* or almoner.[283] It was he who received the poor when they came to the monastery and who gave them a pound of bread and a penny (*iusticia*) when they left. Every day of fasting or without fat in the liturgical calendar, he would give them surplus quantities of bread and wine. Additionally, "prebends" or pensions (from the Latin *praebere*, "to offer") of bread, wine, and beans were provided during the thirty days (tricenary or trental) that followed the death of a professed Cluniac, and every year thereafter on the anniversary of his death. At the abbot's table three daily prebends were given in memory of Odilo and the benefactor-sovereigns of the monastery—Emperor Henry II, King Ferdinand I of Castile-León, and his wife—and this was additional to the eighteen prebendaries whom the community normally provided for daily. Add to these all the passing wretches—children, widows, blind, and paralyzed—to whom the leftovers were served. Daily between All Saints and Ash Wednesday an assistant to the almoner

279. Jotsald, *Vita sancti Odilonis*, 1.9, *PL* 142:904C; also referred to by Peter Damian, *Vita sancti Odilonis*, *PL* 144:929B. On the context and situation of the contemporary peasantry, described as *misérable et asservie*, see Pierre Bonnassie, "Les paysans du royaume franc au temps d'Hugues Capet et de Robert le Pieux (987–1031)," in *Le roi de France et son royaume autour de l'an Mil*, actes du Colloque CNRS Hugues Capet 987–1987, Paris-Senlis, 22–25 June 1987, ed. Michel Parisse and Xavier Barral i Altet (Paris, 1992), pp. 118–29, esp. 117–19.

280. Ulrich, *Antiquiores consuetudines*, 3.11, *PL* 149:751C–753B, and 3.22, 149:764A–765C.

281. Ibid., 3.22, 149:753B.

282. "Le budget de Cluny entre 1080 et 1155," in *Hommes et structures du Moyen Age* (Paris and The Hague, 1973), pp. 63–64. On the deaneries, units of production within the domain of Cluny whose history remains far from clear, see Maria Hillebrandt, "Berzé-la-Ville: la création d'une dépendance clunisienne," in *Le gouvernement d'Hugues de Semur à Cluny"* (Cluny, 1990), pp. 200ff.

283. Bernard, *Ordo Cluniacensis*, 1.13, pp. 157–61; Ulrich, *Antiquiores consuetudines*, 3.24, *PL* 149:765D–767D. On this official and the gradual installation of his duties in the early Cluny, see the basic treatment by Joachim Wollasch: "*Eleemosynarius*: eine Skizze," in *Sprache und Recht. Beiträge und Kulturgeschichte des Mittelalters. Festschrift für Ruth Schmidt-Wiegand zum 60. Geburtstag*, ed. Karl Hauck et al., 2 vols. (Berlin and New York, 1986), 2:972–95, upon which the following remarks are based.

would discharge the *mandatum novum* of John 13:34 and wash the feet of three paupers, thereby echoing the ceremony of Holy (Maundy) Thursday itself, before giving them the same pittance as the monks. Once a week the *eleemosynarius* would go round the *villa* of Cluny, visit the poor who could not get about, and distribute to them bread and wine.

The monks, defining themselves as voluntary poor, necessarily treated the crowd of paupers like themselves. The Cluniac sanctuary was thus a house of benefits. From this point of view, the lexical evolution of the term *eleemosynarius*, closely analyzed by Joachim Wollasch, is highly meaningful. The Rule of Saint Benedict speaks of the duty of care owed to the poor, but lays down no precise office. The Rule of the Master ascribes this duty to the cellarer, while centuries later, at Saint Gall, it had become the office of the *procurator pauperum*. The Cluniacs opted rather for the term *eleemosynarius*, which until the eleventh and twelfth centuries was the term applied to benefactors. Almsgiving had been the particular exercise of mercy taken up by the Carolingian sovereigns in imitation of Christ—the paradigm *eleemosynator* or *eleemosynarius*—and they in their turn were imitated by the princes and aristocrats who became benefactors of the houses of God kept by the "poor" monks. The use of the term at Cluny to denote the functions of the almoner-prebendary was thus a lexical condensation. The monks themselves were both beneficiaries and benefactors. Their function was as intermediaries entrusted with redistributing goods sacrificed to God in a traffic between this world and the next involving the whole order of the world, rich and poor, living and dead. We shall return later to the monks' complex role as "frontiersmen" and to the symbolic dividends of their work. For the present, let us simply note that the Cluniac refuge or asylum represented an intermediate space, an in-between, in which the next world might be anticipated either in the form of personal conversion or by assigning to the monastic community goods or even persons—this last by the oblation of children or indeed by the gift of slaves or serfs having the intermediate status between goods and persons. Both forms of anticipation entailed involvement with the monks, entering into brotherhood with them and becoming their ally. Such was the motivating force that turned traditional monasticism of the Cluniac variety into an *ecclesia mater* destined to include the laity, an ideal reduction of the Christian society.

The *Societas* of the Monks

The Monastery as a "Family of Families"
All individual acts or deeds in the feudal age, whether of conversion or donation, were connected with a family, lineage, or network of fidelity. We might take any number of examples, but one will suffice.[284] An original charter, still extant, dat-

---

284. See also the case of Aquinus and the family of Brancion described by Wollasch, "Wer waren die Mönche von Cluny?" in *Clio et son regard*, p. 671.

ing from Hugh of Semur's abbacy, records the gift of a mill by a certain Oliver, *miles*, who intended to convert to Cluny. Oliver's conversion mobilized the whole network in which his life had been lived. Among the witnesses (*laudatores*) are Oliver's sisters; his uncle Dalmatius of Ginée, from whom Oliver held the mill as a fief and who guaranteed the gift; Baudry of Colchis and his sons from whom Dalmatius himself received the mill and who together with his wife added the land adjoining the mill plus a serf, the serf's wife, and their children present and future; finally, the bishop of Autun, whose man Oliver was (*de cuius capite erat*).[285]

This scale of commitment by an individual and his network in pious deeds of self-giving or donation is comprehensible only in an eschatological perspective. The feudal afterlife was conceived along the lines of the communion of saints. The commonplace *pro remedio animae* recorded in the Cluniac cartularies always expresses an individual's deliberate act in reference to his kinship and others allied in his hope of future joy in common.[286]

Thus on the path to the Last Things the monastery represented a frontier zone where lay seekers after mercy might consolidate their alliances and their relationships of flesh and spirit.[287] Before going into more detail about such consolidations, we need to note the inviolable, eternal nature of the relationship forged between the donor, his network, and the monks, those "administrators" of the afterlife. Many of the deeds recording donations *pro remedio animae* contain restrictive clauses stipulating that goods made over to Cluny shall never be sold, given, exchanged, or granted, but shall ever remain in the use of the brothers who dedicate themselves to God and to assisting the dead.[288] Otherwise the only possible beneficiary of the sale, gift, exchange, or grant of donated property is to be a *propinquus* (relative) of the benefactor.[289]

Being thus fixed for eternity, conversions and donations were a form of widening the family circle. Where a family lacked heirs, the monastery frequently became the final repository of the family wealth. In December 946, a certain Girard and his wife bequeathed to their eldest son, Sigibert, a church and its associated revenues together with a reserve of usufruct. The testators stipulated that the property was not to be alienated. Should Sigibert leave no heir, one of his brothers, Leutald, Richard, or Geribert, was to have it. If none of them

285. *CLU* 2994–96, 4.192–94.

286. E.g., *CLU* 821, a gift *pro remedio animae* of the donor, the donor's parents, and the faithful living and dead, *ut cunctis in commune proficiat*, 1.774–76.

287. E.g., *CLU* 1694, July 984, recording donation of a vine *pro remedio animae* by a certain Sendelenus, on behalf of himself, his father, his mother, his uncle Sendelenus and uncle's wife Odila, his godfather and godmother, whose tenant he is in respect of the vine, 2.718–19.

288. *CLU* 2007, between 1011 and 1030; *CLU* 2749, May 1021, 3.772–74.

289. *CLU* 1433, July 976 or 977, 2.489–90; *CLU* 2934, January 1040, a gift on behalf of one dying in combat financed out of the property of the deceased and containing the following restriction: *Rogamus ergo et precipimus ut nulli homini detur in beneficium, et si hoc factum fuerit, ad heres illius revertatur*, 4.135–36; *CLU* 3612, June 1086, founding deed of the priory of Saint Mary, Cantuario, diocese of Milan, 4.773–75.

had children, then the inheritance would pass to two kinsmen who were priests, Qualpert and Folcher (*iure consanguinitatis*, by right of consanguinity). Then, arriving at the end of the line, it would swell the patrimony of Saint Mary and Saint Peter, Cluny, as a remedy for the donors' souls.[290]

More often still, aristocratic families would ensure the continuation of their identity by endowing the monastery and putting their own members into the community. On a particular level this is a question of relations between individual members of the laity and the monks. But it falls within the more general province of the symbiotic relationship between clergy and aristocracy that was integral to the structure of social and political domination in the feudal age.[291] Two instances drawn from the history of Hugh of Semur, sixth abbot of Cluny (1049–1109), are sufficient to illustrate the question. The first concerns the priory of Paray-le-Monial, founded in 999 by Lambert, count of Chalon and Hugh's maternal great-grandfather.[292] The establishment was maintained by the count's family until the middle of the eleventh century. It was there, at Paray, close to the tomb of Lambert, that the body of Count Thibaud was laid when he died on campaign in the Christian reconquest of Spain in 1065. After the counts, it was the castellans and allied *milites* who invested in the community of Paray, in particular the Busseuil family, whence sprang Prior Hugh, who was placed in that office by his namesake, Hugh of Semur. The prior's brother Atto was similarly placed at Paray, while a third, Geoffrey, was made a canon at Autun. One of his sisters, Agnes, became a nun at Autun, and another, Aelis, joined the Cluniac community at Marcigny-sur-Loire.

Our second example takes us farther still into the kinship network of Hugh of Semur. A quick look at his family tree is enough to show the two sides—lay and ecclesiastical—to the abbot's family in the eleventh and twelfth centuries.[293] Through his father, Dalmatius I, Hugh belonged to the lords of Semur, a line continued by his brother Geoffrey II, as well as his nephew Geoffrey III and great-nephew Geoffrey IV. His sisters' marriages enlarged the circle of aristocratic alliances. Matilda married the lord of Bourbon-Lancy and Adelaide the

290. *CLU* 693, 1.647–48; other examples: *CLU* 802, March 951, 1.754–56; *CLU* 1430, October 976, 2.486–87; CLU 2493, between 999 and 1027, 3.572–75; *CLU* 3746, ca. 1000, 5.100–101.

291. On the clergy-aristocracy symbiosis, and more especially the intermingling of aristocractic families and the monastic communities in Burgundy, see Constance Brittain Bouchard, *Sword, Miter, and Cloister: Nobility and the Church in Burgundy, 980–1198* (Ithaca and London, 1987), the conclusions of which benefit from the finetuning provided in the reviews by: Alain Guerreau, *AESC*, 1990.2: 333–37; Olivier Guillotjeannin, *Francia* 16.1 (1989): 271–72; Neithard Bulst, *Historische Zeitschrift* 259 (1994): 182–84.

292. Maria Hillebrandt, "Le prieuré de Paray-le-Monial au XIe siècle," in *Paray-le-Monial*, pp. 106–24, on which the following remarks are based. On Hugh of Semur's genealogy, see below.

293. Bouchard, *Sword, Miter, and Cloister*, pp. 357–61; Kohnle, *Abt Hugo*, pp. 32–34; Joachim Wollasch, "Parenté noble et monachisme réformateur: observations sur les 'conversions' à la vie monastique aux XIe et XIIe siècles," *Revue historique* 264 (1980): 3–24, esp. 18, and Wollasch, "Wer waren die Mönche von Cluny?" in *Clio et son regard*, p. 673 and n. 44.

lord of Châtel-Montagne; their kinship connections went substantially up in the world with Ermengard's marriage to Robert I, duke of Burgundy. Through his mother Aremburgis, Hugh was descended from Count Lambert of Chalon; subsequent alliances saw the family rise to the level of count (Chalon, Mâcon), then of duke (Burgundy and Portugal), and finally royalty (the Capetians and the sovereigns of Castile-León). The family's connections with the aristocracy of the Church were no less prestigious. Among his ancestors Hugh could count a former abbot of Savigny and an abbess of Peloges on his father's side. His maternal uncle Hugh was both count of Chalon and bishop of Auxerre. His brother Andrew was a deacon. One of his nephews, Reynold, was abbot of Vézelay before becoming archbishop of Lyon (1125–28). Another nephew, Hugh, was successively abbot of Saint-Germain and bishop of Auxerre. Finally, on the distant horizon of his mother's family's alliances came Guy, who was archbishop of Vienne and became pope under the name of Callixtus II (1119–24). All this is apart from the essential: the involvement of the family of Semur in the Ecclesia cluniacensis. Hugh and his brother Geoffrey II used wealth of their own to found the female house of Marcigny-sur-Loire in 1054 in memory of their father, Dalmatius I, and their grandfather, Geoffrey I. From then on the establishment became the refuge, the place of memorial, and the continuation of a lineage, designed to look after the family's destiny, that of its ancestors as much as of its offspring. After the death of his wife, Adelaide, Geoffrey II retired to Cluny and at his death was buried at Marcigny. Hugh and Geoffrey's three sisters, Matilda, Adelaide, and Ermengard, all sooner or later joined the cloister. The two following generations did no differently. Geoffrey III entered Cluny, then went on to become prior of Marcigny, where his wife, Ermengard, and sister Lucy, and then his three daughters, Adelaide, Agnes, and Cecilia, became nuns. The involvement of the family of Semur in the life of the convent demonstrates how it represented a form of family memorial. The cartulary of the establishment, reconstructed by Jean Richard, opens with a genealogical rehearsal of the founders' lineage.[294] In that other memorial of good lay folk, Peter the Venerable's *De miraculis*, Geoffrey III's renunciation of the world is evoked, as is his appointment as prior, and ultimately the tribulations he underwent during the days after his death. On this last theme, Peter tells how Geoffrey appeared to one of his Marcigny nuns, Alberea of Champagne, in order to acquaint her with his lot in the afterlife. At the time of his death, Geoffrey tells her, evil spirits came to snatch him away, but blessed Peter stood in the way to defend him and claim him as one of his own. The Old Enemy thereupon pressed his case, citing the unjust taxes Geoffrey had raised on clothes and on material within the bounds of his lordship. What he requires now is that his son and successor, Geoffrey IV, abolish this bad measure as soon as possible.[295]

294. *Le cartulaire de Marcigny-sur-Loire (1045–1144)*, no. 1, p. 1.
295. *DM*, 1.26, pp. 80–82.

The Monks and the Affairs of (Great) Families

History does not disclose whether Geoffrey IV did as his father's spirit bade. We do know, however, from an extant original charter, about the problems Geoffrey IV caused to the family's religious foundation of Marcigny in the early 1100s.[296] In its preamble, Geoffrey IV's great-uncle Hugh of Semur recalls the history of its foundation as an asylum for men and women desiring to abandon the world's pomp and gain a "safe haven." He goes on to speak of the ups and downs of the house of God, which, he says, is sustained by good people but also attacked by the "adversary of all good," who has managed to inflame the mind of Geoffrey IV. Having neither fear of the Trinity nor reverence for the Virgin—to whom the principal basilica of Marcigny and an adjoining church are dedicated, respectively—Geoffrey has kidnapped a man of the *burgus* that is in the *villa* of the convent. But on the advice of wise and noble men he has come to see reason, and the present assembly has been convened at Montmain, near Cluny, in order to settle the conflict in the presence of Milo, cardinal-bishop of Palestrina and legate sent by Pope Paschal II, Archbishop Raymond of Auch, and "many other doctors." Swearing in public upon the relics and altar, Geoffrey undertakes never again to violate the immunity enjoyed by the *burgus* and *villa* of Marcigny within both its present bounds and any future extension of them. He promises also to impose no tolls within a precisely delimited area. Even outside the *villa* of Marcigny, he swears neither to seize any of the convent's men, nor to lay hands on their property, nor to raise any toll from them. In a final move, Milo seals the peace in the pope's name, promising Geoffrey "a blessed reward with the saints of God" if he observes the terms of the settlement, or "the afflictions of Gehenna and the avenging flames" if he does not. Involved as he is, through kinship, in the community of Cluny, whose patron is the prince of the apostles, Geoffrey IV of Semur must abandon the black designs of the enemy of all good and swear to faithfully (*fideliter*) defend the things of Saint Peter. The term *fideliter* is one of fruitful ambiguity, evoking both the pastoral language of clerics and the vocabulary of the relationships of feudal vassals. This minor episode offers a good illustration of the cycle of confrontation and conflict resolution that moved the world of Burgundian castellans in the seigneurial age, before the Capetians imposed their regulating royal authority at the end of the 1160s. The case we have just looked at is far from exceptional. Its particular interest lies in its "private" nature—or so it seems, at least—involving the two branches, lay and ecclesiastical, of the family of Semur. The monastery, a natural extension of aristocratic kinship, could thus become a theater of family disputes.

By "family disputes" it is possible to understand also conflicts of interests within the monastic community itself, between families of the great allied and represented within it. Its ranks fed by the younger sons of great families, the Ecclesia cluniacensis was a setting for confrontation between rival seigneurial fam-

296. *Le cartulaire de Marcigny-sur-Loire*, no. 288, pp. 165–71.

ilies where abbots needed to exercise dexterity in order to avoid a major crisis. In the 1120s, as we have noted, the schism of Pontius of Melgueil saw the house of Cluny divide into two parties and the abbot resign and leave his church only to return and reimpose his authority by force of arms. Joachim Wollasch's recent thesis is that the schism may have had its source in a conflict of interests between rival seigneurial clans, which engulfed the entire Ecclesia cluniacensis, its head, its monks, and the inhabitants of the *burgus* of Cluny. Bernard Grossus, who opposed Pontius's return and headed the monastery in Peter the Venerable's absence, was doubly implicated in the affair, first, as grand prior of the monastery, and secondly, as representative of the powerful family of Uxelles-Brancion, who were no doubt reluctant to see their hold over the monastery abandoned to others and even less keen to see the rising strength of the burgesses increase further.[297]

The Interweaving of Networks in the Seigneurial System
The names of Semur, Uxelles-Brancion, and so many others suggest the truth: that Cluny and its church in the eleventh and twelfth centuries were primarily the business of great families. The charters of the monastery and its dependencies recount, bit by bit, the story, often several generations long, of properties going back and forth, retained in usufruct, uncertainly granted back to the donor or his heirs, seized by a dishonest kinsman, given back, confirmed anew, and so on. The Cluniac cartularies were effectively the memorial where many aristocratic and princely lines might view the recorded history of their property, their titles, and the acts of devotion constituting their identity.[298] About 1082 Geoffrey, count of Perche, and his wife, Beatrice, granted the monastery of Saint-Denis at Nogent-le-Rotrou to Cluny. Two earlier charters, the first recording the establishment's foundation by Geoffrey's grandfather (also called Geoffrey), and the second, confirmation by his son Rotrocus, father of our Geoffrey, are incorporated into Cluny's Cartulary B. The three charters together make it possible to retrace the family history of the counts of Perche over three generations from the viewpoint of that ideal moment when the powerful, heeding the words of the apostle Paul in 2 Corinthians 6:10, agreed to be as those "having nothing and possessing all things."[299]

297. "Das Schisma des Abtes Pontius von Cluny," *Francia* 23.1 (1996): 31–52, which refers to the large bibliography on the subject.

298. On the definition of aristocratic and princely consciousness in these charters, which meticulously recorded titles and defined powers, see for example *CLU* 3343, 3491, and 3597, as well as studies by Werner Goez, "Mathilda Dei gratia si quid est. Die Urkunden-Unterfertigung der Burgherrin von Canossa," *DA* 47 (1991): 379–94, and Michel Parisse, "Une enquête à mener: la spiritualité des nobles au miroir des préambules de leurs actes," in *Georges Duby: l'écriture de l'Histoire*, ed. Claudie Duhamel-Amado and Guy Lobrichon, Bibliothèque du Moyen Age, 6 (Brussels, 1996), 305–16.

299. *CLU* 2858, ca. 1031, 4.57, mention; *CLU* 3517, 4.633–38; *CLU* 3563, 4.698–702. The quotation from Paul is in the preamble that occurs in all three deeds. On the entry of the monastery of Saint Denis at Nogent-le-Rotrou into the Ecclesia cluniacensis, see Kohnle, *Abt Hugo*, pp. 184 and 315.

In the charter of 1082 Geoffrey granted the monks the right to acquire property by gift or by sale from his own *fideles* (vassals), the closest of these being actually cited as witnesses at the end of the document.[300] Cluny thereby entered the network of loyalties woven by the count's family. Charged with the remembrance of the dead and exchanges with the hereafter, the monastery became heir to the alliances they had secured on earth and was incorporated into their feudal, vassal relationships. Around 1075 a minor nobleman of the southwest, Gerald of Château-Marin, endowed the monks of Cluny and Moissac with a *villa in alodium et feuum* (as alod and fief). As these words implicated the tenant of the fief, the donor laid down that should he wish to renegotiate (*redimere*), he should seek a new grant of the fief from the abbot—whether of Cluny or of Moissac is not clear.[301] This sort of involvement of the monks in networks of seigneurial alliances points up the problem of the complex interconnections between the Church and the laity in the fields of property, legal rights, and power.[302] Let us not, in this regard, be taken in by the slogans of the Church reformers who from the 1050s onward advocated the sharp separation between *temporalia* and *spiritualia*, lay property and Church property. It is true that clerics were preoccupied with getting back "lay" churches in the name of spiritual purity. But it is just as true, and entails no contradiction, that both the aristocracy of the Church and the lay aristocracy belonged to the same social stratum: that dominant class which exploited the fruits of labor and creamed off the surpluses released by the upturn in the countryside during the eleventh century. Let us therefore consign to historical oblivion the curious 1950s notion of a Cluniac monasticism that was "antifeudal."[303]

The Neighborhood of Saint Peter, "Prince of the Earth"
In fact, as Barbara H. Rosenwein has authoritatively shown, the "social logic" of the flow of donations, from which the Burgundian sanctuary benefited massively until the 1050s, argues the depth of the Cluniac involvement in the seigneurial order.[304] History not being a monocausal science, the generosity of lay folk to-

---

300. *CLU* 3563, 4.698–702, here 700.

301. *CLU* 3486, 4.594–95.

302. An excellent example of intense interconnection of networks concerning the priory of Bertrée has been analyzed at length by Giles Constable, "Monasticism, Lordship, and Society in the Twelfth-Century Hesbaye: Five Documents on the Foundation of the Cluniac Priory of Bertrée," *Traditio* 33 (1977): 159–224, rpt. in *Cluniac Studies* (London, 1980), no. 9.

303. Such is the central thesis of Kassius Hallinger, *Gorze-Kluny: Studien zu den monastischen Lebensformen und Gegensätzen im Hochmittelalter, Studia Anselmiana*, 22–25, 2 vols. (Rome, 1950–51).

304. *To Be the Neighbor of Saint Peter: The Social Meaning of Cluny's Property, 909–1049* (Ithaca and London, 1989). The term "social logic"—which encapsulates B. H. Rosenwein's views on the "gift economy"—is taken from the review of this book by Alain Guerreau in *AESC*, 1990.1: 96–101, here 100. This work and the stimulating discussions it aroused have rendered obsolete the thesis of Johannes Fechter, *Cluny, Adel und Volk: Studien über das Verhältnis des Klosters zu den Ständen (910–1049)* (Tübingen, 1966).

ward the monastery may be explained in various ways.[305] Should we discern economic motives? Perhaps such generosity is to be seen as a functional exchange between lands and prayers, a sort of gift and countergift? Or as a necessary gesture dictated by aristocratic prestige?[306] Or again as evidence of family ties uniting monastic brothers with their kinfolk still in the outside world? Alongside all these traditional explanations, Barbara H. Rosenwein suggests that we can view the land that passes from one aristocracy to another, "to the neighborhood of Saint Peter," as a primarily symbolic object. The exchanges of such objects constituted a long cycle, sometimes unending, from one generation to another, during which a property was frequently the object of a donation, then of a counterclaim, and then ultimately of a setting aside of the claim (*werpitio*). The rationale of such a cycle was to create links and maintain them, in short to enable "the social cement" to harden. This thesis is in perfect harmony with the representations nurtured by the Cluniac ideologues, partisans of the inclusion of lay kith and kin in the monastic brotherhood and of their subsequent incorporation in the necrologies as "friends." Thus the possessors of the earth came together in one and the same neighborhood of Saint Peter, Cluny's patron, whom the monastery's very foundation charter described, in a richly ambiguous formula, as together with Paul the "prince of the Earth."[307] The Earth or the earth?

The second part of this book is specifically concerned with analyzing monastic representations of Christian society in the feudal age. For the sake of convenience, those Cluniac writings which aimed at ordering and structuring the world we shall lump together into a single, admittedly ill-defined category under the head of monastic pastoral work. We need to be clear about what this means. It does not mean retracing our steps and looking again at the question of the monastic presence in the parish network and the *cura animarum* exercised by monk-priests, beginning with their responsibilities in respect to Cluny, Vézelay, La Charité-sur-Loire, or elsewhere. Nor—fascinating though such a research exercise would be—is it a question of analyzing the nature of the pastoral activity of the professed Cluniacs who took up episcopal appointments, men like Hugh of Amiens, archbishop of Rouen. What we mean by monastic pastoral effort is rather, with reference to the works of Peter the Venerable, the Cluniacs' magisterial role of engagement in the service of the universal Church, the depth of their identity with it, their labors to purge it and propagate it, and their systematic organization of the abundant images of the *Ecclesia* to define rules constituting Christian society.

305. Such is the object of the first chapter of *To Be the Neighbor of Saint Peter*, pp. 35ff.: "The Problem of Donations"; there is a good résumé of the problem by Patrick Henriet, "La propriété clunisienne comme ciment social (909–1049)," *Le Moyen Age* 98 (1992): 263–70, here 264.

306. Georges Duby, *Guerriers et paysans, VIIe–XIIe siècle: premier essor de l'économie européenne*, Bibliothèque des histoires (Paris, 1973), pp. 60ff. [Eng. trans., *The Early Growth of the European Economy: Warriors and Peasants from the Seventh to the Twelfth Century*, trans. Howard B. Clarke (Ithaca, 1974)].

307. *CLU* 112, 1.124–28, here 127.

II

CHRISTIAN SOCIETY

Peter the Venerable's *Contra Petrobrusianos*
and Its Background

Le souci d'un pouvoir immense et légitime
L'enveloppe. Il se sent rigide, dur, haï.
Il est tel que Moïse, après le Sinaï,
Triste jusqu'à la mort de sa tâche sublime.
Rongé du même feu, sombre du même ennui,
Il savoure à la fois sa gloire et son supplice,
Et couvre l'univers d'un pan de son cilice.
Ce moine croit. Il sait que le monde est à lui.

The cares of a power that is vast and righteous
Close in round him. He feels unbending, harsh, hated.
He is just as Moses was, after Sinai,
Saddened even unto death by his task sublime.
Gnawed by the same fire, sombre with the same ennui,
He tastes at once his glory and his affliction,
And covers the universe with his hair-shirt's tail.
This monk believes. He knows the world belongs to him.[1]

1. Leconte de Lisle. *Les deux glaives, ll. 9–16. First published in the Revue*
européenne, 1 March 1861; included in the Poèmes barbares collection, 1862, ed.
Claudine Gothot-Mersch (Paris, 1985), p. 255.

3

"PURGING" THE CHURCH

CLUNY AND HERESY

A Monk at the Heart of Christendom: Peter the Venerable

The guiding thread of this study of Christian society as seen through monks' eyes comes from the work of Peter the Venerable. Peter was a leading figure in twelfth-century Church life, but first we need to place him in the context of his two interconnected families, that of the Montboissiers and that of Cluny.[1]

Peter's ancestor, Hugh of Paillers, was known as "the Unstitched" on account of his liberality. He was, in truth, the very image of a *miles* (knight) at the close of the first millennium. Embroiled in conflicts between castellans, he did not hesitate to oppress the properties of Sauxillanges, a dependency of Cluny in the Auvergne, and then sought to gain pardon through appropriate gestures of piety.[2] At some unknown date in the last three decades or so of the tenth century, Hugh took his wife, Isengard, on an "expiatory pilgrimage" to Rome. There he was told he should found a monastery. On the way home, he stopped at La Chiusa in Piedmont, where he decided to found an establishment dedicated to the archangel Michael, the patron of warriors.[3] The actual builder of San Michele della Chiusa was perhaps Maurice I, the son of Hugh and Isengard. It was he at all events who gave the family its landed status, building the castle of Montboissier between Ambert and Issoire from which thereafter the Montboissier family would derive its name and prestige. His heir, Maurice II, acquired

---

1. On Peter's family, see *Ep.*, ed. Giles Constable, 2 vols., Harvard Historical Studies, 78 (Cambridge, Mass., 1967), 2:232–46 (appendix A) ; Jean-Pierre Torrell and Denise Bouthillier, *Pierre le Vénérable et sa vision du monde: sa vie, son oeuvre; l'homme et le démon*, Spicilegium Sacrum Lovaniense, Etudes et documents, 42 (Leuven, 1986).

2. The best sketch of Hugh "the Unstitched," in seigneurial context, is Christian Lauranson-Rosaz, *L'Auvergne et ses marges (Velay, Gévaudan) du VIIIe au XIe siècle: la fin du monde antique?* (Le Puy-en-Velay, 1987). I have followed Lauranson-Rosaz's suggested genealogical reconstruction (p. 151), whereby there are four, not three, generations between Peter and his "unstitched" ancestor.

3. The political background to this foundation is excellently described in ibid., pp. 291ff., from which I have taken the term *pèlerinage-expiation*.

the title of *princeps* (noble), thereby indicating that the Montboissiers were by then sufficiently established on the seigneurial scene to renounce the bad customs formerly imposed on Sauxillanges. From then on the destinies of the two families, the seigneurial and the monastic, tended to merge. Maurice III (circa 1040–1116/17) was one of the monastery's benefactors; he was a pious *miles*, who possibly took part in the First Crusade and regularly went on pilgrimage to the tombs of the saints before dying as a monk *ad succurrendum* (converting at the end of life) at Sauxillanges.[4] His wife, Raingard, fascinated by the exceptional personality of Robert of Arbrissel, considered entering the female house of Fontevraud, founded by the former hermit and itinerant preacher. In the event, she followed the monastic logic of the Montboissiers and went instead to Cluny's female house at Marcigny-sur-Loire. Four of the couple's seven surviving sons also opted for Cluny. An eighth almost certainly died when quite young. The eldest, named Hugh like his "unstitched" ancestor, stayed in the world in order to manage and increase the Montboissier estate, a responsibility that passed subsequently to Eustace. The five younger sons all devoted themselves to God. Four entered, at least temporarily, the monastic life of Cluny. In addition to Peter, there was Armannus, Jordan, who became abbot of La Chaise-Dieu (1146–1157/58), and Pontius, who is thought to have gone first to the family foundation of Saint Michael at La Chiusa before entering the Cluniac network and taking charge of Vézelay from 1138 to 1161 with a few years' intermission.[5] The other son, Heraclius, was successively provost of the chapter of Saint-Julien at Brioude, archdeacon of the chapter of Lyon, abbot of Saint-Just, and finally archbishop of Lyon (1150–63).

Hugh III's and Raingard's son Peter became known as "the Venerable" from the end of the 1180s.[6] He was born in 1092 or 1094 and entered the monastery of Sauxillanges as an oblate child. After his education in the monastery *schola* (school), he journeyed to the motherhouse to make his monastic profession there as Cluniac tradition demanded. From there Abbot Pontius of Melgueil sent him on to Vézelay as schoolmaster and claustral prior. The mobility inherent in his career was typically Cluniac. From Vézelay he went as prior to Domène, an establishment not far from La Grande Chartreuse. It was during this period that his affection, not to say veneration, for the Carthusian model codified by Guigo I in his *Consuetudines Cartusiae* was born. Two years later, he left Domène for Cluny in order to succeed Hugh II, the short-lived successor of Abbot Pontius of Melgueil. Peter then was no more than thirty.

Continuing a tradition begun by Abbot Majolus and developed by Odilo,

4. Maurice's crusadership is conjecture based on an allusion by Peter of Poitiers in his panegyric of Peter the Venerable, *BC*, col. 615A. Other biographical details regarding Maurice III and Raingard are taken from the funeral eulogy by their son Peter, *Ep.*, 53, 1:153–73.

5. *Ep.*, 2:243.

6. *Chronique de Robert de Torigny* (died 1186), *MGH SS*, 6.506; Cf. *Dictionnaire de spiritualité*, ed. Viller et al. (1937–), 12.2, cols. 1669–76 (by Jacques Hourlier).

Hugh of Semur, and to a lesser extent Pontius of Melgueil, Peter the Venerable involved himself deeply in contemporary events. He differed from his predecessors, however, in that none was as caught up as he in the pastoral sphere. As he wrestled with the Petrobrusians and Saracens, Peter maintained that it was impossible for him to stay silent. It had been all very well for a man like Odilo, a century earlier, to leave the bishops to police the heretics of Orléans, Champagne, or Aquitaine. But for Peter, in the second quarter of the twelfth century, keeping quiet was not an option. He was the very model of a post-Gregorian monk driven to abandon the silence of the cloister and campaign in the world on every front where the Church needed defending.[7] Such involvement was not just a response to circumstances like the schism of 1130, in which he took the side of Pope Innocent II against Anacletus II, the former Cluniac Peter Pierleone.[8] In a letter to the recluse Gilbert, Peter described the solitary as a *taciturnus praedicator* (quiet preacher).[9] It is a term that aptly describes the abbot of Cluny in his pastoral role; he was present in the world, not directly by preaching but through his many writings. When we analyze them, we get a good idea of the tasks that fell to the monastic *magisterium* between 1120 and 1150.

Peter's works include four sermons that he composed for internal use to satisfy the liturgical needs of the Ecclesia cluniacensis. Two are in honor of Marcellus, pope and martyr, another is for the feast of the Transfiguration, and the fourth is in praise of the sepulchre of Christ. In this fourth sermon, Peter extols the centrality and magnetic power of the Holy Land, a place that, since it once contained the dying and risen Christ, every Christian is supposed to internalize.[10] Peter's Christological devotion is given metrical form in a heavily accented poem, the *Rhythmus in laude sancti Salvatoris*. Also intended for liturgical use are proses (hymns) and Marian sequences as well as a prose in honor of Hugh of Semur;[11] but most important of all is an office for the Transfiguration, a rite that Peter himself originated at Cluny.[12]

Peter's essential work consists of letters, treatises, and a collection of miracles. Some of the letters are occasional texts; others really amount to small treatises. Letter 20, to the recluse Gilbert, is a eulogy of the solitary life. Letters 28

---

7. The best introduction to Peter's works is to be found in the literature by Torrell and Bouthillier, especially *Pierre le Vénérable et sa vision du monde*.

8. On the schism and Peter's encouragement of the recognition of Innocent II, see Aryeh Graboïs, "Le schisme de 1130 et la France," *Revue d'histoire de l'Eglise de France* 76 (1981): 593–612.

9. *Ep.*, 20, 1:27–41, here 39.

10. On editions used of these works, see primary sources in the bibliography.

11. Respectively *Analecta Hymnica*, 48:237–39 (Mary) and 240 (Hugh of Semur).

12. Edited by J. Leclercq, *Pierre le Vénérable*, Figures monastiques (Saint-Wandrille, 1946). The solemnity was inaugurated by Peter's fifth statute, *Statutum* 5, ed. Giles Constable, *CCM*, 6 (Siegburg, 1975), pp. 45–46. On his liturgical work, see Robert Folz, "Pierre le Vénérable et la liturgie," in *Pierre Abélard–Pierre le Vénérable: les courants philosophiques, littéraires et artistiques en Occident au milieu du XIIe siècle*, Abbaye de Cluny, 2–9 July 1972, ed. Jean Châtillon, Jean Jolivet, and René Louis, Colloques internationaux du CNRS, 546 (Paris, 1975), pp. 143–61.

and 111 to Bernard of Clairvaux are lengthy defenses of the Cluniac model of monasticism. Letter 37 is to an anonymous Cluniac monk tainted with Apollinarianism, the belief that Christ was human as to the body, but not the soul. This particular letter is no mere tract on Christological orthodoxy, but an extremely precise deployment of the polemic methods adopted by Peter in his great doctrinal writings against the Petrobrusian heretics (*Contra Petrobrusianos*), the Jews (*Adversus Iudeos*), and the Saracens (*Contra sectam Sarracenorum*). Peter's polemical treatises were written in the spirit and idiom of the burgeoning scholasticism represented by Abelard, whom Peter welcomed to Cluny at the end of his life. Before responding to his opponents, Peter obtained their writings, the Talmud in the case of the Jews, and the Islamic Qur'an (Koran), which he had translated into Latin for the first time. He laid down ground rules for possible debate, blending arguments from authority—where he and his opponents shared authorities in common—with sufficient reason, that is to say the argumentative logic then in vogue in school debates. The quality of Peter's documentary preparation for these tasks, the finesse of his methods of argument, and the novelty of his information, not least in the legal area, raise an issue rarely alluded to by historians of Cluny, namely, our poor knowledge of the schools of the Ecclesia cluniacensis.[13] All we can say, on the basis of the weight and value of the catalogue of the library at Cluny in the eleventh century, is that the education given by such a highly cultured community cannot have been in any way inferior to that offered in the urban schools.[14] Doubtless the same was true of Sauxillanges, where Peter the Venerable received his education at the end of the 1090s.

De miraculis, composed between 1135 and Peter's death in 1156, is virtually the work of a lifetime. Its most recent editor, Denise Bouthillier, has pointed to two distinct collections, each divided into two books: first, a short collection containing eucharistic miracles, appearances of the dead, and apparitions of demons; secondly, a longer collection containing additions and modifications.[15] Among the additions are: the life of Matthew of Albano, originally a freestanding work, then subsequently integrated into the main collection; a number of ghost stories, not least the one in book 1, chapter 27, which Peter wrote amidst the fires of polemic against the Petrobrusians, alongside composition of his *Contra Petrobrusianos*, in 1139–40. *De miraculis* has to be seen as coming from the core of the Cluniac hagiographical tradition. The exemplary stories penned by Peter voice the major themes of the abbatial hagiography of the times of Odilo and Hugh of Semur: phantom appearances; demonology; eucharistic piety; Christological and Marian devotion. But compared with the past, *De miraculis* is different in two essential respects. First, it dispenses with the earlier Cluniac hagiographical

---

13. Some scraps of information are brought together by Pierre Riché, *Ecoles et enseignement dans le haut Moyen Age* (Paris, 1979), pp. 141–42.

14. On the Cluny library catalogue, now redated to Hugh of Semur's abbacy, see the fundamental works by Veronika von Büren listed under secondary works in the bibliography.

15. See Denise Bouthillier's introduction to the edition, *CCCM* 83 (Turnhout, 1988), pp. 57*ff.

tradition that concentrated on the persona of abbots. The saints Peter honors are not abbots but ordinary monks—Gerard (book 1, chapter 8), Alger of Liège (1.17), Benedict (1.20), Matthew of Albano (2.4–23)—and his exemplary models are taken from Cluny and La Chartreuse (2.27–29). Another widening of horizons is the shift of concentration from the very special dead—the saints—to the ordinary dead: the laity. This raises a question of literary typology. Where are we to place *De miraculis*? Jean-Pierre Torrell and Denise Bouthillier consider that it belongs at the confluence of the various streams of "marvelous literature of monastic origin."[16] The term "marvelous" is unfortunate, since it more properly applies to another genre, that of the *Mirabilia*, which are both later than and different from the *Miracula*. The very framework of comparison, "literature of monastic origin," by which is meant the Benedictine, Cluniac, and Cistercian traditions, is too narrow. It is often unclear where the material reworked by Peter the Venerable has actually come from. Indeed, the fact that it is not strictly monastic, but Roman in some cases and above all lay in many others, is quite blatant. From this point of view, *De miraculis* should be sharply contrasted with such contemporary collections as the *Liber miraculorum* from Saint-Benoît-sur-Loire or the *De rebus gestis* of Marmoutier; neither of these strays beyond the borders of the monastic community. The *Liber* centers on the miracles of the saint, while *De rebus* excludes all lay involvement.[17] The portrayal of lay people in *De miraculis* should be seen therefore as a conscious and deliberate act of inclusion in a church system within which Cluny played the role of refuge and asylum.

Taken together, Peter the Venerable's sermons, letters, treatises, and accounts of miracles amount to a coherent system of thought in which the same themes occur and recur. Take the theme of Christian universality: one could quote to equal effect from the *Sermo in transfiguratione domini*, *Adversus Iudeos*, or *Contra sectam Sarracenorum*. The same is true of Peter's concept of the miraculous: between *De miraculis*, *Contra Petrobrusianos*, *Adversus Iudeos*, and *Contra sectam Sarracenorum*, the differences in treatment of this theme are only ones of tone.[18] Numerous other areas could be cited to illustrate the general coherence of Peter's thought. The mid-twelfth century, very roughly the period of Peter's activity, marked a shift in thinking about the Church from images to systems. In other words it saw the elaboration in the prescholastic age of genuine doctrinal syn-

---

16. *Pierre le Vénérable et sa vision du monde*, pp. 196ff.; on the debatable use of the term "marvel" (Fr. *merveille*), see p. 137. A chronological and typological treatment of *miracula* and *mirabilia* may be found in Jean-Claude Schmitt, *Les revenants: les vivants et les morts dans la société médiévale*, Bibliothèque des Histoires (Paris, 1994), pp. 77–78.

17. *Miracula sancti Benedicti*, ed. Eugène de Certain (Paris, 1958; republished, New York and London, 1968); *De rebus gestis in Majori Monasterio*, PL 149:403–20. Others could be cited; the present remarks are based upon Schmitt, *Les revenants*, pp. 82ff.

18. Studied in depth by Jean-Pierre Torrell and Denise Bouthillier, "*Miraculum*: une catégorie fondamentale chez Pierre le Vénérable," *Revue thomiste* 80 (1980): 357–86 and 549–66.

theses conceptualizing a church system.[19] From within the prehistory of the treatises *de vera Ecclesia*, Peter thus had much to contribute to the holistic conception of Christian society that the clerics of the first feudal age were striving to formulate.

Cluniac Notions of the Apocalypse and Demonology

Within this holistic conceptualization, the fight against the various shapes assumed by the Antichrist—heretics, Jews, Saracens—emerged as a major theme. But unlike many of his contemporaries—Norbert of Xanten; Bernard of Clairvaux and the Cistercians, who showed a marked interest in apocalyptic constructions in the context of Church reform; Hildegard of Bingen (1098–1179), waiting for the two last times and the disaster prefacing renewal; Joachim of Fiore (circa 1130–1202), announcing the arrival of the Spirit and the spiritualization of the world[20]—Peter the Venerable was only moderately interested in the theme of apocalyptic expectation. Taking our cue from Bernard McGinn's distinction between "Antichrist *language*" and "Antichrist *application*," we could say that for Peter the Apocalypse constituted more a verbal device to suit a reforming cleric than an overriding conception of the whole of history with its irresistible succession of ages at whose culmination Antichrist was to be freed from his bonds.[21]

In that respect, Peter was following a straight line of Cluniac tradition begun by Odo.[22] Inspired by Gregory the Great, whose *Moralia in Job* he abridged, Odo in his *Occupatio* revealed an undeniable interest in the problem of the Last Days and the advent of Antichrist.[23] To understand the real purpose of Odo's writing, however, one has to take account of the literary and spiritual dimension of the *Occupatio* and not simply, as has been usual since the work of Raoul Manselli, abstract from the text those passages that seem to affirm belief in eschatological expectation in the here and now. Indeed, to labor at such misinterpretation is all the more vain, since Odo's long poem in dactylic hexameters, bristling with rare terms garnered most often from the Greek vocabulary then in fashion in the schools and known only to glossarists, was transmitted in a unique manuscript and its influence upon medieval thought was nil. Addressing

19. Yves Congar, *L'Ecclésiologie du haut Moyen Age de saint Grégoire le Grand à la désunion entre Byzance et Rome* (Paris, 1968), pp. 98–99.

20. Bernard McGinn, *Antichrist: Two Thousand Years of the Human Fascination with Evil* (San Francisco, 1994), pp. 126ff.

21. Ibid., pp. 120–21.

22. The classic study of Odo's apocalyptic is Raoul Manselli, *La "Lectura super Apocalypsim" di Pietro di Giovanni Olivi. Ricerche sull'escatologismo medioevale* (Rome, 1955), pp. 33ff., the conclusions of which are here subjected to considerable qualification.

23. On Odo's précis of Gregory's *Moralia in Job*, see Gabriella Braga, "Problemi di autenticità per Oddone di Cluny: l'epitome dei *Moralia* di Gregorio Magno," *Studi Medievali*, 3d ser., 28 (1977): 45–51.

a "brother," real or supposed, in search of spiritual permanence through the meditation necessary to reveal the unseen forces ordering the world, Odo paints a vast fresco, through seven books, of the history of salvation.[24] The essential purpose of the work is to serve as a mystic primer; by way of glossarial exercises—in other words, rumination on the hidden meaning of pregnant terms that are unintelligible without glosses—the aim is to gain access to a mystic comprehension of History. The *Occupatio* thus wholly defies the possibility of a literalist reading. From gloss to gloss and by a learned shuttling between the narrative and its allegorical or moral interpretation, Odo enables his seeking "brother," and his reader, to apprehend the destiny of the world from the purity of the angels at the Creation to the problematic state of the present contaminated by the devil and his minions. On the way, he considers the fall of Lucifer, the fault and fall of the first among mankind, the emergent light of prophecy, the hope of restoration accomplished by the sacrifice of Christ, and finally Pentecost conceived as the founding moment of monasticism. Odo's all-embracing meditation moreover provided a framework for specific reflection upon the history of the Church. At its origins, the period of persecution, the Church was pure. With peace came the time of corruption foreseen by the apostle Paul and by the author of the Apocalypse (12:1–4), who saw a dragon preparing to devour the son of a "woman clothed with the sun" as soon as she gave birth. The satanic monster then invaded the world, and concupiscence (*libido*) came with him.[25] Before the final unleashing of Antichrist, Abbot Odo of Cluny urges men to amend their lives while there is time. This time "while there is time" was precisely the space that the Cluniac reformers of the tenth to twelfth centuries were eager to occupy in order to amend the life of the world. In so doing they rooted their prerogatives in it as great theocratic lords.

Written less than a century after Odo's work, Rodulfus Glaber's *Historiarum libri quinque* gives a good idea of the Cluniac "ambivalence" regarding apocalyptic expectation.[26] Again the conception of the miseries of the age developed in this work is more deuteronomic than truly apocalyptic; it, too, needs to be seen in the context of an all-embracing meditation on the order of the world, dictated in this instance by the discourse on the divine quaternity with which the book commences.[27] From his viewpoint in the first third of the eleventh cen-

24. On the theme in the *Occupatio* that is of concern here, see Jan Ziolkowski, "The *Occupatio* by Odo of Cluny: A Poetic Manifesto of Monasticism in the Tenth Century," in *Lateinische Kultur im X. Jahrhundert*, Akten des I. Internationalen Mittellateinerkongresses, Heidelberg, 12–15 September 1988, ed. Walter Berschin, Sonderdruck aus *Mittellateinisches Jahrbuch* 24/25 (1989/90) (Stuttgart, 1991), pp. 559–67, upon which the following analysis is based.

25. *Occupatio*, 7.116–22, ed. Antonius Swoboda (Leipzig, 1900), p. 152.

26. There is an excellent analysis of this "ambivalence" (the term is the author's) by Richard Landes, "Radulfus Glaber and the Dawn of the New Millennium," *RM*, n.s., 7 (1996): 57–77.

27. Edmond Ortigues and Dominique Iogna-Prat, "Raoul Glaber et l'historiographie clunisienne," *Studi Medievali*, 3d ser., 26.2 (1985): 537–72.

tury, Glaber notes the signs that could be associated with the millennial anniversary of the birth of Christ (the year 1000) or of his Passion (1033), though these round figures do not in his eyes contain great intrinsic significance.[28] For Glaber, some of these signs are disturbances to the world order—comets, famines, raining blood in Aquitaine, the apostasy of Christians converting to Judaism, invasions of Normans, Hungarians, and Saracens, the destruction of the Holy Sepulchre in 1009, waves of heresy in the 1020s—that testify to the unleashing of Satanic activity. However, other signs proclaim the new alliance between God and his faithful people, through which a renewal of the world is taking place: the discovery of relics; councils of Peace and the setting up of areas free of violence, the construction of a "white mantle of churches," the many pilgrimages to holy places, particularly Jerusalem. Glaber reports, in this connection, the question of "some" who wondered if this recent vogue for Jerusalem should not be seen in relation to the advent of Antichrist, as if "then a way would be opened for all peoples to the east where he would appear, and all nations would march against him without delay."[29] Yet the historian holds his peace on the issue. And rightly so, for at Cluny, in the strict Carolingian tradition formulated by Master Haymo in the prestigious school of Auxerre, the view was that the Apocalypse was a holy book whose meaning was exclusively allegorical: not a "progression in time, but a succession of images."[30] Under these conditions, the eschatological morrow was sufficiently far away to leave space for a possible restoration of humanity. Above all, this "morrow" was *already* prefigured by the monks, whose virginal purity placed them between mankind and the angels. Such spiritual beings already inhabiting the future would see no major difficulty in their contemporaries' having to live a little longer in the present. Apart from the interest shown by Odo and Glaber, the question of the struggle against Antichrist scarcely resurfaced in Cluniac circles until Peter the Venerable entered on the scene. That said, it is worth noting that the *Vitae* of abbots, which account for about four-fifths of Cluny's narrative output prior to the 1120s, point to the emergence, around 1050, of a demonology that quickly became a major hagiographical theme.[31] As we are about to see, some of the *Vitae*

28. Daniel S. Milo, *Trahir le temps (Histoire)* (Paris, 1991), pp. 63ff. and 89ff.

29. Rodulfus Glaber, *Historiarum libri quinque*, 4.21, in *Works*, ed. and trans. John France et al., Oxford Medieval Texts (Oxford, 1989), pp. 204–5.

30. The expression comes from Guy Lobrichon, "Jugement dernier et Apocalypse," in *De l'art comme mystagogie: iconographie du Jugement dernier et des fins dernières à l'époque gothique*, Actes du colloque de la Fondation Hardt, Geneva, 13–16 February 1994, Civilisation médiévale, 3 (Poitiers, 1996), pp. 13ff., upon which article the following remarks are based.

31. Dominique Iogna-Prat, "Panorama de l'hagiographie abbatiale clunisienne (v. 940–v. 1140)," in *Manuscrits hagiographiques et travail des hagiographes*, ed. Martin Heinzelmann, Beihefte der Francia, 24 (Sigmaringen, 1991), pp. 77–118. Alain Guerreau rightly notes the "almost surreptitious appearances" of hell and the devil in the earliest Cluniac abbatial hagiography: "Le champ sémantique de l'espace dans la *Vita* de saint Maieul (Cluny, début du XIe siècle)," *Journal des Savants* (1997): 363–419.

composed to launch the cult of Hugh of Semur reveal the context in which this preoccupation with fighting the deviants, Satan's minions, appeared.

In his *Vita sancti Hugonis*, Gilo records an interesting episode in which Hugh was compelled to play the policeman within the Cluniac community. As narrated, the incident opens with Hugh away at the Cluniac monastery of Saint-Jean at Angély.[32] In a vision the abbot sees a thunderbolt coming from above, dividing the community (*scindere auditorium*) at Cluny and causing desolation (*relinquere exterminium*). It is revealed to him that one of the brothers has offended God, and that if he, Hugh, does not rush back to correct the guilty party, the whole house will be held accountable. Hugh thus returns to Cluny, reprimands the offending brother, a certain Peter of Tournus or Tourniers, and gives point to his judgment with the words: "If I spared you, I would be putting everyone in danger." The episode is not intrinsically remarkable, being essentially a matter of internal monastic discipline, but it does show how Hugh, as abbot, felt answerable for the fate of the community. Peter the Venerable's commitment to the fight against heretics was different only in scale, in that the focus had moved from the level of the religious house to the whole of Christian society, as if the Church were essentially only a vast monastery. As far as Hugh's involvement with Peter of Tournus is concerned, one should note the terms in which the hagiographer chose to couch the situation—*scindere auditorium; relinquere exterminium*—which would not be out of place in an antiheretical context. In the preceding chapter of the same *Vita*, Gilo relates an incident in which Hugh of Semur, on arrival at the priory of La Charité-sur-Loire, refuses the kiss of peace to one of the monks.[33] To the community's utter astonishment, it turns out that the brother concerned is a sorcerer (*mechanicum*) and necromancer. Through the abbot's intervention the "false brother" is discovered and excluded from the community. The same episode is told in another of the *Vitae sancti Hugonis*, that by Hugh of Gournay. But between Gilo's narrative and Hugh's, there is a tangible shift in the choice of words. Hugh of Gournay says:

> As the brothers wondered at his doing, he [Abbot Hugh] anxiously inquired where the man, who had been received as a novice, had come from or what sect [*sectam*] he belonged to. And because "the spiritual man judgeth all things and he himself is judged of no man," he was able to convict the man of being a sorcerer [*mechanicum*] out of his own mouth. Thus the shepherd showed up the wolf with his blot of faithlessness [*infidelitatis*] and drove him away from the sheep; the man of faith [*fidelis*] drove out the faithless one [*infidelem*] from the company of the faithful.[34]

The exorcist power exhibited by the abbot of Cluny in Hugh of Gournay's narrative is corroborated with a quotation taken from the apostle Paul, writing

32. Gilo, *Vita sancti Hugonis*, 1.18, "Two Studies," pp. 67–68.
33. Ibid., 1.17, p. 67.
34. Hugh of Gournay, *Vita sancti Hugonis*, 8, "Two Studies," pp. 125–26.

in 1 Corinthians 2:15. Though Paul's words are not really essential to the author's exorcist context, they nevertheless clearly evoke the pope's power as expressed in the nineteenth chapter of Gregory VII's *Dictatus papae: Quod a nemine ipse iudicari debeat*—"That he is not to be judged by anyone."[35] Thus by means of eloquent mimicry, the power to judge without being judged is translated from Rome to Cluny. But this is not all. Other vocabulary employed here in an exorcist context would be as apt, if not more so, in writing against heresy: not just the words *tenere sectam*, which are obvious enough, but the opposition *fidelis–infidelis* (believer–unbeliever). To crown all, two of the copyists responsible for the four surviving manuscripts of Hugh's narrative have transmitted to posterity the illuminating misreading *manicheum* in place of *mechanicum*.

Having entered Sauxillanges as an oblate child and been educated there while Hugh of Semur was abbot of Cluny, Peter the Venerable no doubt had an early introduction to the demonology then fashioning Cluniac spirituality. Peter's own contribution was to turn the theme of the devil into an obsession, envisioning Cluny as a "celestial citadel" where, as he puts it, "a tireless and unyielding wrestling 'against the spirits of wickedness' [Ephesians 6:12] offers daily palms of victory to the soldiers of Christ."[36]

The Cluniac citadel must have seemed all the more under siege in the early 1100s, given the vivid actuality brought to eschatological expectation by literalist readings of the Apocalypse. As Guy Lobrichon has clearly shown, the masters of the school of Laon were directing meditation on John's work toward a more historical exegesis linking "the ages of the world and the states of the Church with the sevenfold scheme that studded the visions of the Apocalypse."[37] Expectation of imminent Judgment was a spur to numerous evangelical movements anticipating in the here and now the prophecies of Christ and of his beloved disciple. From the late 1120s on, the Church attempted to dampen down apocalyptic surges of too radical a nature and over-frequent expectations of the end of the world. At Cluny it fell to Peter the Venerable to make the rejoinder. His approach was to take at face value the prospect of Antichrist's activities unloosed and thereby to expose, attack, and defeat the three contemporary embodiments, as he saw it, of the unclean beast—heresy, Judaism, and Islam.

THE "POISON" OF THE PETROBRUSIAN HERESY

In Peter the Venerable's eyes, the devil had a number of poisons whereby he sought to gain disciples. Heresy was one of them. In 1139–40, Pe-

35. *Das Register Gregors VII.*, 1.55a, no. 19, *MGH*, Epistolae selectae, 2.1–2, 1:206.
36. *DM*, 1.12, p. 43, ll. 13–14, and 1.9, p. 36, ll. 39–41.
37. Lobrichon, "Jugement dernier et Apocalypse," pp. 13ff., upon which the following remarks are based.

ter composed a long refutation in five chapters of the heresy of Peter of Bruis as transmitted by Henry of Lausanne.[38] The treatise is prefaced by a letter of dedication to the archbishop of Arles, the archbishop of Embrun, the bishop of Die, and the bishop of Gap. In it Peter explains the circumstances that have led him to explore this "poison of heresy" and frame his response. As it happens, it is our only source of precise historical detail about the person of Peter of Bruis.

The phenomenon the abbot of Cluny was combating was already some twenty years old, having begun in 1119–20. At that time, believers were being rebaptized, churches profaned, altars overturned, and crosses thrown onto huge bonfires; meat was cooked on these bonfires and believers were invited to eat of it on Good Friday. Priests were whipped; monks were locked up and forced to marry women.[39] Peter of Bruis's teaching, which had great success within the ecclesiastical jurisdictions of the prelates to whom Peter the Venerable dedicated his treatise, later spread into Septimania and on into the "province of Novempulana, vulgarly called Gascony."[40] The heresy was successfully combated by the bishops concerned, but as he passed through Provence, Peter the Venerable was able to see for himself that the heresiarch's teaching had left its mark. To help his addressees—men busy in Church affairs with little time to read—Peter summarized, in his dedicatory letter, the five heretical propositions that the treatise would refute point by point. These were:

1. rejection of infant baptism, on the ground that salvation was by faith and young children were not sufficiently aware to have belief;
2. nonacceptance of consecrated places, the Church of God being no construction of stone but a purely spiritual reality, the community of the faithful;
3. refusal to revere the cross, since it was the means by which Christ was tortured and suffered and was therefore a hateful object;
4. allegation that the Eucharist celebrated by priests and bishops was a lie, the body of Christ having been eaten once only and by the disciples alone at the Last Supper preceding the Passion, thereby rendering all subsequent eating an empty fiction;
5. insistence on the uselessness of all funerary piety, whether offerings, prayers, masses, or alms, since no deceased person could hope to achieve anything other than what he obtained when he was alive.

To these five points Peter the Venerable added a short defense of the chant of the Church, also rejected by the Petrobrusians, since they espoused interior and silent devotion.

---

38. James Fearns, "Peter von Bruis und die religiöse Bewegung des 12. Jahrhunderts," *Archiv für Kulturgeschichte* 48 (1966): 311–35. I have not had access to P. G. Teruzzi, "Il *Contra Petrobrusianos* di Pietro Venerabile," dissertation, Università Cattolica del Sacro Cuore, Milan, 1969.

39. *CP*, 4, ll. 10–12, and 112, ll. 5–10.

40. *CP, epistola*, 1, ll. 14–16.

At the end of his letter of dedication, the abbot of Cluny recalls the sad end of Peter of Bruis, thrown upon the bonfire of crosses he himself had prepared at Saint-Gilles-du-Gard by "faithful" people infuriated by what he had done. We can make an intelligent guess at who these "faithful" were: possibly the people of Saint-Gilles, or the vassals of the local master, the count. One can imagine the count being concerned to impose law and order within the jurisdiction of a church visited by pilgrims drawn to the remains of Saint Gilles, and even more his interest in exercising control over the profits of the Rhône trade in this strategic location.[41] The political background is all the more relevant in that the troubles provoked by Peter of Bruis and his disciples coincided with the confrontation, during the second decade of the twelfth century, between the families of the counts of Toulouse and Barcelona for control of Provence.[42] Peter the Venerable adds that, after Peter of Bruis's death by burning at Saint-Gilles, his heretical work was continued by Henry of Lausanne. Thus much the abbot of Cluny says he has been able to ascertain directly from a work in which the heresiarch's assertions were related.[43] All the same, he will put off directly answering Henry until he has clearer information as to what he can charge him with; to this end, he begs assistance from the bishops and archbishops to whom he has addressed the present treatise. In the meantime, he asks them to pass on this first antiheretical writing to such as might have need of it, and closes by charging all future transcribers not to omit the introductory letter.

The Shaping of Contra Petrobrusianos

In one of his letters to Bernard of Clairvaux, Peter the Venerable speaks of his intention to send him "chapters written against the heretics of Provence" in order that Bernard should read them and add anything he might deem necessary. Peter was unable to send a copy right away: one had been sent to Provence the year before, and a brother of Cluny, he says, had recently left for the Auvergne with the last available copy.[44] We do not know if Bernard ever received the promised copy; the abbot of Clairvaux made no additions to Peter's text that we know of. Nonetheless Peter's attempt to gain Bernard's input for his project shows how important he regarded the diffusion of Contra Petrobrusianos to be. This was very different from Bernard of Clairvaux's approach to the fight against heresy. Whereas Bernard made his response only when asked,[45] Peter the Ven-

41. Such is suggested by Robert I. Moore, *The Formation of a Persecuting Society: Power and Deviance in Western Europe, 950–1250* (Oxford, 1987), pp. 115–16.

42. Jean-Pierre Poly, *La Provence et la société féodale 879–1160: contribution à l'étude des structures dites féodales dans le Midi* (Paris, 1976), pp. 320ff.

43. *CP*, epistola, 10, ll. 6–8.

44. *Ep.*, 111, 1:274–99, here 299.

45. In his sermons 65 and 66 on the Song of Songs, Bernard responds to an appeal from Everwin, provost of the Premonstratensians of Steinfeld, exhorting him to refute the deviancy of the heretics

erable seems to have composed his treatise on his own initiative. Why? Let us try to answer that question by looking in detail at the opening sections of *Contra Petrobrusianos*, the letter of dedication and the introduction, in which Peter explains what circumstances led him to take up his pen and his purpose in writing.

Peter's Addressees

Peter's prefatory letter dedicates the work, as we have said, to the archbishops of Arles and Embrun as well as to the bishops of Die and Gap. The greeting that opens the treatise itself cites the following names: William, the archbishop of Embrun; Ulric, the bishop of Die; and William, the bishop of Gap; there is no actual mention here of the archbishop of Arles. We therefore cannot be absolutely sure of his identity. If *Contra Petrobrusianos* indeed dates from 1139/40, then he was William I, surnamed "Monge" or "Le Moine," archbishop of Arles from 1139 to 1141, sent as legate to Spain during those years,[46] and listed under 20 October in the necrology of Saint-Gilles-du-Gard, a Cluniac dependency down to the 1130s.[47] His surname "The Monk" was derived from his semi-eremitic experience in a small community at Montrieux in the Var, which around 1133–34 observed the *Consuetudines* of Guigo I of La Grande Chartreuse and between July 1136 and February 1137 was absorbed into the Carthusian order.[48]

William II, archbishop of Embrun from 1135 to 1169(?), is the possible addressee of one of Peter the Venerable's short letters, which is little more than a friendly request to William to receive him as a visitor. However it is possible that the letter was actually addressed to William I, archbishop of Embrun from 1120 to 1134 or 1135.[49] William II attended the Council of Pisa in May–June 1135. He was one of the prelates who, according to another of Peter the Venerable's letters, were captured at Pontremoli, on their way back from Pisa, possibly by partisans of the antipope Anacletus II or of the bishops deposed during the council.[50]

---

of Cologne. Letter 77 responds to the call of Hugh of Saint Victor, concerned by among other things the heretical rejection of infant baptism. See Jean Leclercq, "L'hérésie d'après les écrits de S. Bernard de Clairvaux," in *The Concept of Heresy in the Middle Ages (11th–13th centuries)*, Proceedings of the International Conference, Leuven, 13–16 May 1973, Mediaevalia Lovaniensia, ser. 1, Studia 4, ed. Willem Lourdaux and Daniel Verhelst (Leuven and The Hague, 1976), pp. 24–25.

46. *Gallia Christiana Novissima: histoire des archevêchés, évêchés et abbayes de France, d'après les documents authentiques*, ed. Joseph M. Albanès and Cyr U. J. Chevalier, 7 vols. (Valence, 1899–1920), vol. 3 (1901), no. 62, cols. 239–40. On his legations to Spain: no. 535, cols. 208–9; no. 537, cols. 209–10.

47. Ulrich Winzer, *S. Gilles: Studien zum Rechtsstatus und Beziehungsnetz einer Abtei im Spiegel ihrer Memorialüberlieferung*, Münstersche Mittelalter-Schriften, 59 (Munich, 1988), p. 297.

48. On this pre-Carthusian nucleus led possibly by William, see Raymond Boyer, *La Chartreuse de Montrieux aux XIIe et XIIIe siècles*, vol. 1 (Marseille, 1980), pp. 163–64 and 342.

49. *Ep.*, 12, 1:18 and 2:102–3.

50. *Ep.*, 27, 1:50–52 and 2:114–15.

Ulric (otherwise Ourry or Oudry) was the bishop of Die between 1130 and 1144. It would seem he began his ecclesiastical career as prior of Domène in the Isère, which had been a Cluniac establishment since 1027 or 1028.[51] He was afterward canon and subsequently dean of the chapter of Grenoble during the episcopacy of Saint Hugh, the Carthusians' friend and faithful supporter. In his biography of Bishop Hugh of Grenoble, who died in 1137, Guigo I maintains that Ulric visited the bishop shortly before his death to seek authorization to return to life as a regular.[52] Hence perhaps the tradition—accepted by historians but as far as I know confirmed by no other source and based on reading too much into Guigo's words—that Ulric abandoned his responsibilities as bishop of Die in 1144 and died as a Carthusian at La Grande Chartreuse a year later.[53] Be that as it may, such a career would place Ulric of Die very close to Peter the Venerable, who was himself prior of Domène between 1120 and 1122 and who, after his election as abbot of Cluny in 1122, remained a close friend of the Carthusian order, with which, shortly before his death in 1156, he founded an association of prayer.[54]

With William I, bishop of Gap between 1130 or 1131 and 1149, we remain in the Carthusian orbit. The little we know of him is to be found in the twenty or so charters relating to the charterhouse of Durbon in the Alpes-de-Haute-Provence, of which he seems to have been an active supporter.[55]

At the beginning of the twelfth century, the Gregorians were gaining a firm foothold in the Provençal episcopal hierarchy. Regulars, both canons and monks, contributed widely to this trend.[56] Within an entrenched, reform-minded episcopacy, our limited inquiry into the addressees of *Contra Petrobrusianos* reveals, with the exception of William of Embrun, a somewhat tighter circle of pontiffs who, like Peter the Venerable himself, were part of the Carthusian network. In accordance with a division of labor that was perfectly canonical, Peter addressed himself to those whose "special office" (*singulare officium*)

51. His spell at Domène has been taken for granted—see *Gallia christiana*, vol. 16 (Paris, 1865), col. 259; Ulysse Chevalier, *Répertoire des sources historiques du Moyen Age. Bio-Bibliographie*, vol. 2, 2d ed. (Paris, 1907), col. 4591; Bernard Bligny, *L'Eglise et les ordres religieux dans le royaume de Bourgogne aux XIe et XIIe siècles* (Grenoble, 1960), p. 312 and n. 305—but it is not absolutely justified by the sources. The Domène cartulary, ed. Charles de Monteynard (Lyon, 1859), no. 18, p. 22, mentions only an *Odulricus magister* among witnesses to a deed in 1117; the editor gives, p. xv, a rather unrigorous list of priors of Domène, in which only one Ulric figures, around 1095.

52. *Vita sancti Hugonis* (indexed BHL 4016), PL 153:761–84. Guigo records, col. 782B, a visit by Ulric to Hugh shortly before his death, and the bishop of Die was among three pontiffs present at Hugh of Grenoble's funeral, col. 784.

53. Bligny, *L'Eglise et les ordres religieux*, p. 312 and n. 305.

54. *Recueil des plus anciens actes de la Grande-Chartreuse (1086–1196)*, ed. Bernard Bligny (Grenoble, 1958), no. 24, pp. 67–69, and *Capitulum generale Basilii secundum*, ed. James Hogg, *Die ältesten Consuetudines der Kartäuser*, Analecta Cartusiana, 1 (Berlin, 1970), pp. 136–37.

55. *Gallia Christiana Novissima*, 1 (Montbéliard, 1899), cols. 280–81. Jean-Pierre Poly conjectures that William came from Lérins, *La Provence et la société féodale*, pp. 169ff.

56. Ibid., pp. 269ff.

was, in the apostolic tradition, to fight heresy with the word, even by call to arms, and dispel the doubts of the weak-kneed among the faithful. Peter's object in sending his treatise to these particular archbishops and bishops was not to give them lessons but to consult them (*non docens sed consulens*). Having settled the problem of Peter of Bruis, they were now being asked to send information on Henry of Lausanne. The channel of transmission in both directions doubtless worked all the better for involving ecclesiastical dignitaries who were intimates.

Cluny and Provence

Besides his Carthusian friendships, Peter the Venerable had another good reason to be interested in the "Provençal" heresy.[57] Since the late 970s, Cluny had had a strong presence in Provence and the foothills of the Alps.[58] While Count William II, "the Liberator," was rebuilding Provence, Majolus, the fourth abbot of Cluny, was busily engaged in a policy of monastic foundation and reform. It was for him the spiritual expression of a desire to regain the possessions of his father, Fulcherius of Valensole, dispersed in the unrest of the early tenth century. Majolus's disciple and successor, Odilo, faithfully continued his master's policy in Provence. In the context of the Gregorian reform, Hugh of Semur also saw a few establishments coming under him. But the Cluniac presence in Provence barely exceeded the bounds attained at the end of the tenth century, inasmuch as the most important of these establishments continued to be located north of the Durance river. When Gregory VII recognized the monastery of Saint-Victor at Marseille as a model of exemption on the same lines as Cluny,[59] he encouraged the development of a Victorine "ecclesiastical state." To this "state" were added other local canonical and monastic networks, which blocked further Cluniac development by diverting to themselves the fruits of lay generosity—Saint-Ruf, Montmajour, Saint-André-lès-Avignon, Lérins, and not least Saint-Gilles-du-Gard, which after a bitter struggle managed to throw off the Cluniac yoke in the 1130s.[60] Peter the Venerable had therefore to fight to hold onto Cluny's inheritance in Provence; it was an important source of income the house could not afford to lose.[61]

57. The question of Cluny's presence in Provence has generally escaped the notice of commentators on *Contra Petrobrusianos*; Georges Duby alone has remarked upon the basic normality of the abbot of Cluny's intervention in the region at this time: see the debate around Jean Châtillon's paper "Pierre le Vénérable et les Pétrobrusiens," in *Pierre Abélard–Pierre le Vénérable*, pp. 177–79, here 179.

58. See Barbara H. Rosenwein's recent clarification, "Le domaine de Cluny en Provence," in Dominique Iogna-Prat et al., *Saint Maieul, Cluny et la Provence*, Les Alpes de lumières, 115 (Salagon, 1994), pp. 15–31, and chapter 1 of Eliana Magnani Soares-Christen's doctoral thesis, "Monastères et aristocratie en Provence (milieu Xe–XIIe siècle)," 2 vols., typescript, Université de Provence, Aix-en-Provence, 1997.

59. *Das Register Gregors VII.*, 7.24, 2:502–5, here 504.

60. Winzer, *S. Gilles*, pp. 52ff.

61. Apart from Saint-Gilles, which was ultimately lost, Peter was battling to defend the rights of Piolenc: see *Ep.*, 67, 1:197–8 (to William of Orange) and Poly, *La Provence et la société féodale*, p. 277.

The Provençal inheritance included two establishments in the diocese of Gap that are of relevance to us here: Saint-André at Gap itself, given to Cluny in 1028 or 1029,[62] and Saint-André-de-Rosans, a Cluniac priory from 988.[63] In the introduction to *Contra Petrobrusianos*, Peter the Venerable declares that he has obtained direct knowledge of the heresy, or rather of its remnants (*reliquiae*), on visiting the dioceses of those to whom the treatise is specifically addressed.[64] There are three possible reasons why he had been in Provence. First, he may simply have stopped off there on a journey to Rome in order to pay the *cens* (tribute) due to Saint Peter for the monastery's liberty. Or it may be that his time in Provence was connected with the Council of Pisa in May–June 1135. A third explanation, which is simpler and does not contradict the other two, is that his visit may have had to do with the administration of Cluniac dependencies there. Bruis, the heresiarch's home territory, lay between the two Cluniac priories just mentioned: Gap is just forty kilometers to the northeast; Saint-André-de-Rosans ten or so kilometers to the north. Peter of Bruis was a priest; we know this from words of Peter the Venerable at the end of *Contra Petrobrusianos*. For the sixth proposition of the heretics' teaching, their rejection of ecclesiastical chant, he takes them to task directly, citing the example of the Psalms, which are much used by clerics, especially priests, as "you yourselves were."[65] These words can only refer to Peter of Bruis and Henry of Lausanne. Unfortunately our knowledge of the parochial network in the Hautes-Alpes in the twelfth century does not extend to the status of the church at Bruis, where Peter the heresiarch was priest. In the thirteenth century Bruis was dependent on the archpriest of Rosans.[66] But the study of the temporality of Saint-André-de-Rosans from 988 to 1789 undertaken by Arlette Playoust rules out the possibility that the church at Bruis belonged to the Cluniac priory.[67] Nonetheless the need for strict enforcement of ecclesiastical order in a church so close to a Cluniac dependency would amply explain why the abbot of Cluny should wish to make on-the-spot

------

We know the income Cluny derived from its fifteen Provençal priories in the first half of the twelfth century thanks to the *Census obedienciarum Provincialium*, *CLU* 4395, 5.755–56. Georges Duby presents this exceptional document within the context of the economic crisis affecting Cluny from the 1120s, which Peter the Venerable worked to solve; see "Le budget de Cluny entre 1080 et 1155," in *Hommes et structures du Moyen Age* (Paris and The Hague, 1973), p. 67.

62. *CLU* 2813, 4.16–17.

63. Details in *Saint-André-de-Rosans: millénaire de la fondation du prieuré, 988–1988*, actes du colloque, 13–14 May 1988, in *Bulletin de la Société d'études des Hautes-Alpes*, 1989.

64. *CP*, 1, ll. 17–21.

65. *CP*, 274, ll. 7–12.

66. Only late information is available: accounts of tithes from 1274 and 1350, see *Pouillés des provinces d'Aix, d'Arles, et d'Embrun*, ed. Etienne Clousot, Recueil des historiens de la France, Pouillés, 7 (Paris, 1923), pp. 74B and 86E. The *pouillé* for the order of Cluny (Paris, Bibliothèque Nationale MS, n.a.l. 1502, possibly end of fourteenth century) gives no precise details; see *BC*, col. 1705ff.

67. Arlette Playoust, "Le temporel du prieuré Saint-André-de-Rosans, 988–1789," in *Saint-André-de-Rosans*, pp. 79–103, esp. maps 1–2, pp. 80–81.

inquiries before referring to the ordinary, in this case the bishop of Gap. As we have seen, he was also concerned to involve the other bishops and archbishops along the path by which the poison spread through Provence and thereafter (though Peter names no bishop there) through Septimania and into Gascony.

The Local Significance of Peter the Venerable's Pastoral Effort

Before leaving Provence, we need to ask whether *Contra Petrobrusianos* found an echo locally. In the absence of direct testimony from Peter the Venerable's interlocutors, the answer is not clear. The manuscript tradition is a poor one; no Provençal copy of the treatise is known. All one can cite is a catalogue entry from the library of Saint-Victor at Marseille, which mentions *Contra Sarracenos* and a *Contra hereticos iudeos et paganos* by Peter the Venerable, which would appear to have been a compilation of *Adversus Iudeos* and *Contra Petrobrusianos.*[68]

However, a quick look at some monumental sculpture reveals that local people were clearly interested in showing some aspects of the controversy with the heretics. The facade of Saint-Gilles-du-Gard is normally interpreted as an iconographical representation of the major themes of preaching against the heretics. This interpretation is all the more convincing since Saint-Gilles only left the Cluniac orbit in the 1130s and it was there that Peter of Bruis prepared the fatal bonfire of crosses on which he met his own death. The artists of Saint-Gilles, drilled as they were in antique sculpture, and not least the early Christian sarcophagi at Arles, thus either spontaneously or, more likely, in response to their employers' request fashioned themes that were foreign to the early Christian repertoire: the mysteries of the Incarnation and Redemption and realist representations of the Crucifixion.[69] That said, we must bear in mind Dorothea Diemer's warning about overhasty interpretations of the facade of Saint-Gilles; she has shown convincingly that, while the detail of these themes is not a major problem, it is impossible to offer an all-embracing interpretation in the current state of architectural conservation.[70] Other regional examples, less prestigious but also less disputable and from the twelfth century, argue our case. These include: the representation of the Last Supper and the Crucifixion on the western facade of Saint-Pons at Thomières in Languedoc;[71] the offering of Cain and Abel and the sacrifice of Abraham, both Old Testament prefigura-

68. *Notitia librorum monasterii S. Victoris prope Massiliam*, in J. A. B. Montreuil, *L'ancienne bibliothèque de l'abbaye Saint-Victor* (Marseille, 1854), no. 61, p. 63. I am grateful to Michel Lauwers for this reference.

69. Robert Saint-Jean, "La sculpture à Saint-Gilles du Gard," in *Languedoc roman*, Zodiaque publishers: series La Nuit du Temps, 43 (La Pierre-qui-Vire, 1975), pp. 300–301.

70. Dorothea Diemer, *Untersuchungen zu Architektur und Skulptur der Abteikirche von Saint-Gilles* (Stuttgart, 1978).

71. Dating from the first quarter of the twelfth century: see Robert Saint-Jean, "La sculpture à Saint-Pons de Thomières," in *Languedoc roman*, pp. 294ff. and plates 90–91.

tions of the sacrifice of the Mass, appearing on two capitals of the porch of the tower of Notre-Dame at Die—the seat of Bishop Ulric, one of Peter's named addressees; a representation of the Crucifixion in association with the symbols of the evangelists on the tympanum of one of the facades of the same cathedral.[72] There is another Crucifixion on the tympanum of the church of Saint-Etienne at Condrieu in the Dauphiné.[73] At Champagne-sur-Rhône in the Vivarais[74] and at Vizille, a Cluniac establishment in the Drôme,[75] there are associations between a Crucifixion in the tympanum and a Last Supper in the lintel. Finally, there is a Last Supper in the lintel of the south porch of the church of Notre-Dame at Thines in the Vivarais.[76] The fact is that the area of reference of *Contra Petrobrusianos*—Provence in the broad sense, Languedoc and the foothills of the Alps—possesses a concentration of representations of the Last Supper and the Crucifixion that is highly unusual in Romanesque iconography. At Die and Vizille in particular, it is hard not to imagine that the taste for Christic themes had to do with the pastoral effort against the Petrobrusians.

The Genre and Reception of Contra Petrobrusianos

The surviving manuscript tradition of *Contra Petrobrusianos* is limited to three copies from the twelfth century and a fourth from the mid-fifteenth century;[77] we might add a fifth, from the fifteenth century, but this contains only the letter of dedication.[78] The work was therefore not subject to very widespread literary diffusion in the Middle Ages. Nevertheless it is possible, from the work of its most recent editor, James Fearns, together with Giles Constable's research on Peter the Venerable's collected letters, to retrace the genesis of the text with a degree of certainty. It looks as if *Contra Petrobrusianos* was written before 1138, but that Peter was not happy with it; in 1139–41 he revised it and incorporated it into the collection of his letters and treatises then being put together by his secretary, Peter of Poitiers. Editorially speaking, these were respectively version

72. Guy Barruol, *Dauphiné roman*, Zodiaque publishers: series La Nuit du Temps, 77 (La Pierre-qui-Vire, 1992), pp. 340–41 and plates 124–28. I am grateful to Guy Barruol for pointing out to me these examples of the Crucifixion and Last Supper.

73. Ibid., p. 236.

74. Robert Saint-Jean, *Vivarais, Gévaudan romans*, Zodiaque publishers: series La Nuit du Temps, 75 (La Pierre-qui-Vire, 1991), pp. 199–200.

75. Barruol, *Dauphiné roman*, p. 87 and plate 21; see also Armin Kohnle, *Abt Hugo von Cluny (1049–1109)*, Beihefte der Francia, 32 (Sigmaringen, 1993), p. 152.

76. Saint-Jean, *Vivarais*, pp. 239ff.

77. MSS: Douai, Bibliothèque Municipale 381, 1144/66, Anchin [MS D]; Bern, Bürgerbibliothek 251, twelfth century, France, poss. Fleury [MS B]; Le Mans, Bibliothèque Municipale 8, twelfth century, France or England [MS L]; Le Parc, mid-fifteenth century [MS C]; and see James Fearns's introduction to his critical edition, *CCCM* 10, pp. viii–xiii.

78. MS Le Puy, Cathédrale, early fifteenth century; see *CCCM* 10, p. xiii.

Z and version X represented by manuscript D, a collection of Peter the Venerable's works including *Contra Petrobrusianos* in the corpus of the abbot's letters (folios 66r to 108r). At the end of Peter the Venerable's life, during the 1150s, a second collection was made—version Y, that represented in manuscripts B, C, and L—in which *Contra Petrobrusianos* was separated from the letters and became an autonomous work.[79] There was a shift in literary status. The "letter" integrated into a collection of occasional writings became an independent "treatise" that gained its full significance as part of a triptych of tracts against heretics, Jews, and Saracens. The ideological coherence of this triptych is revealed by Peter of Poitiers in a letter to Peter the Venerable:

> I want them too [the Saracens] to be confounded by you, just as the Jews and Provençal heretics were. For you are the only one in our days to have slain with the sword of the divine word the three greatest enemies of Holy Christendom: the Jews, the heretics, and the Saracens. And you have shown that Mother Church is neither bereft, nor robbed of good sons, but still has such as can, with Christ's favor, answer any inquirer concerning the hope and faith that are in us.[80]

Historians concerned to pay attention to the textual coherence of *Contra Petrobrusianos* will be guided by the manuscript tradition and study the work with an eye to both its epistolary style and its polemical argument.

Manuscript C shows that interest was still being expressed in *Contra Petrobrusianos* in the fifteenth century. The record of early printed editions reveals that interest continued longer still.[81] In 1522 the complete works of Peter the Venerable were published by the Cluniac theologian Pierre de Montmartre. All subsequent editions of *Contra Petrobrusianos* were based on this edition. But most often, Peter the Venerable's treatise was welcomed and raided in the form of excerpts providing ammunition in the Catholic reformation of the sixteenth century. This was particularly so in the case of the important chapter on the Eucharist, which became an authority of choice alongside the works of Lanfranc and Alger of Liège in the theological controversy over the Mass. Enthusiasm for *Contra Petrobrusianos* was such that in 1584 a substantial translation of it was published in Paris by Jean Bruneau, a royal counselor at Giens and onetime Protestant who had returned to the Catholic fold. It bore the title:

> Les oeuvres du bon et ancien Pierre, abbé de Cluny . . . contre les hérétiques de son temps. Ou se void la vraye succession de doctrine, et traditions de

---

79. See stemma established by Fearns, *CCCM* 10, p. xvi.

80. *Epistola Petri Pictavensis*, ed. Reinhold Glei, *Petrus Venerabilis Schriften zum Islam*, Corpus Islamico-Christianum, Series latina, 1 (Altenberge, 1985), p. 228.

81. The researches of Fearns, *PC*, pp. v–viii are complemented by Torrell and Bouthillier, "*Miraculum*," 372–73.

l'Eglise catholique, depuis sa naissance iusques à maintenant. Marque tres-
certaine et excellente qu'elle est la vraye Eglise, contre tous les novateurs de
ce temps.[82]

Under this title, which virtually amounts to a campaign platform in itself, Jean
Bruneau translated and adapted three propositions from *Contra Petrobrusianos:*
(1) on the destruction of altars, churches, and crosses; (2) on the rejection of the
eucharistic sacrifice; (3) on the alleged uselessness of acts performed on behalf
of the dead. In a "letter of exhortation in the form of an epitome," placed right
at the start and not numbered, the translator justifies at length the pertinence of
his undertaking. In so doing, he clearly testifies to the place Peter's work held in
the long-term history of Christianity and the defense of the Church.[83] Bruneau
was defending the classic notion that heresies endlessly repeat themselves in cycles. "Their doctrine," he says, speaking of his sixteenth-century opponents, "is
only a revival, a rewinding of the old heresies, debated and condemned by the
judgment of the Church and the magistracy." Thus in Bruneau's eyes, Peter the
Venerable's work touched on issues that were still relevant to the Church in his
day: the rejection of infant baptism, a Petrobrusian view shared by the sixteenth-
century Anabaptists; the iconoclasm of the Protestants in the wars of religion,
which recalled the burning of crosses by Peter of Bruis; the destruction of
churches and the holding of religious meetings "in woods, lofts, basements, cellars, and barns," which recalled the Petrobrusians' rejection of consecrated
places and support for the converse, the sanctity of all places of assembly. Beyond the historical reductionism inherent in these parallels, which belong to the
repressive amalgam that sees nothing new in Satan's universe, Jean Bruneau
found in Peter the Venerable a position of principle by which to solve the problem of witnesses and their testimony. The "witnesses" were the Gospels and
their record of Christ's work, a part of the Scriptures received by Protestants in
the sixteenth century as it had been by the Petrobrusians in the twelfth. The
"testimonies" were the tradition denied by both: the founding link between the
Gospels and the Church, which Jean Bruneau, relying on Peter the Venerable,
defends by pointing out that the Gospels are "true" only by virtue of the "authority" of this very ecclesiastical tradition. No individual, he says, can arrogate
this tradition by appealing to the Spirit, "for were it possible for any individual

82. Paris, Bibliothèque Nationale, C 3343 octavo: "The works of good, ancient Peter, abbot of
Cluny . . . against the heretics of his time. In which is seen the true succession of doctrine and traditions of the Catholic Church from its birth until now. A most certain and excellent mark that it is
the true Church against all the innovations of this time."

83. For a view of the general use of authorities in Reformation theological controversy, see Jean
Leclerc, *Histoire de la tolérance au siècle de la Réforme* (Paris, 1955; 2d ed., 1994), esp. book 1, chap. 4.
There is as yet no complete study of the reception of Peter the Venerable's works in the sixteenth
and seventeenth centuries. As for the influence of Peter's writings on later forms of iconoclasm (destruction of crosses and sacred places for example), the research of Olivier Christin, kindly undertaken by him at my behest, has as yet yielded only negative results.

PART II. CHRISTIAN SOCIETY

to testify on his own authority under the veil and cover of the Holy Spirit, then this would give ground to the false opinions of the Anabaptists who fabricate for themselves revelations of the Holy Spirit." Thus four centuries later the great danger confronted was the same. Against deviants who testified in their own favor according to so-called direct illumination by the Spirit, it was necessary to defend the "foundations" of the Church: the Scriptures as received by tradition, which, as Bruneau says, bind as "in jurisprudence."

4

POLEMIC METHOD

We have seen how Jean Bruneau and the Catholic reformers of the six-teenth century, inheritors of the medieval struggle against heresy, discovered in Peter the Venerable—a contemporary of the dawn of scholasticism—a useful forerunner and ally in the war of ideas against Protestantism. Now we return to Peter's own times to examine the abbot of Cluny's place within the history of the polemic conducted against the deviants of the eleventh and twelfth centuries and to assess his contribution to that battle.

The antiheretical writings emerging between the years 1000 and 1140 fall into a number of categories. First is historiography, which includes the *Histori-arum libri quinque* of Rodulfus Glaber, the *Chronicon* of Adhemar of Chabannes, the *Historia Mediolanensis* of Landulfus Senior, the Acts of the bishops of Le Mans, and not least the Cartulary/Chronicle of the abbey of Saint-Père, Chartres. A second category is hagiography, such as the *Vita Gauzlini* by Andreas of Fleury. A third comprises biography and autobiography exemplified by the *Monodiae* of Guibert of Nogent. Fourthly, we have letters of denunciation, such as Bernard of Clairvaux's letter *Quanta audivimus*, and conciliar condemnations like that at Arras in 1025 and at Toulouse in 1119. A final category consists of homiletic and exegetical literature, examples being Bernard of Clairvaux's ser-mons on the Song of Songs or Hervé of Déols's commentary on the Epistles of Paul. During the 1130s, a new form of this literature appeared: the treatise. To this new form belong the *Disputatio* of the monk William, written against Henry of Lausanne, and two works that are, broadly speaking, of Cluniac origin: Hugh of Amiens's *Contra hereticos* and Peter the Venerable's *Contra Petrobrusianos*.[1] The emergence of the treatise form represented a new way of dealing with heresy, one that treated the heretics' teachings as a set of propositions put up for debate. This framework allowed the creation of the outline of an ecclesiology, as I shall try to show with the single example of Peter the Venerable, beginning with an analysis of his use of language and rhetoric.

---

1. Given the lack of a typological study of the antiheretical texts of the period 1000–1140, I have followed the outline given by Gerhard Rottenwöhrer, *Der Katharismus*, vol. 3: *Die Herkunft der Katharer nach Theologie und Geschichte* (Bad Honnef, 1990), pp. 131ff.

THE "DEFENSIVE ARGUMENT": DEFINING THE PROBLEM

Peter the Venerable was familiar with the techniques of debate and its legal background. In one of his letters to Bernard of Clairvaux, he refuted Bernard's charges against the Ecclesia cluniacensis point by point, noting that in law a plaintiff had to substantiate his case; he could not content himself with "mere words" (*nudis verbis*), but had to use argument.[2] Against the Petrobrusians, therefore, Peter was concerned to show proof (*auctori probatio*) of his charges against the heretics and to use appropriate forms of argument.

At the outset, we have to accept that very little analytical research has been done on antiheretical discourse. While studies of forms of argument are plentiful in the field of medieval anti-Jewish polemic,[3] this is not true of the field of heresiology, where the overwhelming concentration of interest has been upon the *auctoritates* used, especially those drawn from the Bible.[4] Recent emphasis on the notion of "literacy" in studying heresy, a feature of anglophone historiography following the work done by Jack Goody and Brian Stock, has certainly drawn the attention of medievalists to the emergence of antiheretical polemic as a distinct literary genre.[5] In this approach, the division between orthodoxy and heterodoxy is defined by the confrontation of "textual communities"—with scholars on one side of the line and deviants on the other—based on a particular relationship to the Scriptures.[6] Yet curiously, none of the historians interested in the relationship between "literacy" and heresy has looked in detail at antiheretical polemic as discourse.

The only notable exception, though his work is admittedly of limited scope, is Heinrich Fichtenau, who has written on "heretics and professors."[7] That great Austrian historian had the excellent idea of setting in parallel two contemporary

---

2. *Ep.*, 28, 1:52–101, here 83: *Congruum autem esset. . . .*

3. See especially Gilbert Dahan, *Les intellectuels chrétiens et les juifs au Moyen Age*, Patrimoine judaïsme (Paris, 1990), pp. 423–71, where polemic "method" is discussed. Dahan parallels various anti-Jewish and antiheretical texts, pp. 362ff., in order to present works denouncing Christianity's enemies as a whole (as is the case with Peter the Venerable's triptych), but he does not go into the question of modes of argument.

4. See especially Herbert Grundmann, *"Oportet hereses esse.* Das Problem der Ketzerei im Spiegel der Mittelalterlichen Bibelexegese," *Archiv für Kulturgeschichte* 45 (1963): 129–64, reprinted in *Ausgewälte Aufsätze*, 1 (Religiöse Bewegungen), Schriften der *MGH*, 25.1 (Stuttgart, 1976), pp. 328–63; Robert E. Lerner, "Les communautés hérétiques (1150–1500)," in *Le Moyen Age et la Bible*, ed. Pierre Riché and Guy Lobrichon (Paris, 1984), pp. 597–614.

5. Jack Goody, *The Logic of Writing and the Organization of Society* (Cambridge, 1986); *Literacy in Traditional Societies*, ed. Jack Goody (Cambridge, 1968); Brian Stock, *The Implications of Literacy: Written Language and Models of Interpretation in the Eleventh and Twelfth Centuries* (Princeton, 1983), particularly pp. 88–151.

6. There is a good introduction to the problem in *Heresy and Literacy, 1000–1530*, ed. Peter Biller and Anne Hudson, Cambridge Studies in Medieval Literature, 23 (Cambridge, 1994).

7. *Ketzer und Professoren: Häresie und Vernunftglaube im Hochmittelalter* (Munich, 1992).

historical phenomena that he believes interacted. These are the rise of heresy in the medieval west between the eleventh and thirteenth centuries on the one hand and the "process of rationalization" going on in the world of scholarship on the other. Although Fichtenau does not embark upon a study of antiheretical discourse as such, he nevertheless proceeds by comparative analysis to open a fruitful line of inquiry. How were deviants and infidels answered in the primitive days of scholasticism—according to what rules of rhetoric and upon what axiomatic basis? This is the vital question that concerns us now. Our aim is to understand how Peter the Venerable's discourse works in what is, as far as one can tell at present, the first antiheretical treatise written in the medieval west. I believe the quest to be all the more worthwhile in that Peter was evidently considered by his contemporaries to be a real authority in the area of fighting heresy. Thus Bishop Atto of Troyes, telling Peter in a letter how much he desires to go to Cluny "that I may see you and be with you before I die," addresses the abbot of Cluny in terms that surely exceed the narrow conventions of friendship as

> a second John, of our own age, who have drawn the streams of doctrine from the very fount of our Lord's breast. And from there, to those who are both far and near, you suffice to give utterance [*eructare*—cf. Matthew 13:35] to the hidden things of the heavenly mysteries, the lessons of the Scriptures, the refutation of heretics; so that all who hear say, "Glory to God in the highest, for a great prophet is risen up among us." (Cf. Luke 2:14 and 7:16.)[8]

The Genre of the Epistola disputans

In what form, then, did this "prophet" of later days "give utterance" to the "refutation of heretics"? In his letter of dedication to the prelates of Arles, Embrun, Die, and Gap, Peter the Venerable describes his piece as an *epistola disputans*. In the Gregorian tradition represented by the correspondence of Peter Damian among others, the term *epistola* implied a theological writing with the brevity of a résumé (*compendium*).[9] The object was to brief those who were under pressure and knew little about the question. The epithet *disputans* connoted the modalities of contradictory debate, the first known example of which in the theology of the Latin Middle Ages is the eucharistic controversy sparked by Berengar of Tours in the mid-eleventh century. By the time *Contra Petrobrusianos* came to be written around 1140, the influence of the new urban schools had helped to turn the *disputatio* into a verbal martial art with precise rules of engagement. The mere mention by Peter of the term *epistola disputans* thus assumed a whole discursive background that needs to be taken into consideration if Peter's argument is to be closely understood.

8. *Ep.*, 71, 1:203–6, here 203.
9. Ian S. Robinson, "The 'Colores rhetorici' in the Investiture Contest," *Traditio* 32 (1976): 229–230.

The Polemic Treatise and the Law

One thing needs to be made clear straightaway. *Contra Petrobrusianos* is a polemic treatise, not a legal document of condemnation. The point is a relevant one, since the circle of southern clerics for which Peter wrote contained a number of jurists.[10] Equally, one has only to glance at the catalogue of the library at Cluny to see the interest the monastery showed, from the eleventh century, in the great jurisprudential collections of late antiquity, in particular the *Institutiones* of Gaius, the Theodosian Code, and the collections of Justinian.[11]

Peter the Venerable seems to have been personally familiar with matters of law. In one of his letters, number 174 in Constable's edition, he writes to Pope Eugenius III as to a "special father" on whom Cluny, its abbot and community, directly depends. He speaks of problems affecting the church of Brioude, another establishment placed without intermediary under the direct jurisdiction of Rome.[12] A monstrous crime (*nefarium opus*) had been perpetrated at Brioude: the theft of the church's gold phylactery. But, says Peter, the procedure adopted by the canons in charge of the church in order to unmask and judge the offender was an even greater outrage. Not only had the normal course of ecclesiastical or civil justice not been followed, but even fundamental principles of the Christian religion had been scorned, for instead of proof the prosecution had made use of divination. By such means, comparable in Peter's view to the idolatrous divination denounced in 4 (2) Kings 1:2, a messenger was subsequently charged with the offense. Denying his guilt, the accused man offered to submit to the judgment of God in an ordeal by fire. But before climbing onto the fire, he asked that words of exorcism be uttered. This the canons of Brioude refused, before abandoning the procedure and condemning him without any other form of judgment. As Peter writes, the defendant had no other recourse than to appeal his case to Rome, within whose jurisdiction the church of Brioude lay. Indeed it was

10. For example, William of Orange *tam divinarum quam humanarum legum peritum*, to whom Peter addresses a quotation from the *Digest* in defense of the Cluniac possession at Piolenc: *Ep.*, 67, 1:197–98, here 198. On the influence of Roman law among the Burgundian and southern clerisy, see André Gouron, "Le rôle des maîtres français dans la renaissance juridique du XIIe siècle," in *Comptes rendus de l'Académie des inscriptions et belles-lettres*, 1989, pp. 198–206; reprinted in *Droit et coutume en France aux XIIe et XIIIe siècles* (London, 1983): Gouron considers that the correspondence of Peter the Venerable demonstrates "the evolution of lettered minds faced with the progress of Roman law" (pp. 201–2). See also Jean-Pierre Poly, "*Coheredes legum romanorum:* la renaissance du droit romain dans le midi de la France," in *Historia del derecho privado: trabajos en homenage a Ferran Valls i Taberner*, ed. Manuel J. Pelaez (Madrid, 1990), pp. 2909–45, which gives access to the essential bibliography on the subject. My thanks go to Jacques Chiffoleau for pointing this article out to me.

11. Léopold Delisle, *Inventaire des manuscrits de la Bibliothèque Nationale: fonds de Cluni* (Paris, 1884): no. 285, pp. 353–54 (*Volumen in quo continentur edictum imperatoris Justini de recta fide, et refutationes heresium*), no. 447 (Theodosius), no. 449 (Justinian), no. 450 (Theodosius, Gaius), p. 366, and no. 462 (Theodosius), p. 367.

12. *Ep.*, 174, 1:413–16; Peter's brother Heraclius was provost of Saint Julian's, Brioude, in 1139: see *Ep.*, 2:216.

this appeal that motivated Peter's letter. For, says Peter, the canons would not allow it; in the heat of invective (*contumelia verborum*), they asserted that the pope could not answer on matters "on this side of the Rhône." They therefore challenged the pope's sovereignty (*imperium*) by prejudicial declarations that would in a secular context be pursued as an attack upon the imperial majesty (lese-majesty).

Within the historical literature, this letter is famous above all for its use of the term *imperium* in relation to the pope, as distinct from the emperor,[13] and for its tale of divination and ordeal. With the notable exception of Jacques Chiffoleau, commentators have shown less interest in Peter the Venerable's use of the notion of the crime of lese-majesty. Yet it was precisely during the period in which Peter's letter was written (some time between 1145 and 1153) that canon and civil lawyers with their Roman law school training were salvaging from late antiquity that very legal category intended to condemn any offender whose monstrous act menaced the foundations of order. Peter the Venerable's appeal to Eugenius III thus clearly shows that the abbot of Cluny was perfectly aware of the growing influence of Roman law in the contemporary world of Latin studies.

Such an observation entitles us to make use of an important argument from silence in studying *Contra Petrobrusianos*. In his treatise, Peter at no time resorts to categories of law that are nonetheless entirely familiar to him. Why is this? We must bear in mind that Peter's purpose was to *refute* the Petrobrusian heresy, not *prosecute* it with legal weapons, the latter being the task of the diocesans concerned. The relevant legal weapons, moreover, were not yet those of the repressive system of the end of the twelfth century, since heresy did not pertain to the crime of lese-majesty until Innocent III's letter *Vergentis in senium* of March 1199 to the people of Viterbo.[14] Peter's time was one of prehistory as far as the struggle with heresy was concerned, and we have to be extremely clear and careful about chronology and the circumstances of the protagonists with whom we are dealing. *Contra Petrobrusianos* was not a detailed indictment but a polemical essay whose immediate practical effect was doubtless quite limited. Nevertheless, it gave voice to a system of authorities. The case at the church of Brioude is similarly an excellent illustration of the same process at work during the twelfth century: a movement away from settling conflicts by consensus—as by ordeal—to accusatorial procedures arising from an authority, be it temporal or ecclesiastical.[15]

13. *Ep.*, 2:228–29.

14. *Das Register Innocenz' III.*, ed. Othmar Hageneder, Werner Maleczeck, and Alfred A. Strand (Vienna, 1979), pp. 3–5.

15. On the move from consensus to authority during the twelfth century, see Peter Brown, "Society and the Supernatural: A Medieval Change," in *Society and the Holy in Late Antiquity* (London, 1982), pp. 302–32, here 324.

An Example of Peter the Venerable's Epistolary Technique: His Letter to an Anonymous Apollinarian Monk

Letter 37 in Constable's edition of Peter the Venerable's letters addresses an anonymous monk who has fallen into the heresy of Apollinarianism. It is a short text, serving both to introduce Peter as a letter writer and to highlight the discursive background of *Contra Petrobrusianos*.

In his letter Peter uses several techniques proper to the *disputatio*. We note, first, that his interlocutor is not named. We know only that he is a "certain furious heretic," guilty of Apollinarianism, an ancient Christological heresy according to which Christ's humanity extended only to his body and not his soul. Not only is the heretic unnamed, but Peter deliberately breaks with his own epistolary conventions by placing himself first in the greeting: *Petrus humilis Cluniacensium abbas, nec nominandae feci heresum.* In the introductory flourish, he resorts to invective, stigmatizing the *bestialis insipientia*, the *profunda stultitia* and *ineruditio* of his opponent, to whom he is writing now only because he has to. As abbot of Cluny, he says, he has charge over the other's soul and must take heed that the deviant does not contaminate his brothers. The purpose of the letter is thus disciplinary: unless his correspondent, who "murmurs like a beetle created out of ancient putrescence," amends, he is to perish. Peter was not speaking in purely formal terms. A passage of *De miraculis*, celebrating the "justice" of Matthew of Albano as prior of Saint-Martin-des-Champs, reveals that Cluniac superiors knew how to save a brother against his will, if need be by shutting him up alive in a vault.[16]

Given the disciplinary context, it is rather remarkable that Peter the Venerable should quickly abandon invective in favor of a technique of rational persuasion by which to examine his opponent's thesis. He defines a body of axioms and establishes the framework and modalities by which he will proceed. He proposes to rely not on *auctoritas*, which would have sway with a believer, but on *ratio*, which touches the human being, the faculty of reasoning that a man possesses whether he has faith or not. The discussion implies two questions, arising out of the thesis of Christ's univocal humanity (extending to the body only, and not the soul): first, whether Christ was a man or a beast, and secondly, whether the deity could act within him as a soul (*vice animae*). On the first point, Peter establishes the principle of identity between the Christ-man and the Savior, then proceeds to lock his opponent in a formal contradiction between *dimidium* (half) and *totum* (whole). Would he have Jesus be only half man (*dimidium*) while he is totally (*totum*) Savior? Peter's aim is to confuse the deviant monk by the logic of categories. It is impossible to use synecdoche (expressing the greater to signify the less) and describe as "man" the one in whom the two elements constituting the category of "man"—body and soul—cannot be recognized. To refuse Christ

16. *DM*, 2.9.

an *anima rationalis* (rational soul) is to turn him into a beast, which is an absurdity, as is testified by numerous passages of Scripture that speak of the *spiritus sapientiae* (spirit of wisdom) of Jesus. (Here it will be noted that Peter infringes his rule forbidding appeals to *auctoritas*.) On the second point, Peter proceeds by an argument from evidence of the type "if . . . then." If the deity acted in Jesus in such a way as to take the place of the *anima rationalis*, then it is the deity that suffered throughout the earthly history of Christ from his infant fears to the agonies of the Passion. A final, historical argument ought to convince that Christ had an *anima rationalis*. In what mode did he descend into hell? Not with his body, since history asserts that he was buried for three days. The hypothesis of his deity alone descending into hell is impossible. Only one possibility remains: the descent of his human soul.

The main interest of this letter is that it shows Peter to be an exponent of a conjunction of the two modes that typify antiheretical discourse in the first half of the twelfth century: the imprecatory, arising out of sacred rhetoric, and the argumentative, deriving from use of discourse. This conjunction is what I mean by "defensive argument."

THE SOURCES OF DEFENSIVE ARGUMENT

A Preliminary Example: The Antiheretical Discourse of Bernard of Clairvaux

The sort of conjunction we have just seen in Peter the Venerable's letter against Apollinarianism was actually very exceptional in the twelfth-century monastic world. We need look no further than the antiheretical discourse of Peter's contemporary Bernard of Clairvaux. This was exclusively imprecatory, as a few extracts from his sermon 66 on the Song of Songs may suffice to show.[17]

Sermon 66 forms a unity together with numbers 64 and 65 in the standard collection.[18] According to Giorgio Cracco's recent interpretation, sermon 65 was probably destined for the heretics of Toulouse, alias the Henricians, who were the inheritors of the Petrobrusians.[19] Sermon 66 was written in 1144 in response to an appeal by Provost Everwin of the Premonstratensians of Steinfeld for the abbot of Clairvaux to denounce the heretics of Cologne. The textual peg

17. *Sancti Bernardi Opera omnia*, vol. 2, ed. Jean Leclercq, Charles H. Talbot, and Henri-Marie Rochais (Rome, 1958), pp. 178–88.

18. Ibid., pp. 166–71 and 172–77.

19. Giorgio Cracco, "Bernardo e i movimenti ereticali," in *Bernardo cistercense*, Atti del XXVI Convegno storico internazionale, Todi, 8–11 October 1989, ed. Ernesto Menesto, Accademia Tudertina, Centro di studi sulla spiritualità medioevale dell'Università degli Studi di Perugia, 3 (Spoleto, 1990), pp. 165–86, here 176. See also Beverley M. Kienzle, "Tending the Lord's Vineyard: Cistercians, Rhetoric, and Heresy, 1143–1229," Part I: "Bernard of Clairvaux, the 1143 Sermons, and the 1145 Preaching Mission," *Heresis* 25 (1995): 29–61.

upon which the sermon is hung is Song of Songs 2:15: "Catch us the little foxes that destroy the vines: for our vineyard hath flourished." In sermon 64, Bernard gives a moral interpretation to the text's "little foxes," figures with which heresiologists would have been familiar.[20] These are assimilated to the little vices that can ruin an inner life and drive the most spiritual of persons to their ruin. In sermons 65 and 66, he moves from personal inner sins to the deviances of the heretics who, as "little foxes," ever hidden, destroy the body of the Church. In so saying, Bernard keeps within the field of moral theology, a fact that explains his exclusive recourse to the following forms of discourse: invective; imputation based on rumor; judgments out of context; refutations without appeal on the basis of authority alone; rhetorical refusal to engage in argument. Examples of such usage in sermon 66 are:

1. invective: "Lo, the detractors, behold the dogs!"[21]
2. imputation based on rumor: "The hypocrisy and foxlike cunning in their words are obvious. What they make out to be motivated by love of charity is rather a device to foster and increase filth."[22] The denunciation of false-seeming is a classic figure of antiheretical discourse, claiming to bring into the light of day abominations committed under cover of virtue.
3. judgments out of context: "They rush to banish Christ from the entire human race, from men and from women, from adults and little ones, from living and dead: from children because they say nature makes it impossible; from adults because of the difficulty of continence."[23]
4. refutations without appeal on the basis of authority alone: "They brag about being the apostles' successors and call themselves apostolic, yet they show no sign of His apostleship. . . . The apostles were told, 'You are the light of the world' [Matthew 5:14a]. . . . We have to say to these men, 'You are the shadows of the world.' . . . They say they are the Church, yet they contradict the One who says, 'A city seated on a mountain cannot be hid' [Matthew 5:14b]."[24]
5. rhetorical refusal to engage in argument: "This stupid and foolish people has been persuaded of many other evils by the spirits of error hypocritically uttering falsehood; but I cannot reply to them all. For who knows them all? It would be an unending labor and is hardly necessary. These people are not convinced by reasons, because they lack understanding; they will not be corrected in the light of authoritative

20. The image is used by, among others, Irenaeus of Lyon, *Adversus haereses*, 8.1, to refute Gnostic exegeses; my thanks go to Jean-Daniel Dubois for this information.
21. *Sermones*, 66, III, 9, in *Sancti Bernardi Opera omnia*, 2:183, ll. 24–25.
22. Ibid., I, 3, 2:179, ll. 24–26.
23. Ibid., IV, 2:183, l. 27–2:184, l. 1.
24. Ibid., III, 8, 2:183, ll. 12–19.

texts, because they do not accept them; and they will not be persuaded, because they have been subverted."[25]

Faced with people who preferred death to conversion, Bernard believed that nothing would avail, neither *ratio, auctoritas,* nor *persuasio.* Thus it was not necessary to adduce substantive content in order to denounce heresy. That is why Bernard's response to the heresy denounced by Everwin of Steinfeld was so brief. In 1148, Pope Eugenius III, a former monk of Clairvaux and constant close associate of Bernard, summoned a council at Reims during which a new style of antiheretical canon was drafted: it no longer contained any reference to the content of the deviations it condemned.[26]

Imprecatory Forms and Foundations

The few extracts given above from Bernard of Clairvaux's sermon 66 on the Song of Songs are typical of monastic antiheretical discourse. Its sources were threefold: techniques inherited from doctrinal discussions in the early Church; traditional forms of spiritual justice; the *colores rhetorici,* or instruments of polemic forged during the Gregorian reform and the investiture controversy. Let us look at these three sources now.

The Patristic Legacy

Catholic doctrine was defined little by little in the early centuries through confronting propositions and practices regarded as deviant. Late antiquity thus bequeathed law texts (ecclesiastical and civil), polemic works, and even catalogues detailing the number and nature of heresies encountered. By the eleventh century, the library at Cluny was richly furnished with such texts.[27] This anchorage in the soil of ancient law and doctrine shows why historical references were sought however apt or inapt. Antiheretical polemicists would invoke the *mos maiorum* (customs of the forefathers) in order to denounce their adversaries, whom they conceived as belonging to a long line of strayers. Peter the Venerable thus speaks of "ancient heretics," the "predecessors" of the Petrobrusians: Apelles, Cerinthus, Montanus, Novatian, Sabellius, and Mani—"the most hate-

---

25. Ibid., V, 12, 2:186, ll. 12–17.

26. Mansi, *Sacrorum Conciliorum nova et amplissima collectio,* 21, article 17, cols. 711–18, here 718AB. On this see Monique Zerner, "Hérésie: un discours de l'Eglise," in *Dictionnaire raisonné de l'Occident médiéval,* ed. Jacques Le Goff and Jean-Claude Schmitt (Paris, 1999), pp. 464–82.

27. Delisle, *Inventaire des manuscrits,* nos. 144 and 166 (Augustine, *Contra Manicheos*), nos 146 and 152 (*Contra Iulianum*), no. 148 (*Contra Faustum*), no. 155 (*Contra Arrianos*), nos. 213 and 216 (Jerome, *Adversus Iovinianum*), no. 226 (Tertullian, *Apologeticum, De Sodoma*), no. 285 (*Volumen in quo continentur edictum imperatoris Justini de recta fide, et refutationes heresium*), no. 356 (Irenaeus of Lyon, *Contra diversas hereses,* an extremely rare volume in this period); plus medieval polemical works: no. 234 (Paschasius Radbertus, *De corpore et sanguine Domini*), no. 373 (Jotsald of Cluny's treatise against Berengar of Tours, now lost).

ful of them all."[28] A little later in his treatise, referring to their rejection of church buildings, Peter calls the Petrobrusians "restorers of an ancient error" and places them in a line stretching back to Ahaz, king of Judah, who offered up sacrifices to Baal "on the hills and under every green tree" (2 Chronicles 28:4).[29]

In spite of real novelties among the problems encountered—for the rejection of prayers for the dead and the question of sacred places did not arise in the patristic period—the way in which the early Church treated its deviants remained the frame of reference for dealing with the problem, whether in describing the heresy (right down to the 1150s),[30] denouncing the "novelty of the errors," or attacking them, as Paul and the Fathers had, as pseudoscience (see 1 Timothy 6:20). In the patristic legacy, filtered by the antiquaries of the early Middle Ages, the antiheretical polemicists of the eleventh and twelfth centuries discovered a taxonomy, model replies, and an art of diatribe. What remains to be seen is how they used this legacy in action: Did they retreat within it, in the manner of a Bernard of Clairvaux, or did they, like Peter the Venerable, use it as a launching pad for new-style polemic?

Traditional Forms of Spiritual Justice

What is meant here by traditional forms of spiritual justice is all the resources the liturgy afforded to those in spiritual authority as they strove to affirm their temporal sovereignty—anathema, formulas of excommunication, curses, and clamors.

The notion of anathema within Christianity is as old as the New Testament.[31] The first known pronouncement of anathema as a form of ecclesiastical discipline was made at the Council of Elvira in 305; in the fourth century it consisted of a declaration that excommunicated heretics, like that which excommunicated the Arians at the Council of Nicaea. During the early Middle Ages—and paralleling the evolution of the penitential system—sentences of excommunication multiplied. Anathema became both more specialized and more diverse. Gradually it became a form of supreme excommunication whereby deviants were consigned to eternal death. Heretics were no longer the only category concerned, even if the link between heresy and anathema did not entirely disappear, as is attested by the formulas mentioning the maledictions formerly reserved for Arius.[32] "Malediction" in sum amounted to dispatching an ever-growing variety of deviants "to become companions in hell to the heretical perverters of Holy Church."[33]

28. *CP*, 25, ll. 7–12.

29. *CP*, 98, ll. 18–21.

30. On the problem of the new names given to heretics from the 1150s on, see Zerner, "Hérésie: un discours de l'Eglise."

31. Lester K. Little, *Benedictine Maledictions: Liturgical Cursing in Romanesque France* (Ithaca and London, 1993), pp. 31ff.

32. Ibid., p. 36.

33. A malediction from Jumièges, MS, Rouen, Bibliothèque Municipale, A 293, f. 148v, eleventh century, reproduced by Little, *Benedictine Maledictions*, p. 42.

The tenth and eleventh centuries saw a proliferation of forms of spiritual justice, as public forms of arbitration declined, essentially in western Francia. Expressions of anathema invaded the comminatory clauses of deeds. The formulation of the ritual clamor was a response to the same needs. Originally, the clamor was an insistent call for public justice. In the eleventh century it became "spiritualized," incorporated expressions of excommunication and anathema, and was ritualized into a paraliturgy that imported the use of saints' relics and of the eucharistic elements. By such a performance the monks called upon their divine protectors to act in their defense and effectively demonized their adversaries and contradictors. As Lester K. Little rightly says, liturgy took over from law. It was on such a basis that those occupying spiritual roles sought to guarantee agreements of every sort: gifts, exchanges and sales of land; the ending of disputes; and not least, engagements to say prayers. Let us take a simple example. In one of his letters to Hugh of Semur, Peter Damian recalls how, as papal legate, he helped to defend Cluny's exemption in 1063 against the designs of the bishop of Mâcon. He reminds Hugh that in return the Cluniacs promised to write his name in the community's necrology. In order to underline the binding strength of the obligation, Peter threatens Hugh with anathema should the promise not be carried into effect.[34]

This example reveals how run-of-the-mill expressions of anathema had become. Yet from the second half of the eleventh century, the appeal to forms of spiritual justice in charters grew less frequent. Once current practice, maledictions in the final clauses of charters began to become something of an exception. Again, it is relevant to mention Peter Damian who, in 1069, asked Pope Alexander II to put order into the system. He pointed out that it was neither rational nor efficacious to run penalties together and condemn someone guilty of a minor fault to the same pain "as a heretic."[35] Anathema could not be used so extensively and indiscriminately without eroding its deterrent force. Echoing the Latin Fathers' opposition to the Stoic view of the equal gravity of sins, Peter Damian conceived of a scale of penalties, civil and spiritual, corresponding to the nature of the offense. In this new system of repression, the traditional forms of spiritual justice remained, but their use was better controlled by the pontifical power, which would ensure their full efficacy in extreme cases, not least heresy.

Colores rhetorici of the Gregorian Era

The revival of heresy in the Latin west in the eleventh and twelfth centuries occurred on the following timescale: a first wave in the first half of the eleventh century, followed by a lull from roughly 1050 to 1120, then a renewed

34. *Epistolae*, 113, ed. Kurt Reindel, 4 vols., *MGH*, Die Briefe der Deutschen Kaiserzeit, 4 (Munich, 1983–93), 3:289–95, here 295.
35. Ibid., 164, 4:165–72, here 167–68.

surge from the 1120s. It is interesting to note that the lull of 1050 to 1120 corresponded almost exactly with the years of great politico-ecclesiastical polemic during the Gregorian reform and the investiture controversy. That is why I think it is important to ask what effects the rhetorical tools forged during the reform of the Church and the violent verbal confrontations in the quarrel between the papacy and the empire had upon antiheretical discourse. We shall restrict ourselves essentially to problems of discourse, though plainly the questions studied here were fully meaningful only within a legal framework. In the Gregorian age, the notion of heresy became so wide as to encompass, in effect, any type of disobedience to the decrees of Rome.[36] It was within such a disciplinary perspective that the Gregorian canonists developed the theory of legitimate persecution, which in the short term legitimated the Catholic princes' action against the "Henricians" (the supporters of the excommunicated emperor Henry IV) and beyond it any holy war, including the armed repression of heretics.[37]

The first part of the legacy of these years was the amount of publicity contemporary polemic writings achieved—what the German historian Carl Mirbt terms "Publizistik." Thus Manegold of Lautenbach, a Gregorian writer of the 1080s, was able to say of one of his contemporaries, Wenrich the schoolmaster of Trier, that his writings were "read in every marketplace, nook, and cranny."[38] We do not know if this was exaggeration. But it is clear that the common currency these writings enjoyed meant that the laity, and not just clerics in synod, were able to take part in the great debates then shaking Christendom, whether about the celibacy of priests or matters of investiture. It is interesting to note that some of the anti-Gregorian clerics, like Sigebert of Gembloux, pointed out to their opponents that they were playing with fire. Could not the encouragement given to the faithful to shun priests declared unworthy have the unforeseen effect of undermining the priestly office itself, of short-circuiting all clerical mediation and putting the laity into direct contact with the sacred?[39] In a sense, the Petrobrusians fifty years later were to prove his point.

The second part of the legacy of the years 1050–1120 was the refinement, to an extent hitherto unknown, of techniques of confrontation. This development was characterized by at least three features: first, a battle of words resembling an

---

36. On the importance of the Gregorian influence upon the evolution of heresy as a concept, see Othmar Hageneder, "Der Häresiebegriff bei der Juristen des 12. und 13. Jahrhunderts," in *The Concept of Heresy in the Middle Ages (11th–13th c.)*, proceedings of the International Conference, Leuven, 13–16 May 1973, ed. Willem Lourdaux and Daniel Verhelst, Mediaevalia Lovaniensia, ser. 1, Studia 4 (Leuven and The Hague, 1976), pp. 55–64.

37. Ian S. Robinson, *The Papacy, 1073–1198: Continuity and Innovation*, Cambridge Medieval Textbooks (Cambridge, 1990), pp. 318ff.

38. Quoted by Wilfried Hartmann, *Der Investiturstreit*, Enzyklopädie deutscher Geschichte, 21 (Munich, 1993), p. 62.

39. Sigebert of Gembloux, *Chronica*, 6, ed. L. C. Bethmann, *MGH SS*, 6, p. 363. See also Michel Lauwers's observations in *Inventer l'hérésie? Discours polémiques et pouvoirs avant l'Inquisition*, ed. Monique Zerner, Collection du Centre d'études médiévales de Nice, 2 (Nice, 1998).

armed confrontation behind closed doors; second, the art of wielding an armory of *testimonia* (supporting texts); third, the importance ascribed to rhetoric in the juridico-ecclesiastical arena. The period of the Gregorian reformation and the investiture controversy was one of intense polemic and a total lack of compromise, in which opponents fought each other using biblical quotations as weapons. Hence its description as a *Zitatenkampf* (battle of quotations). One such "battle of quotations" took place on 20 January 1085 at Gerstungen, an obscure corner of Thuringia, between representatives of King Henry IV of Germany and Pope Gregory VII. A notable participant on the papal side was Cardinal-Legate Odo I of Ostia, a former prior of Cluny and future pope Urban II. The spokesman for the Gregorian side, Gerard of Salzburg, began the proceedings by affirming that no loyal Catholic could have dealings with an excommunicated person, a qualification that included Henry IV. In support of this position he cited the Gospels, the Apostolic Canons, decrees of councils (Nicaea and Sardica) and a papal letter drawn from the False Decretals of Isidore Mercator (alias Pseudo-Isidore). This point of law was, Gerard maintained, so inexorable as to apply even when excommunication had been pronounced unjustly in the heat of emotion (*per iracundiam et asperam commotionem*). To the sheer amazement of the Gregorians, the king's representatives replied that they were in complete agreement. They simply rested their case on an "open book"— which was not specifically named, but was the introduction to the False Decretals, also entitled "Inscription by Pope Felix"—with a view to triggering the rule of *exceptio spolii*, whereby no person who had been despoiled might be accused, convicted, or banished. Such was the case of Henry IV, who had been despoiled of a part of his territory through the insurrection of the Saxons and the Swabians.[40] From our point of view, the Gerstungen episode is not simply an example of confrontational polemic behind closed doors. It also yields an interesting insight into the art of assembling *testimonia* in a precise way so as to floor the opposition. In the front rank were the scriptural quotations of which the polemicists of the Gregorian age made such intensive use. One example will suffice, taken from the researches of Max Hackelsperger: the anathema pronounced by the pope against the king.[41] The anti-Gregorian clerics opposed the anathema with a whole battery of scriptural quotations, including Luke 6:37: "Judge not; and you shall not be judged. Condemn not; and you shall not be condemned," and Romans 2:1: "thou art inexcusable, O man, whosoever thou art that judgest.

---

40. Horst Fuhrmann, "Pseudoisidor, Otto von Ostia (Urban II.) und der Zitatenkampf von Gerstungen," *Zeitschrift der Savigny-Stiftung für Rechtsgeschichte, Kanonistische Abteilung* 99 (1982), pp. 53–69, here 54.

41. Max Hackelsperger, *Bibel und mittelalterlicher Reichsgedanke: Studien und Beiträge zum Gebrauch der Bibel im Streit zwischen Kaisertum und Papsttum zur Zeit der Salier* (Bottrop im W., 1934), pp. 69ff. See also Jean Leclercq, "Usage et abus de la Bible au temps de la réforme grégorienne," in *The Bible and Medieval Culture*, ed. Willem Lourdaux and Daniel Verhelst (Leuven, 1979), pp. 87–108.

For wherein thou judgest another, thou condemnest thyself. For thou dost the same things which thou judgest." Against them the Gregorians, anxious to reinforce the pope's jurisdiction, appealed to Matthew 16:19 and 18:18, namely, the power to bind and loose, to which the king was no less subject than any layman. They had equal recourse to all passages of Scripture suited to justifying the use of anathema and cursing, including among others Titus 3:10: "A man that is a heretic, after the first and second admonition, avoid; knowing that he that is such a one is subverted and sinneth, being condemned by his own judgment." In a passage of his *Tractatus de regia potestate et sacerdotali dignitate*, Hugh of Fleury appealed to Paul's words to Titus to justify the rejection of a "heretical king":

> For Holy Church has been wont to make use of divine authority to condemn even a heretical king and gag him with a holy sentence of anathema so as to defend the Catholic faith and prevent the company of Catholic saints from being tainted by association with him. From such the apostle Paul himself separates and divides us [quotation of Titus 3:10–11 follows]. Solomon also pronounces a gentile to be better than a heretic when he says, "A living dog is better than a dead lion" [Ecclesiastes 9:4], calling a gentile "a living dog" and a heretic "a dead lion."[42]

This example is illuminating for at least two reasons: first, the application of Scripture (here the words of Paul) to a present problem; secondly, the glimpse given of the art of scriptural montage (here the juxtaposition of passages from Titus and Ecclesiastes), allowing the writer to slip interpretatively from the heretic to the lion worth less than a dog and on to the king, who at first sight seemed out of the frame.

By far the most important lesson to draw from this extract, however, is the evidence it affords of the increasing role of rhetoric in the juridico-ecclesiastical field. By 1050–1120, the period under review here, rhetoric already had a long history going back to Greek and Roman antiquity. Our problem is to assess how this tradition was received and reoriented. Of what did it consist? There was no Aristotle, at least not yet. His *Topics*, which laid down the rules of discussion, were not really available until the thirteenth century. The tradition employed was made up essentially of the Latin inheritance, in particular Cicero, one of the finest collections of whose works was already at Cluny in the eleventh century, containing his treatise on eloquence, *De inventione*, and his speeches, including *Pro Milone*, *Pro Avito*, and *Pro Murena*, not to mention the *Rhetorica ad Herrenium*, then thought to be by Cicero.[43] In these circumstances it was hardly surprising that Peter the Venerable, lauded by his followers as a new Cicero,

42. Hugh of Fleury, *Tractatus de regia potestate et sacerdotali dignitate*, 8, MGH Ldl, 2, pp. 465–94, here 476.

43. On Cicero's representation in the library catalogue at Cluny in the twelfth century, see Delisle, *Inventaire des manuscrits*, pp. 337–73, here no. 421, p. 363, and nos. 489–501, pp. 368–69;

should in his own *Contra Petrobrusianos* repeat such Ciceronian exclamations as the celebrated formula *O tempora! O mores!* of the *Orationes in Catilinam.*[44] The Ciceronian resurgence of the eleventh and twelfth centuries did not occur in just any context. As Heinrich Fichtenau has noted, Latin rhetoric informed the writings of Church Fathers like Augustine, but long remained an area of specialized activity among technicians of the *ars dictandi* (art of rhetoric). In the eleventh and twelfth centuries, however, rhetoric was imported in a quite striking manner into the fields of law and politics. An example was the *Rhetorimachia* of Anselm of Besate (1046/48), who became Henry III's chancellor and gave rhetoric a noble position in the diplomatic service and in the work of the chancellery. From the rhetoric of antiquity the polemicists of the Gregorian age borrowed techniques of defensive discourse. In Rome, for instance, the work of prosecution was left to young men, but that of defense was always accorded to an experienced lawyer.[45] Among other techniques that grew upon the soil of Latin rhetoric, it is worth mentioning:

1. the *exclamatio,* in the style of *O tempora! O mores!* (Oh, what times! what ways!) or *O inaudita arrogantia hominis!* (Oh, the outlandish presumption of man!);

2. the *dubitatio,* which repeated in an exaggerated and questioning manner an argument of the opponent in order to destroy it;

3. the *contentio,* which turned an image about or upside down. For example, *Qui dicebatur caput, iam est cauda ecclesiae: qui fundamentum, iam detrimentum* (He who was said to be the head is now the tail of the church: he who was the foundation is now the ruination);

4. the *verisimilitudo* or form of imputation based on rumor. Thus the verisimilitude based on *fama* was employed by Lambert of Hersfeld in his *Annales* to denounce the guilty passion and overfamiliar cohabitation of a man (Gregory VII) and a woman (Matilda of Canossa). Meanwhile, on the Gregorian side, Manegold of Lautenbach resorted to the same technique to censure the concubines of Henry IV;

5. the *vituperatio* or *damnatio,* the technique of invective, which played a major role in the art of sacred rhetoric in the Gregorian age. Take, for example, the lengthy harangue delivered by Peter Damian against the

more recently, Veronika von Büren, "Le catalogue de la bibliothèque de Cluny du XIe siècle reconstitué," *Scriptorium* 46 (1992): 260 and 263. At Cluny in 1415 Poggio was to discover an ancient manuscript of Cicero's speeches including two (*Pro Roscio Amerino* and *Pro Murena*) at that time unknown: see Leighton D. Reynolds and Nigel G. Wilson, *Scribes and Scholars: A Guide to the Transmission of Greek and Latin Literature,* 3d ed. (Oxford, 1991), p. 136.

44. Cicero, *Orationes in Catilinam,* no. 1, 1.2, quoted by Peter the Venerable, *CP,* 117. Peter of Poitiers thus likens Peter the Venerable to Cicero: *quis Cicero pulchrius aut copiosius aliquando quicquam disseruit? BC,* col. 619A.

45. A point that Sebastian McEvoy rightly makes in "Rhétorique et sciences sociales," *Sciences humaines: sens social, Critique* 529–530 (June–July 1991): 527–39, here 537.

"wives" of priests in letter 112 of the standard collection. A simple extract in its original Latin will suffice to give an idea of the sophistication of his rhetorical and literary methods:

> *Interea et vos alloquor, o lepores clericorum, pulpamenta diaboli, proiectio paradisi, virus mentium, gladius animarum, aconita bibentium, toxica convivarum, materia peccandi, occasio pereundi. Vos, inquam, alloquor ginecea hostis antiqui, upupae, ululae, noctuae, lupae, sanguisugae, "affer, affer" sine cessatione dicentes* [Proverbs 30:15]. *Venite itaque, audite me, scorta, prostibula, savia, volutabra porcorum pinguium, cubilia spirituum inmundorum, nimphae, sirenae, lamiae, dianae.*[46]

This harangue, composed in rhymed, rhythmic prose, makes use of stressed phonic effects that tend to turn the rich vocabulary employed into what are in effect maledictory formulae. The evil, womankind, is never named. But a whole procession of metaphors (notably involving woman as receptacle) and of animal images (chosen as much for their power to evoke the bestiary as for the richness of their phonic effects) suggests the multiple forms of the feminine that cannot be named. Finally, the hailing by the speaker (*me*) of these creatures, which are condemned yet never directly named (*vos*), belongs to the realm of incantation or exorcism. At the heart of the imprecation, the verb has a conjuring, exorcising, force. To describe what cannot be named—be it female, diabolic, or heretical—is to drive it away.

It is not clear what survived beyond the 1120s from among the books of polemic belonging to the years of the Gregorian reform and the investiture controversy, in particular the famous *libelli de lite*. As Ian Stuart Robinson has shown, these *libelli* had a very weak manuscript tradition.[47] Their transmission in the twelfth century took place in a school context and was due not so much to interest in their content as such, as to their literary features and value as teaching material. The *Codex Udalrici* was one such case among others. It was copied to fulfill the needs of the cathedral school at Bamberg, and assembled a collection of *libelli* from the investiture controversy, for example polemic texts of Gregory VII, Henry IV, Sigebert of Gembloux, and Guy of Osnabrück. This gathering of texts went hand in hand with a certain amount of interpolation in the form of

---

46. Ep. 112, 3:278. The brief commentary following is taken from an analysis of the letter by Monique Goullet, to whom my thanks are due. Trans. of passage quoted: "Meanwhile I address you too, you charmers of the clergy, you titbits of the devil, you refuse of paradise, slime that fouls minds, blade that slays souls, wolfsbane of drinkers, poison of table companions, the stuff of sin, the occasion of death. You I address, you harem of the ancient enemy, you hoopoes, screech owls, night owls, she-wolves, horse leeches saying over and over, 'Produce again, again' (ref. Proverbs 30:15). Come then and hear my words, you whores, harlots, kissing-mouths, sloughs for fat pigs, couches for unclean spirits, nymphs, sirens, bloodsucking witches, dianas. . . ."

47. Robinson, "The 'Colores rhetorici' in the Investiture Contest."

corrections or minor additions, not so as to alter the basic record but to emphasize certain rhetorical figures in the text. Peter Damian's letters, whose manuscript tradition was infinitely richer, were also used for similar purposes of rhetorical training. The harangue against the "wives" of priests in letter 112 quoted above was incorporated around 1075 by the master of the *ars dictaminis*, Alberic of Monte Cassino, in his *Breviarium de dictamine*.[48] With a view to training in rhetoric, these textual compilations turned the serious debates of the years 1050–1120—on simony, the celibacy of the priesthood, respect for ecclesiastical property, and in sum every sort of problem of moral correction—into themes for disputes offered to students as exercises alongside the classic school cases drawn from the Fathers or Scripture.

Ratio *and the Resort to Discourse*

Heinrich Fichtenau has drawn attention to the undoubted synchrony between the heretical surges of the twelfth century and the "process of rationalization"—to use Max Weber's phrase—concomitant with early scholasticism.[49] The eleventh and twelfth centuries witnessed the appearance of *ratio* (reason) in great theological debates. The model was provided by Anselm of Canterbury in his *Cur Deus homo?* in which the author confronted two interlocutors, one Jewish and the other Muslim; the model worked by "establishing an axiomatic structure . . . accepted by both Christians and infidels and, within the system thus defined, convincing the opponent by demonstrative reasons."[50] Anselm's infidel interlocutors were doubtless fictitious, which probably explains why his discussion of the Christian dogma of the Incarnation remained so abstract. However, in the urban world of the twelfth century, the issues were becoming both more concrete and more urgent. Introducing his antiheretical treatise, Peter the Venerable voices his anxiety in the face of the Petrobrusian heresy, once limited to the "poorly inhabited, little cultivated" Alpine foothills yet now gaining the "populous and knowledgeable" cities of the south.[51] In this socially and confessionally mixed context, the clergy were finding it harder and harder to answer not merely the questions put to them by the laity but also the criticisms leveled by Jews at what they saw as the ludi-

---

48. A fact noted by Ian Robinson, but missed by Reindel in his edition of the *Epistolae*. Reindel notes however that the harangue was incorporated by Manegold of Lautenbach in its entirety, *Epistolae*, 3:278, n. 41. The chapter "De vituperatio personarum" reappears in the *Aurea gemma oxionis*, *ars dictiminis* dating from the end of the twelfth century and figuring in the so-called Hildesheim collection of letters: see *Die jüngere Hildesheimer Briefsammlung*, 134, 27, ed. Rolf de Kegel, *MGH* Die Briefe der deutschen Kaiserzeit, 7 (Munich, 1995), p. 214. I am grateful to M. Goullet for bringing this reference to my attention.

49. *Ketzer und Professoren*, p. 273.

50. Dahan, *Les intellectuels chrétiens*, p. 428.

51. *CP*, 6.

crous and irrational dogmas of the Christians, for instance, the Incarnation and the virginity of Mary.

To meet such a challenge, it was necessary to go outside the strict bounds of authorities and argue rationally, even if this particular discursive approach remained quite limited. Preachers and polemicists employed several techniques of argument.[52] They appealed to common sense, using analogies by way of illustration. Thus Alan of Lille likened the Trinity to the three parts of the soul: the memory, the intelligence, and the will. The Virgin Birth was compared to a window through which the sunlight shone. The use of dialectic remained for the most part limited to the construction of syllogisms with terms drawn from Scripture. Such was the treatment given to the "sign" prophesied by Isaiah 7:14: "Behold a virgin shall conceive and bear a son: and his name shall be called Emmanuel." The Messiah's coming was to be marked by a miracle; the virginal incarnation was a miracle: ergo it was the sign of the Messiah's arrival. Prior to the total acceptance of Aristotle's works during the thirteenth century, recourse to philosophy remained extremely tentative. It extended most often merely to questions of language, reflection about the inadequacy of language to portray reality, and reasoning about dogma on the basis of categories. Hence for Abelard and William of Conches the Trinity could be deconstructed according to the theory of appropriations into *potentia* (the Father), *sapientia* (the Son), and *voluntas* (the Holy Spirit).[53] Even so, such a recourse to philosophical verities and excursion outside the field of strict authorities, which was fundamental to speculative theology, went by no means uncontested. The new masters were frequently charged with scientific heresy, their schools likened to "sects" by those who held theology to be practical and moral. The Council of Soissons in 1121 condemned Abelard as "Sabellian" without either reading or refuting his *Theologia summi boni*. The gulf was a wide one. From the other side, a pupil of Gilbert de la Porée reproached Bernard of Clairvaux for knowing nothing of the liberal arts, for failing to understand modes of argument, and for using only rhetorical persuasion (*ornata persuasio*) in his discourse.[54]

The resort to *ratio* amounted in essence to a new attitude toward authority. Attention was given to resolving the apparent contradictions of Scripture. The same spirit was seen at work both in the *sic et non* method adopted by Abelard in his work of that name and in Gratian's *Concordia discordantium canonum* intended to harmonize the contradictions in the canonical writings bequeathed by tradition. It stimulated new technical approaches, for example, studies of context, of textual transmission, of the validity of assertions. It encouraged a whole casuistry of *quaestiones*. As for the area of polemic, interest began to be shown in the writings of opponents. From the twelfth century, certain anti-Jewish polemicists

---

52. The examples following are taken from Dahan, *Les intellectuels chrétiens*, pp. 432ff.

53. Cited by Heinrich Fichtenau, *Ketzer und Professoren*, p. 273.

54. Ibid., p. 254.

made it their business to become acquainted with the Jewish canon of the Old Testament and approach rabbinic literature. They were few and far between, but besides the Spanish Peter Alfonso, there was Peter the Venerable himself, who saw to it that for the purposes of preparing his *Adversus Iudeos* he obtained—by some means unknown to us—a copy of extracts from the Talmud, considered to be the oral law transmitted by God to Moses. He similarly commissioned a translation of the Qur'an (Koran), to enable him to refute Muhammad's sectaries in his *Contra sectam Sarracenorum*.[55] The desire to refute the infidels on the basis of their own texts revealed how little attention had previously been paid to gathering *testimonia* from outside the Christian tradition. Peter the Venerable approached the business of antiheretical polemic in similar fashion, obtaining (as he himself says concerning Henry of Lausanne) a document belonging to the opposition.[56] The problem was that, in contrast to his infidel adversaries, the heretics rejected most of the Christian canon and accepted only the Gospels.

THE TECHNIQUES OF DEFENSIVE ARGUMENT IN *CONTRA PETROBRUSIANOS*

By way of introduction to the fifth proposition of his *Contra Petrobrusianos*, Peter the Venerable makes some general observations about the necessity of heresy, as revealed by the apostle Paul in 1 Corinthians 11:19: "For there must be also heresies; that they also, who are approved, may be made manifest among you." Just as the Church expanded (*dilatatio*) in fighting an external enemy, so also it was purified (*purgatio*) by inner strife. This *purgatio* proceeded through four stages—*investigatio* (also called *quaestio* or question), *discussio* (debate), *inventio* (findings), *defensio* (enforcement). All four stages were equally manifestations of the Holy Spirit, namely, subtlety (in the *investigatio*), application (in the *inventio*), sense of realization achieved (the *perfectio* or accomplishment effected through the *inventio*), and strength (displayed in the *defensio*).[57]

Debating Heresy

The first three of the four phases just mentioned corresponded to operations of the intellect that were well known to practitioners in the schools of the twelfth century. The subject was established by a "question from the adversary or opposing side"—*quaestio* (*ab adversa parte opponitur*). Three stages would ensue: an examination (*investigatio*), discussion (*discussio*), and resolution (*inventio*) of the problem. Then finally came the fourth phase of *defensio*, which in the

55. See below, chaps. 10 and 11.
56. *CP, epistola,* 10, ll. 6–8.
57. *CP,* 212, ll. 15–21.

last resort might call for deeds of justice, even force of arms, but which also found verbal expression in the discourse in the form of preaching and, at the very heart of Peter's treatise, repeated imprecations against the heretics who lie and act as madmen, who speak to the winds. We shall see that this use of imprecation in defense of the truth comes third and last in time, after the heresy has been investigated and explored. At this point, no objection, not even a murmur,[58] can be tolerated: the moment is come when those who stand by their error and continue to invoke it publicly must be condemned, primarily by efficacious words such as are found in an anathema. Besides, such is the canonical definition of heresy: *publice et pertinaciter insistere* (to publicly and obstinately persist).[59]

Peter the Venerable belonged to a period in which a polemical space permitting the debate of heretical propositions still existed. But polemic is not dialogue. Directly descended from Latin rhetoric, Peter's controversial art employed monologue; it was "a school exercise in which the declaimer enjoys a painless triumph over an absent adversary."[60] For all that, the faults laid against Peter of Bruis and his disciples were not—at any rate, not yet—unmentionable. The point is worth making, for in the 1130s and 1140s, the period in which *Contra Petrobrusianos* was composed, scholars of canon and civil law were busy defining the category of the *nefandum*, the unspeakable. This would include all the monstrous crimes that sprang from lese-majesty and was a category that would shortly include heresy.[61]

Investigatio

Peter the Venerable's antiheretical treatment had begun with an inquiry. He had obtained information personally in Provence. But he relied preeminently upon the archbishops and bishops of the provinces tainted with the heretical evil to make their own inquiries and relay information back to him, which is what he asked them to do in the case of the heretic Henry.[62] The inquest enabled him to assemble the various elements of the heretics' argument. Our problem is that our only access to their case is via the abbot of Cluny's refutation and we have no other yardstick by which to measure its coherence. Peter's research contained reported assertions, as is shown by the allusions to heretical preaching—*verba vestra que ad nos pervenire potuerunt . . .* (such words of yours as have reached us . . .);[63] *predicatis, dicitis, asseritis, affirmatis* (you

---

58. For example, concerning the utility of suffrages on behalf of the dead, *CP,* 241, ll. 5–8.

59. *CP,* 247, ll. 1–3.

60. François Desbordes, "La place de l'Autre: remarques sur quelques emplois de 'controversia' dans la rhétorique latine," in *La controverse religieuse et ses formes,* ed. Alain Le Boulluec, Patrimoine, Religions du Livre (Paris, 1995), pp. 29–46 and 405–6, here 406.

61. On this see Jacques Chiffoleau's stimulating study, "Dire l'indicible: remarques sur la catégorie du *nefandum* du XIIe au XVe siècle," *AESC* 1990: 289–324.

62. *CP, epistola,* 10, ll. 13–17.

63. *CP,* 150, ll. 3–4.

preach, you say, you assert, you affirm)[64]—and the echoes of sermons, such as Henry's propositions, which Peter says he learned of "in a work."[65]

Such was the basis upon which Peter built his exposition, first of all denouncing the heretics' violations—the (re-)baptisms, profaning of churches, smashing of altars, burning of crosses, persecution of priests and monks—upon whose truth or likelihood the historian is in no position to pronounce, given the polemical tactic of rumor. Peter's main focus, however, was upon the Petrobrusian propositions that ran counter to the dogma and tradition of the Church. Some of these had scriptural underpinning, like the first, regarding infant baptism. The Petrobrusians denied its validity, basing their view that faith alone saved on Christ's words in Mark 16:16: "He that believeth and is baptized shall be saved; but he that believeth not shall be condemned." The fifth proposition, on the alleged uselessness of suffrages for the dead, rested on a literal reading of two passages from Paul (Galatians 6:5 and 2 Corinthians 5:10), where the apostle speaks of the condemnation or justification of every man according to his own works. The remaining propositions were based on simple affirmations reported to the abbot of Cluny, who sometimes quotes them directly (*Predicatis* . . .).

Discussio et inventio

On the basis of this documentation, Peter the Venerable was able to begin debating, or rather he was ready to launch into a battle of words. For *Contra Petrobrusianos* is strewn with warlike metaphors and injunctions to confrontation. Before tackling the first proposition, Peter takes courage for the fight: "Let me, too, go on the counteroffensive, not as wiser than others but perhaps more unbridled [*effrenatior*]."[66] Before treating the fourth proposition, on the Eucharist, he commands his adversaries to join him on the dueling ground (*campus est*) before witnesses who will judge on the basis of not brute force but weight of argument. [67] His frequent use of the imperative, rooted in the long tradition of classical oratory, is due also to belief in the operative power of words to become deeds in a sacramental context.[68] Thus in the course of his discussion of the Eucharist, Peter urges Christ himself to confound the heretics with his own words: "Speak, Lord Jesus, our savior, our priest, our host. Speak out and answer the adversaries of thy testament."[69]

The duel obeys an axiomatic structure defined at the start of the treatise. Peter's declared intention is to ground the debate on *auctoritas*—assuming the

64. *CP,* 89–92.
65. *CP, epistola,* 10, ll. 6–8.
66. *CP,* 9, ll. 14–16.
67. *CP,* 152, ll. 4–9.
68. This notion of the operative value of language, particularly the liturgical, was theorized a century later by the "intentionalist" grammarians: see Irène Rosier, *La parole comme acte: sur la grammaire et la sémantique au XIIIe siècle* (Paris, 1994), chaps. 5 and 6.
69. *CP,* 168, ll. 5–7.

heretics want to remain Christian, though Peter's aim is equally to strengthen doubting Catholics—or, failing that, on *ratio*, which ought to convince all men. As to the first case, the authority accepted by the two camps calls for definition. For, as Peter explains, the Petrobrusians refute the tradition of the Fathers. They reject all Church tradition and all the biblical books apart from the Gospels.[70] The abbot of Cluny, however, seeks to break out of these limits. From the Gospels alone he attempts to justify importing the whole of Scripture into the argument, not simply the remaining books of the New Testament but the whole of the Old Testament as well—*probatio totius Novi Testamenti ex Evangelio; probatio totius Veteris Testamenti ex Evangelio* (proof of the whole New Testament from the Gospel; proof of the whole of the Old Testament from the Gospel). The same tactic had been used by Augustine against the Manichaean Faustus, who rejected the authority of the Old Testament.[71] The life of Christ, as recounted in the Gospels, thus made it possible to reintroduce the entire matter of Scripture. How was one to deny what Christ himself had ratified? Had he not fulfilled what was announced in the Old Testament? As for the apostles, they were bearers of the Holy Spirit. Their writings, together with the Acts of the Apostles, composed by Luke the evangelist, Peter ventured, were the continuation of the work of Christ, who had commissioned his disciples to bear the good news. Finally, the harmony between the Acts of the Apostles and Paul's Epistles had never been denied by heretics prior to the Petrobrusians; even the pagan Seneca acknowledged it. And if the authority of the Acts and the Pauline Epistles was accepted, then the whole of the Church's tradition, full of the Spirit of God, was authenticated, for the apostles were the conjunction between Christ and His *Ecclesia*: "For if the doctrine or tradition of the Church was received from the apostles, if the same flowed into the apostles from Christ, then it is manifestly true and is to be received by the sons of truth."[72]

Nothing less than all the texts of Scripture and tradition were thus reintroduced into the debate. Moreover, Peter's conception of tradition was an extremely wide one. Unsurprisingly, the Latin Fathers—Peter had no access to the writings of the Greek Fathers—are plentifully quoted in *Contra Petrobrusianos*; but the rich storehouse of hagiographic tradition was also raided. Such a use of hagiography was not entirely unmatched elsewhere in antiheretical writings of the eleventh and twelfth centuries; at the Synod of Arras in 1025, mention was made of the martyrs and of Saint Martin, the prototype of ancient monasticism, in order to bolster ecclesiastical tradition.[73] Yet the massive, reasoned use of *miracula* (the miraculous) by Peter the Venerable is worthy of further remark.

70. *CP*, 231, ll. 1–2.

71. Augustine, *Contra Faustum*, 13.2, *PL* 42:282. I am grateful to Jean-Pierre Weiss for pointing this out to me.

72. *CP*, 29, ll. 8–10.

73. *Acta synodi Atrebatensis*, 11, *PL* 142:1301C–1303C: guidance to this text came from Guy Lobrichon.

He regarded Scripture as a reservoir of *aperta miracula* (openly known miracles), be they miracles performed by Christ or by his predecessors of Old Testament days. These past miracles represented even for the abbot of Cluny the sort of evident proof likely to convince an adversary, an *assertio vallata*—a reinforced assertion. But complementing the *verba divina* (words of God) and adding to the miracles of Scripture, the Church's tradition itself was full of extraordinary happenings that were no less manifestations of God in history. Peter's notion of "extraordinary happenings" comprised, first, the *miracula cotidiana* (everyday miracles), the changes of substance without change of form that happened daily in the Eucharist. To these were added, secondly, all the examples of the saints of former days recorded by tradition and, thirdly, the messages that in Peter's day now came from the world beyond, not least in dreams, the privileged vehicle for manifestations of the dead. In opposition to his friend Abelard, who was persuaded that the age of miracles ended with Christ and that the Church should convince with rational arguments rather than with accounts of miracles,[74] Peter the Venerable stressed the teaching value of miracles and extraordinary events like that of the Eucharist on the ground that "human hearts are moved more by present realities than by absent things."[75] This very principle, defended and illustrated in *Contra Petrobrusianos*, lies at the heart of Peter's major work, *De miraculis*, complementary to his antiheretical treatise.

Peter's recourse to *ratio*, strictly construed as the barring of all use of argument from authority, was limited essentially to the discussion of objections, reasoning from analogy, and examining the logic of propositions, as follows:

1. discussion of objections: *Sed forte aliquis econtra* (Should anyone say in opposition).[76] Familiar with patristic diatribes and contemporary school *quaestiones*, Peter the Venerable knew how to give a voice to possible objections. While refuting the fifth heretical proposition, on suffrages for the dead, he twice interrupts his flow: once, to ask if the life after death is a state of meriting or of recompense; a second time, to ask about the status of dreams and the criteria dividing false from true revelations. In so doing, Peter introduces some classic twelfth-century school cases quite simply into the antiheretical battle.

2. reasoning from analogy. The formula *sed forte aliquis econtra*, just quoted, is employed by Peter at the core of his discussion on the Eucharist. The question was a key one, which Peter refused to solve by appeal to authorities. He refers, at the start of his examination, to the learned works of Lanfranc, Guitmund of Aversa, and Alger, the Liège master who became a monk at Cluny: all are writings that emerged from the controversy with Berengar of Tours in the years 1050–80 but that Peter

74. Cited by Heinrich Fichtenau, *Ketzer und Professoren*, p. 207.
75. *CP*, 201, ll. 34–36 (regarding the Eucharist).
76. *CP*, 182, l. 1.

PART II. CHRISTIAN SOCIETY

opts not to make use of here. His aim is rather to convince men by *ratio* alone of the "reality" of the phenomenon. On what was as yet a narrow, poorly signposted road in the 1130s, Peter makes do with analogies. For him the miracle of the transmuted elements was not without its parallels in everyday life; indeed this was why the notion of *miracula cotidiana* held such sway with him.[77] Does not the air load the clouds, which are transformed into rain, snow, hail, even fire? Are not bread and wine absorbed and transformed into the body of man, the bread into flesh and the wine into blood? And if there are those who object that these are not examples of changed substance without changed form, as is the case in the Eucharist, Peter resorts to an analogy that he himself finds totally convincing: water becomes ice or crystal without changing its form, namely, without losing its transparency.

3. the logic of propositions. The aim is to construct a chain of reasoning in which assertions are linked by logical conjunctions of the type "neither . . . nor" or "if . . . then." There is, frankly, only one instance of the "neither . . . nor" type in *Contra Petrobrusianos*, and it is at the beginning of the *epistola disputans*. The Petrobrusians' literalist reading of Mark 16:16—"He that believeth and is baptized shall be saved; but he that believeth not shall be condemned"—is summed up in the following proposition whose two terms are interdependent: neither is baptism possible without proper faith, nor is proper faith possible without baptism. Peter refutes the second term in the name of common sense. Were the unbaptized martyrs damned? By no means. And if the second term is invalid, why should the first, which is logically dependent upon it, be valid? By means of a logical conjunction of the "if . . . then" type, Peter proceeds to subject the heretics' argument to a logical *reductio ad absurdum* in the matter of infant baptism. If the Petrobrusians' literalist interpretation of Mark were valid, then during all the centuries of infant baptism, no one would have been properly baptized; there would be no Christians, no deacons, no priests to baptize, no bishops to consecrate, and in short no Church. It is when he returns to the territory of scriptural *testimonia*, where he is most at home, that Peter delights in using the "if . . . then" logic; it is an area where he can exploit typological correspondence to the full. The "if . . . then" becomes an indignant interrogative condition. If something was true in the Old Testament, then ought it not to be so in the New? Are Christian infants not to be saved, whereas Jewish children, cleansed of original sin in Old Testament times by circumcision on the eighth day, were? From Peter's point of view it is an unanswerable proof. Let the opponent answer if he can.

---

77. Peter took the notion of *miracula cotidiana* from Augustine, in particular from book 21 of *De civitate Dei*.

A New Attitude toward Authorities

In Peter the Venerable's writing, no less than in other *disputationes* of very early scholasticism, the recourse to *ratio* runs up against the one limiting factor—the unknowable greatness of God. When in his defense of the Eucharist Peter has to respond on the question of consuming the elements (*cur ad manducandum vel bibendum*), he acknowledges the difficulty and counters with a refutation from principle:

> Is not the will of God alone more rational than any human reason? . . . Just as his will cannot be irrational, so reason cannot be other than of his will. As these things are so, his will is sufficient for any reason or rational mind, even if the reason for His will is not made manifest.[78]

At this point in the discussion, Peter transforms Anselm of Canterbury's famous formula *Fides quaerens intellectum* (Faith seeking understanding) in such a way as to make understanding a fruit of faith. Peter's formula is *Credat ut intelligat:* One must believe in order to understand.[79] In these conditions, the "rational" approach followed by Peter the Venerable in order to respond to the Petrobrusians and convince not just "the faithful" but "mankind" is essentially limited to a new treatment of authorities. This consists of widening the notion of authority and attempting to endow the revealed truths of Christianity with universal validity.

Widening the notion of authority amounted to invoking testimonies and examples from the margins of Christian tradition. In opposing the heretics, no less than in countering the Saracens and the Jews, Peter sought to obtain the writings of his heretical adversaries. It is simply unfortunate that whereas the Talmud and the Qur'an are available to us, the writings of Peter of Bruis and Henry of Lausanne are lost, apart from those passages that are directly quoted by the abbot of Cluny. Twice at least Peter appeals to the history of religions. Against the Petrobrusians' rejection of the consecration of particular places for the service of religion, he cites not only the Temple (*templum*) of the Jews but also pagan sanctuaries (*fana*).[80] In discussing the Eucharist, he asks who will sacrifice if the Christians cease to do so: not the Jews, for they need access to Jerusalem to perform their vows; not the Saracens, caught between the Jews and the Christians, who pray but do not sacrifice. Peter then mentions, from an unidentified source, the pagans of the regions of the north (the sea of Azov), who know no idols, rites, or sacrifices, but honor animals as "gods of the day or of the hour."[81] Faced with former priests possibly having a classical education and initiated into scriptural study, Peter sometimes refers to pre-Christian authors. On the eucharistic *commemoratio*, sign of the Redeemer's essential presence, he quotes a

---

78. *CP*, 206, ll. 10–17.
79. *CP*, 189, ll. 5–10 (regarding the Eucharist); the formula was borrowed from Augustine.
80. *CP*, 100, ll. 5–6.
81. *CP*, 161, ll. 23–31.

passage from the *Ars poetica* of Horace (who is referred to simply as *quidam*—"someone") on the usefulness of seeing rather than hearing. A little earlier in the treatise, countering the Petrobrusians' execration of the Cross as the instrument of Christ's torture, Peter asks where the fault lies. One can speak of fault, he says, only where there is *ratio*, namely, in animate beings; such is hardly the case with the wooden crosses burnt by the heretics. Punishment of that sort is no less absurd than the behavior of King Cyrus who, as Herodotus tells in his *Histories* (*1.189*), had three hundred and sixty channels dug in the Gyndes in order to punish the "pride of the river" in which he lost his cherished white horse.[82]

The main aim of *Contra Petrobrusianos* is to portray the revelations of Christianity as universal truths. In order to achieve this, Peter labors to show the present relevance of Christ's teachings through a play between the past on the one hand and the present and future on the other. The model used is the type *non solum . . . sed etiam* (not only . . . but also), *in hoc seculo . . . in futuro* (in this age . . . in the future), or *olim . . . nunc* (once . . . now). It is this logic that lends such importance to *miracula*: not simply to those of hagiographic tradition, in which God makes his presence known in history through the medium of his saints, but also the "miracle" of the Eucharist, in which the unique act of the Redemption is infinitely repeated (*tunc semel . . . semper*—then once . . . for ever). Thereby the historic life and work of Christ are not simply made a present reality and reenacted; his teaching is given universal significance. It is in Christ that all the sacrifices of the history of religions are fulfilled. The Temple (*templum*) of the Jews and the sanctuaries (*fana*) of the pagans have been replaced by the churches (*ecclesiae*), whose multiplicity in unity (in the *Ecclesia*) testifies to the irresistible expansion of Christianity. The seven churches of the Apocalypse, the early Christians in Rome, and then the missions of Trophimus and all the other "streams of Gallic faith" mark out in time and space the essential stages for moving from the unique to the universal, until such time as Cluny, like the vine of the Lord, reaches unto the sea. Such universality, in *Contra Petrobrusianos* at least, is not a matter of simple, narrow proselytism, but is about portraying the revelations of Christianity as universally valid. The principle pursued is that what was true once for one man is (and will be) necessarily true for others. Yet it is essential that that "man" should believe or that someone should have faith on his behalf. In discussing the efficacy of baptizing children, Peter thus invokes the examples of children saved bodily and spiritually by Christ himself.

Peter points out that these miracles, recorded in the Gospels, were a response to requests made of Christ on behalf of a third party—and not just a child, but also a wife or brother, as in the case of Martha, Mary, and Lazarus. From these examples Peter makes what he sees as an obvious point: would Christ have bestowed (*impartit*) so much in return for the faith of one believer and yet given nothing in return for the faith of the entire Church on behalf of the baptized

82. *CP*, 121.

children?[83] This argument based on self-evidence, designed to reinforce the Church's tradition, enables him to close the discussion with a final stroke of all-or-nothing logic: either all men are saved, including the children, or no one is.

BARRIERS TO DEFENSIVE ARGUMENT

How then should we assess the place of *Contra Petrobrusianos* in the history of medieval antiheretical polemic? Peter the Venerable calls his work an *epistola disputans*—a letter of argument. It belongs to the genre of "defensive argument" in the sense that it makes use of both *imprecatio*, normal within sacred rhetoric, and *disputatio*, the discursive method in vogue in contemporary scholastic circles. Such a joint approach was often used by Christian polemicists against the Jews or Saracens in the twelfth century. Its use against heretics was, however, quite exceptional. As we have seen, Bernard of Clairvaux in this field resorted exclusively to imprecation. He took the view that heresy had no content, merited no discussion, and was simply an abomination that had to be exposed and denounced, the linguistic act of imprecation itself having the sacramental power to repress it. For Peter the Venerable, on the other hand, imprecation pertained to the "defense" (*defensio*), coming in the final phase of the four-stage process of *investigatio, discussio, inventio, defensio*. It was only after examination and discussion that it was possible to resort to condemnation in words and if necessary repression. Such a process was symptomatic of a real hope that the minds of deviants could be changed through debating the doctrinal points at issue.

Such optimism, still possible in the 1140s, was short-lived. "The pagans are wrong and the Christians right," exclaimed the *Song of Roland*.[84] In a time of outbursts of violence against the Jews and armed pilgrimages against the Saracens, Christian polemicists, less and less hopeful about being able to persuade opponents by reasoned argument, began to adopt a more aggressive tone.[85] In the same way, after 1200, heresy was no longer a subject for debate. Having become a crime of lese-majesty, the worst of all abominations admitting no amendment, it was no longer a matter for accusation—to be dealt with by imprecation, with or without discussion—but one for inquisition. The aim was no longer to declare and denounce deviations, be they suspected or avowed, but to proclaim the truth through those that were to be condemned.[86] The sort of defensive argument promoted by Peter the Venerable thus was to have no immediate future, a

---

83. *CP*, 69, ll. 15–16.

84. *La Chanson de Roland*, l. 1015: *Paien unt tort e chrestiens unt dreit.*

85. This evolution is clearly seen in Dahan, *Les intellectuels chrétiens.*

86. On this vital development, see the important studies by Jacques Chiffoleau, particularly "*Contra naturam:* pour une approche casuistique et procédurale de la nature médiévale," in [occasional series] *Micrologus*, 4 (1996), *Il teatro de la natura/The Theater of Nature*, pp. 265–312.

fact that goes a long way to explaining the scant manuscript tradition of *Contra Petrobrusianos* during the remainder of the Middle Ages. The discursive approach, represented by Peter's treatise around 1140, had by 1200 given way to the judicial. And it was only later, in the sixteenth century, a period of fire and blood but also of ideas, that Peter's polemic found some resonance.

5

THE CHURCH'S FOUNDATIONS
BAPTISM AND PLACES OF WORSHIP

BAPTISM AND UNIVERSAL SALVATION

The first question debated in *Contra Petrobrusianos* was the logically obvious one of baptism, the rite of admission into the *Ecclesia*.[1] From Augustine's battle with the Pelagians down to that of Peter the Venerable and his clerical contemporaries in defense of the "sacrament" administered to children, the subject of Christian baptism bore out Augustine's adage that the challenge presented by heretics had the happy result of making Catholic doctrine "more clearly understood and more earnestly propounded."[2] By the 1130s, the practice of infant baptism was already ancient, having been insisted upon by the legislators and clergy of the Carolingian age.[3] During the eleventh century, and even more systematically in the twelfth, it became current practice to proceed to the baptismal regeneration of a child as soon as possible (*quamprimum*), without waiting for Easter or Pentecost.[4] It is hard to know whether the practice of baptizing children achieved rapid and universal acceptance. Perhaps not, given the various currents denounced as heretical in the eleventh and twelfth centuries that stoutly

---

1. *CP*, 10–13 and 67–88. This and following refs. to *Contra Petrobrusianos* are to numbered paragraphs in the edition by James Fearns. A general approach to the problem of baptism to the mid-twelfth century is that of Peter Cramer, *Baptism and Change in the Early Middle Ages, c. 200–c. 1150* (Cambridge, 1993), esp. pp. 131ff. Unfortunately, this does not sufficiently elucidate the history of infant baptism in the eleventh and twelfth centuries and so does not replace the older works by Jean-Charles Didier: "La question du baptême des enfants chez saint Bernard et ses contemporains," *Analecta Sacri Ordinis Cisterciensis* 9 (1953): 191–201; *Faut-il baptiser les enfants? La réponse de la tradition* (Paris, 1967).

2. *De civitate Dei*, 16.2; quoted (with incorrect ref.) by Didier, "La question du baptême des enfants," p. 192 and n. 4.

3. See Jean Chelini, *L'aube du Moyen Age, naissance de la chrétienté occidentale: la vie religieuse des laïcs à l'époque carolingienne 750–900* (Paris, 1991), pp. 47ff. On the evolution of the ritual, see *L'Eglise en prière*, ed. Aimé-Georges Martimort, 2d ed. (Paris, 1983–84), 3:76ff.

4. Pierre-Marie Gy, "*Quamprimum*: Note sur le baptême des enfants," *La Maison-Dieu* 32 (1952): 124–28, and "Du baptême pascal des petits enfants au baptême *quamprimum*," in *Haut Moyen Age: culture, éducation et société: études offertes à Pierre Riché*, ed. Michel Sot (Paris, 1990), pp. 353–65.

opposed infant baptism.[5] Bernard of Clairvaux reported that the heretics derided as simpletons those who believed it was possible by baptism alone, without faith, to be cleansed of original sin.[6] On the other hand, it may be that the heretical opposition to infant baptism—like other objections discussed in *Contra Petrobrusianos*—was a sign that the challenged rite was firmly established in a Church sure of itself and of its power over the faithful.

Baptismal ritual was originally designed for adult catechumens who were subjected to "scrutinies": rites of initiation that included, among other things, recital of the Lord's Prayer and the Creed, as well as response to questions put by the priest. Vocal expression of personal commitment was thus needed. During the early Middle Ages infant baptism became general. Its success was due in no small part to the satisfaction it afforded on the problem of the salvation of children dying at birth or very young.[7] An episode in the *Vita sancti Odonis* records the anguished prayer of Odo of Cluny on behalf of an unbaptized nephew who had fallen into the hands of the Normans.[8] When discussing the assistance the living could give the dead, Peter the Venerable cited the example of a sick child who died before Saint Maurilius of Angers was able to baptize him. To assuage his guilt, the saint underwent a penitential exile of seven years; on his return, he was able to resurrect the child, christening him Renatus in order to mark the event.[9]

Carolingian baptismal policy tried to return to the ancient tradition of the rites of late antiquity, in particular the use of "scrutinies." This denoted sensitivity over the issue of personal commitment. How could an infant, etymologically "incapable of speech," be a catechumen and proclaim his or her faith? What value could one assign to the "faith of the others" who committed themselves on the child's behalf at the time of baptism? It was a question asked from the ninth century at least. Augustine's notion of "others' faith" or "faith on another's behalf" was conveniently absorbed into a system using one or more godparents

5. See list of documented cases in James Fearns, "Peter von Bruis und die religiöse Bewegung des 12. Jahrhunderts," *Archiv für Kulturgeschichte* 48 (1966): 311–35.

6. Bernard of Clairvaux, *Sermones super Cantica Canticarum*, 66.4, in *Opera omnia*, vol. 2, ed. Jean Leclercq, Charles H. Talbot, and Henri-Marie Rochais (Rome, 1958), p. 183: *Irrident nos quod baptizamus infantes . . . .*

7. Cramer, *Baptism and Change*, p. 125.

8. The saint's prayer is heard and he baptizes the child himself. The whole episode is bathed in baptismal symbolism: a deep river is crossed dry-foot; the return to Tours takes three days and the child dies three days after his baptism. In John of Salerno, *Vita sancti Odonis*, 2.16, *PL* 133:69D–70A; Nalgodus, *Vita sancti Odonis*, 40, *PL* 133:100D–101A—quoted and commented on by Cramer, *Baptism and Change*, pp. 150–51.

9. *CP*, 245, ll. 15–18, which passage refers to the text of the *Vita sancti Maurilio*, 17, *MGH Auct. Ant.*, 4.2, p. 94. The example is presented and discussed by Cécile Treffort, "Genèse du cimetière chrétien: étude sur l'accompagnement du mourant, les funérailles, la commémoration des défunts et les lieux d'inhumation à l'époque carolingienne (entre Loire et Rhin, milieu VIIIe –début XIe siècle)," doctoral thesis, 4 vols. typescript, Université Lumière-Lyon II, 1994, 1:196–97.

who, by a bond of spiritual parenthood linking them to the child, were able to act as guarantors in the baptismal pact between the child and God.[10] The heretical voices that in the eleventh and twelfth centuries spoke out against infant baptism and insisted on the commitment of adult catechumens as the only valid form of baptism posed, in the first instance, a doctrinal problem. Confronting these critics forced Christian polemicists to go beyond the strictly Augustinian reference to the "faith of others" and grope toward the notion of infused virtue transmitted by the sacrament.[11] But in addition to the purely doctrinal challenge, these critics were throwing doubt upon the very foundations of social practices that relied on the commitments of others however expressed, whether in acts of faith (in both the Christian and the feudal sense) or of charity, or in giving surety (*fideiussio*). Cluny was doubly affected by the issue: indirectly, in the pastoral sphere, as a possessor of churches and parishes; more directly, as a fraternity in which kinships based on personal choice were built up. At the height of the Gregorian reform, that vast undertaking to include the laity in the Church, Hugh of Semur actively forged spiritual links with princely and aristocratic families, for example, when he became godfather to the future emperor Henry IV, or baptized Odo, the son of Count Thibaud I of Champagne.[12] It was thus hardly surprising that Peter the Venerable, in constructing a genuine Church system, should seize the opportunity to debate the nature of the solidarity behind the social links.

All Scripture and the Salvation of All

Infant baptism thus was Peter's point of entry into controversy with the Petrobrusians. His first concern was to define the modalities of the debate, while demonstrating the basic problem posed by Peter of Bruis and his disciples in their polemic. What axiomatic structure could enable debate to take place? What were the bases of Christian society? Upon what ground could one take up position in order to reply to opponents who recognized only the authority of the Gospels? How was one to persuade them that refusing baptism to children was to undermine the all-or-nothing logic upon which the economy of salvation was founded, the notion that what availed for one availed for all?

10. On the notion of a "baptismal pact," see Michel Rubelin, "Entrée dans la vie, entrée dans la chrétienté, entrée dans la société: autour du baptême à l'époque carolingienne," *Annales de l'Est* 34 (1982): 31–51, here 49–50. More generally, on godparents and the vital matter of "spiritual parenthood": Joseph H. Lynch, *Godparents and Kinship in Early Medieval Europe* (Princeton, 1986); Anita Guerreau-Jalabert, "*Spiritus* et *caritas:* le baptême dans la société médiévale," in *La parenté spirituelle*, ed. Françoise Heritier-Augé and Elisabeth Copet-Rougier (Paris, 1995), pp. 133–203.

11. Didier, "La question du baptême des enfants," pp. 199–200.

12. Joseph H. Lynch, "Hugh I of Cluny's Sponsorship of Henry IV: Its Context and Consequences," *Speculum* 60 (1985): 800–826, esp. 816ff. on Thibaud's son. In chapter 6 below we examine a Coincy donation charter documenting the baptism of Odo by Hugh of Semur.

If the abbot of Cluny's word is to be believed, Peter of Bruis and his disciples were impressed by Christ's missionary injunction to the apostles in Mark 16:15–16: "Go ye into the whole world and preach the gospel to every creature. He that believeth and is baptized shall be saved; but he that believeth not shall be condemned."[13] Reading the text *Iudaico more*,[14] according to a literalist interpretation, the Petrobrusians asserted that it was faith that saved, and that children, too young to have faith, could not be saved. The heretics therefore "rebaptized" believers who were old enough to have faith. Of course in their own terms, this was not rebaptism, since they believed infant baptism to be null and void.

To his summary of the Petrobrusian view Peter the Venerable replied with a reductio ad absurdum that reveals the full extent of what was at stake in the debate. If, says Peter, such a literalist interpretation of Christ's words in Mark is true, then for generations there has been no Church, no bishop, no priest or deacon, no Christians; "all our fathers" and "saints without number," incorrectly baptized in infancy, are now "companions of the demons" in hell.[15] Having initially discredited an opposition ill placed to shoulder the consequences of premises so absurdly stated, Peter sets about convincing them more methodically of the necessity of infant baptism. Yet on what ground should the debate take place? Here, one of Peter's main aims is to calmly define the rules of the "dispute," one in which arguments are sometimes based on *ratio* and sometimes on *auctoritates*. Again, there was need for agreement as to the authorities accepted. It was no good for Peter the Venerable to resort to the Fathers, for the Petrobrusians rejected all testimony apart from the words and deeds of Christ as related in the Gospels. Thus in his demonstration, he does not allow himself to quote Augustine in spite of that Father's inescapably important contribution to infant baptism.[16] Peter always tries to start out from the New Testament and end there.[17] Though he accepts this restricted scriptural territory, he nevertheless refuses to be hemmed in by it. Much of his response to the Petrobrusians' first proposition is an effort to prove to them that their cuts in the revealed text make no sense, since all sacred history leads up to and away from Christ.[18] Having thus "proved" the validity of the Old Testament and the whole of the New in the light of the Gospels, Peter prevalidates all future recourse to the Bible as a whole both on the immediate issue of baptism and on the others to be dealt with. One must

13. *CP,* 10, ll. 2–4.

14. *CP,* 77, l. 1.

15. *CP,* 11.

16. Augustine's most important texts on infant baptism are detailed in Jean-Charles Didier, *Le baptême des enfants dans la tradition de l'Eglise,* Monumenta Christiana Selecta, 7 (Tournai, 1959), esp. pp. 55ff.

17. *CP,* 69, ll. 1–4. Earlier, in para. 12, ll. 12–13, Peter makes reference to the theoretical heritage of Ambrose, Augustine, Jerome, Leo the Great, Gregory the Great, "and others."

18. *CP,* 34–66 (*probatio totius Novi Testamenti; probatio totius Veteris Testamenti*).

either accept all the revealed truth of the Scriptures or reject it entirely. In reflecting upon the reasons that make infant baptism necessary, Peter's object is to demonstrate the sociological and ecclesiological implications of this all-or-nothing logic. Either all Christians are saved, including children, or none is.

The Church's Faith

Having established the rules for the debate, Peter can concentrate on the issue of infant baptism itself. He begins by recalling the many miracles in which Christ saved children in both body and spirit.[19] Christ's intervention was in response not so much to a personal request (*pro se*) as to the pleading of a third party, a father for a son, or sisters for a brother, as in the case of Martha, Mary, and Lazarus. Examples thus drawn from the life of Christ, the very head of the body that is the Church, enable Peter to advance an obvious rhetorical question: "Christ having imparted so much to others for the faith of a single believer, shall the faith of the entire Church avail the little baptized ones nothing?"[20] The reference to Christ as head here should be seen as an allusion to the theology of created grace, even then—in the mid-twelfth century—being elaborated in response to questions raised by infant baptism. It enabled the *Corpus Christi* (Body of Christ) to be conceived of as "the domain of *Christ's* grace . . . possessed in full by the Head and spreading throughout *His* entire body."[21]

There then follow miracles drawn from the Acts of the Apostles that also illustrate the efficacy of "others' faith." Following the same chronological and thematic logic, Peter the Venerable adds the Pauline theme of "the unbelieving husband sanctified by the believing wife" and "the unbelieving wife sanctified by the believing husband" (1 Corinthians 7:14).[22] This is an implicit reference to the theorizing about Christian marriage begun by Carolingian clerics and considerably widened in the first three decades of the twelfth century to envisage marriage as a "germ of charity" (*seminarium caritatis*),[23] as a "sacrament" or *sacrae rei signum*, and as a vehicle of grace.[24] The couple is a point of reference for Pe-

19. *CP,* 69: Peter refers to the classic cases of the woman of Canaan (Matthew 15:22–28; Mark 7:24–30), the centurion's servant and the son of the ruler at Capernaum (Matthew 8:5–13; John 4: 46–53), and Jairus's daughter (Matthew 9:18–26; Mark 5:21–24; Luke 8:40–56).

20. *CP,* 69, ll. 14–16.

21. Yves Congar, *L'Eglise, de saint Augustin à l'époque moderne* (Paris, 1970), p. 163 (author's emphasis).

22. *CP,* 72, ll. 14–15. The question of the circulation of grace within marriage based on 1 Corinthians 7:14 and Augustine's commentary on it (*De bono coniugali,* 11.13, CSEL 41, pp. 204–5) was earlier touched upon by Syrus, *Vita sancti Maioli,* 2.21, ll. 8–14, in Dominique Iogna-Prat, *"Agni immaculati": recherches sur les sources hagiographiques relatives à saint Maieul de Cluny (954–994)* (Paris, 1988), pp. 241 and 364.

23. Gratian's definition (*Decretum* 2.35.1.1), erroneously attributed to Augustine. Quoted by Guerreau-Jalabert, *"Spiritus* et *caritas,"* p. 169 and n. 26.

24. Jean Gaudemet, *Le mariage en Occident: les moeurs et le droit* (Paris, 1987), esp. pp. 188–91.

ter, being the basic unit in which the faith of one operates for another. When he writes to his brothers Pontius, Jordan, and Armannus after the death of their mother, Raingard, he reminds them how, on the eve of her departure to enter the nunnery of Marcigny-sur-Loire, she went to meditate at her husband's tomb and in an unbroken stream confessed her own sins and those of the dead man. "She spoke," says Peter, "as it were through the mouth of the deceased, as if, by an exchange of persons, her husband was repenting in the person of his wife."[25] The baptism of children predicated a similar exchange of persons. If the faith of one could operate for the other (*fide mutua*) in the bond that constituted the married couple (*gemina cathena*), why could not the same apply to parents on behalf of their child and with stronger reason to the Church on behalf of her children? The incongruity of the question leads Peter forcibly to enunciate the principle of sacramental mediation. The parent or parent's spiritual substitute (*pro parente*) is a "mediator of the sacrament of faith," which purifies the infant of the original stain transmitted by generation.[26] With remarkable economy, Peter defines the three circles in which "faith on behalf of others" is exercised: the family unit; spiritual parenthood through godparents; the great spiritual family of the Church.[27] It is noteworthy that Peter places these three circles on an equal footing, without dissociating physical parents from spiritual ones; the common view since Carolingian times had been that "those who had carnally engendered the child, thereby transmitting to him the stain of sin, could not be suitable actors in his spiritual regeneration."[28] The examples that follow, taken from the Old Testament, allow Peter to finish his course through sacred history to and from Christ. He names, in passing, Abraham, Moses, David, Samuel, Isaiah, Jeremiah, Daniel, Job, and the Maccabees, who "strove to perfect with the perfection of their faith and charity the imperfections of the imperfect and supplied to others what they lacked." The reference to Old Testament figures is not simply a pretext to quote Christic antecedents. It allows Peter to make a notable verbal elision. These figures were precursory examples of "faith's and charity's perfecting role" (*perfectione fidei et caritatis*).[29] Hitherto Peter has spoken only of faith for others, but by bringing Old Testament prehistory into play he is able to widen the horizon to include solidarity through *caritas* (charity) and leave behind the strictly sacramental reference implied by faith.

From the use of scriptural authority in support of his case, Peter the Venerable moves to the area of sufficient reason. The problem at issue is the thorny one of *propria fides* (an individual's own, proper faith). Peter reduces the Petrobrusian case to a "neither . . . nor" type proposition: neither baptism without

25. *Ep.*, 53, 1:153–73, here 161.
26. *CP*, 72, ll. 17–21 and 22–25.
27. On the problem of *fides ecclesiae* in Peter the Venerable's work, see Jean-Pierre Torrell, "L'Eglise dans l'oeuvre et la vie de Pierre le Vénérable," *Revue thomiste* 77 (1977): 382–84.
28. Guerreau-Jalabert, "*Spiritus* et *caritas*," p. 162.
29. *CP*, 73, ll. 10–12.

one's own proper faith, nor proper faith without baptism, the one being impossible without the other.[30] As Peter sees it, falsification of one part of the proposition will destroy it in its entirety; if the first term is invalid, the second will be and vice versa. Peter raises the case of unbaptized martyrs; they exemplify those who have faith but no baptism in the sacramental sense. Are they damned? Not if the Apocalypse (7:14–15) is to be believed. That passage speaks of martyrdom as a baptism of blood and declares that "they who have come out of great tribulation . . . are before the throne of God; and they serve him day and night in his temple." The conclusion falls like a knife: "If the martyrs are saved by their own faith without baptism, why should not the little ones be saved by baptism without their own faith?"[31] Surely, as the Petrobrusians say, "the one is impossible without the other"!

Having thus turned the tables on his opponents, Peter comes to the word of Christ invoked by them, Mark 16:15: *Ite in orbem universum, predicate evangelium omni creature*—"Go ye into the whole world and preach the gospel to every creature." Peter asks what Christ meant by "every creature." Surely he meant "mankind," for Scripture often employs synecdoche, the figure of speech that intends the part where the whole is expressed? But what is important here is the universality of the commission given to the apostles, expressed by the indefinite *omni* (every) linked to the imperative *predicate* (preach). Not all can be concerned, and yet no one can be excluded from the mission. How could they have faith who have never heard?—"for the Lord is just and . . . has never demanded anyone to pay for what he has not committed."[32] Therefore children cannot be excluded from the "totality" realized in the Kingdom of Heaven, any more than Jewish children were of old. Peter resorts to what he sees as an obvious argument based upon scriptural typology. Is it conceivable for Christian children to be lost whereas Jewish children, circumcised on the eighth day, merited salvation? Peter in this way turns circumcision, envisaged as a rite that in Old Testament times purged original sin, into the typological equivalent of baptism. Like baptism, circumcision was not a matter of the individual's own faith but a rite dictated by the faith of another. The typological interplay between Old and New Testaments enables Peter to return to Christ and the theme of the universality of Christ's redeeming work. By one, Adam, came death: by another, Christ, came life. As Paul says in Romans 5:18, the offense of one brought about the condemnation of all: conversely, the justice of one brought justification to all and washed them not only of their original sin but also of their current sins (*actualia*). The destiny of humanity thus turns on acts of solidarity—the Fall as well as the Redemption—from which no one is exempt. The telescoping of human history, aligning Adam with Christ, permits Peter to conclude by reinvoking the

30. *CP,* 74, ll. 2–4.
31. *CP,* 76, ll. 9–11.
32. *CP,* 79, ll. 25–26.

reductive all-or-nothing law: either all are saved, including the children, or none are. He ends his consideration of this first proposition with the image of Christ bidding the apostles to suffer the little children to come to him that he may bless them. It is a final note that is in harmony with Peter's elaborations on the "universality" of baptism in *Adversus Iudeos*. In that work, he invokes the testimony of Psalm 71(72):8: *Et dominabitur a mari usque ad mare et a flumine usque ad terminos terrae*—"And he shall rule from sea to sea: and from the river unto the ends of the earth." He explains that the river in question is none other than the Jordan, whose water, since Christ's own baptism therein, has poured into the remotest parts of the earth to encompass all peoples.[33]

The Sociological Implications of Peter's All-or-Nothing Logic

In the context of the contemporary debate on infant baptism, Peter the Venerable had a good case based on well-marshaled authorities and adequate reasoning. That said, his importance in this particular area of doctrine remained secondary; the material on baptism was, after all, only a minor part of his work. There were two weighty arguments in favor of infant baptism being formulated in the twelfth century that Peter did not use. The first of these usefully distinguished between the faith of adults (*sacramentum*) and sacramental efficacy (*res sacramenti*). The second one appealed to the notion of *sacramentum fidei* (the sacrament of faith), and was made use of by Hugh of Amiens in his *Dialogues* and *Contra Haereticos*.[34] Archbishop of Rouen and a former Cluniac monk, Hugh set out to demonstrate the universality of the work of salvation in its various modes of operation during sacred history. From Adam to Abraham, he argued, mankind was saved by faith alone, without a "visible remedy." With Abraham came "the mystery of circumcision," though for males only (*masculi*). Finally, with Christ, came "the sacrament of faith," which was a work of charity. Discussing this "sacrament," Hugh carefully distinguished between the efficient *grace* in baptism administered to children and the *works* expected of adults.[35] He thus began the reflections of early scholasticism upon the complementarity of *munus* and *usus*: the grace conferred in baptism was seen as a gift (*gratia in munere*) that would enable the child to grow up and do good (*ex munere usum*).

Peter the Venerable contented himself with the traditional Augustinian thesis of faith on another's behalf. His most original contribution was to place the sacrament of marriage and infant baptism in a genetic relationship. The efficient

33. *AJ*, 2.808–10, and see 4.1294–99.

34. The distinction between *sacramentum* and *res sacramenti* appears in, among other places, the Sentences of the School of Anselm of Laon: see Odon Lottin, *Psychologie et morale aux XIIe et XIIIe siècles*, vol. 5: *Problèmes d'histoire littéraire* (Gembloux, 1959), no. 364, p. 273; I am grateful to Gilbert Dahan for pointing this reference out to me. For Hugh of Amiens, see *Dialogorum libri septem*, 5.7, PL 192:1200AC, and *Contra Haereticos*, 1.11, PL 192:1266B–1268A.

35. *Contra Haereticos*, 1.11, PL 192:1266D.

grace in the couple makes the parents (or their substitutes) into "mediators of the sacrament of faith." From the basic unit represented by the nuclear family to the whole Church, which is itself a great spiritual family, faith on behalf of another is constantly efficient. Somewhat later in the treatise, when he comes to discussing the help given to the dead by the living, Peter recalls the pious (though nonsacramental) act of the early Christians who underwent baptism on behalf of the dead.[36] Similar principles, developed with insistence throughout *Contra Petrobrusianos*, are not simply a doctrinal matter. They lie behind the "holist" conception that Peter has of Christian society, in which the parts complement one another within a whole. Exclude the children from the Redemption, and the whole *Ecclesia* disappears: it would be tantamount to saying that the grace of the Christ-head does not supply the whole of his body, the Church. Expressed in terms of "faith" or "charity," the notion of necessary solidarity runs like a thread through all Peter the Venerable's assertions and is, logically, at the center of his ecclesiology.

THE CHURCH: A CONGREGATION OF BELIEVERS OR A TEMPLE OF STONE?

From one foundation element, the rite of admission into the Church, Peter the Venerable passes to another: the importance of the church of stone, the material representation (*fabrica corporalis*) of the congregation of believers. Having defended the social links upheld by infant baptism and expressions of faith on others' behalf, he has also to defend the physical places of worship, the "basilicas and altars," attacked in the second Petrobrusian proposition debated in *Contra Petrobrusianos*.[37] The Petrobrusians radically contested the use of such places, preaching that it was "vain to build temples, since the Church of God consists not in a multitude of assembled stones, but in the unity of gathered believers."[38] Reinforcing their words with deeds, Peter of Bruis and his disciples had desecrated churches and destroyed altars.[39]

"A Special Privilege: A House Dedicated to God Alone"

In his reply, Peter the Venerable justifies the existence of special places for sacrifice and prayer (*ad sacrificandum et orandum*) in part by pointing out that they are a feature not simply of the Christian tradition but of others too. The

36. *CP,* 237, commenting on 1 Corinthians 15:29.

37. *CP,* 95–111. The best analysis of this part of the treatise is Torrell, "L'Eglise dans l'oeuvre et la vie de Pierre le Vénérable," 374–77. While analyzing this proposition I had the benefit of Alain Guerreau's ever-stimulating ideas, for which I take this opportunity to express my gratitude.

38. *CP,* 89, ll. 13–15.

39. *CP,* 4, ll. 8–9.

Jews had their Temple, pagans have their sanctuaries, and Christians their churches. "For every religion," he asserts, "desires a place where its sacred things can be venerated and more devoted service be given to its established usages."[40] The essence of Peter's refutation is, however, based on Scripture. He reminds his adversaries of the distant witness of the altars Noah and Abraham dedicated to the Lord, the "portable tabernacle" of Moses, and the stone Temple that David and Solomon undertook to build with divine approval. If David "did well"—see 3 (1) Kings 8:18–19—and later tradition did well to follow his example, then the Petrobrusians "do evil" to repeat the ancient error of those who preferred to worship Baal everywhere rather than God in his Temple. In the light of these Old Testament examples, Peter sees an obvious argument. If the Jews had a pure, consecrated place for their sacrifices, how could Christ, in whom all their sacrifices were fulfilled, have no consecrated place? Such a situation would be all the more absurd inasmuch as Jesus, entering the Temple, spoke of it, in Luke 19:45–46, as his house: "My house is the house of prayer." The expansion of Christianity, prefigured by Isaiah's injunction to "enlarge the place of thy tent" (Isaiah 54:2), represents the move from a single place, the Temple, to a multiplicity of churches, cemented together by "one Lord, one faith, one baptism, one Church, one offering."[41] It also represents a change of mode, since henceforth it is "in spirit and in truth" that sacrifice of "a clean offering" is made, and no longer in Jerusalem, but "in every place," as foretold in Malachi 1:11.[42] In *Adversus Iudeos*, Peter returns to this prophecy in order to force his opponents to recognize its fulfillment in the building of churches and altars all over the earth, where, without ceasing, sacrifice is made of "the lamb of God."[43]

Following the course of history, Peter refers next to the consecrated places of the apostolic age: the seven churches of the Apocalypse and the various churches addressed by Paul in his Epistles. The abbot of Cluny points out that by "church" the apostle meant not simply a spiritual association (*congregatio spiritualis fidelium*), but also a material reality (*corporalis structura*). For in 1 Corinthians 11:18 and onward, Paul compared the "human house," in which the body was nourished and in which the activities of this mortal life took place, to the church, "the house of God," dedicated to the Lord's supper, the dwelling of eternal life, in which the soul was fed.[44] Then came the temple that Peter, the prince of the apostles, consecrated to Christ in Rome, the "capital of the world" (*in urbe orbis capite*), amid a multitude of pagan temples. The abbot of Cluny quotes Leo the Great's remark that this temple was "a victory monument to the Cross of Christ among the Roman citadels."[45] From his own firsthand knowledge of

40. *CP*, 100, ll. 3–4.
41. *CP*, 101, ll. 9–12.
42. *CP*, 103, ll. 10–12.
43. *AJ*, 3.899–905. Peter refers to Malachi's prophecy later in *CP*, 163, ll. 28–31.
44. *CP*, 108.
45. *CP*, 109, ll. 10–17; cf. Leo the Great, *Sermones*, 82.5, *PL* 54:425B.

Rome, he reports having seen for himself the oratories and altars of the cata-combs, the places of memory (*monimentum*) of early Christianity. After Peter the apostle, he evokes the names of Trophimus in Arles and "all the streams of Gal-lic faith" that flowed from that "fountainhead." The enumeration is a long one: Irenaeus at Lyon, Crescens at Vienne, Ursinus at Bourges, Paul at Narbonne, Saturninus at Toulouse, Austremonius in the Auvergne, Martial at Limoges, Bordeaux, and Poitiers, Frontus at Périgueux, Eutropius at Saintes, Gatian at Tours, Julian at Le Mans, Denis at Paris, Potentianus and Savinianus at Sens, Lucian at Beauvais, Andochius at Autun, and Benignus at Dijon. They all tore down idols, built new churches, or transformed former pagan temples into churches—proof, if it were necessary, of the permanence of places of worship in history. Other apostles did similar things in the east: Paul and Andrew in Illyria, Greece, and Scythia; John and Philip in Asia; Simon and Jude in the Persian kingdom; Thomas and Bartholomew in India; Matthew in Ethiopia.[46]

Peter the Venerable's purpose in recalling the missionary activity undertaken in the four corners of the earth is to emphasize the antiquity of the monumen-tal tradition. The "temples of stone" being built on ever larger and more lavish lines in the twelfth century—beginning with Cluny III, the *maior ecclesia* of Christendom, consecrated in 1130[47]—are thus not outlandish or vain novelties but rooted in a long line of ancient practice. The notion of unity within a mul-tiplicity of churches is not an issue here, since the Petrobrusian conception of the Church, in its spiritual sense, is of the "congregation of the faithful." What Peter has to do is discuss the material structure of the Church, justify the pres-ence of the divine in consecrated places, and answer the question already asked by Solomon in 3 (1) Kings 8:27: "Is it then to be thought that God should in-deed dwell upon earth? For if heaven, and the heaven of heavens, cannot con-tain thee, how much less this house which I have built?"[48] Peter's answer makes use of the notion of congruent place (*locus congruus*). The history of religions and Scripture teach that the Lord's "singular essence admits no sharing," that con-secrated places are "more intimate," and that it is God's will "to have the special privilege of a house dedicated to him alone that he may infuse the people pray-ing there with greater grace and more effectively grant their prayers."[49]

"The Church Is Not Walls But Believers"[50]

The eleventh and twelfth centuries were a time of unceasing building effort during which Latin Christendom covered itself in a "white mantle of churches." The notion of "congruent place"—a physical location consecrated

46. *CP*, 110–11.

47. Kenneth J. Conant, *Cluny: les églises et la maison du chef d'ordre* (Mâcon, 1968), p. 110.

48. *CP*, 98, l. 27.

49. *CP*, 104, ll. 19–20, and 98, ll. 30–32.

50. The heading is that of Yves Congar, *Sacerdoce et laïcat devant leurs tâches d'évangélisation et de civilisation* (Paris, 1962), p. 295.

to the divine—was, however, far from clear. Analysis of medieval heretical movements shows that the question became particularly insistent from the 1020s on. In his *Vita Gauzlini*, Andreas of Fleury, who died before 1056, reported that heretics at Orléans "did not believe that there was such a thing as the Church or that because there was containment [by a church] it could be said that anything was contained [the Church]."[51] In 1025, the Acts of the Synod of Arras included a lengthy discourse on the problem in an attempt to contradict those heretics who asserted "that there is nothing in the temple of God that makes it any more worthy of the service of religion than the bedchamber of a private house."[52] Speaking of the heretics of Soissons in a chapter of his *Monodiae*, Guibert of Nogent observed, "They make no distinction for cemeteries between sacred ground and any other type of ground."[53] Henry of Lausanne and his disciples for their part treated temples of stone with derision.[54] In the light of such documentation, Peter the Venerable's reply to the Petrobrusians may be regarded as a classic statement. One need only look at the main points of the argument in the Acts of the Synod of Arras. Against the heretics' contention, the Acts insist that the temple of God has nothing in common with a bedchamber. It is a specially (*specialiter*) designated place in which God is "more present" (*praesentius*) and where he gives his grace to petitioners "more richly" (*uberius*).[55] This special presence, which is daily renewed in the eucharistic celebration, has nothing to do with any delight the Lord might have in "the height of the walls or the variety of the paving" but is "because there in particular is the meeting of the faithful."[56] In other words, it is the content (the Church, the congregation of the faithful) that justifies the container (the building). As Peter points out later in his treatise when discussing the Eucharist, it is "for the sacrifices that the temple and altar have been built" and not vice versa.[57]

The case of those defending places of worship was actually rather poorly founded. Christian tradition had not paid huge attention to the issue. In John

51. *Vie de Gauzlin, abbé de Fleury: Vita Gauzlini abbatis Floriacensis monasterii*, 56, ed. and French trans. by Robert-Henri Bautier and Gillette Labory, Sources d'Histoire médiévale publiées par l'Institut de Recherche et d'Histoire des Textes, 2 (Paris, 1969), p. 98.

52. *Acta synodi Atrebatensis*, 3–4, PL 142:1284B–1288C, here 1284C.

53. Guibert of Nogent, *Monodiae*, 3.17, ed. and French trans. by Edmond-René Labande, Les Classiques de l'Histoire de France au Moyen Age, 34 (Paris, 1981), p. 430. Eng. trans., *A Monk's Confession: The Memoirs of Guibert of Nogent*, trans. Paul J. Archambault (University Park, 1996), here p. 196.

54. Raoul Manselli, "Il monaco Enrico e la sua eresia," *Bulletino dell'Istituto Storico Italiano per il Medio Evo e Archivio Muratoriano* 65 (1953): 61–62. Monique Zerner thinks it is unclear whether the heretic denounced in this text is actually Henry of Lausanne. Cf. Bernard of Clairvaux, *Epistolae*, 241, "Quanta audivimus," in *Opera omnia*, vol. 7, ed. Jean Leclercq and Henri-Marie Rochais (Rome, 1974), 125–27, here 125. The denunciation is confirmed in other terms by Geoffrey of Clairvaux in his *Vita prima sancti Bernardi*, PL 185:313.

55. *Acta synodi Atrebatensis*, PL 142:1284CD, 1285B, and 1286A.

56. Ibid., 1286AB.

57. *CP*, 157, ll. 5–7.

4:21–24, Jesus told the Samaritan woman that "the hour cometh, when you shall neither on this mountain, nor in Jerusalem adore the Father," but that "true adorers shall adore the Father in spirit and in truth"—words that play down, even depreciate, all relation to sacred space. The scriptural evidence that the writer of the Acts of the Synod of Arras and Peter the Venerable himself could rely upon was in fact quite insubstantial; both made use of the same references, apart from two Old Testament reports of "holy ground" divinely revealed to Moses (Exodus 3:5) and Joshua (Joshua 5:16), which occur only in the Arras text.[58] Patristic support was meager too; the Christians of the early centuries were more immediately preoccupied with eschatology than with materializing the sacred.[59] In the east, a careful distinction was made between the community of the faithful (the *Ecclesia*) and the ecclesiastical building (*naos, ephtirion*). In the west, however, a curious ambiguity persisted between the container (the church) and the contained (the Church). Even so, for centuries, the word *ecclesia* connoted primarily, even exclusively in some writers' works, the *congregatio fidelium*. Hippolytus of Rome asserted that the Church was not "a house made of stone or clay, but the holy gathering of those who live in justice."[60] Contrasting the Church with Solomon's Temple, Lactantius maintained that the Church "is the true temple of God and is not in the walls but in the heart and faith of the men who believe in him and are called the faithful."[61] Jerome commented that "the Church consists not in the walls, but in the truth of the dogma and true faith,"[62] a slogan that found an echo in Victorinus's amused question to Simplicianus reported by Augustine of Hippo in his *Confessiones*: "Is it the walls that make the Christians?"[63] Augustine left a very unclear legacy on the matter of sacred space. In the seventy-eighth of his *Epistolae*, he recognized that holy places had a certain power; but in *De cura gerenda mortuorum*, he was skeptical about the utility of burial. Again in letter 78, he maintained that God was everywhere and nei-

58. *Acta synodi Atrebatensis, PL* 142:1287B.

59. Outside of issues relating to funerary space, the question of the materiality of the sacred in the early centuries of Christianity and in the Middle Ages has never been studied as a topic in its own right. On funerary space in the early centuries, see Yvette Duval, *Auprès des saints corps et âmes: l'inhumation "ad sanctos" dans la chrétienté d'Orient et d'Occident du IIIe au VIIe siècle* (Paris, 1988). An excellent, though brief, introduction to the materiality of the sacred in the medieval west is in Congar, *Sacerdoce et laïcat*, pp. 295–303. See also Giles Constable, "Opposition to Pilgrimage in the Middle Ages," in *Mélanges G. Fransen*, 1, *Studia Gratiana* 19 (1976): 123–46, esp. 126 on patristic reservations; Alain Boureau, "*Vel sedens, vel transiens:* la création d'un espace pontifical au Xe et XIIe siècle," in *Luoghi sacri e spazi della santità*, ed. Sofia Boesch Gajano and Lucetta Scaraffia (Turin, 1990), pp. 367–79.

60. Hippolyte de Rome, *Commentaire sur Daniel*, 1.17, ed. and French trans. by Maurice Lefèvre, *SC* 14 (Paris, 1947), p. 103.

61. *Institutiones divinae*, 4.13, ed. with French trans. by Pierre Monat, *SC* 377 (Paris, 1992), p. 122.

62. *Tractatos in Psalmos, de Ps. 133*, ed. Germanus Morin, *CCSL* 34, p. 285, ll. 81–85.

63. *Confessiones*, 8.2.4.

ther contained nor enclosed in any place.[64] Acknowledging the expression of such views, Peter the Venerable, in his *Sermo de transfiguratione domini*, concedes that the Lord needs no earthly tabernacle since his dwelling is in heaven.[65] Within the antiheretical literature of the eleventh and twelfth centuries, the redactor of the Acts of Arras appears to be unique in venturing to appeal to patristic authority. He quotes from Augustine's commentary on Psalm 80, in which the bishop of Hippo acknowledged the reality that ecclesiastical buildings (*fabricas*) were necessary for the time being (*ad tempus*), since "without them, we should be unable to do here and now [*hoc tempore*] what we need to do in order to reach heaven."[66] Abelard similarly claimed Augustinian authority in the 1120s, when he maintained that God was omnipresent and that the dwelling of the blessed was independent of all localization.[67] The reservations of the heretics concerning the materiality of the sacred were thus rooted in a long orthodox tradition.

The Slow Emergence of the Notion of "Congruent Place"

Medieval clerics continued to have a reserved attitude toward sacred places at least until the eleventh century. A brief examination of a number of encyclopedic works predating Peter the Venerable or contemporary with him helps to show that the change in attitude took place in the period 1020–1130, as revealed by the antiheretical writings of the times.[68]

In his famous *Etymologiae* (8.1.8), Isidore of Seville (circa 560–636) recognizes the Church only in the spiritual sense of the term, as the *Ecclesia catholica* or the assembly of the faithful (*congregatio, convocatio*). Isidore's chapter (15.4) on "sacred buildings" includes a list of buildings reserved for worship in both pagan antiquity (*fana, propitiatorium*) and Christian tradition (*sacra, sancta, monasterium, basilica* ...). Not the slightest consideration is given to churches or cemeteries as sacred spaces. Rabanus Maurus (780–856), in his *De rerum naturis*, allegorized Isidore's material. According to him, the temple of stone had no special importance. The Church, on its contemporary pilgrimage, was as temporary as the tabernacle constructed by Moses in the wilderness, while the Temple

---

64. *De cura gerenda mortuorum*, 2–3, ed. Gustave Combès, Bibliothèque augustinienne, 2.1 (Paris, 1948), pp. 466–74. *Epistolae*, 78, ed. Alois Golbacher, *CSEL* 34, p. 335. These places are cited by Constable, "Opposition to Pilgrimage," p. 126, n. 4.

65. *PL* 189:966C, responding to the apostle Peter's offer, on seeing Jesus, Moses, and Elijah on the mountain of the Transfiguration, to make for them "three tabernacles" (Matthew 17:4).

66. *Acta synodi Atrebatensis*, PL 142:1287A.

67. Peter Abelard, *Dialogus inter philosophum, judaeum et christianum*, ed. Rudolf Thomas (Stuttgart/Bad Cannstadt, 1970), pp. 140ff., referring to *De doctrina christiana*, 1.10; for Eng. trans. see bibliography.

68. Guidance to the abundant material in this area may be had from Günther Binding, *Der früh- und hochmittelalterliche Bauherr als sapiens architectus* (Darmstadt, 1996), which assembles the necessary bibliography appearing since Joseph Sauer's seminal work, *Symbolik des Kirchengebäudes und seiner Ausstattung in der Auffassung des Mittelalters*, 2d ed.(Freiburg im B., 1924).

built by Solomon in Jerusalem betokened the Church to come, whose form was hidden by the veil separating the sanctuary from the holy of holies.[69] According to this logic, the content (the congregation of the faithful) and the container (the place of worship) bore only a figurative relation to each other, that suggested by the apostle Paul when he described believers in Christ as "God's building" (1 Corinthians 3:9). In his *Liber de officiis*, Amalarius of Metz (circa 775–circa 850) depicted the Church as a symbolic construction, as a Jerusalem whose walls (the faithful) rested on solid foundations (Christ). In the structure of the walls, he pointed to the most advanced, the masters, who were as "stones upon the stones," and ascribed the solidity of the construction to the mortar composed of lime (charity) mixed with the sand and water.[70] It was only around the middle of the eleventh century that the analogy began to be turned around in such a way that the church signified the Church. In his *Tractatus de sacramentis Ecclesiae*, Bruno of Segni characterized the figure as a metonymy, whereby the container signified the content.[71] From then on the way was opened for countless exegetical equivalences to be drawn in either direction: the people representing the paving of the church; hermits, the crypts; the doctors, the windows; the bishops, the columns. Or vice versa—for the changed attitude depended upon the reversibility of the relationships—the paving signifying the people, the crypts the hermits, the doctors the windows, and the columns the bishops. Thus in the age of the Romanesque, the age of cathedral building, God was seen as an architect and Scripture as a building—or, conversely, architecture was seen as a reflection of the doctrinal coherence of the divine word. Similarly, the theological reflections nourished by Scripture would themselves soon take on the monumental shape of the *Summae*.[72] It was not simply a matter of architectural symbolism. In the twelfth century, the buildings of the Bible actually became subjects for representation. In his *Commentary on Ezechiel*, Richard of Saint-Victor (died 1173) did not simply describe the temple spoken of by the prophet; he mapped it out as seen from the front and side, concerning himself with questions of scale and measure. Such a borrowing from contemporary civil architecture is, as Walter Cahn has so neatly described it, "a striking irruption of factual observation in the midst of an exegetical practice that is otherwise overwhelmingly philological in its orientation."[73]

69. *De rerum Naturis*, 14.22, *PL* 111:391–98, here 398B–D

70. *Liber de officiis*, 4.3.4–7, ed. Jean-Michel Hanssens, Studi e Testi, 140 (Vatican, 1950), 2:415ff. Quoted by Binding, *Der früh- und hochmittelalterliche Bauherr*, pp. 383–84.

71. *PL* 165:1092AB. Quoted by Binding, *Der früh- und hochmittelalterliche Bauherr*, p. 377.

72. I am indebted here to Rainer Berndt, "La théologie comme système du monde: sur l'évolution des Sommes théologiques de Hugues de Saint-Victor à saint Thomas d'Aquin," *Revue des sciences philosophiques et théologiques* 78 (1994): 555–72, esp. 556ff.

73. "Architecture and Exegesis: Richard of St.-Victor's Ezechiel Commentary and Its Illustrations," *Art Bulletin* 76 (1994): 53–68, here 62; I am grateful to Guy Lobrichon for bringing this article to my attention.

It is hardly surprising that such a major conceptual shift affected the thinking of liturgists. The *Gemma animae* of Honorius of Autun, who died about 1137, is a long treatise on the *Ecclesia* conceived both as a space and as an institution.[74] Honorius begins by alluding to the holy places of the Old Testament; this enables him to make typological parallels with the Christian church. He notes that Moses' tabernacle was divided into two; transferred to a Christian church context, the first part corresponds to the *domus anterior* (front, or western part of the church) in which the faithful take their place, the second to the *sancta sanctorum* (holy of holies, close to the altar) of the clergy. A chapter on "chapels" allows him to speak of the ancient period of the "little churches made out of hides" before the time when temples were fixed in the earth and made permanent with buildings of stone. The importance attributed to the material structure is perceptible by virtue of the very detail of the monumental exegesis. The altar thus analyzed is an epitome of "ecclesial conjunction." It is constructed from a number of stones, representing the people who are one in the sacrifice of Christ. The relics placed in the altar are a treasury of Christ's wisdom and knowledge. The *capsae* (reliquaries?) placed above are the apostles and martyrs. The ornaments spread upon it are the confessors and virgins who "adorn" the Christ. Although he never classifies the sacred space in a firm, clear-cut fashion, Honorius nevertheless distinguishes the church from its immediate environs. The cemetery is the place where the dead rest in the bosom (*gremium*) of the Church; the cloister, which is assimilated to Solomon's porch in the Temple, where the Apostles "were all with one accord" (Acts 5:12), prefigures paradise. Honorius concludes his allegorical excursions by enunciating the juridical principle that the church is the only place where sacrifice may legitimately be offered to God:

> Therefore, inasmuch as the ritual celebration of the Mass takes place in a consecrated church, so legitimate sacrifice is that made in the Catholic Church and outside of it no sacrifice is accepted by God. And although God justly can and should be blessed and called upon everywhere, in field, in desert, on the seas, in every place of his dominion, the whole world being in a sense his temple, nevertheless it is lawful and right [*iure opportuno tempore*] for the faithful to hasten to the church, so that in that particular place God may be called upon and adored.[75]

In the early 1160s, or thirty years or so after Honorius's *Gemma animae*, came John Beleth's *Summa de ecclesiasticis officiis*. Chapter 2 of that work is concerned entirely with "venerable places and their diversity," and it represents the first attempt in liturgical exegetical tradition to define and classify sacred space.[76] John Beleth defines two sorts of "venerable places": those that holy fathers and

74. *Gemma animae*, PL 172:541–737.
75. Ibid., 1.169: *De certo loco et sacrificio*, PL 172:596BC.
76. *Summa de ecclesiasticis officiis*, ed. Herbert Doubteil (Turnhout, 1976), *CCCM* 41A, pp. 4–7; my thanks are due to Alain Guerreau for directing me to this text.

pious emperors (*religiosi imperatores*) long since established to serve human need (houses for pilgrims, hospices for the sick and old, orphanages) and places given over to prayer. Within this second category, John distinguishes between the *sacra*, the *sancta*, and the *religiosa*. However diverse the vocabulary used to describe them might be (*ecclesia, sacrarium, basilica, oratorium*, and so on), the *sacra* are places ritually consecrated to God to their very foundations by a bishop. John notes that monks equally apply the word *oratorium* to their barns, which implies a "sacralization" of the entire monastic space, not just that strictly assigned to prayer—the *oratorium* intended by rule 52 of the Rule of Saint Benedict—but the whole area of economic activity, here the agricultural. By *sancta* is meant the area of immunity around monasteries, protected by interdict (*sub interminatione*) and offering security to those who take refuge there. Finally, the term *religiosa* is applied to the cemetery, and John Beleth devotes a further whole chapter to this subject.[77] He notes that the term *religiosus* comes not from Church law but from the laws and institutions of Rome; these allowed any body to be buried, provided it was entire (meaning it included a head), regardless of whether it were that of a Christian, a pagan, or an unbaptized infant. But since then, he comments, the Church has limited the accepted meaning of *religiosus* and the right to burial in the cemetery. Excluded thus are Jews, pagans, unbaptized children, excommunicated Christians, and those of the faithful who have died outside the Church's communion by reason of unconfessed faults (for instance, a man dying on his way back from a brothel and, with stronger reason, a suicide).[78] Apart from holy fathers and "patrons and defenders of the entire fatherland," no one may be buried in the church; the commonality of the faithful are to be buried in the cemetery, forming a circle thirty feet around the church. For Beleth it remains unclear whether the burial ground itself should be consecrated: he notes that some say it should be, while others consider a procession by the bishop around the cemetery (*circuitio*) at the church's consecration to be sufficient. At all events, the ground in which the dead lay remained a consecrated space of "second order." On a doctrinal level, the debate begun by Augustine in his *De cura gerenda mortuorum* as to the profit derived from burial was still open. John Beleth merely insisted that wherever there was a Christian tomb, in consecrated or unconsecrated ground, a cross should be planted in order to chase the devil away.

The Structuring of the Space around Places of Worship

Clearly, then, when the heretics of the eleventh and twelfth centuries launched their verbal and physical attacks upon the Church's temples of stone,

77. Ibid., 159, *De officio mortuorum*, pp. 303–310. At the beginning (p. 304, ll. 6–10), the author briefly revisits the distinction between *sacer, sanctus*, and *religiosus*.

78. Under "partially excluded" may be included women dying in childbirth, who are not to soil the church. Their funeral takes place outside the church, and their burial is permitted only once the child has been removed from the body, ibid., p. 309, ll. 138–41.

PART II. CHRISTIAN SOCIETY

it was a particularly fragile part of Christian doctrine that they had in their sights. Until then the question of sacred space had not received any decisive consideration. When, from approximately 1025 to 1130, clerics ventured into that territory, not least in order to fight heresy or, around 1130, for liturgical exegesis, they were more ready to propound principles than discuss fundamentals. By the end of the twelfth century, the dynamic thus created had brought about a reversal of conceptions. At the beginning, in the patristic age, the Church had been reckoned to consist not in walls but in believers; at best the containing walls were seen as symbolizing their content. By the end of the process the Church was seen to be "as much a material place as the gathering of the faithful," to quote Alan of Lille, whose formula achieved canonical status from the 1200s on.[79] Yet how exactly did these two disjunct terms—"church" and "the Church"—end up in a relationship of equivalence? On the basis of our inquiry, it is possible to advance a general hypothesis by way of explanation. By the use of epithets connoting "singularity" (*singularis, specialis*), and by resorting to a range of comparatives (*familiarius, praesentius, uberius*), the anonymous writer of the Acts of the Synod of Arras and Peter the Venerable were able to postulate a conception of "heterogeneous and polarized" space, according to which (to borrow a phrase of Alain Guerreau's) certain points—the consecrated places—were "valorized in opposition to others perceived, from the former and in relation to them, as negative."[80] In response to the undeniable truth of divine omnipresence, Honorius of Autun propounded the rule of the uniqueness of the place of sacrifice, the church and altar, which thereby encapsulated and included all the component parts of the Church. The Church thus was contained within the church, which housed the altar, where the body of Christ was offered, a body that itself both metaphorically and really assembled the different members of the Church. In his *Summa de ecclesiasticis officiis*, John Beleth broadened the system of encapsulations to define different degrees of structuring of the sacred. A first circle housed the "venerable places" intended to assist others. The second contained places intended for the needs of worship and prayer, and these in turn were distinguished from one another in a relationship of diminishing proximity to the divine: the church itself (*sacra*); the area of ecclesiastical immunity (*sancta*), and the space of the dead (*religiosa*), where the Church acknowledged only its own.

"The Heart of the Earth"

In his *Sermo in laude dominici sepulchri*, Peter the Venerable focused upon a precise instance of the structuring of space around a place of worship. The burden of Peter's sermon was the peculiar magnetism exerted by the Holy Sepul-

79. *De fide catholica*, 1.71, *PL* 210:373B: quoted by Congar, *Sacerdoce et laïcat*, p. 299.

80. Alain Guerreau, "Quelques caractères spécifiques de l'espace féodal européen," in *L'Etat ou le roi? Les fondations de la modernité monarchique en France (XIVe–XVIIe siècle)*, ed. Neithard Bulst, Robert Descimon, and Alain Guerreau (Paris, 1996), pp. 87–88.

chre in Jerusalem at the time of the Crusades. Just as it is possible, he says, to speak of men and angels as being "holy" or "saintly" (*sancti*) when they please God, so too it is possible for places to be "holy" (*sancta*) when God sanctifies them. God's agency alone is what makes them so; throughout the history of salvation, men, objects, and places are nothing apart from their relationship to the divine. Whether through a saint, the Cross, or the sepulchre in Jerusalem, God is still the one who is thereby honored. Peter makes this point only in passing, but it is fundamental to the deeply Christological view of sacred places and objects expounded at greater length in *Contra Petrobrusianos*.[81] Peter believes that the relationship these places have with God supposes a greater or lesser proximity to him; among places sanctified by God (*sancta*) a hierarchy obtains. Thus Nazareth, Bethlehem, Capernaum, and other places in Judæa or Galilee are not of equal value; their role in the work of Christ is the important criterion. The place where God was made man—Bethelehem, the virgin's womb—rightly enjoys great glory (*magna gloria*). But the place of Christ's death, the crowning achievement of his work, is worthy of even greater glory (*maior gloria*). The sepulchre was the place where victory was won over death, where corruption yielded to incorruption, whence a man, disempowered, killed, and entombed, rose as almighty God.[82]

The topography of Christian origins thus imposed a set of comparatives having reference to a place of excellence, the "Holy Land," which encapsulated the yet more sacred within it, Jerusalem and the sepulchre of Christ.[83] In *Contra Petrobrusianos*, Peter the Venerable alludes to the slow and gradual way in which God's "own, proper place" became fixed in sacred history, from the altars of Noah, Abraham, and Jacob, the "portable tabernacle" of Moses, the "temple of skin and cloth," to finally the temple of stone built by Solomon.[84] In the *Sermo in laude dominici sepulchri*, Peter speaks at length of the historic sanctification of Jerusalem.[85] Scripture does not divulge where Adam lived after his expulsion from paradise; but we know that his sepulchre was at Hebron (Joshua 14:15). Where the "generation of the just" dwelt until the flood is also unknown, but Genesis 8:4 tells us that Noah's ark ended up on the mountains of "Armenia" (i.e., Ararat). Thereafter Noah and his sons dwelt in that land and cultivated it. Later, Abraham, the father of the Jews and of all Gentiles, left the land of the Chaldeans for the land that he would dedicate to the worship of God. There his descendants lived, and to that "multifariously sanctified" land they returned after the exile in Egypt, in order to see the fulfillment of the word of the Law and the prophecies announcing the coming of the Messiah.

Not only was the work of Christ the crowning moment in the sanctification

81. *CP*, 148, ll. 19–24.
82. *SLD*, pp. 234, 236–37.
83. *SLD*, p. 241.
84. *CP*, 96.
85. *SLD*, p. 240.

of this historically "chosen" land, it also made it a "center." The Christian world has such a center because "the Son of man" was "in the heart of the earth" (Matthew 12:40). Christ's Gospel prophecy that he would be "in the heart of the earth three days and three nights," like Jonah in the belly of the whale, offers Peter the Venerable material for rich elaboration. Accordingly, "heart" signifies middle: the sacrifice of Christ is supposed to sanctify the whole earth from the farthest reaches of India to the limits of Gaul, from the hot south to the frozen north. The sepulchre is in the middle and not in a corner of the earth, since equidistance is a necessary geographical precondition to the work of redemption, which must be truly common and accessible without unequal delays. From here, the center of the earth, the evangelistic effort began as Isaiah prophesied: "For the law shall come forth from Sion: and the word of the Lord from Jerusalem" (Isaiah 2:3). Long before Peter, another "Venerable," the Anglo-Saxon Bede (died 735), had already noted, when reflecting upon the symbolism of Solomon's Temple as an allegory of the Church of Christ, that the twelve oxen of brass that looked out from the structure with their hinder parts enclosed within were a prophetic type of the twelve apostles, united at the center in their communion with Christ, but opening each upon a part of the world to evangelize.[86] A contemporary of Peter, Hugh of Saint-Victor (died 1142), described, in his *De officiis ecclesiasticis*, the blessing of the four corners of the altar when a church was consecrated as signifying the four cardinal points whereby Christianity spread.[87] From one author to another—and one could quote any number of them—evangelization is seen invariably as a centrifugal movement. But by way of balance, Peter also describes a centripetal movement driving the peoples of the earth, be they pilgrims or crusaders, to make their way toward the center, to "that place glorious above all earthly habitation," there to purge Jerusalem, that "place of celestial purity," and thereby fulfill another prophecy of Isaiah (66:19–20): "And I will set a sign among them, and I will send of them that shall be saved, to the Gentiles into the sea, into Africa and Lydia, . . . into Italy and Greece, to the islands afar off. . . . And they shall bring all your brethren out of all nations for a gift to the Lord, upon horses and in chariots and in litters and on mules and in coaches, to my holy mountain Jerusalem, saith the Lord."[88] Like a heart, Jerusalem dilated and irrigated the entire earth, then contracted and gathered itself in its center.

Center and Centers

In his *Adversus Iudeos*, Peter the Venerable tells the Jews to "behold the peoples of the world flocking to the sepulchre of Christ." At the same time— the connection is worthy of note—he bids them "open [their] eyes" to see the

86. Bede, *Quaestiones in Libros Regum, PL* 93:429–56, here 445BCD. [Cf. 3(1) Kings 7:25, 44; Jeremiah 52:20—trans.]
87. *De officiis ecclesiasticis*, 6, *PL* 177:386BCD.
88. *SLD*, p. 247.

sick and crippled who hasten to the "temples of Christ" and depart from them miraculously healed.[89] The missionary work of Christianity is seen as an outward expansion from the Holy Sepulchre into new centers, whose multiplication as reference points constitutes the "enlargement" of "the place of the tent" spoken of in Isaiah 54:2, until such time as it fills the universe. When discussing the second proposition of *Contra Petrobrusianos*, Peter speaks of the earth as sanctified first by Christ, then by the apostolic churches, notably Rome, and thence by the various "streams of Gallic faith." He depicts the advance of Christianity as a gradual seeding, progressively taking over the entire earth, where every point connotes a holy man and a consecrated place.

From the Jewish roots of Christianity Peter retained only the topocentric conceptions implying that Israel was the unique place where the commandments could be kept and sacrifices accomplished. He seems to have known nothing of the "substitutionary strategies" of the Jews in exile after the destruction of the second Temple in Jerusalem.[90] Nor was he apparently aware of the atopism of contemporary Jewish mystics like Abraham Bar Hiya, who conceived the "center" as a spiritual entity, the space for an inner experience.[91] By a curious irony of history, Peter the Venerable espoused a similar spiritualization of space in a passage of his *Sermo in laude dominici sepulchri*, where he likened the "heart of the earth" tropologically to the heart of man.[92] Doubtless unaware of any common ground and convinced of Jewish topocentrism, he contrasted the former days of multiple sacrifices in a single temple with the Christian advent of the unique sacrifice offered in multiple churches. It is a conception that turned the various Christian churches into so many centers or little Jerusalems. Cluny itself was no exception. From its foundation until Peter the Venerable's death, there were three abbey church consecrations: that of Cluny II in 981 by Bishop Hugh of Bourges; that of the major (or high) altar and matutinal (or morning) altar of Cluny III by Pope Urban II in 1095; that of the abbey church of Cluny III as a whole by the Cluniac pope Innocent II in 1130.[93] As the *Liber tramitis aevi Odilonis* and the "Customs" of Bernard reveal, the consecration of Cluny II on 14 Feb-

89. *AJ*, 4.1891–1901.

90. On these "substitutionary strategies," typical of an "economy of absence," especially the talmudic notion of substituting the family table for the altar of sacrifices and replacing sacrifices with ritual prayer and offices, see Schmuel Trigano, "Espaces, ruptures, unités: essai d'introduction à une morphologie générale de la société juive," in *La société juive à travers l'histoire*, ed. Schmuel Trigano (Paris, 1993), 4:15–73, here 63 and 70–72. See also Régine Azria, "La terre comme projet utopique dans les représentations religieuses et politiques juives," *Archives de sciences sociales des religions* 75 (1991): 55–68, esp. 59.

91. Moshé Idel, "*Erets Yisra'el* dans la pensée juive," in *La société juive à travers l'histoire*, 4:77–105, here 87ff.; Leonardo Lugaresi, "'Non su questo monte, né in Gerusalemme': modelli di localizzazione del sacro nel IV secolo. Il tentativo di recostruzione del Tiempo nel 363 d.c.," *Cassiodorus* 2 (1996): 245–65, here 260, cites the conception of "the Torah as the pious Jew's true homeland."

92. *SLD*, pp. 238, 243, 254.

93. Conant, *Cluny*, p. 47.

ruary was an anniversary written into the Cluniac calendar.[94] The forms employed for the occasion were far from mundane. In Psalm 109(110), Cluny was celebrated as the *sedes* (seat or abode) of the Messiah. The words of the hymn "Urbs beata Hierusalem" ("Blessèd city, heavenly Salem") spoke of the dwelling of God, which was also evoked in psalms from the so-called "Songs of Ascents" to Jerusalem (Psalms 119–33). When the monks sang "Angularis fundamentum" ("Christ is made the sure foundation"), they praised the fair city decked with precious stones whose foundation stone was Christ. They sang too of the joy of brethren "dwelling together." The place was proclaimed as *terribilis* (awesome). There, like a latter-day Jacob's ladder, was the "gate of heaven." In short, what the brothers were celebrating was a unique, unchanging place—the center, in one of its replicated forms.

A papal bull records the consecration of the major and matutinal altars of Cluny III by Urban II in 1095 during the tour on which he preached the First Crusade. The bull also defined the limits of the Cluniac "sacred ban," the monastic lordship as a sovereign space within which the high justice of Saint Peter, the patron of the establishment, was exercised.[95] It is worth noting that at the very moment that the pope was calling for the "Holy Land" to be liberated, he was similarly defining the jurisdiction of Cluny as a sacred space. The *maior ecclesia* of Christendom should be regarded as the center of an encapsulated space composed of a number of concentric circles. The very center is the altar, the place of eucharistic sacrifice, containing the relics of Peter and Paul, conveyed from Rome to Cluny at the end of the 980s, and the relics of Stephen, transported from Palestine by Hugh, archbishop of Edessa, during the abbacy of Pontius of Melgueil.[96]

94. *LT*, 136, pp. 196–97; Bernard, *Ordo Cluniacensis*, 2.10, in *Vetus disciplina monastica*, ed. Marquard Herrgott (Paris, 1726), p. 298. The main liturgical texts (and associated themes) were "Urbs beata Hierusalem," in *AH*, no. 102, vol. 51, *Die Hymnen des Thesaurus Hymnologicus H. A. Daniels* (Leipzig, 1908); the Psalms "of Ascents" 121, 131, 132, celebrating Zion, God's chosen dwelling, and the joy of living in common; Psalm 109, the *sedes* of the Messiah; *CAO*, 3.2203 and 5415, evoking Jacob's Ladder, Genesis 28:12–13; *CAO*, 3.5515, on Zachæus welcoming Christ into his house, Luke 19:1–10; *CAO*, 4.6800, on the gate of heaven; *AMS*, 100 (*Terribilis est locus iste*). ["Angularis fundamentum" is the second part of the hymn "Urbs beata Hierusalem" and, as evidenced here, has long enjoyed an independent existence. Both parts of the hymn are well-known in the English-speaking world thanks to John Mason Neale's nineteenth-century translation.—trans.]

95. *Bullarium*, ed. Pierre Simon (Lyon, 1680), p. 25. On Urban II's tour of Gallia and visit to Cluny, see Alfons Becker, *Papst Urban II. (1088–1099)*, 2 vols., Schriften der *MGH*, 19.1–2 (Stuttgart, 1964 and 1988), 1:221. The "sacred ban" reimposed the limits prescribed by Gregory VII's legate Cardinal Peter of Albano in 1080: see Herbert E. J. Cowdrey, "Cardinal Peter of Albano's legation journey to Cluny (1080)," *Journal of Theological Studies*, new ser., 24 (1973): 481–91, reprinted in Cowdrey, *Popes, Monks, and Crusaders* (London, 1984), no. 11. Urban II's privilege was renewed by Honorius II in 1125, Innocent II in 1132, and Lucius II in 1144: see *Bullarium*, pp. 42–43, 46–47 and 52–54.

96. The translation of the relics of Peter and Paul to Cluny is attested in a late account dating from the 1120s, Hugh of Gournay's letter to Abbot Pontius of Melgueil, ed. Herbert E. J. Cowdrey, "Two Studies," pp. 113–17, here 116–17. The translation of Stephen's relics is reported in the *Trans-*

Next is the abbey church itself and the monastery within its walled enclosure, a double space containing the monks' cloister and the areas where the laity were received, both guests and the paupers who were ritually maintained in memory of the dead. Outside the abbey walls lay the monastic *burgus*, where there is evidence of commercial activity from at least the end of the tenth century; here a new community arose, the burgesses "of" Cluny, who derived their identity from the monastery.[97] The Romanesque grandeur of their houses, inspired by the magnificence of Cluny III, put a consecrating touch to the burgesses' opulence and social success.[98] Beyond this, the "sacred ban," protected on the north side by the fortress of Lourdon, represented the core of the monastic lordship; it was at once a demesne swiftly organized into deaneries, a judicial area, and a welfare zone for sick paupers that was visited weekly by the monastic almoner and around which, according to need, relics were ritually conveyed.[99] Beyond these bounds, the Cluniac lordship continued, though limited by and enmeshed within the jurisdictions of lay castellanies. This wide seigneurial circle possibly coincided with the funerary compass within which the brothers of the monastery would collect the bodies of benefactors possessing the right to be buried in the monastery's lay cemetery. Farther out still—sometimes very far away—were the members of the body constituting the Ecclesia cluniacensis, whose head (*caput*), the *monasterium capitale*, was of course Cluny itself. It was an organic entity, defined as such from 1096, naturally identifying itself with the Church of which Christ was the head.[100] At the center of the "head" reigned Stephen, the first deacon and protomartyr, together with the princes of the apostles, Peter and Paul; their presence rooted Cluny securely in the foundations of the Church's history. Indeed the Ecclesia cluniacensis actually saw itself as a summary Church with the aim of integrating into the sacred order the different component parts of the world itself. The Burgundian sanctuary and its dependencies were a perfect model of ecclesiastical incorporation. As Alain Guerreau has shown, the Sanctorale, the relics,

---

latio reliquiarum sancti Stephani Cluniacum (indexed, *BHL* 7894), *RHC, hist. occ.*, 5:317–20; the *Liber tramitis* (*LT,* 189, p. 260, l. 25) attests that the protomartyr's remains were already at Cluny in the 1040s.

97. On the community of the *burgus* of Cluny, see the doctoral research done by Didier Méhu, "Paix et communautés autour de l'abbaye de Cluny (Xe–XVe siècles)," doctoral diss., Université Lumière-Lyon II, 1999.

98. On the outward appearance of the *burgus* in the twelfth century, see Pierre Garrigou-Grandchamp et al., *La Ville de Cluny et ses maisons* (Paris, 1997).

99. Ulrich, *Antiquiores consuetudines cluniacensis monasterii*, 3.24, *PL* 149:767B; Bernard, *Ordo Cluniacensis*, 1.13, p. 159. See Joachim Wollasch, "*Eleemosynarius*: eine Skizze," in *Sprache und Recht: Beiträge und Kulturgeschichte des Mittelalters. Festschrift für Ruth Schmidt-Wiegand zum 60. Geburtstag*, ed. Karl Hauck et al. (Berlin and New York, 1986), 2:988. On the deaneries, see Maria Hillebrandt, "Berzé-la-Ville: la création d'une dépendance clunisienne," in *Le gouvernement d'Hugues de Semur à Cluny*, actes du colloque scientifique international, Cluny, September 1988 (Cluny, 1990), pp. 200ff.

100. *Bullarium*, pp. 26–27, here 26; the "head" (*caput*) mentioned in Urban II's privilege echoes the *capitale monasterium* of which Bernard speaks in his *Ordo Cluniacensis*, 1.16, pp. 167–69, here 168.

and the titles of Cluniac altars during the eleventh and twelfth centuries reveal an effort by Cluny to "assimilate" the major places (from Palestine to Compostela via Rome and Gaul) and principal actors of sacred history: Moses (his staff); Christ (his crib, the True Cross, a stone from his sepulchre, the stone he stood on before his Ascension); the Virgin (a part of her cloak); the raised from the dead (the tomb of Lazarus); the apostles (Peter, Paul, James); the martyrs (the Holy Innocents, Stephen, George, the forty martyrs, Marcellus of Chalon, Denis of Paris and his companions); the virgins and martyrs (Cecilia); the first deacon of the Church (Stephen); popes (Gregory the Great and Marcellus); bishops of Gaul (Martin of Tours; Marcellus, Sylvester, and Agricola of Chalon; Denis of Paris; Taurinus of Evreux); founders of monasticism (Benedict of Nursia, Maurus, Columban) and holy Cluniac abbots (beginning with Majolus).[101]

"White Churches and Black Châteaux"

The structuring of space around sacred places was thus largely the result of a phenomenon of multiplication (one center engendering others) and of aggregation (all places within one). The phenomenon was possible, however, only because the space and social practices in question were perceived as torn between two poles, positive and negative, with the possibility of movement from one to the other in either direction. Let us examine, first, the division between the two poles, before looking at the possible movement.

A "center" was defined in opposition to an environment that was perceived as negative. "White churches and black châteaux": such were the radically opposed terms in which clerics of the eleventh and twelfth centuries described the internal tensions of the seigneurial world.[102] Whatever had not been consecrated was the devil's province: ecclesiastical lords, masters of the rituals, were inspired by this simple principle to demonize their lay opponents. Conversely,

101. Alain Guerreau, "Espace social, espace symbolique: à Cluny au XIe siècle," in *L'ogre historien: autour de Jacques Le Goff*, ed. Jacques Revel and Jean-Claude Schmitt (Paris, 1999), pp. 167–91. In the absence of a synthetic study on the Sanctorale, the relics and titles of Cluniac altars, one has to refer back to the somewhat scattered primary sources. For the titles of altars, see *LT*, 187, pp. 259–60, and Bernard, *Ordo Cluniacensis*, 1. 70, p. 262. The *Liber tramitis*, straight after the passage just cited, gives a first inventory of the Cluniac relics kept *in imagine sancti Petri*, a reliquary in Saint Peter's image, in which a piece of the True Cross had pride of place, *LT*, 189, pp. 260–61. The *Historia abbreviata*, which tells of Odilo's foundation of the priory of Lavoûte-Chilhac, gives an impressive list of relics, including in particular a piece of the True Cross apparently given to Cluny by the Empress Cunegund and remains of the martyr Denis and his companions Rusticus and Eleutherius— ed. Pierre-François Fournier, *Bulletin philologique et historique du Comité des travaux historiques*, 1958 (Paris, 1959): 103–15. The contact with the Holy Land occasioned by the First and Second Crusades enabled Cluny to obtain another piece of the True Cross contained in the *Tabula sancti Basilii* (see *Qualiter tabula sancti Basilii continens in se magnam dominici ligni portionem Cluniacum delata fuerit, tempore Pontii abbatis*, indexed *BHL* 4193, *RHC, hist. occ.*, 5:295–98) and other remains of the protomartyr Stephen (see above, note 96).

102. The expression comes from Dominique Barthélemy, *L'ordre seigneurial XIe–XIIe siècle*, Nouvelle Histoire de la France médiévale, 3 (Paris, 1990), p. 66.

the proper place for the divine was primarily a space removed from the devil. Today we can have only a dim notion of the psychology of insular embattlement obsessing Peter the Venerable and his contemporaries, ready to see the devil endlessly prowling everywhere in search of prey.[103] A constant theme of Peter's *De miraculis* is "the malice that the devil has always harbored against Cluny."[104] The devil and his minions had tried everything to gain control over the monastery; but they could do nothing in a space protected by the Cross, by holy water, relics, and the "whispering of the psalms."[105] Cluny was an impregnable citadel.

Given the missionary drive of Christianity and the logic of ecclesiastical inclusion, it was the citadel's vocation to nibble away at the devil's space, to sow the land ever more densely with consecrated places. From the clerical point of view, every acquisition by the Church was a transfer of property from one to the other of the two opposing spatial poles. Once donated to a monastery, a *castrum* (castle or château) became a sanctuary. Conversely, in *Contra Petrobrusianos*, Peter the Venerable says that Christ's "house of prayer" (*domus orationis*) is being turned by merchants into a "den of thieves" (*spelunca latronum*).[106] In general, however, the age of monastic expansion in which Peter lived was one in which dens of thieves were turned into holy places. The intensity with which the sanctification of space advanced in this "era of conversion" was suggested by Guibert of Nogent in his *Monodiae:*

> Thus one soon began to see, in villages, towns, cities, fortified castles and even in woods and plains, swarms of monks spreading out in all directions. Places that in former times had been the lairs of wild beasts or the dens of robbers were now devoted to the name of God and the worship of the saints.[107]

"Space 'outside Space'"[108]

Asylum, Immunity, Exemption

The definition of a consecrated place as a space apart with its own particular status was as valid in the field of juridical practice as in that of liturgical acts. Ever

103. On Peter the Venerable's demonology, see Jean-Pierre Torrell and Denise Bouthillier, *Pierre le Vénérable et sa vision du monde: sa vie, son oeuvre; l'homme et le démon*, Spicilegium Sacrum Lovaniense, Etudes et documents, 42 (Leuven, 1986).

104. *DM*, 1.12, p. 43.

105. *DM*, 1.14, p. 46, ll. 10–13. Cf. 1.19, pp. 57–58 (the rout of demons going to the infirmary to seize the dying; these last protected by the holy apostles and above all by the sign of the Cross made by an angel of the Lord marking the "place" reserved for the dying) and 2.20, p. 132 (demons put to flight by the sign of the Cross and relics).

106. *CP*, 99, ll. 40–41.

107. *Monodiae*, 1.11, quoted here from Archambault's English trans., *A Monk's Confession*, p. 33.

108. The expression is Alain Guerreau's, "Quelques caractères spécifiques de l'espace féodal européen," pp. 96–97.

since Christianity had acquired the status, first, of a recognized religion, and then of the state religion of the Roman empire, places of worship and the property and revenues attaching to the clergy had become protected enclaves. They were, as has been said, places "of refuge in which persons and things (or at least certain persons and things) were protected from all constraint or seizure by virtue of privilege, custom, or law."[109] From the seventh century onward the right of asylum tended to merge with immunity, an institution that had had entirely separate origins.[110] The main recipients of immunity were ecclesiastical institutions: immunity dispensed them from payments (*in-munus*) and prevented representatives of royal authority from penetrating their jurisdiction "either to judge trials, demand payments of fines, demand lodging, or levy any dues whatever."[111] To asylum and immunity a third procedure was added that put certain monasteries "outside space": exemption.[112] This privilege was accorded by the papacy and in different ways liberated the establishments concerned from episcopal tutelage. Exemption effectively removed the monastery from its diocesan space and attached it instead directly to the center, Rome.

Cluny's history perfectly sums up these different ways in which an establishment could be thus placed "outside space." William of Aquitaine's foundation charter placed the monastery under the patronage of Peter and Paul, removed it from all external ecclesiastical or lay control, including that of William himself, his family, or his network of fidelity, and directly attached it to Rome *ad tuendam non ad dominandum* (for its protection, not domination).[113] These con-

109. *DHGE*, vol. 4, s.v. "*asile*" (Gabriel Le Bras), cols. 1035–47, here col. 1035. For an updated general appraisal, taking into account letters of Augustine unpublished before the 1970s, see Anne Ducloux, *Ad ecclesiam confugere: naissance du droit d'asile dans les églises (IVe–milieu du Ve siècle)* (Paris, 1994).

110. On immunity, reference should henceforth be had to the recent work of Barbara H. Rosenwein, *Negotiating Space: Power, Restraint, and Privileges of Immunity in Early Medieval Europe* (Manchester, 1998); the author's new approach includes valuable contextual studies.

111. A minimal definition suggested by Elisabeth Zadora-Rio, "La topographie des lieux d'asile dans les campagnes médiévales," in *L'Eglise, le terroir,* ed. Michel Fixot and Elisabeth Zadora-Rio, Monographies du Centre de Recherches Archéologiques, 1 (Paris, 1989), p. 12.

112. An introduction may be had from *DIP*, vol. 3, s.v. "*esenzione monastica*," cols. 1295–1306 (Jacques Dubois), which refers to essential bibliography down to the early 1970s; since then Mogens Rathsack's controversial study has appeared, *Die Fuldaer Fälschungen: eine rechtshistorische Analyse der päpstlichen Privilegien des Klosters Fulda von 751 bis ca 1158*, Päpste und Papsttum, 24.1–2 (Stuttgart, 1989)—critically reviewed by Olivier Guyotjeannin, *Francia* 19.1 (1992): 285–86, and Hans Hubert Anton, *CCMé* 35 (1992): 398–99. A convenient summary and review of scholarly debate about the Cluniac exemption, a real paradigm of the *libertas ecclesiae*, is Barbara H. Rosenwein, "La question de l'immunité clunisienne," *Bulletin de la Société des fouilles archéologiques et des monuments historiques de l'Yonne* 12 (1995): 1–2.

113. *CLU* 112, 1.124–28. The expression *ad tuendam non ad dominandum* appears in King Raoul's diploma: *Recueil des actes de Robert Ier et de Raoul rois de France*, ed. Jean Dufour, Chartes et diplômes relatifs à l'histoire de France publiés par l'Académie des Inscriptions et Belles Lettres (Paris, 1978), no. 12, p. 51, ll. 2–3.

ditions were ratified in diplomas of immunity granted by two kings of western Francia, Raoul I in 927 and Lothar III in 955, and in decrees of the Council of Anse in 994. Most important, however, was the role of the papacy, the monastery's protector, which, from John XI in 931 to Urban II and his constitution of the Cluniac "sacred ban" in 1095, confirmed and widened the scope of Cluny's immunity.[114] From 998 on Cluny escaped the bishop of Mâcon's power of order and consecration owing to a bull of exemption granted by Pope Gregory V. In 1024, John XIX extended the privilege to "all Cluniacs wherever they may be," not simply at Cluny but elsewhere. He moreover recognized the sanctuary as a refuge and place of penitence for sinners seeking reconciliation with the Church. Finally, in 1097, Urban II granted exemption to all Cluny's dependent establishments, a measure that was renewed and extended a number of times after that.[115] Thus the Ecclesia cluniacensis fashioned itself into "an entrance to a land of promise" and "a place of total religion," as Jotsald, Abbot Odilo's biographer, termed it.[116]

Ecclesiastical Seigneuries

It is a paradox that the long and complicated history that caused places of worship to be located "outside space" also helped them to become tangible, physical entities. The existence of asylum and immunity presupposed that churches could be defined not simply as temples but also as embodiments of resources and rights requiring preservation. Peter the Venerable had a fondness for the term *fabrica* (building, workshop, or fabric); it was a word with connotations as much of buildings and maintenance as of temporal administration.[117] One needs only to look at the lists of properties granted by royal diplomas and pontifical privileges to Cluny, as to any great ecclesiastical establishment of the period, to see that the word *ecclesia* connoted a double reality, spiritual and material. Thus John Beleth, writing in the 1160s, reported that monks used the word *oratorium* (oratory) to connote their barns. To him it seemed an obvious and natural use of language, though behind it lay the laborious process of the "spiritualization" of

114. Raoul I's diploma, *Recueil des actes de Robert Ier et de Raoul rois de France*, pp. 47–52. Lothar III's diploma, *Recueil des actes de Lothaire et Louis V, rois de France*, ed. Louis Halphen and Ferdinand Lot, Chartes et diplômes relatifs à l'histoire de France publiés par l'Académie des Inscriptions et Belles Lettres (Paris, 1908), no. 7, pp. 15–17. Decrees of the Council of Anse (994): *CLU* 2255, 3.384–88, preserved as a copy in Cluny's "Cartulaire C" (twelfth century). John XI's bull: *Papsturkunden 896–1046*, ed. Harald Zimmermann, 3 vols., Österreichische Akademie der Wissenschaften, Philosophisch-historische Klasse, Denkschriften, 174, 177, 198 (Vienna, 1984–89), vol. 1, no. 64, pp. 107–8. Urban II's bull: *Bullarium*, p. 25.

115. Bulls of Gregory V and John XIX: *Papsturkunden 896–1046*, vol. 2, no. 351, pp. 682–66, and no. 558, pp. 1052–54. Bull of Urban II: *Bullarium*, pp. 30–1.

116. *Vita sancti Odilonis*, 1.3 and 2.23, *PL* 142:899D and 934A.

117. *CP*, epistola, 5, ll. 1–2; 100, l. 13; *Ep.*, 89, 1:229 (regarding Ezelo, architect of Cluny III) and 144, 1:355. See also Jean-Pierre Torrell, "L'Eglise dans l'oeuvre et la vie de Pierre le Vénérable," *Revue thomiste* 77 (1977): 377, n. 24.

ecclesiastical property achieved during the Gregorian reform.[118] One of the main Gregorian ideologists, Humbert of Silva Candida, used spatial references in order to define the contours separating the condition of the laity from the sacred order. The distinction between places "within the sanctuaries" was a tangible mark of the differentiation of tasks within Christian society.[119] This strict regulation of spheres of activity was intended to avoid all possible confusion between the material and the spiritual, which were deemed to be as distinct as body and spirit. Accordingly, the Gregorian clergy took care to differentiate temporal goods (*temporalia*) from spiritual goods (*spiritualia*).[120] They repudiated what they saw as confusions of property rights pertaining to *spiritualia*, which led, for example, to the dissociation of rights over an altar from rights over a church. The malediction in Deuteronomy 27:17—"Cursed be he that removeth his neighbor's landmarks"—they turned into a slogan in their battle to gain such *spiritualia* as still remained in lay hands. The purpose of their demand was to make the Church, together with the goods upon which it depended, a unified, separate space in this world reserved exclusively for administering the business of the next. The many different ways of "fleeing the secular" and of "scorning the world" were radical instances of creating this space "outside space," of which the constitution of the "limits" of the Carthusian wilderness was undoubtedly the paradigm. In order to pursue the model life of unmitigated service to God described in Guigo I's *Consuetudines Cartusiae*, the Carthusians won various privileges from the papacy and episcopacy that strictly bounded their wilderness, barring all access to armed men, women, and herds of animals. They refused to acquire any property outside it. All land within its boundaries was, or was supposed to be, their exclusive possession; hence the frequent and often interminable negotiations with owners of property within the "limits" of Carthusian land to persuade them to renounce their rights. The Carthusians' great admirer, Peter the Venerable, was involved in just such a case, when he ceded land owned by the Cluniac priory of Nantua to the charterhouse of Meyriat.[121]

The construction of this space "outside space" was merely the ecclesiastical version of a wider phenomenon affecting the whole of eleventh- and twelfth-century society: the rooting of power in land. All social orders, whether sacred, princely, or seigneurial, became spatialized. As Alain Guerreau says, "Whereas

118. John Beleth, *Summa de ecclesiasticis officiis, CCCM* 41A, p. 5, ll. 16–18.

119. Humbert of Silva Candida, *Libri tres adversus Simoniacos*, 8, *MGH Ldl*, 1.208.

120. See Giles Constable, "Monastic Possession of Churches and 'Spiritualia' in the Age of Reform," in *Il monachesimo e la riforma ecclesiastica (1049–1122)*, Atti della quarta Settimana internazionale di studio, Mendola, 22–29 August 1968, Miscellanea del Centro di Studi medioevali, 6 (Milan, 1971), pp. 306–7; reprinted in Constable, *Religious Life and Thought (11th–12th centuries)* (London, 1979), no. 8.

121. The question is well presented in Jacques Dubois, "Le désert, cadre de vie des Chartreux au Moyen Age," in *La naissance des chartreuses*, Actes du VIe colloque international d'histoire et de spiritualité cartusiennes, Grenoble, 12–15 September 1984, ed. Bernard Bligny and Gérald Chaix (Grenoble, 1986), pp. 15–35.

up to the tenth century aristocrats owed their position above all to membership of a kinship network, from the twelfth century onward aristocratic status became dependent upon a land base."[122] During the same period, the papacy, seeking to impose itself as a spiritual monarchy, acquired an administration, including a *camera* (chamber of accounts), a chancellery, and a private chapel, and endowed itself with symbols of sovereignty, like a crown. Within the jurisdiction of the Patrimony of Saint Peter, the papacy formed itself into a seigneury that—thanks to skillful use of feudal-vassal institutions and an active policy to increase population and build fortresses—increasingly became a state in its own right.[123] Beyond the boundaries of the Patrimony of Saint Peter, Rome extended (or tried to extend) the secular dominion of the prince of the apostles over monastic churches and even kingdoms, since Spain and Hungary were now dependent upon the "Roman liberty."[124] On a smaller scale, yet entirely comparable to Rome, Cluny offered a similar example of the constitution of an ecclesiastical seigneury. In contradicting the Petrobrusians and proclaiming the necessity of consecrated places, Peter the Venerable was also defending the wider Church of which Cluny was a microcosm.

"An Awesome Place"

The Scope of Spiritual Justice

The period in which the Cluniac seigneury was being built up, around the year 1000, was the high point for the expression of spiritual justice in western Francia. In order to make up for the steady disappearance of royal authority, the clergy endeavored to impose rule on the unruly seigneury in peacemaking assemblies that for the benefit of the "poor"—all who could not resort to arms—proclaimed spaces and seasons during which there should be no violence. Troublemakers who dared break this "peace" or "truce" of God, fight during a prohibited period, or force their way into an asylum were met with all the resources of spiritual justice.

Protection of the Cluniac seigneurial space was the major issue at the Council of Anse in 994.[125] The assembled bishops and abbots confirmed the privileges previously granted to the "most holy place of Cluny" and all the property that the monks had acquired till then, namely, churches with tithes and services

---

122. Guerreau, "Quelques caractères spécifiques de l'espace féodal européen," pp. 88–89.

123. Pierre Toubert, *Les structures du Latium médiéval: le Latium et la Sabine du IXe à la fin du XIIe siècle*, 2 vols., Bibliothèque des Ecoles françaises d'Athènes et de Rome, 221 (Rome: Ecole française de Rome, 1973), vol. 2, book 3, chap. 9: "Du patrimoine de saint Pierre à l'Etat pontifical," pp. 935ff.

124. Brigitte Szabó-Bechstein, *"Libertas Ecclesiae." Ein Schlüsselbegriff des Investiturstreits und seine Vorgeschichte 4.–11. Jahrhundert*, Studi Gregoriani, 12 (Rome, 1986), pp. 144 and 170.

125. Hartmut Hoffmann thinks there were two councils, in 993 and 994, the first summoned at the instigation of Majolus, the second at that of Odilo—*Gottesfriede und Treuga Dei*, Schriften der MGH, 20 (Stuttgart, 1964), p. 46.

due to the monastery or its *burgus*. The prelates forbade all attempts against the power (*potestas*) of the holy place and plundering of its churches, its houses, and its cellars (*cellaria*). In a distant pre-echo of the Cluniac "sacred ban," they proclaimed the "inviolability" of the area. They firmly excommunicated and anathematized those who had seized Lourdon, the fortress protecting the Cluniac seigneury in the north, and listed twenty-one possessions of the monastery in the *pagi* (districts) of Mâcon, Chalon, and Lyon—dependent establishments such as Charlieu and Régny, fortresses such as Huillaux (in addition to Lourdon), and lands (*villae, curtes*). Within the jurisdiction thus defined they banned, on pain of anathema, any civil judge, tax collector (*conductucius*), count, or private army (*exercitus proprius*) from building a fortress (*castrum, firmitas*). They admonished the powerful (*secularis dignitas, militaris sublimitas*) located within the proximity of Cluny and Charlieu not to plunder oxen, cows, pigs, or horses, enjoining them instead to protect "the holy monks."[126] Thus the prelates assembled at Anse provided the first known formulation of Cluny's seigneurial power. The monastic *potestas* was primarily military. In the council's acts, Cluny was described as a *cenobium vel burgus* and a *castrum vel burgus*. The monastery (*cenobium*) thus was viewed also as a fortress (*castrum*). The term *castrum* first appeared in King Lothar III's diploma of immunity dated 20 October 955.[127] *Castrum* should be regarded as a virtual synonym of *castellum* (castle, château), the term used later, in the 1070s, in the customaries of Ulrich and Bernard in connection with taking relics outside the monastery.[128] The use of a military term like *castrum* indicated that the monastery was not simply a space within a walled and gated enclosure dividing interior from exterior, as was the rule within the Benedictine tradition codified during the Carolingian period, for example in the famous plan of the monastery of Saint Gall.[129] It was also a fortified place comprising the monastery itself and a *burgus*. The other element of seigneurial power that the Cluniacs made sure was recognized was their justice. All public judges were excluded from the Cluniac jurisdiction; the monks themselves dispensed justice, at first in conjunction with the count, then entirely on their own. There can be no doubt about this phenomenon, which Georges Duby has studied in detail. Thus in September 998, a certain Stephen made a donation to Cluny *pro remedio animae meae et pro emendatione pro quodam servo cujus pedem amputavi*—"for the remedy of my soul as compensation regarding a certain serf whose foot I cut off."[130] Another example is that of Joceran of Merzé, who in 1023 paid a fine of 600 solidi (silver coins) at Cluny, the tradi-

---

126. *CLU* 2255, 3.384–88.

127. *Recueil des actes de Lothaire et Louis V*, p. 16, ll. 16–20.

128. Ulrich, *Antiquiores consuetudines*, 3.15, *PL* 149:758D–759C, here 759A; Bernard, *Ordo Cluniacensis*, 1.56, pp. 251–52, here 251.

129. Pierre Bonnerue, "Eléments de topographie historique dans les règles monastiques occidentales," *Studia monastica* 37 (1995): 57–77.

130. *CLU* 2464, 3.543–44.

tional penalty for violations of immunity, for having killed a man at the gates of the monastery.[131]

In time the papacy was called upon to help defend the monastery's liberty and the Cluniac seigneurial power against one or another rough-dealing lay castellan. In April 1021 or 1023, Benedict VIII wrote to the bishops of Burgundy, Aquitaine, and Provence to request them to defend the monastery's property against aggression. He named those at fault, cited their titles and lands, and urged their repentance; if they did not comply, he asked his correspondents to pronounce an anathema against them and included a long form of malediction offering a foretaste of the fate they could expect.[132] The Cluniacs themselves made indirect use of anathema. One has only to leaf through the charters of Cluny to notice, at the end of the tenth century and during the first half of the eleventh, a proliferation of comminatory clauses, listing with detail and refinement the spiritual pains—like those of Dathan and Abiram (Numbers 26:9–10) or Judas, blotted out "from the land of the living"—that they could expect to reap who dared infringe the particular agreement recorded. Equally, from Abbot Odilo's time, the Cluniacs perfected a ceremony directly calling down the wrath of God and the thunderbolts of his saints upon the monastery's adversaries—the clamor ritual codified in the *Liber tramitis* and renewed in the "Customs" of Bernard.[133] The ritual took place during Mass. It consisted essentially in placing the saints' relics housed at the monastery together with liturgical objects associated with Christ (the Gospels, the Cross) in the center of the abbey church, before the altar, in order, with appropriate gestures and formulas, to implore the protectors of the place to intervene on behalf of the unjustly violated community. It was in this sense that the place consecrated to God and his saints could be described as "awesome," as an antiphon proclaimed during the annual feast of the consecration of Cluny II.[134]

The Church and Eucharistic Space

It is important to note that the clamor ritual took place in the space (at the altar) and at the time (that of the consecration of the elements) of maximum liturgical efficacy. During the Mass, the reiteration of Christ's sacrifice denoted by the change of the bread and wine into the Savior's body and blood, God was asked to "turn evil into good."[135] In these conditions, the "privileged and singular dwelling of God" was the place where God "would more effectively give

131. *CLU* 2848, 4.48–50. Georges Duby, *La société aux XIe et XIIe siècles dans la région mâconnaise*, 2d ed. (Paris, 1971), p. 146.

132. *Papsturkunden 896–1046*, vol. 2, no. 530, pp. 1008–10.

133. *LT*, 174–75, pp. 244–48; Bernard, *Ordo Cluniacensis*, 1.40, pp. 230–31. For a general treatment of the issues, see Lester K. Little, *Benedictine Maledictions: Liturgical Cursing in Romanesque France* (Ithaca and London, 1993), esp. pp. 20–29 and 262–65.

134. See note 94 above.

135. See chapter 6 below.

heed to prayers."[136] The set of comparatives that Peter the Venerable employed in *Contra Petrobrusianos* to describe the structuring of space around places of worship really made sense only in relation to the eucharistic sacrifice, which represented the supreme manifestation of the divine essence. The church was unique because it was the place of sacrifice. The interior of this unique space focused on an essential point, the altar, the unique within the unique, where the sacrificers officiated. There is a visual image that allows us to understand the attractive force exerted by the altar in this monumental edification of the divine. The church of Zillis in Switzerland has a painted ceiling, dating from the 1120s, composed of panels representing episodes from the Old Testament, the life of Christ, and the life of Saint Martin. The entire work is contained within a "T and O" map of the world, composed of the Cross dividing the ceiling into four equal sections surrounded by a wavy band denoting the ocean on the margins of the earth.[137] The chief message that this erudite composition has for us is the central role played by the altar, inasmuch as it is the only point in the church from which it is possible to decipher the symbolism of the portrayals on the ceiling. The Cross structures the cosmos; the altar, where the sacrifice of the Cross achieves present reality, is at the center of the world. At Cluny, as Anne Baud has pointed out, the doubling of the side aisles in the third abbey church had the main effect of directing the light toward the top of the nave, the transepts, and the apse; the light was thus focused upon the monastic choir and the heart of the building, the high altar, the place of the eucharistic sacrifice.[138] When the Mass was not actually taking place, care was taken nonetheless to maintain the eucharistic presence by reserving the sacrament there: keeping a consecrated host either upon or above the altar.[139] Thus Ulrich and Bernard recorded in each of

136. *CP*, 98, ll. 30–32.

137. Jean Arrouye, "Crux axis mundi," in *Terres médiévales*, ed. Bernard Ribémont (Paris, 1993), pp. 9–20, specifically p. 14. On T and O renderings, see Helma Kliege, *Weltbild und Darstellungspraxis hochmittelalterlicher Weltkarten* (Münster im W., 1991), specifically pp. 24 and 48ff.

138. Anne Baud, "Le chantier de la troisième église abbatiale de Cluny," doctoral diss., 3 vols., typescript, Université Lumière-Lyon II, France, 1996, 1:352.

139. Joseph Braun, *Der christliche Altar in seiner geschichtlichen Entwicklung* (Munich, 1924), 2:582ff. On the history of eucharistic reservation, the increasing care, at least from about 850 A.D., to keep the body of Christ in a proper place—under lock and key as the Fourth Lateran Council in 1215 would stipulate—and the provision of *capsae*, doves, towers, and tabernacles, see Robert Cabié, "L'Eucharistie," in *L'Eglise en prière*, ed. Aimé-Georges Martimort, 2d ed., 4 vols. (Paris, 1983–84), 2:263–65—Eng. trans., *The Eucharist*, trans. Matthew J. O'Connell, The Church at Prayer, 2 (London, 1986)—and Philippe Rouillard in *Catholicisme* 12 (1990), cols. 961–64. In the early thirteenth century the practice of placing the reserved sacrament in a "proper" place was not universally followed; hence for instance Francis of Assisi's insistence that "wherever the most holy body of our Lord Jesus Christ is illicitly laid and abandoned, it shall be removed from that place, put in a precious place, and its presence indicated," *Epistola ad cleros*, 11, in *Ecrits*, ed. K. Esser et al., *SC* 285 (1981), p. 218. On Francis's attachment to churches, see *Testamentum*, 4–5, ibid., p. 204, and *Epistola ad fideles*, 2.33, ibid., pp. 232–33. I thank Jacques Dalarun for bringing these texts to my notice.

their customaries that, at Cluny, the body of Christ, "changed" each Sunday, was deposited after the Mass in a golden pyx that was itself placed in a dove that hung above the altar.[140]

All that remained for Peter the Venerable was to justify the fact that this supreme manifestation should occur in a unique place. The apostle Paul had defined the *Ecclesia* as the assembly of the people for the Eucharist; he therefore had contrasted the "human house" in which the physical body was nourished with the "house of God" dedicated to the Lord's Supper (1 Corinthians 11:18ff.). Peter the Venerable refers to this passage in his justification of temples of stone, seeing the "house of God" as a *corporalis structura* (physical structure), a container necessary for the sustenance of the content, the Church as the communion of the faith in Christ.[141] Though in Peter's time this conception was fast becoming received wisdom, three centuries before it had been far from obvious. The decrees of councils and episcopal capitularies of Carolingian times stressed repeatedly—thereby attesting the prevalence of contrary practice—that "the solemnities of masses are to be celebrated absolutely nowhere else than in church, not in houses of any sort and ignoble places, but in the place that the Lord has chosen."[142] Doubtless the idea of sacred space defined by the presence of relics and the delimiting of a refuge was a very old one. But the opposition to temples of stone voiced by eleventh- and twelfth-century heretics proves that the conception of "proper" or "congruent" place took time to become universally accepted. By the end of the twelfth century, there was no more dispute: Church and church had become interchangeable notions. What happened between 800 and 1150 to account for this evolution in ecclesial conceptions? All we can do here is suggest a hypothesis, which we shall examine in greater depth in relation to the next two propositions of *Contra Petrobrusianos*, on the Cross and the eucharistic sacrifice. What occurred between 800 and 1150 was the great debate over the Eucharist, which opened in the Carolingian era, was relaunched by Berengar of Tours in the 1050s, and was still raging during the first thirty years or so of the twelfth century. The core issue was that of the real presence. Though the matter was not definitively settled in the 1130s, it is possible to say that by then the "realists," who asserted that there was an effective transformation of the elements into the actual body and blood of Christ, had all but won the day against the "symbolists," who believed any transformation to be "figurative." The repercussions of the debate upon the question of places of worship were immense. Belief in the effective transmutation of the elements enhanced both the

---

140. Ulrich, *Antiquiores consuetudines*, 2.30, *PL* 149:723A; Bernard, *Ordo Cluniacensis*, 1.35, p. 226.
141. *CP*, 108.
142. Theodulphus of Orléans, Capitulary I (before 813), c. 11, *MGH Cep*, 1:110, quoted by Treffort, "Genèse du cimetière chrétien," 1:266. The Councils of Mainz in 852 (cap. 24) and 888 (cap. 9) and the Council of Metz in 893 (cap. 8) forbade the celebration of Masses in private houses: see Wildfried Hartmann, *Die Synoden der Karolingerzeit im Frankenreich und in Italien*, Konziliengeschichte, Reihe A (Paderborn, 1989), p. 427.

time and space in which the event took place. Just as the liturgical calendar was structured around Easter and Sunday, so Christian space centered on the church and the altar. The *res* (event) and the *locus* (place) went hand in glove, the sacrifice defining the place and not vice versa.[143] Thus eucharistic realism definitively established the church as the proper dwelling place of God.

143. *CP*, 157, ll. 5–7.

6

THE CHURCH'S CORNERSTONE
THE SACRIFICE OF CHRIST

"THE SACRAMENT OF THE CHRISTIAN PEOPLE"

In his *Sermo de laude dominici sepulchri*, Peter the Venerable honors the center of the universe consecrated by the work of Christ, in particular by his death on the Cross and his three days in the tomb, "the heart of the earth" (Matthew 12:40). We have seen how Peter interpreted this median point, how he viewed it as a center divinely placed to exert its influence upon the four corners of the world and to structure Christian space. He also read the passage in Matthew tropologically, assimilating "the heart of the earth" to the heart of man, who was called upon to internalize the sepulchre of Christ. Thus the faithful themselves, distinguished by the sign of the Cross, were also at the earth's center.[1]

The third proposition of *Contra Petrobrusianos* concerned the very Cross whose majesty was scorned by Peter of Bruis and his disciples.[2] From the heretics' point of view the Cross was an object not to be adored but to be reviled as the instrument of Christ's torture and suffering. Adding injury to insult, the heretics had organized a Paschal "counterritual" in which they made a great pile of crosses, set fire to it, cooked meat upon it, and on Good Friday itself invited people to join them in eating it.[3] Peter saw the devil's cunning at work in this offense to the divine majesty, since such antics were engineered to see the life-giving Cross disappear from the face of the earth. He fought back with an opening question, answering it with a threat akin to exorcism. Peter's question, which was really three linked questions in one, lifted the veil on the main arguments that were to come:

If the name is removed from the middle of the Cross, where will mention of the crucified remain? If the designation of the crucified is taken away, where

1. *SLD*, pp. 238, 243, 254. The subhead is from *CP*, 143, l. 22.
2. *CP*, 112–48.
3. *CP*, 112, ll. 5–10.

will the remembrance of his death or passion be preserved? If the memorial of his death or passion is removed, what hope of salvation will be left for the redeemed, once the price of redemption is reduced to nothing?[4]

Peter thus employed "if . . . then" logic to suggest the disastrous consequences entailed by the heretics' heedless premises. Immediately he was at the heart of a debate whose essence for him may be stated in few words: that the Passion was a present reality and the Cross a memorial of it here and now. He went on to proclaim his belief in the contemporary importance of the Cross by confronting the heretics with words of exorcism designed to convince them of the power and efficacy in the present of the sign of the Cross:

> When the sign of the Cross appears, the spirits of apostasy are put to flight. When they see that sign of abjection which you belittle, the proud angels who strove to raise their head against its undefeated majesty vanish as mist dispersed by the rays of the morning sun.[5]

In his letter of dedication, Peter recalled how the offense Peter of Bruis had given to the majesty of the Cross proved fatal to the heresiarch, thrown by the outraged believers of Saint-Gilles-du-Gard upon the bonfire he had himself prepared.[6] Peter of Bruis having been thus struck down by divine judgment, it now fell to Peter the Venerable to attempt to convince his followers, in particular their leader Henry. Such was the business of this third proposition.

The "Transformation" (Permutatio) Wrought by the Cross

The Petrobrusians held that it was senseless and impious (*stultum et prophanum*) to venerate the Cross; it was better to punish and burn the wood on which Christ was tortured. Peter begins his answer by stating that the Creator himself took responsibility for condemning the instrument of suffering by casting it into Gehenna with Herod, Pilate, Judas, and Caiaphas. Lacking any precise reference, we should perhaps regard this as an indirect allusion to Paul's words in Ephesians 4:8 that Christ "led captivity captive." By triumphing over death, the Savior enchained the devil and sent his minions headlong.[7] It was not man's place to rail against the instrument of his salvation. He might as well similarly abhor the places of the Passion, lay waste the city in which Christ was tor-

4. *CP*, 112, ll. 25–29; the question recurs, 133, ll. 29–30.
5. *CP*, 113, ll. 1–6.
6. *CP, epistola*, 10, ll. 1–3.
7. This was the traditional interpretation of Ephesians 4:8 in the light of Psalm 67:19—among others, see Haymo of Auxerre's commentary, *PL* 117:718D–719A. A familiar theme in the early medieval Latin literature of journeys into the afterlife was the journeying soul's discovery of the devil's minions, such as Herod, Pilate, Judas, and Caiaphas in hell. See Claude Carozzi, *Le voyage de l'âme dans l'Au-delà d'après la littérature latine (Ve–XIIIe siècle)*, Collection de l'Ecole française de Rome, 189 (Rome, 1994), pp. 248, 293, 294, 397, 590, 596.

tured, and destroy his sepulchre. The timing of Peter's words just a few years be-fore the call to the Second Crusade (1146), when energies were being mobilized to liberate the sacred space of Christ's earthly life, was bound to lend conviction to his argument.

Peter continues in a "rational" vein. Logically, he says, there can be fault only where there is reason (*ratio*): in an animate being. Obviously this cannot be true of the Cross.[8] The fault lay in the will of the men who chose to put Christ to death, not in the instrument of his death. How is it possible to confuse the sword with the murderer, arms with those that bear them, inanimate objects with the animate beings who wield them? Echoing Cicero in *In Catilinam*, Peter bristles at having to endure such nonsense.[9] Addressing his remarks directly to the heretical "convent" deceived by their leaders' blindness, he asks them where their anger should be directed: at the blade that killed their brother, indeed their dearest friend, or at the man that committed the murder?[10] A little later, he ex-presses equal derision in recalling the episode recorded in Herodotus's *Histories* where King Cyrus punished the Gyndes river for its "guilt" in drowning his fa-vorite horse![11] Instead of taking vengeance upon inanimate, unfeeling objects, it made better sense to seek out the guilty, who was of necessity a human being, and demand justice of him for his fault.

Having closed the first part of his argument by such an appeal to "sufficient reasons," Peter moves on to important considerations about the sign of the Cross as a divinely chosen mark or token. From being a negative sign, the Cross became a positive one. Peter shows his opponents how the instrument of Christ's torture has become the instrument of his glory. He cites Old Testament prece-dents for this: how David accepted the sword of Goliath, given to him by the priest Ahimelech in 1 Kings (1 Samuel) 21:9; how in 1 Maccabees 3:12 Judas Maccabeus seized his defeated enemy Apollonius's sword "and fought with it all his lifetime." Through a similar "permutation" or transformation (*permutato cruce*) Christ slew the devil with the cross intended for his own execution.[12] This "permutation" or transformation in the role of the Cross, and therefore its sign, is at the heart of Peter's thinking on the sacrifice of Christ conceived of as a great "transmutation" of humanity. With a series of commands (*veniat, mittat*—let it come, let it send) Peter appeals to scriptural examples demonstrating the value of the sign and the necessary discriminations on the way of salvation. He calls upon Moses, "the legislator,"[13] and recalls several episodes from the Exodus.[14] At the first Passover, Jehovah ordered the doorposts and lintel of the Israelites'

8. *CP*, 115, ll. 3–6.
9. *CP*, 117, l. 9.
10. *CP*, 119; *conventum vestrum*, l. 1.
11. *CP*, 121, ll. 1–11, ref. Herodotus, *Histories*, 1.189.
12. *CP*, 118, ll. 14–19.
13. *CP*, 130, l. 4.
14. *CP*, 125.

houses to be sprinkled with blood as a sign that the Exterminating Angel should not enter to kill the firstborn (Exodus 12:7 and 23). In the wilderness of Shur he showed Moses a tree that sweetened the bitter waters of Marah (Exodus 15:25), and in the wilderness of Sin he commanded Moses to "strike the rock, and water shall come out of it"(Exodus 17:6). Peter compares this water, which quenched the thirst of the chosen people, with the water that flowed from the body of Christ for the baptism of the world. He then cites the example of the starving widow of Zarephath in 3(1) Kings 17, whose failing oil and meal Elijah miraculously increased. The two sticks she gathered for fuel (verse 12) symbolized the fire of the Passion that cooked the Bread of Life. Finally, Peter recalls the vision in Ezechiel 9:2–11 in which "the men that sigh and mourn for all the abominations" committed in Jerusalem had their foreheads marked with a cross (*signa tau super frontes*—Ezechiel 9:4) to indicate that they were to be spared. According to Peter's typological logic, these were all types or precedents of the Cross of Christ; they were an overt sign (*signum in aperto*) marking out dwellings and men that were to be saved. Christ inaugurated a new Passover. Peter comments that "Tau," formerly written in the shape of a cross, was to be interpreted in Latin as *consummatio*—fulfillment. It was the final letter of the Hebrew alphabet. It was where all the letters ended, just as in Christ all the former mysteries had an end.[15]

By conquering death Christ turned the Cross, an instrument of torture, into an instrument of glory that reigned over the world and before which "every knee should bow, of those that are in heaven, on earth, and under the earth" (Philippians 2:8–11).[16] The *Liber tramitis aevi Odilonis* and the "Customs" of Bernard reveal that this passage from Paul's Epistle to the Philippians was read at Cluny on the feast of the Exaltation of the Cross (Holy Cross Day, 14 September).[17] The eleventh-century Cluniacs thereby celebrated the universal royalty of Christ, before whom all earthly powers should prostrate themselves.[18] In his argument with the Petrobrusians, however, Peter was less concerned with questions of political theology rooted in devotion to the Cross than with the spiritual significance of the instrument of glorification transforming mankind's destiny. Membership in the suffering Christ opened the way of Redemption. To illustrate the spiritual passage that this implied, Peter refers to the Beatitudes. When the Lord said, "Blessed are the poor," he meant not that poverty was blessed, but that the sufferings endured by the poor would earn them the kingdom of heaven. Similarly those who mourned or hungered were "blessed" because they too suf-

15. *CP,* 129–32.
16. *CP,* 131, ll. 7–12.
17. *LT,* 111, pp.166–68, here 167, ll. 16–17. Bernard, *Ordo Cluniacensis,* 2.31, in *Vetus disciplina monastica,* ed. Marquard Herrgott (Paris, 1726), p. 349.
18. See my "La Croix, le moine et l'empereur: dévotion à la Croix et théologie politique à Cluny autour de l'an Mil," in *Haut Moyen Age: culture, éducation et société: études offertes à Pierre Riché,* ed. Michel Sot (Paris, 1990), pp. 454ff.

fered and their suffering would earn them consolation and abundance.[19] The power of Christ (*virtus Christi*) opened the way from the "although" (*licet*) of an arduous present to the "nevertheless" (*tamen*) of a desirable eschatological future: *although* the Cross was an instrument of suffering, *nevertheless* it was an instrument of glory; *although* men might be poor, mourning, hungry, *nevertheless* their part in the sufferings of Christ would win for them a blessed restoration in the kingdom of heaven.

An "Exclusive" Sign (signum incommunicatum)

Fortified by his reflections on the way opened by the Cross, Peter launches into a long discussion on the "sign of the Son of man" appearing in heaven, as prophesied in Matthew 24:30.[20] How is this sign, with its accompanying cosmic disturbances, to be interpreted? Relying to some extent upon Augustine's definition of "sign," Peter maintains that the "sign of the Son of man" in question cannot mean the Son himself, since "a sign cannot be the thing [*res*] of which it is the sign."[21] Working with the classic case of typological correspondence between the life-giving wood of the Cross and the rod coming forth out of the root of Jesse (Isaiah 11:1), Peter declares that what is signified by the "sign of the Son of man" is the "standard unto the nations" (*signum in nationes*) evoked by Isaiah 11:12. This "standard unto the nations" announced Christ's first advent, when he came to "assemble the fugitives of Israel and . . . gather together the dispersed of Judah, from the four quarters of the earth" (Isaiah 11:12). The Cross, which marks the Second Advent of Christ, is also a "standard unto the nations" because it assembles the elect from the four quarters of the earth. When he sent the Carthusians a crucifix, Peter's accompanying letter said that this "sign of the nations" had become a "sign of friends" who could be compared to Christ.[22] It was a cosmic sign whose "transitive" function was nothing other than to associate mankind with the angels.[23] How astonishing therefore that men could fail to honor what was "life, salvation, honor, love, admiration, felicity, nobility, beatitude, and eternal glory."[24] Such laudatory enumeration was a perfectly familiar theme in the liturgy of the Cross. In his *Sermo de sancta cruce*, Abbot Odilo had borrowed from Pseudo-John Chrysostom a long eulogy celebrating the universality of the Cross, key phrases of which were copied onto the back of the great processional cross described in the *Liber tramitis*. "The Cross

19. *CP*, 135.

20. *CP*, 137–38.

21. Augustine, *De doctrina christiana*, 2.1.1. *CP*, 137, ll. 11–13.

22. *Ep.*, 24, 1:44–47, here 46. Guigo I gives some idea of the power of the comparison in his reply to Peter, saying, "You, being crucified, have sent the crucified to those who must crucify themselves" (*Crucifixum crucifixus et ipse crucifigendis misistis*), ibid., 25, 1:47–48, here 47.

23. *CP*, 138, ll. 10–13.

24. *CP*, 139, ll. 19–22.

the hope of Christians," wrote Odilo; "the Cross the resurrection of the dead; ... the Cross the destruction of the proud; the Cross, the consolation of the poor; the Cross the restraining of the rich," and so on.[25] Such a crescendo of celebration, so arresting a litany sprang from the Augustinian notion of signs, whereby the Cross was the sign of signs subsuming all the possible ways in which the mystery of salvation could be signified.

This allusion to the multiplicity of significations within the uniqueness of the mystery of the Cross allows Peter to close his demonstration with important considerations on the worship due to God and to him alone.[26] Within the general plan of the treatise, Peter's defense of the Cross lays the ground for the argument on the notion of the "exclusive sign" advanced in defense of the Eucharist in the next proposition.[27] He adopts a direct style, borrowing the words of Jehovah and Christ: "The Lord thy God thou shalt adore, and him only shalt thou serve" (Matthew 4:10, cf. Luke 4:8); "Thou shalt not have strange gods before me. Thou shalt not make to thyself a graven thing, nor the likeness of any thing" (Exodus 20:3–4—the first and second of the Ten Commandments); "I will not give my glory to another, nor my praise to graven things" (Isaiah 42:8). Finally, Peter alludes to the "exclusive" or "inalienable" name (*nomen incommunicabile*) of God, which ought never to be given "to stones and wood" (Wisdom 14:21). Following Augustine's lead, he borrows the Greek word *latreia* (service), in Latin *cultus*, to describe the exclusive worship of God.[28]

The Worship (cultus) of God and the "Sacrament of the Christian People"

As is often the case, Peter here provides a neat synthesis of the various elements of a debate that was still raging with some intensity at the time he wrote: the standing of images and iconic mediations.[29] It had been an extremely vexed question in the Carolingian period for two reasons. First there was the influence of the Adoptionist heresy, one of whose features was the refusal to glorify the incarnation of the "adopted" Son and hence opposition to any figure

25. *Sermo de sancta cruce*, PL 142:1031–36, here 1034; *LT*, 188, p. 260; Pseudo-Chrysostom, Homilies, 13, *De cruce dominica*: Latin trans. in *Opera quae hactenus versa sunt omnia* ... (Basle, 1530–31), p. 117.

26. *CP*, 142.

27. *CP*, 158, ll. 4–6.

28. Augustine, *De civitate Dei*, 10.1.

29. For a good overview of the issues see Helmut Feld, *Der Ikonoklasmus des Westens*, Studies in the History of Christian Thought, 41 (Leiden, 1990); Jean-Claude Schmitt, "L'Occident, Nicée II et les images du VIIIe au XIIIe siècle," in *Nicée II, 787–1987: douze siècles d'images religieuses*, Actes du colloque international Nicée II, Collège de France, Paris, 2, 3, 4 October 1986, ed. François Boesflug and Nicolas Lossky (Paris, 1987), pp. 271–301; Schmitt, "Rituels de l'image et récits de vision," in *Testo e immagine nell'alto Medioevo*, Settimane di Studio del Centro Italiano di Studi sull'alto Medioevo, 41, 15–21 April 1993 (Spoleto, 1994), pp. 419–59.

representing God as human. The second factor was the iconoclastic controversy dividing the Byzantine world, which found echoes in the Latin west. Such then was the soil out of which sprang the attacks against that "instrument of vile torture"—the Cross—widely attested in sources relating to heresy around the year 1000 at Arras, Vertus, or Monteforte.[30] It is worth quoting two examples from recently published Aquitainian sources. Adhemar of Chabannes, in his sermon *De eucharistia*, spoke of heretics who "say that God no more wants to recall the Cross of his Passion than a thief released from a pillory wants to recall the hoists by which he hung."[31] The monk Heribert in a circular letter asserted that the heretics "do not adore the Cross or the Lord's likeness and stop others from adoring them so far as they can; they stand before his likeness, saying, 'O how wretched they are that adore thee, as the psalmist says, the idols of the Gentiles . . .'" (Psalms 113:4 and 134:15).[32] A century later the Petrobrusians would express their hatred of the Cross in similar terms. The Jews too would pour scorn upon worship of the Cross; taking their cue from the second commandment (Exodus 20:4), they would accuse the Christians of idolatry.[33]

The polemic brought the person of Christ back onto the field. The attacks made against the Cross were answered by a new presence, that of the Crucified, for representations of the Cross (*signum*) increasingly gave way to those of a crucifix (*imago Christi*). Hand in hand with the iconoclastic surges of heresy went the enrichment of Christic devotion by images of the abused Savior either on his Cross or at the scene of his Passion and shedding streams of tears.[34] The

30. Arras: *Acta synodi Atrebatensis*, 14, *PL* 142:1306A–1307A. Vertus: Rodulfus Glaber, *Historiarum libri quinque*, 2.11.22, in *Works*, ed. with parallel Eng. trans. by John France et al., Oxford Medieval Texts (Oxford, 1989), pp. 88–91, here 90. Monteforte: Landulfus Senior, *Historia Mediolanensis*, 2.27, ed. Georg H. Pertz, *MGH SS*, 8, p. 66, ll. 30–36; Huguette Taviani, "Naissance d'une hérésie en Italie du Nord au XIe siècle," *AESC* 1974: 1229.

31. Ed. and French trans. by Pierre Bonnassie and Richard Landes in *Les Sociétés méridionales autour de l'an Mil: répertoire des sources et documents commentés*, ed. Michel Zimmermann (Paris, 1992), pp. 454–57, here 456.

32. Ibid., pp. 457–59, here 459. On this letter, see the analysis by Guy Lobrichon, who redates to the eleventh century this document previously considered to belong to the twelfth—"The Chiaroscuro of Heresy: Early Eleventh-Century Aquitaine As Seen from Auxerre," in *The Peace of God: Social Violence and Religious Response in France around the Year 1000*, ed. Thomas Head and Richard Landes (Ithaca and London, 1992), pp. 80–103.

33. Schmitt, "L'Occident, Nicée II et les images du VIIIe au XIIIe siècle," pp. 288–89. Peter the Venerable alludes to the Jews' execration of the Cross in *Adversus Iudaeos*, 4.1903–5. Another example is Alan of Lille, *De fide catholica*, 4.11, *PL* 210:427B.

34. Rodulfus Glaber, *Historiarum libri quinque*, 2.8.8, p. 64. Adhemar of Chabannes, *Chronicon*, 3.46, ed. Jules Chavanon, Collection de textes pour servir à l'étude et à l'enseignement de l'histoire (Paris, 1897), pp. 168–69. Richard Landes, *Relics, Apocalypse, and the Deceits of History: Ademar of Chabannes, 989–1034*, Harvard Historical Studies, 117 (Cambridge, Mass., and London, 1995), pp. 299–308, interprets the visions and physical images of the crucified Christ weeping ("the Weeping Crucifix") as an effect of disappointed apocalyptic expectation typifying spirituality around the year 1000.

Christ of Judgment similarly appeared on his Cross, spoke of the sufferings of his Passion, and displayed to the nations his body given for them.[35] This rediscovery of Christ's suffering humanity coincided with a new doctrinal precision about worship, concluding long debates on the notions of "adoration," "veneration," and the signs used to move from the visible to the invisible. This precision came in Peter the Venerable's time. The entire issue turned on resolving the ambiguities inherent in the Latin term *adoratio*, which sometimes could mean "idolatry," sometimes "veneration," and sometimes more broadly "prayer." At the very end of the discussion on the third proposition of *Contra Petrobrusianos*, Peter the Venerable drew a sharp distinction between divine "adoration" and human "reverence."[36] He was able to do so because, like his contemporary Peter Lombard or Alan of Lille a few years after him, he had embraced the Greek notion of *latreia* (worship given to God) as distinct from *douleia* (servitude, submission to men).[37]

According to Peter the Venerable, the worship due to God was signaled by a "proper" or "condign" sign (*congruum signum*) that was also "inalienable" or "exclusive" (*incommunicatum*).[38] It was impious to offer this sort of worship to others, such as angels, prophets, the mother of God, or the apostles. In his *Collationes*, Odo of Cluny reported that the blessed Walbirgis had ceased to perform miracles because her relics had been left "on the Lord's altar, where the majesty of the divine mystery alone should be honored."[39] Peter notes that it is solely in connection with the Cross and as a particular form of the worship due to God that one can "adore" other objects, such as the relics of saints.[40] The Cluniac liturgy made this dependency plain when it displayed the saints' relics in phylacteries hanging from the processional Cross.[41] In *Contra Petrobrusianos*,

---

35. "As I was on the Cross for you, so I am before you now," says the "Christ of Judgment" in the vision of a dying monk reported by Richard of Saint-Vanne and recorded by Hugh of Flavigny, *Chronicon*, 2.15, ed. Georg H. Pertz, *MGH SS*, 8, p. 383, ll. 52–53; the text is translated and commented upon at length by Carozzi, *Le voyage de l'âme dans l'Au-delà*, pp. 396–412.

36. *CP*, 148, ll. 1–4.

37. Peter Lombard, *Sententiarum libri quatuor*, 3.9, ed. by the Franciscans of Quaracchi, vol. 2 (Grottaferrata, 1981), pp. 68–70; Alan of Lille, *De fide catholica*, 4.11–12, *PL* 210:427B–428B: quoted by Schmitt, "L'Occident, Nicée II et les images du VIIIe au XIIIe siècle," p. 296.

38. *CP*, 143. The term *signum incommunicatum* is used a little further on in *CP*, 158, ll. 4–6.

39. Odo of Cluny, *Collationes*, 2.28, *PL* 133:573CD; quoted by Servan Simonin, "Le culte eucharistique à Cluny de saint Odon à Pierre le Vénérable," *Bulletin trimestriel du Centre international d'études romanes* 1961:4. See also Godefridus J. C. Snoek, *Medieval Piety from Relics to the Eucharist: A Process of Mutual Interaction*, Studies in the History of Christian Thought, 63 (Leiden, 1995), p. 217.

40. *CP*, 148, ll. 19–24. In his sermon (*SSMII*) on the relics of Saint Marcellus, Peter makes clear that honoring the saint's body is strictly dependent upon the resurrected body of Christ, in *Sermones tres*, ed. Giles Constable, *RB* 64 (1954): 265–72.

41. *LT*, s.v. "*phylacteria*," esp. 111, p. 167, l. 7 (Feast of the Exaltation of the Cross). Bernard, *Ordo Cluniacensis*, 1.32 (De processionibus pro tribulatione), p. 217. On the phylacteries containing saints' relics, see my "La Croix, le moine et l'empereur," pp. 455–56.

Peter emphasizes that the efficient sign now manifesting God's transcendence, which before Christ was signaled on multiple occasions, is "the sacrament of the Christian people."[42] He here uses the term *sacramentum* in the sense of a sacramental sign or, as defined by Peter's friend and contemporary Abelard, "a visible sign of the invisible grace of God."[43] These considerations about the operant power of a sign that refers to something other than itself, namely, the divine transcendence and the sanctification of believers who are identified with Christ, enable Peter to finish where he began the proposition, with the distinction between the Cross and the crucified one. It is not the Cross as an object in its own right that is adored, but the crucified God-man who came to unite spirit with matter. To emphasize the believer's active association in Christ's work Peter makes use of the evocative power of the present participle. Employing the Cross as a means to adore the Lord's death, resurrection, and ascension is nothing short of adoring the deceased, rising, ascending Lord himself (*mortuum Dominum, resurgentem Dominum, ascendentem Dominum*).

Such "active association" shows how Christological devotion during the eleventh and twelfth centuries, the time of the great debates provoked by heretical iconoclasm, finally passed from simple adoration of the Cross to that of the crucifix; it was a response to questions that had been current since the Carolingian age.[44] The mediation of the "image" of the suffering Christ was especially sought on the deathbed. In his sixty-second statute, Peter the Venerable laid down that a dying monk should be given a crucifix rather than a gold or silver cross and that a piece of the True Cross should be placed under his feet. Peter explained that the very simplicity of the wood of the Cross (*vilitas ligni*) could move souls, though he did not comment further about the recourse to the wood of the True Cross, which demonstrated the necessity of direct contact with the instrument of salvation.[45] The passing of Matthew of Albano, as portrayed in *De miraculis*, offers a small hagiographical illustration of the same phenomenon: "He turned to the Lord's Cross which was there, as if seeing on it the Savior crucified as he once was."[46] The linking "as if" (*velut si*) conveys the power of iconic mediations at the supreme moment of passing. More striking still is the account

---

42. *CP*, 143, ll. 20–22, and cf. 165.

43. Peter Abelard, *Theologia "Scholarium,"* 1.9, *CCCM* 13, p. 321, l. 91: *Sacramentum vero est visibile signum invisibilis gratie dei.*

44. Marie-Christine Sepière, *L'image d'un Dieu souffrant: aux origines du crucifix (IXe–Xe siècles)* (Paris, 1994), sees two decisive points in this development: the eleventh–twelfth centuries, our present interest, and the years around 800, when representations of the Cross gave way to those of the Crucifixion, the symbol to the sign. I thank Daniel Russo for drawing my attention to this work.

45. *Statutum* 62, pp. 93–95, here 94. See Robert Folz, "Pierre le Vénérable et la liturgie," in *Pierre Abélard, Pierre le Vénérable: les courants philosophiques, littéraires et artistiques en Occident au milieu du XIIe siècle*, Actes et mémoires du colloque international, Abbaye de Cluny, 2–9 July 1972, ed. Jean Châtillon, Jean Jolivet, and Reneé Louis, Colloques internationaux du CNRS, 546 (Paris, 1975), p. 158.

46. *DM*, 2.22, p. 137.

Peter gave to his brothers of the death of their mother, Raingard, nun of Mar-cigny-sur-Loire. He describes with remarkable intensity the physical closeness that the dying woman was able to have with Christ through the medium of the crucifix:

> Then anointed at her own request with holy oil, renewed for eternity by the body of Christ, protected by humility and made safe by confession, she asked that a cross with the image of the Lord [*crucem cum domini imagine*] be brought down to her. Having received it, she roused the entire convent to repeated lamentations. The Lord's image she put to her mouth and, licking the feet with her tongue, she pressed it into her face with all the strength of her body. She worshiped the Savior's Passion and swore that his death and wounds would grant her salvation. To all listening she declared that no glory, no hope of salvation existed for her save in the Cross of her Lord. And when, her prayer over, those standing round tried to remove the image of the Lord from her face, her faith blazed up and she declared: "Why do you want to take away my Lord? Leave him to me while I live; I shall go to him as soon as I die." Thus reckoning that she saw not his image but his very self upon that cross, she could not be torn from the embrace.[47]

SEMEL ET SEMPER (ONCE AND ALWAYS): THE SACRIFICE OF CHRIST, THE CHURCH'S CORNERSTONE

To pass directly from attacks on the Cross as an instrument of torture to Christ's sacrificial work was a logical step. Opening discussion on the fourth proposition of *Contra Petrobrusianos*, Peter the Venerable directly quotes the heretics' assertion that the eucharistic views spread by the priests and bishops are "lies."[48] The Petrobrusians, he says, oppose the clerics by saying that "the

---

47. *Ep.*, 53, 1:69.

48. The fourth proposition of *CP* has never been thoroughly studied. The most penetrating analysis of Peter's doctrine of the Eucharist remains Marie-Claude Bodard, "Le mystère du corps du Seigneur: quelques aspects de la christologie de Pierre le Vénérable," *Collectanea Ordinis Cister-ciensium reformatorum* 18 (1956): 118–31. The *table des thèmes principaux* at the end of Jean de Mont-clos, *Lanfranc et Béranger: la controverse eucharistique du XIe siècle*, Spicilegium Sacrum Lovaniense, 37 (Leuven, 1971), pp. 580–606, provides a convenient introduction to the central questions of the Berengarian dispute. Some perspective on Peter's ideas within the context of eucharistic debate in the prescholastic age is briefly given in the general study by Gary Macy, *Theologies of the Eucharist in the Early Scholastic Period: A Study of the Salvific Function of the Sacrament according to the Theologians, c. 1080–c. 1220* (Oxford, 1984), though in his chapter on the ecclesiological dimension of the prob-lem (chap. 4, pp. 106ff.), he strangely ignores *CP*. On the ecclesiological aspect, see Henri de Lubac, *Corpus mysticum: l'Eucharistie et l'Eglise au Moyen Age*, Theologie, 3, 2d ed. (Paris, 1949), esp. 1.4, "Corps sacramentel et corps ecclésial," and Yves Congar, *L'Eglise de saint Augustin à l'époque moderne*,

'body of Christ' was made once only, by Christ himself at the Supper before his Passion, and was bestowed once, namely, on that occasion only, to the disciples."[49]

Having called out his opponents to join him on the "field of combat," Peter refers to the heresy of the cleric Berengar of Tours. If the propositions of the Petrobrusians merely repeated those of Berengar, he might simply refer them to the answers generated by the eucharistic controversy in the period 1050–80. These were in particular the treatises by two bishops, Lanfranc of Canterbury and Guitmund of Aversa, and that by Alger of Liège, who became a "monk and priest at Cluny." But the heresy of Peter of Bruis and his disciples goes beyond that of Berengar and the "Berengarians."[50] Not only do they deny any sort of real presence, they also deny "the sign, form, and figure" of the Eucharist (*sacramentum, speciem et figuram*), imagining that they can be the people of God without sacrifice.[51] New ills call for new remedies. Peter considers it his personal duty to respond to the Petrobrusians' eucharistic temerity. Adopting the "rational" approach that he has explicitly chosen for refutation of the heretics, that which dispenses with appeals to authorities, Peter briefly presents the heterodox view, then gives a general response indicating the full significance of the controversy. The Church, he says, could not exist without the eucharistic sacrifice, and that sacrifice could not consist in anything other than the body and blood given by the Redeemer: "She offers for herself the one who gave himself for her, and what he did once by dying she ever does by offering."[52] The question of the Eucharist is thus introduced here in an ecclesiological perspective. The Church was born and does not cease to renew itself in the sacrifice of Christ, the one who, according to the Epistle to the Hebrews, "offered himself once and for all."[53] The whole difficulty for Peter the Venerable is to justify the fact that the unique sacrifice offered once (*semel*) nevertheless needs to be ever repeated (*semper*).

Sacrifice as a Distinguishing Sign

Peter opens the debate with a question. With no sacrifice, how can God distinguish his own? In answer, Peter recalls the instances, from Adam to Christ, of "saints" offering sacrifices to God and their acknowledgment by God through "signs" such as smoke or clouds. These ancient testimonies proved not only that the sacrifices were pleasing to God but also that he glorified the places that were

---

Histoire des dogmes, 3.3 (Paris, 1970), esp. chap. 7, "L'ecclésiologie dans la scolastique du XIIe siècle": both are indispensable reading, though they make little or no reference to Peter's work.

49. *CP*, 150, ll. 8–11.

50. *CP*, 153, l. 24. On the "Berengarians," see Gary Macy, "Berengar's Legacy as Heresiarch," in *Auctoritas und Ratio. Studien zu Berengar von Tours*, ed. Peter F. Ganz, Robert B. C. Huygens, and Friedrich Niewöhner, Wolfenbütteler Mittelalter Studien, 2 (Wiesbaden, 1990), pp. 47–67.

51. *CP*, 153, ll. 26–29.

52. *CP*, 154, ll. 18–19.

53. *CP*, 167, ll. 49–50: cf. Hebrews 7:27, 9:28, and 10:10.

built and consecrated for sacrifice: "For the sacrifices are not celebrated for the temple's or altar's sake; but it is for the sacrifices that the temple and altar are built, consecrated, adorned, and glorified."[54] The point about sacrifice can therefore be fully appreciated only when linked to the argument on the second proposition of *Contra Petrobrusianos*, where Peter defends sacred places. The two are indeed interconnected in Peter's mind. The sacrifice defined a space set aside exclusively for the divine and within which man's submission in body and soul to God was signaled (*signatur*) by "external" actions. Such a sacrifice was offered only to God; it was the "exclusive sign" (*signum incommunicatum*) that distinguished the Creator from his creatures. Humankind moreover needed to know how to interpret signs, to see the "workman" behind his "works" (Wisdom 13:1) and give not "to graven things" (Isaiah 42:8) the glory due to God alone.

After the Old Testament examples, Peter demands rhetorically whether it could be right to contravene tradition: "Perhaps," he asks ironically, "God approves the sacrifices of the Jews and reproves those of Christians?"[55] In the Old Testament, God's refusal of particular sacrifices was due not to the sacrifice itself but to the depravity of those who sacrificed. As a consequence, to live without sacrifice amounts to living in captivity "without law, without king, without priest, without ephod, and without theraphim," as Hosea said, admonishing his adulterous wife (Hosea 3:4).[56] It is noteworthy that Peter's quotation of Hosea is not a literal one and that he prefers the Septuagint reading "priest" to the Vulgate's "sacrifice." He moreover widens the reference to tradition to embrace the history of religions. If the Christians no longer sacrificed, who in the world would sacrifice among the four "sects"? Not the Jews, for they would need access to Jerusalem. Not the Saracens, in spite of their points in common with Jews and Christians, for though they pray, they do not sacrifice. Not the pagans of the "northern regions" who, knowing nothing of idols, rites, and sacrifices, nonetheless honor animals as "gods of the day or of the hour" (*deos diarios vel horarios*).[57] Peter declares that those living in the Christian era, the one opened up by the Redeemer's sacrifice, have received greater benefits than those of earlier days. Are they therefore less indebted to God? Of course not. The fact is that the Christians have inherited from the Jews the duty to sacrifice all over the world. This *translatio ad gentes* (transfer to the Gentiles) has moreover been accompanied by a change in the forms, the agents, and the nature of the sacrifice. The multifarious has given way to the unique—one God, one people, one faith. Replacing the former plurality of sacrificial victims is the single sacrificial lamb, no longer a servile offering but a liberating victim. The slaves have become sons and friends (John 15:15).[58]

54. *CP*, 157, ll. 5–7.
55. *CP*, 160, ll. 10–11.
56. *CP*, 160, ll. 34–5.
57. *CP*, 161, ll. 30–31.
58. *CP*, 165.

Arriving at this crucial point in the debate, Peter the Venerable considers at length the tradition "prescribed and inaugurated" by Christ whereby his people reenact at the altar (*semper in altari*) the unique sacrifice of the Cross (*tunc semel in cruce*). Resorting to a "prompter approach" (*via expeditior*) using the imperative mode, Peter urges the Lord to intervene in person to confound the deviant detractors and rehearse the words of the Last Supper.[59] This use of the "Christic" imperative was all the more justifiable to Peter and his contemporaries inasmuch as they believed that the efficacy of the Eucharist was due to the very fact that the words of consecration were Christ's own.[60] To Peter's mind Christ's words needed no further commentary: Christ meant what he said. He offered the disciples *his* body and *his* blood, saying to them, "Do this for a commemoration of me." This is Peter's cue to begin a long discussion of the nature of the offering before considering the eucharistic commemoration.

But how could the words mean literally what they said? And how was unceasing obedience to the Lord's injunction to be ensured? Forced by his opponents to explain how what happened "once" (*semel*) can happen "always" (*semper*), Peter embarks on the question of the *commutatio* (change) of the bread and wine into body and blood. He advances the objection that he says he has "heard," the one formerly made by Berengar of Tours, that the body and blood of Christ were modest and finite in quantity and subject to exhaustion over time.[61] Peter's reply begins with an axiomatic argument of vast dimensions: the unfathomable greatness of God is as inaccessible for man as the mystery of mankind may be for a horse.[62] He resorts to a metaphor drawn from his own times and origins, the secular world of knights. A horse may travel or take part in warfare. But what does it understand of the path chosen, the organization of combat, or the peace won at the cost of so much blood? Then returning to domestic tranquillity, what can it grasp of the rules governing husband and wife, the family and household?[63] Is not man a horse in the House of the Lord?

'Continuing his reflections upon the "unfathomable greatness and omnipotence of God," Peter develops a "rational" argument. The institution of the Eu-

<hr/>

59. *CP,* 168.

60. Ludwig Hödl, "Der Transsubstantiationsbegriff in der scholastischen Theologie des 12. Jahrhunderts," *Recherches de théologie ancienne et médiévale* 31 (1964): 231. On the New Testament testimony as "words of eucharistic institution," see also Montclos, *Lanfranc et Béranger, table des thèmes principaux,* s.v. *"Formulation 'évangélique' de la croyance eucharistique."*

61. *CP,* 171. Peter was mistaken in ascribing the extreme formulation of the heretics' "thesis" to Berengar; it is perhaps traceable to Guitmund of Aversa, *De corporis et sanguinis Christi veritate, PL* 149:1450BC, though Macy, "Berengar's Legacy as Heresiarch," pp. 62–63, is inclined to postulate an independent source. The heretics of Arras in 1025 had already evidently expressed doubts on the subject, *Acta synodi Atrebatensis, PL* 142:1280CD.

62. *CP,* 173. The image doubtless comes from Psalm 48:13, "And man when he was in honor did not understand: he is compared to senseless beasts [*iumentis insipientibus*]." There is an exact parallel in Alger of Liège, *De sacramentis corporis et sanguinis dominici, PL* 180:741D.

63. *CP,* 173.

charist was a demonstration of will, power, and execution (*voluit, potuit, fecit*). It would have failed if one of these three terms had been absent. That the Lord "willed" it is attested by the words of the Last Supper. That he demonstrated power and execution is attested by Psalm 134(135):6: "Whatsoever the Lord pleased he hath done." Peter continues with examples of *mutatio* or *transmutatio* (change) drawn from Ambrose of Milan's *De mysteriis*, such as the changing of Moses' staff into a serpent or the waters of Egypt into blood.[64] These were not like the illusory changes performed by the Egyptian magicians Jannes and Jambres in the seventh chapter of Exodus (cf. 2 Timothy 3:8), but true and real (*vera* and *realia*) because works of God. No wonder, then, that in the eucharistic context Peter insists on the *realia*. Indeed his series of examples culminates with Christ's changing of water into wine at the wedding in Cana of Galilee. After this he concludes trenchantly that denial of God's power to change "things into other things and substances into other substances" amounts to an offense against the divine "majesty." According to Peter the subsequent period, the age of the Church, provided a multiplicity of "miracles" testifying to the Truth. Under this head his chief interest is to provide examples of physical phenomena.[65] Thus the sky is the scene of frequent changes of one substance into another, as when, for example, pure air condenses into clouds giving rain, snow, and hail. The eye of the curious may also observe "everyday miracles" on earth: coral, which is a stone born of fire; the "royal powder" of alchemy that changes into gold; the phoenix that is reborn from its own ashes; water that turns into ice and crystal; the bread and wine that is transformed into human body and blood. The last example, taken from Guitmund, makes it possible for Peter to wield an argument from fact.[66] Is it conceivable that God should be unable to accomplish *per virtutem* (through his power) in the eternal world what in the mortal world nature accomplishes by digestion (*per digestionem*)? Is he that created man impotent to restore him? So much for the question of the change of one substance into another. But what of the problem of a substance changing without a change in its outward form? To explain this Peter returns to the example of water, which changes its substance when it becomes ice or crystal but retains its translucid form. In this connection he cites a natural example from the "Spanish orient" (*in orientalibus Hyspanie*): gem salt, a translucid stone produced by rainwater. The eucharistic transmutation from bread into flesh and from wine into blood he considers to be of a similar sort: the substance changes while the form remains (*substantia permutata, specie reservata*). From the objects themselves Peter passes to the problem of how they are perceived. When it is tasted, wine may seem cold and damp, whereas "experts" may describe it as warm and dry. An oar may seem

64. *CP,* 176.

65. *CP,* 177–81.

66. Guitmund of Aversa, *De corporis, PL* 149:1431C, 1444AB, and 1451B. In the last passage, Guitmund refers to medical teaching to assert that only the lightest and most useful of foods and drink are transformed into body and blood.

to "break" the water, though the water remains none the less smooth.[67] Reflections of things in a mirror are not those things, any more than dreams are realities. Such examples from common experience reveal the distance that separates how things seem (*videntur*) from their nature in fact (*in natura rerum*). The change of substance without change of form that takes place in the Eucharist is a similar problem of perception. Divine operation causes to appear what no longer exists, while what does exist is hidden: "The mercy of Almighty God . . . in the sacrament of the altar preserves for human senses the semblance of bread and wine, so that in the sacrament bread and wine appear, though they are not, and the flesh and blood, which are, remain hidden to eyes of flesh."[68] Rather than continue with endless examples Peter concludes this part of the argument by referring his audience to the "founders" of eucharistic doctrine (*de hoc sacramento magnorum voluminum conditores*), probably an allusion to the previous century's apologists, Lanfranc, Guitmund, and Alger, who had brought together all the passages from the Fathers pertinent to the debate. In the very last resort he appeals to the fideist argument that "faith is not the fruit of intelligence" but that the reverse is true.[69]

Having considered the nature of the offering made by Christ, Peter confronts the further questioning of his Petrobrusian opponents. Surely, they argued, the Last Supper was a unique moment without sequels? When Christ said, "Do this for a commemoration of me," was he not simply addressing the apostles there and no one else? In accordance with the all-or-nothing logic so characteristic of him, Peter now seeks to nail his opponents with a reductio ad absurdum. Suppose, he says, the answer to the question were "yes": in that case, no one apart from the apostles would have had the right to preach, teach, baptize, or sacrifice; the Church would have had no existence beyond the apostolic age. So extreme a position was obviously untenable. Instead he applies to the field of ecclesiology a proposition later employed by nominalism as valid in the field of knowledge: *Semel est verum, semper est verum* (A thing once true is always true).[70] Peter confines himself to Christ's words to the apostles as reported in the Gospels, the only part of Scripture accepted by the Petrobrusians. Does one have to limit oneself to the apostles present at the Last Supper? If so, then Paul

67. Two of Peter's recognized sources refer to the comparable optical impression of an oar being "broken" by water: Guitmund, *De corporis, PL* 149:1438CD, who, after Boethius, refers to "everyday experiences" (*experimenta quotidiana*): *Remum in aqua, si interrogas oculos, fractum asserunt, quem mox extractum mansisse integrum testantibus oculis ratio probat;* Alger of Liège, *De sacramentis,* 1.6, *PL* 180:756B: *quamvis ipsis sensibus corporeis per omnia credendum non sit, ut cum oculi in aqua ramum fractum putant.*

68. *CP,* 188, ll. 12–17.

69. *CP* 190, l. 10. Peter is thus faithful to Augustine's warning, repeated by Alger of Liège, *De sacramentis,* 1.9, *PL* 180:767A: *Hoc fides credat, intelligentia non requirat.*

70. William J. Courtenay, "Peter of Capua as a Nominalist," *Vivarium* 30.1 (1992): 157–72, here 161; I am grateful to Irène Rosier for suggesting the connection to me and for details of Courtenay's study.

is excluded. Yet he is the "apostle" who, in the eleventh chapter of his First Epistle to the Corinthians (verses 17 and following), recalls and comments upon the words of Christ at the Last Supper. What Peter sees first in that passage is a distinction between the Lord's chalice and table and those of the devil. His chief interest however focuses upon the two words in Paul's commentary that witnessed to a eucharistic tradition: *quicumque* (whosoever) and *quotienscumque* (as often as). "Whosoever" Peter takes to mean "everyone," while "as often as" means the whole of future history to the Last Judgment. He insists that repetition of the rite is far from superfluous. The commemoration (*memoria*) of the Redemption enacted in the sacrifice of the altar is a means of grace (the *causa sacramenti*—cause of the sacrament). Moreover it was ritualized as a visual act because, as Horace says, men are moved more greatly by what they see than by what they hear.[71] The earlier sacrificial system was a theater of shadows. The Eucharist by contrast entails no prefigurements, no bodies of animals, but the very body and blood of Christ. "The sign itself and what is signified are the same thing" (*Ita signum est, ut sit idem quod signat*).[72] This "same thing" (*idem*) is the essential work wrought by the death of Christ (*Mors Domini maxime representatur*—"It is the death of the Lord that is chiefly represented"). Yet it is not enough to see the sign; participation in the efficacy of Christ's power is also necessary. To see and consume the body of the Redeemer is to be inhabited by him, to be afire with him, to be associated with him in eternal life (*convivere*). As a vehicle of incorporation (*ut habitaret in nobis, habitans etiam corporaliter et in se*—"that he might inhabit us, while bodily inhabiting his own self also"), the Eucharist is indeed a sacrament of the Church (*sacramentum Ecclesiae*), unceasingly renewed "because the human heart is more sensitive to what is present than to what is absent."[73] At all events, the "sacrament of the body and blood of Christ" condenses past, present, and future into one: "By his body he has redeemed us; by his same body he restores us, to the end that, redeemed by his body and restored by his body, we may be nourished and pastured by his humanity until such time as we are utterly satisfied by his deity and glory." Such is "the unique and astonishing miracle" of Christ's hidden presence in the sacrament.[74]

All the same, why are the body and blood of Christ made available for eating and drinking? Should it not be enough to honor and adore them? Peter the Venerable completes his consideration of the fourth proposition of *Contra Petrobrusianos* by addressing this objection. It was, in point of fact, an ancient question

71. Horace, *Ars poetica*, 180–81, quoted by Peter, *CP*, 198, ll. 45–46. Two entries in the eleventh-century Cluny library catalogue attest the presence of all Horace's corpus; see Léopold Delisle, *Inventaire des manuscrits de la Bibliothèque Nationale, fonds de Cluni* (Paris, 1884), nos. 532 (p. 371) and 546 (p. 372): *Volumen in quo continetur Horacius totus*.

72. *CP*, 199, ll. 52–53.

73. *CP*, 201, ll. 11–12, 34–35.

74. CP, 201, ll. 52–55; 202, ll. 5–6. On the Eucharist as "commemoration, anticipation, and presence," see Lubac, *Corpus mysticum*, 1.3.

that had already perplexed the apostles themselves, "scandalized" by Jesus' "hard saying" that they should eat his flesh and drink his blood (John 6:54–62). Peter therefore recalls Christ's own response (verses 62–64) to the apostles' doubts. It is the Spirit that quickens; Christ does not sacrifice his flesh as if it were a corpse to be divided and cut up in agony until there should be none left: he gives it without diminution or destruction because his flesh nourishes not mortal but eternal life.[75] Peter is loath to press the matter further: the divine will exceeds human understanding; it needs no other "reasons" to justify it.[76] He nevertheless advances a "rational" argument. Man needs to eat and drink to sustain mortal life; this includes bread and wine, which hold the "principal place" in his diet and are the "healthiest and commonest" part.[77] Other foods no more than accompany these.[78] Similarly, for a man's spiritual life, he needs to consume the body and blood of Christ. The likeness between the two meals, the bodily and the spiritual, is divinely conceived. "Union" with Christ is a matter not simply of hearing his words but of nourishing oneself with his flesh which he gives of himself. It is the "bread of heaven" which means life to men. Its effects are seen not in the present but in the future: "The sacrament is indeed bodily [*sacramentum corporale*], because it is the true body and true blood of Christ; but the purpose of the sacrament [*res sacramenti*], namely the salutary effect which flows from it, is spiritual."[79] Peter draws attention finally to the universality of the spiritual refreshment that sustains both the disciples (*sequentes*) of Christ and the faithful whose lives were lived before the founding moment of the Last Supper as far back as the world's beginning. But whereas those of pre-Christian times had only spiritual food, those who come later have both physical and spiritual nourishment. It is a sign that Christ has become flesh and has opened the way of eternal life, in which future age the invisible will be made visible and the physical and spiritual united.

The Ecclesia *as the Body of Christ and Sacerdotal Mediations*

In the eucharistic debate of the eleventh and twelfth centuries, Peter the Venerable said little that was new. He represented the orthodox position defined by Lanfranc, Guitmund of Aversa (whose treatises were known at Cluny from the abbacy of Hugh of Semur), and Alger of Liège, himself a Cluniac.[80]

75. *CP*, 205, ll. 20–26.

76. *CP*, 206, ll. 10ff.

77. *CP*, 207, ll. 14–17.

78. See Georges Duby, *L'économie rurale et la vie des campagnes dans l'Occident médiéval*, vol. 1 (Paris, 1962), p. 141.

79. *CP*, 209, ll. 1–5.

80. Hugh of Semur showed early concern about what position he should adopt in the Berengarian controversy, writing to Pope Gregory VII about it, *Das Register Gregors VII.*, 5.21, ed. Erich Caspar, *MGH Epistolae selectae*, 2.1–2 (Munich, 1920), 2:384–85, here 384. The Cluny library cata-

Faithful to a tradition established at Cluny since the abbacy of Odo, he was a resolute "realist" who defended the thesis of a real and material conversion of one substance into another without a change of form.[81] In the discussion about the sacrament as a sign, he opted for the relationship of identity between the sign and what it signified. On the basis of the definition of a sign given by Augustine in *De doctrina christiana*, Berengar had distinguished between *sacramentum* (the sign) and *res sacramenti* (the other matter of the sign).[82] For Peter, on the other hand, the *sacramentum* was the very body and blood of the Lord, Christ being himself, as Guitmund of Aversa had maintained, "the sign of himself,"[83] while the *res sacramenti* was its spiritual effect. Peter's main contribution to the eucharistic debate lay in the ecclesiological reasons adduced against adversaries who did not merely reject the real presence but denied that the sacrifice of the altar had any validity whatever. This is why the discussion of the fourth proposition of *Contra Petrobrusianos* would later attract Catholics opposing Protestants and why it was repeatedly published as a separate piece in the sixteenth and seventeenth centuries.[84] The Petrobrusian concept of the Church as a simple congregation of believers that did not sacrifice was, as Peter saw it, an affront to the divine majesty, to the body of Christ. Against it Peter proclaimed the notion of an incorporating sacrament of the Church and founding sacrifice. In this regard he was not far from Alger of Liège, who in his *De sacramentis* strongly emphasized the notion of *concorporatio* (union in one body), a phenomenon that was realized in the Eucharist and assimilated the faithful into Christ.[85]

---

logue includes the treatises of Lanfranc and Guitmund: Delisle, *Inventaire des manuscrits*, nos. 433 (p. 365) and 565 (p. 373). The same contains a work described as *dicta Jotreldi catholici contra Berengarium hereticum* (no. 373, pp. 360–61), unidentified but ostensibly by Jotsald, Abbot Odilo's disciple and biographer, and an epistle "De corpore et sanguine domini" by the hermit-monk Anastasius inspired by Paschasius Radbertus's "De corpore et sanguine domini" and "Epistula ad Fridugardum": see Mathieu Arnoux, "Un Vénitien au Mont-Saint-Michel: Anastase, moine, ermite et confesseur († vers 1085)," *Médiévales* 28 (1995): 59–64 and 76–78.

81. On Odo's realism and the link between the real presence and Christ's humanity, see Odo, *Occupatio*, 6.50ff., quoted and analyzed by Snoek, *Medieval Piety*, p. 170.

82. Augustine, *De doctrina christiana*, 2.1.1: *Signum est enim res, praeter speciem quam ingerit sensibus, aliud aliquid ex se faciens in cogitationem venire.* See Irène Rosier, "Langage et signe dans la discussion eucharistique," in *Histoire et grammaire du sens. Hommage à Jean-Claude Chevallier*, ed. Sylvain Auroux et al. (Paris, 1996), p. 52.

83. Guitmund, *De corporis*, PL 149:1460D: *Idem igitur Christus sui ipsius est sacrum signum, id est sacramentum.*

84. See James Fearns's comments, *CP*, pp. vi–viii; Jean-Pierre Torrell and Denise Bouthillier, "*Miraculum*: une catégorie fondamentale chez Pierre le Vénérable," *Revue thomiste* 80 (1980): 372–73, n. 44.

85. Alger, *De sacramentis*, PL 180:750D, commenting upon 1 Corinthians 12:27 ("You are the body of Christ and members"). Guitmund, *De corporis*, PL 149:1459C, equally expands on qualifying the members of the body of Christ as *concrucifixos, conmortuos, consepultos*. This ecclesiological interpretation of the Eucharist, inspired by Paul, was already present in Augustine.

The Purity of the Sacrificers

The Petrobrusians' rejection of eucharistic sacrifice went hand in hand with rejection of the power of sacramental mediation. Denunciation of the "lies of priests and bishops" thus also entailed opposition to the mediators, the clerical sacrificers. Significantly, as we noted earlier, Peter preferred to read from the Septuagint version of Hosea 3:4 rather than the Vulgate: in the Septuagint, the prophet admonished those who cease to sacrifice and live in captivity "without law, without king, without *priest* [Vulgate: *sacrifice*], without ephod, and without theraphim." For Peter the essential issue was not so much the principle of mediation as the person and purity of the mediator.

Though merely hinted at in *Contra Petrobrusianos*, the theme is a recurrent one in *De miraculis*, which begins with a series of eucharistic miracles. It is worth reminding ourselves that eleventh- and twelfth-century eucharistic controversy drew richly upon *exempla* furnished by hagiographical tradition.[86] Peter the Venerable refrained from using them in *Contra Petrobrusianos*, restricting the basis of argument to the Scriptures, the Fathers, or "sufficient reasons" taken from common experience. But *De miraculis* was something else entirely. Exemplary stories were woven into that work for the precise purpose of illustrating the doctrine defended in connection with the fourth proposition of *Contra Petrobrusianos*. They consisted of short "true" stories, highly accessible and supportive of faith in the real presence. The discursive strategies of the two texts, each addressed to a different audience, entirely complemented each other. The first story of interest in *De miraculis* concerns a peasant in the Auvergne who wants to conserve his excellent bees indefinitely.[87] Deceived "by the depraved counsel of necromancers," the peasant receives the body of the Lord at church and keeps it in his mouth without swallowing. He returns home to his hives and puts his mouth to a hole in one of them and begins to blow, convinced that in so doing he will transmit to the bees the eternal power contained in the host. The host however falls to the ground. Thereupon the bees, seemingly full of reverence, gather up the Lord's body and transport it into a hive. The peasant finds it there later in the form of a tiny newborn child lying among the honeycombs. When he tries to hold it, it disappears from his "unworthy hands." The main purpose of the story was the lesson that only "worthy hands," those of priests, had authority to handle the body of the Lord.

But those priestly hands also must be pure. The old Cluniac notion of the monks' virginal purity here connected with the ideal of the sacrificer's purity at

---

86. Against Berengar, who rejected the authority of saints' lives, Guitmund of Aversa exclaimed, *De corporis, PL* 149:1479A: "What is more stupid, what more senseless than to invalidate miracles, since absolutely nothing happens without a miracle?" Such *exempla* were drawn from Paul the Deacon's *Vita sancti Gregorii* and the *Vitae patrum*. In his *De corpore*, Lanfranc regarded eucharistic miracles as proofs of the real presence; cf. Montclos, *Lanfranc et Béranger*, pp. 309–10 and 366.

87. *DM*, 1.1, pp. 7–8.

the heart of the Gregorian priestly model.[88] The liturgical codifications of Hugh of Semur's day give a good idea of the horror of pollution that haunted the Cluniac mind. In the chapter of their customaries devoted to making the host, Bernard and Ulrich describe the "diligence and reverence" attaching to this act of the liturgy, which ideally took place before Christmas or Easter, had to be done before breakfast, and used only the best and purest grain, which was selected grain by grain and washed.[89] The servant responsible for carrying the grain sack to the mill was not to be "lascivious." He began by washing the millstones, which he shielded with curtains above and below as he worked. For the task, he was dressed all in white, his head covered by an amice such that only his eyes were visible. He was then allowed to grind the flour and sift it, "diligently washing the sieve beforehand." After lauds, three brethren took over, similarly dressed all in white. They placed the flour on a spotlessly clean table and worked it with water taken from a vessel used during Mass. During their task, the officiants were instructed not to pollute the eventual "Eucharist of the sacrosanct mystery" with their saliva or even their breath. When it came to the Eucharist itself, whether one of the two daily conventual Masses or a private service, the officiating priest washed his hands twice as a sign of purification. The first occasion was, as tradition demanded, before putting on his vestments.[90] The second was just before the consecration, which Ulrich explained by the fact that after the oblation the sacrificer would be touching the actual body of the Lord, really present in the host.[91] This belief in the real presence was so strong that Bernard instructed that if, during the eucharistic sacrifice, a drop of "the Lord's blood" should fall on the altar cloth, the corporal cloth, or chasuble, the area of cloth thus sanctified was to be cut out and placed among the relics.[92]

In the Confiteor (prayer of confession), the priest asked for penitence and purified himself before sacrificing.[93] Peter the Venerable, in his *De miraculis*, re-

88. The insistence on the monk-priest's purity goes back at least to Odo: see Ovidio Capitani, "Motivi di spiritualità cluniacense e realismo eucaristico in Odone di Cluny," *Bulletino dell'Istituto Storico Italiano per il Medio Evo e Archivo Muratoriano* 71 (1950): 1–18. On Cluniac virginal purism, see my own *"Agni immaculati": recherches sur les sources hagiographiques relatives à saint Maieul de Cluny (954–994)* (Paris, 1988), pp. 324ff. On the model Gregorian priestly life centering on sacramental mediation, see Johannes Laudage, *Priesterbild und Reformpapsttum im 11. Jahrhundert*, Beihefte zu Archiv für Kulturgeschichte, 22 (Cologne and Vienna, 1984).

89. Bernard, *Ordo Cluniacensis*, 1.53, p. 249; Ulrich, *Antiquiores consuetudines cluniacensis monasterii*, 3.13, *PL* 149:757A–758A: and see Snoek, *Medieval Piety*, p. 40.

90. Josef A. Jungmann, *Missarum sollemnia: eine genetische Erklärung der römischen Messe*, 4th ed. (Freiburg, 1958), 2:95ff.; for Eng. trans., see bibliography.

91. Ulrich, *Antiquiores consuetudines*, 2.30, *PL* 149:717B.

92. Bernard, *Ordo Cluniacensis*, 1.74, no. 65, p. 278. Equally, infinite precautions were taken when removing any trace of "the Lord's blood" from the pavement or of his "body" from the altar cloth or floor. The customs also took account of soiling by flies and spiders.

93. Ulrich, *Antiquiores consuetudines*, 2.30, *PL* 149:716A. See Jungmann, *Missarum sollemnia*, 1:386ff.

counted some edifying examples of priests who dared to approach the altar without confession. Such was the case of an unworthy cleric carrying on a sexual relationship with a nun. He was miraculously prevented from availing himself of the sacrifice, the consecrated elements disappearing on his three attempts to handle them. It was only after performing a sincere penance that he was able to resume the priestly office, "sacrificing himself to God with tears and contrition of heart." At his first Mass in his restored state, the elements from the earlier three Masses miraculously reappeared on the altar.[94] The picture Peter paints of Matthew of Albano in the second book of *De miraculis* contains an interesting allusion to the necessary purity of sacrificers. Matthew had not long been prior of Saint-Martin-des-Champs. He inquired about the monastery's debts and discovered that some of the creditors were Jewish. He railed against the monks for doing business with those "impious" people:

> With what look on my face, in what state of conscience shall I try to approach the altar of the Savior Christ, with what countenance come to speak with his pious mother, if I have been flattering his blaspheming enemies? How shall I please them, if I have become the friend of their worst enemies? How shall I dare to invoke them or pray to them with the same lips that have fawned upon those others over money or some other cause?[95]

These two examples show Peter the Venerable adopting an aggressive attitude regarding priestly purity that contrasts with the tone of theses, normally defended in eucharistic debates, emphasizing the efficiency of Christ's grace regardless of the merits of his ministers.[96]

Peter's attitude is explained by the ideal Cluniac monk's total identification with the saving sacrament of the altar, whether expressed in the two, and subsequently three, daily conventual Masses—services dedicated exclusively to the Lord—or in the numerous private Masses that also took place.[97] The ideal of the imitation of Christ had imbued Cluniac spirituality since the abbacy of Odilo. The abbot's biographer Jotsald depicted him celebrating the "holy sacrifice of the spotless lamb" with groans, sighs, and tears, and then, on his deathbed,

94. *DM*, 1.2, pp. 9–11.

95. *DM*, 2.15, ll. 19–25, pp. 125–26.

96. For example: Alger of Liège, *De sacramentis*, 3.3, *PL* 180:834–36; Guitmund of Aversa, *De corporis*, *PL* 149:1493D: "But if on account of the unworthiness of the priest there is no change in the bread and wine, then (which God forbid), the wickedness of the priest will have prevailed over the words of the Lord Savior, and the faith of the Church is false that believes the words of the Lord to operate equally whether the ministers be good or evil."

97. The third conventual Mass, that of Our Lady, was instituted by Peter the Venerable, *Statutum* 54, p. 84. Sunday was entirely devoted to the Lord, as prescribed by the *Liber tramitis* (*LT*, 204, p. 283, ll. 18–23) and then Peter's statutes 2 and 3 (*Statutum*, pp. 42–43). See Folz, "Pierre le Vénérable et la liturgie," pp. 156–58.

suffering with Christ, "as if he saw thee once again being crucified and dying!"[98] The abbot who died with Christ in his Passion was succeeded by one, Hugh of Semur, who was "born" in a chalice. Hugh's mother, Aremburgis, when carrying the future saint in her womb, asked a priest to celebrate a Mass for the safe deliverance of herself and her child. During the sacrifice, the celebrant was rapt in contemplation and saw the appearance in the chalice of a child's radiant face. This was little Hugh, destined from adolescence to receive "the chalice of the saving Passion as an imitator of the Lord"; he "crossed in image" to the abiding city and "exchanged the blandishments of the world for celestial harmony."[99] In a short liturgical poem, Peter the Venerable described Hugh's conversion in strongly eucharistic terms that invoke the word *hostia* (eucharistic offering) to designate Hugh as well as Christ:

> For him while yet enclosed within his mother's womb,
> The priest effects the sacrificial offering.
> In the chalice of mighty miracle a sign:
> The image of the little one himself appears.
> If anyone should ask if I know what this means:
> One offering marks out another one to come.[100]

In the early chapters of *De miraculis*, devoted to miracles of the Eucharist, there is one in which Peter the Venerable describes at length the monk Gerard, who "above all else, crowning the body of his virtues, had placed love of the saving sacraments of the altar."[101] Sacrificing almost daily, this Gerard offered himself in tears and achieved such union with Christ that he "penetrated even the very inmost things of heaven":

> For how is one easily to describe how clear was his eye of faith, how beneath the veil of the sacraments he experienced not wonder at a veiled Jesus Christ but contemplation of Christ himself revealed? Outward appearances did not

98. Jotsald, *Vita sancti Odilonis*, 1.6 and 14, PL 142:901C and 910A. See Simonin, "Le culte eucharistique à Cluny de saint Odon à Pierre le Vénérable," 10; Jean Leclercq, "La christologie clunisienne au siècle de saint Hugues," *Studia Monastica* 31 (1989): 267–78 (also reprinted, see bibliography).

99. Gilo, *Vita sancti Hugonis*, 1.1, "Two Studies," pp. 47–49, here 48–49; in 1.6, p. 55, Gilo describes Hugh as a "son of the paschal lamb." The same episode is told in the *Vita Hugonis* by Hildebert of Lavardin, who comments: "It was therefore fitting that he should be dedicated to the ministry of the chalice, who was viewed in the chalice as so promised," PL 159:860A.

100. *Rythmus de sancto Hugone abbate Cluniacensi*, BC, col. 465E. The theme of the personal offering of the sacrificer was a Gregorian tradition: see Gregory the Great, *Dialogues*, 4.61.1, ed. and French trans. by Adalbert de Vogüé and Paul Antin, SC, 265 (Paris, 1980), pp. 202–3. See also Vogüé, "Eucharistie et vie monastique," *Collectanea Cisterciensia* 48 (1986): 126.

101. DM, 1.8, pp. 23–34. This Gerard is not to be confused with Gerard Le Vert, whose eucharistic devotion Peter also celebrates, *Ep.*, 58, 1:179–89, here 189.

darken his understanding, but by spiritual insight he would behold Christ as it were walking with the apostles on earth, hanging on the Cross in the sight of the blessed Virgin, or rising from the dead in the company of Mary Magdalene.[102]

The telescoping of time, whereby the priest could be really present with Christ, see him walking with the apostles, behold him with the Virgin grieving at his Cross or with Mary Magdalene at his resurrection, was a typical eucharistic theme. Gerard was also the witness and protagonist of a miracle supporting belief in the reality of the Eucharist. Introducing the story, Peter recalls having already "read something similar," for the event he describes was not without precedent.[103] But the present case was even more amazing. Around Christmas, Gerard was celebrating Mass. "And when," as Peter puts it, "after the other prayers, he had come to the canon and finished saying the divine words changing the substance of bread and wine into the flesh and blood of Christ," on the altar Gerard saw not bread and wine but a little child.[104] He looked to one side and saw the Virgin accompanied by an angel. And the angel said to Gerard, "Why are you surprised? The child you see rules heaven and earth." After his own death, Gerard appeared to a brother who was in the grip of a demon "small and black like an Ethiopian."[105] In return for defending the monk against the demon, Gerard asked him to go to Abbot Peter requesting that the abbot record the story of yet another brother who had "once upon a time doubted the truth of the body and blood of the Lord." Peter summoned this monk, who told him of a miracle that, with the Virgin's help, had ended his doubts. He had seen a small child appear on the altar inviting him to take him and carry him the length of the church.

Had it been a matter for individual choice, the typical Cluniac monk would have opted to die either at Christmas or at Easter. Such was Hugh of Semur's case. He died at Easter, his last words being a profession of faith in "the Lord's

---

102. *DM*, 1.8, p. 26.

103. Denise Bouthillier, *DM*, p. 28, cites two possible precedents. First is the bleeding host reported by Paschasius Radbertus, *De corpore et sanguinis Domini*, 14, *CCCM* 16, pp. 87–88, a work twice mentioned in the Cluny library catalogue—see Delisle, *Inventaire des manuscrits*, nos. 234 (p. 350) and 272 (p. 352)—and taken from Paul the Deacon, *Vita sancti Gregorii*, 23, ed. H. Grisar, *Zeitschrift für katholische Theologie*, 2 (1887): 162–73, indexed in Frederic C. Tubach, *Index exemplorum: A Handbook of Medieval Religious Tales*, FF Communications, 204 (Helsinki, 1969), no. 2643. The second, more interesting to us, is ibid., no. 2689 ("Host transformed into Christ Child"). There is a Carolingian precedent in the *Miracula Numie episcopi*, 13, ed. Karl Strecker, *MGH PLAC*, 4.2, pp. 943–59, here 957–59, an example cited in the *Acta synodi Atrebatensis*, PL 142:1283C. My thanks go to Guy Lobrichon for these last two references. On the later history of these eucharistic *exempla* in preaching and representation, see Miri Rubin, *Corpus Christi: The Eucharist in Late Medieval Culture* (Cambridge, 1991), esp. pp. 110ff. and 116ff.

104. *DM*, 1.8, pp. 28–29.

105. *DM*, 1.8, pp. 32–34.

---

life-giving flesh."[106] Matthew of Albano "fell asleep in Christ" on Christmas Day 1135. In *De miraculis*, Peter the Venerable tells of the "holy and glorious way" in which his friend left the world. His narrative begins with the dying man's confession as he prepared to eat the body of the Lord:

> I confess (he declared) that this holy body of my Savior is truly and essentially that which he received of the Virgin Mary, that which hung on the Cross for the salvation of the world, which was placed in the tomb, which on the third day rose from the dead, ascended into heaven and will come to judge the living and the dead and the world by fire. I believe that through his body I am incorporated into him and made one with him and have eternal life.[107]

Matthew's deathbed avowal was related to the profession of faith bishops made on entering office in accordance with a tradition dating back to the fifth century and documented by the *Statuta ecclesiae antiqua*.[108] Its use widened in the antiheretical context of the early eleventh century. Abbot Gauzlin of Fleury-sur-Loire made such a declaration after King Robert decided to burn the heretics of Orléans.[109] At the Council of Rouen in 1055(?), Archbishop Maurilius insisted that the participants pronounce against the errors of Berengar; their proclamation was subsequently integrated into the consecration of Norman bishops.[110] The heresy of Berengar of Tours, who was himself summoned on two occasions to read an orthodox profession of faith on the Eucharist, at the Roman synods of 1059 and 1070, marked a vital turning point in the practice of deathbed confession among reform-minded clerics, especially monks and hermits. Bruno of Chartreux thus proclaimed at his dying hour his adherence to the

---

106. Gilo, *Vita sancti Hugonis*, 2.9, "Two Studies," pp. 99–100, here 100. Peter gives us another example, Benedict, *DM*, 1.20, pp. 58–63, here 61, ll. 90–96, and makes the following illuminating general observation: "[His death] occurred at Eastertide when Christ, finding his flock after the forty days of Lent more abstinent, more purified, and as it were a riper crop, drew many away out of this light and stored them away in his celestial granaries. For many at that time were urged on by slight illness, as though instantly following the nod of their beckoning Lord." Peter the Venerable himself died on Christmas Day 1156. On the question of the *dies natalis* of saints in this heyday of the Christian calendar, see Peter von Moos, *Consolatio: Studien zur mittellateinischen Trostliteratur über Tod und zum Problem der christlichen Trauer*, 3, Münstersche Mittelalter-Schriften, 3.3 (Munich, 1972), no. 645a-b.

107. *DM*, 2.22, p. 136, ll. 4–11.

108. *Statuta ecclesiae antiqua*, ed. Charles Munier (Strasbourg, 1960), p. 75. The profession was included in a letter of Gerbert (Pope Sylvester II) (ca. 945–1003), *Correspondence*, Ep. 180, ed. Pierre Riché and Jean-Pierre Callu, vol. 2, Les Classiques de l'Histoire de France au Moyen Age (Paris, 1993), pp. 452–55. I owe knowledge of these two texts to Monique Zerner.

109. *Vie de Gauzlin, abbé de Fleury: Vita Gauzlini abbatis Floriacensis monasterii*, ed. and French trans. by Robert-Henri Bautier and Gillette Labory, Sources d'Histoire médiévale publiées par l'Institut de Recherche et d'Histoire des Textes, 2 (Paris, 1969), pp. 98–101.

110. Herbert E. J. Cowdrey, "The Papacy and the Berengarian Controversy," in *Auctoritas und Ratio: Studien zu Berengar von Tours*, pp. 109–38, here 135 and n. 138.

main articles of the faith, including his belief in the sacrament of the altar, the "true body, true flesh, and true blood of our Lord Jesus Christ."[111] John Gualbert, the founder of Vallombrosa, even had the text of his profession written out, and he was probably buried with it.[112]

The "Miracle" of the Eucharist

The almost obsessional concern shown by Peter the Venerable and the Cluniacs to avoid all impurity in clerics called to sacrifice reflected their belief in the efficacy and importance of sacramental mediation operated by priests. Sacramental efficacy was nowhere more clearly modeled than in the change from one substance to another upon the altar; it lay at the heart of general ideas about the conversion of individuals and the transformation of property in the perspective of the Last Things. If we examine the eucharistic vocabulary that Peter the Venerable uses in *Contra Petrobrusianos* and his other works together with the technical terms used in the charters of Cluny to describe pious donations, we shall see how central the sacrament of the altar and its defense were within the wider context of social practices involving monks and laity in the feudal age.

The Eucharist and the Vocabulary of Essential Transformations

The noun *missa* (mass) occurs countless times in *De miraculis*, sometimes in the singular, sometimes in the plural. When speaking of the Carthusians, who sacrificed only on Sundays, Peter advances an interesting etymology of the term, deriving it from the past participle (*missa*) of the Latin verb *mittere*, "to send." It is thus, he says, a "sacrifice [*sacrificium*] called a 'missa' according to very ancient usage because it is 'sent' to God."[113] Klaus Gamber has distinguished three definitions of *missa* in the Church's early centuries: the *dimissio* or leave to depart given to catechumens in advance of the Eucharist or to all the faithful if no sacrifice was to be offered; *oblatio* or sacrifice; *oratio* (prayer) in the monastic world, where the plural *missae* was used in the sense of prayers, or rather collects, "sent to God," as Smaragdus of Saint-Mihiel is recorded as saying.[114] Peter the Venerable used the term in the sense both of "sacrifice" and of something "sent to God." In his view, sacrificing priests were thus "transmitters."

111. *Confessio fidei magistri Brunonis*, in *Lettres des premiers Chartreux*, vol. 1, *SC*, 88 (Paris, 1962), pp. 90–93.

112. *Vita Iohannis Gualberti*, indexed *BHL* 4399, ed. Friedrich Baethgen, *MGH SS*, 30.2, pp. 1104–10, here 1101. See Patrick Henriet, "*Silentium usque ad mortem servaret:* la scène de la mort chez les ermites italiens du XIe siècle," *MEFRM* 105.1 (1993): 265–98, here 291–92.

113. *DM*, 2.27(28), pp. 151–52, ll. 87–89.

114. Smaragdus of Saint-Mihiel, *Expositio in Regulam sancti Benedicti*, 17.10, *CCM* 8, p. 206. Quoted by Klaus Gamber, "Missa: von den dreifachen Bedeutung des Wortes," *Römische Quartalschrift für christliche Altertumskunde und Kirchengeschichte* 63 (1968): 170–84, here 181. I am grateful to Eric Palazzo for pointing me to Gamber's article.

The commonest term Peter uses is *sacramentum*.[115] He does not use it exclusively to denote the Eucharist; indeed it is instructive to note the other contexts in which he uses it. For Peter, *sacramentum* also meant an oath, a commitment of fidelity (*sacramentum fidelitatis*).[116] It is worth remembering that "sacrifice" was defined in *Contra Petrobrusianos* as a *signum servitutis*, a "mark of submission" by the creature to the Creator.[117] *Sacramenta* were, generally speaking, acts that bound. This was true both ecclesiastically and in social practice, the distinction between the two realms being in practice blurred, especially as oaths of all sorts were sworn at the altar. The expression *sacramenta fidei* (sacraments of faith) was used of the sacramental mysteries of baptism and the Eucharist, which entailed subsequent *opera fidei* (works of faith) because they did not suffice of themselves; otherwise, says Peter, Judas would not have gone out and hanged himself after receiving the body of Christ at the Last Supper.[118] When used by Peter without qualification, the term *sacramentum* invariably refers to the Eucharist, which is equally termed the "sacrament of the altar," "saving sacrament," "saving sacrament of the altar," "sacrament of the body and blood of Christ," which is "taken up" (*sumptum*) at the altar by such priests as the monk Gerard, described in *De miraculis* as contemplating the reality lying "beneath the veil of the sacraments."[119] Beyond these essentially classic uses are more interesting examples of overlapping terms. Thus Peter uses as synonyms or joins up to form doublings such terms as *sacramenta, sacra divina, divina sacrificia*, and above all *divina mysteria*.[120] Thus he appears unconcerned by the usual distinction established for example by Alger of Liège between *sacramentum*, a "visible sign signifying something," and *mysterium*, "something hidden signified by this sign."[121] In other words, Peter treats the signifier as identical with the signified and uses *sacramentum* and *mysterium* one for the other. The same is true of *sacramentum* and *miraculum*.[122] *Miraculum* (miracle) is used by Peter in the very broad sense of the manifestation of a hidden reality. Thus he describes the appearance of the Lord's glorious body at the Transfiguration as a *magnum sacra-*

115. My inquiry is based on the *Contra Petrobrusianos* text and the concordance to the Bouthillier edition of *De miraculis* given in the *Corpus Christianorum, Instrumenta lexicologica latina, series A* (Turnhout, 1988) as well as upon Peter the Venerable's letters.

116. *DM*, 2.12, p. 120, l. 73, concerning an oath of obedience demanded by Abbot Pontius of Melgueil.

117. *CP*, 157, ll. 13ff.

118. *DM*, 1.6, p. 18, ll. 56–60.

119. *Sacramentum* used alone to denote the Eucharist: *DM*, 1.11, p. 42, l. 61. "Sacrament of the altar," "saving sacrament," "saving sacrament of the altar": *DM*, 1.2, p. 10, l. 56; 1.25, p. 7, l. 13; 1.8, p. 29, l. 155, and p. 34, ll. 318–19; 2.2, p. 101, l. 27; 2.8, p. 110, l. 43; 1.8, p. 26, l. 67. *Sacramenta sumere, sumere carnem et sanguinem: DM*, 1.2, p. 9, ll. 2–22, and p. 10, l. 28; 1.25, p. 75, l. 14. Gerard, *DM*, 1.8, p. 26, l. 71.

120. *Sacramenta divina mysteria: DM*, 1.8, p. 26, l. 77, and p. 27, l. 98; 1.14, p. 48, l. 77.

121. Alger of Liège, *De sacramentis*, 1.4, *PL* 180:751C.

122. On this point, see the basic study by Torrell and Bouthillier, *"Miraculum."*

mentum, novum miraculum (mighty sacrament/sign, new miracle).[123] Judged by these criteria, the person and work of Christ are also "miraculous"; thus Christology and eucharistic doctrine are central elements in Peter's thinking about the manifestation of hidden realities.[124] We therefore need look no further to explain Peter's doctrinal interest in the real presence and his pastoral emphasis upon *exempla* containing eucharistic miracles that both revealed hidden realities and tangibly demonstrated the efficacy of the sacraments.

The Effects of Eucharistic Power

We noted earlier the edifying story of the Auvergne peasant who attempted to make his bees immortal by putting them in contact with an unconsumed but consecrated host.[125] Peter's purpose in telling the story was to denounce a wayward form of belief in eucharistic efficacy. Belief in the immediate and tangible effects of the sacrament of the altar was widely shared in the twelfth century. But the clergy, in their role as mediators, endeavored to control and redirect these notions to better effect. *De miraculis* is rich in short *exempla* witnessing to the formidable power of the Eucharist. The dying who failed to make adequate confession or were unrepentant are thus depicted as incapable of consuming the body of Christ. This "accident" is assimilated by Peter to "divine judgment."[126]

It was consistent with this logic that the altar became the place to exercise the spiritual justice that was periodically needed to control secular unrest. In his *Vita sancti Hugonis*, Gilo wrote how Hugh of Semur was forced to defend the Cluniac priory of Saint-Jean-Baptiste at Chaveyriat against an invading castellan, Berard of Riotier.[127] The abbot stood before the altar; in tears he beseeched God for assistance and uttered a malediction. The episode was partly related to the clamor ritual with which the monks defended themselves against their enemies.[128] The first description we have of such a Cluniac ritual is to be found in the *Liber tramitis*, in the chapter on prayers, just after the formulae of prayer for rain.[129] It took place during high Mass. The pavement in front of the altar was covered with a hair shirt, upon which were placed a crucifix, the text of the Gospels, and saints' relics. The clergy prostrated themselves and recited Psalm 73(74), *Ut quid Deus reppulisti in finem?*—"O God, why has thou cast us off unto

123. *STD, PL* 189:962D, quoted by Torrell and Bouthillier, "*Miraculum*," p. 368.

124. In Cluny III, the Chapel of the Virgin, known also as "the Abbot's Chapel," dating from Pontius of Melgueil's abbacy (1109–22), housed a painted cycle of Christ's miracles, as is attested by Peter the Venerable himself, *Ep.*, 86, 1:222–27, here 224; and see Kenneth J. Conant, *Cluny: les églises et la maison du chef d'ordre* (Mâcon, 1968), p. 107.

125. *DM*, 1.1, pp. 7–8.

126. *DM*, 1.3, pp. 11–13, and 1.5, pp. 15–16; the terms quoted are from p. 15, l. 19.

127. Gilo, *Vita sancti Hugonis*, 1.49, "Two Studies," p. 87. I thank Patrick Henriet for drawing my attention to this text.

128. Lester K. Little, *Benedictine Maledictions: Liturgical Cursing in Romanesque France* (Ithaca and London, 1993), esp. pp. 20–29 and 262–65.

129. *LT*, 174–75, pp. 244–48.

the end?" Bells were rung twice. A priest then placed himself "before the Lord's body and blood newly consecrated and before the aforesaid relics of saints" and recited out loud the "clamor" whose text was laid down in the customary. The rite recorded by Bernard in his "Customs" forty years later contained notable differences but confirmed the eucharistic context in which the clamor took place.[130] In order to draw attention to the effects of the aggression suffered, the monks reduced the liturgical service to a minimum. They summoned the people (doubtless the inhabitants of the monastic *burgus*) to the morning Mass said before the crucifix. After the Gospel, creed, and offertory, a brother entered the pulpit. There he recalled the divine precepts, described the troubles endured by the community, and called for prayer that God might calm the offender and "turn evil into good" (*commutet de malo ad bonum*). Then the assembly intoned the response *Aspice, domine* and recited Psalms 3, 45, and 122. The appeal to divine justice enacted in the clamor rite was an expression of profound belief in the immediate and tangible efficacy of the Eucharist. It always took place during Mass. In the earliest case, the priest recited the clamor text at the altar, before the newly consecrated elements. As we have just seen, one of Bernard's touches illustrates well the eucharistic logic of this appeal to God: during the eucharistic reiteration of Christ's sacrifice, the change of the bread and wine into the body and blood of the Savior, there was a parallel plea to God to "turn evil into good." Those few words illustrate how the Eucharist was a paradigm "change" whose wider social relevance we would do well to bear in mind.

Eucharistic Change and Social Practice

In order to provide irrefutable proof of the eucharistic tradition commemorating the Last Supper against the Petrobrusians, Peter goes back over all the precedents from Adam to Christ and then retraces the line leading from Christ to his own time. His treatment of the age of the Church relies exclusively upon "everyday miracles," as he seeks to persuade his opponents on the basis of "sufficient reasons" taken from common experience. The astonishing miracle of the Eucharist he thus portrays as of comparable nature to other physical processes involving changes from one substance to another without change of form, as when water turns to crystal though it retains its translucent form. The recourse to analysis of physical phenomena sets Peter apart from his avowed sources, Lanfranc, Guitmund of Aversa, and Alger of Liège, and places him at the heart of the discussion going on in contemporary scholastic circles about the notion of "accidents" with or without alterations of substance.[131]

130. Bernard, *Ordo Cluniacensis*, 1.40, pp. 230–31.
131. The discussion of "accidents" and "substance" was based upon knowledge—imperfect until the end of the twelfth century—of Aristotle, especially his *Categories;* see Montclos, *Lanfranc et Béranger,* pp. 471–72. On the problem of *accidens sine subiecto,* see David Burr, *Eucharistic Presence and Conversion in Late Thirteenth-Century Franciscan Thought,* Transactions of the American Philosophical Society, 74.3 (Philadelphia, 1984), pp. 2ff. I am grateful to Irène Rosier for knowledge of Burr's work.

The years 1130–40, during which Peter was putting his *Contra Petrobrusianos* together, was the very time when the hunt was on to find the aptest terms to describe the eucharistic change.[132] The term *transformatio* would logically have implied change of form. In preference to *mutatio* or *transmutatio* (mutation or transmutation), partisans of the change of substance chose to use the term *transsubstantio* or *transsubstantiatio* (transubstantiation), which is first attested in the work of Robert Pullen, active in Paris in the 1140s.[133] Pullen taught that *transmutatio* was applicable to a change in quality (or form) with maintenance of the substance, such as in the case of Lot's wife, who was turned into a pillar of salt (Genesis 19:26); *transsubstantio* on the other hand was applicable only to a change of substance with maintenance of the form, as in the Eucharist.[134] Peter the Venerable never used the term *transsubstantiatio*, which it must be said did not receive immediate and universal acceptance.[135] He preferred to describe the reality of the change with more current words like *mutatio, commutatio, transmutatio*. The use of such vocabulary placed the "sacrament of the altar" within the wide category of the "miracles" and "changes" that occurred from day to day. The notions of *mutatio, commutatio, transmutatio* at the heart of Peter's thinking on the Eucharist made it possible to view the essential transformations affecting people and property in general within an eschatological perspective.

Historians of feudal society tend to be greatly interested in the exchanges between monks and lay aristocrats concerned to make provision here for a happy life hereafter. The concept of such a transfer has never been subjected to deep

132. The lexical problems are well presented in Joseph Goering, "The Invention of Transubstantiation," *Traditio* 46 (1991): 147–70. Henri de Lubac's remarks (*Corpus mysticum*, p. 98) on the vocabulary of "eucharistic conversion" remain highly apposite.

133. De Lubac, *Corpus mysticum*, p. 158. The term is also to be found without discussion in a work attributed to Stephen of Baugé, archbishop of Autun (1112–36), who retired to Cluny where he died in 1140: *Tractatus de sacramento altaris, PL* 172:1273–1302, here 1291C and 1293C. The attribution has never been critically established, and I am personally skeptical about his authorship. Peter the Venerable speaks of him admiringly (*Ep.*, 143, 1:352–53, here 353), but without referring to this work, though it would have been an ideal source for *Contra Petrobrusianos*. The distinction it makes around the notion of *sacramentum* (*PL* 172:1296AB: *sacramentum tantum; res sacramenti et sacramentum; res tantum*) also strikes me as slightly later than the 1130s—on which see Marcel Damien van den Eynde, *Les définitions des sacrements pendant la première période de la théologie scolastique (1050–1240)* (Rome, 1950), pp. 18–27.

134. Goering, "The Invention of Transubstantiation," p. 151, n. 13, and appendix C, p. 170: *Et notandum quod magister Robertus Pullus invenit primo hanc dictionem "transubstantiatur" et bene dicebat cum non diceret transmutatur, cum forma remaneat et substantia transeat.*—"It is to be noted that Robert Pullen first invented this term 'transubstantiatur' and did well not to say 'transmutatur,' since the form remains and the substance changes." [The extract is from Cambridge, Peterhouse MS 255, prior to 1250, "Quaestio de eucharistia," from the circle of William de Montibus—trans.]

135. The term was "officially" used in the opening creed of the Fourth Lateran Council in 1215, though transubstantiation was very far from being considered a dogma. For more detail on this aspect, see Gary Macy, "The Dogma of Transubstantiation in the Middle Ages," *Journal of Ecclesiastical History* 45.1 (1994): 11–41.

analysis, but scholars have generally taken for granted Marcel Mauss's notion of "gift" and "countergift," which seems to do justice to the text of Luke 6:38, *Date et dabitur vobis*—"Give, and it shall be given to you."[136] In the present instance we might say that the monks received offerings from the faithful concerned about the afterlife, to whom they in return supplied spiritual services (prayers, Masses, burials in the cemetery, enrollments in their necrology, and so on).[137] Yet such a framework of analysis is both too restrictive and too statistical to satisfy the medievalist. Not only does it focus on two agents in the exchange (the faithful and the monks) to the exclusion of a third (the poor), it obscures a probable evolution in the terms of exchange during the course of the tenth, eleventh, and twelfth centuries. Early on, the faithful would often state that through their gifts they wanted to make the holy patrons of the monastery their "debtors"— especially Peter, who held the keys of heaven—because they would need their intervention as "advocates" at the future judgment.[138] In short the gift was something given today in order to get something back tomorrow. In Marcel Mauss's terms, what motivated the gift was that it created an obligation.[139] From

136. Marcel Mauss, "Essai sur le don: forme et raison de l'échange dans les sociétés archaïques," *L'Année sociologique*, new ser., 1 (1923–24); for reprint and Eng. trans., see bibliography. Mauss's work must now be read alongside Maurice Godelier, *L'énigme du don*. Paris, 1996. [Eng. trans., *The Enigma of the Gift*, trans. Nora Scott (Cambridge, 1999).] Somewhat earlier Georg Schreiber analyzed medieval ecclesiastical dues in terms of gift-countergift (*Gabe-Gegengabe*) or offering-counteroffering (*Leistung-Gegenleistung*), deemed to correspond to the principles of German law. See his "Kirchliches Abgabenwesen an französischen Eigenkirchen aus Anlass von Ordalien," *Zeitschrift der Savigny-Stiftung für Rechtsgeschichte, Kanonistische Abteilung* 36 (1915): 465; for reprint see bibliography. The notion of *Gabe-Gegengabe* has been applied to Cluny by Willibald Jorden, *Das cluniazensische Totengedächtniswesen vornehmlich unter den drei ersten Äbten Berno, Odo und Aymard (910–954)*, Münstersche Beiträge zur Theologie, 15 (Münster im W., 1930), pp. 94ff. On the use of the gift-countergift concept in medieval studies, see Philip Grierson, "Commerce in the Dark Ages: A Critique of the Evidence," *Transactions of the Royal Historical Society*, 5th ser., 9 (1959): 123–40; Georges Duby, *Guerriers et paysans, VIIe–XIIe siècle: premier essor de l'économie européenne*, Bibliothèque des Histoires (Paris, 1973), pp. 60ff; Otto G. Oexle, "Memoria und Memorialüberlieferung im früheren Mittelalter," *FMSt* 10 (1976): 87ff.; Constance Brittain Bouchard, *Sword, Miter, and Cloister: Nobility and the Church in Burgundy, 980–1198* (Ithaca and London, 1987), pp. 217ff. The question of the gift is also studied in a context and with a framework of analysis very similar to ours by Michel Lauwers, *La mémoire des ancêtres, le souci des morts: morts, rites et société au Moyen Age*, Théologie historique, 103 (Paris, 1997), pp. 172–204 and 226–48.

137. See for instance *CLU* 2112, 993/1048, 3.299–300, which contained terms committing the monks.

138. *CLU* 1999, 993/1048, 3.212: *facientes nostri eos debitores quos veraciter novimus et inpresentiarum saluti corporum consulere, et in futuro iudices fore animarum non ambigimus*—"making them our debtors, who in the present we truly know have regard for the health of our bodies and who in the future we do not doubt will be judges of our souls." Similarly: *CLU* 2831, ca. 1021, 4.34–35; 3350, ca. 1055, 4.446–47; 3404, August 1065, 4.507–10. Examination based on original documents prior to 1120 reveals none after 1065 containing this notion of a debt contracted by the saints.

139. Mauss, "Essai sur le don"; and see the presentation and discussion of this central thesis in Godelier, *L'énigme du don*, pp. 20ff.

the Gregorian period on, however, the gift topos underwent modification. What was emphasized increasingly was the inequality of the exchange; the theme of *licet pauca* (though it be but little) began to appear.[140] At the same time, the campaign against simony had the consequence of restricting donations linked to conversion.[141] Finally, and most importantly for our study, the "gift-countergift" model makes no allowance for the "transmutation" of property concerned in transactions for funerary purposes. It also fails to account, more generally, for the process of "transformation" of property in the seigneurial age, whereby an object given, or taken, acquired through its redistribution a greatly enhanced symbolic value.[142]

The vocabulary of exchange found in the charters of Cluny is remarkably varied and difficult to analyze. The category of donation, which Georges Chevrier has described as a "sort of prototype juridical act,"[143] appears to have embraced transactions of different types—freewill grants, restitutions, exchanges, sales— as if the only acceptable tone in which dealings with the afterlife could be couched was that of the "offering." What one has to do is to pick out the abundant terms indicative of the transformation of property: *commutatio, inmutatio,*

---

140. *CLU* 3347, ca. 1054, 4.443–44, a gift by Geoffrey II of Semur, Abbot Hugh's brother: *Quae [bona] si non equalia, et ut dignum est, tamen a suo plasmate cui omnia contulit pro multis non dedignatur recipere breviora*—"Which [goods], though they be not equal, ... nevertheless from His creature, on whom He has bestowed all things, He does not disdain in return for much to receive much less"; *CLU* 3357, ca. 1080, 4.685–87.

141. The culmination of this development was Canon 64 of the Fourth Lateran Council, which opposed payment for conversion. In a statute of 1200, Abbot Hugh V of Cluny sought to avoid the sin of simony at conversion by adopting a position based on Gratian's *Decretum* (1.2), which held that requests for payment were sinful but that freewill gifts were legitimate. On this question, which became an issue only after Peter the Venerable's death, see Joseph H. Lynch, "Efforts to Combat Monastic Simony in the Early Thirteenth Century," *RB* 85 (1975): 126–63, and *Simoniacal Entry into Religious Life from 1000 to 1260: A Social, Economic, and Legal Study* (Columbus, 1976), esp. pp. 163–65.

142. On the "transformation" of property in the seigneurial context, see Joseph Morsel's works on the nobility at the close of the Middle Ages. Several lines of inquiry can already be seen in "Pour une étude du pouvoir de la noblesse à la fin du Moyen Age," *Bulletin de la Mission historique française en Allemagne* 11 (1985): 4–27, esp. 17. Morsel's term "transfiguration" is however best avoided owing to its potential for confusion with the New Testament Transfiguration: the appearance of the Lord in glory during his earthly life (Matthew 17:1–13, etc.).

143. "Evolution de la notion de donation dans les chartes de Cluny du IXe à la fin du XIIe siècle," in *À Cluny*, Congrès scientifique, 9–11 July 1949 (Dijon, 1950), pp. 203–9, here 203: Chevrier traces the gradual fusion during the eleventh century of the notion of the sale with that of the donation, which ceased to be "an act of generosity in the strict sense" but became "a nameless prototype capable of adapting itself to the most varied of dealings," p. 207. In the field of acts of last will, Chevrier's work has been continued by Michel Petitjean, esp. "L'acte à cause de mort dans la France coutumière du Moyen Age à l'époque moderne," in *Actes à cause de mort. Acts of Last Will*, 2, Recueils de la Société Jean Bodin pour l'histoire comparative des institutions, 60 (Brussels, 1993), pp. 85–127.

transmutatio, donare atque transmutare, transfundere.[144] The semantic field in which such terms appear is rich in distinctive oppositions often drawn from the Bible: death and sin versus alms (Tobit 4:10–11 and 12:9; Ecclesiasticus 3:33; Daniel 4:24);[145] sin versus justice (Proverbs 13:6–9);[146] water versus fire (Ecclesiasticus 3:33);[147] wealth that is present, fleeting, and perishable versus treasure in heaven (Matthew 6:20);[148] "having nothing" versus "possessing all things" (2 Corinthians 6:10).[149] The practical value of a believer's earthly goods was thus able to transfer him from one opposing side to the other and decisively change his destiny. This will be clear if we look at a particular instance. In the 1070s, Count Thibaut I of Champagne and his wife, Adelaide, donated a *villa* to Cluny with a view to founding a priory at Coincy.[150] The *memorandum* summarizing the ins and outs of this pious act repays detailed study.[151] At the start, Thibaut is given a title likely to flatter his princely consciousness: "Count of the Franks by the grace of God."[152] The scale of the count's and his wife's act is viewed in relative terms: it is not much (*licet pauca*); the divinely inspired gift does no more than restore temporarily held property to the One from whom it originated (*sua sibi reddimus, non nostra largimur*). Echoing the words of Christ in Luke 16:9, the donors say that their aim is "to make for ourselves friends here and now by whom we may merit to be received after this life into everlasting dwellings." They explain that the "holy community" of Cluny, the recipient of their pious gift, has been chosen because increasingly strong and famous (*potior celebriorque*)—an allusion no doubt to the funerary efficacy of a multibranched body capable of mobilizing all its members.[153] The baptism of one of the cou-

144. Among others: *CLU* 821, 1.774–76; 1639, 2.674–75; 1668, 2.688, mention—*donare atque transfundere* or *tradere atque transfundere*; 3301, 4.396–97—*transmutatio*; 3377, 4.472–73, from 1061/73—*felix commutatio*; 3676, 5.29–30—*commutatio.*

145. *CLU* 1784, 3.39–42; 2815, 4.18–19; 3315, 4.408–10; 3676, 5.29–30.

146. *CLU* 1715, 2.735–38; 3350, 4.446–47; 3506, 4.620–21.

147. *CLU* 2731, 3.755–56; 2997, 4.194–95.

148. *CLU* 1644, 2.674–75, among very many others in this vein.

149. *CLU* 3410, 4.507–10; 3563, 4.698–702.

150. On Thibaut's contribution to the reform movement and the penetration of Cluniac monasticism into Champagne as a result of this donation, see Michel Bur, *La formation du comté de Champagne, v. 950–v. 1150*, Mémoires des *Annales de l'Est*, 54 (Nancy, 1977), pp. 224ff.

151. *CLU* 3557, 4.685–87; and see Armin Kohnle, *Abt Hugo von Cluny (1049–1109)*, Beihefte der Francia, 32 (Sigmaringen, 1993), pp. 180 and 307: Kohnle dates the act prior to 1076.

152. On this title, see Bur, *La formation du comté de Champagne*, p. 130.

153. On the capacity of the Ecclesia cluniacensis to mobilize itself for funerary ends, one may cite among other examples: (1) Odilo's commitment to remember Count Lambert of Chalon with suffrages "in the monastery of Cluny or in all its dependencies," *CLU* 2921, 1037, 4.122–23; (2) Ulrich's stipulations about Cluny's undertaking role for the laity before and after death "not just in our house, but in all the places of our right," *Antiquiores consuetudines*, 3.33, *PL* 149:777; (3) Bernard, to the same effect, *Ordo Cluniacensis*, 1.26, p. 200; (4) Peter the Venerable's commitment to Raoul of Péronne to remember him "throughout the monasteries belonging to Cluny, where the order ob-

ple's sons, Odo, by Hugh of Semur marked the family's entry into the Cluniac fraternity.[154] By this symbolic gesture, which accompanied their donation of Coincy, Thibaut and Adelaide hoped to have, as they said, "our son Odo renewed through the mysteries of holy regeneration by your paternity [the abbot of Cluny, Hugh of Semur], reckoning that through the dispensation of heavenly clemency it will not be vain for him to have had parents in Christ more concerned for religion than for riches."[155]

Their gesture, the noble action of nobles, taught by example that to give was to give back.[156] To make a gift was to pay a due, even if the exchange was fundamentally unequal. As Thomas Aquinas was to say nearly two hundred years later, "Whatever is rendered by man to God is a debt: but it cannot equal what he owes."[157] Humanity was part of a mystic circle facilitating the return of property to its Creator (*Largitor*) or more generally of effects toward their Cause. The mechanism of this return movement was expressed primarily in terms of penitential commutation. It discharged the giver from reparation of a fault in accordance with a dual principle. First, there was the notion of quid pro quo, one thing given for another by way of reparation (hence the use of the term *iusticia* or "justice" to denote the gift).[158] Secondly, the reparation was made by way of a third party symbolically replacing the penitent. Such then was the role of the "friends" mentioned in the foundation charter of the priory of Coincy: the immediate beneficiaries of the gift, the monks, the holy patrons of the monastery, and the poor ritually maintained by the community, who would eventually be welcoming the donors into the "everlasting dwellings." Among these merciful "friends," Thibaut I and Adelaide of Champagne counted above all upon their own son Odo. The redemption of the count's family relied upon the interweaving of two parental relationships: Odo's relationship to his physical parents and his spiritual relationship with his new "father," Hugh of Semur, who renewed him "through the mysteries of holy regeneration." In his role as priest and me-

---

tains," *CLU* 4070, ca. 1140, 5.421–22. Other examples are cited by Herbert E. J. Cowdrey, "Unions and Confraternity with Cluny," *Journal of Ecclesiastical History* 16 (1965): 160, n. 1, namely: *CLU* 3233, 1049/1109, 4.359; 3393, 1063, 4.497–98; 3516, before 1078, 4.632–33; 3652, ca. 1090, 4.821–22; 3765, ca. 1100, 5.117–18.

154. On Odo's baptism, see Joseph H. Lynch, "Hugh I of Cluny's Sponsorship of Henry IV: Its Context and Consequences," *Speculum* 60 (1985): 816ff., where the difference of position between godfather and priest is probably insufficiently stressed.

155. *CLU* 3557, 4.685–87, here 686: *Oddonem filium nostrum sacre regenerationis misteriis innovandum a vestra paternitate destinavimus, rati superna dispensante clementia sibi non inane futurum religiosiores quam ditiores in Christo habuisse parentes.*

156. A phenomenon already noticed by Barbara H. Rosenwein, *To Be the Neighbor of Saint Peter: The Social Meaning of Cluny's Property, 909–1049* (Ithaca and London, 1989), pp. 137–38. On child oblation seen as a "holocaust for the Lord," see Mayke de Jong, *In Samuel's Image: Child Oblation in the Early Medieval West* (Leiden, 1996), esp. pp. 267ff.

157. *Summa Theologiae*, 2.2ae, q. 80, resp., quoted by Godelier, *L'énigme du don*, p. 273 and n. 1.

158. Jorden, *Das cluniazensische Totengedächtniswesen*, p. 90, n. 41.

diator of the sacraments, Hugh was reengendering the child in Christ, who was the bearer of remedies capable of healing the ills of mankind and the pivot of the commutational system that enabled an individual to cross from one side of the oppositions mentioned earlier to the other. It was Christ who opened the way to the great reversal of fortunes; his Pasch or Passover, like his Transfiguration, allowed contemplation of him in his *transitus*, his going across or passing over, the guarantee to the members of his body of their own future passage.[159] The preambles to charters of donation often recalled that the divine Redeemer had freely bestowed on believers the means to attain eternity.[160] According to an early tradition recorded in the Carolingian era, free-will gifts to churches were entered in charters placed on the altar to signify the property's permanent surrender.[161] More symbolic still was the renunciation of the property signaled by the hand on the chalice. In an undated charter probably dating from the 1090s, a Lotharingian aristocrat, Theodore of Saint-Hilaire, gave the church of Vandoeuvre to Bishop Pipo of Toul in order for him to give it in turn to Cluny. The donor thus described his act of relinquishment: "Through [the medium of] the chalice that I held of the same church, I removed my hand, as was just, from the aforesaid church and placed it into the hand of the bishop on the understanding that as I had given it so he should hand it over to Saint Peter and Saint Paul and the lord abbot of Cluny."[162] The chalice was thus a symbolic means whereby such property could pass from lay to ecclesiastical hands.

Allusions to the Redeemer and para-eucharistic acts of relinquishment argue that the monk-priests, to whom the property was delegated, were not considered merely as necessary intermediaries but seen above all as effective transformers. The issue was less one of giving so as to receive than one of granting with a view to the transformation of persons and property "for the better" (*in*

159. On Christ's *transitus* "manifested" in advance through the Transfiguration, cf. *STD, PL* 189:965C: "For he had come not that he might stay here, but that he might pass over [*transiret*] from here. He was crossing [*transibat*] from death to life, crossing [*transibat*] from corruption to incorruption, crossing [*transibat*] from humbleness to glorification, crossing [*transibat*] from the world to the Father." Peter adds that thereby God reversed the destiny of mankind, who were themselves taken into the majesty of the transfigured Christ, 969D: "Thus plainly the love with which I loved the Son was in men, because I loved him for this, that he should call others. For this I loved him, that he might justify the called. For this I loved him, that he should magnify the justified. And because by this love others also are saved through him, since he loved them first, he himself also is loved by them." On the notion of *transitus* in the Transfiguration and Pasch of Christ in Peter the Venerable's writings, see the penetrating analysis by Bodard, "Le mystère du corps du Seigneur," pp. 108 and 112ff.

160. See, for example, *CLU* 1189, 965–66, 2.273–74.

161. *MGH LNG*, 5.1 (*leges Alamannorum*).

162. *CLU* 3445, 4.554–55: *Per calicem quem tenebam ejusdem aecclesie manum meam, ut justum erat, a predicta ecclesia devestivi et in manum episcopi tradidi, eo tenore ut quemadmodum ego dederam, ipse Sancto Petro et Paulo et domno abbati Cluniacensi redderet.* See also Kohnle, *Abt Hugo*, p. 149, and on Theodore of Saint-Hilaire, see Michel Parisse, *Noblesse et chevalerie en Lorraine médiévale: les familles nobles du XIe au XIIIe siècle*, Publications de l'Université de Nancy II (Nancy, 1982), p. 147.

melius transmutare); in the Christian vocabulary of transcendence this amounted to transformation into something socially useful.[163] Where persons were offered—as in baptism, child oblation, or conversion—the process of transformation by regeneration was simple to understand. It meant, as the apostle Paul said in 2 Corinthians 5:17, becoming "in Christ a new creature." More complex was the transformation of property. When it was granted to Cluny and became the sacred property of Peter, its nature changed. Certain last wills stipulate payments to the monks of allowances of grain and wine for the brethren's sustenance; as Willibald Jorden has indicated, such gifts can be regarded as "distant supplies for the eucharistic offering," the supreme moment of "transformation."[164] Assigning such goods to the altar most definitely "converted" them from *temporalia* (worldly goods) into *spiritualia* (spiritual goods). In a letter to Bernard of Clairvaux in defense of the Ecclesia cluniacensis, Peter the Venerable was at pains to explain this phenomenon of the "transformation" of property and dependent persons. To justify the monastic possession of land, Peter begins by quoting from the Rule of Saint Benedict (58.24), the terms of which ("If he has any possessions, . . . he should donate them to the monastery") he maintains envisaged no restriction. As for the Cistercians' objection in favor of the necessary direct exploitation of land, Peter rejects that as "indecent and impossible." Indecent, he says, because the monks' rule of life presupposes that they will devote themselves to prayer and meditation in the isolation of the cloister. Impossible, because abstinence renders the brethren too weak for hard physical toil on their lands. Hence the need for dependents. Several other authorities (Gregory the Great, the *Vita sancti Gregorii*, and the *Vita sancti Mauri*) also sought to justify, in the light of Benedictine history, the possession of land by the monasteries. Peter adds a "rational" demonstration of the transformed nature of property relinquished to monastic establishments. He explains that goods acquired by secular men obey secular laws (*saeculariter disponuntur*); yet if the right (*ius*) that they obey is transferred to men of religion, they too become "religious goods," for henceforth they are used "religiously" by the "religious." Thus Peter could say of one such "transformed" object that "if a fortress [*castrum*] is given to monks, it ceases to be a fortress and starts being a place of prayer [*oratorium*]."[165] Dependents transferred at the same time as the land on which they depended were equally "transformed": they thereby escaped the arbitrary exactions of lay

163. Such is the very expression of original charter *CLU* 3301, 4.396–97, dating from Hugh of Semur's abbacy. There is a good example of personal and material "commutation" in a charter from 1081, *CLU* 3585, 4.732–34, here 732: *dono et commuto sive transfundo memet ipsum cum omnibus rebus et possessionibus et universis que habere possum*—"I give and commute or transmit myself with all goods and possessions and everything that I may have."

164. Jorden, *Das cluniazensische Totengedächtniswesen*, p. 89, citing *CLU* 269, May 926, 1.261–63, here 262.

165. *Ep.*, 28, 1:86: *Nam quamdiu a saecularibus optinentur . . .*

lords, for the monks would demand of them only such tasks and dues as were possible for them. Above all, they ceased to be "serfs and handmaids" (*servi et ancillae*) and became "brothers and sisters" (*fratres et sorores*) who, like the monks, were "as having nothing and possessing all things" (2 Corinthians 2:6).

"Easter" and Monastic Transmigration

The monastery, that space of "transformation for the better," was steeped in eucharistic mysticism. Kenneth J. Conant's reconstitution of the great porch of Cluny III, built during Abbot Pontius of Melgueil's time (1109–22), from sculptured fragments, descriptions, and ancient drawings reveals a central portion containing a Christ enthroned in glory within a mandorla that was sustained by two angels surrounded by two seraphim and the symbols of the four evangelists—the winged man for Matthew, the lion for Mark, the ox for Luke, and the eagle for John. Christ's throne took the form of an altar.[166] The first two bays of the narthex, built in Peter the Venerable's time, roughly between 1145 and 1155, had decorated keystones, one of which had a rose design and the other, that further east and nearer the porch, a paschal lamb.[167] In the second-stage basilica, Cluny II, the narthex was called the "galilee."[168] It was a space of transition where, among other things, the laity would await the monks in procession. But above all, it was where bodies of the deceased coming from outside the monastery were placed before their admission to the church and burial in the cemetery.[169] It was surely no coincidence that the narthex of Cluny III, which played the symbolic role of a space between two worlds, should have offered paschal iconography to observing eyes.

The hagiographic legend of Hugh of Semur celebrated the scale of Cluny III, the greatest church in Christendom until the reconstruction of Saint Peter's in Rome in the sixteenth century. The anonymous author of the *Miracula sancti Hugonis* depicted Hugh's church as a sort of "deambulatory of the angels," a "human habitation to please the inhabitants of heaven." He compared the monks to men "let out of prison," to the apostles after the resurrection of Christ (Matthew 28:7; Mark 16:7):

---

166. Conant, *Cluny*, p. 103 and plate 190. From the fourth century, in Rome, the throne of Christ was assimilated to the *sedes crucis et agni*, cf. *Lexikon der christlichen Ikonographie*, 4 (1972), s.v. "*Thron (Hetoimasia)*," cols. 305–13 (Th. v. Bogyay). By analogy, the throne of the martyrs took the form of an altar, cf. André Grabar, "Le trône des martyrs," *Cahiers archéologiques* 6 (1952): 31–41. My thanks go to Daniel Russo for this last reference.

167. Conant, *Cluny*, p. 113 and plate 228.

168. See *LT*, 142, p. 204, ll. 28ff. On this "galilee," see Conant, *Cluny*, pp. 59ff., and Christian Sapin, *La Bourgogne préromane: construction, décor et fonction des édifices religieux* (Paris, 1986), pp. 68–70.

169. Bernard, *Ordo Cluniacensis*, 1.34, p. 219; and cf. 1.32, p. 217, and 1.74(26), p. 272, for other mentions of the "galilee."

It is as if every day they celebrate Easter, because they have merited to go over [*transire*] into a certain Galilee and be happy in the joy of a new freedom, . . . able to be at liberty to attend to divine contemplation without sadness.[170]

The everyday living of Easter by the monk-priests of Cluny was for them a sort of migration into a new space. We know that contemporary monastic theology ascribed a great deal of importance to the *transitus* represented by the Transfiguration of Christ and his Passover, to which the term *galilea*, in its etymological sense of *transmigratio*, was applied.[171] The assimilation of the "greatest church" in Christendom to Galilee was the translation into spatial terms of the conception of incorporation (*concorporatio*) that was accomplished in the daily Passover of the eucharistic sacrifice. This daily Passover enacted a twofold *transitus:* it commemorated both Christ's passing over from this world to that of the Father (*semel*—once) and the Church's "sacramental" passage in him and through him in anticipation of the General Resurrection (*semper*—always).

Peter the Venerable's argument concerning the fourth proposition of *Contra Petrobrusianos*, the eucharistic anecdotes of *De miraculis*, the practical documents that speak laconically of desires for "transformation for the better," the iconography and monumental symbolism of the great porch and narthex of Cluny II—all this apparently heterogeneous evidence delivered a coherent ecclesiological picture elaborated around the mystery of Christ. The Cluniacs' devotion to the sacrament of the altar turned their monastery into a small-scale model of the Church itself in the corporative and spatial sense of the term. It was the supreme place where mighty transformations took place, where, as Gregory the Great had said, "the heavens open to the priest's voice at the very hour of the sacrifice, . . . the lowest are associated with the highest, earth is joined to the celestial, and visible and invisible things are made one."[172]

170. *Alia miraculorum quorumdam S. Hugonis abbatis relatio, BC,* col. 458BC, a passage that Kenneth Conant sees as alluding to the galilee of Cluny II, *Cluny,* p. 60. Cf. Gilo, *Vita sancti Hugonis,* 2.1, pp. 90–92, esp. 91.

171. Alf Härdelin, "Pâques et Rédemption: étude de théologie monastique du XIIe siècle," *Collectanea Cisterciensia* 43 (1981): 4; my remarks here owe much to Härdelin's penetrating study.

172. *Dialogues,* 4.60.3, p. 202.

7

THE LIVING AND THE DEAD

From the Eucharist, *Contra Petrobrusianos* moved immediately to the question of the dead. In Peter the Venerable's mind the two subjects were intimately linked. In the first place, commemoration was integral to the concept of eucharistic sacrifice, which had been defined as a memorial by Christ himself; secondly, the sacrament of the altar was central to the acts of commemoration actually requested by the dead. Peter followed the same logic in ordering *De miraculis*. He opened book 1 with five chapters devoted to miracles of the Eucharist; in chapters 10 and 11 he dealt with visionary appearances by spirits of the dead; then in book 2, chapter 2, he illustrated the efficacy of the Eucharist offered on behalf of the dead.

The fifth proposition of *Contra Petrobrusianos* summarized the Petrobrusians' challenge to a custom so ancient that it actually predated Christ. The issue was the aid given to the dead in all its forms: Masses, prayers, gifts, and alms.[1] The heretics' view was that such actions were of no profit whatsoever to the dead. Their alleged reason was twofold. First, the afterlife was a place not for earning merit but for recompense. Secondly, and by implication, the deceased could not expect to receive anything in the next world that they had not obtained by the way they had lived here. It was a conception deriving from a literal construction of two passages from Paul's Epistles, Galatians 6:5 and 2 Corinthians 5:10, which taught that everyone (*unusquisque*) was justified or condemned according to his works. The assertions coming from the Petrobrusians were not Peter the Venerable's only worry in this area. He took great care in refuting this position, not just because some Catholics themselves were expressing their own similar doubts, but because aid to the dead represented one of the key features of the Cluniac ecclesial system now coming under criticism not simply from the Petrobrusians but from the newer models of monastic perfection. If we are to appreciate fully Peter's long refutation, we need to understand the issues concerned in assisting the dead during the first thirty years or so of the twelfth century quite apart from heretical opposition. We need also to bear in mind the scale of Cluny's funerary outreach from the turn of the millennium to Peter the Venerable's own time as abbot.

1. *CP*, 211–72.

In his *Dialogues*, Hugh of Amiens offers a handy introduction to the general problem that helping the dead posed for Catholics. Hugh's work, which was dedicated to Matthew of Albano, is a long account, in seven books, of Christian doctrine and the place of monks in the history of salvation, set out in question-and-answer form.[2] Book 5 is devoted to the remission of sins. The anonymous questioner poses the following school problem: God remits sins only in this current life; how therefore can the Church ask him to remit the sins of the dead?[3] Hugh begins by defining the limits of the problem. What is at issue, he says, is not sins as such but penalties for sins; the souls in question are liable not for sins that damn (*damnatoria*), but for purgatorial penalties (*purgatoria*). They are the souls of those who have died after a sincere confession and in communion with the Church, the universal mother who addresses prayers and offerings to God and gives life (*vivificat*) to the mysteries of the Lord's altar. In the sacraments the Church regenerates the faithful and redeems the penalties of the faithful dead. A second question relates to judgment of the merits of everyone (*unusquisque*). Does not Paul say in Romans 14:10, "We shall all stand before the judgment seat of Christ," distantly echoing the words of Jehovah in Ezechiel 24:14, "I will judge thee according to thy ways and according to thy doings"? Is not therefore all external assistance to the dead vain? Hugh agrees that everyone must answer for his own deeds. But mother Church, to whose communion the faithful deceased belong, pays the penalty on their behalf following the example of Christ, the *hostia generalis* (the general sacrificial victim) for the faithful of the past, present, and future. It is this fact that explains the transmission to the dead of the *viaticum salutare* (the saving provisions) of the sacrament of the altar; of such all have need, living and dead, who are *in via* (on the journey of salvation) bound for the Bosom of Abraham. Hugh ends by recalling the twelve thousand drachms of silver collected by Judas Maccabeus in 2 Maccabees 12:39–46 for a sin offering on behalf of those who had died "with godliness" (verse 45), antecedents of those who, in Christian terms, are in communion with the Church and "regenerated" by the body and blood of Christ.

Hugh's was a time of particular awareness of the "individual," an age that had a multiplicity of narratives and images pertaining to the judgment of the soul and that was rethinking traditional eschatological ideas.[4] That is why he

2. *PL* 192:1137–1248.

3. See *Dialogorum libri septem*, 5.19–22, *PL* 192:1212–4.

4. Colin Morris, *The Discovery of the Individual, 1050–1200*, Medieval Academy Reprints for Teaching, 2d ed. (Toronto, 1987), pp. 144ff. On the multiplication of narratives and images around the judgment of the soul and the elaboration during the years 1135–55 of the notion of a *iudicium duplex* (the particular judgment of the soul and the Last Judgment), see Jérôme Baschet, "Jugement de l'âme, Jugement dernier: contradiction, complémentarité, chevauchement?" *RM*, new ser., 6 (1995): 159–203.

spent so much time on a classic school problem that raised questions (quite apart from the issue of heresy) about grace (mediate or immediate) and the function of the sacraments in constituting the community of the Church. It is surely no coincidence that Hugh was a Cluniac by training, for Cluny enjoyed a special relationship with the dead and the afterlife.[5] In the 1030s, Odilo, fifth abbot of Cluny (from 994 to 1049), inaugurated the feast of All Souls on 2 November, the day following All Saints' Day.[6] When Odilo took this step, monastic pastoral care of the dead was a comparatively recent tradition.[7] The Rule of Saint Benedict made no mention at all of commemorating the dead. Rather than Augustine, whose teaching was guarded on the question of suffrages, it was Gregory the Great, pope from 590 to 604 and himself a monk, who provided the primary lead; his work was to exert enormous influence over the monastic communities of the early Middle Ages.[8] Gregory's *Dialogues* contained a refined doctrine of expiation and purgatorial fire that taught that less grave faults were remissible and combustible like wood, hay, and straw. Gregory illustrated these small doctrinal developments of his with stories of miracles and apparitions, popularizing the idea that it was necessary to help the dead with effective liturgical assistance. But it was chiefly the Carolingian period that saw the Church mobilize to help the dead and gather them to the saints. The feast of All Saints appeared in England in the eighth century and spread through the Carolingian empire in the century following.[9] Thereafter the idea arose of linking all the dead with the celebration of all the saints. Such was the conception expressed in particular by Amalarius of Metz in his *Liber de ordine antiphonarii* about 820: "After the offices of the saints, I have inserted an office for the dead. For many pass over from this present age who are not immediately united with the saints."[10] Such a conception moreover accorded with the liturgical logic clearly expressed in the *Communicantes* (intercession in the

5. The extensive bibliography of works on Cluny's relation to the dead, published since Willibald Jorden, *Das cluniazensische Totengedächtniswesen vornehmlich unter den drei ersten Äbten Berno, Odo und Aymard (910–954)*, Münstersche Beiträge zur Theologie, 15 (Münster im W., 1930), may be traced through Joachim Wollasch, "Les moines et la mémoire des morts," in *Religion et culture autour de l'an Mil: royaume capétien et Lotharingie*, Actes du colloque, Hugues Capet 987–1987: la France de l'an Mil, Auxerre 26–27 June 1987, Metz 11–12 September 1987, ed. Dominique Iogna-Prat and Jean-Charles Picard (Paris, 1990), pp. 47–54, and Dominique Iogna-Prat, "Les morts dans la comptabilité céleste des Clunisiens de l'an Mil," ibid., pp. 55–69.

6. *LT*, 126, pp. 186–87, and 138, p. 199.

7. Wollasch, "Les moines et la mémoire des morts."

8. Joseph Ntedika, *L'évocation de l'au-delà dans la prière pour les morts: étude de patristique et de liturgie latines (IVe–VIIIe siècle)* (Leuven and Paris, 1971), esp. pp. 59ff. and 105ff. See also Michel Lauwers, *La mémoire des ancêtres, le souci des morts: morts, rites et société au Moyen Age*, Théologie historique, 103 (Paris, 1997), esp. preliminary chapter.

9. Luce Pietri, "Les origines de la fête de la Toussaint," *Les Quatre fleuves* 25–26 (1988): 57–61.

10. Chap. 65, in *Opera liturgica omnia*, 3, ed. Jean-Michel Hanssens, Studi e Testi, 140 (Vatican, 1950), p. 98.

Canon of the Mass), which during the eucharistic sacrifice placed the deceased in communion with the saints.[11]

Odilo's inauguration of a general commemoration of the dead on the day after All Saints' Day was directly in this tradition. His decree was aimed at Cluny and its dependent establishments. But the text's preamble mentioned the "universal Church," and from the 1050s on Odilo's decree was progressively adopted throughout Latin Christendom. As a result of this blow for Cluniac universality, Odilo was subsequently credited, somewhat dubiously, with originating the weekly commemoration of the dead on Mondays.[12] The institution of All Souls' Day was merely one element in a vast structure of regulation organizing the life of the monastery as a whole, codified in the *Liber tramitis*, a book itself devoted in no small measure to the service of the dead. There in the minutest detail, the various services available were posted: prayers, Masses, enrollment in the necrology, maintenance of paupers. There also were defined the various circles of the community's commemorative horizons: the professed; brethren from other monastic and canonical establishments linked to Cluny by an association of prayer; the parents of professed Cluniacs; benefactors or important lay or ecclesiastical persons entering into the Cluniac fraternity, all entitled to particular memorials; finally, Christendom as a whole. Hugh of Semur continued Odilo's funerary policy. He inaugurated new collective commemorations of the dead in the Cluniac calendar: the Monday after Trinity Sunday and 31 January. He also broadened access to the monastery's *societas et fraternitas* (society and fraternity) and multiplied the undertakings to perform individual commemorations of the monastery's major benefactors, such as the kings of Castile-León Alfonso VI and Ferdinand I, as well as Emperor Henry III and Empress Agnes.[13] Peter the Venerable added two more anniversaries: first, the eve of Michaelmas on behalf of all deceased brethren; secondly, the eve of the Conversion of Saint Paul for the relatives of professed Cluniacs.[14]

11. Josef A. Jungmann, *Missarum sollemnia: eine genetische Erklärung der römischen Messe*, 4th ed., 2 vols. (Freiburg, 1958), 2:213ff. For Eng. trans., see bibliography.

12. *Epistola Burchardi*, ed. Jean Mabillon, *Sancti Odilonis Elogium Historicum, PL* 142:878C–879B; this letter is from Paris, Bibliothèque Nationale, MS latin 5296C, f. 97v (addition by a late-twelfth–early-thirteenth-century hand after the *Vita sancti Odilonis*, listed *BHL* 6281). On the question of the *feria secunda*, see Marie-Anne Polo de Beaulieu, "Recueils d'*exempla* méridionaux et culte des âmes du Purgatoire," in *La Papauté d'Avignon et le Languedoc, 1316–1342, Cahiers de Fanjeaux* 26 (1991): 257–78.

13. Joachim Wollasch, "Hugues Ier abbé de Cluny et la mémoire des morts," in *Le Gouvernement d'Hugues de Semur à Cluny*, Actes du colloque scientifique international, Cluny, September 1988 (Cluny, 1990), pp. 75–92, and Armin Kohnle, *Abt Hugo von Cluny (1049–1109)*, Beihefte der Francia, 32 (Sigmaringen, 1993), pp. 46ff.

14. *Statutum* 8, pp. 47–48; and see Robert Folz, "Pierre le Vénérable et la liturgie," in *Pierre Abélard, Pierre le Vénérable: les courants philosophiques, littéraires et artistiques en Occident au milieu du XIIe siècle*, Actes et mémoires du colloque international, Abbaye de Cluny, 2–9 July 1972, ed. Jean Châtillon, Jean Jolivet, and René Louis, Colloques internationaux du CNRS, 546 (Paris, 1975), p. 157.

From the early 1030s on, therefore, Cluny became a funerary space of prime importance. Odilo's monastery, Cluny II, had two cemeteries, one for the monks and another for the laity.[15] Beyond the sanctuary itself lay the zone within which the Cluniacs accepted the bodies of lay benefactors for burial in their cemetery.[16] We do not know whether this zone, with its imprecise contours, was the same as that of the "sacred ban" enacted by the Cluniac pope Urban II, which defined the limits of the Cluniac seigneury.[17] Its center was the relics of Peter and Paul brought from Rome in the 980s.[18] When lay people demanded burial at Cluny, what they were seeking was the companionship of the princes of the apostles. They hoped, through their gifts, to place the apostles under obligation, to see to it that Peter and Paul would speak up for them on the Day of Judgment.[19] The apostle Peter's spiritual justice made Cluny a space of reconciliation. The monastery was so defined in the privilege of exemption delivered by Pope John XIX in 1024:

> Let the righteous find a place therein, and let not the unrighteous desiring to show penitence be rejected. Let the charity of mutual brotherhood be held out to the innocent, and let not the hope of salvation and indulgence of piety

15. The lay cemetery (*populare cimeterium*) is mentioned in the *Liber tramitis* (142, p. 206; 200, p. 280; 206, p. 284). Kenneth J. Conant, *Cluny: les églises et la maison du chef d'ordre* (Mâcon, 1968), plate 4, conjecturally sites the lay cemetery to the north, against the church of Cluny II. Though the cemetery disappears mysteriously from the archeologists' plans of Cluny III, it is nevertheless clear from the documentary evidence that lay burial was still happening at Cluny at the end of the eleventh century.

16. *CLU* 625, March 943, 1.582–83: "and wherever I shall end this life, the monks shall require my body and arrange its burial in that same monastery of Cluny"; *CLU* 1199, extant original, April 966, 2.281–82: "and after my decease, [my body] shall go to the aforesaid place"; *CLU* 1471, February 979, 2.524–26, in which the donor, Robert, arranges for the burial of his wife, Walburgis: "that they bury my aforesaid wife if she die *in Castello Novo* or in such a place close at hand as allows the monks to undertake for her at Cluny"; *CLU* 2938, extant original, ca. 1040, 4.139–40; *CLU* 3316, ca. 1050, 4.410; *CLU* 3806, extant original, ca. 1100, 5.153–55: "and if he die in the lay state of life, he be taken and buried honorably at Cluny and a due of Masses, prayers, and alms be performed on his behalf by all as for a monk"; *CLU* 3873, 1106, 5.226–27: "that in due measure, just as [when] his wife deceased, he be buried honorably at Cluny, a monk procuring from Berzé carriers and funeral bearers." The *Liber tramitis* (203, p. 282) describes the ceremony whereby the body of a deceased layman was borne to the monastic cemetery. The history of the practice of removing bodies destined for monastic cemeteries remains to be written. It is touched upon by Cécile Treffort, "Genèse du cimetière chrétien: étude sur l'accompagnement du mourant, les funérailles, la commémoration des défunts et les lieux d'inhumation à l'époque carolingienne (entre Loire et Rhin, milieu VIIIe–début XIe siècle)," doctoral thesis, 4 vols. typescript, Université Lumière-Lyon II, 1994, 3:575ff.

17. *Bullarium*, p. 25.

18. According to the belated testimony of Hugh of Gournay's letter to Pontius of Melgueil, ed. Herbert E. J. Cowdrey, "Two Studies," pp. 113–17, here 116–17.

19. *CLU* 1999, 993/1048, 3.212: "making them our debtors, who in the present we truly know have regard for the health of our bodies and who in the future we do not doubt will be judges of our souls"; *CLU* 2831, ca. 1021, 4.34–35; *CLU* 3350, ca. 1055, 4.446–47; *CLU* 3404, August 1065, 4.507–10.

be refused to offenders. And should anyone under any kind of anathema seek admission to the same place either for burial of the body or some other cause relating to his welfare and salvation, let him not be shut out from pardon and desired mercy, but cherished with the oil of health-giving medicine and restored with kindness. For it is also just that in the house of piety [*domus pietatis*], not only the love of holy brotherhood should be shown to the just, but also the medicine of indulgence and salvation should not be denied to the refugee sinner.[20]

The *domus pietatis* (house of piety), the antechamber to the afterlife offered to sinners seeking reconciliation, was at that time limited to Cluny itself. In 1097, however, Urban II revisited this passage in John XIX's bull and extended its application to the monastery's dependencies.[21] Thus the *singulare monasterium* (singular monastery) became an immense ecclesiastical asylum.

In return, the dead were the main contributors to the Cluniac seigneurial economy, which was based almost exclusively upon donation. Evoking the early days of Cluny in the preamble to his *Vita sancti Maioli*, Odilo credited Aymardus with good management of the temporal side of the monastery.[22] Cluny certainly saw remarkable growth from about 950. Analysis of the first five volumes of the *Recueil des chartes de l'abbaye de Cluny* edited by Auguste Bernard and Alexandre Bruel yields the following figures: 29 charters under Abbot Berno, 126 under Odo, 194 under Aymardus; an exponential growth under Majolus and Odilo with 1096 and 1081 respectively; a fallback to 898 under Hugh of Semur; finally a remarkable decline under Pontius of Melgueil and Peter the Venerable with 86 and 229 respectively. The figures do have to be approached with caution, because the dates attributed by Bernard and Bruel are often conjectural.[23] Moreover some of the acts in the *Recueil* refer to transactions predating the assimilation of the property concerned into the Cluniac patrimony. Even making allowances for a certain margin of error, however, one cannot escape the sharp slowdown discernible in the business of the Cluniac chancellery from the 1120s, due partly to a falloff in donations at a time when the Cluniac model of monasticism—in particular its system of making a seigneurial living out of death—no

20. *Papsturkunden 896–1046*, ed. Harald Zimmermann, Österreichische Akademie der Wissenschaften, Philosophisch-historische Klasse, Denkschriften, 174, 177, 198, 3 vols. (Vienna, 1984–99), vol. 2, no. 558, pp. 1053–54.

21. *Bullarium*, pp. 30–31; and see Wollasch, "Hugues Ier abbé de Cluny," pp. 85ff.

22. *BC*, col. 281E.

23. Hence the differences between one historian and another, as for example between Barbara H. Rosenwein in her *To Be the Neighbor of Saint Peter: The Social Meaning of Cluny's Property, 909–1049* (Ithaca and London, 1989), and Dietrich Poeck in his "Laienbegräbnisse in Cluny," *FMSt* 15 (1981): 68–179. Down to Odilo's abbacy I take my figures from Hartmut Atsma and Jean Vezin, "Autour des actes privés du chartrier de Cluny (Xe–XIe siècles)," *BEC* 155 (1997): 45–60, here 48. After Hugh of Semur's abbacy, the figures are given gross and therefore subject to extra caution.

longer attracted the aristocracy as it once had. It is a fact that a large percentage of the transactions recorded in Cluny's archives and cartularies consists of acts of last will. In a highly detailed analysis of the rate of donations made to Cluny from its foundation down to the early years of the twelfth century, Dietrich Poeck has drawn attention to the remarkable growth of acts *pro remedio animae* (for the good of the soul) under Abbot Majolus (72) and above all under Odilo (124), who actively promoted funerary policy, followed by decline under Hugh of Semur (73).[24] The last-mentioned figure corresponds in large measure to a redirection in the flow of wealth; in accordance with Urban II's privilege mentioned earlier, gifts *ad sepulturam* (for burial) could thenceforth be made directly to Cluny's dependent establishments.[25] The real change in the pattern of donations *ad sepulturam* under Abbot Hugh of Semur lay in the increase of alms in the form of cash, such as the Spanish gold with which the kings of Castile-León purchased commemoration at Cluny.[26] In the years 1120–30, Cluny's system of seigneurial profiting from death went into crisis. Though the dead brought in revenue, they were also costly. Joachim Wollasch has calculated that in the early 1100s, the monastery of Cluny had between 300 and 400 monks, but that some ten thousand prebends were distributed to ten thousand paupers, substitutes for deceased brethren.[27] The burden became all the heavier since, in those years, so many churches had already been restored by the laity that there were no more to hand over: as Dominique Barthélemy terms it, the "market" in "Gregorian" restitutions had reached saturation.[28] Equally, the flow of donations was diversifying with the appearance of new fraternities. In a letter to King Roger of Sicily, Peter the Venerable bemoaned such disaffection even as Cluny was being exploited as the "public treasure of the Christian republic."[29] In his description of Matthew of Albano in *De miraculis*, he portrayed the model Cluniac and father of his community being forced to solicit donations from kings and princes.[30] Disaffection of this sort was due in part to early-twelfth-century questioning of the ideals at the root of the Cluniac system of living off the dead. It was a period

24. "Laienbegräbnisse in Cluny."

25. See above, n. 21, and Kohnle, *Abt Hugo*, p. 48.

26. Gilo, *Vita sancti·Hugonis*, 1.9, "Two Studies," pp. 59–60, and Hugh of Gournay, *Vita sancti Hugonis*, ibid., p. 132 (Alfonso VI); *CLU* 3441, ca. 1070, 4.551–53 (Ferdinand I); *CLU* 3509, 10 July 1077, 4.627–28, and *CLU* 3638, Easter 1090, 4.809–10 (Alfonso VI)—both extant in the original. Hugh accepted an exceptional funerary undertaking on Alfonso VI's behalf: see "Two Studies," pp. 159–60, and Charles J. Bishko, "Liturgical Intercessions at Cluny for the King-Emperors of León," no. 8 in *Spanish and Portuguese Monastic History, 600–1300* (London, 1984). Peter the Venerable was still, in his day, recalling the exceptional generosity of the two kings: *DM*, 1.28, pp. 89–92.

27. "Les moines et la mémoire des morts," p. 52.

28. Dominique Barthélemy, *L'ordre seigneurial XIe–XIIe siècle*, Nouvelle Histoire de la France médiévale, 3 (Paris, 1990), p. 170.

29. *Ep.*, 131, 1:330–33, here 332.

30. *DM*, 2.9, p. 111, ll. 15–18.

of general polemic about *spiritualia*, the property that financed spiritual ends.[31] Hermits and newer orders of monks alleged that they did not want to "steal from the priests," meaning the secular clergy, and renounced the possession of churches, altars, burial dues, and tithes as contrary to monastic purity. When addressing the subject of funerary observance in his customary, the Carthusian Guigo I commented: "Rarely indeed here is Mass sung, since our zeal and purpose is preeminently to toil in the silence and solitude of the cell."[32] Guigo here envisaged the service performed for the dead wholly in terms of eucharistic sacrifice, an act of community viewed as out of step with the solitude of the cell. Yet after so many centuries of private Masses, the objection did not entirely hold water. Peter Damian, writing to the hermit Leo, had already pointed out that even hermits did not cease to be at the heart of the ecclesial community, since by saying *Dominus vobiscum* the hermit-priest blessed faithful people who, though absent, were nonetheless real.[33] A little further on in the *Consuetudines Cartusiae*, addressing the question of poverty, Guigo gave the real justification for the refusal to work on behalf of the dead. It was all too easy, he explained, to get drawn into the vicious circle of the economy of gifts, collections, and begging, which was a distraction from contemplation. The religious needed to avoid being tied to the whim of those who provided their sustenance: alliance entailed constraints. As for the necessary duty of mercy toward the poor, this could readily be discharged by distributing surpluses in the villages outside the Carthusian "limits."[34] After a while, some of these new purists no longer systematically refused to be endowed with *spiritualia*; after 1150, burials and anniversary foundations were no longer rare in Cistercian establishments.[35] Yet the criticism of the monastic gift economy was serious enough to engage Peter the Venerable's attention in defending and reordering the Cluniac model. He lowered funeral service charges, reduced to fifty the number of daily prebends "lest the number of dead increasing with time drive out the living,"[36] and had some mixed success in reorganizing the Cluniac economy, with its structural dependence on gifts, by stimulating the demesne's own production. For this task, in 1155, he asked his friend Henry of Blois, bishop of Winchester, to draw up an inventory of the Clu-

31. Giles Constable, "Monastic Possession of Churches and 'Spiritualia' in the Age of Reform," in *Il monachesimo e la riforma ecclesiastica (1049–1122)*, Atti della quarta Settimana internazionale di studio, Mendola, 22–29 August 1968, Miscellanea del Centro di Studi medioevali, 6 (Milan, 1971), pp. 326ff.; for reprint, see bibliography.

32. *Consuetudines Cartusiae*, 14.5, *SC*, 313 (Paris, 1984), p. 196.

33. Peter Damian, *Epistolae*, 28, ed. Kurt Reindel, 4 vols., *MGH*, Die Briefe der Deutschen Kaiserzeit (Munich, 1983–93), 4:248–78, here 274. Commented upon by Michel Grandjean, *Les Laïcs dans l'Eglise: regards de Pierre Damien, Anselme de Cantorbéry, Yves de Chartres*, Théologie historique, 97 (Paris, 1994), pp. 154ff.

34. Guigo I, *Consuetudines Cartusiae*, 20.4–5, p. 209, and 41.5, p. 247.

35. Constable, "Monastic Possession of Churches," p. 330, n. 154; Jacques Dubois, "Les ordres religieux au XIIe siècle d'après la curie romaine," *RB* 78 (1968): 283–309, here 284.

36. *Statutum* 32, pp. 66–67, and *Dispositio rei familiaris*, *CLU* 4132, 5.475–82, here 479.

niac demesnes.[37] On the ideological front, Peter worked to oil the springs of the Ecclesia cluniacensis both as an ecclesiastical seigneury based on alliances and as an inclusive ecclesial system by developing, in *De miraculis*, a whole structure of argument justifying the necessity of acting in solidarity on behalf of the dead. The heretical propositions that he refuted in *Contra Petrobrusianos* did no more than swell, and perhaps slightly misrepresent, a vast internal debate within the Church whose object was of prime importance to Cluny. We therefore can do no better than read Peter's two broadsides in tandem, *Contra Petrobrusianos* followed closely by *De miraculis*.

THE FOURFOLD EXPRESSION OF CHARITY

Peter the Venerable began his refutation of the fifth proposition of the Petrobrusian heresy by recalling, from 1 Corinthians 11:19, the apostle's observation about the necessity of heresy: "For there must be also heresies; that they also, who are approved, may be made manifest among you." Peter believed that Paul's words were no less true in the twelfth century than they had been in the first. Just as the Church expanded through fighting an external enemy (*dilatatio*), so also it was purged by inner strife (*purgatio*). It was no coincidence that Peter the Venerable should recall Paul's classic statement as he considered the dead and the delicate matter of the remission of sins, a case of *purgatio* if ever there was one.

Over against the Petrobrusian individualization of death and salvation deriving from two Pauline passages (Galatians 6:5 and 2 Corinthians 5:10), which attributed to every individual either damnation or justification on the basis of his works, Peter the Venerable invoked the word of Christ in the Beatitudes— "Blessed are the merciful" (Matthew 5:7)—which established a duty of solidarity within the Church. He then defined the time and space within which Christ's teaching on the remission of sins (in Matthew 12:32 and Luke 12:10) operated: not simply in this world but also in the world to come. The abbot of Cluny thus situated the debate squarely in the territory of the Gospels, the only part of Scripture accepted by the Petrobrusians, while taking care to emphasize the teaching's present and future validity. He then argued that the necessary purgation of those good souls who were still imperfect might be abridged and alleviated by the hidden judgment of God—dependent entirely upon the quality of

---

37. *CLU* 4183, 5.490–505. On this see Georges Duby, "Le budget de Cluny entre 1080 et 1155," in Duby, *Hommes et structures du Moyen Age* (Paris and The Hague, 1973), pp. 73ff., and "Un inventaire des profits de la seigneurie clunisienne à la mort de Pierre le Vénérable," ibid., pp. 87–101; Alain Guerreau, "Douze doyennés clunisiens au milieu du XIIe siècle," *Annales de Bourgogne* 52 (1980): 83–128; Mathieu Arnoux and Ghislain Brunel, "Réflexions sur les sources médiévales de l'histoire des campagnes: de l'intérêt de publier les sources, de les critiquer et de les lire," *Histoire et sociétés rurales* 1 (1994): 28–33.

the sinner's penitence—and, by dint of the "inexhaustible goodness" of the Almighty, through the sacrifices, prayers, and offerings of the Church. What Christ the head had done once (*olim*), his body—the faithful—could now do daily (*cotidie*). Peter proposed that such expressions of charity could be divided into four according to their source and destination: from the living for the living, from the dead for the dead, from the living for the dead, and from the dead for the living.

From the Living for the Living

Peter draws attention to the fact that as far back as Old Testament times the living had shown efficacious concern for other living people. Even Elijah's prayer for drought to punish the wicked in 3(1) Kings 17:1 was answered. The apostle Paul, too, had been unambiguous in 1 Timothy 2:1–3: "I desire, therefore, first of all, that supplications, prayers, intercessions and thanksgivings be made for all men. . . . For this is good and acceptable in the sight of God our Savior." It was noteworthy that intercession could be employed efficaciously for or against the one prayed about. The living could pray for the bodily and spiritual well-being of the living; or they could call down upon them the thunderbolts of divine justice. In this connection, Peter the Venerable cites the efficacious prayer of Moses against Dathan and Abiram, "whom the earth, opening her mouth, swallowed up with their households and tents, and all their substance, which they had in the midst of Israel" (Deuteronomy 11:6). Such was the Old Testament foundation upon which rested the whole medieval tradition of malediction and anathema sustaining the spiritual justice that related as much to the dead as to the heretics.

From the Dead for the Dead

The second of charity's four divisions Peter the Venerable introduces by thrusting a self-evident argument into his adversaries' face. Are the prayers of the dead less pleasing to God than the prayers of the living? Are the saints diminished once they are no longer in the body? Is Paul now prevented from doing what he was able to do before death? Of course not. The most perfect among the dead—the saints and martyrs—are able daily to assist those among the dead who are good but less than perfect. Clearly the question of the dead aiding the dead raised the issue of the power of the saints, and thereby the value of their cult as well as the status of *aperta miracula* (overt miracles) compared with that of Scripture. By *aperta miracula*, Peter understood any past event affording "irrefutable" teaching (*assertio vallata*) that complemented the word of God.[38] In this part of *Contra Petrobrusianos*, he makes explicit reference only to examples drawn from Scripture, recalling the prayer of the high priest Onias "for all the

38. *CP,* 229, l. 5.

people of the Jews" in 2 Maccabees 15:12–14, or the returning to life of the dead man cast into the sepulchre of Elisha described in 4(2) Kings 13:21. The remainder of the treatise, however, is sufficient proof that Peter also included Christian hagiography within his category of *aperta miracula*.[39]

Let us recall that Peter the Venerable defined the saints as the "more perfect of the dead," whom those who died good but not wholly perfect would join sooner or later. When discussing the power of these perfect ones, he considers the objection that the afterlife is a place of recompense, not further meriting or demeriting. As we have seen thanks to Hugh of Amiens's *Dialogues*, this was a classic school problem, not an argument proper to antiheretical preaching. Peter's response is unsurprising. It is necessary, he says, not only to distinguish between this world and the next, between meriting and receiving recompense, but also to define what is understood by good and evil. "Evil" may be sin or the penalty attaching to sin. Equally, "good" may refer as much to the work—to the "merit" (*meritum*) earned in pain here—as to the reward of merit (*merces meriti*), the recompense given in the afterlife, synonymous with felicity and beatitude. Given their position, the prayers of the "more perfect dead" cannot fail to be heard; it is indeed a part of their reward to be able to assist others through charity to join them in bliss.[40]

From the Living for the Dead

The third case envisaged, the assistance given by the living to the dead, lay at the heart of the controversy with the Petrobrusians. Peter the Venerable's reply bristles with references to Scripture, Christian hagiography, and the Fathers. He prepared his reply with all the greater care inasmuch as his task was to justify practices that had a firmer basis in custom than in doctrine.[41]

In order to be able to use all the resources afforded by Scripture, Peter subjects his opponents, who recognize only the Gospels, to an instance of all-or-nothing logic: either Scripture must be accepted in its totality or all must be rejected. This permits him to advance his chosen proof texts, commenting if need be on problems of transmission in the sacred text. Thus, quoting Isaiah 8:19, *Numquid non populus a Deo suo requirit pro vivis ac mortuis*—"Should not the people seek of their God, for the living and the dead?"—Peter wonders whether the reading should be *pro vivis a mortuis*, meaning *a mortuis symulachris* (from the shades of the dead), which would confer on the dead the status of ancestral spirits; Peter himself does not rule one way or the other.[42] In addition, he appeals to 2 Maccabees 12:39–46, 1 Corinthians 15:29, and John 14:12. The first of these

39. See for instance *CP*, 109–10, on the saintly founders of churches.

40. *CP*, 226–28.

41. *CP*, 211, l. 31, where Peter speaks explicitly of custom (*mos*), a point made to me by Michel Lauwers.

42. *CP*, 234–36.

texts invokes the example of Judas Maccabeus, an Old Testament type of Christ, who collected twelve thousand drachms of silver to redeem the sins of those who died after sacrificing to idols.[43] Peter requests that this "lesson" (*lectio*) be fully heard.[44] His use of the word *lectio* is possibly an allusion to the liturgy, for the Cluniacs actually took the ninth lesson of their matins for the dead from the 2 Maccabees passage.[45] The apostle Paul's words (1 Corinthians 15:29) allow Peter to explore an extreme example of aiding the dead. In those proselytizing early days of the Church, some unreflecting but well-meaning Christians thought they could aid those who died without baptism by being baptized in their place.[46] As Peter sees it, the apostle did not approve the practice, since baptism is "unique" (meaning it cannot be transferred to another), but was praising the intention behind it, seeing it as a good work without sacramental power useful to the soul in the perspective of the Resurrection. The apostle's words could scarcely fail to comfort Peter the Venerable, confronted earlier in *Contra Petrobrusianos* with the need to justify infant baptism and the role of faithful adults (the parents and godparents) in the act of incorporation on the child's behalf.[47] Finally, in an appeal to the Gospel text of John 14:12, Peter sees the very word of Christ as forging the link between disciples and believers at the Church's inception: "He that believeth in me, the works that I do he also shall do; and greater than these shall he do." The "he" of whom Christ spoke in this passage means, according to Peter, not simply the seventy-two disciples, on whom was conferred the power to raise the dead, but more generally all believers, whether or not they use that power. Such a broad construction of the subject of Christ's sentence enables Peter to import into the argument every example of God's manifestation in history after the Resurrection of Christ, particularly the overt miracles of the apostles' disciples, the miracle-working saints. Under this head, he cites the work of Eucherius in Germania, Frontus in Aquitaine, and Maurilius of Angers, all of whom raised the dead.[48]

After the apostles and their disciples, the miracle-working saints, Peter the

43. *CP*, 232–33.

44. *CP*, 232.

45. Knud Ottosen, *The Responsories and Versicles of the Latin Office of the Dead* (Aarhus, 1993), p. 380, cited by Pierre-Marie Gy, "Bulletin de liturgie," *Revue des sciences philosophiques et théologiques* 78 (1994): 284–86. Another example of the use of the 2 Maccabees 12 passage in the liturgy of the dead is the *Missa pro defuncto* in the Romano-Germanic Pontifical, which continues the tradition of the Gelasian and Hadrianum sacramentaries: see *Le Pontifical romano-germanique du dixième siècle*, ed. Cyrille Vogel and Reinhard Elze, 3 vols. (Vatican, 1963), 2:307–9, here 308. It is worth noting that the Maccabees were a hagiographical as well as scriptural example, having their own feast day of 1 August—within the Cluniac network, see Regina Hausmann, *Das Martyrologium von Marcigny-sur-Loire: Edition einer Quelle zur cluniacensischen Heiligenverehrung am Ende des elften Jahrhunderts*, HochschulSammlung Philosophie Geschichte, 7 (Freiburg im B., 1984), p. 75. I owe this last observation to Jean-Pierre Weiss.

46. *CP*, 237.

47. *CP*, 10–13 and 67–88, esp. 72.

48. *CP*, 245.

Venerable brings forward four doctors, successors to (*vice*) the four evangelists: Ambrose, Augustine, Gregory the Great, and Paulinus of Nola.[49] Of Ambrose's works, it is, as one might expect, the great funerary exhortations that attract Peter's attention: *De obitu Theodosii, De consolatione Valentiniani* and *De excessu fratris sui Satyri*. The first two texts alluded to the Roman tradition of *pietas* (piety, dutifulness, devotion) toward ancestors voiced in the *Aeneid* (notably book 6, from line 883, and book 9, lines 446–49). *De excessu fratris sui Satyri* depicted pauper mourners, "co-heirs" of the deceased, receiving alms and washing away Satyrus's offenses with their redeeming tears. No mean expert himself in the Christianized way of death, Peter the Venerable now passes to Augustine's *De cura gerenda pro mortuis*, in which the Romans' family devotion to their ancestors has become that of the Church to her Catholic sons, for whom "as the pious mother of all" she has "undertaken supplication, even though their names be unuttered," in her general commemoration.[50] In Augustine's *De cura gerenda pro mortuis*, as in the same Father's *Enchiridion* and *Confessiones*, Peter came across thinking that had long been authoritative in Latin Christendom on the utility, yet circumscribed efficacy, of assisting the dead. As to its limited efficacy, the text of the *Enchiridion* recalled Paul's words in 2 Corinthians 5:10, which said that everyone would answer for his deeds before the judgment seat of Christ.[51] The external aid of eucharistic sacrifices, prayers, and alms could at most therefore be only supplementary, profiting above all the "middling" dead, those who were neither very good nor very bad. Peter makes but a passing mention of Gregory the Great, the third doctor of the four called to bear witness. Gregory's life, sermons, and *Dialogues* are well known, says Peter, being "both recited and listened to daily, almost without pause, by countless brothers, including even the simple and less erudite."[52] In the circumstances, there is no reason to accuse Peter of literary negligence. *Contra Petrobrusianos* was addressed to Provençal bishops and archbishops fighting Petrobrusian heresy; its main aim was to furnish them with information to back up their arguments. Peter simply judged that the Gregorian material was so famous it needed no repetition. In the absence of explicit references, it is hard to say what parts of Gregory's funerary message seemed vital to the abbot of Cluny. On the other hand, it is fairly certain that one of the salient passages in his mind would have been the chapter in the *Dialogues* that, in typical Gregorian fashion, blended doctrinal elaboration and hagiographic anecdote to establish the liturgical practice of the "trental."[53] The story was of a monk ill

---

49. *CP*, 249–60. The study by Max Manitius, "Zu Petrus' von Cluny Patristischen Kenntnissen," *Speculum* 49 (1928): 582–87, has been superseded, where *Contra Petrobrusianos* is concerned, by James Fearns's critical edition, *CCCM* 10.

50. *De cura gerenda pro mortuis*, 4.6, quoted in *CP*, 253, ll. 18–21.

51. *CP*, 254.

52. *CP*, 256.

53. *Dialogues*, 4.55, ed. and French trans. by Adalbert de Vogüé and Paul Antin, *SC*, 265 (Paris, 1980), pp. 188–92.

named Justus, who had broken his vow of poverty by hiding two gold pieces. On his deathbed, he sought his brethren's assistance, but none dared approach him. His natural brother Copiosus eventually revealed to him why he was "hated by all." On Gregory's orders, Justus's body was denied burial and thrown into a manure pit. Thirty days later, Gregory requested the monks to help the deceased by means of a liturgical arrangement spread over thirty days, equivalent to the necessary penance. At the end of the period, Justus appeared to Copiosus in order to testify to the efficacy of the liturgical procedure.

The fourth doctor examined, Paulinus of Nola, provided Peter with three letters offering another perspective on the question of family solidarity shown toward the dead. The Church's assumption of duties that were previously the prerogative of family *pietas,* together with the formulation during late antiquity and the early medieval period of the notion of spiritual parenthood, in particular the role of godparents, greatly broadened the scope of "family" solidarity. Peter quotes a letter by Paulinus praising the senator Pammachius for the valuable offerings made on behalf of his deceased wife. An unremarkable piece in itself, its interest lies in its proximity, within Peter's treatise, to another letter by Paulinus, addressed to Delfinus, bishop of Bordeaux, in support of the writer's dead brother, the bishop's "spiritual son." It is hard to know whether the term "spiritual son" means that Paulinus's brother was Delfinus's godson or simply one committed to his charge. At all events, the association of the two letters in Peter's treatise indicates a desire to show the two possible types of Christian kinship operating to assist the dead, the natural and the spiritual.

From the Dead for the Living

The last area in which charity was expressed was where the dead exercised their power to help the living.[54] Peter returns to the passage in 2 Maccabees 15:12–16, already used in support of the suffrages of the dead for the dead. Judas Maccabeus, at war with the evil Nicanor, cheers his companions by describing to them a dream that he has had. In his dream, the deceased high priest Onias appeared with upheld hands praying for the whole Jewish community. The dream then continued with Jeremiah appearing and giving Judas, the dreamer, a holy sword from God with which he should defeat his enemies. Peter draws from the passage a self-evident argument very much in his style. What sense would it make, he asks, if Onias and Jeremiah could pray effectively on behalf of living Jews in Old Testament times and yet the dead Christian saints could not do likewise now? But in order that the episode may be perfectly clear and the consequent argument carry full force, Peter spends some time discussing the standing of dreams. This was an important area, because it bore on the validity

54. *CP,* 263–70.

attributable to all appearances of the dead. Peter accepts that dreams are ambiguous: "They are not always true and they are not always false," he says.[55] Judas's vision in 2 Maccabees allows him to establish the principle that visions are proved one way or another by events. Judas's dream was true because the next day he defeated his enemies as the holy sword of the vision had prefigured. Next, Peter appeals for cogent testimony to a New Testament passage, Apocalypse 6:9–11, the opening of the fifth seal and the appearance "under the altar" of "the souls of them that were slain for the word of God" and who called upon the Lord to "revenge our blood." Peter resorts to another self-evident argument. "Are they," he asks, "to be able to demand vengeance for their blood and yet be unable to pray for mitigation of the vengeance exacted for offenses [*pro mitiganda scelerum vindicta*]?"[56] Of course not. It remains, however, unclear what Peter intended by "mitigation of the vengeance exacted for offenses." Did he mean the effective concern of the more perfect dead in regard to the living, in which case how was such mitigation to be shown? Or was he thinking beyond his immediate context, that of the dead aiding the living, to the purgatorial function of martyrs purging with their blood the "middling" deceased, those neither very good nor very bad?[57] Be that as it may, Peter's last call is to several grand figures of biblical hagiography, including Abraham and David, whose ancestral status is recorded in the Old Testament as weighing with the Almighty on behalf of others still in this world.[58] In so doing, Peter enunciates the principle that underlay the Church's requests for the saints to help the living: that of compensation, whereby the merits of the saints were capable of being weighed against the sins of the living. Again, it was important to distinguish the situation of the saints in this world from their state in the next. Here, the just piously shared the misery of the living: in the next world, they were in glory, freed from this earthly burden, but rejoicing in a capital of merit that the Church was able to mobilize.

Peter ends his long discussion of the fifth Petrobrusian proposition by summarizing the essential possibilities and limits of good works done for the dead. It is not the soul's substance, but its outward state, he says, that is affected by suffrages. "For the prayers of the living can in no way restore [*restaurare*] the lost substance of the dead, but they can reshape the misshapen ornament [*deforma-*

55. *CP*, 264.

56. *CP*, 265.

57. In the tradition of commentaries on the Apocalypse, the passage was often interpreted as a plea for a strict discrimination between the society of the saints and the damnation of the wicked. Haymo of Auxerre, a well-known author in Cluniac circles, commented as follows: "The saints . . . seek vengeance on their enemies in two ways, and this for charity's sake: that those who are predestined to eternal life may be converted from evil to good; but that those who in God's foreknowledge are to be damned may die and stop sinning, so that afterward they may have less pain in hell, where everyone shall have magnitude of pains corresponding to the quality of his works." *Expositio in Apocalypsin*, 2.6, *PL* 117:1030CD.

58. 3(1) Kings 11:11–13; Daniel 3:34–35.

tum speciei decorem] of their outward appearance, while the whole of the substance remains as it was."[59]

THE SOLIDARITY AT THE HEART OF THE ECCLESIAL COMMUNITY

As Jean-Pierre Torrell and Denise Bouthillier have rightly observed, *Contra Petrobrusianos* and *De miraculis* shared a common purpose regarding care for the dead.[60] There is a clear correspondence between the two works, which the author himself planned. Denise Bouthillier has demonstrated the existence within *De miraculis* of two collections of narratives. The first, "short" collection was begun before 1135; Peter subsequently included additions and modifications to constitute a second, "long" collection.[61] Among the additions, it is worth mentioning book 1, chapter 27, the story of a ghostly apparition written in opposition to the Petrobrusians. *De miraculis* was a monumental defense of Cluny as the citadel of heaven, whose struggle against the devil on behalf of the living and above all the dead was held up for its undeniable efficacy. At a time when hagiographic legends were subject to an increasingly critical reception, *Contra Petrobrusianos* afforded *De miraculis* a substrate of doctrine. The discussion around the fifth Petrobrusian proposition contained the key elements: the status of dreams and their proof by events; the power of the saints; the corroborative value of miracles, whose "irrefutable" teaching complemented the testimony of Scripture. Conversely, *De miraculis* was a reservoir of contemporary "overt miracles" confirming the doctrine given form in *Contra Petrobrusianos* and extending it with considerations of prime importance for the sociological implications of Cluny's funerary outreach.

The Doctrinal Foundation of De miraculis

Arriving at chapter 9 of the first book of *De miraculis*, having detailed some important material on the respect due to the divine sacraments of the Eucharist and penance, Peter turns to a group of miracles concerning the dead. Before proceeding to mine this miraculous vein in the following chapters, Peter spends the whole of chapter 9 promoting the monastery of Cluny. That his choreographing of the spirits of the dead should be preceded by so grandiloquent an overture is, of course, no accident. His declamation is intended to recall by antiphrasis why Cluny "is no inferior member of the universal Church."[62]

59. *CP*, 272.
60. Pierre le Vénérable, *Livre des merveilles de Dieu* [French trans. of *De miraculis*], trans., introduction, and notes by Jean-Pierre Torrell and Denise Bouthillier (Freiburg and Paris, 1992), p. 20.
61. *DM*, pp. 56*ff.
62. *DM*, 1.9, p. 36, ll. 64–65.

Peter cites the severity of its discipline; the number of its brothers; its strict observance of the monastic rule; its function as a universal refuge open to all orders, dignities, and professions; its universal reach to the utmost limits of Christendom. At the heart of Cluny's exemplarity Peter cites its liturgical efficacy, measured by the "many losses inflicted on hell" and the "very many gains made for the heavenly realms."[63]

Peter's aim in recording conversations that had taken place with the dead was to provide irrefutable proof of Cluny's efficacy in its undertakings on their behalf. This efficacy was primarily eucharistic. Reading *De miraculis* with an awareness of its closeness to *Contra Petrobrusianos*, the historian will greet the first actor to appear onstage, in chapter 10, as a stroke of perfect casting. It is Stephen Le Blanc, former abbot of Saint-Gilles-du-Gard, who died in 1105 or 1106, more than twenty years before Saint-Gilles broke away from the tutelage of Cluny. Stephen, like his predecessor Odilo, figures in the Cluniac necrologies as a "monk of our congregation."[64] We are dealing, then, with a professed Cluniac seeking the assistance of his brethren. Peter portrays him appearing to one of the brothers, a certain Bernard Savinelle, confessing to him that he sinned much both before and during his abbacy and now suffers cruel pains as a result. The spirit of Stephen pleads with Bernard to "be my ambassador and beseech the lord abbot and all the brothers, that they may pour out prayers to Almighty God for my release and, by as many means as they can, snatch me away from such great ills."[65] In response, as Peter tells us, the Cluniacs gather all their forces to aid the deceased and his messenger. They pour out offerings, supplications, alms, and above all they celebrate the "holy sacrifice." The episode is worthy of two comments, first, on the way apparitions were judged, and second, on the efficacy of the Eucharist. Anxious to prove the story's veracity, Peter relays to the reader Bernard's shock when spoken to by the apparition on the dormitory stairs. How is Stephen's message to be authenticated? As in the case of the Maccabean "holy sword" in *Contra Petrobrusianos*, here too the truth of the vision is proved by events. The truth of the messenger's words becomes apparent when his death, predicted by the apparition, occurs a few days later. Such an "event" is something of a rule in *De miraculis* as a whole: a needy soul makes contact with one of the living who is himself about to depart.[66] As for the power of the Eu-

63. *DM*, 1.9, p. 35, ll. 31–32.

64. See Ulrich Winzer, *S. Gilles: Studien zum Rechtsstatus und Beziehungsnetz einer Abtei im Spiegel ihrer Memorialüberlieferung*, Münstersche Mittelalter-Schriften, 59 (Munich, 1988), pp. 233–36.

65. *DM*, 1.10, p. 38, ll. 31–32.

66. On the dead announcing a coming death, see Jean-Claude Schmitt, *Les revenants: les vivants et les morts dans la société médiévale*, Bibliothèque des Histoires (Paris, 1994), p. 53: example from the *Chronicon* of Thietmar of Merseburg; pp. 124–25: examples from Rodulfus Glaber, *Historiarum libri quinque*, namely visions of Vulcher (2.9.19) and Frotterius (5.1.6), ed. and Eng. trans. John France et al., Oxford Medieval Texts (Oxford, 1989), pp. 80–82 and 222. For Eng. trans. of *Les revenants*, see bibliography.

charist, that was a venerable commonplace of Cluniac hagiography. One needs only to recall the words that Rodulfus Glaber, about 1040, put into the mouth of a hermit living "in the most remote regions of Africa":

> "Know that it exceeds all the monasteries in the Roman world in the number of souls it liberates from the clutches of the devil. The life-giving sacrifice is so often performed there that hardly a day passes without some souls being torn thereby from the power of the devils."[67]

The Cluniac customaries confirm that Glaber's comments were no mere hagiographical propaganda for Abbot Odilo and the institution of All Souls' Day. The *Liber tramitis* attests the importance of the eucharistic sacrifice to the service of the dead. Odilo's Constitution ordered that on 2 November "all the priests shall privately celebrate masses for the repose of all faithful souls."[68] In their service for the dead, the priests of the community formed a eucharistic chain, delivering Masses as a noria continuously delivers buckets of water for irrigation; they celebrated every day except Sunday, when for the sake of reverence and decency most priests celebrated the Lord's Resurrection without any "admixture of some other deceased."[69] The most frequent but also most extreme case was the procedure that was gone through after the death of a professed Cluniac. The *Liber tramitis* laid down that six brothers should, for thirty days without interruption, "daily offer sacred hosts to God for that soul. When each one has completed five Masses, he shall notify the chapter, that another may succeed him."[70] This amounted to the saying of six times five Masses each day for thirty days, a grand total of nine hundred Masses in all! No wonder the services of the monk-priests of Cluny were so popular, and not just with the professed (like Stephen Le Blanc) but also with associates and *familiares*. The importance attached to the power of the eucharistic sacrifice to help the dead was a general feature of western Christendom in the eleventh and twelfth centuries. It was the culmination of an evolving tradition during the early Middle Ages in which eucharistic sacrifice was increasingly seen as "for something," as a means to an end. The development has to be seen in the context of the appearance and spread of votive and private Masses.[71] Whereas formerly the *Memento vivorum* had embraced all the burdens brought along by the participants, the priest now took the place of the former community and sacrificed with a special intention. In the newer context of specialization and professionalization, the requests acquired an individual, noncollective importance, and so the imprecatory and propitiatory

67. Rodulfus Glaber, *Historiarum libri quinque*, 5.1.13, pp. 234–36.

68. *LT*, 126, p. 187, ll. 15–17.

69. *LT*, 204, p. 283, ll. 18–23.

70. *LT*, 195.6, pp. 276–77.

71. Arnold Angenendt, "*Missa specialis*. Zugleich ein Beitrag zur Entstehung der Privatmessen," *FMSt* 17 (1983): 153–221.

character of the Mass was enhanced alongside the evolution of penitential practice to which it corresponded.

The appearance of Stephen Le Blanc's spirit demanding help and the essentially eucharistic service that the Cluniacs gave him in return were directly in this early medieval tradition. All the same, Peter the Venerable's narrative, which comes after a section devoted to the problem of what constituted true confession, contains a novelty that is essential to our subject: the complete avowal by the deceased of his past faults. In an earlier chapter, Peter depicted a monk of Sauxillanges who is interrupted by demons at least forty times in his confession and who directly testifies to the overriding necessity of confessing his own sins himself.[72] The abbot of Cluny does not let the matter drop. Immediately after Stephen Le Blanc's story, he spends an entire chapter on the problem of penitence. The protagonist this time is Bernard II Grossus, one of the recalcitrant castellans of the Mâcon region who gave the Cluniacs so much trouble in the eleventh century. Bernard's family, which in his day acquired the surname "Grossus" (Le Gros), had emerged out of the undocumented darkness in the middle of the tenth century.[73] At that time it was among Cluny's big benefactors. In a charter abandoning oppressive customs, Bernard II, who was apt to forget his duty, hailed the pious deeds of his ancestors (*gesta priorum*).[74] At the start of the eleventh century Bernard was forming a lordship around the knoll of Uxelles. A century later, his grandson, Bernard IV Grossus, succeeded Hugh of Brancion and became, as the head of the castellany of Uxelles-Brancion, one of the greatest lords of the Mâconnais. For more than two hundred years the charters of Cluny chronicled the often stormy and sometimes peaceful relations of the Grossus family with the neighboring sanctuary-lordship. In 1146–47, Peter the Venerable appealed to Pope Eugenius III and his legate Archbishop Amedeus of Lyon to force Joceran IV Grossus to renounce his "grave injuries and exactions" on Cluniac land.[75] The history of the Grossus family and Cluny gives a good idea how enmeshed Mâconnais property and people were with one another in the seigneurial age. The possessions of the two lordships were partly contiguous, partly interlocking.[76] The Grossus family chose the monastery as their necropolis and placed certain of its members at the heart of the community, such as Joceran III and Bernard III, respectively prior and chamberlain of Cluny. The conflicts between the two lordships sometimes have the air of fam-

72. *DM*, 1.6, p. 20, ll. 99–100.

73. Georges Duby, *La société aux XIe et XIIe siècles dans la région mâconnaise*, 2d ed. (Paris, 1971), pp. 336ff.; Constance Brittain Bouchard, *Sword, Miter, and Cloister: Nobility and the Church in Burgundy, 980–1198* (Ithaca and London, 1987), pp. 295–300; Rosenwein, *To Be the Neighbor of Saint Peter*, pp. 59–60 and 115–21.

74. *CLU* 2881, 1031/60, 4.75–76.

75. *CLU* 4106, 5.455–56, and *CLU* 4131, 5.473–74.

76. Duby, *La société aux XIe et XIIe siècles dans la région mâconnaise*, no. 11, p. 518.

ily disputes; thus we read of Bernard III obtaining toll exemptions in Cluny's favor from his brother Landric.[77] Peter the Venerable's narrative in *De miraculis* concerned a typical seigneurial family. Returning as it did to the times of the castellany's founder, the *exemplum* could scarcely fail to carry conviction. Peter's story begins with Bernard II Grossus, after a life of sin, going on a pilgrimage to Rome, where he devotes himself to prayers and alms. On the way back to Burgundy, he falls sick and dies at Sutri. Some years later, a provost of Cluniac lands is making his way through the forest of Uxelles, near a castle that Bernard had built in order to facilitate the pillaging of the surrounding territory. Suddenly the provost is confronted by Bernard's spirit mounted on a mule and wearing a fox-fur cloak. To the astounded and frightened provost, Bernard explains how he is currently expiating his past sins, especially that of building the nearby castle. His repentance toward the end of his life has saved him from eternal damnation, but he still needs Cluniac suffrages. For the moment at least, the fox-fur cloak, yielded in life to a needy pauper, affords him "indescribable relief" (*inerrabile refrigerium*). Peter writes that when Abbot Hugh of Cluny was informed of Bernard's miraculous appearance, he "kindly accepted the deceased's request and, full of the spirit of charity, dispensed many alms and much assistance in divine sacrifices for the soul laboring under eternal judgment."[78] Peter makes clear, however, that the assistance afforded to Bernard by Hugh and his brethren only complemented Bernard's earlier acts of penitence in amending (*mutato spiritu*) his past faults. By confessing his sins while he lived and embarking on works of expiation, he had averted the need to fear the Lord's face on the day of future judgment.[79]

In the view of the abbot of Cluny, the effectiveness of the liturgy was dependent on the inner state of the deceased. Peter's approach was at one with the tradition of Gregorian clerics who questioned the quantitative mentality behind the system of tariffed penance, the notion that so many Masses, alms, paupers fed, and so on were automatically and arithmetically deductible. Peter Damian stressed the necessity of personal preparation for death.[80] He even considered it a cleric's duty to refuse any "unclean offering." For a gift *pro remedio animae* (for the good of the soul) that issued from a sinner who had not, or had incompletely, confessed his faults was not simply useless to him; it was also a form of "leprosy" that risked contaminating the recipients.[81] In the 1060s this was apparently not a universally accepted truth. In one of his letters Peter Damian set

77. *CLU* 3440, ca. 1070, 4.550–51.

78. *DM*, 1.11, p. 42, ll. 52–54.

79. According to the terms ascribed to Count Otto of Mâcon and his son in *CLU* 2979, ca. 1049, 4.176–77: "and [the true penitent must] by forestalling the face of the Lord in confession show zeal to expiate his sins by good works in as great satisfaction as is called for. And [we], bearing this in mind and fearing beforehand the day of future judgment, for a remedy of our souls, give to God . . ."

80. *Sermo in festivitate sancti Stephani Papae, CCCM* 57, pp. 224–31.

81. Peter Damian, *Epistolae*, no. 14, 1:145–50.

about reassuring three archpriests who were scandalized by his opinions and appalled by the notion that aid given to the dead might be useless.[82] The issue boiled down to one of reconciling notions of necessity and sufficiency, of personal salvation and collective responsibility. Thus though personal preparation was necessary, it was normally insufficient to fully discharge the penitent; and while it was an essential duty to assist the dead, it could not suffice for their salvation on its own. *De miraculis* followed this logic by illustrating the Augustinian argument summarized in *Contra Petrobrusianos*, and was at great pains to show that there were limits to what suffrages on behalf of the dead could achieve. Essentially suffrages constituted an extra, a bonus, yet they were necessary to most souls, since the vast majority of the deceased died far from perfect. The dead who appear in the pages of *De miraculis* come to seek that bonus, yet teach how infinite is the distance that separates what is necessary from what is sufficient. Only on behalf of these "middling" souls does the help given by the living do any good. The perfect dead, like the great figures of Cluniac monasticism whose characters are drawn in *De miraculis*, are already within the communion of saints. As for the really bad, no amount of suffrages by the living could save them. To emphasize this point, Peter the Venerable reports the particularly instructive story of a priest of Lusignan. Thoroughly besmirched by sexual sin, this priest had not hesitated frequently to take the body and blood of Christ in his unclean hands. Out of step with his times, he thought that without any personal amendment on his part he could buy himself off through his frequent and enthusiastic association with virtuous men, the monks of Bonnevaux. As he lay dying, he was taken in ecstasy to the scene of his own judgment. At the height of the proceedings, a drop of fire fell from a cauldron of hellfire in the next world onto his hand in this, burning a hole in the flesh down to the bone. As the prior of the monastery attended him in his agony, he screamed out to him in despair: "Stop! Stop praying for me. Tire yourself no more for one on whose behalf you will in no way be heard!"[83]

The Sociological Implications of Cluny's Funerary Outreach

The Testimony of the Absurd: Praying for the Saints

In the spring of 1144, Peter the Venerable went to Pisa and visited the tomb of Matthew of Albano, whose portrait occupies a sizable portion of book 2 of *De miraculis*. For Peter it was an opportunity to honor the "holy ashes" of his friend "as was fitting," and offer "for him the saving host." The reflection that follows attests a degree of perplexity on his part. For he was aware that such a service was of greater benefit to him, Peter, than to the sainted dead Matthew:

82. Ibid., no. 121, 3:392–97, here 393–94.
83. *DM*, 1.25, p. 77, ll. 81–83.

And although I was sure that I could be helped much more by his merits, nevertheless [*tamen*] I commended to the Almighty Creator and most kind Redeemer with all the prayers and tears at my disposal the man whose soul, while he lived, was one with mine.[84]

The intimate union of the two friends merits commentary that would be out of place here. Let us linger simply on the word *tamen*. Being a good Augustinian, Peter was puzzled as to the utility of his prayers and actions for the saints, which were effectively motivated by the desire to give thanks rather than by the duty to show mercy. He "nevertheless" honored "as was fitting" the ashes of his friend. Hugh of Semur's *Imprecatio*, which the abbot addressed to his monastic brethren and which Joachim Wollasch has described as a "text of virtually testamentary character," offers a further illustration of the same phenomenon. In the *Imprecatio*, the abbot founded an obit—an annual memorial to take place on his eventual date of death—laying down that revenues from the obedience of Berzé-la-Ville were to be allocated to defray the expenses entailed in such a celebration.[85] During the 1120s Hugh's cult was officially recognized by the pope.[86] This effectively redefined Hugh's status from that of an ordinary, needy soul to that of a saint. As such he had no need of his brethren's suffrages. All the same, at Cluny, the monks continued to carry out the orders of the *Imprecatio* to the letter. When, in the 1150s, Henry of Winchester was drawing up an inventory of the Cluniac demesnes in the *Constitutio expensae Cluniaci*, he continued to list the revenues of Berzé-la-Ville allocated to Hugh's obit under that head.[87] The evident absurdity of praying *for* the saints signals the sociological importance of what Peter the Venerable portrays elsewhere as a duty of mercy.[88] The dead teach us in a very special way just how tightly woven were the strands of social solidarity constituting the ecclesial fabric of the feudal age.[89] Peter was all the more inclined to idealize this solidarity because he was living at a time when changes in thought were loosening the fundamental ties of the ecclesial community. The total individualization of death and salvation in the fifth proposition of *Contra Petrobrusianos* was one of those changes, and it appears to have been favorably entertained not just in heretical circles but outside them too.

84. *DM*, 2.23, p. 139, ll. 47–51.
85. Ed. Herbert E. J. Cowdrey, "Two Studies," pp. 172–75. On this new practice, see Wollasch, "Hugues Ier abbé de Cluny," p. 81, where the phrase *texte quasi testamentaire* occurs.
86. On Hugh of Semur's cult, see Frank Barlow, "The Canonization and the Early Lives of Hugo I, Abbot of Cluny," *Analecta Bollandiana* 98 (1980): 297–334, and Kohnle, *Abt Hugo*, pp. 250–65.
87. *CLU* 4143, 5.490–505, here 498.
88. *DM*, 1.27, p. 85.
89. The subject is analyzed in detail by Michel Lauwers in his "Le 'sépulchre des pères' et les 'ancêtres': notes sur le culte des défunts à l'âge seigneurial," *Médiévales* 31 (1996): 67–78, and *La mémoire des ancêtres* (see above, note 8).

Family Solidarity and Feudal Solidarity

The duty of mercy to which Peter the Venerable referred was a complex notion operating in different contexts. These were, first, in the narrow circle of the family; secondly, within the ties of spiritual kinship; thirdly, in the relations of fidelity, which were analogues of relationships of kinship.

Among the witnesses called by Peter to testify against the fifth Petrobrusian proposition and in defense of the solidarity of living and dead was Ambrose of Milan. We saw earlier that one of his contributions was the transmission of the ancient Roman notion of family *pietas*, or dutifulness. Peter did not use Ambrosian material simply to be able to claim the ancient and established tradition of a Church Father against the corrosive novelties of Petrobrusian heresy. Family *pietas*, illustrated to perfection in those episodes of *De miraculis* where fathers appeared to their sons or brothers to their brothers, was no mere pastoral theme. It had its place in the Cluniac liturgy. The section of the *Liber tramitis* that deals with interceding on behalf of the dead mentions needy souls making after-death appearances, so that their *familiares*, either brethren who knew them or their blood relations, should promote their cause liturgically.[90] No doubt Odilo and his brethren recalled the passage of Gregory the Great's *Dialogues* where the deceased Justus appeared to his blood-related brother Copiosus. Thus within the Cluniac monastery, prayers and Masses widened the tight circle of close relations. The *Liber tramitis* speaks of Masses and alms "in virtue of which the Lord will undoubtedly be propitiated."[91] Successful outcomes in such cases could be put down primarily to family involvement. It is worth noting that one of the main festivals at Cluny was the feast of Saint Peter *in cathedra in Antiochia*, on 22 February, which was a deliberate Christianization of the *Cara cognatio*, during which the families of pagan Rome had honored their dead. The connotations of this *cathedra*, or chair, of Saint Peter were funerary well before they became episcopal. The liturgy for a long time harked back to these origins. Until 1030, the office lesson on 22 February at Cluny was taken from sermon 190 of pseudo-Augustine.[92] The first half of that text justified the solemnity of the occasion, the feast of the pontiff Peter, the Church's foundation. The tone of the second half was quite different. There the author denounced pagan superstitions still

90. *LT*, 195.8, p. 277.

91. *LT*, 195.6, p. 277, l. 27. On Justus and Copiosus, see above, note 53.

92. As the Cluny office lectionary attests, Paris, Bibliothèque Nationale, MS latin 13371, f. 89v: *In cathedra sancti Petri. Institutio sollemnitatis hodierne* (Dekkers no. 368, *PL* 39:2100–2101). The *Liber tramitis* (*LT*, 39, p. 49, l. 6) says that after 1030, Leo the Great's *Tractatus* 4 was used, *CCSL* 138, pp. 16–21. The Augustinian authorship was rejected by Germain Morin, "Sermons apocryphes du Bréviaire," in *Etudes, textes, découvertes* (Maredsous and Paris, 1913), p. 495, no. 25. The sermon's date is uncertain (ca. 460?); it is integrated into the *Sermo Clementis papae in Petri apostolorum principis sessione qua cathedre sublimatur anthiocena*, transcribed in Paris, Bibliothèque Nationale, MS latin 18304, ff. 137–39v, here 137v–38, an eleventh-century manuscript from the Cluniac priory of Saint-Arnoul, Crépy-en-Valois.

associated with the feast of the Chair of Saint Peter. It was customary to place food and wine on the tombs of the dead, a practice that John Beleth was still re-pudiating in the twelfth century.[93] We have no reason to suppose that such fu-nerary meals were still being laid out in eleventh- and twelfth-century Burgundy. But it is noteworthy that in a very transparent way the liturgy kept the memory alive of the special link that existed between Saint Peter and the deceased rela-tions whose bodies lay in the monastic cemetery.

In Ambrose Peter the Venerable found just the material he needed to justify the ancient Romans' attachment to their ancestors and the devotion of the faith-ful of the twelfth century to theirs. It is worth looking back at what Ambrose said in a little more detail.[94] In *Contra Petrobrusianos*, the first quotation from Am-brose is from *De obitu Theodosii*, a funeral oration in which the bishop of Milan, paraphrasing Psalm 114(116):1–9, promised to follow the deceased with his suf-frages unto the "realm [*regimen*] of the living." There follow two extracts from *De obitu Valentiniani et Gratiani*. Gratian, the son of Emperor Valentinian I (died 375) and his first wife, Marina, was proclaimed Augustus in 367. Through his wife Constantia, the posthumous daughter of Constantius, he belonged to the family of Constantine the Great. Ambrose (339–97), who became bishop in 373 or 374 after the death of the Arian bishop Auxentius, saw Gratian as the Church's military arm, able to restore Catholic order in the face of the Arian heresy and pagan demands. But Emperor Gratian was assassinated in 383. Valentinian II was Gratian's half-brother. He was born in 371, the offspring of Valentinian I's second marriage to the Arian Justina. He was proclaimed emperor at four years old and died in 392. Owing to his mother's lengthy guardianship of him, Valen-tinian II did not die a Catholic. How could he be saved? Ultimately, as we shall see, it was through his brother Gratian that he would be rescued.

Peter the Venerable could not fail to be impressed by the imperial proof of the efficacy of family solidarity. The extract quoted in *Contra Petrobrusianos* comes from chapters 54 to 56 of Ambrose's oration.[95] It is the point where Am-brose beseeches the Lord to grant his servant what he seeks. Although Valen-tinian II was not baptized, he nonetheless (says Ambrose) intended to be baptized before he died, a fact that placed him in the category of a catechumen. Let us observe in passing that this appeal to intention as a moral criterion can-not have failed to interest Peter the Venerable, constrained as he was by his Petrobrusian opponents to recognize the individual dimension of actions in re-gard to salvation. Ambrose goes on to assert that to exclude Valentinian from the Redemption would be as inconceivable as distinguishing between martyrs who had been baptized (who would be saved) and martyrs who had been cate-

93. John Beleth, *Summa de ecclesiasticis officiis*, 83, CCCM 41A, p. 151.

94. Ambrose was regarded as extremely important at Cluny from at least the late tenth century. On the presence of his works there, see Véronika von Büren, "Ambroise de Milan dans la biblio-thèque de Cluny," *Scriptorium* 47 (1993): 127–65.

95. *CP*, 250; *De obitu Valentiniani et Gratiani*, 54ff., CSEL 73, pp. 355ff.

chumens (as if they were to be rejected): just as the martyrs were cleansed by their baptism of blood, so Valentinian was cleansed by his piety and good intention. The passage quoted by Peter begins just after Ambrose has prayed the Lord not to separate Valentinian II from his brother Gratian and not to cut the son's link with his father Valentinian I. In the first case, Ambrose invokes the influence of *pia germanitas* (dutiful brotherhood), whereby the lot of Gratian, "who is already yours" (i.e., the Lord's), might be put in jeopardy if Valentinian II did not join him. It is a difficult passage, which generally puzzles commentators on Ambrose. For us, reading Ambrose through Peter the Venerable's eyes, it is simply a matter of recognizing the strength of the operating logic: saving the one entails redeeming the other, as if *pia germanitas* were itself a means of grace. Ambrose goes on to develop a second strand of family-based argument. All three men, defenders of the Catholic Church, must (argues Ambrose) have been saved together. Valentinian II, like his father and brother, had shown *fides, devotio,* and *pietas* (faith, devotion, and piety) in rejecting the privilege of the temples. Thanksgiving was all the more due for the dead emperor's life since, though he was unbaptized, he had intended his own baptism. Ambrose then invokes the words of Anchises, Aeneas's father, in the sixth book of Vergil's *Aeneid:*

> "Give me lilies in handfuls;
> Purple flowers let me scatter, and upon my offspring's soul
> Heap at least these offerings, discharging my only too vain
> Duty." (lines 883b–86a)

At this point in Vergil's epic, Aeneas has entered the underworld, where he encounters the shade of his dead father. The latter takes him to a mound from which he beholds a succession of souls of great Romans who are yet to come, from the early kings of Alba Longa down to Augustus. The last to arrive in this glorious procession is "a youth of outstanding physique" who has "unjoyous face and downcast eyes." This is Marcellus, Augustus's sister Octavia's son, who was adopted by the emperor but, by the time Vergil wrote, had died tragically in the bloom of youth at the age of nineteen. Late Roman tradition was informed by Servius that Marcellus's funeral was the most sumptuous in Roman history. The request of Anchises for lilies, his urge to scatter purple flowers and act dutifully toward his distant offspring, is thus a family funerary action that Ambrose quite deliberately aligns with his own devotion toward the deceased Valentinian I and his two sons. The implication is that the fates of the three men were inseparable. Thus more than a thousand years after Marcellus's untimely death, Peter the Venerable could still find inspiration in the legacy of Roman *pietas,* as conveyed by the pagan Vergil and the Christian Ambrose, to secure his argument in favor of family solidarity.

Notable in Ambrose's Christianizing reinterpretation of the Roman *pietas* expressed in the Aeneid is the use of allegory. "I do not," says Ambrose regarding Valentinian II, "spread his tomb with lilies; I bathe his spirit with the perfume of Christ." Above all, the virtues of *fides, devotio,* and *pietas* uniting Valentinian II, his father, and his brother were the virtues of monarchs committed to defending the Church. The Christianization of the Roman tradition reached completion in the next patristic generation when Augustine described the Church as a pious spiritual mother caring for all her deceased children. Upon this patristic legacy, the early medieval Church erected the notion of substitute or spiritual kinship.[96] Anxious to show the different pathways of funerary solidarity, Peter the Venerable offers in *De miraculis* an excellent example of how one form of kinship could substitute for another. The story, told in book 1, chapter 23, is of a deceased knight who appears repeatedly to a priest, Stephen. The knight is Guy of the castle of Moras-en-Valloire in the present-day *département* of Drôme; he dies of wounds received in combat. The account opens with his last confession being heard by Archbishop Guy of Vienne (the future pope Callixtus II). Present is his priest Stephen, who is also the storyteller. Stephen explains that a few days later, Guy was buried at the priory of Manthes, a dependency of Cluny. Thus the knight's soul passed from the cure of the archbishop of Vienne to that of the Ecclesia cluniacensis. We have here a good example of Cluny's involvement at the local level and of the practical expression of the funerary policy articulated in *De miraculis*. In Stephen's story, Guy of Moras's confession is not enough, far from it. He appears to his "spiritual father" Stephen (perhaps his godfather as well as his pastor), telling him of the cruel torments he suffers for having forgotten to confess two sins: violating a cemetery and illicit taxation. Guy asks Stephen to go to Anselm, his brother "after the flesh," asking him to restore what Guy has taken unjustly and offer compensation to those he has wronged. But Anselm will have none of it. The objection he makes to Stephen has an oddly Petrobrusian ring:

> What has my brother's soul to do with me? He had what he had while he lived. Why did he not give satisfaction himself to those he wronged? Let him look out for himself! I'll not do penance for *his* sins.[97]

96. On questions of kinship in the Middle Ages, see the important research by Anita Guerreau-Jalabert: "Sur les structures de parenté dans l'Europe médiévale," *AESC* 36 (1981): 1028–49; "La dénomination des relations et des groupes de parenté en latin médiéval," *Archivum Latinitatis Medii Aevi* 46–47 (1988): 65–108; "La parenté dans l'Europe médiévale et moderne: à propos d'une synthèse récente," *L'Homme* 109 (1989): 69–92; "El systema de parentesco medieval: sus formas (real/spiritual) y su dependencia con respecto a la organización del espacio," in *Relaciones de poder, de producción y parentesco en la edad media y moderna,* ed. Reina Pastor (Madrid, 1990), pp. 85–105; "*Spiritus* et *caritas*: le baptême dans la société médiévale," in *La parenté spirituelle,* ed. Françoise Heritier-Augé and Elisabeth Copet-Rougier (Paris, 1995), pp. 133–203. The notion of analogy mentioned in the introductory paragraph under this head comes from this author.

97. *DM,* 1.23, p. 71, ll. 89–92.

In his third and final appearance to Stephen, Guy tells him that as his "spiritual father" it is ultimately up to him, Stephen, to discharge the family duty of mercy. Stephen does so.

The duty of mercy so dear to Peter is particularly well illustrated in chapter 27 of the first book of *De miraculis*. The story concerns the appearance of a deceased knight to Humbert III, lord of Beaujeu. This episode takes us outside the narrow orbit of blood relationships. We even pass beyond that of spiritual kinship, although relations of fidelity were closely analogous to those of the spirit, as the *exemplum* itself shows us. We enter the realm of the seigneurial *familia* with its three concentric circles: the blood family at its core, the wider household of servants around it, and finally the outer network of *fideles*.[98] Humbert is the son of Guichard III, an important castellan who, after a life of worldly vanity, "weaving many woes as spiders weave webs,"[99] died as a monk *ad succurrendum* at Cluny, having had just enough time there to receive the "pilgrim's viaticum," that is, last communion. Like so many others, he lacked much spiritually. But Humbert, his son, as we learn subsequently, is not too worried about the father's lack. Fighting one day in Forez with a troop of his *fideles*, Humbert loses one of his knights, Geoffrey of Oingt. Two months later, Geoffrey's spirit appears to another knight, Milo of Anse, "because lately bound to me in the world by love as well as fidelity."[100] Geoffrey beseeches Milo to intervene with Humbert to remind him of his debt toward him; after all, did he not die fighting for him and, to make Geoffrey's situation worse, "for an insufficiently just cause"? The spirit of Geoffrey goes on to complain that Humbert's ingratitude toward him is hardly surprising in view of his neglect of his own dead father. When Humbert is apprised of Geoffrey's appearance, he displays so little urgency that Geoffrey appears to him directly, charging him that his self-sacrifice on Humbert's behalf has turned his former lord into his greatest debtor.[101] Reminding Humbert of his duty to provide suffrages for both the souls he has neglected, Geoffrey points out to Humbert that he will thereby "provide salvation for your own sake also." The story ends with Humbert finally stirring himself and becoming a Templar.[102] Having told his story, Peter the Venerable states explicitly for whom the narrative is primarily intended: the modern heretics who

98. The bond of fidelity between lord and household servant is seen at work in the next episode (*DM*, 1.28, pp. 87–92), where the servant Sancho appears to his master requesting that wages owing to him at his death be paid in alms for his soul; in the event, the lord adds to this "for a more complete remission."

99. *DM*, 1.27, p. 83, ll. 21–22.

100. *DM*, 1.27, p. 84, ll. 49–50.

101. *DM*, 1.27, p. 85, ll. 97–98.

102. Humbert subsequently came back from the Holy Land and returned to secular life. Peter the Venerable defended his cause against Everard of Barre, Master of the Templars, and Pope Eugenius III: see *Ep.*, 172, 1:407–9, and 173, pp. 410–13. On the episode, see Maria Teresa Brolis, "La crociata per Pietro il Venerabile: guerra di arma o guerra di idee?" *Aevum* 61 (1987): 351ff.

"deny that the aids of the Church can profit the faithful departed," which is proof if any were needed that *De miraculis* and *Contra Petrobrusianos* really did share a common agenda. Peter attacks with equal vehemence the "noxious error" of the heretics who deny the utility of suffrages at one extreme and the "slothful complacency" of those who trust to the "good offices of others" for their salvation at the other.[103] For Peter the truth lay in a middle way: people should do what they could in this world to achieve what was essential for salvation and leave others to make up any deficiencies later. The inestimable value of *De miraculis* compared with *Contra Petrobrusianos* is that it clearly identifies these "others." The example of Humbert, directed at both heretics and doubting Catholics, epitomizes who they were: *fideles*, friends, and kin (both natural and spiritual). We have already looked enough at the role of kin. But we need to stress here the importance of the role attributed to *fideles* in relation to death. The story of Humbert shows that in a society ordered according to the power of reciprocal commitments made through bonds of fidelity, the afterlife was neither a time when ties of solidarity were broken nor a place where society ceased to exist.[104] On the contrary, the story of Humbert reveals how a point of doctrine—taken from the age-old reflections of the Church Fathers—structured relationships (the bonds of fidelity) that at first sight we might have imagined to be purely lay and secular. For *caritas* (charity) was a seigneurial virtue that only the force of ecclesiastical sanction in the form of excommunication or anathema could suspend.[105]

Behind the detail these narratives give of the concern that the living showed their dead, it is possible to detect a historical process at work. It began with the ancient Roman heritage of family *pietas*, allegorized in the fourth and fifth centuries in such a way as to turn the brotherhood of Christians into one vast family. The spiritual kinship thus created played a major role in the early Middle Ages with the institution of godparents and the spread of model communities—guilds and monastic and canonical fraternities. At the end of the process, in the eleventh and twelfth centuries, the relationships of fidelity structuring the society that we call "feudal" were presenting themselves as an analogue of the model of Christian kinship. The evolution from Vergil to Peter the Venerable via Ambrose of Milan and Augustine of Hippo did not lead to social confusion. *Contra Petrobrusianos* and *De miraculis* reveal an author who took the utmost care to distinguish between the various registers of Christian kinship in the feudal age: ties of blood; spiritual kinship, either in the narrow sense of godparenting or monastic and canonical fraternity, or in the wider sense of Christian fraternity as a generality; the seigneurial *familia*, namely, its domestic ties and, above all, the relationships of fidelity. These different registers, which were never confused, corresponded precisely with the different groups whose commemoration was provided for in

103. *DM*, 1.27, p. 87, ll. 140ff.

104. See Schmitt, *Les revenants*, p. 220, which refers in part to the *De miraculis* of Peter the Venerable.

105. Elisabeth Voloda, *Excommunication in the Middle Ages* (Berkeley, 1986), pp. 67ff.

the texts of the liturgy and in the charters that established their practical basis. From Odilo's abbacy on, the Cluniac customaries distinguished between services envisaged for individual commemorations (those of the professed, associates, *familiares*, benefactors), those for kinsfolk, and those for all the faithful. Similarly, the layout of acts *pro remedio animae* followed the classic early medieval template whereby the originator was mentioned first (*ego*, or the person in whose name the act was registered), followed by the *familia* (in any of the accepted senses), and finally by all the faithful, who were entitled to general commemoration. Small wonder, then, that the Petrobrusian proposition strictly individualizing human death was perceived to have dire implications. Peter the Venerable's two rejoinders, *Contra Petrobrusianos* and *De miraculis*, reveal what was at stake sociologically if the Petrobrusian attempt to individualize the funerary sphere should carry the day. To tamper with the bonds of *caritas* linking the living to the dead would have been nothing less than to unravel the finely woven fabric of relationships of kinship and fidelity upholding society in the feudal age.

Between the Living and the Dead: The Poor

The solidarity that bound the powerful members of the aristocracy directly entailed the poor. We noted earlier that when Peter the Venerable quoted Ambrose of Milan's *De excessu fratris sui Satyri* in defense of the concern of the living for the dead, the image given was of paupers, portrayed as the deceased's co-heirs, washing away his offenses with their redemptive tears.[106] But what exactly did this notion of "co-inheritance" amount to in Peter's mind? Throughout the discussion on the fifth Petrobrusian proposition in *Contra Petrobrusianos* and the many chapters of *De miraculis* devoted to the dead, Peter maintained that every believer was responsible for his own salvation, even if satisfying the essential conditions frequently left more to do. "Their works follow them," he said of Alfonso VI of Castile-León, applying to him the words of Apocalypse 14:13 on the blessed dead that die in the Lord. In place of his earthly kingdom, that great benefactor of Cluny had gained the everlasting kingdom; those who benefited from his works were the poor, either the materially poor or else the monks, the "poor in spirit."[107] In his sermon *De eleemosyna*, Abelard explained that charity was not simply conceived in the mind (*mente concepta*) but showed itself in action (*opere exhibita*), with the poor the medium of this necessary exhibition of good works.[108] Hence the many mentions of feeding the poor in funerary contexts, whether in acts *pro remedio animae* or in the liturgy of the dead.[109] Thanks

---

106. *CP*, 251.

107. *DM*, 1.28, pp. 91–92.

108. *Petri Abaelardi Opera*, ed. Victor Cousin (Paris, 1849), 1:547–52; also printed as *Sermo* 30 in *PL* 178:564–9, here 566BC.

109. See for example *CLU* 2110, 993/1048, 3.298, and its contemporary *CLU* 2112, 3.299–300. The latter contains a commitment by Odilo and his brethren to admit the donor and his *familia* into the Cluniac *societas* and allow them all the benefits of that society "in Masses, psalms, prayers, and

to the poor, the needy deceased person remained in contact with this world. Bernard II Grossus, it will be recalled, gained "relief" after death from the fox-fur cloak he had given in life to a pauper as a pious gesture. The shelter from the cold that his good action had given the pauper in this world was thus transformed into the "indescribable relief" (*inerrabile refrigerium*) from the torments he endured supposedly close to the flames of hell. The pauper was the deceased's double in the process of exchange between this world and the next in the sense that he was present at both ends of the journey. He replaced the deceased symbolically in the here and now, just as he would eventually welcome him into the "everlasting dwellings" (Luke 16:9). Having been sustained by earthly things given by the deceased in this world, the pauper would in return give him heavenly things in the next. The pauper was thus more than an intermediary; he was a "transformer." Through him the translation from the kingdom of the devil to the kingdom of God was effected; through him the still unperfected soul of the deceased would be enabled to join the communion of saints. The transforming function of the poor is possibly what lay behind the frequently parallel occurrence of alms distributions to the needy and Masses for the dead.[110] It also helps to explain how the monastery, which received gifts *pro remedio animae* with a view to their "transformation" into eucharistic sacrifices and maintenance of the poverty-stricken "co-heirs" of the deceased, itself came to be a symbolic representation of the afterlife. As certain acts put it, the monastery was a *parvulum habitaculum pro remedio animae* (little dwelling-place for the good of the soul), the future place (*locus*) of the soul, the spot where the hopes of the present merged with their future fulfillment.[111] In his funerary eulogy of his mother, Raingard,

---

in other divine obsequies"; to the donation is added a pauper: "Also we donate to them [provision for] one pauper at all time, whom we shall clothe, shoe, and feed." On the question of the pauper as the symbolic double of the deceased, see Joachim Wollasch, "Toten- und Armensorge," in *Gedächtnis, das Gemeinschaft stiftet*, ed. Karl Schmid, Schriftenreihe der katholischen Akademie der Erzdiözese Freiburg (Munich and Zurich, 1985), pp. 9–38, and "Hugues Ier abbé de Cluny," esp. pp. 78, 81, and 84.

110. See for instance *DM*, 1.23, p. 72, l. 113 and 1.28, p. 91, l. 131. The customaries of Ulrich and Bernard stipulated that at the death of an abbot, twelve paupers were to be fed at the hospice with bread, wine, and meat (if the day allowed); Bernard added that the meal should take place "during Mass," suggesting the parallel established between the eucharistic sacrifice and feeding the poor. See Ulrich, *Antiquiores consuetudines cluniacensis monasterii*, 3.32, *PL* 149:702, and Bernard, *Ordo Cluniacensis*, 1.25, pp. 199ff., in *Vetus disciplina monastica*, ed. Marquard Herrgott (Paris, 1726), pp. 199ff.

111. See *CLU* 3508, 22 May 1077, 4.625–26, extant original diploma of Alfonso VI of Castile-León. *CLU* 3746, ca. 1100, 5.100–101, also an extant original, contains some illuminating wording in which the term *locus* is used both of the monastery (*locus Cluniacensis*) and of the life after death: "For it is established beyond doubt that after death no place of pardon [*nullus locus venie*] is granted to souls, other than to those who in this life endeavor to make an effort with alms and other works of mercy. . . . Wherefore . . . before my death I have conveyed a certain manse for the good of my soul and the burial of my body to the place of Cluny [*loco Cluniacensi*], so that without misrepresentation or disturbance by any person whatsoever after my death the aforesaid place [*prefatus locus*] may possess [it] for ever."

who had spent the last twenty years of her life at Marcigny-sur-Loire, Peter the Venerable depicted her busy caring for the poor, among whom she found "a place for the Lord, a tabernacle for the God of Jacob" (Psalm 131(132): 5).[112]

The Monastic "Purgatory"

Topographical references of this kind deserve to be taken seriously. We know from Jacques Le Goff's work that purgatory took material shape as a new location in the afterlife during the years 1170–1215. It appeared in theological and spiritual literature influenced by the Parisian masters and the Cistercians, and appeared simultaneously in vision literature like *The Purgatory of Saint Patrick*.[113] In the history of the construct, the Cluny of the eleventh and twelfth centuries testified to the urgent need to tie the operation of purgatorial penalties to a definite space. The question of the dead thus brings us back to sacred space, itself an issue central to Peter the Venerable's thoughts on Christian society. At the time when the abbot of Cluny was writing his *Contra Petrobrusianos* and *De miraculis*, the Latin west was in search of an in-between location for the dead who were neither too good nor too bad. Such a refinement was necessary to enable the dead to complete in the next world the purgation begun through penance in this one. But where was it to take place? Were they to be regarded as returning to the scene of their crime, as Gregory the Great had taught and as was shown, even in *De miraculis*, by the spirit of Bernard II Grossus returning to the forest of Uxelles near the castle he had built in his lifetime to pillage the surrounding country?[114] Robert Pullen, the Parisian master who invented the term "transubstantiation" in the 1140s, wondered where such correction could possibly take place, given that physical punishment implied a place in which it could happen. It could not take place in heaven, since no ill was known there; it could not take place in hell, since that was no place for faithful souls with good in them. Logically, there had to be a third, intermediate place or places (*loca purgatoria*, special places of purgation), whose shape gradually became sufficiently distinct to constitute "purgatory."[115]

In the phase of imprecision and questions preceding the invention of purgatory, Cluny made a tangible contribution to the construction of a topography that symbolized the places of purgatorial penalties. All we can do here is to make a general observation and give a couple of examples, the first of which is well known and the second oddly neglected. The general observation that is called for has to do with the development we studied in chapter 5, the restriction of the Eucharist to "proper places." In funerary matters, as we have seen in this

112. *Ep.*, 53, 1:153–73, here 167: *Pausabat in eis mens dedita deo* . . .
113. Jacques Le Goff, *La naissance du Purgatoire*, Bibliothèque des Histoires (Paris, 1981), p. 267.
114. Ibid., p. 192; *DM*, 1.11.
115. Le Goff, *La naissance du Purgatoire*, pp. 177ff., and cf. pp. 203–4 on Robert Pullen, given among the *témoignages mineurs*.

chapter, this translated into an institution of monk-priests and their sanctuary as a space of effective transformations. The vocabulary of purgation employed in *De miraculis* is illuminating in this regard. The monks are characterized as the fruitful branches of Christ—the "True Vine"—that were purged by God the Father (John 15:1–16); they lived "in Galilee," the time and space of Paschal purification. It was there, through the mediation of the pure, the spiritual elite like Benedict—"They need no purgation in whom there is clearly nothing to purge," Peter says of him—that the most effective purgation of all took place, the one sought with insistence by returning spirits, the sacrament of the altar.[116]

Now for the examples. The first takes us to the Cluny of the 1030s, the period during which Abbot Odilo instituted the general commemoration of All Souls' Day, 2 November. Odilo did not simply give the dead their own special, unshared liturgical occasion. If we are to believe his biographer Jotsald, whose authority was regarded as final by Peter Damian, Jacob of Voragine, and Vincent of Beauvais among others, Odilo gave them both a time and a place. Here is Jotsald's narrative:

> There was once a certain religious man from the Rouergue region who was on his way home from Jerusalem. As he was crossing the stretch of sea between Thessalonica and Sicily, he and many others were caught halfway in an extremely strong wind. It drove the ship to a certain island or crag where a servant of God, a hermit, dwelt. Having stayed there some considerable time waiting for the sea to become calm again, the traveler began to talk with the servant of God about many things. Asked by the man of God about his origins, he answered that he was from Aquitaine. The man of God then asked earnestly if he knew of a certain monastery called Cluny and Odilo its abbot. The answer came: "Indeed I do; I know it well; and I'd like to know what makes you ask."
>
> "I'll tell you," he said, "and I advise you to keep in your mind the things you hear. There are places neighboring us, and out of them, by the manifest judgment of God, belch the most dreadful flames of fire in which the souls of sinners pay off varying penalties for a fixed space of time. A multitude of demons is assigned continually to renew their torments. Day in, day out they repeat the souls' punishments, making the suffering ever harder and harder to bear. But I have often heard the demons lamenting and making no little complaint that through the prayers of men of religion and alms given to the poor, as happens in various places of saints, the souls of the condemned are very often released from their pains. And among others they mention especially and complain the most about that congregation of Cluny and its abbot. So I urge you in the name of God: if you manage to return safely to your peo-

116. DM, 1.2, p. 10, l. 56 (the sacrament of the altar is *purgatior*, more purging); 1.9, p. 36, l. 59 (the monks are *palmites purgati*, the purged vine branches of John 15.2); 1.20, pp. 61–63 (Benedict).

PART II. CHRISTIAN SOCIETY

ple, let that congregation know all that you have heard from me. And tell them from me to keep on ever more with their prayers, vigils, and alms, that the souls in pain may have rest and that thereby joy may be increased in heaven and loss and grief inflicted upon the devil."[117]

Jotsald's narrative anticipated the topography of the future purgatory in two respects. First was the reference to physical punishments, with the glosses that the penalties varied, became ever harder to bear, and were for a fixed period. Second was their location in actual physical places, discovered on the way back from Jerusalem, on an island midway between Thessalonica and Sicily. In a sermon, Julian of Vézelay, who was active when Peter the Venerable's brother Pontius of Montboissier was abbot of Vézelay, specified that these places lay at the mouth of Mount Etna, where classical mythology had placed Vulcan and his forges.[118] These places of punishment were counterbalanced by the holy places, of which Cluny was preeminent, spaces in which deliverance became possible through various suffrages—prayers, alms, and, as Jotsald says later, Masses—thanks to the monks and the poor.

A century later, Peter the Venerable was still more definite about the monastery's purgatorial function. In chapter 31 of the second book of De miraculis, he describes the "overt manifestation" of a deceased person that occurred shortly before his time of writing, one Christmas Eve at Charlieu, a dependency of Cluny.[119] The story portrays a monastery child who, excited by the coming feast, cannot sleep. He sees two figures appear at the foot of his bed; they are his late paternal uncle Achard, former prior of Charlieu, and William, another onetime prior. They are deep in conversation. The boy, we are told, never knew them alive, but recognizes them easily from what he has been told of them. It is an incident that gives us yet another example of the familiar commerce that families, in both the blood-related and monastic sense, continued to have with their deceased members. In the story, William and Achard finish their conversation and William goes away; the boy is left alone with the spirit of his dead uncle. Achard asks the boy to go with him to the monks' graveyard "to see some marvelous things." The boy, well aware of the rules governing the monastery children, is fearful and answers that he cannot do anything without his guardian. In the closed world of the cloister with its obsessive fear of homosexual practices, the prepubertal or early adolescent youth were reckoned to be the community's

117. Jotsald, *Vita sancti Odilonis*, 2.13, *PL* 142:926C–927B. Transmission by Peter Damian, *Vita sancti Odilonis*, *PL* 144:935C–936C; Jacob of Voragine, *Legenda aurea*, ed. Thomas Graesse, 2d ed. (Leipzig, 1850), 163(158), pp. 728–39, "De commemoratione animarum"; Vincent of Beauvais, *Speculum historiale*, 25 [24 in Douay edition].105.102–5. I thank Monique Paulmier-Foucard for this last reference.

118. Julian of Vézelay, *Sermo* 11, ed. D. Vorreux, *SC*, 193 (Paris, 1972), pp. 450–55, cited and analyzed by Le Goff, *La naissance du Purgatoire*, pp. 273ff.

119. *DM*, 2.31(27), pp. 158–61.

weakest link in the chain of resistance against all the satanic wiles of sex.[120] In the story, Achard reassures the boy, who finally accepts his invitation. The deceased and his nephew cross the main cloister, then pass by the cloister of the infirmary to arrive at the first of the two gates to the cemetery. Inside are many seats occupied by monks. One is reserved for Achard, but he may not sit down yet. He must first answer for a venial fault, that of being late for the chapter meeting, and do penance for it. In the meantime, he asks the boy to sit down in his place. In the middle of the graveyard is an edifice topped by a lantern, below which are steps leading to a platform. Peter's description is the earliest written record of such a funerary monument, which, as he explains, shines all night "out of reverence for the faithful resting there."[121] On the platform sits a judge, before whom Achard prostrates himself. After a short time, Achard returns to the seat where his nephew is sitting. Shortly after this, the child sees the company rise and leave the graveyard by the second gate. The threshold of this gate burns with fire, and the boy notices that some of the monks take longer than others to pass over it. The spirit of Achard leads his nephew back to his bed in the dormitory and promptly disappears. What we have here is not simply a lesson on the necessary solidarity between the living and the dead, between natural kin (Achard and his nephew) and spiritual kin (the monastic fraternity). More striking is the symbolic topography presented, particularly the blurring of lines between the monastery—the monks' graveyard assimilated to a chapterhouse, the everyday place of penitence and purgation—and a kind of purgatorial place. We do not have purgatory as such here, but it is noteworthy that in this waking dream of the mid-twelfth century the graveyard-cum-chapterhouse of a Cluniac establishment was equipped with a purgatorial fiery threshold. What the dead in the dream were saying was that the monastery was essentially a space of transition between this world and the next, an antechamber or sieve (*sas*) that individuals had to pass through and where they stayed for as long as they had faults to correct. Twenty or thirty years on, this intermediate space would expand and take the name purgatory.

120. See for instance *DM*, 1.14, p. 46, and the study by Isabelle Cochelin, "Enfants, jeunes et vieux au monastère: la perception du cycle de la vie dans les sources clunisiennes (909–1156)," doctoral thesis, 2 vols., typescript, University of Montreal, 1996.

121. On the lanterns of the dead, see René Crozet, "Les lanternes des morts," *Bulletin de la Société des antiquaires de l'Ouest* 13 (1942–43): 115–44; Marcel Plault, *Les lanternes des morts* (Poitiers, 1988); Danièle Alexandre-Bidon and Cécile Treffort, "Un quartier pour les morts: images du cimetière médiéval," in the volume edited by them, *À réveiller les morts: la mort au quotidien dans l'Occident médiéval* (Lyon, 1994), pp. 253–73, here 260.

8

CHRISTIAN SOCIETY REVEALED
BY ITS OUTSIDERS

THE "VOICES" OF THE SPIRIT

With his long defense of the duties of mercy owed by the living to the dead, Peter the Venerable brought to a close his general reflections upon the various ties of solidarity binding members of society to one another. To his discussion of the fifth proposition of *Contra Petrobrusianos* he nevertheless added some complementary material, unannounced in the earlier plan of the treatise, in defense of chanting and liturgical music.[1] Peter of Bruis and his followers had asserted that God was unmoved by words or music and that he would respond only to silent, inner outpourings.[2] The heretics' attack may look relatively minor, but it cast doubt on the efficacy of the Church's entire ritual; Peter the Venerable was therefore at pains to make a brisk reply. Being the head of a monastic church that was both celebrated and criticized for the sumptuousness of its liturgy, he could scarcely do otherwise. He began by reminding his adversaries, once priests themselves, of the value of the Psalms and of the frequent injunctions in Scripture to chant, sing psalms, or shout out loud (*in vociferatione*).[3] He cited the strings and trumpets of the Old Testament. Then there were the examples of David and Elisha. According to 1 Kings (1 Samuel) 16:23, David had played his harp to King Saul, "and Saul was refreshed, and was better, for the evil spirit departed from him." According to 4(2) Kings 3:15, Elisha had summoned a minstrel, and his playing was an occasion for divine prophecy. Music and chant were spiritual media: they chased away the spirit of evil and summoned the Holy Spirit. This last point had all the greater significance in the light of Peter's ear-

1. *CP,* 273–78. The same criticism of Church chant is reported in the monk Heribert's circular letter, ed. and French trans. by Pierre Bonnassie and Richard Landes in *Les Sociétés méridionales autour de l'an Mil: répertoire des sources et documents commentés,* ed. Michel Zimmermann (Paris, 1992), pp. 457–59. See also Guy Lobrichon, "The Chiaroscuro of Heresy: Early Eleventh-Century Aquitaine As Seen from Auxerre," in *The Peace of God: Social Violence and Religious Response in France around the Year 1000,* ed. Thomas Head and Richard Landes (Ithaca, 1992), pp. 80–103.

2. *CP,* 273, ll. 2–4.

3. *CP,* 273, ll. 15ff.

lier consideration of the space within which the liturgy happened. The church or ecclesiastical *fabrica* (building, workshop, forge) was purified by the Spirit's "voices" from all taint of the devil. It was the place of spiritual outpourings, where heaven and earth met, an in-between location reserved exclusively for divine manifestations in a human context through the eucharistic sacrifice. It was the antechamber in which the pilgrim race of humanity transformed itself into something better. Surely such a perspective was worth singing about.

A SOCIOLOGY OF CHRISTENDOM IN THE FEUDAL AGE

At the very end of *Contra Petrobrusianos*, Peter the Venerable once again addressed those to whom his treatise was directed.[4] Appealing to the Church's custom, which had always been to condemn and suppress the lies of heretics, the abbot of Cluny was now ready to dispatch his polemical weapon "so that the religious should not lack authority, nor curious inquirers an explanation."[5] Monks and seculars had their own individual functions; it was now the task of the secular pastors to take action on the ground. Peter believed that his clarifications should enable them to eliminate the heresy whose traces were still evident when he visited their Provençal dioceses. It is the business, he says, of the prelates, holders of the apostolic office, to broadcast the word of truth, to bring the deviants back onto the right path, and condemn the recalcitrant—which in the 1140s meant, as a rule, burning at the stake.[6] "Dispensers of the wheat of the divine word," the bishops and archbishops must weed out the tares and scatter the seed that would provide a good harvest.

Imputations of Heresy and Control of the Social Order

This final, bucolic image of the Lord's "field" implied that Christian society was cultivated land from which weeds were to be utterly removed. Christendom was defined by the beliefs and the individuals it rejected. Hence the importance of antiheretical polemic in establishing the Church and in defining the rules governing society at a time when seigneurial and clerical powers were

4. *CP*, 278.
5. *CP*, 278, ll. 7–11.
6. On the increase in penalties for heresy within the space of a hundred years (1025–1120) and the move from expulsion to the death penalty, see André Vauchez, "Diables et hérétiques: les réactions de l'Eglise et de la société en Occident face aux mouvements religieux dissidents, de la fin du Xe au début du XIIe siècle," *Santi e demoni nell'Alto Medioevo occidentale (secoli V–XI)*, Settimane di Studio del Centro Italiano di Studi sull'alto Medioevo, 36, 15–21 April 1993, 2 (Spoleto, 1989), pp. 597–98.

being settled and populations given boundaries in ordered structures like the village or parish.[7] Peter represented a monastic church that based its exemplary status on its virginal purity and saw itself as a heavenly citadel unassailable by the devil. His very office obliged him as a man of faith to exclude the faithless from the congregation of the faithful. Through his denunciations of the five propositions of the Petrobrusian heretics we see him shaping a sociology of Christendom in the feudal age, even if some essential questions—such as marriage and the sacramental foundations of ordination—are partly or wholly ignored.[8]

Contra Petrobrusianos, which was one of the first, if not the first, of the anti-heretical treatises composed in the medieval west, presented itself as an *epistola disputans*. This particular literary form consisted in an artificial dispute whose aim was to convince, or simply wipe out the opponents with invective: it harked back to the sacred rhetoric of the patristic age and the verbal confrontations behind closed doors of the Gregorian age, yet took advantage of all the procedures current in the school debates of the twelfth century. Such an approach comprised an investigation (*investigatio*) establishing the opponent's case and what supported it, in order to confront him (in a *discussio*) on the basis of shared authorities or, where that was not possible, on the basis of common, universally accepted reasons. The dispute enabled the heresy to be unmasked as such (*inventio*) and the adversary to be confounded. All that remained was to combat the error that had been revealed (*defensio*). This was the business of the prelates to whom the *epistola* was addressed, or indeed the men of arms called upon to silence the recalcitrants. It was an accusatory method of dealing with the problem of heresy in which it fell to the complainant to prove his case. But it had no future. Within fifty years of the writing of *Contra Petrobrusianos*, heresy had ceased to be a matter for discussion. It had become a crime of lese-majesty and a matter for the Inquisition. Peter's treatise lacked influence and had no literary progeny. It was a snapshot that captured the deep reflections of a cleric of the seigneurial age forced by urgent confrontation to define the essential rules of social life. By "rules" we need to understand the term in all its rigor. Peter shows us that his day was one in which people were no longer content with settling conflicts by compromise and had abandoned ad hoc agreements. As a member of a church that regarded itself as a little Rome, the abbot of Cluny illustrates the pivotal moment when the medieval west equipped itself with authorities designed to judge without being judged.

7. On the problems of *encellulement* (compartmentalization) behind the questions raised here, I can do no better than refer the reader to the works of Robert Fossier, especially his *Enfance de l'Europe: aspects économiques et sociaux, Xe–XIIe siècle*, Nouvelle Clio, 17–17 *bis* (Paris, 1982), and *La société médiévale* (Paris, 1991), pp. 196ff.

8. *Contra Petrobrusianos* provides a contrast with Hugh of Amiens's *Contra hereticos*, in which marriage (book 3, chap. 4) and holy orders (book 2) are covered.

The Individual in the Network of Necessary Forms of Solidarity

What did these judging authorities regard as the ideal sociology? Peter's treatise first of all reexamined the fundamental forms of solidarity that constituted the "social bond." In their search for the distant roots of modern identity, medievalists often fasten upon the period 1050–1200 as the time of the "discovery of the individual."[9] A whole range of phenomena is supposed to attest the awakening of a new self-consciousness more than two hundred years before the rise of nominalism and insistence upon the value of what was individual (*individuum*). The following (in no particular order) are a few of the alleged phenomena: the emergence, in Abelard's work, of the notion of the "internal forum" (individual conscience); the definition of a morality of intention; the propagation of autobiographical literature in the twelfth century exemplified by Othlo of Saint Emmeran's *Liber Visionum*, Guibert of Nogent's *Monodiae*, or Abelard's *Historia calamitatum;* the appearance of funerary effigies from the eleventh century; and so on. Yet the views attributed to Peter of Bruis, Henry of Lausanne, and their disciples should most probably be interpreted rather as an expression of resistance to the great ordering of contemporary Christendom by a reforming papacy than as a manifestation of individualism. To see the heretics' views as individualism in that period would be anachronistic and quite unreal, given the context.

In fact the context of these issues is precisely what Peter the Venerable's *Contra Petrobrusianos* enables us to see. By casting doubt upon the basis of infant baptism and suffrages done on behalf of the dead, the Petrobrusians were knocking away at the very vitals of social practices powered by reciprocal undertakings. Peter's defense of infant baptism and suffrages reveals the all-or-nothing—or everyone-or-nobody—principle at the root of Christian sociological holism. Those involved in the plan of salvation shared a common lot. The sin of one had signaled the Fall of all: through the reversal effected by the sacrifice of Christ, the justice of One availed for the redemption of all. Defense of infant baptism revealed the three concentric circles within which the faith of one could operate on behalf of another. At its core was the inner circle of the family based upon the married couple; this was the primary space within which *caritas* (charity) could circulate; it was the *seminarium caritatis* (seedbed of charity), in which the grace pertaining to one member could operate for another by a commutation of persons. Beyond this circle was that of elective kinships, of which the paradigm

9. See Colin Morris, *The Discovery of the Individual, 1050–1200*, Medieval Academy Reprints for Teaching, 2d ed. (Toronto, 1987). The question is ruthlessly examined by Jean-Claude Schmitt, who exposes quite a few historiographical illusions and gauges the anachronism in talking of the medieval "individual": "La 'découverte de l'individu': une fiction historiographique?" in *La fabrique, la figure et la feinte: fictions et statut des fictions en psychologie*, ed. Paul Mengal and Françoise Parot, Sciences en situation: histoire, épistémologie, vulgarisation (Paris, 1989), pp. 213–36, from which the examples mentioned in my text here are taken. See also Jacques Le Goff, *Saint Louis*, Bibliothèque des Histoires (Paris, 1996), pp. 499ff.

was godparenting. Around all was the Church, itself defined as one great spiritual family. However, the duty of mercy toward the dead made it necessary to look wider still. Funerary solidarity was but one application of the *caritas* that bound the living to the dead, the living to the living, the dead to the dead, and the dead to the living. This world and the next were two complementary spaces and two complementary time zones in which and through which the merits of some could avail for others and the pains of some be borne by others, provided always that the recipients had personally done what was necessary to entitle them to reach sufficiency through the efforts of others. Creation was a stake-free gamble in which nothing was ever lost. Whatever good or ill each person accumulated today he would reap tomorrow, and the merits accumulated but unused by the exceptionally meritorious dead, the saints, could be made over to those of the deceased who had not yet reached sufficiency. The next world was therefore not a space in which society ceased to exist. The dead who haunted the nights and visions of the living came to explain social reality. They recalled the fine web of dependences that no individual could escape: the family, in either the narrow sense or the wider one of home and allies; spiritual kinship (godparenting relationships and monastic fraternities); relationships of fidelity, that analogue of the bonds of parenthood; the Church, the fraternity of all the faithful. In social terms, the dead broadened out the teaching that began with baptism by extending the bonds of one person to another that constituted the "feudal" order. In a period with little distinction between the religious and the political, fidelity was about lots of things at once—being a good son, a good brother, a good husband, a good godson, a good vassal, and conversely a good father, a good brother, a good wife, a good godfather (or godmother), and a good lord.

Necessary Mediations

Expressions of faith on another's behalf and the duty of mercy meant that there had to be mediation. In baptism, the mediators were the priest and the godparents. In the offices done on behalf of the dead, they were the pauper—the deceased's symbolic double—and the monk, who was professionally engaged in commemoration of the dead. The Latin Church accorded mediators a position of privilege that cannot be overemphasized. Whereas the baptizing priest in the eastern Church declared, "N is baptized in the name of God," his western counterpart said, "I baptize thee."[10] The social and historical implications of opting for such liturgical formulae were considerable.

The Petrobrusian denunciation of the Cross as an instrument of torture led Peter the Venerable to think about the mediation of signs. His sociology of Christendom was in the first instance a semiology. The Cross had provided the

10. On this point, see Louis-Marie Chauvet, "La fonction du prêtre dans le récit de l'institution à la lumière de la linguistique," *Revue de l'Institut catholique de Paris* 56 (1995): 41–61, here 55.

physical support for the event that founded the Church: the sacrifice of Christ. Through its systematic use to commemorate that event, it had become a sign that pointed to more than itself. It came to signal the crucified himself. Proof that just such an iconic transfer had taken place was given by the advent of the crucifix, which coincided with thinking about the status of images in the eleventh- and twelfth-century Latin west. The way of the sign allowed the individual believer to become one with the crucified and enabled the community as a whole to reverse its destiny in company with the Cross, which had itself been transformed from an instrument of torture into one of triumph: it was the "standard unto the nations" (Isaiah 11:12) that gathered together the elect and associated mankind with the angels.

The focus on the transitive power of the sign of the Cross led Peter logically to meditate deeply on the sacrifice of Christ commemorated in the Eucharist, which he conceived as the going across or passing over (*transitus*) that had founded the Church. In the eucharistic controversy that Berengar of Tours had begun in the 1050s, Peter the Venerable threw his weight resolutely behind the realists, represented at Cluny itself by Alger of Liège. His contribution to the evolution of doctrine on this issue was negligible, but his thinking on the ecclesiological implications of the problem was to gain him a justifiable following in the sixteenth and seventeenth centuries. In the matter of the Eucharist Peter invoked with force the same all-or-nothing or One-for-all logic that he had appealed to in order to justify infant baptism. The "once true, always true" principle adopted as an axiom by the later logicians of scholasticism opened a space for reiteration of the sacrifice. The unique act of the Last Supper could thus be repeated ad infinitum throughout Church history. The infinite time scale was a feature of the universality of Christianity founded by Christ himself, the One for all. The spiritual renewal and sustenance that he had provided passed to all, not merely to those in the present, but also to those in the past (who had lived before the Last Supper), and to those in the future (the remote peoples who had not yet heard the Gospel). The Petrobrusian conception of the Church as a simple, unsacrificing *congregatio fidelium* (congregation of the faithful) was, in Peter's eyes, an insult to the divine majesty, for it insulted the body of Christ. The notion of *congregatio* he countered with that of *incorporatio* (incorporation) through the Eucharist and the notion of the incorporating *sacramentum Ecclesiae* (sacrament of the Church). It was perhaps at this stage in his analysis that the abbot of Cluny's contribution reached its most significant yet least appreciated point. As we have seen, Peter's different writings were the product of a profoundly coherent mind, which focused attention both upon the process of transformation at work in the sacrifice of the altar and upon its agents. Militantly realist in his defense of the thesis of a real conversion of the substance of the eucharistic elements without a change of form, Peter advocated the total identification of the sacrificers with the sacrificed, a transparency to Christ that assumed virgin priests of spotless purity. The terms used to describe the eucharistic process are an unexpectedly rich source for the social historian. Peter was an exact contemporary of the research under way in the twelfth-century Latin west to find an accurate definition of what happened in the eucharistic process, and this research culminated, in the 1140s, with the emergence of the notion of transubstantiation. Peter speaks of the *missa* (Mass) as both a sacrifice and "something sent," an analysis that assigned to the sacrificers a transmitting role. As we noted earlier, the application of overlapping terms—*sacramentum, mysterium, miraculum*—to the Eucharist made it a paradigm of change, of the miraculous, of the awesome manifestation of a hidden, yet present, reality. Concerned not to separate the miracle of the eucharistic sacrifice from other "everyday miracles," Peter did not adopt the term "transubstantiation" and was happy to use the much looser term "mutation" or "commutation." This made it possible for him to envisage the indefinitely reiterated act of Christ within the broad field of social practices. "Commutation" could be applied to the Eucharist and onward to the conversion of persons and property sacrificed to God: the great reversal that fed the monastic communities, converting *temporalia* (things of the secular world) into *spiritualia* (things of the spiritual realm), and enabling effects to unite with their Cause. Such an understanding of the sociological implications of a commutational system having Christ as its pivot threw new light on the exchanges with the afterlife mediated by clerics. Since the exchange between God and humankind was unequal, giving to God came to be seen as simply the repaying of a debt. No longer was the donor seen as giving temporal goods (as a gift) so as to receive spiritual goods in exchange (as a countergift). Rather the aim of the exercise was to well manage the gifts received in this life, so as to recover them in the next world transformed into something better. The clerics—in this case the monk-priests extolled by Peter the Venerable—were necessary mediators because through their transparent purity the sacrificed could be seen and through their selflessness effective transformations were guaranteed. The return of effects toward their Cause was reckoned to be achieved through the Church's material fabric, the place where the sacrifice that created humankind's great debt to Christ was daily repeated.

Social Space

The importance attributed to these essential transformations explains the extreme attention given to the time and, more particularly, the place of sacrifice. The eucharistic controversies of the eleventh and twelfth centuries provided a stimulus to thinking about the organization of space or, in other words, the spatialization of the fundamental hierarchies of Christian society.

Preoccupied as they were with immediate eschatology, early Christians paid little attention to materialization of the sacred in a specific place. Among the Fathers, the term "Church" referred unambiguously to the congregation of the faithful, and confusion with the building was impossible. By the end of the twelfth century, however, Church and church had become interchangeable notions. How had this come about? Eleventh- and twelfth-century antiheretical polemic offers a good guide to the complexities of the question. In opposition to the assertion of the heretics of Arras in 1025 that "the temple of God is no more worthy . . . than a bedchamber," and that of the Petrobrusians, who in line with the Fathers were convinced that "the Church of God consists not in a multitude of assembled stones, but in the unity of gathered believers," was the notion of proper place, the privileged dwelling of God, a space where spiritual outpourings were greater and prayer was more effective. The church was this unique place, dedicated exclusively to the divine; it was a center with a center of its own, the altar, where sacrifice took place of the One for all. In the structuring of space around places of worship, the influence of eucharistic realism was decisive. The church was unique because it was the framework within which the real transformation of the eucharistic elements took place. The container (the church) could be confused with the content (the Church), because the awesome revelation of the body of Christ was the *sacramentum Ecclesiae:* the very rite that effected the incorporation of the faithful.

This major doctrinal development had profound sociopolitical repercussions—if indeed there is any sense in using such a distinction at a time when Church and society were coextensive notions. The definition of a eucharistic center allowed space to be ranked hierarchically and sovereignty to be conceived in geographic terms. At a time when the monastic sanctuaries were also lordships, the experience of clerics mirrored a general phenomenon in which powers became rooted territorially. Returning to Peter the Venerable's work, let us remember the important lessons given by the men of God in this area. First of all, they contributed the notion of space that was withdrawn or set aside from ordinary use, conceived as an inner circle comprising the church and its altar, with further concentric circles encompassing it of varying size, among which was the cemetery, the space of the dead who sought, close to the *fabrica* (building, workshop, forge) in which the Eucharist was wrought, an effective purgatorial setting. The whole space was located "outside space," in that all was dedicated to the divine, however the phenomenon might be technically described (refuge, asylum, immunity, exemption, and so on). It was a place free of secular entanglements, where *temporalia* (earthly things) became *spiritualia* (spiritual things). It was one in which the different encapsulated zones that constituted the sanctuary could all be described as a part of the "church," not merely the space of prayer and sacrifice but even the material property whose governance derived from the altar. Yet this withdrawal of space "from space" was a dynamic process. The center of Christendom was Jerusalem, the place of the sacrifice that founded it. In a centrifugal movement deriving not simply from the historic reality of the apostles' mission but from the infinite reiteration of the Passion in the sacrament of the altar, that center had engendered others. Jewish topocentrism (or what eleventh- and twelfth-century clerics imagined to be such) with its many sacri-

PART II. CHRISTIAN SOCIETY

fices in a single temple was succeeded by a single sacrifice enacted in many churches. The multiplication of so many centers from the prime center revealed an institution, the Church, which saw itself as an island within territory still subject to the devil's power. Christendom's historic mission was no less than this: the extension, by slow but irreversible erosion, of the space of the kingdom of Christ.

Aliens as Foils

The ever-expanding space withdrawn from the world—whether in the guise of the Cluniac monastic institution that merged its identity with the universal Church or of the Gregorian "mountain" intended to fill the universe—defined itself as much by what it excluded as by what it sought to transform and include. Woe betide those who refused to go through the center, the space of exchange with the divine in the sacrifice and hence the *fabrica* (workshop) in which the links of society were forged. When the two centuries studied here had run their course, one of the circles dependent on the center, the cemetery, could be spoken of as "Christian" because from it were excluded unrepentant sinners, suicides, heretics, and infidels.[11] Among the encapsulated spaces constituting the Church, the cemetery, that space of funerary inclusion and exclusion, was a microcosm of the Christian society theorized by the clerics in which medieval people lived their lives. The eleventh- and twelfth-century heretics left no writings of their own. Their voices are like those of the Jews, whose own challenge is also perceptible now and then as part of the subtext of *Contra Petrobrusianos*: no more than ghostly echoes in a scenario scripted by others using them as easy foils to demarcate their own collective, and contrasting, identity. Yet defining social identity in this way came with a price: the emergence of a society of intolerance.

11. On the Christianization of the cemetery, the latest studies to consult are: Cécile Treffort, "Genèse du cimetière chrétien: étude sur l'accompagnement du mourant, les funérailles, la commémoration des défunts et les lieux d'inhumation à l'époque carolingienne (entre Loire et Rhin, milieu VIIIe–début XIe siècle)," doctoral thesis, 4 vols. typescript, Université Lumière-Lyon II, 1994; the various contributions in *Archéologie du cimetière chrétien*, actes du 2e colloque A.R.C.H.E.A., Orléans, 29 September–1 October 1994, ed. Henri Galinié and Elisabeth Zadora-Rio (Tours, 1996).

III

CHRISTIAN UNIVERSALITY

Peter the Venerable's *Adversus Iudeos*
and *Contra sectam Sarracenorum*
and Their Background

>   —*Kommt,*
> *Wir müssen, müssen Freunde sein! —Verachtet*
> *Mein Volk so sehr Ihr wolt. Wir haben beide*
> *Uns unser Volk nicht auserlesen. Sind*
> *Wir unser Volk? Was heißt denn Volk?*
> *Sind Christ und Jude eher Christ und Jude,*
> *Als Mensch? Ah! wenn ich einen mehr in Euch*
> *Gefunden hätte, dem es gnügt, ein Mensch*
> *Zu heißen!*

>   Come,
> We must, we really must be friends. Despise
> My people as much as you like. Neither you
> Nor I have chosen our people. Are
> We our people? What does it mean, "people"?
> Christian or Jew, are they Christian or Jew before
> They are men? Oh, if only I had found in you
> One more for whom it was enough to own the name
> Of man![1]

1. Gotthold Ephraim Lessing, *Nathan der Weise*, 2.5: many editions, including ed. Joachim Bark (Munich, 1994), here p. 62.

9

THE UNSTOPPABLE SPREAD
OF CHRISTENDOM

In the course of *Contra Petrobrusianos*, Peter the Venerable followed Pauline and patristic tradition by drawing attention to the two complementary movements whereby the Church established and continued itself—purgation (*purgatio*) and expansion (*dilatatio*).[1] Elsewhere he described the pope and martyr Marcellus (died 308) as "the head of the members of Christ," ordering the Church with one hand and fighting its external enemies with the other.[2] Having seen how Christian society structured itself during the eleventh and twelfth centuries through a slow process of identifying and eliminating dissidence, let us now see how it sought to extend its territory in confronting the other religions of the Book, Judaism and Islam.

THE TURNING OF THE TIDE

As an apprentice historian in 1970s France , I went to the "Destins du monde" series in order to learn about the fate of mankind between the fifth and the fifteenth century, and found no little inspiration in Roberto S. Lopez's *Naissance de l'Europe*.[3] I remember how taken aback I was by the maps inside the front and back covers. The first of these was of the invasions of Europe from the fourth to the tenth century. The background showed how densely wooded Europe was at the time. Brown, green, and blue arrows led out from sources of population dispersal located in the north, in the Asian steppes to the east, and in the Arab south, revealing a Europe invaded by wave upon wave of "barbarian" insurgents both by land and by the sea routes of the North Sea, the Atlantic coast, and the Mediterranean. The second map showed the precise opposite. This time the

1. *CP*, 212, ll. 15–21.
2. *SSMI*, p. 259.
3. Roberto S. Lopez, *Naissance de l'Europe* (Paris, 1962), being volume 6 of the collection "Destins du monde," edited by Lucien Febvre and Fernand Braudel. The maps were by Serge Bonin. Published in English as *The Birth of Europe* (New York, 1967).

source areas were located in the west and the colored arrows went eastward to show the "expansion of Europe from the tenth to the fourteenth century," as it exported its faith, its arms, and its merchandise to Scandinavia and Russia and to Asia via the Black Sea, turning the Mediterranean into a Christian sea and absorbing the Holy Land (at least partly and temporarily) into the Latin world. Two green points marked the two great Burgundian sanctuaries, Cluny and Cîteaux; their names were printed in the same font as those of the great trading cities, Venice, Genoa, Pisa, and so on, and their corresponding arrows showed their irresistible influence in the spread of Christendom north, east, and south.

The map recalled Peter the Venerable's image of Cluny spreading over the surface of the earth like vine branches reaching "unto the sea."[4] Peter's image exaggerated the reality somewhat; Cluny indeed participated in and encouraged the spread of Christendom in the eleventh and twelfth centuries, but on nothing like the scale of the Cistercians. Under Peter the Venerable, the Cluniac presence on the pioneering fronts of Latin Christendom was uneven.[5] In Scandinavia, which was definitively won over to the Christian faith in the mid-twelfth century after missions in Finland, the Cluniacs had outposts only in Lund and in Nidarholm near Trondheim.[6] Central Europe—Poland, Bohemia, and Hungary—lay outside their main area of direct activity. But they were present in force on the Reconquista front in the Iberian peninsula, and set foot in the Holy Land during the First Crusade.

But for Peter the Venerable the theme of expansion (*dilatatio*) exceeded the strict bounds of the Ecclesia cluniacensis. His holist conception of Christian society held good for the entire ordering of the world; his all-or-nothing logic, that of the One for all, was applicable to the whole universe. Nothing could or should stand in the way of converting and baptizing the peoples of the earth. In an unstoppable centrifugal movement, the influence at the heart of the earth—the sepulchre of Christ, multiplied into myriad small centers, all of them places of eucharistic sacrifice—was predestined to fill all the representable space of the world, from the extremest confines of India to the Atlantic seaboard of Gaul, and from the deserts of the south to the ice of the northern pole.

The horizon of the apostolic commission was, in Peter the Venerable's thinking, all the more clearly defined in so far as he perceived Christendom as a single entity. He believed that in spite of the schism of 1054, the Greek and Latin

---

4. *DM*, 1.9, p. 36 (alluding to Psalm 79:12).

5. The only way to avoid the old historiography largely dominated by "pan-Clunyism" and lacking any real basis is to start from the incomplete results summarized in the *Lexikon des Mittelalters*, 2, s.v. "Cluny": B: "Der Einfluß Clunys außerhalb Frankreichs," cols. 2177–89.

6. On eleventh- and twelfth-century Christian missions in Scandinavia and central and eastern Europe, see Gert Haendler, *Geschichte des Frühmittelalters und der Germanenmission*, and Günther Stökl, *Geschichte der Slavenmission*, Die Kirche in ihre Geschichte, vol. 2, part E (Göttingen, 1961); *Les Vikings: les Scandinaves et l'Europe de 800 à 1200*, Catalogue, XXIIe Exposition de l'art (Paris, 1992), esp. pp. 152ff.

Churches continued to share a common faith.[7] In a letter to Bernard of Clairvaux dating from the spring or summer of 1144, the abbot of Cluny raised the question of the tolerance of differences within the Church, referring to those separating black and white monks. Observing to Bernard that they were mere nuances, he proceeded to reflect on other examples. He began by recalling the ancient debates over the date of Easter, mentioning the peculiarities of the British Isles on the subject. He then passed to the contemporary divergences in eucharistic practice between the unleavened host adopted by the Latins and the leavened bread used by the Greeks. Peter minimized the gravity of the problem. What importance have "clashes of uses," he asked, when "faith and mutual charity" draw us into one harmony?[8] So, two years before the Second Crusade, Christendom presented a united front that bade fair to take over the rest of the earth in a single leap. A mere half a dozen years later, however, the unitary ideal was cracking apart. Between 1148 and 1152 Peter the Venerable wrote to the Norman king Roger II of Sicily, urging him to join Emperor Conrad III in an expedition whose aim was to wreak revenge on the Greeks held responsible for the failure of the Second Crusade.[9]

IMAGES OF THE CHRISTIAN MISSION

This conception of the Christian mission was given visual expression, with all the synthetic power of iconographic programming, in the large central tympanum of the narthex at Vézelay, an abbey closely connected with Peter the Venerable.[10]

Founded by Count Gerard of Vienne and his wife, Bertha, between 857 and 874, Vézelay owed its fame to the rise, during the first three decades or so of the eleventh century, of the cult of Mary Magdalene, the apostles' apostle supposed to have her resting place on the "eternal hill" in the Morvan.[11] Around

7. Jean-Pierre Torrell and Denise Bouthillier, *Pierre le Vénérable et sa vision du monde: sa vie, son oeuvre; l'homme et le démon*, Spicilegium Sacrum Lovaniense, Etudes et documents, 42 (Leuven, 1986), p. 84.

8. *Ep.*, 111, 1:274–99, here 279: *Testes sumus . . .*

9. *Ep.*, 162, 1:394–95.

10. The following rapid analysis owes much to suggestions and observations from Kristin Sazama, to whom I express my thanks.

11. On the history of the first Vézelay and the launch of the cult of Mary Magdalene, see Victor Saxer, *Le culte de Marie Madeleine en Occident des origines à la fin du Moyen Age*, Cahiers d'archéologie et d'histoire, 3 (Auxerre/Paris, 1959). The traditional attribution of the *Sermo in veneratione sanctae Mariae Magdalenae*, which was a major landmark in the development of the saint's cult, to Odo of Cluny is mistaken: see Dominique Iogna-Prat, "'Heureuse polysémie': la Madeleine du *Sermo in veneratione sanctae Mariae Magdalenae* attribué à Odon de Cluny," in *Marie Madeleine dans la mystique, les arts et les lettres*, Actes du colloque international, Avignon, 20–22 July 1988 (Paris, 1989), pp. 21–31. On Vézelay as a "place of memorial," see Guy Lobrichon, "Vézelay," in *Les lieux de mémoire*, ed. Pierre Nora, 3 (Les France).3 (De l'archive à l'emblême), Bibliothèque illustrée des Histoires (Paris, 1992), pp. 317–57.

1026–27, the Cluniacs made a first attempt to bring Vézelay within the Ecclesia cluniacensis.[12] However, it was not until 1058—a time when huge numbers of pilgrims were already flocking to Vézelay for sanctification through contact with Mary Magdalene's relics—that Pope Stephen IX entrusted the establishment to the abbot of Cluny, Hugh of Semur.[13] Peter the Venerable was schoolmaster and claustral prior there between 1116 and 1120 under Abbot Reynold of Semur, Hugh of Semur's nephew and biographer.[14] Peter's own brother Pontius of Montboissier was in charge of the abbey between 1138 and 1161—in other words during the period immediately prior to the abbey's throwing off Cluniac tutelage in 1162. The scheme of the tympana that interest us here belongs to the Romanesque building begun perhaps by Reynold of Semur; progress on the building was interrupted by fire in 1120. The ten-bay nave was built between 1120 and 1132, when it was consecrated by Pope Innocent II, visiting France at the time to gain support in his struggle against the antipope Anacletus II. The three bays belonging to the narthex were built between 1132 and 1138, but the accompanying scheme of sculpture was possibly not completed in its entirety before 1145. The slightly projecting transept and the choir, both in the Gothic style, followed.[15] The relevant dates place the construction of the abbey church and its decoration within the chronology of Peter the Venerable's writings, though exegetes of Vézelay's sculpture have curiously neglected his testimony.[16]

It was at Vézelay in 1146 that Bernard of Clairvaux, accompanied by King Louis VII, made the appeal to launch the Second Crusade. What lesson did people draw at that time (or a few years later) from the representations on the tympana?[17] The entire series constitutes a Christological cycle. Largely defaced and

12. Neithard Bulst, *Untersuchungen zu Klosterreformen Wilhelms von Dijon (962–1031)*, Pariser Historische Studien, 11 (Bonn, 1973), pp. 190–92.

13. *Bullarium*, p. 16. Armin Kohnle, *Abt Hugo von Cluny (1049–1109)*, Beihefte der Francia, 32 (Sigmaringen, 1993), pp. 173ff.

14. *Ep.*, 2:243–44 and 257.

15. For an initial examination of the building of the Romanesque edifice, see Raymond Oursel, "Vézelay," in *Bourgogne romane*, 6th ed. (La Pierre-qui-Vire, 1974), pp. 257–85, the chronology of which needs revision in the light of Lydwine Saulnier and Neil Stratford, *La sculpture oubliée de Vézelay* (Paris, 1984).

16. The relationship between the works of Peter the Venerable and the scheme of the Vézelay tympanum has long since been a commonplace of art historians, but always in very vague, general terms. See Francis Salet, *La Madeleine de Vézelay: étude iconographique par Jean Adéhmar* (Melun, 1948), p. 134 (referring to *De miraculis*); Adolf E. M. Katzenellenbogen, "The Central Tympanum at Vézelay: Its Encyclopaedic Meaning and Its Relation to the First Crusade," *Art Bulletin* 26 (1944): 141–51 (referring to the *Sermo in laude dominici sepulchri*).

17. In addition to the titles given in the two previous notes, sure guidance within a dense and often contradictory bibliography full of byways and false trails will be found in Pieter Diemer, "Das Pfingstportal von Vézelay—Wege, Umwege und Abwege einer Diskussion," *Jahrbuch des Zentralinstituts für Kunstgeschichte* 1 (1985): 77–114, which is of assistance for fragments "forgotten" by Saulnier and Stratford, *La sculpture oubliée de Vézelay*, pp. 33ff., 76ff., and annex 1, pp. 245ff. The

destroyed, the scheme of the tympanum on the western façade is hard to recon-
struct in detail. Christ reigns there in majesty surrounded by the symbols of the
evangelists and, in the archivolts, angels and the elders of the Apocalypse. In all
likelihood this is a prefigurement of the Last Judgment as depicted in Apocalypse 4:2–9. The lintel displays scenes from the life of Lazarus (especially his
raising from the dead, an allegory of penitence) and of Mary Magdalene, the
penitent who washed Christ's feet with her tears. Inside the narthex, the nave
façade has three portals. The small side portal on the right contains scenes from
the childhood of Christ (the Annunciation, the Visitation, the Declaration to the
Shepherds, the Nativity, the Adoration of the Magi); the left-hand side portal
depicts the disciples of the Emmaus road and Christ appearing to the apostles
after the Resurrection. The central tympanum combines the two complementary themes of Pentecost and the commissioning of the apostles. Here again,
Christ is enthroned in majesty. The imagery extends down the central supporting pier, where John the Baptist stands on a plinth holding a plate bearing the
mystic Lamb of God. A missing fragment, between the feet of Christ and the
head of John the Baptist, probably represented Mary. From the Lord's hands,
rays of light diffuse upon the heads of the apostles sculpted on either side. Some
of them, like Peter—on Christ's immediate right and easily identified from his
keys—look toward him. The others, bearers of the Book—the Gospel proclaiming the teaching of Christ—have their back turned to the Lord's majesty
and look outward to the edge. The substitution of Christ for the Holy Spirit here
ought not to surprise us. It is a typically Cluniac theme, which is to be found
with minor variations in the twelfth-century office-lectionary and refers to
Christ's promise in John 14:16 to send "another Paraclete," who would empower
the apostles to testify.[18] The main Gospel passage attesting this promise, John
14:23–31, was read on the feast of Pentecost (Whit Sunday), underpinning the
ecclesial conception that Peter the Venerable, strongly attached to the direct link
with Christ and the apostles, developed in his *Contra Petrobrusianos*.[19] The commission of the thus-illumined disciples is signified in two ways. Just above
Christ's right hand and the rays illumining the apostles in the central part of the
tympanum is a wave motif. In exactly the same position on Christ's left, we see
a tree. What does it all mean? The conventional view is to see here inspiration
from Apocalypse 22:1–2, which speaks of the water of life proceeding from the

<hr />

analysis that follows also draws its inspiration from Kristin Sazama's as yet unpublished "The Assertion of Monastic Spiritual and Temporal Authority in the Romanesque Sculpture of Sainte-
Madeleine at Vézelay," doctoral thesis, typescript, Northwestern University, Evanston, 1995.

18. Paris, Bibliothèque Nationale, MS n.a.l. 2246, f. 79v2. Another example is in a sacramentary
of Saint-Martial at Limoges, Bibliothèque Nationale MS latin 9438, f. 87r; see Danielle Gaborit-
Chopin, *La décoration des manuscrits à Saint-Martial de Limoges et en Limousin du IXe au XIIe siècle*,
Mémoires et documents publiés par la Société de l'Ecole des Chartes, 18 (Paris and Geneva, 1969),
pp. 128–40 and plate 164.

19. *CP*, 16, ll. 19ff., and 29, ll. 8–10; also chapter 5 above.

1. The Childhood of Christ. Tympanum of the right side portal of the nave, Ste. Madeleine, Vézelay, France. By permission of the Bridgeman Art Library International.

2. Apparition of Christ to the Apostles, Supper at Emmaus, Road to Emmaus, and Noli Me Tangere. Tympanum of the left side portal of the nave, Ste. Madeleine, Vézelay, France. Copyright Giraudon/Art Resource, New York. Reproduced by permission.

throne of God and of the tree whose leaves were for the healing of the nations. Marcel Angheben even argues, convincingly, that the entire iconography of the tympanum is contained within Apocalypse 21 and 22 and their associated commentaries. He points out in particular that the theme of the tree fruiting twelve times may explain the signs of the zodiac and labors of the month represented in the band arching over the tympanum.[20] But Jean and Bernard Poulenc, in a recent contribution, relate the wave motif to a passage in Jerome's Commentary on Habakkuk.[21] In his hymn (Habukkuk 3:3–9) the prophet exalts the majesty of Jehovah, whose "glory covered the heavens: and the earth is full of his praise. His brightness shall be as the light: horns [of light] are in his hands" (verses 3–4). The light metaphors are followed by the image of rivers—"Thou wilt divide the rivers of the earth" (verse 9). In his Commentary, traditionally read during lauds on Friday, Jerome gave an apostolic interpretation of these rivers:

> See Peter and Paul and you will have no doubts about the wells and rivers of Christ. Behold all the apostles, and you will realize that now no longer four but twelve rivers flow out of the paradise of the Scriptures.[22]

20. Marcel Angheben, "Apocalypse 21–22 et l'iconographie du grand portail de Vézelay," *Cahiers de civilisation médiévale* 41 (1998): 209–40.

21. Jean and Bernard Poulenc, *Le Christ soleil de justice: le tympan du narthex à Vézelay* (Paris, 1996).

22. Jerome, *Commentarii in Prophetas minores, In Abacuc*, 2.3.8.9, CCSL 76A, p. 633.

3. Ascension of Christ. Central tympanum of the narthex, Ste. Madeleine, Vézelay, France. Copyright Giraudon/Art Resource, New York. Reproduced by permission.

The four rivers of paradise (Genesis 2:10) had become the twelve apostolic rivers and their associated streams that watered all the earth. Peter the Venerable used a similar image in his *Contra Petrobrusianos*, where he described the main landmarks of the Christian mission: the seven churches of the Apocalypse, the underground Christianity of the Roman world, the preaching of Trophimus, and the various "streams of Gallic faith."[23]

The representations on the lintel and the eight compartments in the curve of the tympanum defined the horizon of the apostles' commission, which, as Kristin Sazama has shown, included the monks of Vézelay and Cluny as continuers of the apostles' work. Along the lintel, on either side, is a file of peoples of the earth making their way toward John the Baptist and the apostles represented to left and right of him around the central pier. Some of these were familiar, like the pagan Romans participating in the ritual sacrifice of a bull. Others were more exotic and seem straight out of the pages of Pliny the Elder's *Historia naturalis*, such as the Panotii, a Syrian people with huge ears, the Pygmies and the "Maritimi," bearers of bows and arrows, or the Macrobians, giants of Nubia.[24] The eight compartments in the curve are occupied by other remote peoples, some of them poorly identified, as well as by characters who are deformed, sick, or possessed; among these are a Jew in the second compartment from the extreme left (as we face the tympanum), who has a sick arm, and cynocephali (dog-headed men) in the fourth compartment from the left.[25] As a whole, these eight compartments would have drawn attention to the commission of the apostles and their disciples to convert all the peoples of the earth by preaching and above all subdue them by the miracle-working power they held from Christ. This last theme was central to the thinking on Christian universality that Peter the Venerable, faced with problems of internal deviance within the Church, Judaism's survival, and Muslim proselytism, deployed not only in his *Contra Petrobrusianos* but also in his *Adversus Iudeos* and *Contra sectam Sarracenorum*.[26] The double movement—inward and outward—animating the central tympanum of the narthex at Vézelay was also at the core of Peter's conception of the diffusion of the word of Christ. Along the lintel, we see the peoples of the earth converging upon John the Baptist, among the closest of which are the Romans participating in the ritual bull sacrifice, a type of the pagan sacrifices superseded by the universal sacrifice of Christ. From John the forerunner, who shows forth the mystic Lamb, the onlooking eye travels upward to Christ, toward whom half the

---

23. *CP*, 109, ll. 23ff.

24. The identification of the Maritimi comes from Kristin Sazama, "Assertion of Monastic Spiritual and Temporal Authority," p. 62, n. 131, citing Pliny, *Historia naturalis*, 6.35.

25. The Jew with the sick arm is a traditional interpretation since Salet, *La Madeleine de Vézelay*, p. 125. The other peoples represented are hard to identify—Arabs, Cappadocians, Armenians, Ethiopians, Byzantines, and Phrygians?

26. On the question of miraculous powers conferred on all believers, see *CP* 245, being commentary upon John 14:12.

apostles represented direct their gaze. The other half look outward toward the territory to be evangelized, heeding the direction initiated by the hands of Christ himself. It is possible, as Marcel Angheben remarks, that three medallions interrupting the zodiac cycle on the upper arch of the tympanum and representing respectively a siren, a dog, and a man refer to the banned "dogs and sorcerers, and unchaste, and murderers, and servers of idols" of Apocalypse 22:15. If so, the implication is that the theme of universal preaching by the apostles went hand in hand with the notion of a trash element, hostile to the Christian message and cast out into the portion of the accursed. Such indeed, according to Peter the Venerable, was the lot reserved for the heretics who persisted in their error. And with the rarest exceptions it was the fate also of the Jews, regarded as dogs, and of the Saracens, who were the minions of Antichrist.

"O JEW, I DARE NOT CALL
THEE MAN ..."

Et la Confession commence. Sur le flanc
Se retournant, le Roi, d'un ton sourd, bas et grêle,
Parle de feux, de juifs, de bûchers et de sang.

"Vous repentiriez-vous par hasard de ce zèle?
Brûler des juifs, mais c'est une dilection!
Vous fûtes, ce faisant, orthodoxe et fidèle."[1]

And the Confession starts. Onto his side
He rolls, the King. His muffled, low, strained voice
Cites fires, Jews, burnings at the stake, and blood.

"Do you by any chance repent such zeal?
To burn Jews—that's an act of love!
Both orthodox and faithful were you then."

On 3 September 1079, Cluny's great benefactor King Alfonso VI of
Castile-León gave to the monastery's patrons Peter and Paul the house of Santa
Maria de Nájera, an establishment founded by King Garcias IV of Navarre in
1052. The gift to Cluny explains why the Nájera foundation act was recorded in
one of the Burgundian house's cartularies.[2] In the preamble to his act, Garcias

---

The chapter title is a quotation from Peter the Venerable: "Iudee, . . . Hominem enim te profiteri
ne forte mentiar, non audeo"—O Jew . . . I dare not call thee man, lest I lie", Peter the Venerable,
AJ, 5.3, 6; cf. nn. 4 and 112 below.

    1. Paul Verlaine, *La mort de Philippe II*, ll. 98–103, in *Poèmes saturniens* (1866). There are many
editions of this collection.

    2. *CLU* 3343 (Cartulary C, no. 104), 4.431–40: foundation act of Santa Maria de Nájera; *CLU*
3540, 4.665–66: donation to Cluny. See Peter Segl, *Königtum und Klosterreform in Spanien: Untersuchungen über die Cluniacenserklöster in Kastilien-León vom Begin des 11. bis zur Mitte des 12. Jahrhunderts* (Kallmünz, 1974), p. 211. Cartulary C (Paris, Bibliothèque Nationale, MS n.a.l. 2262), compiled
from 1100 on, assembles all the documents—pontifical bulls, royal diplomas, conciliar decrees,

lengthily justified its testamentary significance. The community installed through his generosity were to keep his memorial. Those of his descendants who dared infringe his pious dispositions were liable to "be excluded from the communion of Christians, like the Jew and the heretic."[3]

In the mental universe of a mid-eleventh-century Spanish monarch, the Jew, like the heretic, was the very model of an outsider, a paradigm of the excluded. Around 1100, when the foundation charter of Santa Maria de Nájera was copied into Cluny's cartulary, Latin Christendom was becoming less and less tolerant of the Jewish communities "encysted" in its midst. The history of Cluny in the eleventh and twelfth centuries reveals the intolerance slowly taking hold of Christian society at the time of the first two Crusades, in 1095–99 and 1146–49. Peter the Venerable's works reflect in microscopic detail the mechanisms whereby the Jews were excluded and demonized.[4] The Jews' rejection by a high-flying intellectual schooled in all the subtleties of verbal combat was more than mere rhetoric. How can the historian from the age of the Shoah not be alarmed in retrospect when he sees the abbot of Cluny railing against the Jews as the murderers of Christ and wondering if they really belonged to the human race? "The Human Race"—is that not the title of Robert Antelme's haunting account of his journey through the "birchwoods" of Buchenwald, where in former times Goethe had meditated?[5]

---

etc.—establishing the monastery's independence and full possession of its property; on the complex issue of the Cluniac cartularies, see Maria Hillebrandt, "Les cartulaires de l'abbaye de Cluny," *Mémoires de la Société pour l'histoire du droit et des institutions des anciens pays bourguignons, comtois et romans* 50 (1993): 7–18.

3. *CLU* 3343, 4.439.

4. Peter's writings, viewed in the context of the anti-Judaism of the eleventh- and twelfth-century west, have given rise to an abundant literature, now partly made obsolete by Yvonne Friedman's critical edition of *Adversus Iudeorum inveteratam duritiem*, CCCM, 58 (Turnhout, 1985). Only essential reading can be cited here: Gilbert Dahan, *Les intellectuels chrétiens et les juifs au Moyen Age* (Paris, 1990); Yvonne Friedman, "An Anatomy of Antisemitism: Peter the Venerable's Letter to Louis VII, King of France," in *Bar-Ilan Studies in History*, 1 (Ramat Gan, 1978), pp. 87–102, and "Peter the Venerable, a Twelfth-Century Humanist or an Anti-Semite," in *Proceedings of the Seventh World Congress of Jewish Studies* (Jerusalem, 1981), pp. 1–8, which ignorance of Hebrew has prevented me from accessing directly; Manfred Kniewasser, "Die antijüdische Polemik des Petrus Alfonsi (getauft 1106) und des Abtes Petrus Venerabilis von Cluny († 1156)," *Kairos: Zeitschrift für Religionswissenschaft und Theologie* 22 (1980): 34–76; Gavin I. Langmuir, "Peter the Venerable: Defense against Doubts," in *Toward a Definition of Antisemitism* (Berkeley, 1990), pp. 197–208; Jean-Pierre Torrell, "Les Juifs dans l'oeuvre de Pierre le Vénérable," *CCMé* 30 (1987): 331–46. A general overview of Jewish history during the first two Crusades is to be found in Salo W. Baron, *A Social and Religious History of the Jews: the High Middle Ages, 500–1200*, 2d ed., vol. 4: *The Meeting of East and West* (New York, 1957), esp. pp. 122–23.

5. Robert Antelme, *The Human Race*, trans. Jeffrey Haight and Annie Mahler (Evanston, 1998). Orig. title: *L'espèce humaine* (Paris, 1957; rev. ed., 1991). Robert Antelme is a French man of letters and a one-time companion of Marguerite Duras; he was deported by the Nazis to Buchenwald.

THE LATTER-DAY MALIGNITY OF CAIN

Cluny and Its Jewish Neighbors

Things had started out well. According to its most recent editors, Cluny's foundation charter included mention of a "Count Aron" (*Aroni comitis*) among its signatories.[6] It seems that the Duke of Aquitaine's entourage contained a dignitary whose name was of Old Testament origin: Aaron. Such a choice of patronym at the beginning of the tenth century does not indicate whether the bearer was a Christian or a Jew. Yet this very fact is significant. Two hundred years later, no confusion would be possible.

When Cluny was founded, there had long been Jews in Burgundy. Their origins were far from clear. Were they exiles, as everyone assumed? Or were they, as Robert-Henri Bautier has recently speculated, converts from the former Gallo-Roman population?[7] Perhaps, as Robert Chazan postulates, they were migrants to northwestern Europe from the Mediterranean world, responding to the economic growth that began in the Latin west at the end of the tenth century?[8] Their mode of settlement and activities in the early medieval period are no easier to determine. Georges Duby, inspired by André Deléage, regards the Jewish communities as essentially urban—settled in places like Mâcon, Chalon, or Tournus—even if such citizens, being descendants of late-empire merchants, often owned land in the countryside.[9] Bernhard Blumenkranz, on the other hand, maintains that the Jews of Burgundy were cultivators and winegrowers who had long been established on their land. The first act confirming their presence in the city of Mâcon dates only from 1051.[10] From some indeterminate date they had their own cemetery, a fact attested by its mention in the necrology of the church of Saint-Pierre, copied in the twelfth century.[11] The diver-

---

6. *Les plus anciens documents originaux de l'abbaye de Cluny conservés à la Bibliothèque nationale de France*, 1, Collection de Bourgogne, ed. Hartmut Atsma and Jean Vezin, Monumenta Paleographica Medii Aevi Gallica (Turnhout, 1997), no. 4, p. 35, l. 44.

7. "L'origine des populations juives de la France médiévale: constatations et hypothèses de recherche," in *La Catalogne et la France méridionale autour de l'an Mil*, ed. Xavier Barral i Altet, Dominique Iogna-Prat, Anscari Manuel Mundó, et al. (Barcelona, 1991), pp. 306–16. Bob Moore considers the hypothesis likely: Robert I. Moore, *The Formation of a Persecuting Society: Power and Deviance in Western Europe, 950–1250* (Oxford, 1987), p. 82.

8. "The Deteriorating Image of the Jews—Twelfth and Thirteenth Centuries," in *Christendom and Its Discontents: Exclusion, Persecution, and Rebellion, 1000–1500*, ed. Scott L. Waugh and Peter D. Diehl (Cambridge, 1995), p. 220.

9. *La société aux XIe et XIIe siècles dans la région mâconnaise*, 2d ed. (Paris, 1971), pp. 48–49, 94, 110–11, and sketch 5, p. 510.

10. *Juifs et chrétiens dans le monde occidental 430–1096* (Paris and The Hague, 1960), pp. 27–29.

11. *Martyrologe-obituaire de Saint-Pierre de Mâcon*, in *Obituaires de la province de Lyon*, 2, ed. Jacques Laurent and Pierre Gras, Recueil des Historiens de France, Obituaires, 6 (Paris, 1965), p. 496 (3 September): *Ipso die ob. Gauffredus subdiaconus, S. Vincentii canonicus, qui dedit huic ecclesie unam vineam iuxta Hebreorum sepulturam et unum pratum.*

---

gence of analysis is not without significance. Were they urban or rural, merchants or peasants? Within a Latin world deeply rooted in the countryside until the rebirth of cities in the twelfth and thirteenth centuries, were the Jews distinctively early urban settlers? It would not seem so. Wherever the truth lies, Cluny's charters reveal Jews in exchange relations connected with the monastery, already a large landowner in the second half of the tenth century. In August 949, two Jews, a certain Joshua and his wife, Tensoretis, used their farm at Sennecé as security for a loan of twelve solidi from the abbey of Cluny. Evidently the lenders were not—at least not yet—the ones one might suppose. In the act, Joshua's name and that of a witness, Samuel, appear in Hebrew characters.[12] In June 1022, a Jew, Solomon, and the monks exchanged land.[13] Other acts simply make mention, when defining boundaries, of "the Jews' land."[14] It is a definition that similarly leaves traces in place-names styled "of the Jews."[15] The owners were thereby placed within the anonymous setting of their ethnic community. The impression given is of Christians and Jews living harmoniously together. Within 150 years, the Jews had become enemies. Invited by King Louis VII to back the Second Crusade against the Saracens, Peter the Venerable replied to the king that although the enterprise was praiseworthy, Christendom's enemies within, the Jews, should not be forgotten.[16] But for the earlier witness of Rodulfus Glaber and the passage in his *Historiarum libri quinque* where he records the destruction, in 1009, of the Holy Sepulchre in Jerusalem by the "prince of Babylon" at the instigation of the Jews of Orléans and the "just reprisals" that followed, the change of perspective would seem sudden and violent.[17]

Cain and Abel

Trained like all Christian intellectuals to fit the world to a scriptural framework, Peter the Venerable lived his life alongside a double who was both respected and hated, who was the heir to the Old Testament but equally the betrayer of that heritage, and who was stuck in a perspective of insurmountable literalism. The story of their problematic cohabitation, likened to that of the two

---

12. *CLU* 749–50, 1.706–7.

13. *CLU* 2762, 2.783–84, extant original.

14. *CLU* 1474, March 979, 2.528–29; *CLU* 1640, December 983, 2.675; *CLU* 2364, 996/1031, 3.469–70; *CLU* 2603, 1004 or 1005, 3.655; *CLU* 2699, 1016, 3.725.

15. *CLU* 1272, 969 or 970, 2.351–52: *in villa qui dicitur iudaeis.*

16. *Ep.*, 130, 1:327–30, here 327; on the context in which it was written, see Yves Sassier, *Louis VII* (Paris, 1991), pp. 153ff.

17. Rodulfus Glaber, *Historiarum libri quinque*, 3.7.24–25, *Works*, ed. John France et al., Oxford Medieval Texts (Oxford, 1989), pp. 132–36. The preceding chapter deals with the count of Sens, Raynard II, dubbed the "king of the Jews," whose Judaizing tendencies led to his downfall. On the event and its treatment in the sources, see John France, "The Destruction of Jerusalem and the First Crusade," *Journal of Ecclesiastical History* 47.1 (1996): 1–17.

enemy brothers Cain and Abel, recurs as an obsessive theme throughout Peter's work. It is as if twelfth-century Christendom, in order to define itself, needed first to identify what was to be rejected in its own prehistory updated by the presence of contemporary Jews.[18]

The Jew was a sort of boundary figure, a foil, who enabled the excluder thereby to shape his own identity. In his *Sermo in laude dominici sepulchri*, Peter glorified Christian universality, its ineluctable spread from the center of the earth in Jerusalem. He contrasted Jewish topocentrism with the multiplicity of Christian centers, the multiple sacrifices in the one Temple with the unique sacrifice of Christians in multiple locations all identified with the sepulchre of Christ. Two contrary destinies were thus defined in spatial terms. In his sermon, the abbot of Cluny spoke of the annual miracle of fire falling from heaven upon the sepulchre of Christ on the anniversary of the Passion. He likened this sign to the divine distinction between the offerings of Cain and Abel in Genesis 4:4–5. Just as Cain's sacrifice was rejected while Abel's pleased God, the fire of the Lord set Abel ablaze, but not so Cain. Abel's sacrifice symbolized that of the Christians; Cain's prefigured those of the Jews and the Gentiles who sacrificed to Baal. The Christians were bearers of the light that illuminated the world from the center of the earth, while the Jews had wandered in darkness ever since their expulsion from the unique place of their sacrifices.[19] In his *Rythmus in laude Salvatoris*, Peter envisaged the end of this wandering, damned, benighted race. The poem finishes with an enactment of the Last Judgment. Christ appears, bearing his Cross. The entire world beholds the glorious spectacle, not just those who believed, but those who mocked the Savior. Peter upbraids the Jew, ordering him to look at Jesus, the despised, blasphemed, and crucified One who now sits in authority over him. In that final moment, the Jew recognizes God in the one who now dispatches him to his destiny, the flames of hell.[20]

That, then, was how contempt for Christ would be recompensed. Peter did not simply denounce the historic execution of the "King of the Jews," as all the Christian writers of anti-Jewish polemic since the Church's early centuries had done. His approach to the Jews was rarer in that he was keen to demonstrate the ongoing nature of their deicide. In 1135, the abbot of Cluny wrote to Henry of Blois, bishop of Winchester, to thank him for his generosity toward Cluny. In the letter, Peter likens the attitude of the bishop, a son and brother to kings, to the largesse of Cyrus and the concern of Ezra. But, significantly, he goes on to observe that Henry's gifts have restored to Christ the clothes that today's Jews

18. On the allegory of the two enemy brothers, see Dahan, *Les intellectuels chrétiens et les juifs*, pp. 339 and 395; similarly his "L'exégèse de l'histoire de Caïn et d'Abel du XIIe au XIVe siècle en Occident," *Recherches de théologie ancienne et médiévale* 49 (1982): 21–89, and 50 (1983): 5–68.

19. *SLD*, p. 252.

20. *Rythmus in laude Salvatoris*, ed. Udo Wawrzyniak, in *Philologische Untersuchungen zum "Rythmus in laude Salvatoris" des Petrus Venerabilis*, Lateinische Sprache und Literatur, 22, (Bern and Frankfurt am Main, 1985), pp. 53–63, ll. 193–96.

have ripped from Christ, as if seeking to crucify him anew.[21] There is no reason to take the image at face value and infer that Peter, when short of funds, had been forced to deal with Jewish usurers, pawning a crucifix and other precious liturgical objects from the Cluniac sacristy.[22] It nonetheless clearly refers to Jewish involvement in sacrilegious economic parasitism. Peter needed to say no more to his friend Henry of Blois. Henry was perfectly aware of Cluny's material difficulties. He knew that Peter had been working from his early years as abbot to reorient the monastery's economy of structural dependence upon gifts toward a direct and more rational exploitation of its lands. Henry had experience of the modern management methods developed in the kingdom of England, and had helped Peter's plans by drawing up for him an inventory, demesne by demesne, of the Cluniac seigneury.[23] But Henry knew also that such efforts might not be enough and that Cluny would periodically need to approach lenders. But what sort of lenders? Could spiritual men, however wary, go to the Jews, the murderers of Christ, in order to get the House of God out of difficulties?

An Affront to Christ

Peter's answer was no. Although there is good evidence that he made approaches to Christian financiers like Pierre de Montmin, nothing to my knowledge proves that he ever turned to the Jews. His own ideal monk, Matthew of Albano, whose life he sketched in *De miraculis*, refused to do so. Peter tells how Matthew, having become prior of Saint-Martin-des-Champs, investigated the financial health of the monastery. He discovered that it was crippled by debts and that, in order to maintain the monastery's life of hospitality and care for the poor, the monks had borrowed from the Jews. Indignantly Matthew asked the brethren how, as Christians and more particularly monks, they could have borrowed money from the impious Jews. How could light treat with darkness, he countered, quoting the apostle Paul in 2 Corinthians 6:14–15: "What concord hath Christ with Belial? Or what fellowship hath light with darkness? Or what part hath the faithful with the unbeliever?" Matthew insisted that the monks repay their debts without delay and cut all links with the "reprobate society" of the Jews. Otherwise, he asked, "In what state of conscience shall I try to approach the altar of the Savior Christ?"[24] The monk-priest whose office it was to sacrifice must flee the taint of the Jews.[25]

Peter the Venerable follows a similar line in his letter to King Louis VII.

---

21. *Ep.*, 56, 1:177–78.

22. Georges Duby's interpretation; see his "Le budget de Cluny entre 1080 et 1155," in Duby, *Hommes et structures du Moyen Age* (Paris and The Hague, 1973), p. 76 and n. 64.

23. *CLU* 4183, 5.490–505.

24. *CLU* 4012, 5.366–67. [Peter's quotation of 2 Corinthians differs very slightly from the Vulgate, and this is reflected in the English here—trans.]

25. *DM*, 2.15, pp. 125–26.

Called upon to support the Crusade, the abbot of Cluny begins in true feudal fashion by assuring the king of the "prayer, counsel, and aid" that are his due. How can Peter refuse, since Louis VII is seeking not earthly gain but the glory and honor due to the King of kings? Without suspecting for a moment that disaster was in the making, Peter maintains that victory is certain, since Christ says, "All power is given to me in heaven and in earth" (Matthew 28:18). He then raises the question of the fate reserved for the "enemies within." The abbot of Cluny's position was not unlike that of the crusaders of Rouen who, as Guibert of Nogent reports in his *Monodiae*, pointed to the irony of going so far east to attack the enemies of God, when in their midst they had the Jews: "No race is more hostile to God than they are."[26] Peter writes to the king that the Jews, who have "with impunity blasphemed, trampled underfoot, and disfigured Christ and all the Christian mysteries," are "far worse than the Saracens," who live "in foreign or remote lands." He invokes one of the classic anti-Jewish texts, Psalm 138(139): 21-2: "Have I not hated them, O Lord, that hated thee, and pined away because of thy enemies? I have hated them with a perfect hatred." Peter concedes that the Saracens are indeed odious. Yet they do share certain beliefs with Christians, for example the truth that Christ was born of a virgin. The Jews, on the other hand, are more detestable because they deny all truths relating to Christ and blaspheme him. Peter does not urge, however, that they be put to death. Taking his instruction from another verse in the Psalms, Psalm 58:12 (in other versions Psalm 59:10–11), Peter urges abandoning them to the greater torment recommended there. Like their fellow fratricide, Cain, the Jews, he says, are destined to wander through the world, abject and groaning, till the end of time. The king's duty is to punish them with penalties appropriate to their crime, and what better way than one "whereby both their iniquity is condemned and charity assisted"? They should be left alive, but "stripped of what they have fraudulently acquired." Let us be clear what these terms mean. "Assisting charity" meant that the duties of the king's office included contributing to the redistribution of wealth characterizing a functioning Christian society within which each order worked for the good of all. Diametrically opposed to the long tradition of royal protection of the Jews, which he violently denounces as "a now old yet truly devilish law," Peter the Venerable maintains that the king will contribute to the good functioning of Christian society by quite simply robbing those whom previously he has protected.[27] The punishment fitted the crime be-

26. Guibert of Nogent, *Monodiae*, 2.5, ed. and French trans. by Edmond-René Labande, Les Classiques de l'Histoire de France au Moyen Age, 34 (Paris, 1981), p. 246. Eng. trans., *A Monk's Confession: The Memoirs of Guibert of Nogent*, trans. Paul J. Archambault (University Park, 1996), here p. 277.

27. *Ep.*, 130, 1:328–29. See also Jean-Pierre Torrell, "Les Juifs dans l'oeuvre de Pierre le Vénérable," *CCMé* 30 (1987): 341, n. 50; like many others before him, Torrell links this observation to the privilege given to the Jews of Speyer by Emperor Henry IV on 9 February 1090, which provided that stolen goods bought by Jews in good faith could not be removed from them.

cause the property in question was held to be ill-gotten. Peter hesitates a moment before reminding the king of something known to all. What is this? The property of the Jews is ill-gotten because they perform no useful function: they appropriate (*subtrahunt*) from others.

> For their barns are not stuffed with fruit, their cellars with wine, their purses with money, and their coffers with gold or silver as a result of simple agriculture, legal service (*de legali militia*), or any sort of honest and useful activity, but through what they have craftily appropriated from Christians.[28]

By "appropriated," Peter did not merely mean that a usurer was able to take from another's honest production and that Jewish creditors ended up acquiring it at a very low price. Foremost in his mind was the "theft" of ecclesiastical objects that passed into the hands of the Jews and which were hidden by them and sold to the "synagogues of Satan." Was he saying that pawning liturgical objects with the Jews amounted to theft and that the Jews were criminal receivers? In all likelihood he was. The fastidious Gregorian reformer Peter Damian had already compared the alienation of ecclesiastical property to theft and homicide inflicted on the Christian community, represented by the poor who were thereby plundered and made to starve.[29] But what upset Peter the Venerable here was that, whether stolen or pawned, chalices that had contained the body and blood of Christ ended up in the hands of "the murderers of Christ's body and shedders of his blood," who injured and insulted him in life and continued to blaspheme him now. Although Peter noted that the objects themselves were without feeling, this firm believer in eucharistic realism held that Christ was aware of the injury that was thereby done to him.[30] For the instruments of the sacrifice, through which the Redeemer really made himself manifest, just like those who sacrificed, must be strictly kept from the taint of the Jews.

The Jews in the Seigneurial Order

The full meaning of Peter the Venerable's letter to Louis VII becomes clear only when viewed in the context of the political turmoil of the 1140s and, more generally, that of the gradual strengthening of Capetian royal authority. Behind the issue of royal protection of the Jews just touched on here lay some bitter power struggles.

Who controlled the Jews and the wealth generated by their dynamic economic activity? In late antiquity and throughout the early Middle Ages, their sta-

---

28. *Ep.*, 130, 1:329. Torrell, "Les juifs dans l'oeuvre de Pierre le Vénérable," p. 340, translates *de legali militia* by *ni d'une pratique de juriste.*

29. Ep. 74, in *Epistolae*, ed. Kurt Reindel, 4 vols., *MGH*, Die Briefe der Deutschen Kaiserzeit, 4 (Munich, 1983–93), 2:369–75, here 370–71.

30. *Ep.*, 130, 1:329.

tus was that of Roman citizens of the Hebraic religion.[31] They were free men, with rights and duties, placed directly under the emperor's protection and his local representatives in the Carolingian period. The first two Crusades were the turning point in the attitudes of Christians toward Jews. Excluded from the Peace and the Truce of God, the Jews were not simply persecuted and massacred during sudden outbursts of local or regional violence.[32] As the seigneurial order came into being in the eleventh and twelfth centuries, there was a slow but highly significant change in their status, linked to the appropriation of royal prerogatives and the territorialization of rights.[33] The onetime free Roman citizens became "our Jews" (*Iudei nostri*), the possessions of the castellans, counts, or kings on whose land they lived, like some sort of chattels. A little later the civil law began to record the real situation, even if the earlier status of the Jews as "Roman citizens" was never explicitly abolished. Oldradus de Ponte, who died in perhaps 1337, maintained that the death of Christ had turned the Jews into serfs. The prince who owned them was entitled to sell them, expel them, or dispossess them at will.[34] Their changed fate simply followed from the territorialization of the sociopolitical order, either seigneurial or royal, and the control of the men belonging to it. In the Germanic empire and the Anglo-Norman kingdom, the Jews stayed within the emperor's or king's jurisdiction; he was their protector, just as the Carolingian emperors had been. The Plantagenets, with whom Peter the Venerable was in contact, regarded the English and Norman Jews as subjects, entitled to go where they chose, own land and earn income, make exchanges without paying customs dues, "to receive and buy at any time whatever may be brought to them, except church items and bloodstained(?) clothing" (probably a reference to liturgical objects and eucharistic relics, i.e., cloth splashed with consecrated wine). In 1201, the community of Rouen had an official representative known as its "presbyter" or "archpresbyter" together with independent jurisdiction. Accordingly, it was a recognized corporate body.[35] In western Francia, the situation was much more complex and decidedly less favorable to the Jews. Our period of interest was characterized by the slow increase of Capetian royal power. From Louis VI (1108–37) to Philip II Augustus (1180–1223), the Capetian kings anchored their suzerainty in the feudal hierarchy and

31. The following remarks are based on Dahan, *Les intellectuels chrétiens et les juifs*, pp. 64ff.

32. On the Jews' exclusion from the movements of Peace and Truce of God, see Aryeh Graboïs, "Les juifs et leurs seigneurs dans la France septentrionale aux XIe et XIIe siècles," in *Les juifs dans l'histoire de France*, Premier colloque international de Haïfa, ed. Myriam Yardeni (Leiden, 1980), p. 16; reprinted in Graboïs, *Civilisation et société dans l'Occident médiéval* (London, 1983), no. 18.

33. Alain Boureau, "L'inceste de Judas: essai sur la genèse de la haine antisémite au XIIe siècle," *Nouvelle Revue de Psychanalyse* 33 (1986): 25–41.

34. Oldradus de Ponte, *Consilia*, 87, in Norman P. Zacour, *Jews and Saracens in the* Consilia *of Oldradus de Ponte*, Pontifical Medieval Studies (Toronto, 1990), pp. 83–84.

35. Norman Golb, *The Jews in Medieval Normandy: A Social and Intellectual History* (Cambridge, 1998), pp. 208–16; the quotation, translated by Golb (p. 213), comes from a charter of Richard I (1190), renewing rights and privileges granted by Henry II to the Jewish community of Rouen.

defined their "majesty" in terms of the "fatherland" and "kingdom," which soon took the name "France."[36] The Jews, like any other "possession," were at the center of power disputes between the king and the seigneurial powers, among whom were ecclesiastical lordships like the monastery of Saint-Denis-en-France or the Cluniac priory of Saint-Martin-des-Champs (Paris), the house presided over by Matthew of Albano.[37] Right through the twelfth century, agreements were made that defined the jurisdictional boundaries between "our Jews" and "your Jews" or "others' Jews"—patrimonial vocabulary typical of the demesne system—even if the complexities of inheritance and economic mobility often upset the delicate settlement of jurisdictional limits.[38] The abbot of Cluny was himself a grand lord and was well aware, when he wrote to Louis VII, of where the power lay. This aristocrat of the Church, rooted by his very office in the world of social realities, saw the Jews not as a simple theological abstraction but first and foremost as agents in everyday life, whose status varied according to the geopolitical space they inhabited: in some places they were protected subjects, in others serfs. In his doctrinal writings, Peter was anxious to justify the second of these conditions. He never contemplated the possibility of integrating Jewish free men into the feudal system, because they could not swear oaths, and hence could neither do homage nor pledge their faith.[39]

DEFENSE OF CHRISTIANITY AND DEMONIZATION OF JUDAISM IN *ADVERSUS IUDEORUM INVETERATAM DURITIEM*

Peter the Venerable's letter to Louis VII, in which he violently denounced the Jews as economic parasites, asked the king to expropriate his Jewish "protégés," and warned priests against all contact with deicides, was not his

36. See Jacques Krynen, *L'empire du roi: idées et croyances politiques en France XIIIe–XIVe siècle*, Bibliothèque des Histoires (Paris, 1993), pp. 36ff.

37. Graboïs, "Les juifs et leurs seigneurs," p. 14 (on the Jews of the *burgus* of Saint-Denis-en-France). Graboïs, "L'abbaye de Saint-Denis et les juifs sous l'abbatiat de Suger," *AESC* 24 (1969): 1187–95; reprinted in his *Civilisation et société dans l'Occident médiéval*, no. 17. An original bull of Callixtus II, dated 27 November 1119, reveals that the property of Saint-Martin-des-Champs included a Jewish *burgus* and *villa* (*vicus Judeorum, villa Judea*) in the *pagus* of Paris; see Ulysse Robert, *Bullaire du pape Callixte II (1119–1124): essai de reconstitution*, 1 (Paris, 1891), no. 110, pp. 162–65, here 162–63.

38. Gavin I. Langmuir, "*Judei nostri* and the Beginning of Capetian Legislation," *Traditio* 16 (1960): 203–39, meticulously reconstructs the history of this legislation to the 1230s. The evolution he describes ends with a royal law that, with the aid and assent of the great, covered the entire kingdom: no one could move against the "Jews of others." See also Langmuir's "*Tamquam servi*: The Change in Jewish Status in French Law about 1200," in *Les Juifs dans l'histoire de France*, pp. 24–54. Both articles are reprinted in the same author's *Toward a Definition of Antisemitism*, pp. 137–66 and 167–94.

39. On questions relating to the Jews' integration into the feudal system, see the brief treatment by Aryeh Graboïs, "La société urbaine chrétienne dans la France septentrionale du XIe siècle vue à travers les *Responsa* de Rashi," *Revue historique* 600 (1996): 241–52, here 245–46.

first writing on this theme. Already in 1143–44, he had written extensively against the Jews in an important polemical treatise, *Adversus Iudeorum inveteratam duritiem.*[40] The treatise's very title betrayed its agenda. It did not merely continue the long tradition of treatises *Contra Iudeos*, which were defenses of Christian truth by tight doctrinal argument; it was a violent attack on the "inveterate obduracy" of the Jews. As the text's most recent editor, Yvonne Friedman, rightly stresses, the abbot of Cluny's violence throughout the treatise was primarily a matter of tone and style: the coarse, deliberately insulting style of written sermons intended to back up tangible grievances and end in the rout and obliteration of the opponent. But additionally, Peter gradually left debate about ideas behind in order to indulge in frontal attack. The textual tradition, extant only in three twelfth-century manuscripts and one of the fifteenth century, and associated internal criticism (particularly of the prologue) reveal that *Adversus Iudeos* was written in two stages.[41] In stage one, Peter found enough material in anti-Jewish polemic to write a classic treatise of Christology. Having completed his initial project, he apparently felt the need to go further. The second part of the fourth chapter and the whole of the fifth therefore constitute a second stage in which the abbot of Cluny set about denouncing the "ridiculous fables" of the Talmud, demonizing his opponents, and proving the universality of the Christian faith on the irrefutable basis of miracles. No room was left for debating ideas; Peter allowed himself to score even the lowest points. Here, Peter's mode of discourse also changes. He abandons defensive argument in favor of imprecation, using language intended to demolish the opponent. Yvonne Friedman assigns this second part, undertaken at the latest in 1144, to the context of the Second Crusade. That would explain both its aggressive tone and the crossover of themes and quotations between *Adversus Iudeos* and *Contra sectam Sarracenorum*, which Peter wrote several years later.[42] Modern criticism of *Adversus Iudeos* needs to recognize the treatise's distinctly bipartite character and understand the themes linking the Jews and the Saracens.

Christological Considerations

"You, I address—you, O Jews" (*Vos ego, vos, inquam, convenio, o Iudei*). Such is the theatrical rhetoric with which Peter the Venerable, opening the pro-

40. The analysis that follows owes much to Yvonne Friedman's introduction to her critical edition (*CCCM*, 58) of *Adversus Iudeorum inveteratam duritiem*, otherwise known as *Adversus Iudeos* (herein abbreviated as *AJ*, all refs. being to chapter and line).

41. MS Douai, BM 381, originally from the abbey of Anchin, copied by Siger between 1156 and 1166; MS Le Mans, BM 8, from the charterhouse of Le Parc-en-Charnie, ca. 1180; MS Paris, Bibliothèque Nationale, lat. 12410 and n.a.l. 1436, originally from Cluny, twelfth century; MS Madrid, BN, lat. 4464 (Conde del Miranda 144), used by a mendicant in Spain, very early fifteenth century. See *AJ*, pp. xxviiiff.

42. *AJ*, pp. lviiff., where two dates are offered (p. lxiii) for *Contra sectam Sarracenorum*, 1148–49 and 1154.

logue to *Adversus Iudeos*, accosts the Jews, whose fierce denial of the Son of God is the source of their wretchedness.[43] Peter borrowed this opening from a sermon by Quodvultdeus (died about 450), which was used as an office lesson in the Cluniac liturgy four days before Christmas.[44] The Jews were therefore periodically rebuked in the monks' choir and called to account for their culpable blindness. A little later, this sermon gave rise, in dramatic form, to the *Ordo prophetarum*, a liturgical play assembling the prophets of the Old Testament who foretold the coming of Christ into the world.[45] Peter's aim was similar. He wished to persuade his opponents that all further resistance to triumphant Christianity was vain, that the Jews were lonely, isolated, blind, deaf, seemingly petrified in a faith restricted to their own writings and prophets. Yet those very Scriptures of theirs and their prophets supported the Christian faith. The first movers of Christianity, Christ himself, the Virgin, and the apostles, were Abraham's descendants. Peter repeats the words of Christ announcing the kingdom of heaven. He calls the Jews to repentance, assuring them that their offense— the Savior's murder—is reparable. They need only recognize the godhead of the king they once refused to acknowledge. The abbot of Cluny's purpose is to help them see this truth. He ends his prologue by mentioning a point shared by all: that the coming of Christ was repeatedly foretold by the prophets. But there are, he says, four differences in their interpretations. The Jews say, first, that Christ is not the Son of God, secondly, that he is not God, thirdly, that he is a king like earthly kings, and fourthly, that the Messiah is yet to come. Peter's plan is to overturn these four assertions in as many chapters. There is nothing in the prologue to suggest that they will be followed by discussion of miracles (in the second part of chapter 4) and the legends of the Talmud (in chapter 5).

Christ the Son of God[46]

Discussion of the first point of difference opens with a question taken from Isaiah 66:9: "Shall not I that make others to bring forth children, myself bring forth, saith the Lord?"[47] This, Peter asserts, was the solemn prophecy that there would be a divine childbirth. The principle of generation assumes that there is a father, God, and a son, Christ. Yet this divine engendering cannot be defined or represented; it is in no way comparable to carnal generation. Peter takes his cue from the Fathers, especially Tertullian and Lactantius, to assert that

43. *AJ*, prologue, pp. 1–3.

44. Quodvultdeus (confused with Augustine), *Contra Iudeos, Paganos et Arianos*, 11.1–2, ed. René Braun, CCSL 60 (Turnhout, 1976), p. 241. For the office lesson, see CCM, 7.4, p. 126.

45. Dahan, Les intellectuels chrétiens et les juifs, p. 377.

46. The index of scriptural quotations given in ibid., pp. 613ff., is a guide both to the biblical basis of Peter the Venerable's Christological arguments and to the wider context of his (mostly very classic) scriptural justifications within medieval anti-Jewish polemic.

47. *AJ*, 1.7–8.

the only viable physical comparison is that of light issuing from light, like the ray from the sun and the brightness (*splendor*) yielded by fire.

Other "bright" examples (*lucidiora exempla*) follow, designed to support this interpretation of Isaiah's text. First is David's proclamation in Psalm 2:7–8: "The Lord hath said to me: Thou art my son; this day have I begotten thee. Ask of me, and I will give thee the Gentiles for thy inheritance, and the uttermost parts of the earth for thy possession."[48] Do these verses apply to the person of Christ, as Peter argues? Or are the Jews correct to apply them only to David, seeing them as containing traditional scriptural imagery, whereby both men and inanimate objects are termed sons or creatures of God, as when Job (Job 38:28–29) calls the Creator "the father of rain." Pointing out that language sometimes connotes "accidents" and sometimes "essentials," Peter retorts that in the present case, the expressions "I have begotten a son" and "father of rain" do not belong to the same level of reference.[49] God "begets" men in loving, sustaining, and saving them. But the begetting referred to in Psalm 2 is of a totally different order. In that case, God begets of his "own substance." Moreover, the following verse—"I will give thee . . . the uttermost parts of the earth for thy possession"— cannot apply to David or any other kings of Israel, who neither received the Gentiles for their inheritance nor dominated the earth. David's kingship stretched for only a short time over a part of Syria, while the rest of the earth— India, Persia, the Gallic and German lands, Scythia—all escaped his dominion. The psalmist's words therefore must mean Christ, the Son of God, before whom, as the apostle said in Philippians 2:10, "every knee should bow, of those that are in heaven, on earth, and under the earth."

Peter's next, "even more obvious" scriptural proof comes from Psalm 109(110): 3, "In the brightness of the saints, from the womb before the daystar I begot thee" (*In splendoribus sanctorum ex utero ante luciferum genui te*).[50] Convinced of the power of scriptural testimony, the abbot of Cluny defies his opponents to contradict him. The begetting in question cannot apply to the angelic spirits or mankind, since the stars and light-bearing heavenly body (*Lucifer*) were not created until the fourth day and man not until the sixth. What "the Lord said to my Lord," according to David's words in verse 1 of the same psalm, can therefore apply only to God, the first "Lord" referring to God the Father and the second to God the Son. The verse continues with the invitation spoken by the one Lord to the other: "Sit thou at my right hand." God alone can sit on the "seat of God" (*sedes Dei*). On this basis, Peter refutes the Jewish commentators, including perhaps Rashi, who thought that Psalm 109(110) referred not to David but to Abraham.[51] Peter concedes that Genesis 22:18 speaks of the multiple

48. *AJ*, 1.33ff.
49. *AJ*, 1.80–81.
50. *AJ*, 1.160ff.
51. *AJ*, 1.270–72

grace enjoyed by Abraham. Yet Abraham was but a man. Only Christ, both man and God, can "sit at God's right hand." Furthermore the way Psalm 109(110): 1 ends—"Until I make thy enemies thy footstool" (*Donec ponam inimicos tuos scabellum pedem tuorum*)—does not fit Abraham, who had no enemies.

Peter ends this series of "evident" testimonies with Daniel 3:91–92 [24–25] and Proverbs 30:4.[52] The first of these texts had the merit of demonstrating to Peter's opponents that even a pagan like Nebuchadnezzar could recognize the Son of God. In the fiery furnace into which the three men had been cast, the king discerned a fourth whose form was "like the Son of God." The final discussion, on Proverbs 30, is intended to persuade the Jews that Solomon had greater perception than they, in that he perceived what they denied, when he alluded to the "science of saints" and asked, "Who hath ascended up into heaven, and descended? . . . Who hath raised up all the borders of the earth? What is his name, and what is the name of his son?" The answer is God and his Son, who is no less God than the Father.

Christ, True God

Peter's aim in the second chapter of *Adversus Iudeos* is to prove that Christ is truly and specially God. Men and angels are both sometimes described as "sons of God." But what is a simple figure of speech (*vocaliter*) should not be confused with the fact of nature (*naturaliter*) whereby Christ is God. Peter means that Christ is not distinct from the Father. Just as a man is identical to a man, a bird to a bird, and light to light, so God is identical to God.

The discussion opens with an examination of Genesis 19:24: "And the Lord rained upon Sodom and Gomorrah brimstone and fire from the Lord out of heaven."[53] The "Lord" in question does not mean the angels honored by Lot in this same chapter of Genesis, but the one Lord (*Dominus unus*), Father and Son, whose power "to reward the just, punish sinners, glorify the good, and condemn the ungodly [*prophanos*]" is demonstrated by the sulfur and fire rained down on Sodom and Gomorrah. Peter observes that these natural events came from God's power alone, and could be revealed again if the Jews persist in their ungodliness and blasphemy. He considers the objection that "Lord" is not the same as "God."[54] However, he points out that verse 8 of Psalm 44(45) contains a similar double mention, using "God" (*Deus*): *Propterea unxit te Deus Deus tuus oleo laetitia* (Therefore God, thy God, hath anointed thee with the oil of gladness). The Christians see this as a reference to God the Father and God the Son, while the Jews read it as referring to David and his son Solomon. Yet, says Peter, this last interpretation is impossible, since the "throne" referred to in the preceding verse 7 of the psalm—*Sedes tua Deus in saeculum saeculi* (Thy throne, O God, is

52. *AJ*, 1.380ff.
53. *AJ*, 2.40ff.
54. *AJ*, 2.122ff.

for ever and ever)—is eternal. Turning again to verse 8, Peter suggests that it is possible to see the first *Deus* as a vocative and the second as a nominative: "O God, thy God hath anointed thee." Moreover, the passage should be interpreted as the Father (*Deus*) anointing the Son (*Deum*) not as God but as man. Since he is God, the Son is the equal of the Father, and nothing can be added to him. This is not the anointing of a king, but an anointing of grace (*oleo laetitiae*).

Peter goes on to discuss the Son's humanity with reference to Baruch 3:36–38: "This is our God, and there shall no other be accounted of in comparison of him. . . . He was seen upon earth and conversed with men."[55] Peter distinguishes this appearance from the experiences of Jacob or Moses (Exodus 33:20): they saw only images of God and heard a voice; they did not truly see him. Moses and the Hebrews were also enjoined not to overstep the mark. But the prophet Baruch speaks of God perfectly visibly appearing on earth. This can only refer to the Incarnation. At this point in the discussion, in order to confound and isolate the Jews, Peter invokes the word of Isaiah, observing that "though a tiny number of unbelievers reject it, the infinite mass of the world shall receive and revere it."[56] The prophet Isaiah (Isaiah 9:6) clearly foretold the birth of a wondrous child, whom he described as "Wonderful, Counselor, God the Mighty, the Father of the world to come, the Prince of Peace." Peter holds that "Prince of Peace" properly refers to God, since a man can only be a "lover," "friend," or "son" of peace, not its "author" (*auctor*). The kingdom (*imperium*) and peace of the prophesied Child-God shall have no end. Peter asks what king is meant in the following verse (Isaiah 9:7): "He shall sit upon the throne of David, and upon his kingdom." No king in fact, says Peter, not even Josiah, as the abbot of Cluny says he has heard certain Jews allege—Peter thus briefly alludes to a debate or at least an exchange with Jews on this subject.[57] How could Josiah be described as "the Father of the world to come" or "the Prince of Peace"? According to 2 Chronicles 35:20ff., Josiah was killed at Megiddo by Necho, king of Egypt; a few years later, the Temple was destroyed and the Babylonian Captivity began. Peter concludes that Isaiah's prophecy does not apply to a Jewish or even Gentile king, but to Christ, to whom alone the words of Isaiah 9:7 about strengthening the kingdom with judgment and justice for ever can possibly apply.[58]

Christ's humanity in no way detracts from God's greatness. Having appealed to the decisive authority of Isaiah, Peter devotes space to determining the depth of the gulf dividing him and his interlocutors.[59] Since they cannot acknowledge the humanity of Christ, they cannot see the two dimensions of the Christian God or understand the fundamental dialectic of Christianity: humility-greatness, humanity-divinity. Contrary to what the Jews imagine, the one does not cancel

55. *AJ*, 2.217ff.
56. *AJ*, 2.295ff.
57. *AJ*, 2.388.
58. *AJ*, 2.400ff.
59. *AJ*, 2.426ff.

out the other. The new message of Christianity is that the one is approached through the other. Likening the Incarnation to the divine "work" referred to by the prophet Habakkuk (Habakkuk 3:2), Peter asks what is so scandalous about God's wish to speak to men through a man.[60] He begins by citing the example of the Lord appearing to Moses in a flame of fire (Exodus 3:2–4), and expresses his astonishment that the Jews can have faith in such minor manifestations and yet ignore a major manifestation like the Incarnation! Are the Jews bothered, perhaps, by notions of bodily pollution, deemed unworthy of a God who cannot suffer, be hungry or thirsty, or die? The Christians maintain that the God of the Incarnation is in no way damaged by all these human miseries. Peter explains by means of a "natural" school case. Can the light of the stars, the sun, or the moon be polluted by the dirty places into which it shines? God's essence, like light, cannot be impaired. The Son of God, born of a virgin, has suffered no pollution, but on the contrary has purified the flesh, glorifying and exalting mankind.

Having established the divine humanity, Peter finishes by tackling the problem of Christ's royal status. This passage serves as a link to the next chapter, on the kingdom of heaven. The Christian polemicist again invokes David, whom no one ever successfully resisted, in order to fight the Jews who had become his enemies.[61] The discussion centers on Psalm 71(72), concerning the Messiah's reign. To whom is Solomon alluding when he prays, "Give to the king thy judgment, O God"? Is he referring to himself, as son of David, as the Jews believe? Yet there is nothing in the rest of the psalm that could apply to Solomon. The king reigned for only forty years and therefore cannot be said to "continue with the sun, and before the moon, throughout all generations" (verse 5). His kingdom did not extend beyond Syria, whereas the Messianic king is called to dominate the whole earth "from sea to sea" (verse 8). Solomon was not worshiped by "all kings of the earth" (verse 11). Finally, the name of a man cannot have been "blessed for evermore," as verse 19 says. In venturing such an interpretation, the Jews blaspheme the name of God. Magnanimously Peter concedes that it is possible to see one man in the king's son to whom Solomon makes allusion. Christ belonged to David's line. He is a "king's son"; the whole psalm indeed refers to him. He dominates the entire world "from sea to sea, and from the river unto the ends of the earth," inasmuch as the Jordan and its baptismal waters are everywhere.[62] Thus, apart from the Jews, all the peoples of the earth believe in Christ, worship him, and honor him. Among the Gentiles, the Sibylle—believed by many Christian writers since Lactantius and Augustine to have prophesied the Passion of Christ—similarly foretold the truth of this universal conversion.[63]

60. *AJ*, 2.528ff.
61. *AJ*, 2.637ff.
62. *AJ*, 2.807–10.
63. *AJ*, 2.847ff. See Dahan, *Les intellectuels chrétiens et les juifs*, pp. 410 and 470.

Christ's Eternal and Heavenly Kingdom

Peter now contradicts the Jews' belief that Christ would be an earthly king like David or Solomon. He counters that Christ's kingdom is not limited to Jerusalem, Judea, and Galilee. Nor is Christ the Messiah who they believe is yet to come in order to release them from their captivity, gather them together, and enable them to dominate virtually all the peoples of the earth. Such fables, says Peter, are proof of a damnable attachment to worldly goods and daily cause the Jews to forgo the kingdom of heaven.

Peter the Venerable immediately goes to the heart of Jewish messianism. He refers to the prophecy of Jeremiah 23:5ff., which speaks of a wise, just king who will save Judah, and that of Ezechiel 37:21ff.: "I will take the children of Israel from the midst of the nations whither they are gone, and I will gather them on every side and will bring them to their own land." These he links with Zechariah 9:9, which speaks of a king who is "the just and Savior. He is poor and riding upon an ass." This last prophecy is too late to refer to David or Solomon, Zechariah being a contemporary of Darius. Appealing to Flavius Josephus, Peter considers that the prophecy relates neither to Aristobulus, who reigned later but only for one year, nor to Herod, who was not Jewish or humble, nor to his successors, who came to a sorry end under the Roman domination.[64] Finally he rejects the hypothesis that it could refer to some contemporary Jewish king. He mentions a lowly king mounted on an ass who had recently come out of Africa, one of the multitude of Muhammad's sectaries and whom certain Jews recognized as their own prophet.[65] Peter is thinking of the Berber Ibn Tumart (1078/81–1130), the "one led aright" (*Mahdi*), who came to restore the original purity of Islam; he founded the Almohads, the politico-religious movement that opposed the Almoravids in the Maghreb and subsequently in Spain (1130–1269).[66] The source of Peter's information on the Almohads is unknown, but it is significant that he should regard the Mahdi as a prophet recognized by the Jews, as if all contemporary infidels were really the same. Peter's error is all the more poignant inasmuch as we do know that the Almohads forced the Jews to choose between conversion and exile.

Having dismissed these pretenders to a kingship of poverty and humility, Peter calmly concludes that the king referred to by the prophets must be Christ.

64. *AJ*, 3.75ff. (Flavius Josephus, *The Jewish War*, 1.6).

65. *AJ*, 3.96–108: "But perhaps in order to reveal anew to the whole world what a mockery you are, you will say that this prophecy [Zechariah 9:9] was fulfilled in that asinine king of our own times who in Africa rose up against the newly named king of Morocco. And for the sake of the unspeakable Mohammedan sect, he recruited an infinite multitude of that lost people . . . , often fought with the aforesaid king, and frequently won in battle. . . . When the Jews heard report of this, they immediately raised their hopes and some of them said that that king of theirs had come who the aforesaid prophet had foretold would ascend upon an ass."

66. Maurice Drouard-Adda, "Eléments historiques dans un traité de polémique antijuive: l'*Adversus Judaeos* de Pierre le Vénérable," *Archives juives* 1 (1971–72): 1–6, here p. 2. On Ibn Tumart, see *Encyclopaedia of Islam*, 3 (1969), pp. 958–60 (J. F. P. Hopkins).

Yet this is no earthy king, whose functional insignia are gold, purple, and pomp.[67] Christ's kingship is the precise opposite. Instead of royalty, he presents poverty; instead of abundance, penury; instead of exaltedness (*sublimitas*), humility. He is the king without glory (*inglorius*) spoken of by Isaiah (Isaiah 52 and 53). This is precisely what places Christ higher than men. The kingdom of the despised and sacrificed Christ is "not of this world," as Jesus says in John 18:36. Or rather, Christ's kingdom represents the overthrow of one kingdom by its opposite. Exchanging exaltedness for humility, glory for contempt, power for weakness, and royal power (*regnum*) for dejection is what grants access to the eternal kingdom.[68]

As a sort of counterpoint to Isaiah's prophecy, Peter makes sport of the Talmudic story of the "Messiah" born under Vespasian, who was transported to Rome, thrown to the dogs, hidden in crypts and caves, and who suffered pains and wounds for the sins of the Jews before making a triumphant return to the Promised Land, where he assembled all the Jews dispersed over the face of the earth.[69] Adopting a line that becomes systematic in the fifth chapter of *Adversus Iudeos*, the abbot of Cluny does not bother to quarrel with an authority—the Talmud—that he does not recognize. He makes do with a bitter commentary designed to unsettle his opponents. Quoting Psalm 21(22): 17 and Matthew 27:25, Peter observes that the Messiah was indeed thrown to the dogs. And were not the Jews the dogs in question?[70]

At this point, Peter wonders whether his interlocutors are really men: Are they rational beings?[71] How else can one explain that after so many arguments drawn from their own scriptures, their "heart of stone" still resists the divine spirit that leads to Christ? Yet the Christian polemicist presses on with his task. He now invokes the authority of Daniel 7:9ff., which speaks of an "everlasting power" and a "kingdom that shall not be destroyed": a celestial realm. Having reminded the Jews of their belief in the resurrection of the body and defended the idea that Christ must be everlasting in order to command the living and the dead, Peter links Daniel's prophecy of "everlasting power" to the eternal reign with neither "day nor night" prophesied in Isaiah 60:19–20 and Zechariah 14:5–7. Since it is impossible to imagine the earthly Jerusalem without sun or moon, day or night, the prophecy must be a glorification of the reign of Christ and the

67. *AJ*, 3.123ff.

68. *AJ*, 3.489–90.

69. *AJ*, 3.493ff. (cf. Babylonian Talmud, Sanhedrin, 98a). See Dahan, *Les intellectuels chrétiens et les juifs*, p. 499.

70. *AJ*, 3.540–42: *Nonne canes fuistis, quando canum more sanguinem sititis ac nimia rabie pene linxistis, dicentes, 'Sanguis eius super nos et super filios nostros'?* —"Were you not dogs, when like dogs you thirsted for blood and so very rabidly almost licked it up, saying [of Jesus Christ], 'His blood be upon us and upon our children'?"

71. *AJ*, 3.562ff.

saints, the everlasting nature of which is fundamental to the law of the prophets and indeed the whole canon.[72] No other interpretation is conceivable. Or is one to think that the infinite marvels of Creation have no other end but earthly finiteness? Such short-term thinking is typical of the Jews, with their earth-centeredness, their preoccupation with filling their bellies, drinking, yielding to the delights and pleasures of the flesh, material wealth, filling their coffers with gold or silver and thereby subjecting the world to themselves.[73] All this is contrary to reason and justice—unless man is no more than an animal limited to passing things, with no perspective on eternity. These brief considerations of the "animality" of his opponents help to explain how, when he wrote to Louis VII denouncing the Jews as economic parasites, Peter believed he was defending the divine order, humanity's only reason for existence. To depart, in the manner of the Jews, from the cycle of exchanges of property intended, from the Christian point of view, for transformation "into something better" amounted to a descent into animality. It was the prospect of eternity that "transformed" men, helped them to obey and raise themselves.[74] Though rarely mentioned in the early books of sacred history, eternity became an insistent theme of the prophets and the Gospel of Christ. Even if the Jews will not listen to the Gospel, Peter would have them at least listen to their own prophets. These are clear enough. Let them believe Moses, who spoke of the "everlasting hills" (Deuteronomy 33:15), or Isaiah, who foretold "the new heavens and the new earth" (Isaiah 66:22). For all that, these prophecies are not for the Jews alone. At the end of chapter 3, Peter the Venerable amasses the Old Testament authorities that speak of "all peoples" to prove—against the "brutish reasoning" of the Jews—how fitting it was that he who had created mortal humanity should assume it fully in his sacrifice.[75]

The Messiah Has Already Come to Save the World

Peter's last point concerns the realized fact of the saving sacrifice. The Christians assert that it has been accomplished by Christ, while the Jews still await their Messiah. Has he come (*venit*) or will he come (*veniet*)? From an earlier confrontation with "some Jews," Peter understands that his opponents agree that, as Jacob foretold in Genesis 49:10, "the scepter shall not be taken away from Judah" and that the text is about a single mission.[76] Yet is Christ the "root of David" [*sic*] and "ensign of the people" foretold by Isaiah (11:10), or does the text refer to some other prince of the tribe of Judah? In order to show that it is indeed Christ, Peter looks at all other possible hypotheses and proceeds to demolish them. The first hypothesis to be eliminated concerns the contemporary

72. *AJ*, 3.745–46.
73. *AJ*, 3.757–64.
74. *AJ*, 3.779ff.
75. *AJ*, 3.835ff.—Psalm 85(86):9; Psalm 21(22):28; Isaiah 65:1; Malachi 1:10–11.
76. *AJ*, 4.29–30.

Jewish kings of Narbonne and Rouen.[77] The Narbonne reference is to the Todros, leaders (*Nassi*) of the Jewish community there in the ninth to the thirteenth century, in whom tradition saw descendants of King David.[78] In the case of Rouen, Peter hastily dubs "kings" the "presbyters" or "archpresbyters" who represented the city's Jewish community, although it is not known whether the office was actually the responsibility of a particular family.[79] Peter does not dwell on these cases, which he regards as aberrant. Earlier, Fulbert of Chartres (circa 960–1028) had already considered the question of the "kings of Judah" in his *Contra Iudeos*. He asserted that the only true kings of Judah were those born of the tribe of Judah, who had been chosen and anointed by a legitimate priest to reign over the people dwelling in the land of Judah—conditions that were impossible to fulfill after the destruction of the Temple at Jerusalem and the scattering of the Jews.[80] Like Fulbert, Peter considers that the text can only refer to kings of the kingdom that the Jews have no hope of recovering: the former Hebrew kingdom, now, at the time of writing *Adversus Iudeos*, under the sovereignty of Frank princes and kings.[81] Peter uses the Old Testament, evidence from the Gospels, Flavius Josephus, and even pagan writers to make a lengthy list of kings of Judah from David to Herod.[82] He emphasizes the breaks and the culmination of the kingdom in the time of Christ. He quotes Haggai 1:1 to show that during the Persian domination it was forbidden to bear the royal title and that the kings took over the priestly role that by rights belonged to the sons of Levi. From Zerubbabel to Herod it is uncertain whether the various princes actually came from the tribe of Judah. On the other hand, there is no doubt that Herod had an Arab mother and was therefore not Jewish; moreover, he became king by a decision of the Roman senate. Since then, down to Peter's own time, no king or prince has ever been supplied by the tribe of Judah. Less than sixty years after Herod, in the year 70 A.D., began the period of wretchedness marked by the destruction of the Temple in Jerusalem, the time of Jewish exile and servitude.

77. *AJ*, 4.77–79. As Drouard-Adda suggests, "Eléments historiques," p. 2, Peter may have received information direct from the archbishop of Narbonne, Arnold of Levenon (1121–49), and the archbishop of Rouen, Hugh of Amiens (1129/30–64), with both of whom he was in close contact. On Arnold, see *Ep.*, 105, 1:268, in which Peter invites the archbishop to retire to Cluny. [In citing Isaiah 11:10, Peter or his scribes substituted "root of David" for "root of Jesse"—trans.]

78. Aryeh Graboïs, "La dynastie des 'rois juifs' de Narbonne (IXe–XIIIe siècle)," in *Narbonne, archéologie et histoire*, 2: *Narbonne au Moyen Age* (Montpellier, 1973), pp. 49–54. The oldest surviving seal belonging to a member of the community, that of Kalonymos (very early thirteenth century), represents a lion rampant evoking the Davidic ascendency of the Todros; see Brigitte Bedos, "Les sceaux," in *Art et archéologie des Juifs en France médiévale*, ed. Bernhard Blumenkranz, Collection Franco-Judaïca, 9 (Toulouse, 1980), pp. 207–28, here 209, fig. 5–5 *bis*.

79. Golb, *The Jews in Medieval Normandy*, pp. 202ff.

80. Fulbert of Chartres, *Tractatus contra Iudeos*, 3, PL 141:316C–317A, cited by Golb, *The Jews in Medieval Normandy*, p. 203.

81. Peter thus was in correspondence with a Frankish king of Jerusalem, Fulk of Anjou (1131–43) or Baldwin III (1143–62), *Ep.*, 82, 1:219.

82. *AJ*, 4.127ff.

The land given them by God in days of old has rejected them as filth (*inutilia purgamenta*). They are the trash of history, scattered across the world and exposed to humiliation. Peter looks finally at the prophecy of seventy weeks made in Daniel 9:22–27: seven weeks will pass until the arrival of an "anointed Saint of Saints"; after a further sixty-two weeks, during which Jerusalem will be rebuilt, the anointed one will be slain and the holy city destroyed; in the final week of the seventy will come "the abomination of desolation," and this desolation "shall continue even to the consummation and to the end."[83] The abbot of Cluny is in no doubt about the identity of the anointed one: it can only be Christ. The problem lies with fitting the prophecy within a reliable historic framework. Peter devotes much attention to the prophet's symbolic figures, converting them into years corresponding exactly with the Savior's life and death, the destruction of the Temple in Jerusalem by Titus and Vespasian, and the beginning of the endless desolation of the Jews; he refers to a number of authorities, some of which are still unidentified.[84] Peter's interpretation of the "desolation" that "shall continue . . . to the end" (verse 27) includes past history from the desolation of the Holy City down to the writing of his own *Adversus Iudeos* and beyond, right until the end of the world. Henceforth, the Jews have no hope of freedom on earth and still less the prospect of returning to the Promised Land of old. Christ's work thus marked a reversal in their condition. Since then, there has been neither any Jewish king or prince, nor any Jew who was not servile.[85] The chosen people have become an enslaved people. They have gone from being the head (*caput*) to being the tail (*cauda*). Their destiny is that of Cain: eternally wandering, eternally humiliated and subservient.

Proof by Miracles

After his historical commentary on Daniel's prophecy, Peter pauses. His judgment, as a polemicist, is that the four points declared in the prologue have been aired and the adversaries' objections swept away. The Jews have only to submit to their own authorities or sufficient "reasons," if indeed they are endowed with reason.[86] The debate is over—unless those who contradict him now seek proof by miracles, for "the Jews require signs" (1 Corinthians 1:22). Moving beyond the original framework of the four Christological questions examined in the light of the opponents' authorities, the discussion now takes on new life. Peter is drawn, in the second part of chapter 4 and throughout chapter 5, into a long and fascinating excursion.

It really is a second treatise. At the outset, Peter affirms the superiority of

---

83. *AJ*, 4.228ff.

84. *AJ*, 4.270–325, a passage from an unidentified commentary on Daniel. For commentaries on this prophecy, see Dahan, *Les intellectuels chrétiens et les juifs*, pp. 495–96.

85. *AJ*, 4.97–101.

86. *AJ*, 4.521ff.

Christian miracles. "Your time," he tells his adversaries, referring to the Hebrew antiquity of the Old Testament, was indeed one of miracles, but the "works of the Christian faith" are more numerous and more powerful still. His apostolic namesake, the apostle Peter, who commanded demons, raised the dead, and ministered to the sick, was far superior to Moses. The apostles, who responded to Christ's injunction, and the disciples of Peter also exercised miracle-working powers across the world. If Christ's words in Mark 16:17–18 can be trusted, all who believe can work signs. The abbot of Cluny asserts that the universal spread of Christianity down to his own time has been marked by countless extraordinary happenings whose missionary effect he impresses upon his readers.[87] The success of Christian proselytism he puts down to the miracle-working of Christ's close and more distant disciples.

The Finite and Eternal Nature of the Law

The new things (*nova*) that God dispensed by means of signs well before the coming of Christ—though inferior in number and quality to those accompanying the founding of the "New" Covenant—raise the question of the Law's eternal nature. Is there proof that the Law of Moses had to change?[88]

Peter begins by pointing to texts that speak of God rejecting his people's sacrifices: Psalm 49(50):13; Isaiah 1:13. He mentions the foundation of a new covenant foretold in Jeremiah 31:31–32, by which Christ, according to John's testimony (John 9:39), would perform the dual action of opening the eyes of those who did not see and making blind those who saw—the Jews. Jeremiah's prophecy contrasts with the everlasting character of the Law of Moses, as proclaimed in Exodus 12:14. But since God is incapable of contradiction, it is necessary to discriminate. Peter, who naturally leans toward Jeremiah, undertakes to show that the eternality of which Exodus speaks is perhaps less eternal than appears at first sight. Scriptural quotations at the ready, Peter endeavors to show that the words *perpetuus, aeternus, sempiternus* do not mean "unending." Sometimes, he says, Scripture speaks of eternity, while actually connoting a finite duration. Such is the case in Exodus 15:18, where God is said to "reign for ever and beyond" (*et ultra*). Secular authors are also cited, especially the Roman poets Horace and Vergil, to confirm this notion of finite eternity. There is therefore, says Peter, no reason to see Moses and Jeremiah as contradictory; it is more useful to examine what Moses meant by "an everlasting observance" (Exodus 12:14). Affirming the mutually noncontradictory stance of these two biblical figures enables Peter to follow Augustine's authority and employ the classic theme of the New Testament fulfilling the Old.[89] He repeats the argument Augustine used in *Contra Faustum* (6.6), that the prescriptions of the Old Testament were always

---

87. *AJ*, 4.546–51.
88. *AJ*, 4.651ff.
89. *AJ*, 4.1029ff.

valid for Christians, not as rules for leading life (*ad modum agendae vitae*), but as symbols (*ad modum significandae vitae*). Thus the physical circumcision of the Old Testament was significant for Christians on a spiritual level, and the multiple, finished sacrifices of the Old Covenant were forerunners of the unique sacrifice of Christ, which sealed the New.

The next question to ask is whether the New Testament and its observances—baptism, unique sacrifice, sacraments, and various commandments—are eternal.[90] Yes and no, says Peter. No, because the prescriptions of the New Testament, no less than those of the Old, will end when the world ends. Yes, because they are a preparation for eternal realities. Indeed, that is the only real meaning of the term "eternal Law." These considerations concerning the overtaking of the one testament by the other are enough, says Peter, to show that the Christians have stayed true to the injunction in Deuteronomy 4:2 to leave the divine word unchanged, neither adding to it nor subtracting from it. For the Christians have kept the Scriptures in their original, uncorrupt state, using translations that are faithful to the Hebrew.[91] Peter's remark was timely. For this was a period when Latin and Hebrew biblical manuscripts were increasingly being compared by Christian clerics like Stephen Harding, the abbot of Cîteaux (1109–33), concerned to have a reliable text of the Old Testament.[92] Here Peter merely touches on the vexing question of the reliability of the Scriptures communicated to the peoples of the earth. It is something that he treats at length in *Contra sectam Sarracenorum*.[93] Jews and Christians, he continues, read the same text, but differently. As the apostle Paul says in 2 Corinthians 3:6, the Jews follow the letter that "killeth," while the Christians are imbued with the Spirit that "quickeneth." The Jews content themselves with the outer shell (*cortex*); the Christians feed upon the innermost part (*medulla*). Thus the Christians escape the curse mentioned in Deuteronomy 27:26: "Cursed be he that abideth not in the words of this law." Their focus is not what signifies (*significans*) but what is signified (*significatum*), not physical sacrifices but the spiritual virtues contained within them.[94] Such is the way opened by Christ: from circumcision to baptism; from the Sabbath to the repose from sin; from countless sacrifices to the offering of the unique Lamb of God, pure, innocent, and spotless. Such is the transforming power of the Creator God.[95] A growing movement crowned by Christian universality, the history of the righteous is viewed by Peter as having three stages. In the first, before the Law, such men as Abel, Enoch, Noah, or Abraham

90. *AJ*, 4.1052ff.

91. *AJ*, 4.1093–97, and cf. 5.720–23.

92. Aryeh Graboïs, "The *Hebraica veritas* and Jewish-Christian Intellectual Relations in the Twelfth Century," *Speculum* 50 (1975): 613–34, here 617ff.; reprinted in his *Civilisation et société dans l'Occident médiéval*, no. 13.

93. *CS*, 58–86, pp. 110–46.

94. *AJ*, 4.1129–32.

95. *AJ*, 4.1195ff.

had knowledge neither of circumcision nor of Sabbath observance, and yet they were justified by their works—like many (*plurimi*) of those who later lived under the Law. Now finally, after the period of the Law, all mankind (*universi*) can qualify for salvation. Christ has opened an era of general justification, for in him the generality of the prophets' foretellings is fulfilled.[96]

The Rational Evidence of Miracles

This fulfillment of the prophets by Christ is in Peter's mind itself a miracle that ought to convince the Jews. In the last part of chapter 4, Peter examines this miracle and the signs irrefutably proving the truth of Christ's teaching.[97]

In order for the demonstration to work, it is a prerequisite to have a definition of what constitutes a miracle. Is what is not seen to be regarded as fictitious? The Jews have not seen the miracles wrought by Moses, Joshua, and many others. But they do not consider these to be a fiction. Likewise, they cannot consider Christian miracles to be fictitious simply because they have not seen them. It is a case of all or nothing. Either all miracles, Jewish and Christian, are acceptable or they must be rejected in their entirety. Peter thereby insists that his adversaries respect the writings that recount the miracles recognized by Christians. He concludes: "We believe your prophets; so you should believe our apostles."[98] Peter's view is that Christian universality is itself a miracle; it is the world's response to extraordinary events. Yet how did a world formerly dominated by idolatry, where signs were nonexistent, come to believe in Christian miracles? Idolatry, says Peter, was only a preliminary stage in human history. The quest of innate reason (*innata ratio*) for the divine is characterized by experimentation in which man first adores what the Creator has made: images. By the time of Christ, the ardor of schools of philosophy, the study of human and divine realities, the blossoming of natural reason, written law, and science made it less possible for men to be deceived. They had become sufficiently mature to set aside the adoration of images. They could understand the meaning of the signs and embrace Christianity.

Having forged a link between the miraculous and conversion, Peter is confronted by a sizable objection: Islam.[99] He regards the problem as vitally requiring examination and devotes space to it accordingly. How is it that Muhammad's heresy has been so successful in establishing itself in several parts of the world, yet without recourse to the miraculous? Arriving at this point in *Adversus Iudeos*, the reader begins to see why this treatise should be read in conjunction with *Contra sectam Sarracenorum* and vice versa. How could such a learned age, the early centuries of Christianity, fall into the Muslim error? Pe-

96. *AJ*, 4.1270ff.
97. *AJ*, 4.1360–2001.
98. *AJ*, 4.1392.
99. *AJ*, 4.1447ff.

ter starts by minimizing the damage: he will show a greater measure of concern (and certainly more realism) in *Contra sectam Sarracenorum*.[100] For the moment, he observes that although a few areas of the world are affected, this is not the whole world. There is no period in history, apart from the very beginning and the very end, in which darkness has not mingled with the light, and error with truth. Unlike Islam, Christianity dominates the entire world:

> I said "the whole world," because, although Gentiles or Saracens may exert tyranny over some parts of it and Jews lurk [*laceant*] among Christians and pagans, there is little or no part of the earth, even remote islands of the Mediterranean Sea or the ocean itself, that are not inhabited by Christian rulers or subjects, that the truth may be plain which Scripture says concerning Christ: "And he shall rule from sea to sea: and from the river unto the ends of the earth" (Psalm 71[72]: 8).[101]

Like all errors before and after Christ, Muhammad's heresy is limited. There is no comparison between this "devilish falsehood" and the "divine truth of the Gospel." What then explains the success of Islam? In order to get a clear picture, Peter examines the various possible grounds of conversion: authority, reason, miracles, force, sensuality. From the Qur'an (Koran) 3.18–19 and 17.61, and al-Kindi's *Apologia*, he "proves" that neither miracles nor reason has anything to do with Islamic conversion.[102] Authority is no explanation, since the supposed prophecy of Muhammad is a fiction passing itself off as divine revelation.[103] Force and sensuality are all that remain. In fact, al-Kindi refers to the "strength of the sword" as an instrument of submission to Islam. Al-Kindi also asserts that the God of the Muslims does not demand hardship or lofty behavior but encourages the easy life. This deity urges his adherents to eat, drink, and sleep with women all night; he allows them to have a minimum of four wives and an infinite number of concubines.[104] Peter scarcely returns to these issues in *Contra sectam Sarracenorum*; the essential is said here, in *Adversus Iudeos*. Briefly, Islam's success is due partly to the power of arms, but above all to the irrepressible thirst for sex that abases mankind.

Peter points out that Christianity by contrast has come to dominate the whole world by the power of signs alone.[105] In the process of conversion, authority plays no part. There is belief in Christ, followed by acceptance of the Scriptures which declare him. Reason is one thing, but faith too has a contribution to make. All the reasoning of philosophers is not enough to explain the immensity of divine mysteries like the Word made flesh. The humility of the Most High is in-

100. *CS*, 11, p. 46.
101. *AJ*, 4.1466–73.
102. On the authorities cited, see chapter 11 below.
103. *AJ*, 4.1531ff.
104. *AJ*, 4.1541ff.
105. *AJ*, 4.1559ff.

accessible to minds swollen with pride; it reveals itself to the "humble." And what of force? Christianity does not employ it. What does violence achieve? Prison and torture have never forced Christians to abjure. So says Peter. But what are we to make of these affirmations of his? At best, the abbot of Cluny's sin is unconscious; at worst, it is blind. He was not ignorant of the phenomenon of Christians falling away during the great persecutions of the early Church. Moreover, was he not a contemporary of the first two Crusades, during which Christian universality tried to impose itself by fire and blood? Perhaps he sees only the other's sword? Finally, when it comes to sensuality, it is easy for Peter, the spiritual man whose profession is based on renouncing the flesh, to recall the words of Christ in Matthew 19:12, "There are eunuchs who have made themselves eunuchs for the kingdom of heaven." But he insists that there is no room in Christianity for the sensuality procured by worldly goods either, since Christians force themselves to give them up, so as to reverse their destiny, the greatest becoming the least and the master the servant. Thus, having eliminated four of the five possible causes of conversion—authority, reason, force, and sensuality—Peter reckons he has proved that the only explanation for Christianity's success necessarily lies in miracles.

In order to make a just appraisal of the extraordinary events that compel recognition of Christianity, it is equally necessary to distinguish between miracles and magic.[106] Magic is a matter for the literate and learned, whereas the apostles were uncultivated men. Peter observes that even the "science" of illiterate stage players and mimes of his own day requires years of apprenticeship; the disciples of Christ had nothing like it. The power to work miracles was granted by Christ to those who believed in him, as evidenced in Matthew 10:1. It was a divine power, which manifested itself in true, tangible (*solida*), useful signs, while magic is always false and delusive. A magician, for all his skill, can do little for the blind, the dumb, the paralyzed, the dead. But Christ and those who believe in him have power to heal the body to save the soul, that thereby "the whole man, snatched from all death, corruption, or misery, might enter eternally into the beatitude of the angels."[107]

Peter passes rapidly over the countless miracles of Christ, the apostles, the martyrs and confessors, then the bands of monks and hosts of hermits. He contents himself with drawing attention to the miracle-working power of this long line of Christians in life and after death. He similarly describes himself walking toward "the busts and sepulchres." Sacred relics, he says, reveal the beatitude and glory that the souls of the saints (*spiritus*) acquire betweentimes in the presence of the Almighty.[108] This time "betweentimes" (*interim*) functions to express the passing of the saints from life to death and the bipolarity of their presence.

---

106. *AJ*, 4.1672ff. The question is also touched on earlier, 4.1375ff.
107. *AJ*, 4.1859–61.
108. *AJ*, 4.1880–83.

They reign in the afterlife, while remaining in this world. But Peter focuses essentially upon contemporary Christian miracles. The Jews know nothing like it. Peter taunts them with the spectacle of crowds flocking to the tombs and temples of the Christians, hoping there to find cure and leaving healed. He evokes the person of the Virgin, the object of the Cross, and the holy places as so many memorials to Christ. For the sake of brevity, he refers his interlocutors to another book, indicating thereby his *De miraculis*.[109] He makes as if to pass over the one example that he chooses nevertheless to mention here, a miracle witnessed by Christians, pagans, and Saracens. Every year, on the anniversary of his Passion, Christ visits his tomb in the form of lightning sent from heaven. This extraordinary phenomenon, which has not ended with the Saracen domination of the holy places, demonstrates how death gives birth to life and how the darkness of the tomb gives birth to the light of the world.[110]

"The Ridiculous and Most Stupid Fables of the Jews"[111]

Opening the fifth and final chapter of *Adversus Iudeos*, Peter the Venerable ponders the nature of his opponents. As he sees it, the weight of authorities and reason in the Christological content of the first four chapters, plus the evident proof of miracles given in the second part of chapter 4, ought to be enough to convince anyone. Recalling the words of Psalm 48(49): 21, which compare men to "senseless beasts" (*iumenti insipientes*), Peter seriously questions whether his opponents possess rationality or whether they are beasts and not really members of the human race. Everywhere, he says, they seem like asses, the most stupid of animals, which hear but have no understanding.[112] The fifth chapter, "concerning the ridiculous and most stupid fables of the Jews," aims to expose to the world "the monstrous beast" (*portuentuosa bestia*) and deride it. The purpose is no longer to debate, however formally, but to attack head-on.

Discovery of the Talmud

The "monstrous beast" that Peter denounces is actually the Talmud, the book that makes the Jews dull, "like beasts." Peter the Venerable appears to be the first western author to employ the term "Talmud" and, alongside Peter Alfonso, a Spanish Jew converted and baptized in 1106, to use it in a polemical treatise. In the history of confrontation between Christian intellectuals and Jews in the twelfth century, this was exceptional. Not until the middle of the thir-

109. *AJ*, 4.1953–54.
110. *AJ*, 4.1967–68 (and *SLD*, p. 252).
111. *AJ*, 5.2 (chapter title).
112. *AJ*, 5.6–8: *Hominem enim te profiteri ne forte mentiar, non audeo, quia in te extinctam, immo sepultam quae hominem a caeteris animalibus vel bestiis separat eisque praefert rationem agnosco.*—"I dare not call thee man, lest perchance I lie, for I perceive that in thee is extinguished, nay buried, what separates man from the other animals or beasts and sets him before them: reason."

teenth century and the action brought against the Talmud and the rabbinic texts in Paris in 1240 did postbiblical Jewish literature receive slightly more than superficial examination from Christian censors.[113] On this front, as on others— the struggle against heretics and more especially the ideological war against Islam—Peter the Venerable was something of a forerunner.

It is hard to know where Peter obtained his information in this new field. Normally, when handling an opponent's polemical authorities, he gave precise details. He followed this rule in *Contra Petrobrusianos* and in his writings against Islam. In *Adversus Iudeos*, he strangely avoided doing so in the case of the Talmud. He anticipated his opponents' surprise that a non-Jew should have access to "the secrets of the Jews," but offered no more than a vague reference to Christ's inspiration to explain it.[114] Peter's secrecy about his own discovery only served to play up the secret character of the unveiled object, thereby launching the long-running theme of the Talmud's occult character.[115] We ourselves are reduced to conjecture.[116] It is impossible that Peter had access to a Latin translation of the Talmud, as Max Manitius has surmised, since no manuscript even of simple extracts is known about before the thirteenth century, if not the fourteenth.[117] The most probable hypothesis is that Peter had the services of a converted Jew. He was also probably acquainted with Peter Alfonso's *Dialogue*. Intermediaries of this sort, which cannot be precisely identified, would have provided Peter the Venerable with access, if not to the Talmud itself, to what Gilbert Dahan describes as a "smattering of Jewish literature," including extracts from the Talmud and other texts, such as the *Alphabet of Ben Sira*, a satirical work possibly composed in the eastern Mediterranean basin in the seventh century, foreign to the Talmud and indeed vigorously contested within the medieval Jewish tradition.[118] If this is correct, then Peter would have had a somewhat hazy notion of the object hastily dubbed "Talmud." In order to get the measure of his uncertainties and misunderstandings, readers from the Christian tradition need to know what Jews understood by the term "Talmud."[119] The word meant

113. Dahan, *Les intellectuels chrétiens et les juifs*, pp. 457ff.

114. *AJ*, 5.35–39.

115. A point made by Kniewasser, "Die antijüdische Polemik des Petrus Alfonsi," p. 57.

116. Yvonne Friedman gives a good summary of the question, *AJ*, pp. xvff.

117. Max Manitius, *Geschichte der lateinischen Literatur des Mittelalters*, 3, Handbuch der Altertumswissenschaft, 9.2 (Munich, 1931), p. 138. On the manuscript file assembled at the Paris trial of 1240, see Dahan, *Les intellectuels chrétiens et les juifs*, pp. 461–62.

118. Dahan, *Les intellectuels chrétiens et les juifs*, p. 459 (*échantillonnage de littérature juive*). On *Ben Sira*, whose textual tradition is very unclear, see *Encyclopedia Judaica*, 4B, s.v. "Ben Sira, Alphabet of," cols. 548–50, and Isaac Levi, "La nativité de Ben Sira," *Revue des études juives* 29 (1894): 197–205. Peter distinguishes *Ben Sira* from the Talmud, but ascribes to it an authority it did not possess in Jewish tradition—*AJ*, 5.2150–52: "Although this tale is not from the Talmud, it is taken from a book that enjoys no less authority among the Jews than the Talmud."

119. The short description that follows is based on Adin Steinsaltz, *The Essential Talmud* (London, 1976).

"teaching" or "study," the object being the Torah. In Jewish tradition it was a rather formal term connoting the summary of the oral law, of which there were two groups. First was the Mishnah, a treatise of *halakhah* (law), whose systematization into six orders (*sedarim*), divided into treatises (*massekhtot*) and then further into chapters (*praqim*), went back to the second century A.D. The commentary on the Mishnah, the Gemara, represented the Talmud in the strict sense of the term. It was a compendium of discussions on the Mishnah and explanations of it, an accumulation of juridical and legendary texts. Down to the ninth century, the directors of Babylonian academies (*Geonim*), asked about this or that obscure passage or difficult question, supplied commentaries (*responsa*). The rabbis of the Maghreb or western Europe then took over this task. Talmudic exegesis reached its height in the eleventh and twelfth centuries with the works of Gerschom of Mainz (ca. 960–1028) and preeminently Rashi of Troyes (1040–1106), who wrote numerous *responsa* as well as commentaries on the Bible and Talmud further developed by his pupils in the literature of "additions" (*tosefta*).[120] This corpus in turn became a sort of "Talmud on the Talmud."[121] Did Peter the Venerable, as a contemporary of this Talmudic renaissance, have the wherewithal to grasp the complexity and richness of its textual tradition, understand its linkages and thrust? He would have needed to be able to distinguish the *halakhah*, a juridical corpus lacking the constraining force of the canon law or civil law of Latin Christendom, from the generically termed *haggadah*, texts of a very different nature, including in particular sermons and legends whose conclusions had no sort of authority. This complex whole was an indiscriminate collection of important questions and minor problems. It was a search for truth without any necessarily immediate practical application. Hence the sorts of stories that might seem strange to a reader brought up in the traditional system of Christian authorities. Eliette Abécassis, for instance, evokes rabbinic discussions on such Talmudic subjects as "a tower floating in the air, a mouse taking breadcrumbs into a house at Passover, a fetus transplanted from one womb to another, an automaton participating in a prayer group."[122] Yet what we today might find merely amusing or strange would have horrified a twelfth-century Christian intellectual like Peter the Venerable, for whom the Law was not to be discussed humorously or in the absence of immediate practical application. The abbot of

120. See Aryeh Graboïs, *Les sources hébraïques médiévales*, 2: *les commentaires exégétiques*, Typologie des sources du Moyen Age occidental, 66 (Turnhout, 1993), pp. 19ff.; Simon Schwarzfuchs, *Rashi de Troyes*, Présence du judaïsme (Paris, 1991); *Rashi 1040–1990: hommage à Ephraïm E. Urbach*, Congrès européen des Etudes juives, ed. Gabrielle Sed-Rajna, Patrimoines judaïsme (Paris, 1993), esp. contributions by Elazar Touitou, "L'oeuvre de Rashi: exégèse biblique et éthique juive," pp. 21–27, Charles Touati, "Rashi, commentateur du Talmud," pp. 29–32, and Gilbert Nahon, "Les Tosafistes," pp. 33–42.

121. On the expansion and transformation of Jewish exegesis from the second half of the eleventh century, see Dahan, *Les intellectuels chrétiens et les juifs*, pp. 290–92.

122. Eliette Abécassis, *Qumran* (Paris, 1996), p. 81. There is a translation by Emily Read, entitled *The Qumran Mystery* (London, 1998).

Cluny's limited and confused grasp of rabbinic literature, together with his ignorance of its cultural habits and mental processes, led him up a blind alley. Such was the mental place in which he formulated his anti-Judaism; its tone and themes were without precedent in the earlier tradition of treatises *contra Iudeos*.

Sure enough, Peter the Venerable's work reveals an inability to achieve an overview of the Talmudic content, its structure or purpose. He manifestly failed to appreciate the difference between *halakhah* and *haggadah*. In concentrating on the "fabulous" content of the latter, Peter ascribed to it a normative value that the Jews themselves had never given to this collection of legends and short stories. Peter thought that the Jews "believed" in the Talmud and "followed its prescriptions" as if it were the Torah.[123] Peter's misapprehension derived from his belief that the Christian equivalent, hagiography, was an extension and actualization of the Scriptures, that its teaching had normative force within the Church and the status of proof in any doctrinal discussion. He made the mistake of likening Jewish fabulous material to Greek and Latin fables in order to belittle it, pointing out that the Jewish fables were no different from the purely moral or humorous sketches of classical authors who had desired them "to be understood otherwise than according to plain speech."[124] It was not surprising that the Jews should have such tales. But since they took theirs literally, they were probably incapable of understanding anything figuratively. By such standards, even the "true and sacred page" that contained scriptural imagery was ridiculous, for example Jotham's apologue in Judges 9:8–16 about the trees choosing their king. The trees chose first the olive tree, the fig, then the vine, and ultimately the thorn. Taken literally, the fable was absurd: no one ever heard trees speak. Yet as a parable the story made perfect sense, the fruits of the trees standing for the sons of Gideon and the thorn tree referring to the fratricidal Abimelech.[125] The Jews, says Peter, are incapable of parables. As the apostle Paul asserted in 2 Timothy 4:3–4, they "will indeed turn away their hearing from the truth, but will be turned unto fables." Peter's incomprehension is total. He reproaches his adversaries for their literalism, while we can see that the Talmud's interpretative portions are actually a notable effort at exegesis. Perceiving no coherence in his contradictors' stories, Peter is able to manipulate at will the rabbinic literature at his disposal. He summarizes the stories and gives the legends a consistently anti-Christian spin. Such manipulation stems from a defensive strategy that is as perceptible in Peter's treatise as in the manuscripts of it that have come down to us. Siger, the scribe of the Douai manuscript, indicates all the borrowings from the Talmud (or reckoned to be such) so as to distinguish them from Bible quotations and thereby avoid any confusion on the reader's part. He radically abridges the tale of the prophet Jeremiah's incest, the content

123. See Friedman's introduction, *AJ*, p. xvii, referring to 5.1106–79.
124. *AJ*, 5.1134–35.
125. *AJ*, 5.1145ff.

of which no doubt revolted him.[126] The margins of the Le Mans manuscript contain unsympathetic observations along the lines of "Note the ignominy of this fable."[127] The strategy of the author himself was to contrast the Bible and Talmud, as if to defend the Jews against themselves. In the first part of the treatise, the Christological dispute on the basis of Old Testament evidence, Peter relied on authorities that he shared with his opponents. In the latter part of *Adversus Iudeos*, his aim is to show that the Talmud and its monstrous fables marked a departure from the inherent truths of the Old Testament. His literary treatment of the Jewish problem is explicable within the wider context of the relations between ecclesiastical authority and the Jews in the twelfth century, and more particularly the thirteenth. Although the Jews were outside the Church on issues arising from the New Testament, they surely could and should be judged by the Church if they abandoned the truths of the Old Testament.[128] The alternatives were well stated by Peter the Venerable in his treatise: either the Jews returned to their own history or they must be reckoned less than human, since believers in the Talmud could only be beasts.[129] The denunciation of the Talmud that closes *Adversus Iudeos* is intended to detail an important contrast. Using carefully chosen narratives, Peter draws a contrast between the elect humanity of Christianity and the monstrosity of Judaism. Let us now summarize the main terms of this radical contrast by concentrating on three areas that were bound to stir up the theorists of twelfth-century Christendom: the omnipotence of God; the afterlife; morals.

Doubts about the Omnipotence of God

The first "fable" Peter cites comes from a *midrash* (interpretation of a Bible verse); this is followed by two passages from the Babylonian Talmud.[130] In heaven, God passes his time reading and discussing the book—the Talmud—with the Jewish sages who have put it together. As a preliminary, Peter wonders about the propriety of even replying. He masters his revulsion in the hope that some at least—the tiny number that the divine mercy has garnered from the crowds of the lost—will hearken to his words and be converted.

Such a fable, he counters, is not merely a sin; it is a blasphemy against God's

126. In MS Douai, BM 381, the nonbiblical or patristic quotations are marginally indicated in both *Adversus Iudeos* (extracts from the Talmud, ff. 161v, 162v–63r, 166v, 167v–68r, 169r, 170v–71v, 175, 176v) and *Contra sectam Sarracenorum* (refs. to the Qur'an or al-Kindi's *Apologia*, ff. 182, 185, 187, and to Bede's *Historia ecclesiastica*, f. 184v). On the passage abridged from the *Alphabet of Ben Sira* (*AJ*, 5.2005–55, i.e., MS Douai, BM 381, ff. 175v–76r), see my remarks later in this chapter.

127. Yvonne Friedman in *AJ*, introduction, pp. xxx–xxxi (MS Douai, BM 381) and p. xxxv (MS Le Mans, BM 8).

128. Dahan, *Les intellectuels chrétiens et les juifs*, pp. 105–6.

129. Kniewasser, "Die antijüdische Polemik des Petrus Alfonsi," pp. 75–76.

130. *AJ*, 5.56ff. (cf. Midrash Gen. Rabbah 64.4; Babylonian Talmud, Berakhot 8a and Avodah Zarah 3b).

omnipotence. Why would God spend time reading? To become wiser or remind himself of what he has forgotten? God is all wisdom. He does not forget. Did he not remember Noah and his ark amid the floods (Genesis 8:1)? Nor does God read in order to instruct disciples or entertain them, as with tragedy, comedy, or satire. Is not this Talmud which is said to interest him a material book, made of parchment, papyrus, or paper (incidentally, we have here a very early reference to the use of paper in the medieval west)?[131] Does God read these Jewish writings to learn, teach, or enhance his knowledge? The implication is that God still has things to learn and needs counselors or doctors. All these are absurd questions and hypotheses, since God created all minds and contains all wisdom.

Another passage from the Babylonian Talmud reveals the object of the supposed conversation between God and his rabbinic company in heaven.[132] The discussion turns on the various types of leprosy mentioned in Leviticus 13–14. The question asked is whether alopecia (sudden loss of hair and beard) should be considered a form of leprosy. The assembly is divided: God says yes; the rabbis say no. After a long and heated confrontation, it is decided to consult a Jewish sage, Rabbi Nehemiah, and abide by his decision. God dispatches the angel of death to earth with orders to bring back the sage's soul to heaven. The angel finds Nehemiah absorbed in reading the Talmud. In answer to the angel's injunction, the terrified sage says that he has no intention of dying. The heavenly legation gets nowhere. The angel fails to convince Nehemiah that he would be better off in heaven with God and other rabbis. He returns to heaven alone and tells God that nothing could tear the sage away from his reading of the Talmud. God sends the angel of death back to earth with instructions to use deception— frightening phenomena like a rock fall—to drag Rabbi Nehemiah away from his book and ravish his soul. This second tactic is a brilliant success. When he arrives in heaven, the rabbi adjudicates in the debate, declaring that alopecia is an earthly illness and not leprosy. God therefore is wrong. Red-faced, God admits to having been confounded and "defeated by his sons."

Peter's response to the story is revealing of his artistry in demonizing the Jews. First, he displays his anger, finding no words to describe such nonsense.[133] Then, after the initial display of shock, he challenges his opponents with their own Scriptures, beginning with Isaiah, which Isaiah 1:2–4 shows to be no longer the Jews' property but "ours." Isaiah himself foretold the coming of Christ and the blasphemies of the Jews who preferred to turn away from God. Thereafter they went from bad to worse. While most of the early Jews had a strong faith in God, those of later times do not fear to trot out rubbish like the idea of God debating in heaven with dead Jews. The entire story is incredible. Does polemic take place in heaven, that place of rest and beatitude? Could a man challenge

131. *AJ*, 5.194: *ex rasuris veterum pannorum.* The Islamic world discovered paper, a Chinese invention, at the beginning of the eighth century; it was not used in Spain until the thirteenth century.

132. *AJ*, 5.239ff. (cf. Babylonian Talmud, Baba Metzia 86a).

133. *AJ*, 5.275ff.

PART III. CHRISTIAN UNIVERSALITY

God's injunction, brought by the angel of death? Would the Almighty need to resort to a trick to take away a soul? Finally, would God be thus conquered and admit defeat with a red face? To realize what nonsense all this is, says Peter, it is sufficient to draw from the authority of the Old Testament. As Psalm 93(94):8 shows, God teaches man and not the contrary. Ecclesiasticus 1:1 says that "all wisdom is from the Lord God." Genesis 18:25 says that God is the judge of all the earth, not that he is judged.[134] As for God's resort to trickery, Peter appeals to common sense. Instead of needlessly provoking a "natural" disaster, would the Deity not simply have waited for the sort of propitious moment afforded by the human condition—by the need to sleep or eat, for instance—when Nehemiah would be distracted from his reading of the Talmud? Peter appeals again to common sense a little further on, when he denounces another "fable" that infringes "the most sublime and incomprehensible majesty of Almighty God." The story supposes that the Creator has left the northern part of the firmament unfinished in case some rival should appear who also claimed to be God and who would be called upon to prove it by completing the work begun. The abbot of Cluny asks his adversaries who, apart from them, sees the firmament unfinished.[135] These two examples represent the only "rational" discussion in the chapter. After his commentary on the fable about Rabbi Nehemiah, Peter descends into violent invective. To him the idea of the Almighty's being defeated is utterly intolerable. He explodes with rage against the Jews, the laughingstock (*ludibrium*) of the Christians, the Gentiles, the Saracens, and even the demons. Barely can he stay the hands of his own people who would spill Jewish blood. But Peter recalls the injunction of Psalm 58(59):12—"Slay them not"—the classic anti-Judaic text justifying the survival of that murderous people as a memorial to the sacrifice of Christ.[136] Such was the humiliation willed on the Jews by God: not death, but to be made by their wandering a spectacle of degeneration and malediction for the world, an abomination to men on earth and the playthings of the demons in the life to come.

God in Man's Image

The following two fables concern the nature of God, whom the Talmud depicts expressing anger and crying tears like a man. The first tale, from the Babylonian Talmud, portrays God displaying anger every morning at the first hour against the kings of iniquity, who wear their diadems and worship the sun.

134. *AJ*, 5.410ff.
135. *AJ*, 5.685ff.
136. *AJ*, 5.599–605: "Who should stay his hands, still less his words? Since for eleven hundred years now you have groaned under the feet of those whom you hate above all else, the Christians, and are become not only their sport but also the sport of the Saracens and all peoples and demons, who shall curb the hands of our men from shedding your blood save the precept of the One who cast you out and chose us, God speaking by your prophet, 'Slay them not'?" On the theme of the survival of the Jews as a witness, see Dahan, *Les intellectuels chrétiens et les juifs*, pp. 574ff.

The story asserts that the only beings to know the exact timing of the divine wrath are Balaam and the cock.[137] Against the story, Peter points out, first of all, that the Talmud's notion of God's wrath totally contradicts Psalm 7:12: "God is a just judge, strong and patient: is he angry every day?" Anxious to use scriptural argument to the full, Peter, "albeit a Latin," excludes any notion that his version of the biblical text is faulty, resting his case on "the copious erudition of many experts in both languages," Hebrew and Latin. This simple remark, made in passing, testifies to the concerns of a western Christian intellectual faced with Hebrew truth and to the stimulus given to textual criticism by the needs of anti-Jewish polemic.[138] The equable portrait voiced in the psalm is, declares Peter, a way of emphasizing the unchangeability of God, who is not affected either essentially or outwardly by humanlike movements of joy or anger. Peter's commentary continues with the observation that the effect, the anger of God, presupposes a cause. What can it be? It sounds like a sort of golden age, this time when kings were always available at the day's first hour to wear their diadem and worship the sun! After the spark of irony, the abbot of Cluny, with his usual concern for history and minor ethnographical observation, says that he is aware that certain eastern kings used to worship the sun, but they also waged war. They therefore were not available every day at the first hour. Besides which, no king worships the sun in the twelfth century, in either the Christian world or Islam. As for the few pagans that remain, Peter denies ever hearing of their doing so. Since the practice is unattested, the cause is unsustainable, and, consequently, the effect is nil. There remains the question of Balaam and that of the cock. Is it likely that Balaam's knowledge would surpass that of the prophets? Numbers 31:16 speaks of Balaam as an ungodly man who offended God by giving evil counsel to the children of Israel. The knowledge attributed to him by the Talmud therefore contradicts the truth of Scripture. Peter similarly asks whether the cock, a mere animal, would be given knowledge of divine acts before men? That idea is contradicted by Job 38:36: "Who gave the cock understanding?" Peter declares that the animal has only a simple natural intelligence enabling it to perceive the coming of day.

The subject of the second story is the Deity's supposed daily weeping, which is held to form a great sea of luminosity that is the source of the light that falls from the stars at night. The divine sobbing is reckoned to be occasioned by the Jews' captivity. The grief God suffers causes him to roar three times a day like a lion and moan like a dove. In his misery, he is said to bewail his abandoned house, his burned down Temple and dispersed sons. The Jewish doctors hear "in a certain ruined place" the voice of God asking mercy for his people.[139] Going beyond mere rhetoric, Peter asks whether it is seemly to respond to these "dogs

137. *AJ*, 5.710ff. (*Babylonian Talmud, Berakhot*, 7a).
138. *AJ*, 5.720–3 and cf. 4.1093–7.
139. *AJ*, 5.919ff. (Babylonian Talmud, Berakhot 59a, 3a, and 7a); see Dahan, *Les intellectuels chrétiens et les juifs*, p. 493.

and pigs" who blaspheme God. Yet perhaps he may save some. There is, says Peter, no Old Testament passage that permits the attribution of dovelike moans to God. Peter admits that Scripture on occasions describes God as roaring, grieving, shouting, hissing, or screeching. But the abbot of Cluny's use of present participles (*rugientem, dolentem, vociferantem, sibilantem, stridentem*) helps to make his point that these are not states but divine actions; such language is, moreover, not intended to be interpreted literally. Being neither physical nor confinable, God cannot fall into physical states. How should he weep without eyes or roar without a voice? How should he exclaim "Woe is me!" like those who suffer, since he is never unhappy? Besides, to ascribe physicality to God amounts to a form of idolatry condemned in Deuteronomy 4:15–19. Peter's accusation sounds a bit like tit for tat, given that, in their disputes with Jews, the Christians were often pilloried by their opponents for worshiping images and practicing idolatrous devotion to the Cross.[140]

A Jewish Excursion into the Afterlife

A little further on in his narrative, Peter the Venerable mentions the story of Iozah ben Levi (Joshua, the son of Levi), who thought he could escape death by means of the Book.[141] The tale begins with God desiring to take to heaven the soul of a wise and good Jew called Joshua; this Joshua is very learned in the Talmud. When the angel of the Lord appears, Joshua declares that he has come in vain. The sage is absorbed in the Talmud and swears on the Book that God's envoy has no power to take him away. When the angel returns to God alone, God orders him to return and invite Joshua back to heaven, where he will be able to eat better and enjoy himself more than on earth. Joshua agrees on the sole condition that he is left alive and can see the gates of paradise and of hell. This is agreed. Joshua mounts on the angel's back and demands the angel of death's sword lest the angel kill him on the way. They travel first to the gate of hell, where Joshua sees various people of different nations: Christians, Amorites, Jebusites, and Moabites, plus a pharaoh and some kings. The visitor asks why the Christians are damned. The reply given is that they believe in Jesus, son of Mary, do not observe the Law of Moses, and reject the Talmud. The kings are in hell because they did not believe in the Talmud and persecuted the Jews, as is the case of the pharaoh, whose eye is used as the hinge of the door to hell. They continue to paradise. The angel sets down his passenger on the wall of paradise, where Joshua can easily see the souls of saints, patriarchs, prophets, and other blessed. He sees, among others, Pharaoh's daughter sitting on a throne. She is there because she saved Moses from death, fed him, and raised him. All the others in paradise have merited this glory because they found and wrote the Tal-

140. Dahan, *Les intellectuels chrétiens et les juifs*, pp. 500ff.
141. *AJ*, 5.1336ff. Immediately preceding comes the tale of Og the king of Bashan (5.1088ff.), which I have not included in my survey. In that passage (1106ff.), Peter makes interesting observations (noticed earlier) about Jewish fables compared with those in Greek and Latin.

mud in their hearts, being unable to study it as their successors did. The angel asks Joshua to come down from the wall. But Joshua refuses, and jumps with the sword into paradise. The arrival of a living man, clothed and armed, causes major astonishment. Joshua finds nowhere to sit and remains standing. He ends up with Pharaoh's daughter and, in order to get her off her throne, tells her that her father is at the gate. A little later, she angrily returns and accuses Joshua of telling lies. He retorts that he spoke the truth, but simply did not specify which gate her father was at, that of heaven or hell! The angel reports back to God on the unexpected turn of events. Believing that he is master in his own house, God instructs Joshua to get out quickly. The sage refuses "by God and the Talmud." What is God to do? He demands that inquiry be made "throughout the library" to see whether Joshua has ever been guilty of false swearing. If he has, he will have to go. If not, as is ultimately the case, he can stay on account of his piety and constancy in studying the Talmud. The story ends with the angel asking the triumphant Joshua for his sword back and Joshua refusing unless the angel promises no longer to kill men with it. This final outrage on the part of Joshua is accepted by God, and the angel of death is made redundant.

As he starts his commentary on this Jewish journey into the afterlife, Peter the Venerable observes that such fables have never yet been uttered by the mouths of men or demons.[142] The idea that a human being could escape death is especially intolerable to him. He gives the appearance of being completely thrown by the ways in which the Jews play about with the afterlife. In the tale about Rabbi Nehemiah, God was forced to use a trick in order to get hold of a soul. Now, in the case of Joshua, a man is able to use tricks to outwit the infinite wisdom of God. The abbot of Cluny responds point by point. As Peter sees it, the stakes are high. The Jews have turned the world order upside down: it needs righting. Through a series of astonished questions, he points to unbelievable elements in the story. Would Joshua have mounted on an angel, as upon a mare? Did he really need to take the angel of death's sword in order to stop it from being used on him? Why, in hell, were so many peoples forgotten? What about the Gauls, the Iberians, the Germans—or indeed Elam, Asshur, and the multitude spoken of in Ezechiel 32:22–24? Perhaps the prophet saw better than the sage of the Talmud? What of Dathan, Abiram, and the other accursed ones of the Old Testament who are known with certainty to have been swallowed up by the earth and buried in hell? Curiously, Joshua did not see his own people (*proprios indigenas*), yet managed to clearly recognize the Christians, who were foreign to him. And why were these last damned? The answer given by the Talmud, says Peter, is the exact opposite of the reality. It is the Jews who are destined to hell precisely because they have not believed in Jesus, son of Mary, and reject the Gospel and blaspheme it. The two positions are thus poles apart. Nevertheless, Peter considers that his earlier demonstrations—the first four chapters of his

142. *AJ*, 5.1431ff.

treatise, devoted to the person of Christ—reveal the truth of his position over that of his opponents.

Peter then gives some rapid thought to the physical side of the afterlife. To say that Pharaoh's eye is a hinge of the gate to hell is senseless and "bestial." This world and the afterlife, says Peter, are in no way comparable. It is impossible for houses and gates to be the same in an incorporeal world as in the physical world. Moreover, hell is not a human prison: why should it need a gate? God's will is sufficient to contain the damned. Equally, why should paradise require a wall? In the context of new Christian conceptions of a spatialized afterlife, Peter is cautious about attributing too physical a character to paradise, hell, or the purgatorial places (purgatory as such coming only a generation later).[143] How could a living man, clothed and armed, enter paradise? Peter thinks the inhabitants of heaven would have had every right to be surprised on finding Joshua in their midst. Although Christ spoke of violent men bearing away the kingdom of heaven by force (Matthew 11:12), he did not talk of arms. Finally, has it ever been said that paradise might be entered fraudulently? On the contrary, the way that leads there is that of the virtues: penitence, humility, continence, and seeking after truth. Peter now tackles the point that has irritated him the most in the fable of Joshua, the Deity's supposed order to search "throughout the library." This is trifling not simply with the angel of death but with God himself. Would he who knows all truth need to carry out an inquiry into Joshua's oath-swearing history? Would he resort to trickery to expel an interloper from paradise? Would a man swearing by God make himself thereby higher than God? Could the Talmud be higher than the Creator? Would God have to bow to the Book? At issue is the question of divine omnipotence. Are we to believe that the field of divine dominion evoked by the psalmist in Psalm 71(72): 8—"from sea to sea and from the river unto the ends of the earth"—stops short of paradise? Does not another Psalm, 134(135): 6, say, "Whatsoever the Lord pleased he hath done, in heaven, in earth, in the sea, and in all the deeps"? So it is false that man can escape the divine will in paradise. The matter of the Book of life also raises the question of the divine omniscience. The mere consulting of a book (*suffragium biblorum vel pellium*) to investigate Joshua's works presupposes that God's memory is fallible. If such were true, how many books would be needed to supplement the divine memory and record all the misdeeds of human history? Would not the other world need to consist of one huge library? The verdict delivered after consultation of the book is equally incredible. How come Joshua has been saved alive, while David, Moses, and Abraham did not merit the same treatment? And what about the sword? Could not God have got it back, or else find or make another? Has the sword of death always been one and the same?

---

143. A good example of such hesitancy, cited by Jacques Le Goff for "his fierce criticism of viewing spiritual life spatially" (*sa vive critique d'une vision spatiale de la vie spirituelle*), is Honorius Augustodunensis (early twelfth century), *Scala coeli maior, PL* 172:1237–38: see Le Goff, *La Naissance du Purgatoire* (Paris, 1981), p. 185.

Scripture, in Exodus 12:29–30 and 4(2) Kings 19:35, makes clear that there were a number of angels of death. Did they all use the same sword? Is one to believe that through Joshua's action there is only one—the one abusively put out of action by the Jewish sage? Peter concludes his commentary on this "monstrous" story by demanding that his opponents restore to God the pilfered sword. Should they refuse, he defies them to demonstrate the capacity to make mortal men immortal.

Peter adds no further commentary on this fable. In order to gauge the effect produced by such a tale on contemporary Christian minds, it is helpful to look outside the confines of *Adversus Iudeos*. Immediately before transcribing the abbot of Cluny's treatise, the copyist of the Douai manuscript, Siger, inserted three vision narratives wrongly ascribed by tradition to Peter the Venerable.[144] Why were they added next to *Adversus Iudeos*? In part, we can point to the attraction of themes. The most important of the three narratives, the *Vision of Gunthelm*, recounts the journey of a soul into the Christian afterlife. Whether consciously intended or not, the proximity is worthy of note. Perhaps the scribe wished to preface the Talmudic fantasies occupying the final section of Peter's treatise, not least Joshua's journey into the afterlife, with a reminder from this small exemplary narrative of the rules applying to similar journeys in the Christian environment. The *Vision of Gunthelm* was composed within English Cistercian circles between 1128 and 1161.[145] The main protagonist, Gunthelm, is a layman who has much offended God and decides to go off to fight Christ's enemies in Jerusalem. On his return, he becomes a novice in a Cistercian monastery; then again he is stirred by the call of the Holy Land. But because his abbot is away, he is obliged to defer his departure. At this point the vision occurs. The hesitant novice is visited by Benedict of Nursia, the father of the monks, who bids him follow him and climb a ladder leading to heaven. Accompanied by the saint, he first visits a chapel where he meets the Virgin. She makes the novice promise never to leave her service. A little later, he goes through a pleasant place peopled with monks. With Benedict's permission, he talks to a former brother of his own monastery, Matthew, who teaches him that the way to the afterlife is one of aridity, and that the abode of the blessed is attained by abandoning all personal will. Later, the archangel Raphael takes over from Benedict in order to show Gunthelm the remainder of paradise, conduct him on a visit to the deepest darkness, and lead him to contemplate the torments of bad layfolk and reprobate

144. MS Douai, BM 381, ff. 127v2–131r1. On the manuscript diffusion of these texts, which partly coincides with that of Peter the Venerable's *De miraculis*, see Giles Constable, "The Vision of Gunthelm and Other Visions Attributed to Peter the Venerable," *RB* 66 (1956): 92ff.

145. Text edited by Giles Constable, "The Vision of Gunthelm and Other Visions Attributed to Peter the Venerable," *RB* 66 (1956): 105–13. The following remarks are based on Claude Carozzi, *Le voyage de l'âme dans l'Au-delà d'après la littérature latine (Ve–XIIIe siècle)*, Collection de l'Ecole française de Rome, 189 (Rome, 1994), pp. 475–91.

monks. The account ends with the novice's soul being reunited with its body on earth. If indeed the copyist of the Douai manuscript wished his readers to make the connection, then the journey of Gunthelm stands in opposition to that of Joshua. Anticipating the Jewish fantasy of a living man in clothes and arms visiting the afterlife in a willful and capricious manner, and settling there regardless of the wishes of the angel of death or God, the Christian *exemplum* of the soul's journey responds in advance with a preparatory lesson on the renunciation of all self-will.

The Incestuous Prophet

Peter the Venerable finds the four fables that follow no less stupefying than the narrative of Joshua's journey.[146] However, their content does not revolt him as much as what went before and what will follow. At this point in chapter 5 he treats the Jews as overgrown children. Here what they maintain is seen as ridiculous but of no consequence. One example will suffice: the Talmudic tale of the infinite propagation of people to fill the Promised Land, each Jewish woman giving birth to 366 children a year, or one a day.[147] Peter limits himself to asking one amused question: What do the women who have to go through the daily pains of labor think about it? In a world where extraordinarily large numbers of women died in childbirth, it was a sensible remark. But what the abbot of Cluny, reading the tale literally, failed to realize was that the Jews themselves were not taken in by their fable. Sometimes the very point of the *haggadah* was to ask ostensibly incredible questions due to a taste for the paradoxical and the unforeseen answer.

In contrast, the story that closed Peter's treatise had plenty to scandalize a twelfth-century cleric with delicate feelings about sex. It was a curious tale of biblical morals with the prophet Jeremiah playing a leading role. The story came not from the Talmud but from the *Alphabet of Ben Sira*, a suspect text that Peter the Venerable erroneously considered a Jewish authority. It was as if a rabbi had asked the abbot of Cluny to reply to fables contained in the *Life of Merlin*.[148] The summary of the story provided by Peter opens with a scene of onanism. Young men bathing indulge in masturbation. Jeremiah arrives and scolds them for it, but they care little for his reprimand and invite the prophet to join them. Jeremiah allows himself to be tempted. He masturbates and his semen falls into the water. Further down river, Jeremiah's own daughter is bathing. Unwittingly she is impregnated by her father's sperm, and a singular son, Ben Sira, is born. He astounds from his birth on. He refuses his mother's milk, demanding more

146. *AJ*, 5.1906–93.
147. *AJ*, 5.1906–23.
148. *AJ*, 5.1994–2152 (on the status attributed to the text, 2150–52). The comparison with the *Life of Merlin* is made by Levi, "La nativité de Ben Sira," p. 199.

substantial food like bread, seasoned meat, honey, and butter. Very soon, he is able to answer the most learned questions. His mother, who is continually surprised by her son, begins to worry. Finally, the boy prodigy reveals to her that he is her own father's son, the fruit of incest. To think that Jeremiah is a fornicator! Choking with rage, Peter considers that the perverseness of this story exceeds even Satan's accusations. Pursuing his defensive line of leading the Jews back from the blindness caused by the Talmud to the original truth of the Old Testament, Peter contents himself with responses drawn from the canonical Jeremiah. Although he might easily have gone to Leviticus 19–20 to confront his opponents with their own law's prohibitions of incest, he totally sidesteps the core problem in the story. But we must not allow ourselves to be taken in by his silence. Like all clerics of the eleventh and twelfth centuries, the abbot of Cluny was concerned about the excesses of the flesh. He was a contemporary of the Church's great effort to control sexuality within marriage, defined in his own time as a sacrament, an efficacious sign of grace. Though male masturbation was a minor offense generally punished by fifteen days on bread and water, incest was something else. It was a major problem, the object of hairsplitting ecclesiastical regulation, which long wavered between the fourth and seventh degree of consanguinity before fixing on the seventh degree during the eleventh century. Even then it was only the rule. Coming from the aristocracy, Peter was well aware of the uncertain, ephemeral unions that took place within domestic sexual life. He feared those moments of overexcitement in which the master of the house would choose a playmate from among his "forbidden" kinswomen.[149] In this context, the fornication of father and daughter was the most horrendous of all. The monstrousness contained in the story from the *Alphabet of Ben Sira* was for Peter an utter lie and calumny. By challenging the story's foundations, Peter could both nullify its effects and avoid all debate with the Jews on the essentials of sexuality. Where in the Bible, he asks, does it say that Jeremiah had a daughter? In fact, Scripture says that Jeremiah was told by God to take no wife, nor have sons or daughters (Jeremiah 16:2). It is impossible that such a holy man should have fallen and had children by another woman—Peter means extramaritally. The story of impregnation without intercourse is still more incredible. Peter adopts a "rational" argument to oppose it. Would not river-borne semen be diluted to the point where it lost all generative power? The discussion ends with this appeal to common sense; Peter deems it unnecessary to continue, given the absence of any proof. He contents himself with summarizing the end of this unlikely story. It is as follows. Nebuchadnezzar sends a thousand men in arms to examine the child prodigy. The king does not come in person, but sends

149. On these major points, which need not be labored here, see Georges Duby, *The Knight, the Lady, and the Priest: The Making of Modern Marriage in Medieval France*, trans. Barbara Bray, introduction by Natalie Zemon Davis (London, 1984); originally published as *Le chevalier, la femme et le prêtre* (Paris, 1981). On the prohibited degrees of consanguinity, see Jack Goody, *The Development of the Family and Marriage in Europe* (Cambridge, 1983), pp. 134–46.

a hare with questions written on its brow. Finally, the king recognizes that the child is the greatest of sages.

The Topsy-Turvy World of the Jews

Peter ends the fifth chapter of his *Adversus Iudeos* by denouncing his adversaries' "mysteries" and "sacraments" (*mysteria, sacramenta*).[150] What the abbot of Cluny is referring to are the extraordinary events reported in the rabbinic literature whose reality he has set about destroying. Humiliated like Cain and condemned to endless wandering, the Jews are incapable of genuine miracles. The stories of the Talmud are but fables. By "believing" in them, the Jews have abandoned the authority of the Old Testament and all reason with it. They no longer belong to humanity. In their dehumanized state, "they have broken [open] the eggs of asps and have woven the webs of spiders" (Isaiah 59:5), works of iniquity that are the fruits of the Antichrist. With their Talmud the Jews have quit sacred history, sealing their fall whose end will be in hell.

By polarizing so radically the Bible and the Talmud, the human and the demonic, Peter aims to right the world order turned upside down by the Jews. In their topsy-turvy world God is fallible. He reads and goes on learning to improve his knowledge. He uses the celestial library to plug the gaps in his memory. His sons manage to beat him in discussions in heaven. He has to resort to tricks in order to impose his will on living men whose souls he wishes brought to him. He weeps and rages like an ordinary human being. Man, by contrast, is all-powerful. He refuses to die, moves freely through an afterlife world of walls and gates like the world here below, refuses to leave it, and ends up in control. Confronted by such a perversion of the laws governing Creation, Peter understandably focuses on the "monstrous" story of Jeremiah and his daughter to complete his chapter. Incest was, for Peter, a very paradigm of disorder. Inasmuch as the Jews had no respect for the order governing human society, they were excluded from it. It is interesting to note that the years in which Peter worked on his *Adversus Iudeos* saw the shaping of a legend that held that Judas had murdered his father and had sex with his mother.[151] Dehumanized, reduced to the level of animals, and demonized, the Talmudic Jews became figures of pure antithesis. In contrast to their fables, the world could be shown to be the exact opposite. God was essentially incorporeal, uncontainable, and almighty. Man was his creature and faithfully obeyed his orders. Access to the afterlife was strictly regulated. It could not be obtained fraudulently, but could be achieved only by following the arid way of virtue, through the abandonment of all personal will. Finally, the faithful must respect the rules of kinship instituted by the Church. Just as in the world of the physical sciences matter presupposes antimatter, so in the twelfth century world the Christian order postulated the disorder of the Jews.

---

150. *AJ*, 5.2153ff.

151. Boureau, "L'inceste de Judas," pp. 32ff.

Given his commitment to a Church system designed to take account of Christian society's constitutive parts, modes of functioning, and ultimate purpose, Peter the Venerable ran up against real difficulties with the Jews. The question confronting Peter, like all the apprentice sociologists of his time, has been extremely well formulated by Richard W. Southern and Gilbert Dahan. What place was to be assigned to the Jewish "outsiders," who were "in society but outside the Church" in a period when it was impossible "to give a secular definition of society"?[152] In a world where Church and society merged, could the development of the Jews be anywhere but on the margins?

How to Dispose of This Alter Ego?

Peter the Venerable's anti-Jewish writings are exemplary because they reveal in magnified detail a twelfth-century Latin cleric's unease when faced with an impossible alter ego. Rejections like his were to play a large part in the elaboration of future Jewish identity. The stereotypes forged then still largely influence our mental images. It is worth taking a closer look at them before we end this chapter.

As a theoretician of Christian society, Peter would have come up against the embarrassing question of his common origins with the Jews. He shared with the Jews the scriptural authorities that anchored Christianity in "intellectual Semitism," as Jean-Pierre Weiss has usefully called it. Was there also a common racial overlap? In his *Antiquities of the Jews*, the Jewish historian Flavius Josephus (circa 37–circa 100) quotes the Greek geographer Strabo's description of the cities of Cyrenaica to the effect that "it is difficult to find a place where this people has not been accepted and become master."[153] Robert-Henri Bautier makes a connection between this statement and the success of Jewish proselytism in the Roman empire of late antiquity.[154] If correct, Peter the Venerable's Jewish neighbors would have been at least in part descendants of Gallo-Roman converts. In either a racial or a literary form, the notion of a shared heritage was evidently hard for the abbot of Cluny to bear. How could the Jews be like him and his coreligionists? His defense consisted in fixing his adversaries in time and space. The Jews had no other history than their biblical past. In contradistinction to Christian universality, the Jewish religion of exile had no future to offer new peoples. Peter denied both the existence and the efficacy of Jewish prose-

---

152. Dahan, *Les intellectuels chrétiens et les juifs*, p. 104; the term "outsiders" is used by Richard Southern, *Western Society and the Church in the Middle Ages* (Harmondsworth, 1970), p. 17, to which Dahan refers.

153. Josephus, *Antiquities of the Jews*, 14.7.2 (many editions).

154. Robert-Henri Bautier, "L'origine des populations juives de la France médiévale: constatations et hypothèses de recherche," in *La Catalogne et la France méridionale*, pp. 306–16.

lytism—although we know that in fact it did exist.[155] He pictured these wandering sons of Cain, exiled after the destruction of the Temple in Jerusalem, as outside time, indefinitely awaiting their eternal damnation. Their sovereign space was limited to the eternally lost kingdoms of David or Solomon. They were a people with no center, no direction, and no present. Hence Peter's vehement denial of any hint of a contemporary Jewish kingdom, be it at Narbonne or Rouen. How could serfs be kings? Treated thus, the question took another turn. If the Jews were so alien and different, how was their presence to be tolerated? In 1182, the "most Christian" king, Philip II Augustus, expelled the Jews for the first time from the kingdom of France, intending thereby to purify it. Less than forty years earlier, in 1146, Peter the Venerable was writing to Louis VII to denounce the Jews as Christendom's enemies within. For Peter, the reality was inescapable: it was impossible for disciples of Christ to live with the Jews and not be tainted by them. It was equally impossible to integrate them into the system of exchange, since they produced nothing of their own and lived as parasites, even when they did not act simply as receivers of Church goods.

What, then, was the way out of the Jewish problem? In his polemical works, Peter envisaged various solutions. While confessing that he sometimes found it difficult to stay the hands of his own people, he rejected the hypothesis of physical elimination. The Jews should remain, so as to witness to the murder of Christ. Two other solutions offered themselves: containment and exclusion. One form of containment was to force contemporary Jews to return to their origins, their biblical past, and confine themselves to it. The only exit from the confines of their history would be conversion to Christianity. Though skeptical, Peter had not totally given up hope on this front. In at least two passages of *Adversus Iudeos*, he dares to imagine his arguments convincing some of his opponents. Conversions of Jews had happened in the past. The other form of containment was the heavy-handed one of treating the Jews as serfs. In this respect, the great lord abbot's polemical treatise did no more than confer doctrinal justification upon the factual reality. The Jews were serfs—"your" Jews, "our" Jews, the Jews "of others"—and a seigneurial possession. Faced with the protected subjects of the English king, the Jews of Rouen, Peter was bemused to the point of confusing their community's autonomy with sovereignty, their presbyter with the "king of the Jews." To a great ecclesiastical lord of the twelfth century, reduction to a servile condition already amounted to a form of distancing. The Jew was not "one of us." *Adversus Iudeos*, analyzed at length in this chapter, throws a very exact light on the intellectual mechanics of such a rejection. First and foremost was

155. Lucien Musset, "Un prêtre normand converti au judaïsme en 1102: Jean d'Oppido," *Bulletin de la Société des antiquaires de Normandie* 53 (1955–56): 363–66; Bernhard Blumenkranz, "La conversion au judaïsme d'André, archevêque de Bari," *Journal of Jewish Studies* 14 (1963): 33–36; Norman Golb, "Notes on the Conversions of European Christians to Judaism in the Eleventh Century," *Journal of Jewish Studies* 16 (1965): 69–74. I am grateful to Véronique Gazeau for the first two references.

the ascent out of "intellectual Semitism." Although the cradle of Christianity had been Jewish, the Jews had failed to recognize the expected Messiah; by their denial of Christ, they had missed the second half of history, the coming of Christianity and its unstoppable spread throughout the world. Their literalism made them incapable of all symbolic understanding of divine teaching. Bound to the earth and mired in fleshly defilements, they had lost the way to humanity's destined bliss. Worse, the text of Jewish exile, the Talmud, challenged the ancient truths of the Bible. Forced to respect the Hebraic truth of the Old Testament, Peter the Venerable gave recognition to the Hebrew past but demonized the Jewish present. He radically distinguished between the two "textual communities," the biblical and the Talmudic, which to him were as different from each other as heaven and earth. As long as they had remained within the confines of the Old Testament, the Jews were still men. But when they adopted the Talmud, they became beasts that had lost all access to original truth.[156] Their own prophets became exclusively "Christian" prophets and inimical to them. The Jews' acceptance of the Talmud was fraught with bias and traps: it took them away from their own history and consigned them to bestiality; it was the theological mark of an actual reduction of status, to that of servility. It was, in sum, a fine example of a development with both an epistemological and a sociological dimension.

The radical separation of the two textual communities (Christian and Jewish) was expounded in the Christological part of *Adversus Iudeos* in terms of reversed destinies. Christ came to work a double transmutation. His kingly character comprised distinctive oppositions between humanity and divinity, humility and greatness, poverty and royalty, penury and abundance. By his human sacrifice, the long-awaited Messiah opened the way from one term of these opposites to the other. He was a figure of transition from an earthly kingdom to a heavenly one. The Jews had not simply missed out on the transition provided by Christ. For having despised, calumniated, and killed him, theirs was a reversal of fortunes. The sighted became blind (John 9:39). The chosen people became henceforth the humiliated people. The head became the tail. The Jews' reversal of destiny lay behind Peter's perplexity when, in writing to Louis VII, he attempted to assess their economic activity within a Christian society. We saw earlier how his understanding of the economy of Christianity (in every sense) was rooted in the mystery of the Redemption. The purpose of earthly property and of the men who used that property was their conversion and transformation "into something better," the paradigm of conversion and commutation being accomplished in the eucharistic sacrifice. Being doubly removed from the great transforma-

156. For perspective on this problem in the context of the twelfth-century renaissance, see Anna Sapir Abulafia, *Christians and Jews in the Twelfth-Century Renaissance* (London and New York, 1995), esp. pp. 127ff. For the term "textual community" and its ramifications, see Brian Stock, *The Implications of Literacy: Written Language and Models of Interpretation in the Eleventh and Twelfth Centuries* (Princeton, 1983).

PART III. CHRISTIAN UNIVERSALITY

tion at Christianity's heart, the Jews had no place in cycles of exchange other than as serfs, being themselves reduced to the status of chattels. What else indeed could be open to them in an economy rooted in eschatology?[157]

From Anti-Judaism to Anti-Semitism?

In considering the long-term history of western stereotypes and ways of conceiving otherness, it is useful to take one last look at the problem of Jewish "humanity." By asking apparently rhetorically whether the Jews were really human, Peter the Venerable unwittingly laid one of the essential stones in the road that led from anti-Judaism to anti-Semitism. Concerned to clarify terms that are currently used indiscriminately and to emphasize the radical novelty of the rejection of the Jews in the modern world, Hannah Arendt has suggested that a careful distinction be made between "antisemitism, a secular nineteenth-century ideology," and anti-Judaism, whose origins were religious, "inspired by the mutually hostile antagonism of two conflicting creeds."[158] Some historians, by contrast, look much further back for the transition from anti-Judaism to anti-Semitism. Gavin I. Langmuir dates it from when the Jews became an "institutionalized minority": the twelfth and thirteenth centuries. In his examination of the famous question of *limpieza de sangre* (purity of blood) posed by forced conversions in Spain at the end of the Middle Ages, Yosef H. Yerushalmi casts doubt on the notion that racial anti-Semitism was unknown in the Middle Ages and that it was a specifically modern, secular phenomenon.[159] Is it possible to say more on the basis of twelfth-century documentation, beginning with Peter the Venerable's *Adversus Iudeos*?

A contemporary of the abbot of Cluny, the Spanish Jew Judah Halevi (1075–1141), formulated the notion of natural difference, an idea with a future before it.[160] In his *Kuzari*, an imaginary dialogue between a rabbi and the king of the

---

157. See the judicious remarks of Brigitte M. Bedos-Rezak, "Les juifs et l'écrit dans la mentalité eschatologique du Moyen Age chrétien occidental (France 1000–1200)," *AHSS* 1994/95: 1049–63, here 1052.

158. Hannah Arendt, *The Origins of Totalitarianism* (London, 1986), p. xi. The literature on this question is huge, but see Yves Chevalier, *L'antisémitisme: le Juif comme bouc émissaire* (Paris, 1988), whose ample bibliography includes Léon Poliakov's classic *Histoire de l'antisémitism*, 3 vols. (Paris, 1955–68) [Eng. trans., *The History of Antisemitism*, trans. Miriam Kochan, Littman Library of Jewish Civilization (London, 1974–75)].

159. Gavin I. Langmuir, "Anti-judaism as the Necessary Preparation for Antisemitism," *Viator* 2 (1971): 383–89, here 387; reprinted in his *Toward a Definition of Antisemitism*, pp. 57–62. Yosef H. Yerushalmi, *Assimilation and Racial Antisemitism: The Iberian and the German Models*, Leo Baeck Memorial Lecture 26 (New York, 1982); I am indebted to Anne Levallois for bringing this lecture to my attention. The question was reexamined in Benzion Netanyahu's somewhat diffuse survey, *The Origins of the Inquisition in Fifteenth-Century Spain* (London, 1995).

160. Judah Hallévi, *Le Kuzari: apologie de la religion méprisée*, trans., introduction, and notes by Charles Touati (Leuven, 1994), esp. pp. 11, 13, 33, and 39.

Khazars, converts to Judaism in the eighth century, he considered the natural order, in which it was possible to differentiate between minerals, plants, animals, and men within Creation. Within mankind, he singled out an elite of "eminent wise men," a community descended from the twelve sons of Jacob, representing the core of humanity, occupying the central point of the earth, Palestine, a land distinguished by the presence of the divine. These elect persons, who made their first appearance as isolated individuals, were issue of the purified sperm of Adam, a noble seed inhabited by God, which made them a different species. Though his ideas were far from unanimously shared by his coreligionists, Judah Halevi thought that conversion to Judaism was possible, even desirable, but that no convert, such as the king of the Khazars, could ever equal a Jew by birth. The difference between the two—and hence the difference between a Jew and a Christian—was species-linked. It was impossible to escape the divisions fixed by nature. Prior to its reception of Aristotelian anthropology, the Latin west was a long way from clear-cut formulations of otherness in terms of natural differences. When Peter the Venerable wondered whether the Jews were really human beings, he was stating a simple problem of classification in an effort to discover the created order. Positioned between angels and beasts, men were characterized by their possession of reason and obedience to instituted authorities. Uncovering the Talmud and its "bestial" legends led Peter to exclude the Jews from humanity thus defined. His attitude was not widely shared at the time. More conciliatory spirits, like his friend Abelard, continued to regard the Jews as men.[161] Nonetheless, an enduring insinuation had been made. The worm was in the fruit, however long it might take to gnaw its way out.

A politico-religious dispute of Peter's own times revealed the racist turn that anti-Jewish polemic began to take in the first half of the twelfth century. This was the schism of Anacletus II.[162] Assembling in Rome on 14 February 1130 to choose a successor to Pope Honorius II, the College of Cardinals could not agree. They were divided between Gregory of Papareschi, who ultimately triumphed as Pope Innocent II, not least because of the support of the Cluniacs,

161. Peter Abelard, *Dialogus;* see Aryeh Graboïs, "Un chapitre de tolérance intellectuelle dans la société occidentale: le 'Dialogus' de Pierre Abélard et le 'Kusari' d'Yehudah Halévi," in *Pierre Abélard, Pierre le Vénérable: les courants philosophiques, littéraires et artistiques en Occident au milieu du XIIe siècle,* Actes et mémoires du colloque international, Abbaye de Cluny, 2–9 July 1972, ed. Jean Châtillon, Jean Jolivet, and René Louis, Colloques internationaux du CNRS, 546 (Paris, 1975), pp. 641–54.

162. Aryeh Graboïs, "Le schisme de 1130 et la France," *RHE* 76 (1981): 593–612; reprinted in his *Civilisation et société dans l'Occident médiéval,* no. 2. Graboïs, "From Theological to Racial Antisemitism: The Controversy of the Jewish Pope in the Twelfth Century," *Zion* 47 (1982): 1–16 (in Hebrew, inaccessible to me). Mary Stroll, *The Jewish Pope: Ideology and Politics in the Papal Schism of 1130,* Brill's Studies in Intellectual History, 8 (Leiden, 1987), esp. pp. 156ff. For a synthesis of the question and fuller bibliography, see Ian S. Robinson, *The Papacy 1073–1198: Continuity and Innovation* (Cambridge, 1990), pp. 69ff.

and Peter Pierleone, who lasted as Antipope Anacletus II until 1138. Peter speaks of this schism in *De miraculis*, right in the middle of his biographical sketch of Matthew of Albano and straight after his depiction of the former prior of Saint-Martin-des-Champs denouncing the taint of Jewish moneylenders.[163] The placing of Peter's comments was no chance matter. Anacletus II came from a great Roman family, the Pierleoni, founded by a Jewish convert to Christianity (the antipope's great-grandfather) under Pope Leo IX (1049–54).[164] Although his rise via Cluny to the office of cardinal in 1113 was rapid and brilliant, he never managed to rid himself of the original stain. At the height of the struggle between Innocent II and Anacletus II, Innocent's partisans did not hesitate to denounce the "Jewish" pope, protesting that conversion and baptism could never remedy the racial defect. The most extreme, such as Arnoul of Lisieux, described him as becoming as mindless as a dog through sexual vileness and plunging into incest with his own sister.[165] A historian close to Cluny, Orderic Vitalis, went so far as to denigrate the physique of the Jewish Pierleone family as exemplified by one of the future Anacletus's brothers. In book 12 of his *Historia ecclesiastica*, he speaks of the Council of Reims in 1119, where the envoy of the archbishop of Cologne "pointed out with his finger a dark-haired youth, more like a Jew or a Saracen than a Christian, dressed in splendid garments, but physically deformed." Orderic describes how the Franks, "at the sight of him seated beside the Pope . . . laughed scornfully and called down shame . . . out of hatred for his father whom they knew as an infamous usurer."[166]

Less than two centuries later, the Jew would be portrayed in Christian art as a definite physical type, with a hooked nose and thick lips. Before being applied exclusively to representations of Jews, these features were sometimes used in the Middle Ages to represent a variety of embodiments of otherness or exclusion—pagans, infidels, and heretics.[167] In the early 1300s, one of the many school questions whose purpose was to examine the pros and cons of a problem (*quodlibetum*) asked whether there was a natural difference between Christians and Jews, similar to that between men and women.[168] The question hinged on whether Jewish men were subject to periodic bleeding like the menstrual flows of women. The answer given was affirmative. Being under the sign of Saturn, Jews were of

163. *DM*, 2.15–16.

164. On this great Roman family, see Pierre Toubert, *Les structures du Latium médiéval: le Latium et la Sabine du IXe à la fin du XIIe siècle*, Bibliothèque des Ecoles françaises d'Athènes et de Rome, 221 (Rome, 1973), pp. 15, 675–76, 1049, and 1069.

165. *Tractatus de schismate orto post Honorii II papae decessum*, PL 201:173–94, here 182A.

166. Orderic Vitalis, *Historia ecclesiastica*, 12.21, ed. and Eng. trans. by Marjorie Chibnall, 6 vols., Oxford Medieval Texts (Oxford, 1969–80), 6:266–69.

167. Bernhard Blumenkranz, *Le juif médiéval au miroir de l'art chrétien* (Paris, 1966), esp. p. 32; Ruth Mellinkoff, *Outcasts: Signs of Otherness in Northern European Art of the Late Middle Ages*, California Studies in the History of Art, 32 (Berkeley and Oxford, 1993), esp. 1:127–30.

168. Dahan, *Les intellectuels chrétiens et les juifs*, pp. 528–29.

melancholic temperament. The corollary was that all women were, at least periodically, somewhat Jewish.[169] Having been first cast out among the beasts and subsequently differentiated by nature, the Jew was increasingly viewed by medieval intellectuals as an out-and-out Other, with its own peculiar species. These medieval considerations were still a long way from the anthropological taxonomy of the Age of Enlightenment or the systematization of racial theory in the nineteenth century.[170] They were no more than the prelude to a long history whose tragic developments are well known, not simply in the realm of ideas but in practice, where Jews would face both exclusion and elimination.

169. On the development of the equivalence Jews–women in traditional European societies, see Claudine Fabre-Vassas, *La bête singulière: les juifs, les chrétiens et le cochon*, Bibliothèque des Sciences humaines (Paris, 1993), pp. 140 and 228. Eng. trans., *The Singular Beast: Jews, Christians, and the Pig*, trans. Carol Volk (New York, 1997).

170. Guidance on the subject is to be had from Michel Wieviorka, *L'espace du racisme* (Paris, 1991), pp. 26ff., and from the number of *Mots. Les langages du politique* 33 (1992), ed. Simone Bonnafous, Bernhard Herszberg, and Jean-Jacques Israël, devoted to the term "race" under the head "Sans distinction de . . . race." I am grateful to Anne Levallois for these two references.

ISLAM AND THE ANTICHRIST

In tracing the course of Peter the Venerable's polemic against the Jews, we have seen his attention slip on several occasions from one group of infidels to another, from the Jews to the Saracens. His asides against the Saracens indicate a perception that the enemies of Christ needed to be dealt with as a whole. In *Adversus Iudeos*, Peter blamed the deceitful fables of the Jews for inspiring the false teaching of Muhammad, depicted Ibn Tumart, the Almohad Mahdi, as a prophet recognized by Jews, and worried about the power of Muslim proselytism, which either subjected men by force of arms or seduced them with a permissive attitude to sex.[1] Several years after finishing *Adversus Iudeos*, Peter turned directly to the problem of the Saracens. In a group of writings that included an important treatise entitled *Contra sectam Sarracenorum*, he attacked the falseness of Muhammad and attempted to erect a dam of words against the surge of Islam. In so doing he completed his denunciation of the Church's enemies—the heretics, the Jews, the Saracens—and in his own radical way helped to forge the intolerant society that emerged during the time of the first two Crusades.

CLUNY AND THE HISTORY OF THE CRUSADES

Like the history of the Gregorian reform, the history of the Crusades was long subject to "Panclunism."[2] This took two forms. First was that represented by the French theses advanced by Anouar Hatem, Ferdinand Chalandon,

---

1. See *AJ*, 5.2087–88, 3.96–108, 4.1541ff.

2. The term belongs to Etienne Delaruelle, "L'idée de croisade dans la littérature clunisienne du XIe siècle et l'abbaye de Moissac," *Annales du Midi* 75 (1963): 419 (for reprint, see bibliography), whose historiographical panorama (pp. 419–21) may be supplemented by reference to Maria Teresa Brolis, "La crociata per Pietro il Venerabile: guerra di arma o guerra di idee?" *Aevum* 61 (1987): 327–33; Ambrogio M. Piazzoni, "*Militia Christi* e Cluniacensi," in "*Militia Christi*" *e Crociata nei secoli XI–XIII*, Atti della undecima Settimana internazionale di studio, Mendola, 28 August–10 September 1989, Publicazioni dell'Università Cattolica del S. Cuore, Miscellanea del Centro di studi medievali, 13 (Milan, 1992), pp. 241–69.

and Pierre Boissonnade. They viewed Cluny as directly involved in the first crusading movements, in Spain and then in the east.[3] Such views, however, long ago became obsolete. Second was the altogether more subtle conception of Carl Erdmann, who pointed to Cluny as indirectly influencing the notion of a holy war, its precursor being the movement of the Peace of God, in which Cluny possibly played a leading role. More generally, Erdmann's view stressed the reform of the Church in the eleventh century and the domination of the laity, particularly those with hands on the levers of military power, by a largely "monkish" clergy.[4]

Today, it seems a mighty exaggeration to ascribe even an indirect role to Cluny in either the ideological prehistory of the Crusades or the practical prosecution of the first two of them. All the same, the arguments used do need to be aired here and can be summarized as follows. First, in his *Vita sancti Geraldi* (Life of Saint Gerald), Odo provided the early decades of the tenth century with a prototype *miles christianus* (Christian knight). The capture of Abbot Majolus by the Saracens of La Garde-Freinet in 972 and the ensuing war to "liberate" Provence were a sort of "pre-Crusade." Then, under abbot Odilo, Cluny was active in the movements of the Peace and Truce of God, which aimed to control the violence of men of arms and redirect it toward the margins of Christendom, against the infidels. Urban II, the pope who launched the First Crusade, was a former Cluniac. Lastly, the Ecclesia cluniacensis had a strong presence in Spain, notably contributing to the ecclesiastical élites in the kingdoms that emerged from the Reconquista. In this first theater of operations against the Saracens, the Cluniacs were preachers of the holy war, bringing about what Jean Flori has described as "the fusion of pilgrimage and meritorious warfare."[5] The current tendency, represented by Herbert E. J. Cowdrey, Jean Flori, and Marcus Bull, is to relativize Cluny's role and view it as a part of the religious communities' general contribution toward creating a lay ideal of penitence.[6] Given Peter the Venerable's very active role in the war of ideas against Islam, let us now briefly retrace the historical record in order to understand better the sources of his ideas.

3. Anouar Hatem, *Les poèmes épiques des croisades, genèse, historicité, localisation: essai sur l'activité littéraire dans les colonies franques de Syrie au Moyen Age* (Paris, 1932). Ferdinand Chalandon, *Histoire de la première croisade* (Paris, 1925). Pierre Boissonnade, "Cluny, la papauté et la première croisade internationale contre les Sarrasins d'Espagne, Barbastro (1064–1065)," *Revue des questions historiques* 97 (1932): 257–301.

4. Carl Erdmann, *Die Entstehung des Kreuzzugsgedankens,* 2d ed. (Darmstadt, 1980); for Eng. trans. (1977), see bibliography.

5. Jean Flori, "Du nouveau sur les origines de la première croisade," *Le Moyen Age* 101 (1995): 108.

6. Herbert E. J. Cowdrey, "Cluny and the First Crusade," *RB* 83 (1973): 285–311; for reprint, see bibliography. Marcus Bull, *Knightly Piety and the Lay Response to the First Crusade: The Limousin and Gascony, c. 970–c. 1130* (Oxford, 1993).

Did Cluny Contribute to the Ideological Prehistory of the Crusades?

The reality is that there is no reason to see Gerald of Aurillac as a prototype *miles christianus*. In the *Vita sancti Geraldi*, Odo was pursuing a similar agenda to that of the Carolingian "Mirrors of Princes": he was enunciating rules of behavior that bearers of arms should follow in service of the Church.[7] His was a new hagiographic model whose purpose was to instruct the order of fighting men how to sanctify themselves within the lay world. But Odo's teaching was still a long way from the "new way of meriting salvation" that Guibert of Nogent would declare to men of arms becoming crusaders at the end of the eleventh century.[8] Odo was doing no more than dealing with a subject of statutory morality within a Christian society divided into functional *ordines* (orders)—which respectively prayed or fought or produced—that they might together win paradise.

From around the year 1000, the Cluniacs developed a strong theology of the Cross. In a context of devoted service to the Cross from both the clerical and the military orders, Odilo and his disciples were drawn toward the notion of "holy war."[9] Majolus was famously captured by the Saracens of La Garde-Freinet in 972. Many Cluniac texts refer to this episode, not least the various biographies of the holy abbot. In the second *Vita sancti Maioli* (Life of Saint Majolus), Syrus develops the theme of Majolus's "martyrdom" in a surprising way. He precedes the holy abbot's own story with the martyrdom (date unknown) of Porcarius and the five hundred monks of Lérins. The abbot of Lérins walked to his death, bearing aloft the "standard of the Cross," here explicitly assimilated to the willing sacrifice of the monk. Majolus's sacrifice prefigures Porcarius's martyrdom, but it also brings reparation for it: Syrus describes at length how God wrought vengeance by the sword of the Christian warriors.[10] A few years later, Odilo too, in his own *Vita sancti Maioli*, took up the theme of holy war.[11] As an appendix to

7. For description of the manuscript and textual tradition, with useful references to the huge bibliography, see Anne-Marie Bultot-Verleysen, "Le dossier de saint Géraud d'Aurillac," *Francia* 22.1 (1995): 173–206. The text is contextualized within the long evolution of chivalric ideology by Jean Flori, *L'idéologie du glaive: préhistoire de la chevalerie* (Geneva, 1983), pp. 108ff.

8. Guibert de Nogent, *Gesta Dei per Francos, RHC, hist. occ.*, 4, p. 124.

9. For further detail, see my "La Croix, le moine et l'empereur: dévotion à la Croix et théologie politique à Cluny autour de l'an Mil," in *Haut Moyen Age: culture, éducation et société: études offertes à Pierre Riché*, ed. Michel Sot (Paris, 1990), pp. 449–75, on which the discussion following is based— I was no doubt wrong to make use there of the notions of *précroisade* and *esprit de croisade*. More generally, Cluny's devotion to the Cross is dealt with in Robert G. Heath, *"Crux imperator philosophia": Imperial Horizons of Cluniac "Confraternitas," 964–1109* (Pittsburgh, 1976).

10. Syrus, *Vita sancti Maioli*, 1.1 and 3.8–9, in my *"Agni immaculati": recherches sur les sources hagiographiques relatives à saint Maieul de Cluny (954–994)* (Paris, 1988), pp. 178–82 and 257–60; French trans. in Dominique Iogna-Prat et al., *Saint Maïeul, Cluny et la Provence*, Les Alpes de lumières, 115 (Salagon, 1994), p. 36.

11. Latin text printed in *BC*, cols. 279–90, and *PL* 142:943–62; French trans. in *Saint Maïeul, Cluny et la Provence*, pp. 37–38.

his spiritual eulogy of Majolus, Odilo supplies a short *exemplum* with an obvious moral. Early-tenth-century Provence was plagued with wolves; Fulcher of Valensole, Saint Majolus's father, got rid of them. Odilo highlights a number of instructive correspondences. The father, Fulcher, prefigured the son, Majolus, and the wolves a still more fearsome plague, the Saracens. Majolus, having been captured and then freed, was a new Christ, and the Saracens were new Jews. The saint's capture brought ruin on the Saracens, just as the death of Christ had signified the Jews' ruin. The Saracens were dealt with by the sword of Count William II, "the Liberator," just as the emperors Titus and Vespasian had dealt with the Jews.

The story of "Saint Majolus's War," fought on behalf of the Cross, found expression in stone in Provence. In an act drawn up between 1031 and 1048, Ledger, monk of Cluny and the son of Letgar, a powerful lord in the southern Alps, made a donation for the building of a church in the *villa* of Sarrians.[12] The preamble states that Sarrians had previously been donated to Cluny *ad sepulturam* (as a burial donation) by William the Liberator, who is described in the Roman manner, with imperial grandeur, as the *pater patriae* or "father of the fatherland." The enduring memory of the reconquest of Provence by troops led by the "most Christian prince," William, very likely explains why the dedication of Letgar's church gave prominence to the "memory of the Lord's most victorious Cross." The building remains a good example of early Provençal Romanesque art. Even today it bears testimony to the ideal of serving the Cross that informed the aristocratic "reconstructors" of Provence in their devotion to the monasteries around the turn of the first millennium.[13] The same theme appears in Odilo's epitaph in honor of Emperor Otto the Great, who labored "to make conspicuous the triumph of the Cross."[14] Writing shortly after Odilo, Rodulfus Glaber linked the symbolism of the Cross with the name of another emperor, Henry II. Speaking of Henry's coronation in Rome by Pope Benedict VIII in February 1014, Glaber focuses on the symbolism of the insignia given to the emperor by the pope. Benedict had ordered an orb "to be made in the form of a golden apple set around in a square with all the most precious jewels and surmounted by a golden cross." Glaber explains that the orb was an "allegorical form" (*species intellectualis*) and that "the different stones set in it as decoration indicated that the head of the empire ought to be decorated with many virtues." The emperor should "never forget, whether in war or government, that he ought to conduct himself here only in a manner worthy of the protection of the standard of the life-giving cross." Henry took the words of the consecrating pope to heart. At his coronation, says Glaber, he praised the pope for indicating "to our

12. *CLU* 2866, 4.63–64, extant in the original.

13. Guy Barruol, *Un témoin du premier art roman méridional: le prieuré clunisien de Sarrians*, in *Hommage à André Dupont: études médiévales et languedociennes* (Montpellier, 1974), pp. 13–24.

14. *Epitaphium Ottonis*, in *MGH Pl*, vol. 5 (Die Ottenzeit), part 2, ed. Karl Strecker (1939), esp. ll. 15–16.

monarchy by a symbol how it should be exercised." So impressed was the emperor by the lesson contained in the orb that he immediately donated it to the monks of Cluny, because they "trample underfoot the pomps of this world and blithely follow the cross of Our Saviour."[15] From that time on, the processions connected with the major feasts in Cluny's calendar (the Nativity, the Purification of Mary, Palm Sunday, the Ascension, and the Assumption) included display of the "imperial apple," so as to celebrate the royal status of Christ and the Virgin.[16]

Cluny's devotion to the Cross thus nurtured a political theology that made the emperors guarantors of the Church's peace. This conception, however, did not stand up to events. After Odilo's death, Christendom was riven between the papacy and the empire. More precisely, even during Abbot Odilo's own lifetime, the Church's peace was far from complete in Burgundy and southern Gallia. There, the waning power of the king meant that the higher clergy had to look to their own spiritual arms to defend themselves against the unruly aristocrats whose lives coincided with the establishment of the seigneurial "order." We need not go into Cluny's (often exaggerated) contribution to the movements of the Peace and the Truce of God, for the role of these assemblies in the genesis of the Crusades is far from clear.[17] Although Urban II declared a general Peace in Christendom prior to the First Crusade, we may well ask how the Peace and Truce of God, proclaimed to control seigneurial violence and take it out of certain spaces and times of the Christian calendar, could prepare men of arms for a "new way of meriting salvation." A "good" layman bearing arms is not even

15. Rodulfus Glaber, *Historiarum libri quinque*, 1.5.23, ed. with parallel Eng. trans. by John France et al., Oxford Medieval Texts (Oxford, 1989), pp. 38–41.

16. *LT* 13.4, p. 23 (Nativity); 31.2, p. 42 (Purification); 54.2, p. 68 (Palm Sunday); 72, p. 108 (Ascension); 100.3, p. 151 (Assumption).

17. See the general treatment by Hartmut Hoffmann, *Gottesfriede und Treuga Dei*, Schriften der *MGH*, 20 (Stuttgart, 1964), whose theses have been refined, extended, or corrected by numerous subsequent studies. Guidance on the extensive bibliography and an overview of recent interpretations are provided by Jean-Pierre Poly and Eric Bournazel, *La mutation féodale Xe–XIIe siècle*, Nouvelle Clio series, 2d ed. (Paris, 1991), pp. 235–51, although they probably overstate the role of Cluny's abbots and the influence of the network of Cluniacs deeply implanted in the episcopal hierarchy after the 1040s. Two studies by Hans-Werner Goetz need also to be considered: "Kirchenschutz, Rechtswahrung und Reform: zu den Zielen und zum Wesen der frühen Gottesfriedensbewegung in Frankreich," *Francia* 11 (1983): 194–239, abridged in "Protection of the Church, Defense of the Law, and Reform: On the Purposes and Character of the Peace of God, 989–1038," in *The Peace of God: Social Violence and Religious Response in France around the Year 1000*, ed. Thomas Head and Richard Landes (Ithaca, 1992), pp. 259–79; "La Paix de Dieu en France autour de l'an Mil: fondements et objectifs, diffusion et participants," in *Le Roi de France et son royaume autour de l'an Mil*, Actes du colloque, Hugues Capet 987–1987: la France de l'an Mil, Paris-Senlis 22–25 June 1987, ed. Michel Parisse and Xavier Barral i Altet (Paris, 1992), pp. 131–45. New documentation on Odilo has surfaced; see Roger Reynolds, "Odilo and the *Treuga Dei* in Southern Italy: A Beneventan Manuscript Fragment," *Medieval Studies* 41 (1984): 450–62; reprinted in *Law and Liturgy in the Latin Church, 5th–12th Centuries* (London, 1994).

potentially a Crusader. At the very most, the prescriptions of the Peace and Truce encouraged fixing names to social groups, such as *caballarii* (horsemen), *milites* (soldiers), *vilani* (villeins), *clerici* (clerics), and so on, defining statutory morality for each function, and calling to mind the social order's divine origin and purpose. Such a program of action in the world was of itself deeply Cluniac. Yet it had to do only with Christian society's internal functioning. There was nothing to suggest that men of arms loyal to the order of Christian society would move against the Church's external enemies, or indeed that a "new militia," as Saint Bernard called the Templars, would be set up at the Holy Places.

The Reconquista was not a Crusade—it would be an inappropriate term to use about that period in any event.[18] The various expeditions undertaken in Spain during the eleventh century were not encouraged by the Church as meritorious wars conferring indulgence upon men of arms engaged in the struggle against "infidels."[19] Nonetheless, whatever we may think of the contribution of the Spanish front to the genesis of the idea of Crusade and Cluny's role in that genesis, it is undeniable that Spain gave the brethren of the Ecclesia cluniacensis their first direct confrontation with Islam. From around the year 1000, Odilo was in contact with King Sancho III the Great of Navarre, who sent the monk Paternus of San Juan to Burgundy for training in the ways of Cluny. In a diploma of 1033 in favor of the monastery of Oña, the king made Cluny the source of the monastic genealogy that would thereafter give light to his "fatherland."[20] A little later, extremely close links were formed between Cluny and kings Ferdinand and Alfonso of Castile-León.[21] The annual *cens* or tribute of one thousand (and later two thousand) pieces of gold obtained from the infidels contributed greatly to the financing of Latin Christendom's "major church," the *maior ecclesia*, Cluny III. Years later, in *De miraculis*, Peter the Venerable recalled the "zeal" of Alfonso VI, who "obtained, after his temporal kingdom, a second, eternal one, as it is fitting to believe."[22] Hugh of Semur guaranteed Alfonso exceptional liturgical benefits both in his life and after death. Among other things, the monastery sang daily after terce Psalm 19(20), the *Exaudiat te Dominus* (May the Lord hear thee in the day of tribulation), an appeal to God "to give the king victory."[23] Hugh

18. The late emergence of the term "crusade" and historians' understanding of it are studied by Ernst Dieter Hehl, "Was ist eigentlich ein Kreuzzug?" *Historische Zeitschrift* 259 (1994): 297–336, esp. 298ff.

19. This view is expressed by Bull, *Knightly Piety and the Lay Response to the First Crusade*, p. 112, in distinct contrast with the traditional conceptions defended by Carl Erdmann, *Die Entstehung des Kreuzzugsgedankens*, pp. 267ff.

20. *CLU* 2891, 4.89–95.

21. Peter Segl, *Königtum und Klosterreform in Spanien: Untersuchungen über die Cluniacenserklöster in Kastilien-León vom Begin des 11. bis zur Mitte des 12. Jahrhunderts* (Kallmünz, 1974).

22. *DM*, 1.28, p. 92.

23. The statute on Alfonso VI's behalf is edited by Herbert E. J. Cowdrey, "Two Studies," pp. 159–60. On the Cluniacs' liturgical commitment to the kings of Castile-León, see Charles J.

of Semur was no less active on the pastoral front. Writing to the Cluniac Bernard of Sahagún, who had become archbishop of Toledo and primate of the Church in Spain, his advice was: "An irreproachable life and a demonstration of good works accompanied by scrupulous morals will prevail over all preaching in inspiring and converting the infidels."[24] According to his biographer, the hermit Anastasius was asked to go to Spain by Hugh of Semur and Pope Gregory VII in order to help with the business of conversion. In order to "demonstrate the sureness of the Christians' faith and eradicate the harsh cruelty of the Saracens," God's champion offered to "cross a blazing funeral pile after celebrating Masses." The Saracens, however, would not agree to the test, because, "if he crossed unhurt, they would resort to the grace of baptism."[25] Lastly, Cluniac circles were long considered to be the source of the anonymous letter by the so-called "monk of France," a conversion document of the 1080s addressed to King al-Muqtadir Billah of Zaragoza. The attribution is, however, pure conjecture. No less plausible is Abdel Magid Turki's suggestion that the letter was in fact written simply as a vehicle for al-Bayi's response.[26]

The First Crusade

Cluny's contribution to the First Crusade was extremely modest. It is true that Urban II was a professed Cluniac and that his 1095 tour of Gallia included many member houses of the Ecclesia cluniacensis.[27] But, as far as we know, Hugh of Semur and his Cluniac brethren did not work directly to launch the expedition.[28] The only known Cluniac appeal came from Moissac, where shortly after Urban II's departure a false encyclical attributed to Pope Sergius

---

Bishko, "Fernando I and the Origins of the Leonese-Castilian alliance with Cluny," no. 2 in *Spanish and Portuguese Monastic History, 600–1300* (London, 1984), and Bishko, "Liturgical Intercessions at Cluny for the King-Emperors of León," no. 8 in ibid.; Cowdrey, "Cluny and the First Crusade," pp. 297–300.

24. Text in "Two Studies," pp. 145–49, here 147.

25. Galterius, *Vita sancti Anastasii*, 5, *PL* 149:429A: cited by Mathieu Arnoux, "Un Vénitien au Mont-Saint-Michel: Anastase, moine, ermite et confesseur († vers 1085)," *Médiévales* 28 (1995): 65.

26. Abdel Magid Turki, "La lettre du 'moine de France' à al-Muqtadir Billah, roi de Saragosse, et la réponse d'al-Bayi, le faqih andalou," *Al-Andalus* 31 (1966): 73–83; rpt. in *Théologiens et juristes de l'Espagne musulmane*, Islam d'hier et d'aujourd'hui, 16 (Paris, 1982), pp. 233–43. More recently, Turki's conclusions have been confirmed by Maribel Fierro, "Su relación con otras religiones," in *Los reinos de Taifas: Al-Andalus en el siglo XI*, ed. Maria Jesùs Viguera Molíns (Madrid, 1994), pp. 471–79: I thank J. L. Senra Gabriel y Galán for drawing the latter to my attention.

27. Alfons Becker, *Papst Urban II. (1088–1099)*, vol. 1, Schriften der *MGH*, 19.1 (Stuttgart, 1964), pp. 213ff.; Cowdrey, "Cluny and the First Crusade," pp. 300–301. On Cluny and the First Crusade, see, lastly, Giles Constable's subtle assessment in *Le Concile de Clermont de 1095 et l'appel à la croisade*, Collection de l'Ecole française de Rome, 236 (Rome, 1997), pp. 179–93.

28. Already Carl Erdmann's analysis in *Die Entstehung des Kreuzzugsgedankens*, p. 304, n. 73.

IV (1009–12) was fabricated calling for extermination of the enemies of God, guilty for destroying the Holy Sepulchre.[29] At Cluny itself, the mood was one of acquiescence. A few, very rare, acts speak of laymen from the Mâconnais leaving for Jerusalem. Thus a charter dated 12 April 1096 recalls the "enormous excitement" of Achard of Montmerle as he left to "wage war for God against the pagans and Saracens."[30] Achard entered into a contract with Cluny whereby he pledged his goods against two thousand solidi in Lyon currency and two mules. One of the act's clauses stipulated that the property pledged would become permanently the monastery's if Achard died during the expedition, chose to remain in the Holy Land, or died without issue after returning. In June 1100, Stephen of Neublans confided to Hugh of Semur his intention to leave for Jerusalem and made a donation to the monastery. Receiving him in chapter, the abbot blessed him, made the sign of the cross on the pilgrim's shoulder, and put a ring on his finger. From then on, Stephen considered the Cluniacs his "brothers" and entrusted them to remember him.[31] Going on crusade thus entailed a definitive entry into the monastic fraternity, and the contract recording it might be regarded as a variant of the act of last will.

The success of the First Crusade and the creation of the Latin world's eastern states put Cluny in direct touch with the Holy Land. Hugh of Semur's biographer Gilo, who wrote during the abbacy of Pontius of Melgueil, was promoted to cardinal bishop of Tusculum and subsequently sent as a papal legate to the eastern Latin states. He has left us his *History of the First Crusade*.[32] Two other contemporary texts tell of the translation to Cluny of a portion of the True Cross and of the relics of the protomartyr Stephen.[33] The first of these narratives recalls

29. Aleksander Gieysztor, "The Genesis of the Crusades: The Encyclical of Sergius IV (1009–12)," *Medievalia et Humanistica* 5 (1948): 3–23 and 6 (1950): 3–34 (text edited, 33–34); on this text, henceforth see *Papsturkunden 896–1046*, ed. Harald Zimmermann, Österreichische Akademie der Wissenschaften, Philosophisch-historische Klasse, Denkschriften, 174, 177, 198, 3 vols. (Vienna, 1984–89), vol. 2, no. 445, pp. 845–48. Axel Müssigbrod, *Die Abtei Moissac 1050–1150: zu einem Zentrum cluniacensischen Mönchtums in Südwestfrankreich*, Münstersche Mittelalter-Schriften, 58 (Munich, 1988), pp. 150–51, correctly notes that this false encyclical, viewed within the documentary record of Moissac as a whole, both narrative and diplomatic, is a unique piece.

30. *CLU* 3703, 5.51–53, original extant; another contemporary example is *CLU* 3712, 5.59. A general treatment of the contribution of lords from the Mâconnais to the Crusades is that of Georges Duby, *La société aux XIe et XIIe siècles dans la région mâconnaise*, 2d ed. (Paris, 1971), pp. 283–84.

31. *CLU* 3737, 5.87–91. Other contemporary or slightly later examples are *CLU* 3804, 5.152; *Le Cartulaire de Marcigny-sur-Loire (1045–1144): essai de reconstitution d'un manuscrit disparu*, ed. Jean Richard, *Analecta Burgundica*, 4 (Dijon, 1957), nos. 109, 161, 286, 306, pp. 79–80, 96, 164–65, 184–85. Research remains to be done on the charters of the Ecclesia cluniacensis's dependent establishments as a whole.

32. *Historia Gilonis cardinalis episcopi de via Hierosolymitana*, RHC, hist. occ., 5.2, pp. 721–800.

33. *Translatio tabulae sancti Basilii*, indexed *BHL* 4193, text BC, cols. 561–64, and RHC, hist. occ., 5.295–98. *Translatio reliquiarum sancti Stephani Cluniacum*, indexed *BHL* 7894, text BC, cols. 565–68, and RHC, hist. occ., 5.317–20. These texts are known from only two MSS: Paris, Bibliothèque

that Basil of Caesarea had obtained a relic of the True Cross for which he had commissioned a *tabula*, a reliquary in the form of a Gospel book. During the Turkish conquest of the eleventh century, the archdeacon Mesopotamius, nephew of the deceased archbishop of Caesarea, decided to transfer the holy relics to safety in Constantinople. There Mesopotamius became acquainted with Emperor Michael and married his niece. When Mesopotamius died, his widow inherited the relics. She then encountered Maurice, the archbishop of Braga, who was passing through Constantinople on his return from Jerusalem. Finding her there, living in great privation, Maurice persuaded her to part with the precious relic. Once back home, he placed the *Tabula sancti Basilii* in the Cluniac monastery of Carrión de los Condes and then had it transferred to Cluny itself. The second narrative covers the translation of the relics of the protomartyr Stephen. The aristocrat Hilduin (or Gelduin) of Le Puiset converted to Cluny and became prior of Lurcy-le-Bourg. With the consent of Abbot Pontius, he took two brethren with him to Jerusalem and became abbot of Our Lady at Jehosaphat, a Cluniac dependency. Accompanied by his cousin, King Baldwin II of Jerusalem, Hilduin journeyed to Antioch and then to Edessa, where the two men were received by Hugh, the archbishop. Hugh inquired after Cluny, to which he said he was linked by a confraternity of prayer formed during Hugh of Semur's abbacy. The archbishop maintained that Cluny had of old been consecrated to the apostles Peter and Paul as well as to "the blessed protomartyr Stephen." Fearing lest the city should fall into the hands of the Saracens, Archbishop Hugh decided after some hesitation to entrust the distinguished relics of Stephen to Hilduin of Le Puiset, with instructions to pass them on to Cluny, where they ended up in 1120. After his abdication in 1122, Pontius of Melgueil himself went to the Holy Land. While he was there, he visited the monastery of Mount Tabor. At first associated with Cluny by simple links of confraternity, the brethren at Mount Tabor regarded themselves as entirely Cluniac from the 1130s; this is clear from one of Peter the Venerable's letters.[34] In addition to Our Lady at Jehosaphat and Mount Tabor, the twelfth-century Ecclesia cluniacensis included three other establishments in the eastern Latin states. One was Civitot, near Constantinople, a priory of La Charité-sur-Loire.[35] After 1170 came also Akkon and Palmarea near Haifa.[36] Lastly in connection with Cluny's relationship with the Holy Land, we ought to mention the donation to Moissac-Cluny by Sergius

---

Nationale, latin 12603 (date: 1140–50); Paris, Bibliothèque Nationale, latin 17716, a liturgical-historical collection most probably composed by Abbot William II of Cluny at the beginning of the thirteenth century.

34. *Ep.*, 31, 1:80; see also *Ep.*, vol. 2, appendix 1, pp. 291–92.

35. Known only from a mention in a letter of Peter the Venerable to Emperor Alexis I, *Ep.*, 75, 1:208–9, here 209.

36. On these last two foundations, see Hans E. Mayer, *Bistümer, Klöster und Stifte im Königreich Jerusalem*, Schriften der *MGH*, 26 (Stuttgart, 1977), pp. 403–5.

of Jerusalem of the priory of the Saint-Sépulcre at La Salvetat-de-Lauragais in the diocese of Toulouse in return for the payment of an annual *cens* (tribute) to God, the Holy Sepulchre, and the Patriarch's envoys.[37]

PETER THE VENERABLE AND THE SARACENS

Peter the Venerable, whose birth in 1092 or 1094 virtually coincided with the First Crusade, remained faithful to the Cluniac position of reserve. He believed that the liberation and administration of the Holy Places was the business of the pope and the order of fighting men, not of monks. If indeed monks had a role to play, then it was a pastoral, "lecturing" one.[38] Among those who have studied Peter the Venerable, virtually only Virginia Berry sees Peter as an active and unfailing partisan of the Crusades; the overwhelming majority support the "pacific interpretation," namely, that he was simply participating in a debate of ideas.[39] Jean-Pierre Torrell's thesis that there were "two levels" to Peter the Venerable's approach is doubtless closer to the reality.[40] While on one level Peter's intervention took the shape of a refutatory debate in the style of early scholasticism, his desire on another was to wage a real ideological war and carry off the trophy. And if his adversaries could not be won over, then he would demonize them.

37. Text, transmitted by a late copy, edited and introduced by Müssigbrod, *Die Abtei Moissac*, pp. 233–35.

38. This attractive term (*voie de conférence*), now somewhat outdated, was used by Jacques Hourlier in discussion of Delaruelle, "L'idée de croisade dans la littérature clunisienne du XIe siècle," p. 440.

39. Virginia Berry, "Peter the Venerable and the Crusades," in *Petrus Venerabilis 1156–1956: Studies and Texts Commemorating the Eighth Centenary of His Death*, ed. Giles Constable and James Kritzeck, Studia Anselmiana, 40 (Rome, 1956), pp. 141–62. Brolis, referring to this as the "irenic hypothesis," gives a good overview of its proponents in "La crociata per Pietro il Venerabile," see n. 2 above. The irenicism that Peter has been boxed into has been deemed as valid for his writings against Islam as for his polemic against the Jews; clerical commentators on Peter have descended to astonishing levels of misreading, as, for example, Jean Leclercq, who, in *Témoins de la spiritualité occidentale* (Paris, 1965), p. 257, speaks of Peter's benevolence and scrupulousness toward the Muslims! More accurate assessments of Peter's writings within the general framework of Christian polemic against Islam are those of Norman Daniel, *Islam and the West: The Making of an Image*, rev. ed. (Oxford, 1993), and Benjamin Z. Kedar, *Crusade and Mission: European Approaches toward Muslims* (Princeton, 1984).

40. Jean-Pierre Torrell, "La notion de prophétie et la méthode apologétique dans le *Contra Sarracenos* de Pierre le Vénérable," *Studia monastica* 17 (1975): 278; for reprint, see bibliography. Jean-Pierre Torrell and Denise Bouthillier, *Pierre le Vénérable et sa vision du monde: sa vie, son oeuvre; l'homme et le démon*, Spicilegium Sacrum Lovaniense, Etudes et documents, 42 (Leuven, 1986), pp. 78ff., 180, and 185.

Reserve about the Crusades

Peter was absent from the gathering at Vézelay in 1146 that launched the Second Crusade. He was equally absent from the one at Chartres called in 1150 to instigate a third Crusade.[41] During this period Bernard of Clairvaux, at the request of the Cistercian pope Eugenius III, was throwing all his energies into mobilizing the Latin Church.[42] Peter stood back. Replying to Bernard's invitation to attend the Chartres gathering, Peter acknowledged that it was impossible to remain unmoved by the fall of the Holy Land into infidel hands again after the stinging defeat of the Second Crusade. Likening Christ's body, the Church, to a human body, Peter reflected on the necessary solidarity of the members with the suffering head:

> Just as in human flesh one spirit quickens all the members, so in the body of the Church one Holy Spirit gives life to all its members. He therefore who is insensitive to the wounds of the Body of Christ is not alive with the Spirit of Christ.[43]

As a member of Christ's body, Cluny contributed financially to the Second Crusade—even if Peter the Venerable did suggest to King Louis VII that he should rather make the Jews pay, as the murderers of Christ.[44] However, Cluny's contribution ended there. In contrast to Bernard of Clairvaux, who personally exhorted men of arms to march to Jerusalem and, above all, enlist in the Templars' "new chivalry," Peter remained true to the traditional logic of the *ordines* (orders). Writing to his brother Pontius, abbot of Vézelay, about a pilgrimage Pontius had made to the "tombs of the martyrs of Christ" (perhaps Rome), he recalled that it was proper "for a monk to live with monks, a cleric with clerics, a layman with laymen, and for them not to confuse their orders."[45] Each to his own. Laymen could go on pilgrimage or become crusaders. Indeed, Peter did not omit from his *De miraculis* the story of pilgrims who were exemplary for one reason or another. Bernard II Grossus d'Uxelles went to Rome for forty days; Armannus and Peter de la Roche each went to Jerusalem.[46] But the vocation of

41. Brolis, "La crociata per Pietro il Venerabile," gives an excellent presentation and analysis documenting Peter's reserve toward the Crusades; the following remarks owe much to that study.

42. André Seguin, "Bernard et la seconde Croisade," in *Bernard de Clairvaux*, Commission d'histoire de l'ordre de Cîteaux, 3 (Paris, 1953), pp. 379–409, and Pierre-Yves Emery's introduction to his edition of Bernard of Clairvaux, *De laude novae militiae*, SC, 367 (Paris, 1990), pp. 32ff.

43. *Ep.*, 164, 1:396–98, here 397.

44. *Ep.*, 130, 1:327–30, here 328.

45. *Ep.*, 16, 1:23–24, here 24. On Peter's opposition to monks' going on pilgrimage, see Giles Constable, "Opposition to Pilgrimage in the Middle Ages," in *Mélanges G. Fransen*, 1, *Studia Gratiana* 19 (1976): 137; for reprint, see bibliography.

46. *DM*, 1.11, p. 40 (Bernard II Grossus of Uxelles); 1.18, p. 55 (Armannus); 2.26, p. 147 (Peter de la Roche).

a monk or cleric was different. In a letter to Theobald, abbot of Sainte-Colombe at Sens, tempted to join the expedition of 1146, Peter reminded him that a monk who emulated men of arms ran the risk of vainglory and was acting "against his purpose and order."[47] In his *De laude novae militiae* (In Praise of the New Military), Bernard of Clairvaux extolled the alliance of the two swords. But Peter the Venerable urged him on the contrary to draw a sharp distinction between the "pastor's staff" (*virga pastoris*) belonging to the Church and the "king's sword" (*gladius regis*).[48] The direct use of armed force was not the office of clerics. Peter always held very firmly to this principle. During the schism of Pontius of Melgueil he refused to have recourse to arms. In the struggle that Cluny had in the 1150s with the lord of La Bussière, Hugh Deschaux, he resisted calls to use arms in self-defense, arguing that an armed monk was a monstrosity.[49] It is true that, by creating a bourgeois Cluniac militia some years earlier, in 1145, Peter had managed to square his principles with the need to afford the monastery realistic physical protection.[50] Awareness of the Church's need to defend itself also led him to warn his contemporaries against allowing huge numbers of men of arms to leave for the Holy Land, as the following example of Humbert III of Beaujeu and others show.

Humbert was a lord of the Mâconnais. Between 1148 and 1153, Peter the Venerable intervened on his behalf before Pope Eugenius III and Everard of Barre, the grand master of the Order of Templars.[51] In *De miraculis*, Peter describes how, by taking the road to Jerusalem, Humbert aimed to expiate, among other offenses, his culpable neglect of his father's memory (Guichard III), as well as that of one of his *fideles*, Geoffrey of Oingt, who gave his life in battle on Humbert's behalf "for an insufficiently just cause."[52] Having become a Templar monk-soldier, Humbert rather late in the day called to mind that he had matrimonial obligations and seigneurial interests. He determined to return to his former state. The Templars had at the outset been regarded as mere lay auxiliaries, a sort of third order of Augustinian canons regular. Now, in Humbert's day, they had very recently acquired the status of an actual order of religious knights.[53]

47. *Ep.*, 144, 1:353–60, here 359.·

48. *Ep.*, 192, 1:443–48, here 446.

49. *Ep.*, 191, 1:442–43 (to Pope Eugenius III), beginning *Aderant econverso longe plures*. On this conflict and its resolution, see Hoffmann, *Gottesfriede und Treuga Dei*, pp. 138ff. (referring to Hugh of "Lachaux").

50. *CLU* 4098 *bis*, 6.958–60, and Jean Leclercq, *Pierre le Vénérable*, Figures Monastiques (Saint-Wandrille, 1946), pp. 372–74. On this episode, see, lastly, Giles Constable, "The Abbot and Townsmen of Cluny in the Twelfth Century," in *Church and City, 1000–1500: Essays in Honour of Christopher Brooke*, ed. David Abulafia, Michael J. Franklin, and Miri Rubin (Cambridge, 1992), p. 161.

51. *Ep.*, 172, 1:407–9 (to Everard of Barre), and 173, 1:410–13 (to Eugenius III).

52. *DM*, 1.27, pp. 82–86.

53. The Order of the Temple was founded in 1118; its Rule dates from 1129; Bernard of Clairvaux wrote his *De laude novae militiae* between 1129 and 1136; Innocent III confirmed the order in 1139. On this period of the order's genesis, see Rudolf Hiestand, "Kardinalbischof Matthäus von Albano, das Konzil von Troyes und die Entstehung des Tempelordens," *Zeitschrift für Kirchengeschichte*

Peter the Venerable favored clear-cut walks of life and opposed intermediate situations like that, for example, of the canons regular. He was torn between a certain admiration for the "military of the eternal King, the army of the Lord of Sabaoth," which he grandly honored as "like the gleaming body of a new star," and the consequences of wrenching men of arms from their traditional policing role at home.[54] He thus pleads Humbert's cause in terms of the Church's own interests. Is it right, he asks, so to focus the energy of Christian society on the Holy Land that it leaves "our land . . . without king, duke, prince, or defender, exposed to the teeth of wild animals"—in other words, the whetted appetites of the castellans?[55] This remark is accompanied by reservations about the spiritual interests of laymen called to fight and defend the Holy Places. Why choose the good when one could opt for the better? Men of arms could become crusaders so long as they did not leave the "home front" undefended, and above all if crusading was not an alternative to becoming a monk. To the *miles* (knight) Hugh Catula, who went through Cluniac conversion only to want to go off to Jerusalem, perhaps at the time of the Second Crusade, Peter remarked, "It is all well and good to visit Jerusalem, where the feet of the Lord stood, but better by far to look longingly toward heaven, where he is gazed upon face to face."[56] In a letter to the Cluniacs of Mount Tabor, he maintained, "Salvation comes from holy deeds, not holy places," recalling Horace's dictum, "They change the sky above them, and not their inmost being, who rush across the sea."[57] Such sentiments contrast with those expressed by Bernard of Clairvaux, writing in his *De laude novae militiae:* "I think that . . . no little profit accrues to the one who beholds, even with his bodily eyes, the physical place where the Lord rested."[58] Ultimately, Peter appears to have been more strongly attracted to the Holy Land as a symbol than to the Holy Places as physical entities. Odilo's biographer, Jotsald, had similarly described the deaths of Majolus and Odilo in terms of their arrival in Jerusalem after crossing from Egypt.[59] Documents honoring the

---

99 (1988): 295–325, esp. 323; Marie Luise Bulst-Thiele, "Die Anfänge des Tempelordens. Bernard von Clairvaux. Cîteaux," *Zeitschrift für Kirchengeschichte* 104 (1993): 312–27.

54. *Ep.*, 172, 1:407, beginning *Feci hoc a primordio institutionis vestrae.* Is such homage enough to place Peter the Venerable, with Suger and Bernard of Clairvaux, among representatives of the "Temple lobby," as Alain Demurger has done? See his *Vie et mort de l'ordre du Temple*, Point Histoire, 123 (Paris, 1989), p. 126. Marie Luise Bulst-Thiele, *Sacrae domus militiae templi Hierosolymitani magistri: Untersuchungen zur Geschichte des Tempelordens, 1118/9–1314* (Göttingen, 1974), p. 51, describes Peter as, like Bernard, a "great extoller of the Order."

55. *Ep.*, 173, 1:410, beginning *Est enim misera illa terra nostra.*

56. *Ep.*, 51, 1:151–52, here p. 152. This episode seemed important enough to Cluniac tradition to be included in the abbey's *Chronicon* at the beginning of the sixteenth century, *BC*, col. 594A.

57. *Ep.*, 80, 1:214–17, here 216, citing Horace, *Epistulae*, 1.11.27: *Caelum non animum mutant qui trans mare currunt.*

58. Bernard of Clairvaux, *De laude novae militiae*, 11.29, *SC* 367, pp. 120–21.

59. Jotsald, *Vita sancti Odilonis*, 1.4 (death of Majolus) and 17 (death of Odilo), *PL* 142:900B and 914B.

building of Cluny III by Hugh of Semur evoke the "Easter" henceforth lived by the monks in "Galilee" with Christ.[60] Finally, in his own *Sermo in laude domini sepulchri*, Peter the Venerable internalized the religious significance of Jerusalem by assimilating Matthew's reference (Matthew 12:40) to Christ's burial in the "heart of the earth" to his indwelling in the "heart of man."[61]

The War of Ideas

For all his attachment to the symbolic Jerusalem of the contemplatives, the abbot of Cluny nonetheless contributed effectively by his writings to the struggle against the Saracens. In a letter to Bernard of Clairvaux, he urged Bernard to follow the example of the Fathers and in the name of the "charisma of edification and instruction" passed on by Augustine use the written word to confound the heretics, the Jews, and the pagans.[62] Peter prefaced his *Contra sectam Sarracenorum* with indignation about the Latins' ignorance. For ignorance of the opponent translated into inexpertise and the inability to defend oneself.[63]

The Two Ways: Insult or Debate?

But what form should the defense take? In the Latin west around 1100, the simplest, commonest, and doubtless most effective approach to the Saracens was the frontal attack, demonizing the opponent, bombarding him with insults and distortions. Hence the stereotypes that would for centuries bias western views of Islam as a religion for lechers and idolaters.[64] Yet in the twelfth century, after centuries of what has been described as "closed doors" and "total ignorance of the adversary," abundant information began to circulate in the zones where there was contact—in Spain, in Sicily, even in Palestine.[65] One of the earliest

---

60. Gilo, *Vita sancti Hugonis*, 2.1, "Two Studies," pp. 90–92, here 92; on the *Miracula sancti Hugonis*, see chapter 6 at n. 171 above.

61. *SLD*, pp. 238 and 243. Virginia Berry ("Peter the Venerable and the Crusades," pp. 152–3) hypothesizes, on the basis of pure conjecture, that this sermon was preached in Paris, while Pope Eugenius III was there, during the preparation of the Second Crusade.

62. *Ep.*, 111, 1:274–99, here 298, beginning *Propono inde vobis patres omnes*.

63. *CS*, 17, p. 54, ll. 9–12.

64. The best overview of the assembling and solidifying of these stereotypes during the twelfth century is to be found in Daniel, *Islam and the West*.

65. On this ignorance and the subsequent opening up to cultural exchanges, see Nikita Eliséef, "Les échanges culturels entre le monde musulman et les croisés à l'époque de Nur ad-Din b. Zanki (m. 1174)," in *The Meeting of Two Worlds: Cultural Exchange between East and West during the Period of the Crusades*, ed. Vladimir P. Goss, Studies in Medieval Culture, 21 (Kalamazoo, 1986), pp. 39–52; Henri Bresc, "Les chocs des reconquêtes et la Croisade," in Jean-Claude Garcin et al., *Etats, sociétés et culture du monde musulman médiéval Xe–XVe siècle*, vol. 1 (Paris, 1995), pp. 197ff. These use the quoted terms *huis clos* (Eliséef, p. 39) and *ignorance complète de l'adversaire* (Bresc, p. 197). Palestine played nothing like the same role as Spain in cultural exchanges; some historians—for instance, Claude Cahen, *Orient et Occident au temps des Croisades* (Paris, 1982), p. 211—even consider the eastern Latins to have been totally ignorant of Islam.

signs that western Latins were gaining knowledge of Islam comes from Cluniac circles in the first three decades or so of the eleventh century. Writing in his *Historiarum libri quinque* of the capture of Majolus by the Saracens of La Garde-Freinet, Rodulfus Glaber reports that one of the Saracen jailers inadvertently stepped on the abbot's traveling Bible. The abbot's groans were answered by indignation on the part of the "less ferocious" Saracens, who hastened to amputate the guilty foot. Glaber comments, by way of explanation, that the Saracens respected the Hebrew and Christian Scriptures as part of their own heritage. They believed, however, that the Old Testament prophecies were fulfilled not by Christ but by Muhammad.[66] Glaber was one of the first in the medieval west to put a name to the prophet of Islam and to mention the genealogy linking him to Abraham by ancestry through Ishmael.[67] Almost a century later, the passage of information had become louder and more diverse, yet essentially stereotypical. A mind as questioning and reflective as that of Guibert of Nogent could well appreciate that many of the stereotypes conveyed in the small change of Crusade writings and songs of brave deeds were pure propaganda—not least the imputation of idolatry, an absurdity in the case of a religion that was so openly monotheistic. Although he took care not to denounce the Muslims for polytheism or the worship of idols, he did not hesitate to repeat many of the common rumors that were current. Even if he knew such allegations to be false when looked at in detail, the effect created was to depict Islam as generally deviant and erroneous.[68] By now polemicists were making their points by false assimilation, forcing the "other" into preordained categories. The twelfth-century fantasy of the "other" simply insisted that he must start out or end up as idolatrous and lascivious.

Peter the Venerable was one of the tiny minority who chose another approach toward Islam, that of the lecturer. His aim was combat, but through debate, without recourse to the commonplace distortions with which the Saracens were usually taxed. The abbot of Cluny turned his back on the personalized attacks on Muhammad—as lascivious, adulterous, idolatrous, a false prophet and fake god—that his Muslim interlocutors considered blasphemous. He therefore denounced the legend that traced Muhammad back to Nicholas, one of the first seven deacons of the Church, whose sectaries maintained that fornication was

---

66. Rodulfus Glaber, *Historiarum libri quinque*, 1.4.9, pp. 20–21.

67. Richard W. Southern, *Western Views of Islam in the Middle Ages* (Cambridge, Mass., 1962), p. 28. The very earliest mention comes in Anastasius Bibliothecarius's ninth-century translation of Theophanus's *Chronographia tripartita*: I owe this information to François Bougard.

68. Guibert of Nogent, *Gesta Dei per Francos*, 1.4, *RHC, hist. occ.*, 4, pp. 127–30. On the ambiguity of Guibert's position and his play between "objective truth" and "ideological truth," see Jean Flori's penetrating article, "La caricature de l'Islam dans l'Occident médiéval: origine et signification de quelques stéréotypes concernant l'Islam," *Aevum* 66.2 (1992): 245–56. I do not share the optimistic view of Norman Daniel, *Islam and the West*, pp. 338–43, who sees the imputation of idolatry as mere literary convention.

lawful.[69] Or rather, Peter went on the attack only after he had argued and displayed the basis of his accusations. In the complex and chaotic history of western concern about Islam, his approach was without doubt a qualitative leap forward, even if its limits and blind alleys ought not to be glossed over. Let us not confuse one age with another, or read into Peter's writings on Islam a pacific attitude inspired by today's post–Vatican II ecumenism.

Creation of a Christian Armory

By a happy chance, we know how Peter the Venerable and his secretary, Peter of Poitiers, prepared and conducted the war of ideas against Islam. Between March and October 1142, Peter was on a long visit to Spain. There he visited Cluny's dependencies and saw Alfonso VII, the "victorious emperor" of Castile-León, whom he reminded of his family duty to give tribute to the Ecclesia cluniacensis.[70] On the front of the Christian Reconquista, he was in the eye of the struggle between the two branches of Abraham's descendence: the opposition between Hagar and Ishmael on the one hand and Sarah and Isaac on the other, a scene that is represented on the tympanum of the southern door of the church of Saint Isidore at León.[71] During his stay, Peter encountered two men of letters who had learned Arabic to further their work on astronomy, Robert of Ketton (or Chester) and Hermann of Dalmatia.[72] Investing an important sum in the enterprise, the abbot of Cluny decided to commission a translation of the Qur'an (Koran) into Latin together with other books documenting "the heresy of Muhammad."[73] Meanwhile literate Muslims in Baghdad and al-Andalus had had Arabic versions of the Christian Scriptures for over two centuries.[74] When Peter sent the translation of the Qur'an to Bernard of Clairvaux, encouraging him to "refute that pernicious error," he justified his initiative by

69. *Summa*, 3, p. 4. Marie-Thérèse d'Alverny, "Pierre le Vénérable et la légende de Mahomet," in *A Cluny*, Congrès scientifique, 9–11 July 1949 (Dijon, 1950), pp. 161–70, here 165–66; rpt. in *La connaissance de l'Islam dans l'Occident médiéval* (London, 1994).

70. Charles J. Bishko, "Peter the Venerable's Journey to Spain," in *Petrus Venerabilis 1156–1956*, pp. 163–75; Damien van den Eynde, "Les principaux voyages de Pierre le Vénérable," *Benedictina* 15 (1968): 58–110. The title "Emperor Victorious" used by Peter the Venerable in *CS*, 17, p. 54, ll. 25–26 had been adopted since the reign of Alfonso VI.

71. John Williams, "Generationes Abrahae: Reconquest Iconography in León," *Gesta* 16.2 (1977): 3–14, connects the iconography of the tympanum with Peter the Venerable's activities and work, although it is impossible to say whether the tympanum's iconography influenced Peter or the writings of Peter influenced the tympanum. Everything depends on the tympanum's date: Williams dates it to the late 1140s, while most art historians place it in the 1110s.

72. On Hermann, see *A History of Twelfth-Century Western Philosophy*, ed. Peter Dronke (Cambridge, 1988), pp. 386–404.

73. *Summa*, 18, p. 20; *CS*, 17, p. 54, ll. 14–22.

74. In his reply to the "monk of France," al-Bayi confirms that he has read the Gospels translated into Arabic; see Abdel Magid Turki, "La lettre du 'moine de France' à al-Muqtadir Billah," p. 140 (reprint, p. 268, see bibliography) and n. 130 for earlier attestations.

the need to make available a "Christian armory" (*armarium christianum*).[75] This *armarium* consisted of a corpus of texts on Islam usually referred to as the *Corpus toledanum* or *Collectio toledana* after the founder of the Spanish "school" of translation, Raymond, archbishop of Toledo (1125–52).[76] The corpus is made up of the following items:[77]

1. the *Fabulae Sarracenorum*, translated by Robert of Ketton from an unknown Arabic original, comprising a collection of Judaeo-Muslim legends on the creation of the world and mankind, a chronology of the patriarchs and prophets, the story of Muhammad, and biographical sketches of the first seven caliphs;

2. the *Liber generationis Mahumeth* (of Kitab Nasab Rasul Allah de Sa'id ibn-'Umar), translated by Hermann of Dalmatia, recording the legend of the prophetic light (*nur Muhammadi*) passed down from Adam to Muhammad via Noah;

3. the *Doctrina Muhammad* (of Masa'il 'Abdallah ibn-Salam), translated by Hermann of Dalmatia, telling the story of four Jews led by Abdia asking Muhammad one hundred questions about the Jewish Law;

4. the *Lex Sarracenorum*, the Qur'an as translated by Robert of Ketton;

5. the *Epistola Sarraceni et Rescriptum Christiani*, a translation by Peter of Toledo and Peter of Poitiers of the *Apologia* or *Risala* of al-Kindi, possibly written in the first half of the ninth century and summarizing the main points of Islamic doctrine in the form of correspondence between a Christian and a Muslim.[78]

The *Collectio toledana* survives in complete form in Paris Arsenal Manuscript 1162, accompanied by two writings by Peter the Venerable that serve to introduce it. The first of these, the *Epistola de translatione sua*, mentioned earlier, was addressed to Bernard of Clairvaux. Its contents appear in extract form in another of Peter's letters (no. 111 in Constable's edition); this contains material on various subjects and was similarly addressed to Bernard.[79] Peter evidently wanted

75. *Epistola de translatione sua*, 4, p. 26, ll. 7–8.

76. On the "school" of Toledo—or rather the nebula of translators somewhat arbitrarily grouped under this common head—see Roger Lemay, "Dans l'Espagne du XIIe siècle: les traductions de l'arabe au latin," *AESC* 18.4 (1963): 639–68; Marie-Thérèse d'Alverny, "Translations and translators," in *Renaissance and Renewal in the Twelfth Century*, ed. Robert Louis Benson and Giles Constable (Oxford, 1982), pp. 421–62, here 444ff.

77. On this collection, see Marie-Thérèse d'Alverny, "Deux traductions latines du Coran au Moyen Age," *Archives d'histoire doctrinale et littéraire du Moyen Age* 16 (1947–48): 69–131.

78. For more details on this corpus, see Reinhold Glei's introduction to his edition, *Petrus Venerabilis Schriften zum Islam*, Corpus Islamico-Christianum, Series latina, 1 (Altenberge, 1985), pp. xv–xix. The *Apologia*'s date of composition—ninth or tenth century—is controversial.

79. The relationship of Letter 111 to the *Epistola de translatione sua* and *Summa* is controversial—see *CS*, p. xix, and Constable's Appendix F in *Ep.*, 2:275ff.

Bernard to be the first to read his translation; he sought to persuade Bernard to follow in the Fathers' footsteps and fight against heresy. Peter urges on Bernard the useful nature of this "Christian arsenal" and invokes the examples of Solomon and David. Solomon helped to preserve the republic by building up arms (*ad tutelam*) in advance, though his own days were peaceful; David devoted resources to "ornament" (*ad decorem*) in the form of a Temple for God. Although their preparations seemed of little immediate use, they turned out to be of enormous value. Modifying Paul's words in 2 Corinthians 10:5, Peter the Venerable urges Bernard that it is essential to fight with the spoken and written word against "every knowledge that exalteth itself against the height of God." Even if it fails to win converts, the effort at refutation ought to strengthen the least secure members of the Church.

The second text by Peter the Venerable, entitled *Summa totius haeresis Sarracenorum*, is a summary of the manuscript's contents. A short introductory rubric sets the tone. Muhammad is "the greatest forerunner of Antichrist and the Devil's chosen disciple," his genealogy "most foul and false," his life and doctrine "impure and unspeakable," his "fables . . . utterly derisory and insane."[80] Rubrics and marginal notes, written in a contemporary hand, maintain this unpleasant, not to say vengeful, theme throughout the manuscript. The *Summa totius haeresis Sarracenorum* is, as its title clearly shows, a summary or compendium of the "absurdities" to which "the most wretched and most impious man, Muhammad . . . has delivered . . . almost a third of humanity."[81] Peter begins his eighteen-part argument with the most serious charge. The Saracens or Ishmaelites reject the Trinity and acknowledge only God and his soul; the God of the Qur'an expresses himself in the first person plural, as "we" (1). Christological deviations follow (2). Muhammad's sectaries deny that Christ is the Son of God, because it is impossible to be a father without begetting. Jesus, they say, is simply a sinless prophet, born of Mary without a father. He did not die, but escaped the murder planned for him by the Jews and flew to heaven, where he now lives bodily in the Creator's presence until Antichrist should come. At that time he will come and kill the faithless with the power of his sword; he will convert the remainder of the Jews and restore the Christians, who, after the death of the apostles, turned aside from the teaching of the Gospels. Like all creatures,

---

80. MS Paris, Arsenal 1162, f. 1r: *Si vis scire quis fuerit vel quid docuerit maximus precursor Antichristi et electus discipulus diaboli Muhamet, prologum istum intente lege, in quo breviter continentur omnia que liber iste continet, sive de genealogia eius turpissima et mendosissima, sive de vita ipsius vel doctrina incestissima et nefanda, sive de fabulis tam ab ipso quam a sequacibus eius confictis omni ridiculositate et deliramento plenis.*—"If you want to know who the greatest forerunner of Antichrist and the devil's chosen disciple, Muhammad, was or what he taught, read this prologue attentively, in which are briefly contained all this book contains: his most foul and false genealogy, his most impure and unspeakable life and doctrine, and the utterly laughable and insane fables produced by him and his followers."

81. *Summa*, 2, p. 4, ll. 22ff. The following analysis refers directly to the paragraphs of Reinhold Glei's edition, *Petrus Venerabilis Schriften zum Islam*, pp. 2–22, which follows the original MS, Paris Arsenal 1162.

Jesus is destined to die and then be resurrected. At the Last Judgment, he is to assist God in his work, though he himself will not judge. The essential part of the *Summa* is a succinct presentation of Muhammad's vile doctrine and life (3–16). Peter's intention is not to use untrue allegations, like the legend declaring that Muhammad was a Nicolaitan (3). The abbot of Cluny depicts Muhammad as a man of low extraction, uneducated, scheming, and violent, who sought to rule through terror (4). Realizing that he could not attain his ends by the sword, he tried to become king under the cover of religion, declaring himself to be God's prophet. The Arabs, though ignorant of idolatry, were not led by Muhammad to know the true God. They were simply led astray into the illusions of his heresy (5). Using a Nestorian heretic called Sergius as his intermediary, Satan conveyed to Muhammad a corrupt reading of the Scriptures, which taught that the Savior was not God, and other apocryphal fables (6). The perdition became total when the Jews, too, contributed their nonsense. For Muhammad based his conceptions on the "best" Jewish and heretical Christian doctors, maintaining that Gabriel, whose name he knew from Scripture, transmitted the Qur'an to him "volume by volume" (*per tomos*) (7). His Christological teaching is (continues Peter) derisory. It fails to take account of the mystery of the Incarnation. Muhammad sees Jesus as simply the greatest of the prophets and not God. At the hour of Judgment, Jesus, like Muhammad himself, simply intervenes to defend humankind (8). Paradise is not an angelic society unified in the vision of God and the supreme good, but a place flowing with milk and honey, a sensual world of infinite couplings with virgins and magnificent women. A whole series of notes copied further on in the manuscript, in the margins or between the lines of the translation of the Qur'an, reveals the extent of the scribe's (or a reader's) incomprehension. When, in the opening section (Sura 2:23), the Qur'an speaks of "wives of perfect purity" inhabiting this paradise, a well-informed observer has clarified: "purified of menstruation and excretion." The implied objection, which quickly became a classic of Christian criticism of Allah's paradise, derived from reading literally the Qur'an's description of human existence there.[82] If the blessed feasted in the afterlife, what did they do with their bodily waste products? Islam thus revived Christian discussion about the materiality of the resurrected body. In the tradition of the Fathers, particularly Augustine, the clerics of the Latin west gradually evolved the concept of a glorious body that was wholly physical, one possessed of all its members. Yet they emphasized that the Resurrection would change that body, in some way "shutting it down," rendering its sexual and alimentary functions obsolete.[83]

82. Paris, Arsenal 1162, f. 26r2. On this question, see Daniel, *Islam and the West*, pp. 172–76.

83. Peter directly tackles the question of the incorruptibility of holy bodies in his sermon on Saint Marcel's relics: *SSMII*, esp. pp. 266 and 269. On the history of this complex problem, see Caroline W. Bynum, *The Resurrection of the Body in Western Christianity, 200–1336* (New York, 1995). The term "shut down" (*fermé*) is used by Jérôme Baschet in his excellent review of Bynum's book in *AHSS* 1996.1:135–39, here 138.

The *Summa* meanwhile continues with Muhammad, the devil's creature, who represents the sum of all heresies. Like Sabellius, he denied the Trinity; like Nestor he denied the divinity of Jesus. Finally, like Mani, he put the Savior to death (9). With the practice of circumcision, said to be taken from Ishmael, he unleashed all kinds of lasciviousness, setting a polygamous example with his own eighteen wives. As he evokes these damnable teachings and practices, Peter the Venerable equally recalls Muhammad's piety in teaching charity and showing mercy. Rather like the unnatural monster depicted by the poet Horace, Muhammad has a human head with an equine neck and bird feathers.[84] As Marie-Thérèse d'Alverny points out, a small ink drawing is inserted at this point in MS Arsenal 1162, depicting "a long rectangular head extending into a feathered body and ending in a sort of fish's tail."[85] Muhammad was able to persuade rustic and uneducated populations to abandon their multiplicity of gods to worship one alone (10). He thereby managed to become a king, mixing good and evil, truth and falsehood, providing fuel for the everlasting fire. After the fall of the Roman empire and with the consent of him "by whom kings reign" (Proverbs 8:15), the Arabs and Saracens took over most of Asia, the whole of Africa, and a part of Spain, all subjected to the empire of Muhammad and his error (11)— "now almost half the world."[86]

Are Muhammad and his sectaries heretics or pagans? Peter acknowledges that they share several points of belief with Christians and proclaim several truths about the Lord. But the teaching they propagate is essentially false; they do not recognize baptism, the sacrifice of the Mass, penance, or any other Christian sacrament. They have therefore rejected more than any heretics before them (12). Muhammad stands between Arius and Antichrist. The long rubric prefacing the *Summa* in MS Arsenal 1162 describes him as "the greatest precursor of Antichrist" and "the devil's chosen disciple." Like Arius, Muhammad refused to see Christ as the true son of God. Although Antichrist will own Christ neither as God, as Son of God, nor even as a good man, Muhammad did at least reckon the Savior to be a prophet (13). Yet Peter sees this as a further cause for mistrust, since Augustine taught that the subtleness of the Evil One led him always to speak some little truth and good about the Savior (15).

Peter ends his short *Summa* by stating its aims. His notes are meant not as debating material but in order to sound an alert (*contremiscere*), to brief anyone willing and able to write against this heresy. Response is essential. Muhammad's teaching is the only heresy to have gone unopposed, even though it affects the greater part of the world. No one has even taken trouble to define it (17). Hence Peter's acceptance of the task, taking advantage of visits to Spain to commission, at great expense, translators exposing "that whole impious sect and the execrable

---

84. *Ars poetica*, 1–4.

85. D'Alverny, "Deux traductions latines du Coran au Moyen Age," 81.

86. *Summa*, 16, p. 18, l. 13. On Latin Christendom's obsessive fear in the face of the Muslims' great numbers, see Daniel, *Islam and the West*, pp. 152 and 211.

life of its most wicked inventor." Peter waited long for another person to take up the pen, but in vain. In the end, it has fallen to him to raise a Christian voice against Muhammad and his sectaries (18).

Contra sectam Sarracenorum[87]

The final words of the *Summa* are perhaps a passing shot at Bernard of Clairvaux, who, in spite of Peter's urging, failed to launch into the expected refutation. Having supplied Bernard with Islam's foundation authorities in translations declared to be "very faithful," the abbot of Cluny believed that the main obstacle had been overcome.[88] Information would lead to refutation. Yet Peter's optimism was ill judged. Modern criticism has shown that the *Collectio toledana* texts are far from faithful to the Arabic originals. In particular, the translation of the Qur'an by Robert of Ketton, though never downright incorrect, was sufficiently inexact to trap Latin commentators in baleful interpretations. One instance, mentioned by Norman Daniel, will suffice to show the scale of the problem. Robert never managed to translate the word "Muslim"; he avoided it by resorting to circumlocutions mostly drawn from the verb *credere* (to believe). He failed to understand that in Islam the "Muslim" "surrendered," "resigned," "submitted" to God. He could only conceive of a Muslim as adhering to a corpus of beliefs.[89] His translation also contained some significant changes and omissions. Thus the Prophet's "unchanging word" that "has never harmed men" was truncated to the Prophet's "unchanging word": Robert could not conceive that Muhammad's preaching was capable of anything but harm.[90]

Peter of Poitiers's Capitula

Peter the Venerable had no option but to work on the longed-for refutation himself. It was his final work, written at the very end of his life.[91] His secretary, Peter of Poitiers, who had revised Peter of Toledo's translation of al-Kindi's *Apologia*, mapped out the treatise for him, envisaging four books divided into a varying number of chapters (*capitula*). The first task was to defend the validity

---

87. The present analysis refers to Reinhold Glei's edition in *Petrus Venerabilis Schriften zum Islam*, which is based on one manuscript, Douai, BM 381, ff. 177–95, copied between 1156 and 1166. *CS* is also partially transmitted in a fifteenth-century manuscript, Madrid, BN 4464 (Conde del Miranda, 144), used by a mendicant active in Spain (on this, see Yvonne Friedman's introduction to her edition of *AJ*, pp. xxxviiiff.).

88. *CS*, 17, p. 54, l. 17.

89. Daniel, *Islam and the West*, p. 43.

90. *Verbum enim mei nunquam hominibus nocui, non mutabitur,* as opposed to *Verbum enim meum non mutabitur.* Presented and commented upon by d'Alverny, "Deux traductions latines du Coran au Moyen Age," 101.

91. Yvonne Friedman, in an attempt to elucidate the textual relationship between *AJ* and *CS*, proposes two dates for *CS*, namely 1148 or 1154 (*AJ*, p. lxiii). She does not appear convinced by her own arguments for an early date. We shall therefore keep to the later date, long held by historians of Peter the Venerable.

of the Jewish and Christian Scriptures, which had never been lost and whose tradition was extremely trustworthy. The abbot of Cluny would then proceed to a personal attack on Muhammad, who was no prophet but a deviant, a homicide, parricide, adulterer, and sodomite. Thirdly and fourthly, the treatise was to note the total lack of miracles performed by Muhammad and define precisely what prophecy consisted in. Thereby it would be proved that Muhammad's activity was not prophetic and that his "writing" (*scriptura Mahumeti*) consisted simply of variations on already known heresies, especially Manichaeism, and of nonsense found in the Talmud. The treatise was to end with an exhortation to conversion. A letter by Peter of Poitiers accompanied this sketch. In it the secretary made clear that the *Capitula* was only a plan, which his master could expand or prune as he wished. He hoped that the abbot of Cluny would not be shocked by the chapter concerning the "shameful abuse of women" attested both in the Qur'an and in the daily practice of the Saracens in Spain.[92] He ended by stressing the importance of refuting Christ's enemies as a whole. After the Jews and the "Provençal heretics" (the Petrobrusians), refutation of the Saracens would close the series.

It is hard to say whether Peter the Venerable fully accomplished the task sketched out in Peter of Poitiers's *Capitula*. There is no obvious answer. Peter's extant treatise, *Contra sectam Sarracenorum*, consists only of two books, whereas the secretary's sketch called for four. It was long believed that two books had been lost. The scribe who copied the collection of Peter the Venerable's works contained in manuscript 381 of the Municipal Library at Douai notes at the end of the treatise, folio 195r2: "Two books are missing, which I have not been able to find" (*Desunt duo libri quos invenire non potui*). The sixteenth-century *Chronicon cluniacense* actually speaks of a treatise in five books.[93] Modern criticism has come to reject these venerable observations, concluding that the known version of *Contra sectam Sarracenorum* most probably contains the totality of Peter's script.[94] Did the abbot of Cluny perhaps leave the work unfinished when he died? Commentators generally think so. Jean-Pierre Torrell and Denise Bouthillier have pointed to several internal references to later material that does not actually appear. They observe that *Contra sectam Sarracenorum* is barely a third of the length of *Adversus Iudeos* and *Contra Petrobrusianos*.[95] Without reopening the problem here, it is nevertheless noteworthy that, compared with Peter of Poitiers' sketch, the supposed gaps in the text as we have it would scarcely constitute two more books; far from it. On the contrary—though this

92. *Epistola Petri Pictavensis*, 3, in *Petrus Venerabilis Schriften Zum Islam*, p. 228, ll. 8–14; *Capitula Petri Pictavensis*, 2.6, in ibid., p. 234. On this point, see Daniel, *Islam and the West*, pp. 164ff.

93. *BC*, col. 591C.

94. James Kritzeck, "Peter the Venerable and the Toledan Collection," in *Petrus Venerabilis 1156–1956*, pp. 176–201, here 188–89, and *Peter the Venerable and Islam*, Princeton Oriental Studies, 23 (Princeton, 1964), pp. 155–56.

95. Torrell and Bouthillier, *Pierre le Vénérable et sa vision du monde*, pp. 182–83.

is only a working hypothesis—it would seem that Peter the Venerable actually did complete his set task. Once he had demonstrated the robustness of the Jewish and Christian Scriptures and proved it with lengthy treatments on the nature and history of prophecy, Muhammad's "imposture," the essential issue, had been dealt with. Having established that Muhammad was no prophet, what need had he to discuss further? The lack of biographical detail could be explained by the desire on Peter's part not to get enmeshed in personal attacks against Muhammad and thereby give gratuitous offense to the Saracens. Hence the neglect of Muhammad as homicide, parricide, adulterer, and sodomite, and, more generally, of the "shameful abuse of women." This absence is all the more understandable since the *Summa* had already said what needed communicating in criticism of Saracen morals, and the question of "Saracen lasciviousness" had already been raised in *Adversus Iudeos*. If this hypothesis is valid, then *Contra sectam Sarracenorum*, with its limits and silences, should be regarded as the work Peter the Venerable intended. Such, in any event, is the reading offered here.

The Prologue: The Impossibility of Silence

The prologue to *Contra sectam Sarracenorum* sets out to justify the long-contemplated enterprise of refuting Muhammad and his sectaries, those "most dreadful adversaries" (1).[96] Having called upon the spirit of wisdom and the Paraclete, Peter refers to the tradition of the Church Fathers who, possessed by the Spirit, "subverted, trod down, destroyed" anything inimical (*iniqua*) to the knowledge of God. He begins with an inventory of the chief heretics who were answered by the Fathers: Manichaeans, Arians, Macedonians, Sabellians, Donatists, Pelagians, Nestorians, Eutychians (3–4). Relying on Jerome's *De viris illustribus*, he pictures the men who became illustrious in their defense of orthodoxy: he labors to show that never in the Church's history did any heresy go unanswered (5–7). Although no refutation of Sabellianism is known—the heretical belief in a single divine person with three names—those who fought the Arians have sufficiently answered it. Moreover heresies can contradict one another. Thus the Arians and the Macedonians were in opposition to the Sabellians; the first two groups acknowledged only the Father's divinity, while the last named repudiated the divinity of the Spirit. Alongside the Fathers gathered in Church councils, the illustrious men of orthodoxy even opposed errant individuals who failed to give their names to sects: Jovinian, who denied that virginity was a higher state than marriage; Helvidius, who argued against the perpetual virginity of Mary; Vigilantius, who mocked the veneration of holy bodies and relics. In the name of Church unity, made real in one faith, one baptism, one God, and one life eternal, Peter believes it to be impossible to do less than these illustrious predecessors. Being in communion with them means doing battle as

96. The numbers in parentheses refer to the textual divisions in Reinhold Glei's edition, pp. 30–224.

they did. The iron law of tradition obliges Peter the Venerable and his contemporaries to fight against Islam, just as the Fathers fought heresy. The Fathers, he says, were never silent; they refuted all error, even the "barely heretical." Otherwise the Church, identified with the bride of the Song of Songs, could not be presented to Christ as "fair" and "spotless" (Song of Songs 4:7) (8–9). Peter believes it to be even more dangerous to remain silent now, inasmuch as Muhammad's "error" is more widespread than was Arianism, though that heresy contaminated numerous barbarian and Roman princes in many countries. Muhammad's "frenzy," more dangerous than all other known heresies put together, has gained kingdoms for the devil in three parts of the world, especially in Asia. Now Europe is at stake; Spain is already affected (10–11).

Yet these "dreadful adversaries," are they "of us"? Are they such as "went out from us" (1 John 2:19)? Ought one simply to answer errors arising within the Church and ignore "alien, extra-ecclesiastical errors"? How, though, are Muhammad and his sectaries to be characterized? Are they heretics or pagans? There is no clear answer. They are like heretics when they lose themselves in Christological deviations; they are like pagans when they reject and deride the Church's sacraments. Peter had already touched on this issue in *Contra Petrobrusianos*, when he noted that the Muslims did not sacrifice.[97] The question therefore remained open. Now, Peter decides to adopt a dual strategy: oppose them as heretics and resist them as pagans. Again, tradition in the shape of Justin, Irenaeus, Augustine, and many others offer numerous examples of resistance, with their various writings *contra Gentiles* (against the Pagans)(12–16).

Within the perspective of a thus-defined dual struggle, is not the linguistic barrier insurmountable, given the Latins' ignorance of their heretical and pagan adversaries' language? Peter is undaunted. Ignorance means inability to resist. Such was the overriding necessity that drove him directly to the Arabic sources themselves, translation of which he commissioned in 1142, while visiting Spain.[98] Moreover, what can work in one direction might also work in the other. Peter's own treatise can be translated into Arabic and help to bring Muhammad's sectaries out of error. Are not the Scriptures translated into Latin and Latin Fathers translated into Greek (19)? Peter's declaration of intent does not seem to have been accompanied by a real effort to have *Contra sectam Sarracenorum* translated into Arabic.[99] Even so, the translations into Latin will serve the Church as an *armarium christianum*: to aid the struggle against the "hidden thoughts" of Christians inclined to the view that the impious Muslims are not absolutely without piety or wholly outside the truth (20). Here Peter acknowledges the temptations of Islam and hints that the Christian body is already infected here and there by the Islamic disease. He does not specify, but no doubt had in mind the

97. *CP*, 161, ll. 10ff.
98. *CS*, 17, p. 54: here, Peter is speaking of 1141.
99. Daniel, *Islam and the West*, p. 278.

zones of contact between Christians and Muslims, especially in Spain, where adherents of the two religions lived side by side.[100] There, combating Islam was a matter of internal policing. Peter recognizes that "the Spirit breatheth where he will" and the success of his refutation is in the hands of God. Yet the abbot of Cluny does not doubt that he will succeed. Following his predecessors on this inspired route, he cannot imagine being wrong and his work fruitless. It will be a means of conversion, a help in fighting the enemy, or simply useful to Christians (21).

Book One: The Impossibility of Not Hearing
The main aim of the first book of *Contra sectam Sarracenorum* is to determine the bounds of the argument. On what ground are Muslim and Christian to meet? Such is the question Peter begins with, having briefly introduced himself as "Gallic by tribe, Christian by faith, abbot by office" and declared a real willingness to meet with Islam across the geographical, religious, and cultural divide:

> It seems strange, and perhaps indeed it is, that I, a man in a place far from you, speaking a different language, divorced from you by creed and customs, leading a life alien from yours, should write from the utmost parts of the west to men in the east and south, addressing verbally those whom I have never seen and perchance never shall. I do indeed address you, not as our men often do, with arms, but with words, not with violence but reason, not with hate but love.[101]

This declaration of intent, the touchstone of the rose-tinted legend of Peter the Venerable as the apostle of nonviolence, is too famous and has been too often overinterpreted to be allowed to pass without some placing in context. What lies behind the appeal to "words . . . reason . . . love"? Peter proceeds immediately to explain the two driving forces behind this expression of "reasoned love" (24–33). First is the need to obey the "Christian authority" that teaches that the Creator loves his creatures before they come to know him, as Matthew 5:45 says: "[God] maketh his sun to rise upon the good and the bad." Second is the need to conform to reason. Scripture says (Ecclesiasticus 13:19): "Every beast loveth its like; so also every man him that is nearest to himself." Animate beings, like man, "seek out [*consectantur*] those whom they sense to be similar or of like form to themselves."[102] The use of the verb *consector*, a frequentative form of *consequor*, is significant: it means as much "to seek after eagerly" as "to pursue," "to chase," "to follow with hostility." The desire to seek out those like one thus has as much to do with attraction within the species as with rejection of those outside it. Peter addresses his adversaries as fellow "rational men," whom nothing of itself will

---

100. On conversion to Islam, see ibid., pp. 294–96.
101. *CS*, 24, p. 62, ll. 1–8.
102. *CS*, 25, p. 64, ll. 9–10.

deceive, not even the strong ties of friendship and kinship or passionate love. Do not the arts teach as much, beginning with philosophy, as practiced in Greece and among the Latins, Persians, Indians, and all the sages who do not keep silent but talk and argue in seeking after truth, the nature of God, and the "noncreated essence"? Such, too, is the message of Christ, who, through his apostle Peter (1 Peter 3:15), urged his followers to be ready always "to satisfy everyone that asketh you a reason of that hope which is in you."

The search for truth is an open matter. Error alone seeks to hide. The refusal to discuss leads to darkness. Does not this exactly describe the situation of Muhammad and his sectaries? The rumor is that they will hear nothing that goes against their laws and customs, and that the merest word is met instantly with stones and swords.[103] Their very law forbids discussion: *Nolite disputare cum legem habentibus. Melior est enim caedes quam lis*—"Do not argue with those possessing the law. For bloodshed is better than a dispute." Peter says much about this recommendation, which he holds to be "asinine stupidity" contrary to human reason (35–48). In fact, Peter's horror stems from misunderstanding. The first sentence quoted ("Do not argue with those possessing the law") comes from al-Kindi's *Apologia*.[104] The second ("For bloodshed is better than a dispute") is a faulty reading of Suras 2:191 and 2:217 of the Qur'an, which in reality are far from recommendations to kill infidels rather than debate with them.[105] Peter wonders who these "possessors of the law" (*legem habentibus*) might be. They cannot be the pagan Saracens who lived before Muhammad; nor the Greeks and Romans, who had simply human laws to keep order and help run the republic. The law referred to here is divine law; therefore only Jews and Christians are meant. The words are Satan's, for who else could declare "such absurdities"? Satan knows that he cannot effectively challenge the divine law, even with arms. He is familiar with both the constancy of the Maccabees and the valor of the Christian martyrs. He knows that nothing can oppose the outward spread of the divine word, as taught by Psalm 18(19):5 and the apostle Paul's words in Romans 10:18. All Satan can do is interpose arms and thereby remove those who might have heard and been saved, This is why Satan-Muhammad teaches that "bloodshed" (*caedes*) is better than a dispute (*lis*). Moreover, such an assertion defies the rules of logic, for it is possible to compare two good things or two bad things, but not a good thing with a bad thing or a bad thing with a good thing.

Having drawn strength from this rule, Peter prevails on his adversaries not to impede the free circulation of the "charity" that unites all men (*ethnici*), not just Christians. They are not asked to agree, but simply to listen without resorting to stones or arms. They need only follow the example of the Christians

103. *CS*, 29, p. 68, ll. 10–14.

104. *Apologia del Cristianismo*, ed. José Muñoz Sendino, in *Miscelanea Comillas*, 11–12 (Madrid, 1949), p. 426.

105. See Glei's commentary, *CS*, n. 278, pp. 273–74.

who argue with Jews. Hearing the Jews blaspheme, the Christians do not go into a fury, but listen patiently and make scholarly, wise reply (49–50). Displaying a most sanguine view about the condition of slaves in the Christian world, Peter goes so far as to mention Muslim prisoners of war: they may have lost their freedom to return home, but they have not forfeited their freedom of speech.[106] All he seeks is a hearing, along the lines so often seen in the history of Christian missions. Drawing liberally on chapter 25 of the first book of the Venerable Bede's *Ecclesiastical History*, Peter cites the example, virtually contemporary with Muhammad's own lifetime, of the conversion of the English under King Ethelbert (561–616). He reports in detail how the mission, sent by Pope Gregory the Great and led by Augustine, was received in England. When the missionaries landed on the Isle of Thanet, Ethelbert received them in the open air, taking care not to let them in anywhere for fear of sorcery. In response to Augustine and his companions' enthusiastic news of eternal bliss in heaven, an endless paradise, the king said that these were very fine promises but "new and uncertain" and that he could not abandon overnight what he had long since honored. Even so, he offered to let them stay in the country at his expense and preach conversion as they wished. The story is a godsend to Peter. He is able to make out that Ethelbert's example typifies all kings' behavior. Why should the Saracens exempt themselves from this universal rule and refuse a hearing to the Christians' missionary appeal (51–54)?

Defense of the Scriptures
Now that Muhammad's sectaries have been forced to listen, "combat" can be joined.[107] Peter starts by attacking Muhammad's law, now available to him in his own language. How astonished he is to discover this mix of borrowings from the Hebrews' Law and that of the Christians! If Muhammad accepts some part of the Scriptures, then why not all? Either the Scriptures are bad, in which case they should be rejected; or they are true and should be taught. Unlike the fallible, perfectible laws of men, the law of God is to be accepted or rejected in its totality (55–57).

Next, Peter answers an objection put out by his adversaries concerning the reliability of the Scriptures. They allege that the original text was lost long ago and that the modern text is a reworking by subsequent generations, mixing truth and falsehood (58–86); an early task of Islam was thus to filter out the true and condemn the false. Peter was probably aware of the boast by educated Muslims, like al-Bayi, that the whole of Islam, regardless of geography, read the same

---

106. *CS*, 50, p. 98, ll. 11ff.

107. *CS*, 55, p. 104: *Iam ad proposita sermo festinet et primo contra pessimum hostem adiutus spiritu dei ad prelium accingatur.*—"Now to the main points, and first against the worst enemy let aid be furnished for the battle by the Spirit of God."

"Book"—"without adding a single word, diverging by so much as a vowel or a diacritic dot."[108] The Muslims saw the Christians as corrupters or, as the anonymous marginal hand of Arsenal manuscript 1162 put it, "variatores."[109] What is the basis, asks Peter, for this assertion that the Christian Scriptures have been falsified? In the collection of translated texts at his disposal, Peter can see no foundation for such talk. What he does see, however, is fables unworthy of men so expert in the things of this world. The first of these ludicrous fables tells the story of the Jews' loss of their sacred books on the way back from captivity in Babylon, the ass "carrying the Law" having wandered off (64). Now suppose, for argument's sake, says Peter, this absurd story were true. The obvious question to ask then would be whether in the entire exiled Jewish world there was no other written copy of the Law. Would a single volume have been enough to serve so many scattered people? The example of contemporary European Jewry, he says, contradicts this hypothesis. Peter maintains that every community of fifty, even twenty inhabitants, keeps a complete copy of the Law, the Prophets, and other Hebrew writings at the synagogue. Long before the destruction of the Temple by the Romans and their expulsion from Jerusalem, the place of sacrifice, the Jews had copies of their sacred books in cities throughout the Diaspora. One might equally suggest that the Qur'an is to be found only at Mecca (66–69)! Moreover, Scripture itself proves the story of the errant ass to be a fable. Ezra, one of the erstwhile captives, is depicted in Nehemiah 8:1–6 opening and reading the book of the Law of Moses. Are we to deem the holy Ezra a falsifier? If the story is a fable, how can people go on pretending that Scripture, which is so old and widespread, has been falsified? And where is the falsification supposed to be—in the Law, in the Prophets? Muhammad refers to both. Peter thus arrives at the "probable and necessary" conclusion that the rumor casting doubt on the validity of the Old Testament is baseless (74–75).

What is true of the Old Testament is equally so of the New. Peter now addresses the false notion that the foundation Scriptures of Christianity were lost during the persecutions of the early centuries, then rewritten on the basis of surviving scraps and conjecture centuries later (77). To be sure, says Peter, there were persecutions, particularly under Diocletian, who required by edict the destruction of churches and Christian books. Yet how is one to believe that all the books were destroyed? When the edict was given out, did no one think to hide a copy? There were Christians throughout the empire. What about the Persians, Medes, Arabs, and other kingdoms not under Rome? No part of the world remained ignorant of the Gospel message, which was spread in every language and written down everywhere (80). Peter asserts that the texts of the evangelists and

108. Abdel Majid Turki, "La lettre du 'moine de France' à al-Muqtadir Billah," p. 141; reprint, p. 269.

109. Folio 89r2: *Christianos legum variatores appellat, volens dicere illos evangelium corrupisse et ad libitum commutasse.*—"He calls the Christians variers of the laws, meaning that they have corrupted the Gospel and changed it at will."

apostles have been transmitted without interruption down to his own day and "by most sure intermediaries."[110] The apostle Peter, instructed directly by Christ, and Paul, the beneficiary of an invisible revelation, spread the Gospels of Mark and Luke from Jerusalem to the bounds of the west. The Gospel of John was revealed in Asia Minor, and the Gospel of Matthew in the regions of the south. Rome, "the head of the world's churches," kept these writings pure of all falsification from Peter down to the present (81–82). The same is true of the apostles' writings; these went throughout the world, have come down to the present, and must be preserved "as long as the heaven hangeth over the earth" (Deuteronomy 11:21). In so far as all or any part of the universally diffused Christian Scriptures have suffered corruption, this can have occurred only among some, not among all the peoples of the earth. Otherwise the conclusion would have to be that all the earth's books have been corrupted and no one realizes except—an even greater absurdity—the Saracens: "The Saracens know the business of others, while the Christians don't even know their own!"[111] Declarations of this sort, says Peter, are but "the emptiest of jests" (83–85). Finally, if the Gospel is false, it must be admitted that the Qur'an must be too, since a falsified book can only spread errors. At the end of book 2, Peter will return to this matter, maintaining that it needs only one falsehood to contaminate the totality of a text. Peter's all-or-nothing logic is intended to force the Saracens to accept the books in the Jewish and Christian canons, from which Muhammad himself drew inspiration. Basing his argument on these writings, whose authority he believes he has now fully established, Peter now prepares to demonstrate to his opponents in book 2 that their law is false and that Muhammad is neither a prophet nor an envoy of God, but a falsifier (87–88).

Book 2: What Is Prophecy?
Book 2 opens with an appeal to the humanity of those to whom it is addressed, according to the principle enunciated earlier, that man seeks out those like him (89). Out of love for humanity, Peter the Venerable echoes Isaiah 44:18–21 to warn his interlocutors against the sin of idolatry. He admits that Muhammad's sectaries do not worship wood or stone; but those who follow Satan will inevitably drift in that direction, as so many Jewish and indeed Christian examples testify. Failing to worship the true God or ceasing to obey him amounts to idolatry. It is a dereliction that will end in the same darkness and the same reign of Antichrist, which will swallow up pagans, Jews, and heretics alike (90–93).

Peter's aim is to show his adversaries their error so that they may realize the risk they run. He goes to the heart of the debate. Was Muhammad really a prophet, the "seal of the prophets," the transmitter of revelation, the Lord's messenger? The abbot of Cluny means to prove the opposite. Calmly, he proceeds

110. *CS,* 80, p. 138, ll. 12–15.
111. *CS,* 85, p. 144, ll. 4–5.

to define what prophecy is.[112] He begins with his namesake, the apostle Peter, who, drawing strength from the Lord's Transfiguration and Resurrection, taught that prophetic inspiration lay not in the human being but in the Holy Spirit (2 Peter 1:21). Building on this, Peter the Venerable gives prophecy a broad definition that goes well beyond the etymological:

> Prophecy is the proclaiming of unknown things, be they past, present, or future, made not by human invention but by divine inspiration.... The prophet is the one who manifests to mortals unknown things of past, present, or future time, not having been taught by human cognition but inspired by the Holy Spirit.[113]

As an example of retrospective prophecy, Peter cites the example of Moses speaking of the Creation. As "a certain great man of ours"—Gregory the Great—put it, "A man has spoken about that time when there was no man" (98).[114] The Book of Numbers reports Moses' prophecies about the then present, accurately predicting, first of all in Numbers 16:30–33, the damnation of Korah, Dathan, and Abiram (99). Then the episode ends with Moses announcing to Aaron, "Already wrath is gone out from the Lord" (verse 46), a statement vindicated by events. Regarding future prophecy, Peter has a plentiful choice of examples from before and after Moses: Enoch, Noah, Jacob, Joseph, Samuel, David, Isaiah, Elijah, Elisha, Jeremiah, and many others (100–101). Among them Isaiah prophesied "from afar" the coming of the virgin-born Lord, as well as Christ's baptism, miracles, and Passion (104–5).[115] Isaiah and Jeremiah both prophesied events that took place before and after their own deaths (107–8). A little later, Peter cites the example of Elisha, in 2(4) Kings 6:8–12, warning the king of Israel about traps set by the king of Syria. Peter points out that Muhammad's inability to foresee the outcome of his various military exploits is a perfect counterexample of this (118–19).[116]

The Qur'an, says Peter, contains no prophecy by Muhammad. Does his prophetic reputation rest on some other text? According to Muhammad's "genealogy"—Peter's reference is to the *Liber generationis Mahumeth*—the "Prophet" is supposed to have foretold that twelve caliphs would descend from his family and to have given the names of the first three of them, Abu-Bakr, 'Umar, and 'Uthman. Yet the Qur'an, says Peter, contradicts such a prophecy. Actually, what Peter cites as a warning from the Qur'an comes from al-Kindi's

112. The best clarification of the issue is Torrell, "La notion de prophétie" (see above, n. 40).

113. *CS*, 97, p. 158, ll. 9–11, and p. 160, ll. 17–19. Peter relies on Gregory the Great's classic definition of the prophecy given in his first Homily on Ezechiel (see next ref.).

114. *Homilia in Ezechiel*, 1.1, ed. Charles Morel, *SC*, 327 (Paris, 1986), pp. 50–52.

115. Respectively Isaiah 7:14, 35:5–6, 53:7–12. Regarding the baptism of Christ, Peter confuses Isaiah with Ezechiel (36:25).

116. *CS*, 119, p. 186, ll. 1–3.

Apologia: "Reject everything that does not concur with these words."[117] As the Qurʾan contains no prophecy, Peter maintains that the episode from the *Liber generationis Mahumeth* should be rejected as inconsistent with the revelation. Even if he had had access to other sources, like the *hadith* reporting signs intended to prove the sincerity of Muhammad's prophecy, Peter would still have held to the same negation based on the Qurʾan. Schooled in the Christian continuum between scriptural miracles and extraordinary signs recorded in the hagiographic tradition, Peter manifestly failed to conceive that Islam could distinguish between the Muhammadan prophetic model—which essentially allowed little space for miracles—and hagiographic models.[118]

Then comes the supposed Muslim defense that God did not have Muhammad accomplish any miracles because his audience would not have believed it. Peter again relies on al-Kindi's *Apologia:* "They would not have believed thee, just as they did not believe the others."[119] The abbot of Cluny makes an immediate challenge. What "others" are these? Surely not Moses or Christ, for these both accompanied their prophetic words with signs (124–26). In any case, such could not be the will of God, since it is impossible to get anyone to believe by simple faith in words. Religious utterance needs to be efficacious and accompanied by tangible proof. In *Adversus Iudeos,* Peter had already declared his utter perplexity at Islam's success in the absence of any miracle.[120] How could mere palaver like that command belief? Because it promised sensual pleasure in all its forms in paradise? Peter denies that Muhammad was a prophet, even if he did claim to be one; real prophets, like Amos, have refused the name of prophet out of humility.[121] Muhammad has revealed nothing about things that have happened or are to happen. His views on the *voluptuosa* (sensual pleasures) of heaven or on hell are not based on any proof. What witnesses, dead or alive, did Muhammad advance to support his prophecies about the Last Things? Being a specialist in accounts of spirits and visions of the afterlife, sometimes false and sometimes veridical, Peter knows this territory. Hence the efforts deployed in

117. P. 410, 7–9.

118. On the prophetic signs of Muhammad discussed in a polemic context, see the refutation of the "Monk of France" by al-Bayi in Abdel Majid Turki, "La lettre du 'moine de France' à al-Muqtadir Billah," 126ff.; reprint, p. 254. On the distinction between the Muhammadan prophetic model and hagiographic models in Islam, I am indebted to stimulating ideas heard at the colloquium "Les saints et leurs miracles à travers l'hagiographie chrétienne et islamique (IVe–XVe s.)," organized by Denise Aigle, Paris, 23–25 November 1995; proceedings published as *Miracle et Karama: hagiographies médiévales comparées,* ed. Denise Aigle, Bibliothèque de l'Ecole pratique des Hautes Etudes, Section Sciences religieuses, 109 (Turnhout, 2000).

119. P. 408, 5–6, 27–28.

120. *AJ,* 4.1448–52. Quoted and commented upon by Torrell and Bouthillier, *Pierre le Vénérable et sa vision du monde,* p. 189.

121. On criticism of Islam, general on the part of Latin commentators, for the absence of miracles from the life of Muhammad, see Daniel, *Islam and the West,* pp. 88–99.

Contra Petrobrusianos to distinguish false from true visions and the precautions taken in *De miraculis* to verify the reliability of testimonies to the supernatural.

Since he was no prophet, Muhammad cannot, says Peter, have been the "seal of the prophets." Book 2 of the whole treatise (in the state in which we have it, at least) ends by examining this matter. Peter clarifies and widens the definition of prophecy given earlier. Good prophets, he says, need to be distinguished from bad. Bad prophets lead blameworthy lives and their preaching is false, even if they manage to speak truth on occasion in the manner of diviners, augurs, haruspices, or magi. Good prophets, whose lives are praiseworthy and whose preaching is true, fall into three categories: those who announce universalities, those who predict particular events, and those who are capable of both, such as Isaiah, Jeremiah, and Daniel. Their common feature is that their pronouncements are borne out by events (131–32). Bearers of universal truths speak of universal salvation, namely, the work of Christ (133). From the time of Christ to the end of time, says Peter, there cannot be any further universal prophets. With the Savior, all universal prophecy was given; some things were accomplished then, and some events are yet to come. The "seal of the prophets" was not therefore Muhammad but John the Baptist, whom the Saracens call "the son of Zacharias" (136–37). The only prophets that were left were particular prophets, whose pronouncements were intended for certain people or individuals, such as the apostle Paul, who foretold many events that have happened or are yet to come in the Church of Christ. Among the things that have happened, Peter points to Paul's prophecy in 2 Timothy 4:3–4: "There shall be a time when they will not endure sound doctrine," a prediction that the "fables" of Muhammad and of the Talmud have proved right (138).

Having spoken of Paul, Peter the Venerable says that he will not speak of the many other examples of particular prophecy that he could mention. His pretext is that his opponents would refuse to believe him; they do not even believe in God (139–40). Beyond these convoluted justifications, it is possible to suspect, along with Jean-Pierre Torrell, a certain embarrassment on Peter's part in the face of the ever-vexed question of prophecy in the postapostolic age, when the Church became institutionalized and there were fewer inspired voices.[122] His silence nevertheless begs the question of why the majority of prophets cited are Hebrews. Peter extricates himself with a remark that to him seems sensible. He explains to his interlocutors that these prophets are also in fact theirs. Ishmael, their forebear, was born, like Isaac, of Abraham, who had sired Ishmael by Hagar and Isaac by Sarah. Thus ties of consanguinity—not to mention language, writing, and the practice of circumcision—included the Saracens within the prophetic tradition of the Hebrews (145–46). Yet again Peter's all-or-nothing logic comes into play: the teachings of the prophets are to be either accepted in their entirety or totally rejected. Peter then winds up the long discussion on

122. Torrell, "La notion de prophétie," p. 269.

prophecy by concluding that Muhammad cannot have been a prophet in either the universal or the particular sense, or else he was a bad prophet, reprobate and false (151–54).

A Debate of the Deaf

Norman Daniel has successfully traced the history that made meaningful debate between Islam and Christianity an impossibility in the Middle Ages. He points to the "air of unreality" in Latin literature concerned with the Muslims.[123] The debate between "fellows," the meeting of minds sought by Peter the Venerable between men united by reason and charity, was actually unrealizable. The "discussion" was abortive almost from the start. The necessary conditions for a proper exchange were far from being fulfilled. Peter thought that obtaining a translation of the corpus of Islam's fundamental authorities would put him in a position to challenge his adversaries. Yet he demonstrably failed to see the limitations inherent in his approach. The rubrics and glosses accompanying the texts compiled in the *Collectio toledana*, "inspired," as Marie-Thérèse d'Alverny has commented, "by a spirit of systematic denigration," betray a manifest lack of serenity in the face of the adversary.[124] Blighted by approximation, his translations led Peter into some dire misunderstandings. Above all, he seems not to have gauged the necessity of two expository efforts that were indispensable if he was to have an even minimal chance of connecting with his interlocutors. Unable to gain an overall view, Peter always quoted the Qur'an out of context and failed to distinguish, in the Islamic legacy, between revealed text and tradition.[125] Peter behaved like the "monk of France," whom al-Bayi had refuted in the 1080s, charging him with moving his quotations "out of their proper place" and "using them outside of their meaning."[126]

It is, as Jean Jolivet thinks, unclear whether the abbot of Cluny was involved in an "exchange" of views—which would imply the recognition of an interlocutor.[127] Debate was an unrealistic expectation. Peter does not hide his irritation in the face of blocking procedures that, by an extremely eloquent projection mechanism, he puts down to adversaries supposedly unwilling to engage in debate. The circumstances leave him with no alternative but to verbally abuse these poltroons and, incidentally, enrich the rhetorical arsenal necessary to Latin

---

123. Daniel, *Islam and the West*, p. 287.

124. D'Alverny, "Deux traductions latines du Coran au Moyen Age," p. 99.

125. Daniel, *Islam and the West*, p. 56.

126. Abdel Majid Turki, "La lettre du 'moine de France' à al-Muqtadir Billah," p. 151; reprint, p. 279.

127. Jean Jolivet, "Philosophie au XIIe siècle latin: l'héritage arabe" and "L'Islam et la raison, d'après quelques auteurs latins des XIe et XIIe siècles," in *Philosophie médiévale arabe et latine. Etudes de philosophie médiévale* (Paris, 1995), pp. 47–76, here 47–49, and 155–67, here 164–67. These articles appeared previously in the *Revue de synthèse*, 4th ser., 3–4 (1987) and *L'art des confins. Mélanges offerts à Maurice de Gandillac*, ed. Annie Cazenave and Jean-François Lyotard (Paris, 1985), pp. 153–65.

Christendom in order to defeat Islam or at worst resist it. Contrary to the pacific declaration of intent placed at the start of book 2 and cited ad nauseam by historians of the twelfth-century Renaissance—words rather than arms, reason not force, love not hate[128]—Peter sees himself compelled to make war. For a twelfth-century Christian intellectual and a black monk to boot, there was only one war, the fierce, ever uncertain war against the devil. Regardless of the dialectical nuances that here and there adorn *Contra sectam Sarracenorum*, the struggle with Islam came down in the end to demonizing Muhammad and his sectaries. In a mental universe that was divided, in anticipation of the Last Things, into the "good" and "evil" part, to fail to follow the path of obedience to the true God was to fall into the territory of the Evil One. No more room, then, for fine distinctions: Jews, heretics, and pagans all belonged in the bottomless abyss of all the abominations. Compared with this, did it really matter if declared monotheists were presented as idolaters?

In the history of demonizing the other in the west, Peter the Venerable's treatment of Islam is interesting from two points of view. First, he shows the place ascribed to Islam in the scale of gradually increasing power attributed to the Ancient Enemy. Muhammad represented an intermediate stage between Arius, the worst of heretics, and Antichrist. That final satanic manifestation before the last great unloosing was Peter's justification for dealing with Muhammad and his sectaries by a process of accumulation. In accordance with a conception developing in Hispanic apocalyptic thought since the ninth century, Islam was thus presented as the sum of all heresies.[129] It contained every possible bad influence, including Christian heresies and Jewish Talmudic fables. With their ambiguous identity, the Muslims were at once heretical and pagan. One sees therefore why Peter could not avoid confronting these worst possible enemies. Despite his generally steely personality, Peter was eaten up with anxiety when he beheld in his interlocutors the inverse image of himself. No mean member of the Church establishment, the abbot of Cluny found himself brutally confronted by a religion with neither priests nor sacramental mediation. Moreover, what could be more insufferable to a Cluniac virgin, who saw renunciation of the flesh as the very way to transform humanity into an angelic society, than the sexual debauch promised in Allah's paradise? Entering the monastery as a child, Peter was the living incarnation of the sexual phobia inhabiting the contemplatives, men of the spirit, intent on keeping women beyond the bounds of the monastery and repressing any sexual awakening among the boys within.[130] The demons pervading Peter's *De*

128. *CS*, 24, p. 62.

129. Paul Alphandéry, "Mahomet-Antichrist dans le Moyen Age," in *Mélanges H. Derenbourg* (Paris, 1909), pp. 261–77, esp. 261–62; Bernard McGinn, *Antichrist: Two Thousand Years of the Human Fascination with Evil* (San Francisco, 1994), pp. 85ff.

130. On this point see Isabelle Cochelin, "Enfants, jeunes et vieux au monastère: la perception du cycle de la vie dans les sources clunisiennes (909–1156)," doctoral thesis, 2 vols. typescript, University of Montreal, 1996, 1:295ff.

miraculis cause lay folk to commit adultery in the world and adults inside the monasteries to fornicate with their child charges.[131] Obsession with Islam as a religion "of the lascivious" was the shadow thrown by insecurity of identity. Would the blessedness of the afterlife perhaps not include the sublimation of sex? It would be centuries before this leaden cope would lift, enabling Verlaine to sing of "endless harems" and Grantaire to proclaim that "Mahom has some good."[132]

As he watched for signs of Antichrist's advance, Peter the Venerable revealed on several occasions how worried he was to witness the gains made by Islam; it had already come to dominate half, if not two-thirds, of the earth. His preoccupation was all the greater as Islam's expansion was coming to block Christian proselytizing during a period when the Latin west too was in a fully conquering phase. Several times in *Contra sectam Sarracenorum*, Peter defines Christianity as a universal religion. In the *Sermo de transfiguratione domini*, he thrills to the voice of God sounding from the clouds (Matthew 17:5) and exhorts not simply the faithful but pagans and infidels to hearken to so clear a message.[133] Within this perspective, Peter's war of ideas against Islam came down to one proselytism against another. What was important for him was to have an "arsenal" of information and proven responses at hand in case there was confrontation. This was far from a missionary effort, which did not come to the fore before the activities of the mendicant orders in the thirteenth century. This was an attempt to steady the faithful.[134] Hence his reaffirmation of the basic principles of the *unitas Ecclesiae* (unity of the Church)—imitate the Fathers in fighting the least deviation and, above all, acknowledge the Church's deep roots in a body of writings faithfully transmitted by tradition. Whatever Peter wanted to come of it, his effort was for internal consumption. Yet even reduced to this one front, Peter's impact seems to have been faint. The medieval reception of *Contra sectam Sarracenorum*, of which there are only two known surviving manuscripts, was very limited.[135] The attempt at an interpretative, reasoned, lecturing approach to Islam was short-lived. Though his resources were more sophisticated than those of many other twelfth-century clerics, the abbot of Cluny, too, ended up feeding the stereotypes of Islam as an empire of the devil.

131. *DM*, 1.14, p. 46.

132. Verlaine, "Résignation," in *Poèmes saturniens* (1866), many eds.; Victor Hugo, *Les Misérables*, 4.12.2, many eds.

133. *STD*, PL 189:968B.

134. Cahen, *Orient et Occident au temps des Croisades*, p. 187; Daniel, *Islam and the West*, pp. 140ff.; Christoph T. Maier, *Preaching the Crusades: Mendicant Friars and the Cross in the Thirteenth Century*, Cambridge Studies in Medieval Life and Thought, 28 (Cambridge, 1994).

135. See above, n. 87. The weak influence of Peter the Venerable's work is noted by Daniel, *Islam and the West*, pp. 259–60, and recalled more recently by M. Vandecasteele, *Etude comparative de deux versions latines médiévales d'une apologie arabo-chrétienne: Pierre le Vénérable et le rapport grégorien*, Overdruk uit Academiae Analecta, Mededelingen van de Koninklijke Academie voor Wetenschappen, Letteren en Schone Kunsten van België, Klasse der Letteren, Jaargang 53, 1991, Nr. 1 (Brussels, 1991), pp. 81–134. My thanks to Benoît-Michel Tock for obtaining this work for me.

12

"CONCERNING REPRESSED
THINGS WHICH ENABLE
HUMANS TO LIVE IN SOCIETY"

—*D'où viennent les idées justes?*
—*Elles tombent du ciel!*
—*D'où viennent les idées justes?*
—*Des pratiques sociales . . .* [1]

"Where do the right ideas come from?"
"They fall from heaven!"
"Where do the right ideas come from?"
"Social practices . . ."

THE TYRANNY OF THE SINGLE RING

Inquiring into what constituted society, Gotthold Ephraim Lessing (1729–81) noted that paradoxically what united people, like the state and religion, was also what divided them. Hence his search for the "natural" man beneath the social animal, a theme he expressed in his theatrical fiction *Nathan der Weise*, a fable that recounts the story of human divisions. The action takes place in Jerusalem, where the three monotheistic religions meet; the time is that of the Third Crusade, during the years of truce declared by Saladin (1189–92). The plot surrounding the play's three main characters facilitates the beginnings of a peaceful exchange between the three religions of the Book. Saladin represents Islam, a Templar Christianity, and the sage Nathan Judaism. The middle of the play (act 3, scene 7) contains a dialogue in which Nathan tells Saladin a parable about three rings. Once upon a time, a man who lived in the Orient had a ring of inestimable worth. Thinking of his death and succession, he decided to

The title of this chapter is taken from Maurice Godelier, *The Enigma of the Gift*, trans. Nora Scott (Cambridge, 1999), p. 177; originally published as *L'énigme du don* (Paris, 1996), p. 246.
    1. Jean-Luc Godard, *La Chinoise* (1967).

bequeath the ring to the son who was most dear to him and stipulated that his inheritors should do likewise. There came a generation in which the father equally cherished his three sons. Unable to decide between them, he had two perfect replicas of the ring made before his death. Each of the three sons thought he was the sole possessor of the father's love, and they fell out with one another. Which was the authentic ring and which of the sons therefore the head of the household? Nathan replies that it is as impossible to answer that question as to say which—Judaism, Christianity, or Islam—is the single true religion of the Father. Like the three sons, Jews, Christians, and Muslims must accept their share of indeterminacy and live as three equal sons within the one original family. Furthermore, the plot of *Nathan der Weise* goes on to show that the characters of the play are related. The Templar is in fact nephew by blood to Saladin, and Nathan's adopted daughter is the Templar's sister. The human beings involved in the Crusades are but members of a single family ignorant of the reality! Behind this fable and the role play that sees Jews, Christians, and Muslims tear one another apart, Lessing, like the sage Nathan, probes what it is to be human.

CHRISTIAN SOCIOLOGY AND CHRISTIAN ANTHROPOLOGY IN THE FEUDAL AGE

The literary theme of Saladin and the three rings used by Lessing had a long, complex medieval prehistory traceable to at least the first half of the thirteenth century.[2] For our purposes it is enough to point out that there were two main versions of the legend. One, attested in Boccaccio's work in particular, revealed a precocious deism together with prudent indeterminacy about which of the three religions of the Book was the authentic one. It was this distant version that underlay Lessing's reflections. The other version, attested in a thirteenth-century *fabliau* (tale or fable), *Li dis dou vrai aniel* (The Tale of the True Ring), recounted how, on the contrary, the good son, he who possessed the one authentic ring, successfully challenged the waywardness of his two evil brothers. A good century before, this was the thesis that Peter the Venerable had sought to defend through the less poetic medium of polemical writing. The abbot represents a watershed period, the eleventh and twelfth centuries, in which western society began to define itself in terms of what it rejected as nonhuman. The concept of "religion" was as yet unformulated, and it would be some time yet before mankind could define itself in terms of "nature." For the moment, human life was impossible outside of society, and the only society possible was

---

2. On this complex history, see Americo Castro, "The Presence of the Sultan Saladin in the Romance Literatures," in *An Idea of History: Selected Essays of Americo Castro*, trans. from Spanish and ed. by Stephen Gilman and Edmund L. King (Columbus, Ohio, 1977), pp. 241–69. I thank Maurice Kriegel for drawing my attention to this article.

Christian. As the member of a monastic Church identifying itself, in the dynamic of its expansion, with the universe, Peter could not but be drawn logically into establishing the tyranny of a single ring. On the inside, the contours of the ring allowed him to define Christian society by what it cast out to the margins (heretics and Jews); on the outside, the ring's uniqueness necessitated exclusion of the Jews and Muslims from human status. Peter's Church system had both a sociological and an anthropological base. Let us quickly recall what they were.

The long refutation of the Petrobrusian heresy held a mirror up to the elements that constituted the Church's system as conceived by Church authorities in the first half of the twelfth century. First, Peter recalled the fundamental forms of solidarity underlying the social bond. The triple logic of all or nothing, everyone or no one, and the One for all was essential to a Christian sociological holism that operated through the commutation of persons and the force of reciprocal engagements entered into in marriage, baptism, and expressions of funerary solidarity. From its basic unit, the couple, via intermediate circles of the seigneurial order's wider family, spiritual parenthood, and relations of fidelity, to the structure embracing all things—the great spiritual family of the Church—we see that charity nourished the whole social body, which was identified with the body of Christ, regardless of degrees of hierarchy. The logic of all or nothing and of the One for all was moreover defined as eternal and universal truth. The sacrifice of Christ, the foundation of Christianity, availed for ever and for all: *semel verum, semper verum* (once true, always true). It signaled to all mankind, participators in a universal destiny, what mediations made social life possible. It was a question not so much of joining as of becoming incorporated into the Church, taking the way (*transitus*) opened by Christ. The mystery of the Eucharist (in the sense of hidden reality and efficacious sign) was the forum of the great commutation enabling the divine to reveal itself in the human and conversely the people and goods waiting in this world to return to their origins in the world beyond. The exchange between the two realms was conceived in terms of transformation and circular dynamics enabling effects to go back toward their Cause. Yet the process needed a spatial center. This was provided by the ecclesiastical *fabrica* (building, fabric, workshop), the sacred, set-aside space determined by the church and the altar or (in functional terms) by the priests, efficacious transformers because purified from the stain of sex and therefore transparent to the divine.

The Cluniac Church system's logic of embracing everything, expressed in the dynamic form of space set aside yet ever expanding, envisaged eventual inclusion of the universe and all mankind on earth. It entailed, in the age of the Crusades, a head-on collision between Christianity and the two other religions of the Book, Judaism and Islam.

In the process of defining the identity of Christian society in the eleventh and twelfth centuries, the Jew occupied an ambiguous position. He was both an insider and an outsider, in society but outside the Church, at a time when clerics were striving hard to make the two coterminous. After centuries of cohabitation, the moment of Christian truth had come for the Jewish communities who were heirs either of the period of exile or of the conversions of late antiquity in the west. Dealing with the Jewish question meant, for Christians, ridding themselves of an alter ego, breaking from the constraints of the intellectual Semitism at the root of Christianity. The way out of the Christian identity crisis lay in reducing the Jews to detritus of history, relegating them outside time to the role of witnesses. Fixing them in the past was the theological counterpart of a process of social isolation. The Jews could not pretend to political sovereignty in a context of discrete kingdoms. In the seigneurial order systematized by Peter the Venerable, they were serfs with the status of chattels, whose evolution lay outside the circuits of exchange constituting Christian society. Their exclusion from such exchange expressed itself in two complementary ways that it would be erroneous to treat separately. Expelled from all agricultural activity and confined to usury, the Jews did not produce, at least not directly; in the eyes of a cleric living off domanial production they produced nothing at all. Above all, as exiles from the Temple, the Jews no longer sacrificed. Yet sacrifice lay at the heart of the construction of Christian sociology in the feudal age. How was it possible to ascribe a social existence to people who did not go through a sacrifice, the place of exchange with the world beyond, the forge (*fabrica*) of the social bond?

Such indeed was the basic question that led the abbot of Cluny to reflect on Christianity as an anthropology. The great contribution of *Adversus Iudeos* consisted in linking a refutation of the Talmud (or a group of extracts deemed to be such) to a classic treatise of Christology occasioned by confronting Christ's murderers. The Jews' move from Scripture to rabbinic literature seemed to Peter a turning point in the history of Creation. With just the Old Testament, the Jews had still been men, even if their obsessional literalism bound them to the earth and mired them in carnal filth. Of course, their ancestors' crime forced them to face the wretched heritage of an errant people, once elect and now humiliated, once humanity's head but now the tail. Yet they had still been men. But when they adopted the Talmud and its fables, the Jews of the exile fell headlong into bestiality. They abandoned at once their authorities and reason. Placed by God between the angels and the beasts, mankind was characterized by reason and obedience to established authorities. The Talmudic Jews therefore no longer belonged to humankind. They were beasts distinguished by abnormal sexual ardor.[3] Peter presented their exit from humanity as a simple intellectual mechanism. But it is notable that the first known example of racial characterization of a Jew as a small dark being—the brother of the Jewish pope Anacletus II—came

---

3. Such is the image of the "red Jew" analyzed by Claudine Fabre-Vassas, *The Singular Beast: Jews, Christians, and the Pig*, trans. Carol Volk (New York, 1997), pp. 105ff.; originally published as *La bête singulière: les juifs, les chrétiens et le cochon*, Bibliothèque des Sciences humaines (Paris, 1993), pp. 122ff.

in Peter's time. The twelfth century thus provided a first marker in the history of the change from anti-Judaism to anti-Semitism, the exclusion of the Jews being glossed in terms of species difference. Those who did not belong to the only society possible, Christian society, were quite simply not human.

Such a denial of humanity applied, though differently, to the Saracens. In Peter the Venerable's conception of history and the final great unloosing of the Antichrist, the emergence and rising power of Islam marked a last stage, a prelude to the great chaos. Before the one side, that of God, could definitely triumph over the other, that of the devil, there was a heightened apocalypse to live through. As preliminary to the great expected conflagration, Islam was seen as a concentration of the devilish. Muhammad and his sectaries recapitulated all the heresies and deviations possible of Judaism and Christianity. To confront them was to attack the sum of all the ills inflicted on humanity. It was irrelevant to ask whether the Saracens were men or not. They were the last offspring of the supreme beast, Antichrist.

REPRESSED SEXUALITY AND THE CONTROL OF EXCHANGES

From heretics to infidels, from Peter of Bruis to Muhammad, taking in the anonymous Talmudic Jews on the way, the topology of exclusion enabled the Cluniac monk-priest to define a sociology of Christianity that was also an anthropology. Belonging to humankind and constituting society were one and the same thing. The deviations that this Christian society denounced were a sort of mirror image of the rules that constituted it. Let us therefore end by recapitulating the rules of this society that saw itself as coterminous with humanity.

First, man's social existence implied sexual repression. The renunciation of the flesh and aspiration to the unblemished, eunuch-like state of angels represented one of the original marks of Christian anthropology; it withdrew the human body from the time-honored great chain of being. As Peter Brown has powerfully demonstrated, the Fathers and athletes of God of the early Christian centuries made a radical break with the ancient view; now "sexuality was not seen as a cosmic energy that linked human beings to the fertile herds and to the blazing stars."[4] However, it was not until the age of the Gregorian distinctions, the eleventh and twelfth centuries, that the institutional Church managed to impose on contemporary practice its concept of order, and functionally distinguished social roles according to differentiations of sexuality. It was by sacrificing their sexuality that henceforth clerics were able to define themselves as an exclusive order, that part of society which was devoted purely to the divine and which saw

4. Peter R. L. Brown, *The Body and Society: Men, Women, and Sexual Renunciation in Early Christianity* (New York, 1988), p. 432.

to the running of the eucharistic *fabrica* and social machinery in general. Purified of this blemish, the sacrificer was distinct from that other part of society comprising laymen, who married. Above all, the cleric was demarcated from women, the posterity of Eve, the ancestor through whom humanity became what it was, sexualized. Direct manipulation of the sacred was barred to women; at best, women might be consecrated to God by being shut up in the cloister or, more commonly, confined to the role of passing on the gift of life, the early education of children, and the management of ancestral memory.[5]

Within this perspective, the infidel and the heretic were perfect antitypes of the Christian priest. Those whom the priest rejected were identified fundamentally with what he sought to escape: the body. In the traditional European societies studied by Catherine Fabre-Vassas for her book *The Singular Beast*, the unbaptized child was no more than a "piece of flesh," a "piglet," a "little Jew," a "Moor," a "Saracen," who needed to be transformed in nature by the grace of baptism.[6] The Jew, with his attachment to the letter that "killeth" the spirit, was not merely bogged down in the human. Carnal defilement had made him bestial. The Saracen was a lecher, rendered senseless by sexual debauchery. Allah's paradise, in which males endlessly abandoned themselves to the flesh, eating, drinking, and copulating with ravishing virgins, was the diametric opposite of the vision of blessed humanity returning to a state beyond sex that Christian ideologists like Robert of Arbrissel, and a few enthusiastic individuals (quickly denounced as deviants because exceeding their role), attempted to realize in the here and now, living in a mixed community of men and women in anticipation of the afterlife.[7] Heretics, too, were most often regarded as sexually deviant. Hence the progressive lumping together of Jews, Muslims, heretics, and sodomites during the eleventh and twelfth centuries. All of them were opposed by the institutional Church with a view to defending the organic unity of the social body and the order of nature.[8]

5. The rich and complex subject of women's access to the sacred cannot be explored here in its own right. A refined approach with all necessary bibliography is Michel Lauwers's study, "L'institution et le genre: à propos de l'accès des femmes au sacré dans l'Occident médiéval," in *Clio, Histoire, Femmes et Sociétés* 2 (1995): 279–317. The whole subject is raised in Georges Duby's *The Knight, the Lady, and the Priest: The Making of Modern Marriage in Medieval France* and *Dames du XIIe siècle*, 3: *Eve et les prêtres* (see bibliography).

6. Fabre-Vassas, *The Singular Beast*, pp. 198ff. and 274 (quoted here); *La bête singulière*, pp. 225ff. and 305.

7. On these anticipatory movements, well documented in the eleventh and twelfth centuries, see (on the hermits of Bas-Maine only) Jacques Dalarun, *L'impossible sainteté: la vie retrouvée de Robert d'Arbrissel (v. 1045–1116), fondateur de Fontevraud* (Paris, 1985), and Dominique Iogna-Prat, "La femme dans la perspective pénitentielle des ermites du Bas-Maine (fin XIe–début XIIe siècle)," *Revue d'histoire de la spiritualité* 53 (1977): 47–64.

8. Jean Chiffoleau, "*Contra naturam:* pour une approche casuistique et procédurale de la nature médiévale," in the occasional series *Micrologus*, 4 (1996), *Il teatro de la natura/The Theater of Nature*, pp. 279 and 306 (about Jewish usury, *contra naturam*). The subject of heretics' sexual deviancy is never

Their transcendence of sexuality and consequent reservation to themselves of the part (*sors*) allotted to the divine underpinned clerics as an institution and put them in a position to control exchanges with the other world forged through the Eucharist. They possessed the power to achieve the transformation that gave Christian society its reason for existence. They had the authority to define what was human, to reveal the conditions necessary for man to live in a society destined to return to the pastures of the Lamb. That is why the fault line between Christendom and the devil's territory—be it that of heretics or infidels—was formed by the conception and practice of sacrifice. Peter the Venerable could not envisage a viable form of humanity that did not sacrifice. In modern anthropological language, he might have said that every society was formed by its exchanges between this world and the next. What Petrobrusians, Jews, and Saracens had in common was that they did not sacrifice. The Petrobrusians thought that it was possible for men to associate together without sacrificing to God—in other words without joining the circuit of exchanges that involved not only God and man but also man and man, living or dead. Bereft of their Temple and center, the Jews were no longer able to sacrifice. The Saracens simply did not sacrifice. The eleventh- and twelfth-century Christendom envisioned by a great abbot of Cluny thus had the historic role of saving humanity. By convincing mankind of the iron law of their condition—sacrifice, exchange with the other world—the disciples of Christ could hope to spread across the whole world, turning it all into Christendom.

The tyranny of the single Christian ring in the eleventh and twelfth centuries thus imposed on the world the certainties of clerics charged with the blessed morrows of humanity. However, as Peter Brown says, "even today, these notions still crowd in upon us, as pale, forbidding presences."[9] The exclusion of difference between 1000 and 1150 discussed in this book continued beyond those years. Ours has been a microhistorical analysis of a monastic Church that merged with the universal Church and sought to dominate all Christian society, if not indeed all mankind. Yet it shows very clearly how our own intolerances, those of the age of the Shoah and the desecration of cemeteries, of appeals for crusades and fundamentalist fervor, have distant origins in the demonization of the other in the Latin west of the eleventh and twelfth centuries. Our present-day ebbs and flows are signs of deeper currents. With a little effort and from good observation posts, the history of the Middle Ages can help us piece together the genesis of our stereotypes and throw light upon the infernal mechanisms like anti-Semitism that alienate human beings from their fellows. We

---

raised as such by Peter the Venerable, though it is a theme of Bernard of Clairvaux's: see Beverley M. Kienzle, "Tending the Lord's Vineyard: Cistercians, Rhetoric, and Heresy, 1143–1229," part 1: "Bernard of Clairvaux, the 1143 Sermons, and the 1145 Preaching Mission," *Heresis* 25 (1995): 42.

9. Brown, *The Body and Society*, pp. 446–47.

cannot draw neat, unequivocal routes from the alienation of the twelfth century to our own problems of collective identity. No doubt our relationship to the past is more a matter of residues than of permanence. Yet whatever the discontinuities that make the Middle Ages seem distant and exotic, it is worthwhile to seek to identify their residues and project a little light into the theater of our shadows.

BIBLIOGRAPHY

PRIMARY SOURCES

Acta synodi Atrebatensis. PL 142:1269–1312.

Alan of Lille. *De fide catholica contra haereticos. PL* 210:305–430.

Alger of Liège. *De sacramentis corporis et sanguinis dominici. PL* 180:739–854.

Bernard. *Ordo Cluniacensis.* In *Vetus disciplina monastica,* ed. Marquard Herrgott, pp. 133–364. Paris, 1726.

Bernard of Clairvaux. *De consideratione ad Eugenium papam.* In *Opera omnia,* vol. 3, ed. Jean Leclercq and Henri-Marie Rochais. Rome, 1963.

——. *De laude novae militiae.* Ed. and French trans. by Pierre-Yves Emery. Vol. 31 of *OEuvres complètes. SC* 367. Paris, 1990.

——. *Sermones super Cantica Canticarum.* In *Opera omnia,* vol. 2, ed. Jean Leclercq, Charles H. Talbot, and Henri-Marie Rochais. Rome, 1958.

Bullarium sacri ordinis cluniacensis. Ed. Pierre Simon. Lyon, 1680.

Le Cartulaire de Marcigny-sur-Loire (1045–1144). Essai de reconstitution d'un manuscrit disparu. Ed. Jean Richard. Vol. 4 of *Analecta Burgundica.* Dijon, 1957.

Galterius. *Vita sancti Anastasii. PL* 149:425–32.

Gilo. *Vita sancti Hugonis.* Ed. Herbert E. J. Cowdrey. Included in Cowdrey's "Two Studies in Cluniac History." In *Studi Gregoriani,* 11:45–109. Rome, 1978.

Guibert of Nogent. *Monodiae (De vita sua).* Ed. and trans. into French by Edmond-René Labande. Les Classiques de l'Histoire de France au Moyen Age, vol. 34. Paris, 1981. [English trans., *A Monk's Confession: The Memoirs of Guibert of Nogent,* trans. Paul J. Archambault. University Park, 1996.]

Guigo I. *Consuetudines Cartusiae.* In *Coutumes de Chartreuse,* ed. and French trans. by "un Chartreux." *SC* 313. Paris, 1984.

Guitmund of Aversa. *De corporis et sanguinis Christi veritate. PL* 149:1427–94.

Hildebert of Lavardin. *Vita sancti Hugonis. PL* 159:857–94.

Historia Compostellana. Ed. Emma Falque Rey. *CCCM* 70. Turnhout, 1988.

Hugh of Amiens. *Contra haereticos. PL* 192:1255–98.

——. *Dialogorum libri septem. PL* 192:1137–52.

Hugh of Gournay. *Vita sancti Hugonis.* Ed. Herbert E. J. Cowdrey. Included in Cowdrey's "Two Studies in Cluniac History." In *Studi Gregoriani,* 11:121–39. Rome, 1978.

Iotsaldus [Jotsald]. *Vita sancti Odilonis.* Ed. Johannes Staub. *MGH, SS,* 68. Hanover, 1999. [Replaces *PL* 142:897–940.]

John Beleth. *Summa de ecclesiasticis officiis.* Ed. Herbert Doubteil. *CCCM* 41A. Turnhout, 1976.

John of Salerno. *Vita sancti Odonis. PL* 133:43–86.

al-Kindi. *Apologia del Cristianismo.* Ed. José Muñoz Sendino. In Miscelanea Comillas, 11–12, pp. 375–460. Madrid, 1949.

Liber tramitis aevi Odilonis. Ed. Peter Dinter. *CCM* 10. Siegburg, 1980.

Miracula sancti Odonis. BC, cols. 447–62.

Nalgodus. *Vita sancti Odonis. PL* 133:85–104; see also Fini, Maria Luisa, under secondary works.

Odilo of Cluny. *Epitaphium domne Adalheidae auguste.* Ed. Herbert Paulhart. In *Die Lebensbeschreibung der Kaiserin Adelheid von Abt Odilo von Cluny.* Mitteilungen des Instituts für Österreichische Geschichtsforschung, Ergänzungsband, 20.2, pp. 27–45. Graz/Cologne, 1962.

——. *Vita sancti Maioli. BC*, cols. 279–90. [Text also printed in *PL* 142:943–62.]

Odo of Cluny. *Collationes. PL* 133:517–638.

——. *Vita sancti Geraldi. PL* 133:639–704.

Orderic Vitalis. *Historia ecclesiastica.* In *The Ecclesiastical History of Orderic Vitalis*, ed. and Eng. trans. by Marjorie Chibnall. 6 vols. Oxford Medieval Texts. Oxford, 1969–80.

Papsturkunden 896–1046. Ed. Harald Zimmermann. 3 vols. Österreichische Akademie der Wissenschaften, Philosophisch-historische Klasse, Denkschriften, 174, 177, 198. Vienna, 1984–89.

Peter Abelard. *Dialogus inter philosophum, judaeum et christianum.* Ed. Rudolf Thomas. Stuttgart/Bad Cannstadt, 1970. [Eng. trans., *A Dialogue of a Philosopher with a Jew and a Christian*, trans. Pierre J. Payer. Pontifical Institute of Mediaeval Studies. Toronto, 1979.]

Peter Damian. *Epistolae.* Ed. Kurt Reindel. 4 vols. *MGH*, Die Briefe der Deutschen Kaiserzeit, 4. Munich, 1983–93.

——. *Vita sancti Odilonis. PL* 144:925–44.

Peter of Poitiers, *Epistola.* Ed. Reinhold Glei. In *Petrus Venerabilis Schriften zum Islam.* Corpus Islamico-Christianum, Series latina, 1, pp. 226–30. Altenberge, 1985.

Peter the Venerable. *Adversus Iudeorum inveteratam duritiem* [cited here and elsewhere also as *Adversus Iudeos*]. Ed. Yvonne Friedman. *CCCM* 58. Turnhout, 1985.

——. *Contra Petrobrusianos hereticos.* Ed. James Fearns. *CCCM* 10. Turnhout, 1968.

——. *Contra sectam Sarracenorum.* Ed. Reinhold Glei. In *Petrus Venerabilis Schriften zum Islam.* Corpus Islamico-Christianum, Series latina, 1, pp. 30–225. Altenberge, 1985.

——. *De miraculis libri duo.* Ed. Denise Bouthillier. *CCCM* 83. Turnhout, 1988. [French trans., *Livre des merveilles de Dieu (De miraculis)*, trans., introduction, and notes by Jean-Pierre Torrell and Denise Bouthillier. Freiburg and Paris, 1992.]

——. *Epistola de translatione sua.* Ed. Reinhold Glei. In *Petrus Venerabilis Schriften zum Islam.* Corpus Islamico-Christianum, Series latina, 1, pp. 22–28. Altenberge, 1985.

——. *Epistolae.* In *The Letters of Peter the Venerable*, ed. Giles Constable. 2 vols. Harvard Historical Studies, 78. Cambridge, Mass., 1967.

——. *Rythmi, prosae, versus et hymni.* Ed. Guido M. Dreves. In *Lateinische Hymnendichter des Mittelalters.* Analecta Hymnica Medii Aevi, 48. Leipzig, 1905.

——. *Rythmus in laude Salvatoris.* Ed. Udo Wawrzyniak. *Philologische Untersuchungen zum "Rythmus in laude Salvatoris" des Petrus Venerabilis.* Lateinische Sprache und Literatur, 22, pp. 53–63. Bern and Frankfurt am Main, 1985.

——. *Rythmus de sancto Hugone abbate. PL* 189:1020–21.

——. *Sermo cuius supra in honore sancti illius cuius reliquiae sunt in praesenti. RB* 64 (1954): 265–72.

——. *Sermo in laude dominici sepulchri.* In *Sermones tres*, ed. Giles Constable. In ibid., pp. 232–54.

——. *Sermo de sancto Marcello papa et martyre.* In ibid., pp. 255–65.

——. *Sermo de transfiguratione domini. PL* 189:953–72.

——. *Sermones tres.* Ed. Giles Constable. *RB* 64 (1954): 232–72.

——. *Statuta.* Ed. Giles Constable. *CCM* 6, pp. 21–106. Siegburg, 1975.

——. *Summa totius haeresis Sarracenorum*. Ed. Reinhold Glei. In *Petrus Venerabilis Schriften zum Islam*. Corpus Islamico-Christianum, Series latina, 1, pp. 2–22. Altenberge, 1985.

Ralph of Sully. *Vita Petri Venerabilis*. *PL* 189:15–28.

Recueil des chartes de l'abbaye de Cluny. Ed. Auguste Bernard and Alexandre Bruel. Vols. 1–6. Collection de documents inédits sur l'Histoire de France. Paris, 1871–1903.

Das Register Gregors VII. Ed. Erich Caspar. 2 vols. *MGH*, Epistolae selectae, 2.1–2. Munich, 1920.

Reynold of Vézelay. *Vitae sancti Hugonis*. Ed. R. B. C. Huyghens. In *Vizeliacensia II: textes relatifs à l'histoire de l'abbaye de Vézelay*. *CCCM* 42, Supplementum, pp. 39–60 and 61–67. Turnhout, 1980.

Rodulfus Glaber. *Historiarum libri quinque*. In *Works*, ed. with parallel Eng. trans. by John France et al. Oxford Medieval Texts. Oxford, 1989.

Les Sociétés méridionales autour de l'an Mil: répertoire des sources et documents commentés. Ed. Michel Zimmermann. Paris, 1992.

Statuts, chapitres généraux et visites de l'ordre de Cluny. Ed. Gaston Charvin. 9 vols. Paris, 1965–82.

Synopse der cluniacensischen Necrologien. Ed. Wolf-Dieter Heim et al. and Joachim Wollasch. 2 vols. Münstersche Mittelalter-Schriften, 39. Munich, 1982.

Syrus. *Vita sancti Maioli*. Ed. Dominique Iogna-Prat. In *"Agni immaculati": recherches sur les sources hagiographiques relatives à saint Maieul de Cluny (954–994)*, pp. 163–285. Paris, 1988.

Ulrich. *Antiquiores consuetudines cluniacensis monasterii*. *PL* 149:635–778.

Vita sancti Hugonis. Listed, *BHL* 4012b. Ed. L. M. Smith. *English Historical Review* 27 (1912): 96–101.

Vita sancti Morandi. Listed, *BHL* 6020. Text in *BC*, cols. 501–6.

Vita sancti Odonis. Ed. Maria Luisa Fini. In *"L'editio minor della 'Vita' di Oddone di Cluny e gli apporti dell'Humillimus. Testo critico e nuovi orientamenti."* *L'Archiginnasio* 63–65 (1968–70): 132–259.

SECONDARY WORKS

À Cluny. Congrès scientifique, 9–11 July 1949. Dijon, 1950.

d'Alverny, Marie-Thérèse. "Deux traductions latines du Coran au Moyen Age." *Archives d'histoire doctrinale et littéraire du Moyen Age* 16 (1947–48): 69–131.

Angenendt, Arnold. *"Missa specialis*. Zugleich ein Beitrag zur Entstehung der Privatmessen." *FMSt* 17 (1983): 153–221.

Angheben, Marcel. "Apocalypse 21–22 et l'iconographie du grand portail de Vézelay." *Cahiers de civilisation médiévale* 41 (1998): 209–40.

Arnoux, Matthieu. "Un Vénitien au Mont-Saint-Michel: Anastase, moine, ermite et confesseur († vers 1085)." *Médiévales* 28 (1995): 55–78.

Arnoux, Mathieu, and Ghislain Brunel. "Réflexions sur les sources médiévales de l'histoire des campagnes: de l'intérêt de publier les sources, de les critiquer et de les lire." *Histoire et sociétés rurales* 1 (1994): 11–35.

Auctoritas und Ratio: Studien zu Berengar von Tours. Ed. Peter Ganz, Robert B. C. Huygens, and Friedrich Niewöhner. Wolfenbütteler Mittelalter Studien, 2. Wiesbaden, 1990.

Barlow, Frank. "The Canonization and the Early Lives of Hugo I, Abbot of Cluny." *Analecta Bollandiana* 98 (1980): 297–334.

Barthélemy, Dominique. *L'ordre seigneurial XIe–XIIe siècle*. Nouvelle Histoire de la France médiévale, 3. Paris, 1990.

Baud, Anne, and Gilles Rollier. "Abbaye de Cluny: campagne archéologique 1991–1992." *Bulletin monumental* 151.3 (1993): 453–68.

Bautier, Robert-Henri. "L'origine des populations juives de la France médiévale: constatations et hypothèses de recherche." In *La Catalogne et la France méridionale autour de l'an Mil*, ed. Xavier Barral i Altet, Dominique Iogna-Prat, Anscari M. Mundó, et al., pp 306–16. Barcelona, 1991.

Becker, Alfons. *Papst Urban II. (1088–1099)*. Vols. 1–2. Schriften der *MGH*, 19.1–2. Stuttgart 1964 and 1988.

Berlière, Ursmer. "L'exercice du ministère paroissial par les moines du XIIe au XVIIIe siècle." *RB* 39 (1927): 227–50.

Berry, Virginia. "Peter the Venerable and the Crusades." In *Petrus Venerabilis 1156–1956* (listed below), pp. 141–62.

Binding, Günther. *Der früh- und hochmittelalterliche Bauherr als sapiens architectus*. Darmstadt, 1996.

Bishko, Charles J. "Fernando I and the Origins of the Leonese-Castilian Alliance with Cluny." No. 2 in *Spanish and Portuguese Monastic History, 600–1300*. London, 1984.
——. "Liturgical Intercessions at Cluny for the King-Emperors of León." No. 8 in ibid.

Bligny, Bernard. *L'Eglise et les ordres religieux dans le royaume de Bourgogne aux XIe et XIIe siècles*. Grenoble, 1960.

Bloch, Marc. *La société féodale*. 1939–1940; 3d ed., Paris, 1970.

Bodard, M.-Claude. "Le mystère du corps du Seigneur: quelques aspects de la christologie de Pierre le Vénérable." *Collectanea Ordinis Cisterciensium reformatorum* 18 (1956): 118–31.

Bouchard, Constance Brittain. *Sword, Miter, and Cloister: Nobility and the Church in Burgundy, 980–1198*. Ithaca and London, 1987.

Boureau, Alain. "L'inceste de Judas: essai sur la genèse de la haine antisémite au XIIe siècle." *Nouvelle Revue de Psychanalyse* 33 (1986): 25–41.
——. "*Vel sedens, vel transiens:* la création d'un espace pontifical au Xe et XIIe siècle." In *Luoghi sacri e spazi della santità*, ed. Sofia Boesch Gajano and Lucetta Scaraffia, pp. 367–79. Turin, 1990.

Brolis, Maria Teresa. "La crociata per Pietro il Venerabile: guerra di arma o guerra di idee?" *Aevum* 61 (1987): 327–54.

Brown, Peter R. L. *The Body and Society: Men, Women, and Sexual Renunciation in Early Christianity*. New York, 1988.

Bull, Marcus. *Knightly Piety and the Lay Response to the First Crusade: The Limousin and Gascony, c. 970–c. 1130*. Oxford, 1993.

Bulst, Neithard. *Untersuchungen zu Klosterreformen Wilhelms von Dijon (962–1031)*. Pariser Historische Studien, 11. Bonn, 1973.

Büren, Veronika von. "Ambroise de Milan dans la bibliothèque de Cluny." *Scriptorium* 47 (1993): 127–65.
——. "Le catalogue de la bibliothèque de Cluny du XIe siècle reconstitué." *Scriptorium* 46 (1992): 256–67.
——. "Le grand catalogue de la bibliothèque de Cluny." In *Le gouvernement d'Hugues de Semur à Cluny* (listed below), pp. 245–63.

Cahen, Claude. *Orient et Occident au temps des Croisades*. Paris, 1982.

Cantarella, Glauco M. "Cultura ed ecclesiologia a Cluny (sec. XII)." *Aevum* 55.2 (1981): 272–93.
——. "Per l'analisi di una fonte cluniacense: l'*Epistola ad domnum Pontium cluniacensem abbatem*." *Bulletino dell'Istituto Storico Italiano per il Medio Evo e Archivo Muratoriano* 87 (1978): 54–87.

———. "Un problema del XII secolo: l'ecclesiologia di Pietro il Venerabile." *Studi Medievali*, 3d ser., 19 (1978): 159–209.

Capitani, Ovidio. "Motivi di spiritualità cluniacense e realismo eucharistico in Odone di Cluny." *Bulletino dell'Istituto Storico Italiano per il Medio Evo e Archivo Muratoriano* 71 (1950): 1–18.

Carozzi, Claude. *Le voyage de l'âme dans l'Au-delà d'après la littérature latine (Ve–XIIIe siècle)*. Collection de l'Ecole française de Rome, 189. Rome: Ecole française de Rome, 1994.

Les Cartulaires. Actes de la Table ronde organisée par l'Ecole des chartes et le GDR 121 du CNRS, Paris, 5–7 December 1991, ed. Olivier Guyotjeannin, Laurent Morelle, and Michel Parisse. Mémoires et documents de l'Ecole des Chartes, 39. Paris, 1993.

Chachuat, Germaine. "L'érémitisme à Cluny sous l'abbatiat de Pierre le Vénérable." *Annales de l'académie de Mâcon* 58 (1982): 89–96.

Chaume, Maurice. "Observations sur la chronologie des chartes de l'abbaye de Cluny." *RM* 16 (1926): 44–48; 29 (1939): 81–89 and 133–42; 31 (1941): 14–19, 42–45, and 69–82; 32 (1942): 15–20 and 133–36; 38 (1948): 1–6; 39 (1949): 41–43; 42 (1952): 1–4.

Chazan, Robert. "The Deteriorating Image of the Jews—Twelfth and Thirteenth Centuries." In *Christendom and Its Discontents* (listed below), pp. 220–33.

Chelini, Jean. *L'aube du Moyen Age, naissance de la chrétienté occidentale: la vie religieuse des laïcs à l'époque carolingienne, 750–900*. Paris, 1991.

Chiffoleau, Jacques. "*Contra naturam:* pour une approche casuistique et procédurale de la nature médiévale." In [occasional series] *Micrologus*, 4 (1996), *Il teatro de la natura/ The Theater of Nature*, pp. 265–312.

———. "Dire l'indicible: remarques sur la catégorie du *nefandum* du XIIe au XVe siècle." *AESC* 1990: 289–324.

Christendom and Its Discontents: Exclusion, Persecution, and Rebellion, 1000–1500. Ed. Scott L. Waugh and Peter D. Diehl. Cambridge, 1995.

Cluniac Monasticism in the Central Middle Ages. Ed. Noreen Hunt. Readings in European History. London, 1971.

Die Cluniazencer in ihrem politisch-sozialen Umfeld. Ed. Giles Constable, Gert Melville, and Jörg Oberste. Münster im W., 1998.

Cluny: Beiträge zu Gestalt und Wirkung der cluniazensischen Reform. Ed. Helmut Richter. Wege der Forschung, 241. Darmstadt, 1975.

Cluny in Lombardia. Atti del Convegno storico celebrativo del IX Centenario della fondazione del priorato cluniacense di Pontida, 22–25 April 1977. 2 vols. Italia benedettina, 1. Cesena, 1979–81.

Cochelin, Isabelle. "Enfants, jeunes et vieux au monastère: la perception du cycle de la vie dans les sources clunisiennes (909–1156)." 2 vols. Typescript. Doctoral thesis, University of Montreal, 1996.

Conant, Kenneth J. *Cluny: les églises et la maison du chef d'ordre*. Mâcon, 1968.

The Concept of Heresy in the Middle Ages (11th–13th century). Proceedings of the International Conference, Leuven, 13–16 May 1973, ed. Willem Lourdaux and Daniel Verhelst. Mediaevalia Lovaniensia, ser. 1, Studia 4. Leuven and The Hague, 1976.

Congar, Yves. *L'ecclésiologie du haut Moyen Age de saint Grégoire le Grand à la désunion entre Byzance et Rome*. Paris, 1968.

———. *L'Eglise, de saint Augustin à l'époque moderne*. Histoire des dogmes, 3.3. Paris, 1970.

———. *Sacerdoce et laïcat devant leurs tâches d'évangélisation et de civilisation*. Paris, 1962.

Constable, Giles. "The Abbot and Townsmen of Cluny in the Twelfth Century." In *Church and City, 1000–1500: Essays in Honour of Christopher Brooke*, ed. David Abulafia, Michael J. Franklin, and Miri Rubin, pp. 151–71. Cambridge, 1992.
——. *Cluniac Studies*. London, 1980.
——. "The Disputed Election at Langres in 1138." *Traditio* 13(1957): 119–52. Reprinted in Constable, *Cluniac Studies*, no. 10.
——. "Entrance to Cluny in the Eleventh and Twelfth Centuries according to the Cluniac Customories and Statutes." In *Mediaevalia Christiana XIe–XIIe siècles. Hommage à Raymonde Foreville de ses amis, ses collègues et ses anciens élèves*, ed. Colomon Etienne Viola, pp. 335–54. Tournai, 1989.
——. "Monastic Possession of Churches and 'Spiritualia' in the Age of Reform." In *Il monachesimo e la riforma ecclesiastica (1049–1122)* (listed below), pp. 304–31. Reprinted in Constable, *Religious Life and Thought*, no. 8.
——. *Monastic Tithes from Their Origins to the Twelfth Century*. Cambridge, Mass., 1964.
——. "Monasticism, Lordship, and Society in the Twelfth-Century Hesbaye: Five Documents on the Foundation of the Cluniac priory of Bertrée." *Traditio* 33 (1977): 159–224. Reprinted in Constable, *Cluniac Studies*, no. 9.
——. "Opposition to Pilgrimage in the Middle Ages." In *Mélanges G. Fransen*, 1. *Studia Gratiana* 19 (1976): 123–46. Reprinted in Giles Constable, *Religious Life and Thought*, no. 3.
——. "The Reception Privilege of Cluny in the Eleventh and Twelfth Centuries." In *Le gouvernement de Hugh de Semur à Cluny* (listed below), pp. 59–74.
——. *The Reformation of the Twelfth Century*. Cambridge, 1996.
——. *Religious Life and Thought (11th–12th centuries)*. London, 1979.
——. "*Seniores* et *pueri* à Cluny aux Xe, XIe siècles." In *Histoire et société: mélanges offerts à Georges Duby* (listed below), 3:17–24.
——. *Three Studies in Medieval Religious and Social Thought*. Cambridge, 1995.
——. "The Vision of Gunthelm and Other Visions Attributed to Peter the Venerable." *RB* 66 (1956): 92–114. Reprinted in Constable, *Cluniac Studies*, no. 6.
Corbet, Patrick. *Les saints ottoniens: sainteté dynastique, sainteté royale et sainteté féminine autour de l'an Mil*. Beihefte der Francia, 15. Sigmaringen, 1986.
Cowdrey, Herbert E. J. "Cardinal Peter of Albano's Legation Journey to Cluny (1080)." *Journal of Theological Studies*, new ser., 24 (1973): 481–91. Reprinted in Cowdrey, *Popes, Monks, and Crusaders*, no. 11.
——. *The Cluniacs and the Gregorian Reform*. Oxford, 1970.
——. "Cluny and the First Crusade." *RB* 83 (1973): 285–311. Reprinted in Cowdrey, *Popes, Monks, and Crusaders*, no. 15.
——. *Popes, Monks, and Crusaders*. London, 1984.
——. "Two Studies in Cluniac History," I: "Memorials of Abbot Hugh of Cluny (1049–1109)." In *Studi Gregoriani*, 11, pp. 13–175. Rome, 1978.
——. "Unions and Confraternity with Cluny." *Journal of Ecclesiastical History* 16 (1965): 152–62.
Cramer, Peter. *Baptism and Change in the Early Middle Ages, c. 200–c. 1150*. Cambridge Studies in Medieval Life and Thought. Cambridge, 1993.
Current Studies on Cluny. In *Gesta* 27 (1988).
Cygler, Florent. "L'ordre de Cluny et les *rebelliones* au XIIIe siècle." *Francia* 19.1 (1992): 61–93.
——. "Règles, coutumiers et statuts (Ve–XIIIe siècle): brèves considérations typologiques." In *La vie quotidienne des moines et chanoines réguliers au Moyen Age et Temps modernes* (listed below), 1:31–48.

Dahan, Gilbert. *Les intellectuels chrétiens et les juifs au Moyen Age.* Patrimoine judaïsme. Paris, 1990.

Daniel, Norman. *Islam and the West: The Making of an Image.* Rev. ed. Oxford, 1993.

Delaruelle, Etienne. "L'idée de croisade dans la littérature clunisienne du XIe siècle et l'abbaye de Moissac." *Annales du Midi* 75 (1963): 419–40. Reprinted in *Cluniac Monasticism in the Central Middle Ages* (listed above), pp. 191–216, and Delaruelle, *L'idée de croisade*, pp. 129–52.

——. *L'idée de croisade au Moyen Age.* Turin, 1980.

Delisle, Léopold. *Inventaire des manuscrits de la Bibliothèque Nationale, fonds de Cluni.* Paris, 1884.

Didier, Jean-Charles. *Le baptême des enfants dans la tradition de l'Eglise.* Monumenta Christiana Selecta, 7. Tournai, 1959.

——. *Faut-il baptiser les enfants? La réponse de la tradition.* Chrétiens de tous les temps, 21. Paris, 1967.

——. "La question du baptême des enfants chez saint Bernard et ses contemporains." In *Saint Bernard théologien*, Actes du congrès de Dijon, 15–19 September 1953. *Analecta Sacri Ordinis Cisterciensis* 9 (1953): 191–201.

Diener, Herbert. "Das Verhältnis Clunys zu den Bischöfen vor allem in der Zeit seines Abtes Hugo (1049–1109)." In *Neue Forschungen über Cluny und die Cluniacenser*, ed. Gerd Tellenbach, pp. 219–393. Freiburg im B., 1959.

Drouard-Adda, Maurice. "Eléments historiques dans un traité de polémique antijuive: l'*Adversus Judaeos* de Pierre le Vénérable." *Archives juives* 1 (1971–72): 1–6.

Dubois, Jacques. "Le désert, cadre de vie des Chartreux au Moyen Age." In *La naissance des chartreuses*, Actes du VIe colloque international d'histoire et de spiritualité cartusiennes, Grenoble, 12–15 September 1984, ed. Bernard Bligny and Gérald Chaix, pp. 15–35. Grenoble, 1986.

Duby, Georges. "Le budget de Cluny entre 1080 et 1155." In Duby, *Hommes et structures*, pp. 61–82.

——. *Le chevalier, la femme et le prêtre: le mariage dans la France féodale.* Paris, 1981. [Eng. trans., *The Knight, the Lady, and the Priest: The Making of Modern Marriage in Medieval France*, trans. Barbara Bray with introduction by Natalie Zemon Davis. London, 1984.]

——. *Dames du XIIe siècle.* 3 vols. Bibliothèque des Histoires. Paris, 1995–96. [Eng. trans., *Women of the Twelfth Century*, trans. Jean Birrell. Oxford, 1997–98.]

——. *Guerriers et paysans, VIIe–XIIe siècle: premier essor de l'économie européenne.* Bibliothèque des Histoires. Paris, 1973. [Eng. trans., *The Early Growth of the European Economy: Warriors and Peasants from the Seventh to the Twelfth Century*, trans. Howard B. Clarke. Ithaca, 1974.]

——. *Hommes et structures du Moyen Age.* Paris and The Hague, 1973. [Most articles translated into English by Cynthia Postan in Georges Duby, *The Chivalrous Society.* Berkeley, 1980.]

——. "Un inventaire des profits de la seigneurie clunisienne à la mort de Pierre le Vénérable." In Duby, *Hommes et structures*, pp. 87–101.

——. *La société aux XIe et XIIe siècles dans la région mâconnaise.* 2d ed. Paris, 1971.

——. *Les trois ordres ou l'imaginaire du féodalisme.* Bibliothèque des Histoires. Paris, 1978. [Eng. trans., *The Three Orders: Feudal Society Imagined*, trans. Arthur Goldhammer, with foreword by Thomas N. Bisson. Chicago, 1982.]

Dumont, Louis. *Essays on Individualism: Modern Ideology in Anthropological Perspective.* Chicago, 1986. [Revised and extended English version of *Essais sur l'individualisme: une perspective anthropologique sur l'idéologie moderne.* Paris, 1991 and 1993.]

L'Eglise en prière. Ed. Aimé-Georges Martimort. 2d ed. 4 vols. Paris, 1983–84.

L'Eglise, le terroir. Ed. Michel Fixot and Elisabeth Zadora-Rio. Monographies du Centre de recherches archéologiques, 1. Paris, 1989.

Erdmann, Carl. *Die Entstehung des Kreuzzugsgedankens.* Stuttgart, 1935; 2d ed., Darmstadt, 1980. [Eng. trans., *The Origin of the Idea of Crusade*, with updated bibliography by Marshall D. Baldwin and Walter Goffart. Princeton, 1977.]

Etaix, Raymond. "Le lectionnaire de l'office à Cluny." *Recherches augustiniennes* 11 (1976): 92–159. Reprinted in *Homélaires patristiques latins: recueil d'études de manuscrits médiévaux*, pp. 137–205. Collection des Etudes augustiniennes, Série Moyen Age et Temps modernes, 29. Paris, 1994.

Fabre-Vassas, Claudine. *La bête singulière: les juifs, les chrétiens et le cochon.* Bibliothèque des Sciences humaines. Paris, 1993. [Eng. trans., *The Singular Beast: Jews, Christians, and the Pig*, trans. Carol Volk. New York, 1997.]

Fearns, James. "Peter von Bruis und die religiöse Bewegung des 12. Jahrhunderts." *Archiv für Kulturgeschichte* 48 (1966): 311–35.

Fichtenau, Heinrich. *Ketzer und Professoren: Häresie und Vernunftglaube im Hochmittelalter.* Munich, 1992.

Fini, Maria Luisa. "L'editio minor della 'Vita' di Oddone di Cluny e gli apporti dell'Humillimus. Testo critico e nuovi orientamenti." *L'Archiginnasio* 63–65 (1968–70): 132–259.

———. "Studio sulla 'Vita Odonis reformata' di Nalgodo. Il 'fragmentum mutilum' del Codice latino NA 1496 della Bibliothèque nationale di Parigi." *Rendiconti dell'Accademia di Scienze dell'Istituto di Bologna: Classe di scienze morali*, Bologna 63.2 (1975): 33–147.

Flori, Jean. "Du nouveau sur les origines de la première croisade." [Review article on Marcus Bull, *Knightly Piety and the First Crusade.*] *Le Moyen Age* 101 (1995): 103–11.

———. *L'idéologie du glaive: préhistoire de la chevalerie.* Geneva, 1983.

Folz, Robert. "Pierre le Vénérable et la liturgie." In *Pierre Abélard, Pierre le Vénérable* (listed below), pp. 143–61.

Fonseca, Cosimo D. "Typologie des réseaux monastiques et canoniaux des origines au XIIe siècle." In *Naissance et fonctionnement des réseaux monastiques et canoniaux* (listed below), pp. 11–20.

Fossier, Robert. *Enfance de l'Europe: aspects économiques et sociaux, Xe–XIIe siècle.* Nouvelle Clio, 17–17 *bis.* Paris, 1982.

Frugoni, Arsenio. *Arnaldo da Brescia nelle fonte del duecento.* Rome, 1954; 2d ed., Turin, 1989. [French trans., *Arnaud de Brescia dans les sources du XIIe siècle.* Paris, 1993.]

Garand, Monique-Cécile. "Une collection personnelle de saint Odilon de Cluny et ses compléments." *Scriptorium* 33 (1979): 163–80.

———. "Copistes de Cluny au temps de saint Maieul (948–994)." *BEC* 136 (1978): 5–36.

———. "Les plus anciens témoins conservés des *Consuetudines Cluniacenses* d'Ulrich de Ratisbonne." In *"Scire litteras": Forschungen zum mittelalterlischen Geitesleben*, ed. Sigrid Krämer and Michael Bernard, pp. 171–82. Munich, 1988.

———. "Le scriptorium de Cluny carrefour d'influences au XIe siècle: le manuscrit Paris, BN n.a.l. 1548." *Journal des savants* 1977:257–83.

Godelier, Maurice. *L'énigme du don.* Paris, 1996. [Eng. trans., *The Enigma of the Gift*, trans. Nora Scott. Cambridge, 1999.]

Goering, Joseph. "The Invention of Transubstantiation." *Traditio* 46 (1991): 147–70.

Golb, Norman. *The Jews in Medieval Normandy: A Social and Intellectual History.* Cambridge, 1998. Revised and augmented edition of *Les Juifs de Rouen au Moyen*

Age: portrait d'une culture oubliée. Publications de l'Université de Rouen, 66. Rouen, 1985.

Goody, Jack. *The Development of the Family and Marriage in Europe*. Cambridge, 1983.

Le gouvernement d'Hugues de Semur à Cluny. Actes du colloque scientifique international, Cluny, September 1988. Cluny, 1990.

Graboïs, Aryeh. *Civilisation et société dans l'Occident médiéval*. London, 1983.

———. "Les juifs et leurs seigneurs dans la France septentrionale aux XIe et XIIe siècles." In *Les juifs dans l'histoire de France* (listed below), pp. 11–23. Reprinted in Graboïs, *Civilisation et société*, no. 18.

———. "Le schisme de 1130 et la France." *Revue d'histoire de l'Eglise en France* 76 (1981): 593–612. Reprinted in Graboïs, *Civilisation et société*, no. 2.

———. *Les sources hébraïques médiévales*, 2: *les commentaires exégétiques*. Typologie des sources du Moyen Age occidental, 66. Turnhout, 1993.

Grandjean, Michel. *Les laïcs dans l'Eglise: regards de Pierre Damien, Anselme de Cantorbéry, Yves de Chartres*. Théologie historique, 97. Paris, 1994.

Guerreau, Alain. "Espace social, espace symbolique: à Cluny au XIe siècle." In *L'ogre historien: autour de Jacques Le Goff*, ed. Jacques Revel and Jean-Claude Schmitt, pp. 167–91. Paris, 1999.

———. "Quelques caractères spécifiques de l'espace féodal européen." In *L'Etat ou le roi? Les fondations de la modernité monarchique en France (XIVe–XVIIe siècle)*, ed. Neithard Bulst, Robert Descimon, and Alain Guerreau, pp. 85–101. Paris, 1996.

Guerreau-Jalabert, Anita. "*Spiritus* et *caritas*: le baptême dans la société médiévale." In *La parenté spirituelle*, ed. Françoise Heritier-Augé and Elisabeth Copet-Rougier, pp. 133–203. Paris, 1995.

Hageneder, Othmar. "Der Häresiebegriff bei der Juristen des 12. und 13. Jahrhunderts." In *The Concept of Heresy in the Middle Ages* (listed above), pp. 42–103.

Hallinger, Kassius. "*Consuetudo*: Begriff, Formen, Forschungsgeschichte, Inhalt." In *Untersuchungen zu Kloster und Stift*, pp. 140–66. Veröffentlichungen des Max-Planck-Instituts für Geschichte, 68. Göttingen, 1980.

———. *Gorze-Kluny: Studien zu den monastischen Lebensformen und Gegensätzen im Hochmittelalter*. 2 vols. Studia Anselmiana, 22–25. Rome, 1950–51.

———. "Klunys Brauche zur Zeit Hugos des Grossen (1049–1109). Prolegomena zur Neuherausgabe des Bernhard und Udalrich von Kluny." *Zeitschrift der Savigny-Stiftung für Rechtsgeschichte, Kanonistische Abteilung* 45 (1959): 99–140.

Härdelin, Alf. "Pâques et Rédemption: étude de théologie monastique du XIIe siècle." *Collectanea Cisterciensia* 43 (1981): 3–19.

Hausmann, Regina. *Das Martyrologium von Marcigny-sur-Loire. Edition einer Quelle zur cluniacensischen Heiligenverehrung am Ende des elften Jahrhunderts.* HochschulSammlung Philosophie Geschichte, 7. Freiburg im B., 1984.

Heintz, Cornelia. "Anfänge und Entwicklung des Cluniazenser-Priorates St.-Martin-des-Champs in Paris (1079–1150)." Dissertation, Münster im W., 1982.

Henriet, Patrick. "Saint Odilon devant la mort. Sur quelques données implicites du comportement religieux au XIe siècle." *Le Moyen Age* 96 (1990): 227–44.

Hillebrandt, Maria. "Albertus Teutonicus, copiste de chartes et de livres à Cluny." In *Etudes d'histoire du droit médiéval en souvenir de Josette Metman*, pp. 215–32. *Mémoires de la Société pour l'histoire du droit et des institutions des anciens pays bourguignons, comtois et romans* 45 (1988).

———. "Berzé-la-Ville: la création d'une dépendance clunisienne." In *Le gouvernement d'Hugues de Semur à Cluny* (listed above), pp. 199–229.

——. "Les cartulaires de l'abbaye de Cluny." *Mémoires de la Société pour l'histoire du droit et des institutions des anciens pays bourguignons, comtois et romans* 50 (1993): 7–18.

——. "The Cluniac Charters: Remarks on a Quantitative Approach for Prosopographical Studies." *Medieval Prosopography* 3 (1982): 3–25.

——. *Neudatierung von Urkunden der Abtei Cluny.* Münstersche Mittelalter-Schriften. Munich, forthcoming.

——. "Le prieuré de Paray-le-Monial au XIe siècle: ses rapports avec le monde laïc et l'abbaye de Cluny." In *Paray-le-Monial*, Premier Colloque scientifique international, 28–30 May 1992, pp. 106–24. Paray-le-Monial, 1994.

——. "Stiftungen zum Seelenheit durch Frauen in den Urkunden des Klosters Cluny." In *Vinculum societatis* (listed below), pp. 58–67.

Histoire et société: mélanges offerts à Georges Duby. 3 vols. Aix-en-Provence, 1992.

Hödl, Ludwig. "Der Transsubstantiationsbegriff in der scholastischen Theologie des 12. Jahrhunderts." *Recherches de théologie ancienne et médiévale* 31 (1964): 230–59.

Hoffmann, Hartmut. *Gottesfriede und Treuga Dei.* Schriften der *MGH*, 20. Stuttgart, 1964.

Hofmeister, Philipp. "Mönchtum und Seelsorge bis zum 13. Jahrhundert." *SMGBOZ* 65 (1955): 245–62.

Hüls, Rudolf. *Kardinäle, Klerus und Kirchen Roms 1049–1130.* Bibliothek des deutschen historischen Instituts in Rom, 48. Tübingen, 1977.

Hunt, Noreen. *Cluny under Saint Hugh.* London, 1967.

Inventer l'hérésie? Discours polémiques et pouvoirs avant l'Inquisition. Ed. Monique Zerner. Collection du Centre d'études médiévales de Nice, 2. Nice, 1998.

Iogna-Prat, Dominique. *"Agni immaculati": recherches sur les sources hagiographiques relatives à saint Maieul de Cluny (954–994).* Paris, 1988.

——. "Le 'baptême' du schéma des trois ordres fonctionnels: l'apport de l'école d'Auxerre dans la seconde moitié du IXe siècle." *AESC* 1986.1:101–26.

——. "Cluny à la mort de Maieul (994–998)." *Bulletin de la Société des fouilles archéologiques et des monuments historiques de l'Yonne* 12 (1995): 13–23.

——. "Coutumes et statuts clunisiens comme sources historiques (ca. 990–ca. 1200). *RM*, new ser., 3 (1992): 23–48.

——. "La Croix, le moine et l'empereur: dévotion à la Croix et théologie politique à Cluny autour de l'an Mil." In *Haut Moyen Age: culture, éducation et société: études offertes à Pierre Riché*, ed. Michel Sot, pp. 449–75. Paris, 1990.

——. "La geste des origines dans l'historiographie clunisienne des XIe–XIIe siècles." *RB* 102 (1992): 135–91.

——. Les morts dans la comptabilité céleste des Clunisiens de l'an Mil." In *Religion et culture autour de l'an Mil* (listed below), pp. 55–69.

——. "Ordre(s), transcendance et mobilité sociale dans l'Occident médiéval (IVe–XIIe siècle)." In *Dictionnaire raisonné de l'Occident médiéval*, ed. Jacques Le Goff and Jean-Claude Schmitt, pp. 845–60. Paris, 1999.

——. "Panorama de l'hagiographie abbatiale clunisienne (v. 940–v. 1140)." In *Manuscrits hagiographiques et travail des hagiographes*, ed. Martin Heinzelmann, pp. 77–118. Beihefte der Francia, 24. Sigmaringen, 1992.

Iogna-Prat, Dominique, Barbara H. Rosenwein, Xavier Barral i Altet, and Guy Barruol. *Saint Maieul, Cluny et la Provence.* Les Alpes de lumières, 115. Salagon, 1994.

Iogna-Prat, Dominique, and Christian Sapin. "Les études clunisiennes dans tous leurs états." *RM*, new ser., 5 (1994): 233–58.

Jorden, Willibald. *Das cluniazensische Totengedächtniswesen vornehmlich unter den drei*

ersten Äbten Berno, Odo und Aymard (910–954). Münstersche Beiträge zur
Theologie, 15. Münster im W., 1930.

Les juifs dans l'histoire de France. Premier colloque international de Haïfa. Ed. Myriam
Yardeni. Leiden, 1980.

Jungmann, Josef A. *Missarum sollemnia: eine genetische Erklärung der römischen Messe*. 4th
ed. 2 vols. Freiburg, 1958. [Eng. eds.: (1) *The Mass of the Roman Rite: Its Origins and
Development (Missarum sollemnia)*, trans. of 2d ed. (Vienna, 1949) by Francis A.
Brunner. 2 vols. New York, 1950. (2) same Eng. title, Brunner's version updated
from 1958 German ed., one-volume abridgment by Charles K. Riepe. London,
1959.]

Kienzle, Beverley M. "Tending the Lord's Vineyard: Cistercians, Rhetoric, and Heresy,
1143–1229," Part 1: "Bernard of Clairvaux, the 1143 Sermons, and the 1145
Preaching Mission." *Heresis* 25 (1995): 29–61.

Kniewasser, Manfred. "Die antijüdische Polemik des Petrus Alfonsi (getauft 1106) und
des Abtes Petrus Venerabilis von Cluny († 1156)." *Kairos: Zeitschrift für
Religionswissenschaft und Theologie* 22 (1980): 34–76.

Kohnle, Armin. *Abt Hugo von Cluny (1049–1109)*. Beihefte der Francia, 32.
Sigmaringen, 1993.

Kritzeck, James. *Peter the Venerable and Islam*. Princeton Oriental Studies, 23.
Princeton, 1964.

Langmuir, Gavin I. *History, Religion, and Antisemitism*. Berkeley, 1990.

———. *Toward a Definition of Antisemitism*. Berkeley, 1990.

Laudage, Johannes. *Gregorianische Reform und Investiturstreit*. Erträge der Forschung.
Darmstadt, 1993.

———. *Priesterbild und Reformpapsttum im 11. Jahrhundert*. Beihefte zu Archiv für
Kulturgeschichte, 22. Cologne and Vienna, 1984.

Lauranson-Rosaz, Christian. *L'Auvergne et ses marges (Velay, Gévaudan) du VIIIe au XIe
siècle: la fin du monde antique?* Le Puy-en-Velay, 1987.

Lauwers, Michel. *La mémoire des ancêtres, le souci des morts: morts, rites et société au Moyen
Age*. Théologie historique, 103. Paris, 1997.

Leclercq, Jean "La christologie clunisienne au siècle de saint Hugues." *Studia Monastica*
31 (1989): 267–78. Reprinted in *Le gouvernement d'Hugues de Semur à Cluny* (listed
above), pp. 523–35.

———. "L'hérésie d'après les écrits de saint Bernard de Clairvaux." In *The Concept of
Heresy in the Middle Ages* (listed above), pp. 12–26.

———. *Pierre le Vénérable*. Figures Monastiques. Saint-Wandrille, 1946.

———. "Pierre le Vénérable et l'érémitisme clunisien." In *Petrus Venerabilis 1156–1956*
(listed below), pp. 99–120.

Le Goff, Jacques. *La naissance du Purgatoire*. Bibliothèque des Histoires. Paris, 1981.
[Eng. trans., *The Birth of Purgatory*, trans. Arnold Goldhammer. Chicago, 1984.]

Lemarignier, Jean-François. "L'exemption monastique et la réforme clunisienne." In *À
Cluny* (listed above), pp. 288–334.

Levi, Isaac. "La nativité de Ben Sira." *Revue des études juives* 29 (1894): 197–205.

Little, Lester K. *Benedictine Maledictions: Liturgical Cursing in Romanesque France*. Ithaca
and London, 1993.

Lobrichon, Guy. "The Chiaroscuro of Heresy: Early Eleventh-Century Aquitaine As
Seen from Auxerre." In *The Peace of God: Social Violence and Religious Response in
France around the Year 1000*, ed. Thomas Head and Richard Landes, pp. 80–103.
Ithaca and London, 1992.

———. "Jugement dernier et Apocalypse." In *De l'art comme mystagogie: iconographie du*

Jugement dernier et des fins dernières à l'époque gothique, pp. 9–18. Actes du colloque de la Fondation Hardt, Geneva, 13–16 February 1994. Civilisation médiévale, 3. Poitiers, 1996.

———. *La religion des laïcs en Occident.* La vie quotidienne. Paris, 1994.

Lubac, Henri de. *Corpus mysticum: l'Eucharistie et l'Eglise au Moyen Age.* 2d ed. Théologie, 3. Paris, 1949.

———. *Exégèse médiévale: les quatre sens de l'Ecriture.* 4 vols. Théologie, 41, 42, and 59. Paris, 1959, 1961, and 1964.

Lynch, Joseph H. *Godparents and Kinship in Early Medieval Europe.* Princeton, 1986.

———. "Hugh I of Cluny's Sponsorship of Henry IV: Its Context and Consequences." *Speculum* 60 (1985): 800–826.

Maccarrone, Michèle. *Vicarius Christi: storia del titolo papale. Lateranum,* new ser., 18. Rome, 1952.

McGinn, Bernard. *Antichrist: Two Thousand Years of the Human Fascination with Evil.* San Francisco, 1994.

Macy, Gary. "Berengar's Legacy as Heresiarch." In *Auctoritas und Ratio* (listed above), pp. 47–67.

———. "The Dogma of Transubstantiation in the Middle Ages." *Journal of Ecclesiastical History* 45.1 (1994): 11–41.

———. *Theologies of the Eucharist in the Early Scholastic Period: A Study of the Salvific Function of the Sacrament according to the Theologians, c. 1080–c. 1220.* Oxford, 1984.

Magnani Soares-Christen, Eliana. "Monastères et aristocratie en Provence (milieu Xe–XIIe siècle)." 2 vols. Typescript. Doctoral thesis, Université de Provence, Aix-en-Provence, 1997.

Manselli, Raoul. "Il monaco Enrico e la sua eresia." *Bulletino dell'Istituto Storico Italiano per il Medio Evo e Archivio Muratoriano* 65 (1953): 1–63.

Martimort, Aimé-Georges. *Les "Ordines," les ordinaires et les cérémoniaux.* Typologie des sources du Moyen Age occidental, 56. Turnhout, 1991.

Das Martyrolog-Necrolog von Moissac/Duravel: Facsimile-Ausgabe. Ed. Axel Müssigbrod and Joachim Wollasch. Münstersche Mittelalter-Schriften, 44. Munich, 1988.

Mauss, Marcel. "Essai sur le don: forme et raison de l'échange dans les sociétés archaïques." *L'Année sociologique,* new ser., 1 (1923–24). Reprinted in *Sociologie et anthropologie,* pp. 143–279. Sociologie d'aujourd'hui. 4th ed. Paris, 1968. [Eng. trans., *The Gift: The Form and Reason for Exchange in Archaic Societies,* trans. W. D. Halls. London, 1990.]

Mehne, Joachim. "Cluniacenserbischöfe." *FMSt* 11 (1977): 241–87.

Melville, Gert. "Die cluniazensische *Reformatio tam in capite quam in membris:* Institutioneller Wandel zwischen Anpassung und Bewahrung." In *Sozialer Wandel im Mittelalter: Wahrnehmungsformen, Erklärungsmuster, Regelungsmechanismen,* ed. Jürgen Miethke and Klaus Schreiner, pp. 249–97. Sigmaringen, 1994.

———. "Cluny après 'Cluny': le treizième siècle, un champ de recherche." *Francia* 17.1 (1990): 91–124.

Memoria: der geschichtliche Zeugniswert des liturgischen Gedenkens im Mittelalter. Ed. Karl Schmid and Joachim Wollasch. Münstersche Mittelalter-Schriften, 48. Munich, 1984.

Memoria in der Gesellschaft des Mittelalters. Ed. Dieter Geuenich and Otto G. Oexle. Veröffentlichungen des Max-Planck-Instituts für Geschichte, 111. Göttingen, 1994.

Memoria als Kultur. Ed. Otto G. Oexle. Veröffentlichungen des Max-Planck-Instituts für Geschichte, 121. Göttingen, 1995.

Milis, Ludo J. R. *Angelic Monks and Earthly Men: Monasticism and Its Meaning to Medieval Society*. Woodbridge, 1992.

Il Monachesimo e la riforma ecclesiastica (1049–1122). Atti della quarta Settimana internazionale di studio, Mendola, 22–29 August 1968. Miscellanea del Centro di Studi medioevali, 6. Milan, 1971.

Montclos, Jean de. *Lanfranc et Béranger: la controverse eucharistique du XIe siècle*. Spicilegium Sacrum Lovaniense, 37. Leuven, 1971.

Moore, Robert I. "A la naissance d'une société persécutrice: les clercs, les cathares et la formation de l'Europe." *Heresis* 6 (1993): 11–37.

——. *The Formation of a Persecuting Society: Power and Deviance in Western Europe, 950–1250*. Oxford, 1987.

——. "Heresy, Repression, and Social Change in the Age of Gregorian Reform." In *Christendom and Its Discontents* (listed above), pp. 19–46.

Morris, Colin. *The Discovery of the Individual, 1050–1200*. 2d ed. Medieval Academy Reprints for Teaching. Toronto, 1987.

Müssigbrod, Axel. *Die Abtei Moissac 1050–1150: zu einem Zentrum cluniacensischen Mönchtums in Südwestfrankreich*. Münstersche Mittelalter-Schriften, 58. Munich, 1988.

——. "Die Beziehungen des Bischofs Petrus von Pamplona zum französichen Mönchtum." *RB* 104 (1994): 346–78.

——. "Quellen zum Totengedächtnis der Abtei Moissac." *RB* 97 (1987): 253–88.

——. "Zur Necrologüberlieferung aus cluniacensischen Klöstern." *RB* 98 (1988): 62–113.

Naissance et fonctionnement des réseaux monastiques et canoniaux. Actes du premier colloque international du CERCOM, Saint-Etienne, 16–18 September 1985. CERCOR, Travaux et Recherches, 1. Saint-Etienne, 1991.

Neiske, Franz. "Concordances et différences dans les nécrologes clunisiens: aspects d'une analyse statistique." *Revue d'histoire de l'Eglise de France* 68 (1982): 257–67

——. "Der Konvent des Klosters Cluny zur Zeit des Abtes Maiolus. Die Namen der Mönche in Urkunden und Necrologien." In *Vinculum societatis* (listed below), pp. 118–56.

——. "Reform oder Kodifizierung? Päpstliche Statuten für Cluny im 13. Jahrhundert." *Archivum Historiae Pontificiae* 26 (1988): 71–118.

Neue Forschungen über Cluny und die Cluniacenser. Ed. Gerd Tellenbach. Freiburg im B., 1959.

Oberste, Jörg. "*Ut domorum status certior habeatur* . . . Cluniazensischer Reformalltag und administratives Schriftgut im 13. und frühen 14. Jahrhundert." *Archiv für Kulturgeschichte* 76.1 (1994): 51–76.

Oexle, Otto. "Memoria als Kultur." In *Memoria als Kultur* (listed above), pp. 9–78.

——. "Memoria und Memorialüberlieferung im früheren Mittelalter." *FMSt* 10 (1976): 70–95.

——. "Les moines d'Occident et la vie politique et sociale dans le haut Moyen Age." *RB* 103 (1993): 255–72.

——. "Stand, Klasse." *Geschichtliche Grundbegriffe* 6 (1990): 155–200.

Ohly, Friedrich. "Die Kathedrale als Zeitenraum: zum Dom von Siena." *FMSt* 6 (1972): 94–158. Reprinted in *Schriften zum Mittelalterlichen Bedeutungsforschung* (Darmstadt, 1977), pp. 172–273.

Ortigues, Edmond. "Haymon d'Auxerre, théoricien des trois ordres." In *L'Ecole carolingienne d'Auxerre, de Muretach à Remi, 830–908*, ed. Dominique Iogna-Prat, Guy Lobrichon, and Colette Jeudy, pp. 181–227. Entretiens d'Auxerre, 1989. Paris, 1991.

Ortigues, Edmond, and Dominique Iogna-Prat. "Raoul Glaber et l'historiographie clunisienne." *Studi Medievali*, 3d ser., 26.2 (1985): 537–72.

Pacaut, Marcel. "La Formation du second réseau monastique clunisien (v. 1030–v. 1080)." In *Naissance et fonctionnement des réseaux monastiques et canoniaux* (listed above), pp. 45–51.

——. *L'ordre de Cluny*. Paris, 1986.

——. "Recherche sur les églises paroissiales monastiques: l'exemple de Cluny." In *Historia de la Iglesia y de las instituciones ecclesiásticas. Trabajos en homenaje a Ferran Valls i Taberner*, pp. 4025–42. Barcelona, 1990.

——. "Recherche sur les revenus paroissiaux: l'exemple des églises clunisiennes." In *Histoire de la paroisse*, pp. 33–42. Publications du Centre de recherches d'histoire religieuse et d'histoire des idées, 11. Angers, 1988.

La Parole du prédicateur Ve–XVe siècle. Ed. Rosa M. Dessi and Michel Lauwers. Collection du Centre d'études médiévales de Nice, 1. Nice, 1997.

Patschovsky, Alexander. "Der Ketzer als Teufeldiener." In *Papsttum, Kirche und Recht. Festschrift für Horst Fuhrmann zum 65. Geburtstag*, ed. Hubert Mordek, pp. 317–34. Tübingen, 1991.

Petke, Wolfgang. "Von der klösterlichen Eigenkirche zur Inkorporation in Lothringen und Nordfrankreich im 11. und 12. Jahrhundert." *RHE* 87 (1992): 34–72 and 375–404.

Petrus Venerabilis 1156–1956: Studies and Texts Commemorating the Eighth Centenary of His Death. Ed. Giles Constable and James Kritzeck. Studia Anselmiana, 40. Rome, 1956.

Peuchmaurd, Paul. "Le prêtre ministre de la parole dans la théologie du XIIe siècle." *Recherches de théologie ancienne et médiévale* 29 (1962): 52–76.

Pierre Abélard, Pierre le Vénérable: les courants philosophiques, littéraires et artistiques en Occident au milieu du XIIe siècle. Actes et mémoires du colloque international, Abbaye de Cluny, 2–9 July 1972, ed. Jean Châtillon, Jean Jolivet and René Louis. Colloques internationaux du CNRS, 546. Paris, 1975.

Poeck, Dietrich. *"Cluniacensis Ecclesia": der cluniacensische Klosterverband (10.–12. Jahrhundert)*. Münstersche Mittelalter-Schriften, 71. Munich, 1997.

——. "Formgeschichtliche Beobachtungen zur Entstehung einer necrologischen Tradition." In *Memoria als Kultur* (listed above), pp. 727–49.

——. "Laienbegräbnisse in Cluny." *FMSt* 15 (1981): 68–179.

——. *Longpont: ein cluniacensisches Priorat in der Ile-de-France*. Münstersche Mittelalter-Schriften, 38. Munich, 1986.

——. "La synopse des nécrologes clunisiens: un instrument de recherche." *RM* 60 (1983): 315–29.

Poly, Jean-Pierre. *La Provence et la société féodale 879–1160: contribution à l'étude des structures dites féodales dans le Midi*. Paris, 1976.

Poly, Jean-Pierre, and Eric Bournazel. *La mutation féodale Xe–XIIe siècle*. Nouvelle Clio series. 2d ed. Paris, 1991.

Religion et culture autour de l'an Mil: royaume capétien et Lotharingie. Actes du colloque, Hugues Capet 987–1987: la France de l'an Mil, Auxerre 26–27 June 1987, Metz 11–12 September 1987, ed. Dominique Iogna-Prat and Jean-Charles Picard. Paris, 1990.

Riche, Denyse. "L'Ordre de Cluny de la mort de Pierre le Vénérable à Jean II de Bourbon: le 'Vieux Pays clunisien.'" 4 vols. Typescript. Doctoral thesis, Université Lumière—Lyon II, 1991. Now published as *L'ordre de Cluny à la fin du Moyen Age*. Saint Etienne, 2000.

Robinson, Ian S. "The 'Colores rhetorici' in the Investiture Contest." *Traditio* 32 (1976): 209–38.
———. "L'Eglise et la Papauté." In *Histoire de la pensée politique médiévale*, ed. James H. Burns, pp. 241–90. Paris, 1993.
———. *The Papacy 1073–1198: Continuity and Innovation*. Cambridge Medieval Textbooks. Cambridge, 1990.
Le Roi de France et son royaume autour de l'an Mil. Actes du colloque, Hugues Capet 987–1987: la France de l'an Mil, Paris-Senlis 22–25 June 1987, ed. Michel Parisse and Xavier Barral i Altet. Paris, 1992.
Rosenwein, Barbara H. *Negotiating Space: Power, Restraint, and Privileges of Immunity in Early Medieval Europe* (Manchester, 1998).
———. "La question de l'immunité clunisienne." *Bulletin de la Société des fouilles archéologiques et des monuments historiques de l'Yonne* 12 (1995): 1–11.
———. "Reformmönchtum und der Aufstieg Clunys. Webers Bedeutung für die Forschung heute." In *Max Webers Sicht des okzidentalen Christentums: Interpretation und Kritik*, ed. Wolfgang Schluchter, pp. 276–311. Frankfurt am Main, 1988.
———. *Rhinoceros Bound: Cluny in the Tenth Century*. Philadelphia, 1982.
———. *To Be the Neighbor of Saint Peter: The Social Meaning of Cluny's Property, 909–1049*. Ithaca and London, 1989.
Rosier, Irène. "Langage et signe dans la discussion eucharistique." In *Histoire et grammaire du sens. Hommage à Jean-Claude Chevallier*, ed. Sylvain Auroux et al., pp. 42–58. Paris, 1996.
———. *La parole comme acte: sur la grammaire et la sémantique au XIIIe siècle*. Sic et Non. Paris, 1994.
Rottenwöhrer, Gerhard. *Der Katharismus*, vol. 3: *Die Herkunft der Katharer nach Theologie und Geschichte*. Bad Honnef, 1990.
Sackur, Ernst. *Die Cluniacenser und ihrer kirchlichen und allegemeingeschichtlichen Wirksamkeit bis zur Mitte des elften Jahrhunderts*. 2 vols. Halle, 1892–94.
Saint-André-de-Rosans: millénaire de la fondation du prieuré, 988–1988. Actes du colloque, 13–14 May 1988. In *Bulletin de la Société d'études des Hautes-Alpes*, 1989.
Salet, Francis. *La Madeleine de Vézelay: étude iconographique par Jean Adéhmar*. Melun, 1948.
Sapin, Christian. *La Bourgogne préromane: construction, décor et fonction des édifices religieux*. Paris, 1986.
———. "Cluny II et l'interprétation archéologique de son plan." In *Religion et culture autour de l'an Mil* (listed above), pp. 85–9.
Sauer, Joseph. *Symbolik des Kirchengebäudes und seiner Ausstattung in der Auffassung des Mittelalters*. 2d ed. Freiburg im B., 1924.
Saulnier, Lydwine, and Neil Stratford. *La sculpture oubliée de Vézelay*. Paris, 1984.
Sazama, Kristin. "The Assertion of Monastic Spiritual and Temporal Authority in the Romanesque Sculpture of Sainte-Madeleine at Vézelay." Typescript. Doctoral thesis, Northwestern University, Evanston, 1995.
Schluchter, Wolfgang. *Religion und Lebensführung*, vol. 2: *Studien zu Max Webers Religions- und Herrschaftssoziologie*. Frankfurt am Main, 1988.
Schmid, Karl, and Joachim Wollasch. "*Societas et Fraternitas*: Begründung eines kommentierten Quellenswerkes zur Erforschung der Personen und Personengruppen des Mittelalters." *FMSt* 9 (1975): 1–48.
Schmid, Paul. "Die Entstehung des Marseiller Kirchenstaats." *Archiv für Urkundenforschung* 10 (1928): 176–207 and 11 (1930): 138–52.
Schmitt, Jean-Claude. "L'Occident, Nicée II et les images du VIIIe au XIIIe siècle." In

Nicée II, 787–1987: douze siècles d'images religieuses, pp. 271–301. Actes du colloque international Nicée II, Collège de France, Paris, 2, 3, 4 October 1986, ed. François Boesflug and Nicolas Lossky. Paris, 1987.

——. *Les revenants: les vivants et les morts dans la société médiévale.* Bibliothèque des Histoires. Paris, 1994. [Eng. trans., *Ghosts in the Middle Ages: The Living and the Dead in Medieval Society*, trans. Teresa L. Fagan. Chicago, 1998.]

——. "Rituels de l'image et récits de vision." In *Testo e immagine nell'alto Medioevo*, pp. 419–59. Settimane di Studio del Centro Italiano di Studi sull'alto Medioevo, 41, 15–21 April 1993. Spoleto, 1994.

Schreckenberg, Heinz. *Die christlichen Adversus-Judaeos-Texte (11.–13. Jh.).* Europäische Hochschulschriften, Theologie, 335. Frankfurt am Main, 1991.

Schreiber, Georg. "Kirchliches Abgabenwesen an französischen Eigenkirchen aus Anlass von Ordalien." *Zeitschrift der Savigny-Stiftung für Rechtsgeschichte, Kanonistische Abteilung* 36 (1915): 414–83. Reprinted in *Gemeinschaften des Mittelalters. Recht und Verfassung. Kult und Frömmigkeit*, pp. 151–212. Gesammelte Abhandlungen, 1. Münster im W., 1948.

——. *Kurie und Kloster im 12. Jahrhundert.* 2 vols. Kirchenrechtliche Abhandlungen, 65 and 66. Stuttgart, 1910.

Segl, Peter. *Königtum und Klosterreform in Spanien: Untersuchungen über die Cluniacenserklöster in Kastilien-León vom Begin des 11. bis zur Mitte des 12. Jahrhunderts.* Kallmünz, 1974.

Simonin, Servan. "Le culte eucharistique à Cluny de saint Odon à Pierre le Vénérable." *Bulletin trimestriel du Centre international d'études romanes* 1961:3–13.

Snoek, Godefridus J. C. *Medieval Piety from Relics to the Eucharist: A Process of Mutual Interaction.* Studies in the History of Christian Thought, 63. Leiden, 1995.

La Société juive à travers l'histoire. Ed. Schmuel Trigano. Vol. 4. Paris, 1993.

Sohn, Andreas. *Der Abbatiat Ademars von Saint-Martial de Limoges (1063–1114): ein Beitrag zur Geschichte des cluniacensischen Klosterverbandes.* Beiträge zur Geschichte des alten Mönchtums und des Benediktinertums, 37. Münster im W., 1989.

Stratford, Neil. "Les bâtiments de l'abbaye de Cluny à l'époque médiévale: état des questions. *Bulletin monumental* 150.4 (1992): 383–411.

Sydow, Jürgen. "Cluny und die Anfänge der Apostolischen Kammer: Studien zur Geschichte der päpstlichen Finanzverwaltung im 11. und 12. Jahrhundert." *SMGBOZ* 63 (1951): 45–66.

Szabó-Bechstein, Brigitte. *"Libertas Ecclesiae": ein Schlüsselbegriff des Investiturstreits und seine Vorgeschichte 4.–11. Jahrhundert.* Studi Gregoriani, 12. Rome, 1986.

Taviani, Huguette. "Naissance d'une hérésie en Italie du Nord au XIe siècle." *AESC* 1974:1224–52.

Tellenbach, Gerd. *Ausgewählte Abhandlungen und Aufsätze.* 4 vols. Stuttgart, 1988–89.

——. *The Church in Western Europe from the Tenth to the Early Twelfth Century.* Cambridge Medieval Textbooks. Cambridge, 1993. [Updated trans. of *Die westliche Kirche vom 10. bis zum frühen 12. Jahrhundert.* Die Kirche in ihrer Geschichte, 2, F 1. Göttingen, 1988.]

Teske, Wolfgang. "Bernardus und Jocerannus Grossus als Mönche von Cluny: zu den Aufstiegsmöglichkeiten cluniacensischer 'conversi' im 11. Jahrhundert." In *Ordensstudien I: Beiträge zur Geschichte der Konversen im Mittelalter*, ed. Kaspar Elm, pp. 9–24. Berliner Historische Studien, 2. Berlin, 1980.

——. "Laien, Laienmönche und Laienbrüder in der Abtei Cluny: ein Beitrag zum 'Konversen-Problem.'" *FMSt* 10 (1976): 248–322 and 11 (1977): 288–339.

Tolan, John V. "Mahomet et l'Antéchrist dans l'Espagne du IXe siècle." In *Orient und*

Okzident in der Kultur des Mittelalters: Monde oriental et mode occidental dans la culture médiévale, pp. 167–80. Greifswalder Beiträge zum Mittelalter. Études médiévales de Greifswald, 68. Greifswald, 1997.

——. "Peter the Venerable on the 'Diabolical Heresy of the Saracens.'" In *The Devil, Heresy, and Witchcraft in the Middle Ages: Essays in Honor of Jeffrey B. Russell,* ed. Alberto Ferreiro, pp. 345–67. Leiden, 1998.

Torrell, Jean-Pierre. "L'Eglise dans l'œuvre et la vie de Pierre le Vénérable." *Revue thomiste* 77 (1977): 357–92 and 558–91.

——. "Les Juifs dans l'oeuvre de Pierre le Vénérable." *CCMé* 30 (1987): 331–46.

——. "La notion de prophétie et la méthode apologétique dans le *Contra Sarracenos* de Pierre le Vénérable." *Studia monastica* 17 (1975): 257–82. Reprinted in *Recherches sur la théorie de la prophétie au Moyen Age, XIIe–XIV siècle: études et textes,* pp. 75–100. Dokimion, 13. Fribourg (Switzerland), 1992.

Torrell, Jean-Pierre, and Denise Bouthillier. "*Miraculum:* une catégorie fondamentale chez Pierre le Vénérable." *Revue thomiste* 80 (1980): 357–86 and 549–66.

——. *Pierre le Vénérable, abbé de Cluny: le courage et la mesure.* Chambray-lès-Tours, 1988.

——. *Pierre le Vénérable et sa vision du monde: sa vie, son oeuvre; l'homme et le démon.* Spicilegium Sacrum Lovaniense, Etudes et documents, 42. Leuven, 1986.

——. "Une spiritualité de combat: Pierre le Vénérable et la lutte contre Satan." *Revue thomiste* 84 (1984): 47–81.

Toubert, Pierre. *Les structures du Latium médiéval: le Latium et la Sabine du IXe à la fin du XIIe siècle.* Bibliothèque des Ecoles françaises d'Athènes et de Rome, 221. Rome, 1973.

Treffort, Cécile. *L'Eglise carolingienne et la mort: Christianisme, rites funéraires et pratiques commémoratives.* Centre interuniversitaire d'histoire et d'archéologie, Collection d'histoire et d'archéologie médiévales, 3. Lyon, 1996.

——. "Genèse du cimetière chrétien: étude sur l'accompagnement du mourant, les funérailles, la commémoration des défunts et les lieux d'inhumation à l'époque carolingienne (entre Loire et Rhin, milieu VIIIe–début XIe siècle)." 4 vols. Typescript. Doctoral thesis, Université Lumière—Lyon II, 1994.

Turki, Abdel Majid. "La lettre du 'moine de France' à al-Muqtadir Billah, roi de Saragosse, et la réponse d'al-Bayi, le faqih andalou." *Al-Andalus* 31 (1966): 73–153. Reprinted in *Théologiens et juristes de l'Espagne musulmane,* pp. 233–81. Islam d'hier et d'aujourd'hui, 16. Paris, 1982.

Tutsch, Burkhardt. "Die Consuetudines Bernhards und Ulrichs von Cluny im Spiegel ihrer handschriftlichen Überlieferung." *FMSt* 30 (1996): 248–93.

Valous, Guy de. *Le monachisme clunisien des origines au XVe siècle.* 2d ed. 2 vols. Paris, 1970.

Vauchez, André. "Diables et hérétiques: les réactions de l'Eglise et de la société en Occident face aux mouvements religieux dissidents, de la fin du Xe au début du XIIe siècle." *Santi e demoni nell'Alto Medioevo occidentale (secoli V–XI),* pp. 573–601. Settimane di Studio del Centro Italiano di Studi sull'alto Medioevo, 36, 15–21 April 1993, 2. Spoleto, 1989.

——. *Les laïcs au Moyen Age: pratiques et croyances religieuses.* Série Histoire. Paris, 1987. [Eng. trans., *The Laity in the Middle Ages: Religious Beliefs and Devotional Practices,* trans. Margery J. Schneider. Ed. and with an introduction by Daniel E. Bornstein. Notre Dame, Ind., 1993.]

——. *La spiritualité du Moyen Age occidental (VIIIe–XIIe siècle).* L'historien, 19. Paris, 1975. [Eng. trans., *The Spirituality of the Medieval West: From the Eighth to the Twelfth*

Century, trans. Colette Friedlander. Cistercian Studies series, 145. Kalamazoo, 1993.]

La vie quotidienne des moines et chanoines réguliers au Moyen Age et Temps modernes. Actes du premier colloque international du LARHCOR, Wroclaw/Ksiaz, 30 November–4 December 1994, ed. Marek Derwich. Publications of the University of Wroclaw, Institute of History. Wroclaw, 1995.

Vinculum societatis: Joachim Wollasch zum 60. Geburtstag. Ed. Franz Neiske, Dietrich Poeck, and Mechthild Sandmann. Sigmaringendorf, 1991.

Vogüé, Adalbert de. "Eucharistie et vie monastique." *Collectanea Cisterciensia* 48 (1986): 120–30.

Voloda, Elisabeth. *Excommunication in the Middle Ages*. Berkeley, 1986.

Winzer, Ulrich. *S. Gilles: Studien zum Rechtsstatus und Beziehungsnetz einer Abtei im Spiegel ihrer Memorialüberlieferung*. Münstersche Mittelalter-Schriften, 59. Munich, 1988.

Wischermann, Else M. "L'abbé Hugues de Cluny et le début du monachisme clunisien de femmes." In *Le gouvernement d'Hugues de Semur à Cluny* (listed above), pp. 231–43.

——. *Grundlagen einer cluniacensischen Bibliotheksgeschichte*. Münstersche Mittelalter-Schriften, 62. Munich, 1988.

——. *Marcigny-sur-Loire: Gründungs- und Frühgeschichte des ersten Cluniacenserinnenpriorates (1055–1150)*. Münstersche Mittelalter-Schriften, 42. Munich, 1986.

Wollasch, Joachim. "Ein cluniacensisches Totenbuch aus der Zeit Hugos von Cluny." *FMSt* 1 (1967): 406–43.

——. *Cluny, Licht der Welt: Aufstieg und Niedergang der klösterlichen Gemeinschaft*. Zürich and Düsseldorf, 1996.

——. "*Eleemosynarius*: eine Skizze." In *Sprache und Recht: Beiträge und Kulturgeschichte des Mittelalters. Festschrift für Ruth Schmidt-Wiegand zum 60. Geburtstag*, ed. Karl Hauck et al., 2:972–95. Berlin and New York, 1986.

——. "Hugues Ier abbé de Cluny et la mémoire des morts." In *Le Gouvernement d'Hugues de Semur à Cluny* (listed above), pp. 75–92.

——. "Konventsstärke und Armensorge in mittelalterlichen Klöstern." *Saeculum* 39 (1988): 184–99.

——. "Les moines et la mémoire des morts." In *Religion et culture autour de l'an Mil* (listed above), pp. 47–54.

——. *Mönchtum des Mittelalters zwischen Kirche und Welt*. Münstersche Mittelalter-Schriften, 7. Munich, 1973.

——. "Les obituaires, témoins de la vie clunisienne." *CCMé* 22 (1979): 139–71.

——. "Das Projekt 'Societas et Fraternitas.'" In *Memoria in der Gesellschaft des Mittelalters* (listed above), pp. 11–31.

——. "A propos des *fratres barbati* de Hirsau." In *Histoire et société: mélanges offerts à Georges Duby* (listed above), 3:37–48.

——. "Prosopographie et informatique: l'exemple des Clunisiens et de leur entourage laïque." In *Informatique et prosopographie*, ed. Caroline Bourlet, Jean-Philippe Genêt, and Lucie Fossier, pp. 209–18. Table ronde du CNRS, Paris, 1984. Paris, 1986.

——. "Das Schisma des Abtes Pontius von Cluny." *Francia* 23.1 (1996): 31–52.

——. "Toten- und Armensorge." In *Gedächtnis, das Gemeinschaft stiftet*, ed. Karl Schmid, pp. 9–38. Schriftenreihe der katholischen Akademie der Erzdiözese Freiburg. Munich and Zürich, 1985.

——. "Die Wahl des Papstes Nikolaus II." In *Adel und Kirche. Gerd Tellenbach zum 65*.

Geburtstag dargebracht von Freunden und Schülern, ed. Josef Fleckenstein and Karl Schmid, pp. 205–20. Freiburg im B. and Basle, 1968.

——. "Zur Datierung des *Liber tramitis* aus Farfa anhand von Personen und Personengruppen." In *Person und Gemeinschaft im Mittelalter. Karl Schmid zum fünfundsechzigsten Geburtstag*, ed. Gerd Althoff et al., pp. 237–55. Sigmaringen, 1988.

——. "Zur Datierung einiger Urkunden aus Cluny." *RM*, new ser., 3 (1992): 49–57.

——. "Zur Verschriftlichung der klösterlichen Lebensgewohnheiten unter Abt Hugo von Cluny. *FMSt* 27 (1993): 317–49.

Zadora-Rio, Elisabeth. "La topographie des lieux d'asile dans les campagnes médiévales." In *L'Eglise, le terroir* (listed above), pp. 11–16.

Zerfaß, Rolf. *Der Streit um die Laienpredigt: eine pastoralgeschichtliche Untersuchung zum Verständnis des Predigtamtes und zu seiner Entwicklung im 12. und 13. Jahrhundert.* Freiburg im B., 1974.

Zerner, Monique. "Hérésie: un discours de l'Eglise." In *Dictionnaire raisonné de l'Occident médiéval*, ed. Jacques Le Goff and Jean-Claude Schmitt, pp. 464–82. Paris, 1999.

ADDENDA

The following important studies have appeared since the original publication of this book in French. They may be found useful, but were not available to the author during the writing of the present work.

Abulafia, Anna Sapir. *Christians and Jews in Dispute: Disputational Literature and the Rise of Anti-Judaism in the West (c. 1000–1150).* Variorum Collected Studies Series, 621. Aldershot, 1998.

Le brûlement du Talmud à Paris 1242–1244. Ed. Gilbert Dahan. Nouvelle *Gallia Judaica*. Paris, 1999.

Chazan, Robert. *Medieval Stereotypes and Modern Antisemitism.* Berkeley, 1997.

Cowdrey, Herbert E. J. *Pope Gregory VII 1073–1085.* Oxford, 1998.

Juden und Christen zur Zeit der Kreuzzüge. Ed. Alfred Haverkamp. Vorträge und Forschungen, 47. Sigmaringen, 1999.

Moore, Rebecca. *Jews and Christians in the Life and Thought of Hugh of St. Victor.* South Florida Studies in the History of Judaism, 138. Atlanta, 1998.

Moore, Robert I. *The First European Revolution c. 970–1215.* Oxford, 2000.

INDEX

141; on sacred space, 160–61; on signs, 186, 187, 199; on spiritual kinship, 244, 246

Augustus (Roman emperor), 243

Aujoux, 49–50

Austremonius (saint), 158

authority: arguments from, 102, 124, 127, 140–41, 151–53, 347; and conversion, 299–300; Peter's widened notion of, 144–46, 305; vs. power, 1, 11; and reason, 137–38

Autun, 89, 90, 158

Auxentius (Arian bishop), 242

Auxerre, 91, 106

Aymardus (Cluniac abbot), 26, 224

Azov, Sea of, 144

Baal, 129, 157, 279

Babylonian Talmud. *See* Talmud

Balaam, 308

Baldwin II (king of Jerusalem), 331

baptism: on another's behalf, 230; and Christian sociological holism, 360; intention and, 242–43; and martyrdom, 154; ritual of, 149; as sacrament, 19, 207; universality of, 154–55; unrecognized by Islam, 342. *See also* infant baptism

Barcelona, 110

Barthélemy, Dominique, 225

Bartholomew (apostle), 158

Baruch, 289

Basil (prior of La Grande Chartreuse), 51

Basil of Caesarea, 331

Baud, Anne, 179

Baudry of Colchis, 89

Baume-les-Messieurs, 26, 29

Bautier, Robert-Henri, 277, 316

al-Bayi, 329, 349, 355

Beatrice (countess of Perche), 93

Beaulieu, 59

Beaumont (priory of Saint-Martin-des-Champs), 66

Beaumont-sur-Grosne, 49

Beauvais, 158

Bede the Venerable, 167, 349

Benedict (Cluniac monk), 46, 50, 51, 52, 103, 205n. 106

Benedict VIII (pope), 80, 178, 326

Benedict of Aniane, 55

Benedict of Nursia, 171, 312

benefactors, 222

Benignus (saint), 158

Ben Sira, 302, 313–15

Berard of Riotier (castellan), 208

Berengar of Tours, 49, 122, 142, 180, 192, 194, 199, 205, 258

Bernard, Auguste, 224

Bernard (author of Cluniac customs): on care of the poor, 248n. 110; on clamor rituals, 178, 209; on Cluny's organization, 57; on consecration of Cluny II, 168–69; customs of, 27, 62, 63; on Eucharist, 179–80, 201; on festivals, 185; on lay memorials, 71; on monastery as fortress, 177

Bernard II Grossus of Uxelles, 237–38, 248, 249, 333

Bernard III Grossus of Uxelles, 237–38

Bernard IV Grossus (lord of Uxelles and Brancion), 78, 237

Bernard Grossus, 93

Bernard of Clairvaux: antiheretical discourse of, 24, 126–28, 129, 137, 146; and apocalyptic constructions, 104; approach to heresy, 110–11; on armed monks, 334; and Cluniac hospitality, 86; and Crusades, 24, 268; on Holy Land, 335; on opposition to infant baptism, 149; and parochial network, 74; Peter's letters to, 73, 75, 102, 121, 267, 336; on pope's multiple roles, 19–20; and Qur'an translation, 338–40, 343; and Second Crusade, 333; on Templars, 328, 334–35n. 53; writings of, 120

Bernard of Sahagún (archbishop of Toledo), 329

Bernard of Tiron (hermit), 24, 47

Bernard Savinelle, 235

Berno (Cluniac abbot), 26, 27, 35–36, 55, 224

Berry, Virginia, 332

Bertha of Vienne (countess), 267

Bertrada of Montfort, 39

Berzé-la-Ville, 240

Bethlehem, 166

biography/autobiography, 120

bishops, nomination of, 20

blasphemy, accusation of, against Jews, 281–82, 290, 305–6, 308–9, 310, 349

Blumenkranz, Bernhard, 277
Boccaccio, Giovanni, 359
body, glorious, 341
body of Christ: Church as, 10, 12, 78–79, 152, 198–99, 258, 333, 360; Cluny as, 57–60, 78–79, 170; and Eucharist, 109; heretical views on, 191–92; and infant baptism, 152
Boethius, 15
Boissonnade, Pierre, 324
Bollschweil, 48
Bonnevaux, 239
Bordeaux, 158
Bourbon-Lancy, 90
Bourges, 158
Bouthillier, Denise, 102, 103, 234, 344
Breme, 76
Brioude, 44, 100, 123–24
Brown, Peter, 362, 364
Bruel, Alexandre, 224
Bruis, 114
Bruneau, Jean, 117–19, 120
Bruno (Carthusian founder), 24–25, 50
Bruno of Chartreux, 205–6
Bruno of Segni, 162
Buchenwald, 276
Bull, Marcus, 324
Bulst, Neithard, 68
Burchard the Venerable (count), 56
burgesses, 170, 177
burial, right of, 57
Busseuil family, 90
Bussière, La, 334
Byzantium, 1, 188

Cahn, Walter, 162
Caiaphas, 183, 183n. 7
Cain, 115, 278–80, 295, 315
Calcidius (translator), 12
Callixtus II (pope), 91, 244
canonization, 20–21
canons regular, 37, 44–45, 69, 335
Canossa, 21
Cantarella, Glauco Maria, 32
Capernaum, 166
caritas. See charity (*caritas*)
Carrión de los Condes, 331
Carthusians, 186; boundaries on land of, 175; cenobitism and eremitism combined in, 24–25, 51–52; Cluny and, 30,

50–51; as eremitic model, 35; and fight against heresy, 112–13; and monastic hospitality, 85; Peter's veneration of, 100; sacrifices of, 206
cartularies, 27, 76, 91, 93, 120
castellans, 23, 178
castrum, 177
catechumens, 242–43
categories, logic of, 125
Cathars, 22
Cava, 63
Cecilia (Hugh of Semur's great-niece), 91
Cecilia (saint), 171
celibacy, 136
cemeteries: at Cluny, 41, 223; heretics and, 159; Jewish, 277; lay, 70, 170, 223, 223n. 15; significance of, 163–64, 260; as space of inclusion and exclusion, 164, 261
cenobitism, 35, 46–47, 50–51
Centullus IV (viscount of the Béarn), 39
Cerinthes, 128
Chaise-Dieu, La, 100
Chalandon, Ferdinand, 323–24
Chalon, 91, 177, 277
Champagne-sur-Rhône, 116
chant, 114, 253–54
chapters-general, 30, 32, 33
Charité-sur-Loire, La, 107, 331
charity (*caritas*): fourfold expressions of, 227–34; and marriage, 152; and sacred space, 162; as seigneurial virtue, 246; and solidarity, 153, 156, 247, 256–57, 360; toward the poor, 86–88
Charlemagne, 12
Charles the Bald, 12, 13, 14
Charlieu, 57, 58, 177, 251
Chartres, 76, 333
Châtel-Montagne, 91
Chazan, Robert, 277
Chevrier, Georges, 212
Chiffoleau, Jacques, 124
Christ: as fulfillment of prophecy, 296–98, 354; and Islam, 337, 342; as king, 291–93; linked to the apostles, 269; as Messiah, 293–95; prophecies of, 353; as son of God, 286–88; *transitus* of, 215, 218, 258, 360; as true God, 288–90
Christendom: anthropology of, 361–62;

Christianity remodeled into, 1–2; defined, 2; defined through exclusion, 23, 254, 265, 279; expansion of, 261, 265–74, 364; ordering of, 9–25; sociology of, 254–61, 359–61

churches: desecration of, 156; as places of Eucharistic sacrifice, 178–81; significance of, 163–64, 360

church system: all-or-nothing logic of, 42; anthropological base of, 361–62; defined, 31–32, 33; sociological base of, 360–61

Cicero, 133–34, 184

circumcision, 154, 155, 297, 298, 342, 354

Cistercians, 24, 30, 32, 35, 85, 312; and apocalyptic constructions, 104; and Christendom's expansion, 266; and monastic possession of land, 216

Cîteaux, 33, 266, 297

Civitot, 331

Clairvaux, 33, 41, 126

clamors, 129, 178, 208–9

Claudius of Turin (theologian), 12

clergy: distinguished from laity, 10–11, 17–19, 175; order of, 11–12; sacramental mediation of, 200–206; symbiotic relationship with aristocracy, 90, 93–94, 210–12, 213–15; and transformation of property, 215–17, 360

Cluny: as asylum, 37–52, 86–88, 172–74; bourgeois militia at, 334; burgesses near, 170; and Christendom's expansion, 266; as "church system", 31–37; and ecclesiastical hierarchy, 75–78; economic dependence on gifts, 224–27, 280; in 11th and 12th centuries, 26–31; eucharistic mysticism of, 217–18; expansion of, 52–53; festivals at, 241, 327; funerary efficacy of, 213–14, 213–14n. 153, 235–37; as hospice, 84–86; and Jews, 277–78; meaning of, 53–54; mimicry of Rome, 78–84, 108; pastoral work of, 39–40; and Provence, 113–15; relics at, 330–31; sacred ban at, 28, 169–70, 174, 177, 223–24; as seigneury, 176–78; structuring of space at, 168–71, 179–80. See also Ecclesia cluniacensis

Cluny II, 27, 61, 81, 168–69, 217–18, 223

Cluny III, 28, 50, 80, 158, 168–71, 179–80, 217, 328

Codex Udalrici, 135–36

Coincy, 213–15

College of Cardinals, 77, 79, 320

Cologne, 126

Columban, 171

commendam system, 30–31

commutation (*commutatio*), 194–95, 210, 212–13, 214, 259, 318–19, 360–61

Conant, Kenneth J., 217

Concordat of Worms, 21

Condamine-sur-Arve, 82

confession, 201–2, 205, 237, 238, 244

confirmation, 19

confraternities, 65, 76, 246, 331

Congar, Yves, 32

congregatio fidelium, Church as, 258, 260

congruent place, Church as, 158–65, 180–81, 259–61

conjurations, 65

Conrad III (emperor), 267

consanguinity, 18, 39, 314

Constable, Giles, 116

Constance (queen), 71

Constantia (Gratian's wife), 242

Constantine the Great (Roman emperor), 242

Constantius (Roman emperor), 242

Contra Petrobrusianos (Peter the Venerable), 23, 30; authority used in, 144–46, 151–53; and *De miriculis*, 234, 245–46; as *epistola disputans*, 122, 146, 255; genre and reception of, 116–19; influence of, 32, 146–47; polemic method of, 102, 138–43, 150–55; as polemic treatise, 123–24; and Provence, 113–16; purpose of, 145; reason used in, 142–43, 151, 153–55, 183–84, 194–98; shaping of, 110–16; sociological significance of, 3, 255. See also Cross, the; dead, the; Eucharist; funerary suffrages; infant baptism; sacred space; sacrifice of Christ

Contra sectam Sarracenorum (Peter the Venerable), 23, 343–55; and *Adversus Iudeos*, 285, 298–99; as anthropology of Christianity, 3–4; demonization of Islam in, 30; driving forces behind, 347–49; dual strategy of, 345–47; influence

Gregory VII (pope), 12, 35, 39, 134; career of, 77n. 226; Cluny's abbacy declared holy by, 58; on Cluny's excellence, 79; on Cluny as model, 60, 113; and Henry IV, 29; on Hugh I's conversion, 40; in investiture controversy, 132; on order, 16–17; on papal power, 108; polemic texts of, 135; privileges granted to Cluny, 59; radicalization of church reform, 21; and Reconquista, 329; register of, 78; and tithes, 74

Gregory of Papareschi, 320. *See also* Innocent II (pope)

Grenoble, 112

Guerreau, Alain, 165, 170–71, 175–76

Guibert of Nogent, 38, 120, 159, 256, 281, 325, 337

Guichard III of Beaujeu, 245, 334

Guigo I, 24–25, 85, 100, 111–12, 175, 226

guilds, 65, 246

Guitmund of Aversa, 142, 192, 195, 196, 198–99, 209

Gundrada (countess of Warenne and Surrey), 82

Gunthelm (Cistercian novice), 312–13

Guy (archbishop of Vienne), 91, 244–45

Guy (bishop of Beauvais), 38

Guy (count of Domène), 84

Guy I (count of Albo and Vienne), 40

Guy de Valous, 42

Guy of Faucigny (bishop of Geneva), 82

Guy of Moras (knight), 244

Guy of Osnabrück, 135

Habakkuk, 290

Hackelsperger, Max, 132

hadith, 353

Hagar, 338, 354

haggadah, 303–4, 313

hagiography, 233; antiheretical writings, 120; and arguments from authority, 141; Christian knight as model, 325; of Cluny, 27, 102; and eucharistic controversy, 200; eucharistic power in, 235–36; as extension of scripture, 304; and Islamic prophetic models, 353

Haifa, 331

halakhah, 303–4

Hallinger, Kassius, 42, 60, 61, 62

Hatem, Anouar, 323–24

Haymo of Auxerre, 14–15, 106

Hebrews, prophecies of, 354

Hebron, 166

Heiric of Auxerre, 15

Helvidius, 345

Henricians, 126, 131

Henriet, Patrick, 82

Henry (archbishop of Sens), 45

Henry (bishop of Soissons), 38

Henry I (king of England), 28

Henry II (emperor), 63, 87, 326–27

Henry III (emperor), 48, 71, 134, 222

Henry IV (emperor), 21, 29, 131, 132–35, 139

Henry of Blois (bishop of Winchester), 226–27, 240, 279–80

Henry of Burgundy (duke), 55

Henry of Lausanne, 109, 114, 120, 159, 183; heresy of, 22, 110, 113; and monastic reform, 256; writings of, 144

Henry of Winchester, 30

Heraclius (Peter's brother), 100

heresy/heretics: and anathema, 129–30, 133; as Antichrist, 104, 108; Cluny and, 99–108; debating, 138–43; in early Church, 128–29, 345–46; exclusion of, 21–22, 34, 274, 363; Islam as, 356–57; and lese-majesty, 124, 146, 255; necessity of, 227; Peter's response to, 3, 4; in Provence, 113–15; and rationalization process, 121–22, 136; reason used against, 136–38; rhetorical tools used against, 130–36; scientific, 137; and social control, 254–55. *See also* Petrobrusians

Heribert (monk), 188

Hermann of Dalmatia, 338, 339

Hermann of Metz, 12

hermits, 30, 46-52

Herod, 183, 183n. 7, 294

Herodotus, 145, 184

Hervé of Déols, 120

hierarchies: Dionysian, 12–13; dyarchy, 11; three functional orders, 13–16

Hildebert (count of Auvergne), 40

Hildegard of Bingen, 104

Hilduin (translator), 13

Hilduin of Le Puiset (prior of Lurcy-le-Bourg), 331

Hippolytus of Rome, 160

Hirsau, 28

historiography: antiheretical writings, 120; conceptual ambiguity in, 4

Holy Cross Day (September 14), 185

Holy Land: Cluny and, 330–32; First Crusade in, 28, 266; Islam confronted in, 2; Peter the Venerable on, 101, 335–36

holy war, 325–26

homilitic/exegetical literature, 120

homosexuality, 251–52

Honorius II (pope), 46, 320

Honorius of Autun, 162, 165

Horace, 145, 197, 296, 335, 342

Hosea, 193

hostia (eucharistic offering), 203

Hourlier, Jacques, 75

Hugh (archbishop of Edessa), 169, 331

Hugh (bishop of Auxerre), 91

Hugh (bishop of Bourges), 81, 168

Hugh (bishop of Grenoble), 112

Hugh (prior of Paray-le-Monial), 90

Hugh (saint), 40, 112

Hugh I (duke of Burgundy), 40

Hugh II (Cluniac abbot), 30

Hugh V (Cluniac abbot), 30, 212n. 141

Hugh Capet (king of Francs), 56

Hugh Catula (knight), 335

Hugh Deschaux (lord of La Bussière), 334

Hugh of Amiens (archbishop of Rouen), 31, 54, 73; antiheretical writings of, 120; on assistance to the dead, 220–21, 229; on salvation by faith, 155

Hugh of Brancion, 237

Hugh of Die (papal legate), 38, 39

Hugh of Fleury, 133

Hugh of Gournay, 81, 107

Hugh of Montboissier (Peter's brother), 100

Hugh of Paillers (Peter's ancestor), 99

Hugh of Saint Victor, 110–11n. 45

Hugh of Saint-Victor, 167

Hugh of Semur (Cluniac abbot), 27, 30, 36, 47, 48–49, 64, 238; abbacy under, 55; abbatial hagiography under, 102; admonishes Philip I, 39; becomes saint, 240; birth of, 203; building of Cluny III under, 335–36; charters under, 224–

25; and Cluniac demonology, 106–8; Cluny's development under, 57; Cluny's influence under, 28–29; Cluny's synchrony with Rome under, 75–76; on Cluny as substitute for Rome, 81; concern with monastic purity under, 201; conversions under, 38; customs composed under, 62–63; death of, 204–5; and First Crusade, 329–30; foundation of Marcigny-sur-Loire, 37–38, 52, 91, 92; funerary policies of, 222; gifts to Cluny under, 70, 88–89, 213–15; hagiographic legend of, 217; involvement in contemporary events, 100–101; kinship network of, 90–91; lay conversions under, 40; lay memorials under, 71; malediction uttered by, 208; miracle performed by, 80; monastic reform under, 113; necrologies under, 67; and Reconquista, 328–29; and Rome, 59, 78; threatened with anathema, 130

Huillaux, 177

Humbert III (lord of Beaujeu), 245, 334–35

Humbert of Silva Candida, 16, 175

Ibn Tumart (Mahdi), 291, 323

iconoclasm, 118, 188, 190

iconography, 218; at Vézelay, 267–74

identity, 2, 5, 360–61, 364

idolatry, 123, 188, 298, 309, 337, 341, 351

Idung, 60

Imar (cardinal-bishop of Tusculum), 77

immunity, 173–74, 177–78

imprecation, 126, 146

incantation, 135

Incarnation, 115, 136–37, 341

incest, 39, 304–5, 313–15

inclusion, 33–34; all-or-nothing logic of, 42; in Cluniac necrologies, 64–68; Cluny as structure of, 68; donations and, 94–95; of laity, 70–71, 84–88, 103; modes of, 35

incorporation, 74–75, 170–71; Eucharist as vehicle of, 197, 218, 260; infant baptism as vehicle of, 230

infant baptism, 143, 145, 148–56; and adult catechumens, 149–50; all-or-nothing logic of, 150–52, 154–56; and faith, 152–55; heretical rejection of, 2–

Judaism/Jews (*continued*)
361, 364; in seigneurial system, 282–
84, 361; stereotypes of, 104, 108, 202,
280–82, 293, 301, 310, 315–16, 321,
361–62; survival of, 273, 307, 317;
topocentrism of, 260–61, 279. *See also
Adversus Iudeos* (Peter the Venerable)
Judas, 178, 183, 183n. 7, 207, 315
Judas Maccabeus, 184, 220, 230, 232–33
Jude (apostle), 158
Julian (saint), 158
Julian of Vézelay, 251
Justin (martyr), 346
Justina (Valentinian I's wife), 242
Justinian, 123
Justus (monk), 232, 241

al-Kindi, 298, 339, 343, 348, 352–53
Korah, 352
Koran. *See* Qur'an

Lactantius, 160, 286, 290
laity: conversions of, 38–40, 42–44; distinguished from clergy, 10–11, 17–19,
175; dominated by "monkish" clergy,
324; donations of, 94–5, 213–15; funeral ceremonies for, 70–71, 222–23;
inclusion of, 70–71, 84–88, 103; op-
tions open to, 44; participation in ecclesiastical debates, 131
Lambert (count of Chalon), 90, 91, 213n.
153
Lambert of Hersfeld, 134
Landulfus Senior, 120
Lanfranc (archbishop of Canterbury), 64,
117, 142, 192, 196, 198, 209
Langmuir, Gavin I., 319
Langres, 75
Languedoc, 116
Laon, school of, 108
Last Supper, 115–16, 180, 194, 196–97,
207, 209, 258
Lateran IV Council, 212n. 141
latreia, 187, 189
law: divine, 348; Old Testament vs. New
Testament, 296–98; Roman, 123–24
lawsuits, ecclesiastical, 20–21
Lazarus (brother of Martha and Mary),
145, 152, 171, 269
Leclercq, Jean, 110–11n. 45

Ledger (Cluniac monk), 326
legitimate persecution, theory of, 131
Le Goff, Jacques, 249
Leo (hermit), 226
Leo I, the Great (pope), 157
Leo IX (pope), 21, 321
leprosy/lepers, 21, 306
Lérins, 56, 113, 325
lese-majesty, 124, 146, 255
Lessing, Gotthold Ephraim, 358–59
Letgar (lord of Alps), 326
Lézat, 59
Limoges, 158
limpieza de sangre, 319
literacy, 42–44
Little, Lester K., 130
Lobrichon, Guy, 108
Longpont, 45, 66, 67
Lopez, Roberto S., 265
Lot, 210, 288
Lothar III (king of Francia), 174, 177
Louis VI (king), 283
Louis VII (king), 278, 280–81, 282, 284,
293, 317, 333
Lourdon, 170, 177
Lucian (saint), 158
Lucifer, 105, 287
Lucy (Hugh of Semur's sister), 91
Luke (apostle), 351
Lund, 266
Lurcy-le-Bourg, 331
Lusignan, 239
Lyon, 22, 100, 158, 177

Macarius (prior of Longpont), 45
Maccabees, 153, 348
Macedonians, 345
McGinn, Bernard, 104
Mâcon, 26, 44, 76, 91, 130, 174, 177, 277
Mâconnais, 57, 237, 330, 334
magic, vs. miracles, 300
Maisons-Alfort, 56
Majolus (Cluniac abbot), 26–27, 53, 81,
171; captured by Saracens, 324, 325–
26, 337; charters under, 224–25;
Cluny's influence under, 28; Cluny's
structure under, 55; death of, 335; as
holy, 58; involvement in contemporary
events, 100–101; monastic reform un-
der, 56, 113; offered papacy, 77n. 226

malediction, 129–30, 175, 178, 208–9, 307

Manegold of Lautenbach, 131, 134

Mani, 128, 342

Manichaeans, 141, 344, 345

Manitius, Max, 302

Mans, Le, 120, 158

Manselli, Raoul, 104

Manthes, 244

Marcellus (Augustus's son), 243

Marcellus I (pope and saint), 101, 171, 265

Marcellus of Chalon, 171

Marcigny-sur-Loire, 30, 35, 48; as asylum, 37–38; Cluniac reclusion at, 52; and Cluny's synchrony with aristocracy, 76–77; foundation of, 91, 92; lay penances at, 39; necrologies of, 66, 67; Peter's mother at, 100, 153, 190–91, 248–49; relics at, 81

Marina (Valentinian I's wife), 242

Mark (apostle), 351

Marmoutier, 103

marriage, 19; and Christian sociological holism, 360; and consanguinity, 18, 39; and faith, 152–53

Martha (sister of Mary and Lazarus), 145, 152

Martial (saint), 158

Martimort, Aimé-Georges, 61

Martin (bishop of Tours), 171

Martin (saint), 46, 141, 179

martyrdom/martyrs, 154, 233, 348

Mary (sister of Martha and Lazarus), 145, 152

Mary (virgin), 20, 90, 137, 171, 340, 345

Mary Magdalene (saint), 267–68, 269

Mary the Egyptian (saint), 49

masturbation, 313–14

Matilda (Hugh of Semur's sister), 90–91

Matilda of Canossa, 134

Matthew (apostle), 158, 336, 351

Matthew (Cistercian monk), 312

Matthew of Albano, 220; as canon regular, 44–45; and Cluny's dependence on gifts, 225; Cluny and, 46, 54, 77; death of, 190, 205; in De miraculis, 102, 103; exclusion of Jews, 202, 280; Peter's prayers for, 239–40; at Saint-Martin-des-Champs, 125, 284

Maurice (archbishop of Braga), 331

Maurice I of Montboissier, 99

Maurice II of Montboissier, 99–100

Maurice III of Montboissier, 42, 100

Maurilius (archbishop), 205, 230

Maurus, 171

Mauss, Marcel, 211

Maximus the Confessor, 54

Mecca, 350

mediations, 257–59; iconic, 190–91, 257–58

Megiddo, 289

Mehne, Joachim, 75

Melchizedek, 20

Melfi, Council of, 74

Melville, Gert, 32, 57–58, 60

Mesopotamius (archdeacon), 331

Méyriat, 50

Michael (archangel), 50, 99

Michael (emperor), 331

Michaelmas, 222

miles christianus, 324, 325

Milis, Ludo J. R., 23–24

Milo (cardinal-bishop of Palestrina), 92

Milo of Anse (knight), 245

miracles: aperta miracula, 228–29; and Christian sociological holism, 103–4; Christian vs. Jewish, 295–96; and Cluny's mimicry of Rome, 80; and the dead, 234–35; defined, 207–8; Eucharist as, 209–10, 259; eucharistic, 200, 203–5, 208, 219; as evidence of Christianity's superiority, 295–96, 298–301; lack of, in Islam, 353; and transmutation of elements, 195–96; used in antiheretical debate, 141–42, 145–46, 152

Mirbt, Carl, 131

missa, 206, 259

missionary work, 167–68

Moissac, 58, 66, 67, 94, 329, 331

monasteries: and Cluniac archabbacy, 58–59; defined, 37; donations to, 94–95; as ecclesiastical asylums, 223–24; family disputes at, 92–93; as "family of families," 88–91; as fortresses, 177; purgatorial function of, 249–52; as symbolic representation of afterlife, 248–49

monasticism: emergence of, 11, 33; and exclusion, 23–24; as model of inclu-

monasticism (*continued*)
sion, 35; Pentecost as founding mo
ment of, 105
monastic reform, 26, 55–56, 60, 113, 256,
324
monks, 43; *ad succurrendum*, 41–42, 100;
and aristocratic family disputes, 92–93;
arming of, 333–34; black vs. white,
267; conversion of, 38–40, 41–42; and
cura animarum, 68–70, 72; distinctions
among, 41–44; duties of, 24–25, 36,
70–71, 73; novices, 41, 58; and the
poor, 88; and priesthood, 69–70; rights
of admittance, 37; and seigneurial system, 93–94; and tithes, 71–74. *See also*
purity, monastic
Montanus, 128
Montaut, 76
Montboissier family, 99–100
Monte Cassino, 70
Monteforte (Italy), 22, 188
Montierneuf (Poitiers), 66, 67
Montmain, 92
Montmajour, 113
Montrieux, 111
Mont-Saint-Michel, 48, 68
monumental sculpture, 115–16
Moore, R. I., 21
Morandus (Cluny patron), 36
Moras-en-Valloire, 244
Morigny, 45
Moses: Law of, 296–98, 309, 350; male-
diction uttered by, 228; and papacy, 20;
prophecies of, 293, 352, 353; and sa-
cred space, 160; and salvation, 311; and
signs, 184–85, 289, 290; and solidarity
through charity, 153; staff of, 171;
tabernacle of, 157, 161, 163, 166
Mount Tabor (monastery), 331, 335
Moûtier-en-Puisaye, 53
Muhammad (Islamic prophet): as fulfillment of prophecy, 337; and Ibn Tumart, 291; inspired by Christian and
Jewish teachings, 323, 351; lack of
prophecy by, 351–55; legends of, 4,
339; stereotypes of, 298–99, 340,
342–43, 348, 356–57, 362
al-Muqtadir Billah (king of Zaragoza), 329
music, liturgical, 114, 253–54

Muslims. *See* Islam/Muslims
Müssigbrod, Axel, 68

Nantua, 50
Narbonne, 158, 293–94, 317
Nazareth, 166
Nebuchadnezzar, 288, 314–15
Necho (king of Egypt), 289
necrologies, 45; Cluniac, 49, 76, 130; in-
clusion in, 44, 64–68, 95; laity in, 71
necromancy, 107, 200
Nehemiah (rabbi), 306–7, 310
Nestor, 342
Nestorians, 341, 345
Nicaea, Council of, 129, 132
Nicanor, 232
Nicholas (deacon), 337
Nicolaitism, 17, 341
Nidarholm, 266
Noah, 20, 157, 166, 297, 306, 339, 352
Norbert of Xanten, 104
Notre-Dame at Die, 116
Notre-Dame at Thines, 116
Nouaillé, 63
Novatian, 128

Octavia (Augustus's sister), 243
Odilo (Cluniac abbot), 26–27, 38, 39, 44,
76, 235, 241; abbatial hagiography under, 102; All Souls' Day inaugurated
under, 221–22, 250; and aristocracy,
327; charters under, 224–25; clamor
ritual under, 178; Cluny's development
under, 57; Cluny's influence under, 28;
and contemporary events, 100–101; on
the Cross, 186–87; customs composed
under, 61, 64; death of, 202–3, 335; funerary suffrages of, 213n. 153, 247;
gifts *pro remedio animae* under, 70; as
holy, 58; on holy war, 325–26; monastic reform under, 55–56, 113; and purgatory, 250–51; and Peace and Truce
of God, 324; and the poor, 87; and Reconquista, 328
Odo (Cluniac abbot): on adoration of
relics, 189; apocalyptic poetry of, 104–
5, 106; and baptism, 149; as canon regular, 44; charters under, 224; and
Christian knight prototype, 324, 325;

Cluny and, 26, 55; pastoral work of, 39; and transmutation of elements, 199
Odo I (cardinal-bishop of Ostia), 132. *See also* Urban II (pope)
Odo II (cardinal-bishop of Ostia), 77
Odo of Champagne, 213–15
Odo of Saint-Maur, 56–57
Oldradus de Ponte, 283
Oliver (knight; Cluniac monk), 88–89
omnipotence, divine, 305–7
omniscience, divine, 311
Oña, 328
Onias (high priest), 228–29, 232
order: during Carolingian period, 12–16; categories excluded from, 21–25; Cluny as, 30, 32–33; cosmic vs. social, 9–21; Dionysian hierarchies, 12–13; in early Christian society, 10–12; 11th to 13th centuries, 16–21; Gregorian divide, 17–19; Gregory VII's definition of, 16–17; and inclusion, 34–35; and Jewish "disorder," 310, 315–16; papal primacy in, 19–21; three-functions theory of, 13–16
Orderic Vitalis, 54, 321
orders, society of, 33
ordination, rite of, 18, 19, 69, 73
Orléans, 22, 101, 159, 205, 278
Ostia, 77–78
otherness: as anathema, 4–5; Christian identity defined against, 2, 360–61, 364; demonization of, 364–65; and natural differences, 320; twelfth-century versions of, 337
Othlo of Saint Emmerman, 256
Otto (count of Mâcon), 238n. 79
Otto II (emperor), 77n. 226
Otto III (emperor), 44
Otto the Great (emperor), 39, 326
Our Lady at Jehosaphat, 331

Pacaut, Marcel, 71
pagans, 193, 241–42, 273
Palmarea, 331
Pamiers, 49
Pammachius (senator), 232
"Panclunism," 323–24
papacy: becomes seigneury, 176; as head of Cluny, 78–79; power of, 108; pri-macy of, 19–21; role played at Cluny, 59–60; title of, 19; tutelage of Cluny, 30–31
Paray-le-Monial, 90
parenthood, 230; godparents, 153, 230, 232, 246, 256–57; and infant baptism, 153. *See also* spiritual kinship
Paris, 5, 158
Paschal II (pope), 57, 77, 92
past, imagined, 5
Pataria, 24
Paternus of San Juan, 328
Patrimony of Saint Peter, 176
Paul (apostle), 14; and aristocracy, 93; on charity, 228; on Church as community, 10, 18, 44; churches established by, 157, 158; as Cluny's patron, 26, 39, 59, 170, 171, 173, 275, 331; on congregations as churches, 162; and the Cross, 183; on *Ecclesia*, 180; evangelism of, 351; and heretics, 129, 133, 138; on Jews vs. Christians, 297; and judgment of merits, 220, 231; and Last Supper, 196–97; organicism of, 12; and papacy, 107–8; and parables, 304; on proper response to dissenters, 340; prophecies of, 105, 354; relics of, 27, 81, 169, 223; on transformation by regeneration, 216; on universality, 154
Paul (bishop of Narbonne; saint), 158
Paulinus of Nola, 231, 232
Payerne, 76
Peace and Truce of God, 283, 324, 327–28
Pelagians, 345
Peloges, 91
penance, 19, 342; at Cluny, 38–39
penitence, 237–38
Pentecost, 105, 148, 269
Pérec, Georges, 4
Périgueux, 158
persecution, 350; legitimate, 131
Peter (apostle): and Cluny's mimicry of Rome, 78; as Cluny's patron, 26, 39, 59, 90, 170, 171, 173, 275, 331; depicted at Vézelay, 269; evangelism of, 1, 351; feast of the Chair of, 241; and inclusion, 52, 94–95; as mediator, 211;

Peter (apostle) (*continued*)
  miracles of, 80, 296; and papacy, 20;
  Patrimony of Saint Peter, 176; relics of,
  27, 81, 169, 223; and Rome, 157; on
  search for truth, 348; and transformation of property, 216; tributes to, 114
Peter (archdeacon), 47
Peter (bishop of Pampeluna), 68
Peter Abélard: on charity, 247; and Jews,
  4, 320; on miracles, 142; on omnipresence of God, 161; on order, 9; philosophical method of, 137; retreat to
  Cluny, 86; on sacraments, 190; as
  scholastic, 102; and social bond, 256
Peter Alfonso, 138, 301–2
Peter Damian, 250; and anathema, 130;
  and Cluny, 67, 76; on ecclesiastical
  property, 282; on involvement of hermits, 51–52, 226; on preparations for
  death, 238–39; rhetorical method of,
  122, 134–35, 136
Peter de la Roche, 333
Peter Gloc, 29, 78
Peter Lombard, 18, 189
Peter of Bruis: death of, 115, 183; dese-
  cration of sacred space, 118; on Eu-
  charist, 192; exclusion of, 362; heresy
  of, 2–3, 22, 109–10, 139, 187; on in-
  fant baptism, 149–50; on liturgical music, 253; and monastic reform, 256; in
  Provence, 113, 114; writings of, 144.
  See also Petrobrusians
Peter of Montboissier. *See* Peter the Venerable (Cluniac abbot)
Peter of Montmartre, 117
Peter of Montmin, 280
Peter of Poitiers, 116–17, 338, 339, 343–
  45
Peter of Toledo, 339, 343
Peter of Tournus (Cluniac monk), 107
Peter Pierleone. *See* Anacletus II (antipope)
Peter the Venerable (Cluniac abbot), 2,
  46; all-or-nothing logic of, 42, 149,
  150–52, 154–56, 266, 351, 354; anti-
  Judaism of, 304; as apostle of nonvio-
  lence, 347; approach to Islam, 337–43;
  on canons regular, 44–45; charters under, 224; "Christian armory" of, 338–
  43, 357; and Cluniac demonology, 108;

on Cluny's assistance to poor, 87; on
  Cluny's hospitality, 85, 86; Cluny's influence under, 30; and contemporary
  events, 101; and conversions, 38; death
  of, 205n. 106; ecclesiology of, 82–84,
  156; epistolary technique of, 125–26;
  familiarity with writings of adversaries,
  138, 301–4; holist conception of Christian society, 266; influence of, 32–33;
  life and work of, 99–104; on model
  Cluniacs, 44–47; on parochial income,
  73; and Provence, 113–16; on recruit-
  ing of Cluniac pastors, 75; role in
  Church's exclusionary efforts, 23–24;
  and sexuality, 356–57; on "silent
  preaching," 25, 101; statutes of, 63, 67.
  See also Adversus Iudeos; antiheretical
  discourse; *Contra Petrobrusianos*; *Contra
  sectam Sarracenorum*; specific issue
Petke, Wolfgang, 74
Petrobrusians, 101; and arguments from
  authority, 141; on the Church, 199,
  260; on the Cross, 188; on Eucharist,
  191–92, 200; and Henricians, 126;
  heresy of, 108–10, 128–29, 136; individualization of death and salvation,
  219, 227, 229, 240, 247; on infant baptism, 150; Peter's response to, 3, 33;
  and sacrifice, 364; and solidarity, 256–
  57; violations committed by, 140
Philip (apostle), 158
Philip I (king of Franks), 39, 45
Philip II Augustus (king of France), 22,
  283, 317
pietas, 231, 241, 243–44, 246
Pilate, 183, 183n. 7
pilgrimages: and apocalyptic expectation,
  106; to Cluny, 81–82; and Crusades,
  333–34; to Jerusalem, 29, 82, 106; to
  Rome, 82, 99, 238; to Saint-Gilles-du-
  Gard, 110; against Saracens, 146
Pipo (bishop of Toul), 215
Pisa, 239, 266; Council of, 111, 114
places of worship. *See* sacred space
Plantagenets, 283
Plato, 12–13
Playoust, Arlette, 114
Pliny the Elder, 273
Poeck, Dietrich, 32, 55, 58, 59, 67, 70,
  225

relics (*continued*)

   300; heretical rejection of, 345; sacred space defined by, 180; as sign, 106; significance of, 163

Renouf (abbot of Mont-Saint-Michel), 48

renunciation vs. world: as "ordered dichotomy," 34

res publica christiana, 87

resurrection, 341

Reynold of Semur (abbot of Vézelay), 91, 268

Rhineland, 22

Richard, Jean, 91

Richard of Saint-Victor, 162

Robert I (duke of Burgundy), 91

Robert II (king of Franks), 56–57, 205

Robert of Arbrissel (hermit), 24, 100, 363

Robert of Ketton, 338, 339, 343

Robert of Paris, 80

Robert of Tombelaine, 48

Robert Pullen, 210, 249

Robinson, Ian Stuart, 135

Rodolfus Glaber, 44, 52–54, 105–6, 120, 278, 326–27, 337

Roger II (king of Sicily), 84, 85, 267

Rome, 1, 168; Christianization of traditions, 242–44; classification categories, 13–14; Cluny's mimicry of, 78–84, 108; Cluny's relationship with, 29, 59–60, 75–78, 79–80, 173–74; Empire, 11; festivals of, 241; law, 123–24; pilgrimages to, 82, 99, 238; places of worship in, 157–58; and reliability of Scripture, 351; rhetorical tools of, 133–35; synods, 17, 74, 79, 205

Romulus, 14

Rosans, 114

Rosenwein, Barbara H., 60, 94

Rostagnus, 81

Rouen, 54, 281, 283, 293–94, 317; Council of, 205

Rudolph IV of Habsburg (emperor), 36

Rule of Saint Benedict, 27, 43, 50–51, 84–85, 88, 164, 216, 221

Rule of the Master, 88

Sabellians, 345

Sabellius, 128

Sabina (Italy), 61

Sackur, Ernst, 31

sacraments (*sacramentum*), 234; and the dead, 220; defined, 207; efficacy of, 155, 297; and incorporation, 258; infused virtue transmitted by, 150; of Jews, 315; and sacred space, 218; as signs, 190, 192, 198; and solidarity, 221; synthesis of, 18–19; unrecognized by Islam, 342. *See also* Eucharist; *specific sacrament*

sacred space, 156–81; as congruent place, 158–65, 180–81, 259–61; and Eucharist, 178–81, 217–18; heretical rejection of, 3, 109, 118, 129, 156, 159; heritage of, 156–58; protection of, 176–78; purgatorial function of, 249–52; special status of, 172–76; structuring of, 165–72, 193, 260

sacrifice of Christ, 105, 191–218; eucharistic space for, 178–81; and exclusion, 364; and Jews, 293–95, 307; pagan precedents for, 273; as sign, 192–98; spatialization of, 167; universality of, 360; unrecognized by Islam, 342. *See also* Cross, the; Eucharist

Saint-André at Gap, 114

Saint-André-de-Rosans, 114

Saint-André-lès-Avignon, 113

Saint-Antonin at Fredelas, 49

Saint-Bénigne at Dijon, 53–54

Saint-Benoît-sur-Loire, 103

Saint-Bertin, 59

Saint Blaise, 28

Saint-Claude, 40, 64

Saint-Cyprien at Poitiers, 47, 59

Saint-Denis at Nogent-le-Rotrou, 93

Saint-Denis-en-France, 56, 284; Council of, 74

Sainte-Colombe at Sens, 334

Sainte Maria-in-Schola-Graeca, 77

Sainte Maria in Trastevere (Rome), 77

Sainte-Marie-sur-l'Aventin, 77n. 226

Saintes, 158

Saint-Etienne at Condrieu, 116

Saint-Evroult, 54

Saint Gall, 88, 177

Saint-Germaine at Auxerre, 53–54, 55, 59

Saint-Gilles-du-Gard, 29, 59, 110, 111, 113, 183, 235; facade of, 115

Saint Isidore at León, 338

Saint-Jean at Angély, 107

Solomon, 157, 161–62, 163, 166, 167, 288, 290, 291, 317, 340
Solomon (Sennecé Jew), 278
Song of Roland, 146
sorcery, 107
Southern, Richard W., 316
Souvigny, 58
sovereignty: and eucharistic center, 260
spiritualia, 72, 94, 175, 216, 225–26, 259, 260
spiritual justice, 129–30, 176–78, 208–9, 223
spiritual kinship, 244–45, 246, 257
statutes, 62–63
Staub, Johannes, 64
Stephen (abbot of Saint-Rigaud at Ancise), 47
Stephen (Cluny benefactor), 177
Stephen (priest), 244–45
Stephen (protomartyr), 169, 170, 171, 330–31
Stephen IX (pope), 57, 79, 268
Stephen Harding (abbot of Cîteaux), 297
Stephen Le Blanc (abbot of Saint-Gilles-du-Gard), 235–37
Stephen of Neublans, 330
stereotypes: of Islam, 336–37, 357; of Judaism, 321, 361–62; medieval genesis of, 364–65
Strabo (Greek geographer), 316
sun worship, 307–8
Suppo (abbot of Fruttuaria and Mont-Saint-Michel), 68
Sutri, 238
syllogisms, 137
Sylvester I (pope), 12
Sylvester II (pope), 44
Sylvester of Chalon (saint), 171
synods: 1025, 141, 159–61, 165; 1059, 17, 205; 1070, 205; 1078, 74; 1080, 79; as assemblies of the pope, 20
Syrus (biographer), 325
Szabó-Bechstein, Brigitte, 78

Talmud: on afterlife, 309–13; contrasted with Bible, 305, 315, 318–19; and exclusion of Jews, 361–62; on nature of God, 307–9; on omnipotence of God, 305–7; Peter's familiarity with, 102, 138, 144, 301–4; Peter's misunder-

standing of, 292, 304–5; Peter as first to address, 3–4
Tanchelm, 22
Taurinus (saint), 36, 171
Templars, Order of, 328, 333, 334, 334–35n. 53
Tensoretis (Sennecé Jew), 278
Tertullian, 10–11, 286
Teske, Wolfgang, 42–43
testimonia, 132, 143
Teuto (abbot of Saint-Maur-des-Fossés), 56–57
Thanet, Isle of, 349
Theobald (abbot of Sainte-Colombe at Sens), 334
Theobald (bishop of Paris), 46
Theodore of Saint-Hilaire, 215
Theodosian Code, 11
Theodosian Code, 123
Thibaud (abbot of Corméry), 56
Thibaud (count of Chalon), 90
Thibaud I (count of Champagne), 213–15
Thomas (apostle), 158
Thomas Aquinas, 19, 214
tithes, 71–74
Titus (Roman emperor), 295, 326
Todros (Nassi of Narbonne), 294
Toledo, Council of, 73
Tombelaine, 48
Torrell, Jean-Pierre, 32, 103, 234, 332, 344, 354
Toul, 74
Toulouse, 49, 110, 120, 126, 158, 332
Tournus, 277
Tours, 44, 158
Tours-sur-Marne, 74
Transfiguration, 101
transformation, 183–86, 212n. 141, 215–17, 360
transmutation of elements, 143, 180–81, 194–98, 209–10
treatises, ecclesiastical, 31–32
trental, 231
Trinité, La (Vendôme), 41
Trinity, 137, 340, 342
Troeltsch, Ernst, 34
Trophimus (saint), 158, 273
Turki, Abdel-Magid, 329
Tusculum, 77
Tutsch, Burkhardt, 60, 63